Poetry for Students

National Advisory Board

Susan Allison: Head Librarian, Lewiston High School, Lewiston, Maine. Standards Committee Chairperson for Maine School Library (MASL) Programs. Board member, Julia Adams Morse Memorial Library, Greene, Maine. Advisor to Lewiston Public Library Planning Process.

Jennifer Hood: Young Adult/Reference Librarian, Cumberland Public Library, Cumberland, Rhode Island. Certified teacher, Rhode Island. Member of the New England Library Association, Rhode Island Library Association, and the Rhode Island Educational Media Association.

Ann Kearney: Head Librarian and Media Specialist, Christopher Columbus High School, Miami, Florida, 1982–2002. Thirty-two years as Librarian in various educational institutions ranging from grade schools through graduate programs. Library positions at Miami-Dade Community College, the University of Miami's Medical School Library, and Carrollton School in Coconut Grove, Florida. B.A. from University of Detroit, 1967 (magna cum laude); M.L.S., University of Missouri–Columbia, 1974. Volunteer Project Leader for a school in rural Jamaica; volunteer with Adult Literacy programs.

Laurie St. Laurent: Head of Adult and Children's Services, East Lansing Public Library, East Lansing, Michigan, 1994–. M.L.S. from Western Michigan University. Chair of Michigan Library Association's 1998 Michigan Summer Reading Program; Chair of the Children's Services Division in 2000–2001; and Vice-President of the Association in 2002–2003. Board member of several regional early childhood literacy organizations and member of the Library of Michigan Youth Services Advisory Committee.

Heidi Stohs: Instructor in Language Arts, grades 10–12, Solomon High School, Solomon, Kansas. Received B.S. from Kansas State University; M.A. from Fort Hays State University.

Poetry for Students

Presenting Analysis, Context, and Criticism on Commonly Studied Poetry

Volume 21

Anne Marie Hacht, Project Editor

Foreword by David Kelly

THOMSON
GALE

Detroit • New York • San Francisco • San Diego • New Haven, Conn. • Waterville, Maine • London • Munich

THOMSON
GALE

Poetry for Students, Volume 21

Project Editor
Anne Marie Hacht

Editorial
Mark Milne and Michelle Kazensky

Rights Acquisition and Management
Lori Hines, Sue Rudolph, Ann Taylor

Manufacturing
Rhonda Williams

Imaging and Multimedia
Lezlie Light, Dan Newell, Robyn Young

Product Design
Pamela A. E. Galbreath

Vendor Administration
Civie Green

For more information, contact

Thomson Gale
27500 Drake Rd.
Farmington Hills, MI 48331-3535
Or you can visit our Internet site at
http://www.gale.com

ISBN 0-7876-6960-1
ISSN 1094-7019

Printed in the United States of America
10 9 8 7 6 5 4 3

Table of Contents

Just a Few Lines on a Page

I have often thought that poets have the easiest job in the world. A poem, after all, is just a few lines on a page, usually not even extending margin to margin—how long would that take to write, about five minutes? Maybe ten at the most, if you wanted it to rhyme or have a repeating meter. Why, I could start in the morning and produce a book of poetry by dinnertime. But we all know that it isn't that easy. Anyone can come up with enough words, but the poet's job is about writing the *right* ones. The right words will change lives, making people see the world somewhat differently than they saw it just a few minutes earlier. The right words can make a reader who relies on the dictionary for meanings take a greater responsibility for his or her own personal understanding. A poem that is put on the page correctly can bear any amount of analysis, probing, defining, explaining, and interrogating, and something about it will still feel new the next time you read it.

It would be fine with me if I could talk about poetry without using the word "magical," because that word is overused these days to imply "a really good time," often with a certain sweetness about it, and a lot of poetry is neither of these. But if you stop and think about magic—whether it brings to mind sorcery, witchcraft, or bunnies pulled from top hats—it always seems to involve stretching reality to produce a result greater than the sum of its parts and pulling unexpected results out of thin air. This book provides ample cases where a few simple words conjure up whole worlds. We do not actually travel to different times and different cultures, but the poems get into our minds, they find what little we know about the places they are talking about, and then they make that little bit blossom into a bouquet of someone else's life. Poets make us think we are following simple, specific events, but then they leave ideas in our heads that cannot be found on the printed page. Abracadabra.

Sometimes when you finish a poem it doesn't feel as if it has left any supernatural effect on you, like it did not have any more to say beyond the actual words that it used. This happens to everybody, but most often to inexperienced readers: regardless of what is often said about young people's infinite capacity to be amazed, you have to understand what usually does happen, and what could have happened instead, if you are going to be moved by what someone has accomplished. In those cases in which you finish a poem with a "So what?" attitude, the information provided in *Poetry for Students* comes in handy. Readers can feel assured that the poems included here actually are potent magic, not just because a few (or a hundred or ten thousand) professors of literature say they are: they're significant because they can withstand close inspection and still amaze the very same people who have just finished taking them apart and seeing how they work. Turn them inside out, and they will still be able to come alive, again and again. *Poetry for Students* gives readers of any age good practice in feeling the ways poems relate to both the reality of the time and place the poet lived in and the reality of our emotions. Practice is just another word for being a student. The information given here helps you understand the way to read poetry; what to look for, what to expect.

With all of this in mind, I really don't think I would actually like to have a poet's job at all. There are too many skills involved, including precision, honesty, taste, courage, linguistics, passion, compassion, and the ability to keep all sorts of people entertained at once. And that is just what they do with one hand, while the other hand pulls some sort of trick that most of us will never fully understand. I can't even pack all that I need for a weekend into one suitcase, so what would be my chances of stuffing so much life into a few lines? With all that *Poetry for Students* tells us about each poem, I am impressed that any poet can finish three or four poems a year. Read the inside stories of these poems, and you won't be able to approach any poem in the same way you did before.

David J. Kelly
College of Lake County

Introduction

Purpose of the Book

The purpose of *Poetry for Students* (*PfS*) is to provide readers with a guide to understanding, enjoying, and studying poems by giving them easy access to information about the work. Part of Gale's "For Students" Literature line, *PfS* is specifically designed to meet the curricular needs of high school and undergraduate college students and their teachers, as well as the interests of general readers and researchers considering specific poems. While each volume contains entries on "classic" poems frequently studied in classrooms, there are also entries containing hard-to-find information on contemporary poems, including works by multicultural, international, and women poets.

The information covered in each entry includes an introduction to the poem and the poem's author; the actual poem text (if possible); a poem summary, to help readers unravel and understand the meaning of the poem; analysis of important themes in the poem; and an explanation of important literary techniques and movements as they are demonstrated in the poem.

In addition to this material, which helps the readers analyze the poem itself, students are also provided with important information on the literary and historical background informing each work. This includes a historical context essay, a box comparing the time or place the poem was written to modern Western culture, a critical overview essay, and excerpts from critical essays on the poem. A unique feature of *PfS* is a specially commissioned critical essay on each poem, targeted toward the student reader.

To further aid the student in studying and enjoying each poem, information on media adaptations is provided (if available), as well as reading suggestions for works of fiction and nonfiction on similar themes and topics. Classroom aids include ideas for research papers and lists of critical sources that provide additional material on the poem.

Selection Criteria

The titles for each volume of *PfS* were selected by surveying numerous sources on teaching literature and analyzing course curricula for various school districts. Some of the sources surveyed included: literature anthologies; *Reading Lists for College-Bound Students: The Books Most Recommended by America's Top Colleges*; textbooks on teaching the poem; a College Board survey of poems commonly studied in high schools; and a National Council of Teachers of English (NCTE) survey of poems commonly studied in high schools.

Input was also solicited from our advisory board, as well as educators from various areas. From these discussions, it was determined that each volume should have a mix of "classic" poems (those works commonly taught in literature classes) and contemporary poems for which information is often hard to find. Because of the interest in expanding the canon of literature, an emphasis was also placed on including works by international, multicultural, and women poets. Our advisory board members—educational professionals—helped pare down the list for each volume. If a work was not selected for the present volume, it was often noted as a possibility for a future volume. As always, the editor welcomes suggestions for titles to be included in future volumes.

How Each Entry Is Organized

Each entry, or chapter, in *PfS* focuses on one poem. Each entry heading lists the full name of the poem, the author's name, and the date of the poem's publication. The following elements are contained in each entry:

- **Introduction:** a brief overview of the poem which provides information about its first appearance, its literary standing, any controversies surrounding the work, and major conflicts or themes within the work.
- **Author Biography:** this section includes basic facts about the poet's life, and focuses on events and times in the author's life that inspired the poem in question.
- **Poem Text:** when permission has been granted, the poem is reprinted, allowing for quick reference when reading the explication of the following section.
- **Poem Summary:** a description of the major events in the poem. Summaries are broken down with subheads that indicate the lines being discussed.
- **Themes:** a thorough overview of how the major topics, themes, and issues are addressed within the poem. Each theme discussed appears in a separate subhead and is easily accessed through the boldface entries in the Subject/Theme Index.
- **Style:** this section addresses important style elements of the poem, such as form, meter, and rhyme scheme; important literary devices used, such as imagery, foreshadowing, and symbolism; and, if applicable, genres to which the work might have belonged, such as Gothicism or Romanticism. Literary terms are explained within the entry, but can also be found in the Glossary.
- **Historical Context:** this section outlines the social, political, and cultural climate *in which the author lived and the poem was created.* This section may include descriptions of related historical events, pertinent aspects of daily life in the culture, and the artistic and literary sensibilities of the time in which the work was written. If the poem is a historical work, information regarding the time in which the poem is set is also included. Each section is broken down with helpful subheads.
- **Critical Overview:** this section provides background on the critical reputation of the poem, including bannings or any other public controversies surrounding the work. For older works, this section includes a history of how the poem was first received and how perceptions of it may have changed over the years; for more recent poems, direct quotes from early reviews may also be included.
- **Criticism:** an essay commissioned by *PfS* which specifically deals with the poem and is written specifically for the student audience, as well as excerpts from previously published criticism on the work (if available).
- **Sources:** an alphabetical list of critical material used in compiling the entry, with full bibliographical information.
- **Further Reading:** an alphabetical list of other critical sources which may prove useful for the student. It includes full bibliographical information and a brief annotation.

In addition, each entry contains the following highlighted sections, set apart from the main text as sidebars:

- **Media Adaptations:** if available, a list of audio recordings as well as any film or television adaptations of the poem, including source information.
- **Topics for Further Study:** a list of potential study questions or research topics dealing with the poem. This section includes questions related to other disciplines the student may be studying, such as American history, world history, science, math, government, business, geography, economics, psychology, etc.
- **Compare and Contrast:** an "at-a-glance" comparison of the cultural and historical differences between the author's time and culture and late twentieth century or early twenty-first century Western culture. This box includes pertinent parallels between the major scientific, political, and cultural movements of the time or place the poem was written, the time or place the poem was set (if a historical work), and modern Western culture. Works written after 1990 may not have this box.

- **What Do I Read Next?:** a list of works that might complement the featured poem or serve as a contrast to it. This includes works by the same author and others, works of fiction and nonfiction, and works from various genres, cultures, and eras.

Other Features

PfS includes "Just a Few Lines on a Page," a foreword by David J. Kelly, an adjunct professor of English, College of Lake County, Illinois. This essay provides a straightforward, unpretentious explanation of why poetry should be marveled at and how *Poetry for Students* can help teachers show students how to enrich their own reading experiences.

A Cumulative Author/Title Index lists the authors and titles covered in each volume of the *PfS* series.

A Cumulative Nationality/Ethnicity Index breaks down the authors and titles covered in each volume of the *PfS* series by nationality and ethnicity.

A Subject/Theme Index, specific to each volume, provides easy reference for users who may be studying a particular subject or theme rather than a single work. Significant subjects from events to broad themes are included, and the entries pointing to the specific theme discussions in each entry are indicated in **boldface**.

A Cumulative Index of First Lines (beginning in Vol. 10) provides easy reference for users who may be familiar with the first line of a poem but may not remember the actual title.

A Cumulative Index of Last Lines (beginning in Vol. 10) provides easy reference for users who may be familiar with the last line of a poem but may not remember the actual title.

Each entry may include illustrations, including a photo of the author and other graphics related to the poem.

Citing Poetry for Students

When writing papers, students who quote directly from any volume of *Poetry for Students* may use the following general forms. These examples are based on MLA style; teachers may request that students adhere to a different style, so the following examples may be adapted as needed.

When citing text from *PfS* that is not attributed to a particular author (i.e., the Themes, Style, Historical Context sections, etc.), the following format should be used in the bibliography section:

"Angle of Geese." *Poetry for Students.* Eds. Marie Napierkowski and Mary Ruby. Vol. 2. Detroit: Gale, 1998. 5–7.

When quoting the specially commissioned essay from *PfS* (usually the first piece under the "Criticism" subhead), the following format should be used:

Velie, Alan. Critical Essay on "Angle of Geese." *Poetry for Students.* Eds. Marie Napierkowski and Mary Ruby. Vol. 2. Detroit: Gale, 1998. 7–10.

When quoting a journal or newspaper essay that is reprinted in a volume of *PfS,* the following form may be used:

Luscher, Robert M. "An Emersonian Context of Dickinson's 'The Soul Selects Her Own Society.'" *ESQ: A Journal of American Renaissance* Vol. 30, No. 2 (Second Quarter, 1984), 111–16; excerpted and reprinted in *Poetry for Students*, Vol. 1, eds. Marie Napierkowski and Mary Ruby (Detroit: Gale, 1998), pp. 266–69.

When quoting material reprinted from a book that appears in a volume of *PfS,* the following form may be used:

Mootry, Maria K. "'Tell It Slant': Disguise and Discovery as Revisionist Poetic Discourse in 'The Bean Eaters,'" in *A Life Distilled: Gwendolyn Brooks, Her Poetry and Fiction.* Edited by Maria K. Mootry and Gary Smith. University of Illinois Press, 1987. 177–80, 191; excerpted and reprinted in *Poetry for Students*, Vol. 2, eds. Marie Napierkowski and Mary Ruby (Detroit: Gale, 1998), pp. 22–24.

We Welcome Your Suggestions

The editor of *Poetry for Students* welcomes your comments and ideas. Readers who wish to suggest poems to appear in future volumes, or who have other suggestions, are cordially invited to contact the editor. You may contact the editor via E-mail at: ***ForStudentsEditors@thomson.com.*** Or write to the editor at:

Editor, *Poetry for Students*
Thomson Gale
27500 Drake Rd.
Farmington Hills, MI 48331–3535

Literary Chronology

1821 Charles Baudelaire is born on April 9 in Paris, France.

1857 Charles Baudelaire's "Hymn to Beauty" is published.

1867 Charles Baudelaire dies on August 31.

1897 Louise Bogan is born on August 11 in Livermore Falls, Maine.

1909 Anna Swir (Anna Swirszczyńska) is born on February 7 in Warsaw, Poland.

1920 Paul Celan (Paul Antschel) is born on November 23 in Czernowitz, Romania.

1923 Louise Bogan's "Words for Departure" is published.

1924 Claribel Alegría is born on May 12 in Esteli, Nicaragua.

1926 Robert Creeley is born on May 21 in Arlington, Massachusetts.

1931 Tomas Tranströmer is born on April 15 in Stockholm, Sweden.

1935 Foroogh (also spelled Forough or Faroogh) Farrokhzaad is born on January 5 in Tehran, Iran.

1935 Claire Malroux is born on September 3 in the rural town of Albi in southwestern France.

1939 Stephen Dunn is born on June 24 in the Forest Hills section of New York City.

1941 Eamon Grennan is born on November 13 in Dublin, Ireland.

1952 Elizabeth Spires is born in Lancaster, Ohio.

1952 Paul Celan's "Late and Deep" is published.

1953 Ana Castillo is born on June 15 in Chicago, Illinois.

1954 Sarah Arvio is born in Philadelphia, Pennsylvania.

1958 Robin Behn is born.

1964 Faroogh Farrokhzaad's "A Rebirth" is published.

1967 Foroogh Farrokhzaad dies in a car accident on February 14.

1969 Joelle Biele is born in the Bronx, New York.

1970 Paul Celan commits suicide by drowning himself in the Seine in Paris.

1970 Anna Swir's "Maternity" is published.

1970 Louise Bogan dies on February 4 in her New York apartment.

1983 Tomas Tranströmer's "Answers to Letters" is published.

1984 Anna Swir dies of cancer.

1986 Elizabeth Frank is awarded the Pulitzer Prize for biography for *Louise Bogan: A Portrait.*

1988 Robert Creeley's "Fading Light" is published.

1991 Eamon Grennan's "Station" is published.

1993 Claribel Alegría's "Accounting" is published.

1993 Robin Behn's "Ten Years after Your Deliberate Drowning" is published.

1996 Claire Malroux's "Morning Walk" is published.

2000 Stephen Dunn's "The Reverse Side" is published.

2000 Stephen Dunn is awarded the Pulitzer Prize for poetry for his collection *Different Hours.*

2001 Joelle Biele's "Rapture" is published.

2001 Ana Castillo's "While I Was Gone a War Began" is published.

2002 Elizabeth Spires's "Ghazal" is published.

2002 Sarah Arvio's "Memory" is published.

Acknowledgments

The editors wish to thank the copyright holders of the excerpted criticism included in this volume and the permissions managers of many book and magazine publishing companies for assisting us in securing reproduction rights. We are also grateful to the staffs of the Detroit Public Library, the Library of Congress, the University of Detroit Mercy Library, Wayne State University Purdy/Kresge Library Complex, and the University of Michigan Libraries for making their resources available to us. Following is a list of the copyright holders who have granted us permission to reproduce material in this volume of ***Poetry for Students (PfS)***. Every effort has been made to trace copyright, but if omissions have been made, please let us know.

COPYRIGHTED MATERIALS IN *PfS*, VOLUME 21, WERE REPRODUCED FROM THE FOLLOWING PERIODICALS:

Asheville Citizens-Times, March 22, 2002. Reproduced by permission.—***Booklist***, v. 98, February 1, 2002. Copyright © 2002 by the American Library Association. Reproduced by permission.—***Centennial Review***, v. 36, fall, 1992. © 1992 by The Centennial Review. Reproduced by permission of the publisher.—***Georgia Review***, v. 54, winter, 2000. Copyright © 2000 by the University of Georgia. Reproduced by permission.—***Magill Book Reviews***, June 1, 1997. Reproduced by permission.—***New England Review***, v. 11, spring, 1993 for "Eamon Grennan: To Leave Something Bright and Upright Behind," by Richard Tillinghast. Copyright © 1993 by Middlebury College. Reproduced by permission of the author.—***NuCity***, June 18-July 1, 1993. Reproduced by permission.—***Ploughshares***, v. 25, winter, 1999/2000 for "About Elizabeth Spires," by Elizabeth Spires and A. V. Christie. Reproduced by permission of A. V. Christie.—***Poetry***, v. 161, January, 1993 for "Review of 'As If It Matters,'" by Ben Howard; v. 177, October–November, 2000 for "From Intimism to the Poetics of Presence: Reading Contemporary French Poetry," by John Taylor; v. 179, January, 2002 for "Down from the Tower: Poetry as Confabulation," by Bill Christophersen. © 1993, 2000, 2002 by the Modern Poetry Association. All reproduced by permission of the Editor of Poetry and the respective authors.—***Prairie Schooner***, winter, 1998. Copyright © 1998 by University of Nebraska Press. All rights reserved. Reproduced from Prairie Schooner by permission of the University of Nebraska Press.—***Publishers Weekly***, August 12, 1996. Copyright 1996 by Reed Publishing USA. Reproduced from Publishers Weekly, published by the Bowker Magazine Group of Cahners Publishing Co., a division of Reed Publishing USA., by permission.—***The Southern Review***, winter, 2001 for "The Collective Unconscious," by C. E. Murray. Copyright, 2001, by the author. Reproduced by permission of the author.—***World Literature Today***, v. 64, autumn, 1990; v. 71, summer, 1997. Copyright 1990, 1997 by the University of Oklahoma Press. Both reproduced by permission of the publisher.

COPYRIGHTED MATERIALS IN *PfS*, VOLUME 21, WERE REPRODUCED FROM THE FOLLOWING BOOKS:

Aldritch, Marcia. From "Lethal Brevity: Louise Bogan's Lyric Career," in ***Aging and Gender in Literature: Studies in Creativity***. Edited by Anne M. Wyatt-Brown and Janice Rossen. University Press of Virginia, 1993. Reprinted with permission of the University of Virginia Press.—Alegría, Claribel. From "Accounting," in ***Fugues***. Translated by D. J. Flakoll. Curbstone Press, 1993. Copyright © 1993 by Claribel Alegría. Translation © 1993 by D. J. Flakoll. All rights reserved. Reproduced by permission.—Arvio, Sarah. From "Memory," in ***Visits from the Seventh***. Alfred A. Knopf, 2002. Copyright © 2002 by Sarah Arvio. All rights reserved. Reproduced by permission of Alfred A. Knopf, Inc., a division of Random House, Inc.—Behn, Robin. From "Ten Years after Your Deliberate Drowning," in ***The Red Hour***. HarperPerennial, 1993. Copyright © 1993 by Robin Behn. All rights reserved. Reproduced by permission of HarperCollins Publishers.—Biele, Joelle. From "Rapture," in ***White Summer***. Crab Orchard Review and Southern Illinois University Press, 2002. Copyright © 2002 by Joelle Biele. All rights reserved. Reproduced by permission.—Castillo, Ana. From "While I Was Gone a War Began," in ***I Ask the Impossible: Poems***. Anchor Books, 2001. Copyright © 2000 by Ana Castillo. All rights reserved. Reproduced by permission.—Creeley, Robert. From "Fading Light," in ***Just in Time: Poems 1984-1994***. New Directions, 2001. Copyright © 1982-1994, 2001 by Robert Creeley. All rights reserved. Reproduced by permission.—Crosby, Margaret B. From "Claribel Alegría," in ***Dictionary of Literary Biography, Vol. 145, Modern Latin-American Fiction Writers, Second Series***. Edited by William Luis and Ann Gonzalez. Gale Research, 1994. Copyright © 1994 by Gale Research Inc. All rights reserved. Reproduced by permission.—Davis, William V. From "Elizabeth Spires," in ***Dictionary of Literary Biography, Vol. 120, American Poets Since World War II, Third Series***. Edited by R. S. Gwynn. Gale Research, 1992. Copyright © 1992 by Gale Research Inc. All rights reserved. Reproduced by permission.—De La Fuente, Patricia. From "Ana Castillo," in ***Dictionary of Literary Biography, Vol. 122, Chicano Writers, Second Series***. Edited by Francisco A. Lomeli and Carl R. Shirley. Gale, 1992. Copyright © 1992 by Gale Research Inc. All rights reserved. Reproduced by permission.—Doak, SuAnne. From "Stephen Dunn," in ***Dictionary of Literary Biography, Vol. 105, American Poets Since World War II, Second Series***. Edited by R. S. Gwynn. Gale Research, 1991. Copyright © 1991 by Gale Research Inc. Reproduced by permission.—Engelbert, Jo Anne. From "Claribel Alegría and the Elegiac Tradition," in ***Claribel Alegría and Central American Literature***. Edited by Sandra M. Boschetto-Sandoval and Marcia Phillips McGowan. Ohio University Center for International Studies, 1994. Reproduced by permission.—Faas, Ekbert. From "Robert Creeley," in ***Dictionary of Literary Biography, Vol. 16, The Beats: Literary Bohemians in Postwar America*** . Edited by Ann Charters. Gale, 1983. Copyright © 1983 by Gale Research Company. Reproduced by permission.—Farrokhzaad, Foroogh. From "Rebirth," in ***A Rebirth***. Translated by David Martin. Mazda Publishers, 1997. Reproduced by permission.—Ford, Arthur L. From "Form as Fact," in ***Robert Creeley***. Twayne Publishers, 1978. Copyright © 1978 G. K. Hall & Co. All rights reserved. Reproduced by permission of The Gale Group.—Gómez-Vega, Ibis. From "Ana Castillo," in ***Dictionary of Literary Biography, Vol. 227, American Novelists Since World War II, Sixth Series***. Edited by James R. Giles and Wanda H. Giles. Gale, 2000. Copyright © 2000 by The Gale Group. All rights reserved. Reproduced by permission.—Grennan, Eamon. From "Station," in ***Relations: New and Selected Poems***. Graywolf Press, 1998. Copyright © 1998 by Eamon Grennan. All rights reserved. Reproduced by permission.—Gunn, Thom. From "Small Persistent Difficulties," in ***Robert Creeley's Life and Work***. Edited by John Wilson. University of Michigan Press, 1987. Copyright © 1987 by The Times Supplements Limited. Reproduced from The Times Literary Supplement by permission.—Lyon, James K. From "Paul Celan," in ***Dictionary of Literary Biography, Vol. 69, Contemporary German Fiction Writers, First Series***. Edited by Wolfgang D. Elfe and James Hardin. Gale, 1988. Copyright © 1998 by Gale Research Inc. Reproduced by permission.—Malroux, Claire. From "Morning Walk," in ***Edge***. Translated by Marilyn Hacker. Wake Forest University Press, 1996. Copyright © 1996 by Claire Malroux. Translation copyright © 1996 by Marilyn Hacker. All rights reserved. Reproduced by permission.—Millier, Brett C. From "Louise Bogan," in ***Dictionary of Literary Biography, Vol. 169, American Poets Since World War II, Fifth Series***. Edited by Joseph Conte. Gale, 1996. Copyright © 1996 by Gale Research. All rights reserved. Reproduced by permission.—Mills, Kathryn Oliver. From "Charles Baudelaire," in ***Dictionary*** *of Literary Biography, Vol. 217, Nineteenth-Century French Poets*. Edited by Robert Beum. Gale, 1999. Copyright © 2000 by The Gale Group. All rights reserved. Reproduced by permission.—Pequeño Glazier, Loss. From "Robert Creeley," in ***Dictionary of Literary Biography, Vol. 169, American Poets Since World War II, Fifth Series*** . Edited by Joseph Conte. Gale, 1996. Copyright © 1996 by Gale Research. All rights reserved. Reproduced by permission.—Rodríguez, Ana Patricia. From "Claribel Alegría," in ***Dictionary of Literary Biography, Vol. 283, Modern Spanish American Poets, First Series***. Edited by María. Salgado. Gale, 2003. Copyright © 2003 by Gale. All rights reserved. Reproduced by permission.—Shloss, Carol. From "Louise Bogan," in ***Dictionary of Literary Biography, Vol. 45, American Poets, 1880-1945, First Series***. Edited by Peter Quartermain. Gale, 1986. Copyright © 1986 by Gale Research Inc. Reproduced by permission.—Swir, Anna. From "Maternity," in ***Talking to My Body***. Translated by Czeslaw Milosz and Leonard Nathan. Copper Canyon Press, 1996. Copyright © 1996 by Czeslaw Milosz and Leonard Nathan. All rights reserved. Reproduced by permission.—0Tranströmer, Tomas. From "Answers to Letters," in ***New Collected Poems***. Translated by Robin Fulton. Bloodaxe Books, 1997. Copyright © Tomas Tranströmer 1987, 1997. Translations copyright © Robin Fulton 1987, 1997. All rights reserved. Reproduced by permission.

PHOTOGRAPHS AND ILLUSTRATIONS APPEARING IN *PfS*, VOLUME 21, WERE RECEIVED FROM THE FOLLOWING SOURCES:

Alegría, Claribel, photograph by Joe Kohen. AP/Wide World Photos.—Arvio, Sarah. © Judith Vivell.—Behn, Robin, photograph. Courtesy of Robin Behn.—Biele, Joelle, photograph. © Kirk Siegwarth.—Bogan, Louise, photograph. © Bettmann/Corbis.—Breaking wave, photograph by David Pu'u. © David Pu'u/Corbis.—Castillo, Ana, photograph. Arte Publico Press Archives, University of Houston. Reproduced by permission of the publisher.—Creeley, Robert, photograph. © Christopher Felver/Corbis.—Dunn, Stephen, April 16, 2001, in Port Republic, N. J., holding his Pulitzer poetry prize volume of original verses, photograph by Chris Polk. AP/Wide World Photos.—Fumes and smoke fill the air and Israeli artillerymen hold their ears while laying down a barrage on Syrian positions, Syrian-Israeli border, October 12, 1973, photograph. © Bettmann/Corbis.—Grennan, Eamon, photograph. Francis G. Mayer.—Lodz ghetto Jewish people, walking to the train station, where they will be deported by Auschwitz, August, 1944, photograph. USHMM Photo Archives.—Machu Picchu, Peru, ca. 1970-1995, photograph by Roman Soumar. © Corbis.—Malroux, Claire, photograph. © Jerry Bauer. Reproduced by permission.—Portrait of French poet, Charles Baudelaire, photograph. © Bettmann/Corbis.—Sailor sails towards an island in the San Blas Archipelago, photograph. © Richard Hamilton Smith/Corbis.—Spires, Elizabeth, photograph. © Jerry Bauer.—Swir, Anna, photograph. Copper Canyon Press.—The central square of Hamadan, Iran, 1950, photograph. Hulton Archive/Getty Images.—Transtromer, Tomas Goesta, photograph. © Bassouls Sophie/Corbis Sygma.

Contributors

Bryan Aubrey: Aubrey holds a Ph.D. in English and has published many articles on twentieth-century literature. Entry on *Station. Original essay on Station.*

Laura Carter: Carter is currently employed as a freelance writer. Original essays on *Late and Deep, Maternity,* and *Rapture.*

Kate Covintree: Covintree is a graduate student and expository writing instructor in the Writing, Literature, and Publishing department at Emerson College. Original essay on *Ghazal.*

Patrick Donnelly: Donnelly is a poet, editor, and teacher. His first book of poems titled *The Charge* was published by the Ausable Press in 2003. Entry on *The Reverse Side.* Original essay on *The Reverse Side.*

Joyce Hart: Hart has degrees in English and creative writing and is a freelance writer and author of several books. Entries on *A Rebirth* and *Ten Years after Your Deliberate Drowning.* Original essays on *A Rebirth* and *Ten Years after Your Deliberate Drowning.*

Pamela Steed Hill: Hill is the author of a poetry collection, has published widely in literary journals, and is an editor for a university publications department. Entries on *Ghazal* and *Rapture.* Original essays on *Ghazal, Memory, Rapture,* and *Ten Years after Your Deliberate Drowning.*

Anna Maria Hong: Hong earned her master of fine arts degree in creative writing from the University of Texas's Michener Center for Writers. Her poems have appeared in several literary journals. Entry on *Morning Walk.* Original essay on *Morning Walk.*

David Kelly: Kelly is an instructor of creative writing and literature. Entry on *Hymn to Beauty.* Original essay on *Hymn to Beauty.*

Lois Kerschen: Kerschen is a freelance writer and part-time English instructor. Entries on *Maternity* and *While I Was Gone a War Began.* Original essays on *Maternity* and *While I Was Gone a War Began.*

Sheri E. Metzger: Metzger has a doctorate in English Renaissance literature and teaches literature and drama at the University of New Mexico, where she is a lecturer in the University Honors Program. Entries on *Accounting* and *Words for Departure.* Original essays on *Accounting* and *Words for Departure.*

Frank Pool: Pool is a published poet and reviewer and a teacher of high school English. Entries on *Fading Light and* Late and Deep. Original essays on *Fading Light and Late and Deep.*

Mary Potter: Potter is a university writing instructor and fiction writer living in San Francisco. Original essay on *Accounting.*

Lisa Trow: Trow is a published poet and writer. Entry on *Memory.* Original essay on *Memory.*

Scott Trudell: Trudell is a freelance writer with a bachelor's degree in English literature. Entry on *Answers to Letters.* Original essay on *Answers to Letters.*

Accounting

Claribel Alegría

1993

Claribel Alegría's poem "Accounting" was first published in English by Curbstone Press in 1993 as part of a collection of poems in her book, *Fugues*. Although only twenty-six lines in length, the poem is saturated with a collection of autobiographical images as diverse as her happiness as a child, playing in puddles of water, and her grief at her mother's death. Alegría refers to the vignettes in her poem as "electrical instants." These snapshots of her life are only brief moments, but they tell the poet's own story. The title, "Accounting," can refer to the systematic presentation of the data that comprises her life. That is what accountants do. They examine financial data, list and interpret it, and balance the account. This is what Alegría has done with this poem. Her poem is an elegy that provides an accounting of her memories over a large span of years. The events and people mentioned in the poem are representative of several of the locations in which she has lived, and thus her memories become the source material for the poem. When Alegría wrote "Accounting," she had been writing poetry for sixty-two years. This poem appears in one of her latest collections of poetry, and so its publication also serves as a reflection of her creative life.

Author Biography

Claribel Alegría was born May 12, 1924 in Esteli, Nicaragua. When Alegría was nine months old, the

Claribel Alegría

family fled the occupation of Nicaragua for El Salvador. Alegría grew up in Santa Ana, El Salvador, and attended a progressive school, Jose Ingenieros, which was named after the Argentinean philosopher. From the time she was nine months old until she was eighteen, Alegría and her family lived as exiles from their native Nicaragua.

When Alegría was only six years old, she began to create her own poems. Her mother carefully wrote down the poems that Alegría dictated. Then, when she was fourteen, Alegría read Rainer Maria Rilke's, *Letters to a Young Poet*. Rilke's letters, written in 1903, had a profound effect on Alegría's young life. In virtually every interview ever given, she has recounted how, upon reading Rilke's letters, she suddenly knew that she wanted to be a poet. By the time she was sixteen, Alegría was writing poetry with all the seriousness of an established poet, even though she was still unpublished. Finally, in 1941, when she was seventeen years old, she published her first poems in *Repertorio Americano*, a Central American newspaper's cultural supplement. Then, two years later, Alegría was admitted to a girls' finishing school in Hammond, Louisiana.

In 1944, Alegría moved to Washington, DC, and enrolled at Georgetown University. She found a job as a translator at the Pan-American Union, studied for her classes at night, and three afternoons a week, studied with the poet, Juan Ramon Jiménez. As part of her study, Alegría was forced to concentrate on learning formal poetic forms. She also worked on becoming a more disciplined poet. After three years of studying with Jiménez, he chose twenty-two of her poems, and they became her first published book of poetry, *Ring of Silence*, which was published in 1948. Also in 1948, Alegría graduated from George Washington University with a bachelor's degree in philosophy and letters.

In December 1947, she had married Darwin J. Flakoll, a student at Georgetown University, who was completing a graduate degree. In time, Alegría and Flakoll had four children: Maya, Patricia, Karen, and Erik. During the next thirty years, Alegría and her family moved many times, but even through all the moves, she continued to write poems and short stories. Some of the works that she published during these years include several poetry collections, such as *Vigils* (1953), *Aquarius* (1955), and *Guest of my Time* (1961). Alegría also wrote novels, but even with a creative change to writing novels, Alegría never abandoned her poetry. A 1978 book of poems, *I Survive*, won the Casa de las Americas Prize in 1978.

Alegría was finally able to return to Nicaragua to live in 1979, when the Sandinista rebels gained power. After the move, Alegría and her husband wrote a history of the revolution titled *Nicaragua: The Sandinista Revolution; A Political Chronicle 1855–1979* (1982). A pivotal event in Alegría's life occurred in 1980 when Archbishop Romero was assassinated in El Salvador. Alegría spoke out against this assassination and the death squads in El Salvador. As a result, she was forbidden to return to El Salvador to visit her parents. Alegría continued to write poetry and in 1993 published *Fugues*, from which the poem "Accounting" is taken. Her husband's death in April 1995 was depicted by Alegría in *Sorrow* (1999). *Casting Off*, a collection of poems, was published in 2003. Alegría lives in Managua, Nicaragua.

Poem Text

In the sixty-eight years
I have lived
there are a few electrical instants:
the happiness of my feet
skipping puddles
six hours in Macchu Pichu
the ten minutes necessary

to lose my virginity
the buzzing of the telephone
while awaiting the death of my mother
the hoarse voice
announcing the death
of Monsignor Romero
fifteen minutes in Delft
the first wail of my daughter
I don't know how many years
dreaming of my people's liberation
certain immortal deaths
the eyes of that starving child
your eyes bathing me with love
one forget-me-not afternoon
and in this sultry hour
the urge to mould myself
into a verse
a shout
a fleck of foam.

Poem Summary

Overview

Alegría's poem "Accounting" is an accounting of the important events of her life. The first few lines tell the reader that the poem's author remembers certain events in her life that she defines as "electrical instants." What follows are vignettes from the author's memory, beginning with her childhood recollections. Alegría's memories make the leap from skipping puddles to losing her virginity in only a few lines. She also recalls painful memories—the death of her mother, the assassination of Archbishop Romero, and the occupation of Nicaragua. Coupled with memories of loss are memories of love. Alegría compresses a lifetime of events into the few moments that a reader takes to study the poem. She dissolves the barrier of time and reduces her existence into twenty-six lines.

It is sometimes a mistake to assume the author and the poem's narrator are one person, but in this case, there are several clues that indicate that Alegría is offering autobiographical details from her own life in this poem. The speaker of the poem tells the reader that she is sixty-eight years old, and Alegría would have been sixty-eight when the poem was written. Because Alegría relied upon her husband, Darwin Flakoll, to translate her books from Spanish into English, the publication date would be at least a year after the poem's composition, and so the reader can assume that "Accounting" was written in 1992, although not published until 1993. There are other confirmed autobiographical details present in the poem, as well. Alegría had been prohibited from returning to El Salvador after she spoke out publicly and condemned the assassination of Archbishop Romero. She was not permitted to re-enter the country even to visit her dying mother, and thus, Alegría would have been forced to wait for news of her mother's death by telephone. Alegría was also a vocal critic of the military occupation of Nicaragua. All of these details suggest that Alegría and the poet narrator are the same person. Knowing this information makes appreciating and understanding the poem as an autobiographical accounting easier for the reader.

Lines 1–3

The opening lines of "Accounting" offer the background information needed to understand the poem. These three lines also explain the narrative that follows. Alegría tells the reader that she is sixty-eight years old. As people age, they often reminisce about the life they have led. Alegría is engaging in this process of reflection. At the same time, the title makes clear that the poem is an accounting of her life. She will chronicle her life and list "a few electrical instants." "Electrical" suggests these are moments of power, perhaps moments that shocked her. They are also moments that left a mark upon her psyche. The use of "instants" makes clear that the memories are just moments of time, vignettes of events that when recalled pass through her mind in an instant.

Lines 4–8

The first of Alegría's memories is the happiness she felt skipping through puddles. Presumably, this first memory is of her childhood, when playing in puddles after a fresh rainfall brings the sort of carefree enjoyment that the poet describes as "happiness." Alegría quickly jumps to another memory, this time a visit to the Inca ruins at Macchu Pichu in the mountains of Peru. It would be possible to consider that a childhood trip, perhaps a vacation taken with parents, created wonderful memories that are recalled many years later. However, there is no evidence that this poem's accounting is chronological. Alegría's husband was with the United States foreign service for many years and the family moved frequently, visiting many different countries. The family lived in Chile for a period of time. While there is no record that they lived in Peru, they did live in Central America, and so the visit that the author recalls might have occurred during her marriage, rather than during childhood. The ruins of Macchu Pichu are breathtaking, and regardless of whether Alegría visited as an adolescent or as an adult, the visit would have been unforgettable. Her six hours at the site indicates a day trip, though, and that she did not spend the night there. Whether taking the train and bus or walking the Inca Trail, the trip is a long one, and with transportation, a visitor has only five or six hours to actually spend at the ruins if trying to do the trip in one day. Visitors who spend the night near the site can enter at dawn and spend all day.

Lines 7 and 8 recall the memory of the author's loss of virginity. No age is given, but the small amount of time, only ten minutes, suggests that perhaps she was young. The quick fumbling of youth might be brief, but Alegría counts it as one of the moments that left a mark upon her. It is the awakening of sexuality, and it marks the end of childhood and the transition to being an adult. Such an event is "electrical," since sexuality also brings greater responsibilities and, eventually, children who will change her life forever.

Lines 9–13

In lines 9 and 10, Alegría jumps ahead to the death of her mother. The buzzing of the telephone has special significance for Alegría, since it has been the instrument of bad news on several occasions. Because the government has forbidden her to reenter Nicaragua, the author must await the phone call that will tell her of her mother's death. She wanted to be with her mother, who had asked for her daughter, but Alegría's brothers telephoned and told her not to come since they feared she would be arrested and murdered. The telephone also brought her news of the death of Monsignor Romero. The voice is hoarse, grief-stricken at the assassination of this brave man. When Archbishop Oscar Arnulfo Romero was assassinated on March 24, 1980, Alegría was in Paris, preparing to give a poetry reading at the Sorbonne. She abandoned her reading and instead spoke about the murder of the prelate. Romero had spoken out against the El Salvadorian death squads that functioned with government acquiescence. Alegría admired Romero and was distraught at his death. She lists this event immediately after the death of her mother, and like her mother's death, it is an event that marked her permanently. Romero's death was also the beginning of Alegría's protest writing, and so it is crucial in defining her as a writer. One other aspect of Archbishop Romero's death proved to be very crucial to Alegría's life. When she spoke at the Sorbonne, Alegría's tribute to the slain churchman and her condemnation of the death squads angered the El Salvadorian government. The result was a twelve-year self-imposed exile. If she returned, she would be arrested. As mentioned previously, Alegría did not even dare return for her mother's funeral in 1982.

Lines 14–17

Line 14 remains a mystery. Since Alegría has not published her memoirs, not all events in her life are known. Since she and her husband traveled extensively, they may have visited Delft, Holland, at some period. They may even have lived there briefly, but the brevity of the period mentioned indicates that it is an event in Delft, perhaps something intensely personal that warrants mention. Such a brief time, "fifteen minutes in Delft," does suggest an event important enough to be one of the "few electrical instants" in the poet's life. Of line 15, Alegría gave birth to three daughters, but it seems most likely that in this line she is reflecting on the birth of the first. She says, "my daughter," and thus signifies only one, likely the first. Readers will note the use of "my" and ponder its meaning, but mothers often feel a special connection to a daughter that is revealed in the possessive use of "my" rather than "our."

The next two lines signal an abrupt change of thought. Lines 16 and 17 capture Alegría's commitment to Nicaragua's liberation. Nicaragua was the country of her birth, and although she was only an infant when her family was forced to flee, she had always felt a deep connection to the country. Her father worked to support rebellions in their homeland, and Alegría grew up knowing that all Nicaraguans bore a special responsibility to oppose the oppression in that country. She was associated with the Sandinista National Liberation Front, the guerilla movement that took control of the Nicaraguan government in 1979. After the rebels gained control, Alegría and her family were finally able to move back to Nicaragua. The move was the culmination of many years of hard work, and as she notes in line 17, "dreaming."

Lines 18–21

These four lines offer an opposition in images. Alegría wrote poetry that exposed the injustice of government, the inequities of economy, and the inequitable results of a patriarchal system that repressed one half of the population. The "immortal deaths" of line 18 are the deaths that endure forever. They are not forgotten, nor are "the eyes of that starving child." The poet cannot forget the injustice of the world. This poem lists a "few electrical instants," but it also lists the events that marked the poet and that cannot be erased. She has seen political oppression's effects on the individual, thus an oppressive state is no longer a vague entity but a child starving to death.

In contrast to starvation and death, Alegría moves now to the opposite image, that of love. After his death in 1995, Alegría wrote another book of poetry, *Sorrow*, a book filled with a longing for what had been lost that defies description. These poems are filled with immense pain and grief. Alegría's husband is clearly the "your" in line 20. It is his eyes that bathe her in love. Line 21 is a continuation of the previous line and the two lines should be read as one sentence: the poet remembers "your eyes bathing me with love / one forget-me-not afternoon." There were many moments of love in a marriage that lasted nearly forty-eight years, but some moments are always more intense, more memorable. Readers cannot know what "electrical instant" the poet cites, but its importance to the writer is made very clear by its inclusion in this poem.

Lines 22–26

The last four lines of the poem recall that Alegría is also the poet. This poem is the autobiographical musing of a poet, a craftsman of words. Lines 23 and 24 tell the reader of the poet's urge to make her life a poem. The reader also learns that the poet is writing in the heat of the day, in the afternoon. But we also learn more about this period of composition, since the poet refers to this time as "sultry," a romantic connotation rather than the description of oppressively hot or sweltering temperatures that the word suggests. The writing of Alegría's life is, therefore, linked to a more intimate atmosphere. It is more personal than just composing a list of events. The composition of this poem was an "urge," a force that impelled her to compress her life into these few lines, perhaps a need to escape the heat and mould herself into her poem. She used the British spelling of mold, to "mould" these events. Her use of the British spelling may reflect only that her international background centers her language. On the other hand, this spelling of mould is most often associated with death and the return to earth. Perhaps as Alegría nears seventy years of age, she also begins to reflect on death. Certainly there have been several references to death in this poem, and in this case, the poet may "mould" herself into the poem, as the dead moulder into earth. The poet becomes the poem and is thus preserved for eternity.

The final two lines continue this evolution into the void. Initially, the voice is "a shout." The poet's words can be heard clearly, but the words have been compressed into just one sound. Just as she had compressed her life, she now compresses her poem. But even that shout is transitory. Soon all that remains of the poet is "a fleck of foam," as she dissolves into nothingness. The end of the poem is cyclical. Alegría began this confessional by noting her age, and she ends it by disappearing into the void. The poem now contains her life, it reveals her story, and finally, the poet has been dissolved into the language of poetry.

Themes

Change

Alegría's poem, "Accounting," assembles the major events in the poet's life. Because these events occur over a wide space of time, they reflect the author at different periods of her life. The young girl who skipped puddles is also the same woman who later grieved at the death of loved ones and who worked so resolutely for her country's freedom. The poet has not only grown older, she has changed from a child to a woman, from lighthearted play to social activism. In the final lines of the poem, the poet prepares for one last change—her own death. At that hour, she will not cease to be. Like many poets before her, she has seen that she will live on in her work. More than her memories are preserved; she is preserved within the poem's lines. When she moulds herself into these lines, she follows in the footsteps of poets as great as William Shakespeare, who also recognized in his Sonnet 55 ("Not marble nor the gilded monuments") that he would live forever in verse.

Endurance

Alegría's poem is a testament to her ability to endure and to the power that it takes for anyone to endure tragedy. She was born into a country of conflict. As an infant, Alegría's father opposed the United States marine occupation of Nicaragua. The family was harassed and even fired upon by armed soldiers. Even though Alegría was only an infant when the family finally fled Nicaragua, she grew up understanding that she was a refugee and an exile from the country of her birth. In lines 16 and 17, the poet poignantly recalls the wait for her country's liberation to become a reality: "I don't know how many years / dreaming of my people's liberation." The use of "dreaming" signifies the depth of yearning as she endured this long wait. She waited fifty-five years.

Topics For Further Study

- Make a list of ten to twelve of your own memories. These should be the things that first come to mind when you think of your life. You might try to pick one or two items from each of the past several years. After you have a list, arrange them in some order of importance. This order does not have to be chronological, but it can be. When you have brought some sort of order to your list, rewrite it as a poem. Alegría writes her poem as a narrative lyric, but you can use a different poetic format, if you wish.
- Research the life of Archbishop Oscar Romero, whom Alegría mentions in her poem. Consider why she thought him such an important figure in trying to call attention to human rights violations in El Salvador.
- Choose one poem by another Central American poet, and compare his or her work to the poetry of Alegría. What similarities do you notice? Are there differences in theme or content? You might consider using poetry by Magdalena Gomez, Sandra Maria Esteves, or Ricardo Morales.
- Research the role of both men and women in the Nicaraguan revolution. Consider in what ways the contributions of women differed from those of men.
- Alegría's poem is a memoir, recounting the events of her life. Most people who write memoirs do so as prose writing. Choose a memoir by any other writer and discuss the differences between prose and verse memoirs.

Identity

Few people think at great depth about the elements that make up their identity. And yet, we are all the composite identity of the important events of our lives. Alegría acknowledges this fact in her poem, "Accounting." In the opening lines of the poem she reveals her age and that she will list the defining moments of her life, the "few electrical instants" that marked her. These moments that marked her forever are the moments that created the adult who emerged from that moment of happiness in which the child skipped puddles. Alegría's identity is an accumulated self-awareness that she is the result of a multifaceted life lived in many places, whether Delft or Macchu Pichu. She is the result of the events that occurred in her life, whether the birth of a child or the death of a parent. All events that occurred in Alegría's life are considered collectively and become essential components of her self-identity. Alegría's poem reveals her identity to her readers in an intensely personal manner.

Human Rights

Lines 12 and 13, as well as lines 17, 18, and 19 of "Accounting" reveal what a huge part of Alegría's life has been devoted to human rights issues. In a poem of 26 lines, almost one fifth of the lines that comprise the poet's life are centered on her concern for the peoples' right to exist freely, to protest injustice, to offer aid to those most in need. The description in line 11 of "the hoarse voice" that telephoned Alegría to announce the death of Archbishop Romero reveals both the anguish that the caller felt at having to make this call, and the poet's commitment to the ideals for which the archbishop worked. Alegría was in Paris when she was called. The effort to locate her at this place suggests that her work was important within the context of Archbishop Romero's human rights work. The remaining three lines in the poem, which deal with human rights issues, are equally convincing of Alegría's resolution to improve her country. She has dreamed "of my people's liberation" and is equally aware of the "immortal deaths" and the "starving child" who need an advocate. Alegría is as marked by her commitment to human rights as she is by any other event of her lifetime.

Memory

Memory is the foundation of Alegría's poem, "Accounting." The poem is a list of the poet's most important memories, drawn from a lifetime of memories. Each human being forms new memories almost constantly, but only certain memories are retained and recalled as significant. The reader knows that the memories recalled for this poem are important because the poet has written in line three that these are the "few electrical instants" of a lifetime of memories. Memory can be a powerful tool of growth and change, and Alegría's list of memories reveals how she has grown from child to woman, from happiness to grief, and finally, to love.

Wisdom

Alegría never mentions knowledge or the growth of wisdom in her poem, and yet this theme is implicit in any discussion of this poem. The poet tells readers that "In the sixty-eight years / I have lived / there are a few electrical instants" worth recalling. The poet is reflecting on a lifetime of events, places, and people. The title of the poem, "Accounting," suggests something about this process of having reached a position of wisdom in the author's life. The process of accounting is the systematic presentation and interpretation of accumulated data. For Alegría the process of amassing memories—sifting though them, choosing those of singular importance, the "electrical instants," and finally understanding their importance in her life—is similar to the work that an accountant does in assessing financial worth. Alegría is assessing her worth and defining it by key events. To finally understand the work of a lifetime, she also needed to have gained the wisdom to appreciate all that she had accomplished.

Style

Committed Generation

La generacion comprometida, also known as the Committed Generation, was created as an attempt by the intellectual sectors of the middle and upper classes of Central America as a way to use literature to achieve social justice. Alegría's ideological approach to her poetry reflects this literary movement. "Accounting" contains references to both social justice and human rights issues.

Elegy

In its origins in Greek and Latin poetry, the elegy was a meditation that might focus on death, but might equally call to mind love or almost any list of events. During the Elizabethan period, the English used the elegy as a love poem, often as a lover's complaint. During the seventeenth century, the elegy was most commonly used as a poem of mourning to honor the dead and to reflect upon a life that had ended. Since that time, the elegy has also been used as a poem to reflect on solemn events. In "Accounting," Alegría uses the elegy to reflect on her life. Just as an elegy might honor the dead, for this poem, the poet uses the format to evaluate and consider the events of her life.

Imagery

Imagery refers to the described images in a poem. The relationships between images can suggest important meanings in a poem; with imagery, the poet uses language and specific words to create meaning. For instance, "skipping puddles" suggests an image of a child at play, perhaps just after a rain. The "first wail of my daughter" creates an image of birth and the joy that a new child brings. Images allow the reader to "see" the events of a poet's life, rather than just read about them.

Memoir

A memoir is a form of autobiographical writing that deals with the memories of someone who has either witnessed important events or has taken part in significant events. Alegría's poem is an abbreviated form of the memoir, in the form of a poem rather than prose. However, the meaning is the same. The author is revealing her life to an audience of readers, who will use this material to learn something about the writer. In general, memoirs are told in chronological order; however, Alegría has chosen to list the important events of her life in an order than has special significance to her.

Narrative Poem

A narrative poem is a poem that tells a story. In "Accounting," the poem tells the story of Alegría's life. She offers small vignettes of her life, memories of the most "electrical" moments that shaped the adult she became. In this case, Alegría's narrative poem functions very much like an autobiography, except that the poet does not always list these events in chronological order.

Free Verse

The word "poem" is generally assigned to mean a literary composition distinguished by emotion, imagination, and meaning. But the term *poem* may also fit certain designated formulas, such as a sonnet or a couplet, which are defined by a specific length and or a particular rhyme scheme. A poem may also include divisions into stanzas, a sort of paragraph-like division of ideas, and may also include a specific number of stressed or unstressed syllables in each line. Alegría's poem is not divided into separate sections; instead it flows from one word and phrase into the next, without breaks for punctuation or stanza in a free verse form. Not one word is wasted in this poem. At just over 100 words, each word has to have significance as it flows to the next word. Modern poetry offers the poet a chance to experiment with style, since poetic style is no longer defined by the strict formulas of the early poets, but even the contemporary poet still strives for an impassioned response to his or her poem. Like the earliest poetry, modern poetry is still highly individualistic.

Historical Context

A Long History of Civil Conflict

Alegría's "Accounting" is the poet's reflection upon the events and people that fill a lifetime. The content of the poem reflects an indeterminate point in time and the locations are many. Because of this, one way to approach her poetry is to try and understand the place that Alegría most closely identifies as her homeland, as well as its crucial influence on her work. Nicaragua was colonized by the Spanish early in the sixteenth century, but it gained its independence from Spain in 1821, as did all of Central America. After 1855, the United States took an active part in controlling Nicaragua, with U.S. troops actively training and supervising the Nicaraguan military forces, which in turn controlled the government of Nicaragua. Alegría's father opposed this U.S. military interference and supported the rebel forces, and as a result, the family was forced to flee in 1925. The rebellions in Nicaragua did not end with the establishment of a U.S.-supported dictator, General Somoza, in 1934, but they were better suppressed under his leadership. After Somoza was assassinated in 1956, his sons continued as dictators, and like their father, bled the country of its wealth and resources. As the Somoza regime became wealthier, the people became poorer and more ravaged by the lack of the most basic necessities. The Samozas allocated little money to education, and since most Nicaraguan children needed to work to help support their families, few children were able to attend the few schools that were available. The government spent almost no money on basic infrastructure. Besides the malnutrition that afflicted the poor, lack of proper sanitation and limited access to health care led to many outbreaks of dysentery, which was a leading cause of death. Children also died of many of the diseases that modern medicine now prevents, such as tetanus and measles. Because of the economic oppression of the people, opposition to the Samoza regime increased.

Alegría actively supported the Sandinista rebels, who succeeded in overthrowing the old Somoza dictatorship and seizing control in July 1979. In response, the United States funded a counter-revolutionary group, the Contras, withheld economic aid, and imposed a trade embargo that further decimated the Nicaraguan economy. The civil wars in Nicaragua did not end until 1990. The rebellion cost was high, with at least 50,000 dead during the years of fighting. There were also more than 100,000 wounded, and as many as 40,000 children were orphaned. It is little wonder that Alegría mentions the "eyes of that starving child" in her poem.

Education and Health Care

After the Somoza period ended, the new Sandinista government set about to improve life for the citizens of Nicaragua. This is when Alegría returned to help rebuild her country. One area that received immediate attention was education. Before the Sandinista government took control, only about 22 percent of children completed the minimum six years of primary schooling. Because secondary education was private and very expensive, very few children enrolled in secondary schools. Within five years, the new government had doubled the number of students enrolled in schools. With an increased budget for education, new schools were built and new teachers added. There was even an outreach program to educate adults through informal night schools, called Popular Education Cooperatives. The number of students continuing on to university study more than tripled in this short space of time. The emphasis on university study focused more on technology, agriculture, and medicine, rather than on the humanities or art.

It is worth noting that the U.S.-supported Contra wars forced cuts in education that eliminated many of the early gains created by the Sandinista government. This was also true of health care spending, which initially created improvements for the Nicaraguan people. Under the Somoza regime, wealthy upper-class Nicaraguans had access to private physicians or could go abroad to receive their medical care. A very small number of government workers comprised the middle class and had access to the Nicaraguan Social Security Institute, a sort of health maintenance organization that appropriated

Compare & Contrast

- **1990s Nicaragua:** In May 1997, university students begin a more than two-month protest of the government's decision to cut university budgets by nine million dollars. While the protests are initially peaceful, they soon escalate into street wars with many injuries and arrests resulting.

  1990s United States: While in the past there have been some localized student protests on U.S. campuses, most frequently about tuition raises or cuts in student aid, few students undertake a lengthy months-long protest over budget concerns. In recent years, protests over U.S. involvement in foreign wars elicit the strongest non-economic based protests on university campuses.

- **1990s Nicaragua:** In 1998, Nicaragua has the highest teen pregnancy rate of any country in Central America. It is thought that forty to forty-five percent of all pregnancies involve girls aged fourteen to nineteen. Pregnant girls are not able to complete their education, and are thus unable to find employment to support their children. Teenage pregnancy also results in social exclusion and rejection by the girl's family.

  1990s United States: Teenage and unwed pregnancies also increase in the United States during the last two decades. Many school districts encourage pregnant teenagers to stay in school and, in many instances, offer special programs to adapt schooling needs to fit the requirements of the pregnant teenager. In addition, several local community programs work to provide health care and social services to single mothers.

- **1990s Nicaragua:** In 1997, the government of Nicaragua is accused of trying to silence opposition radio and newspaper outlets. In part, this practice results from broadcast and print accounts of the student protests, which are marked by episodes of police brutality. This effort to close down opposition media outlets fails after the public demands an investigation.

  1990s United States: While the government does not try and close down media outlets that provide criticism of the government, there is questioning of the large corporate ownership of media outlets that are thought to restrict free speech. For instance, in many cities, multiple radio stations, multiple television stations, and local newspapers are often owned by the same large corporations. The result is that diverse opinions are oftentimes not heard.

- **1990s Nicaragua:** While abortion is illegal in Nicaragua, it is actually quite common. Wealthier women have easier access to medical abortion, while poor women are at greater risk in seeking more dangerous alternatives.

  1990s United States: Abortion continues to be legal in the United States, although it continues to be a controversial topic. In addition to legal challenges, there are also a number of violent attacks on abortion clinics and doctors who perform abortions.

- **1990s Nicaragua:** The number of women who are employed outside the home in Nicaragua continues to increase since the early 1980s. In general, women work in low-wage jobs, especially in service-type employment, as domestic workers and as agricultural workers. In spite of so many women now in the work force, few men assist in the domestic chores of home, and so women continue to be responsible for maintaining the household even if they choose to also work outside the home.

  1990s United States: More women than ever hold managerial positions or serve as directors of major corporations. However, wages for women are still roughly 30 percent less than for men performing comparable jobs.

The ruins of Macchu Pichu in Peru

about half of the national health care budget. The remainder of the population, about 90 percent of all Nicaraguans, made due with public clinics, which were poorly funded and staffed. The Sandinista government unified the health care system, increased the budget for public health care, and improved access for the poorest members of the population. Community health care also improved and treatments for dysentery and inoculations against common childhood diseases were put in place. Unlike the improvements in education, many of the improvements in health care survived the Contra wars. Although there were some setbacks, infant mortality decreased and the population as a whole was healthier. In particular, issues relating to improving education and healthcare were priorities of the Sandinista government, which Alegría had worked so hard to support.

Critical Overview

Alegría's book of poetry, *Fugues*, received a generally unfavorable review by the anonymous writer at *Publishers Weekly*, who reviewed the book for the October 18, 1993 publication. Among this writer's criticisms was the length of many of the poems, which are described as "mere aphorisms." This reviewer also stated that the poems in this book were "[s]parse on imagery." The reviewer referred to these poems as "tidbits" that "ask little from readers, and give little back." An additional complaint focuses on the poet's use of classical figures from Greek mythology, whom according to the reviewer "seem wholly out of place in both her [Alegría's] physical and emotional landscape." The poems in *Fugues* were translated by the author's husband. This reviewer cites Flakoll's translation as one aspect of the book that does not work, calling the translation "littered with cliches." This review of Alegría's book ends with the admonition that readers who "open this book expecting the work of a master" will instead find a book that "reads like a naive first collection." At the end of the review, the book is given a D grade.

Alegría's publisher, Curbstone Press, also provides limited reviews of the books they publish, and while they are not an unbiased source, they do include a review of *Fugues* written by poet Luisa Valenzuela, who says, "Illumination is the word that comes to mind when reading these poems." Valenzuela explains that Alegría's "simple words ... allow us to see the duality of life as one single luminous flow of love." While it would be easy to dismiss the reviews provided by Curbstone as just an effort to sell books, they support the general view of Alegría's poetry. The review of *Fugues* published by *Publishers Weekly* also contradicts the most common assessment of Alegría's body of work. In her essay, "The Volcano's Flower," Chilean poet Marjorie Agosín calls Alegría's poetry "clear and defined." Her poetry is "stirring" and it "moves us and liberates us, not just to feel but also to think." In a 1991 interview with Marcia Phillips McGowan, Alegría stated that her poetry was "subjective." Clearly, reviews of her poetry are also subjective, and so perhaps that accounts for the wide disparity in opinions of reviewers of her work.

Criticism

Sheri E. Metzger

Metzger has a doctorate in English Renaissance literature and teaches literature and drama at the University of New Mexico, where she is a lecturer in the University Honors Program. In this essay, Metzger discusses Alegría's appropriation of the classical elegiac form to memorialize her own life.

As she approaches the period that she calls "old age," Claribel Alegría responds by composing her own elegy, "Accounting," for which she uses a traditional poetic form to reflect upon the events of her life. In an interview with Bill Moyers, Alegría described this poem as having been created as a result of a period of reflection in which she asked herself, "what have been the crucial moments in my life?" In reflecting on her life, she chose "a few electrical instants" so that she could create a poem that would, as she related to Moyers, "sum up *all* my life." This poem accomplishes this goal, transforming determinate elements of time—"six hours in Macchu Pichu," "the ten minutes it took / to lose my virginity," and "fifteen minutes in Delft"—into a timeless eternity. The poet ensures with this poem that the indeterminate moments of her lifetime will not be lost when she has died. "Accounting" demonstrates Alegría's ability to transform the elegiac form to not only reflect upon the life she has lived, but also to honor that life. While the traditional mourning elegy can be used to honor and defend a life, Alegría demonstrates how the elegy can be altered to proclaim the poet's own life within the lines of her poem.

In "Accounting," Alegría composes a list of the crucial moments of her life. The people and places and the moments of joy and sorrow show individual moments from a lifetime of nearly seventy years. She inventories places she has visited, her love for a newborn child and for her spouse, and the deaths of those individuals whose presence in her life was critical in defining her experiences. In writing down these memories, Alegría reveals them to all her readers, even as she keeps them vibrant in her own life. The process for keeping her memories alive is the same for Alegría, regardless of the format used to reveal them. For instance, in a 1991 interview with Marcia Phillips McGowan, Alegría explained that one way she has been able to keep her family's memories alive was through the characters that she creates in her novels. She does this through telling stories and examining pictures, and then she incorporates these memories into her stories. Alegría does much the same thing in this poem. Alegría sifts through the memories of a lifetime, chooses fewer than a dozen, and then examines them, as she would a photo, studying each one as she arranges them into a montage that signifies her life. In this interview, Alegría tells McGowan that one of her "pervasive themes is nostalgia," and indeed, the title of one of the poems in *Fugues*, from which "Accounting" is taken, is "Nostalgia." The poet's nostalgia for the past, for the memories that she recalls in "Accounting," is an important component in defining her life. Alegría claims that it is "a great richness to recover memories" and preserve them in her writing. With "Accounting," she chooses to preserve her memories in an elegy that also honors and preserves her life for as long as her poems endure. Traditionally, an elegy can become an effective way to honor someone's life after death, but for Alegría, the elegy serves to reflect upon her life and anticipate her death.

"Clearly Alegría is four-hundred years and far removed from Renaissance English poetry, and yet, the recognition by the poet that verse can give life to that which death has removed is a view that extends beyond time and space."

Although Alegría is comfortable expressing her thoughts using an elegy, she makes it uniquely her own by challenging both the classical English and the Spanish elegiac traditions. In the classical elegiac tradition, the poem consists of a specific arrangement of lines that was notable for its use of the elegiac meter—an alternating hexameter and pentameter arrangement of stressed and unstressed syllables. Alegría dispenses with this classical form to use free verse, which is her accustomed mode of expression. She deviates from the traditional form in other ways, as well. In her essay, "Claribel Alegría and the Elegiac Tradition," Jo Anne Engelbert explores how Alegría uses the elegy in her poetry as a means to celebrate life rather than death. Engelbert begins her essay by quoting poet Pedro Salinas, who outlines some of the ways in which Central American poets use the elegiac tradition. According to Englebert, Salinas claimed that the elegy was "always, in the last analysis, a protest, a struggle against death." In fact, even if the poet appears accepting of his or her death, his or her use of poetry is designed "in order that something not perish." Thus the very use of poetry itself, counters the

What Do I Read Next?

- Published by Curbstone Press and edited and translated by Alegría and her husband, Darwin J. Flakoll, *On the Front Line: Guerilla Poems of El Salvador* (1996) is an anthology of poetry written by El Salvadorian revolutionaries.
- *Sorrow* (1999) is a collection of poetry that Alegría wrote after the death of her husband.
- In Alegría's collection *Casting Off* (2003), many of the poems deal with death and with the poet's thoughts about approaching the end of her life.
- *The Language of Life: A Festival of Poets* (1995) contains the transcripts of more than 30 interviews that Bill Moyers conducted with contemporary poets. This book is a companion to Moyer's public television series *The Language of Life*.
- *Nicaragua: The Sandinista Revolution; A Political Chronicle 1855–1979* (1982) is a nonfiction account of the revolution, written by Alegría and her husband, Flakoll.
- *Latin American Poetry: A Bilingual Anthology* (1996), edited by Stephen Tapscott, includes poetry by more than 75 Latin American poets.
- *After the Revolution: Gender and Democracy in El Salvador, Nicaragua, and Guatemala* (2001), written by Ilja A. Luciak, provides data and interviews about the democratization of guerilla movements and the link to gender inequality in this region.
- *Mothers of Heroes and Martyrs: Gender Identity Politics in Nicaragua, 1979–1999* (2001), written by Lorraine Bayard de Volo, is the story of how women who did not fight in the revolution supported it through the sacrifice of their sons.

"serene resignation" of the elegy. This inconsistency is evident in Alegría's personal elegy. "Accounting" captures the author's ambivalence to the recognition that she will be preserved for all eternity in her poem. The resignation is present but so is the urge to fight. For example, in lines 24 and 25, she writes that she is "a shout" before she disappears in "a fleck of foam."

In her interview with Moyers, Alegría explains that while the poem "would sum up" her life, "I also wanted to cry out to everybody, a desperate cry telling them what has happened." At the same time, she wants to become "a fleck of foam," and as she tells Moyers, just "disappear and float in the air." In just these last few lines of "Accounting," Alegría exemplifies the paradox that Salinas had noted—the need to "survive that very death whose acceptance is being extolled." Alegría's poem defies the traditional elegy in other ways, as well. Engelbert explains that the Spanish elegiac tradition begins with laments, an expression of grief at the life that has ended. In contrast, Alegría's elegy begins with a celebration of her life. Since her elegy seeks to preserve the memories of her life, there is no need to lament the past. Even as she subverts the Spanish tradition, Alegría claims that she does not intentionally set out to defy or rewrite traditional genres. But she does tell McGowan that "maybe I do so unconsciously." When critics tell her that she is defying traditions, Alegría does not dissent and accepts this judgment even while she explains that "I myself am never conscious of it." Engelbert is one of the critics who has observed Alegría's efforts to challenge and transform modes of traditional poetry. Englebert claims that Alegría's "absence of verbal opulence," the brevity of language, transforms the traditional elegy. Rather than the conventional response to the bereaved, Alegría's elegy memorializes her own life as a celebration of endurance and change. The need for excess, for expressions of grandeur and superfluous accomplishments, are not necessary devices for Alegría to memorialize her life in an elegy.

In her interview with McGowan, Alegría mentioned that she had recently completed a new collection of poetry called *Fugues*. She explained that the book's "main themes are love, death, and the encounter with old age." All of the themes from this book are captured in the one poem that is the subject of this study: "Accounting." In the final lines of the poem, Alegría considers the concluding event of her life—her death. She describes how she has "the urge to mould myself into a verse," and so not only will her memories be preserved—she will be preserved within the poem's own lines. In recognizing the poet's ability to memorialize a life, in this case her own, Alegría follows in a long tradition of poets who acknowledged that poetry was one way to cheat death.

William Shakespeare was one of the first poets to recognize that his own work would transcend the "gilded monuments / Of princes." In Sonnet 55, Shakespeare tells the object of the poem, the young man, that this poem shall be "The living record of your memory." Long after marble monuments have been "besmeared with sluttish time," the young man will live on, since his "praise shall find room / Even in the eyes of all posterity." Shakespeare returns to this theme in Sonnet 81, when he again tells the young man that "your memory death cannot take" because "Your monument shall be my gentle verse." As Gerald Hammond notes in his text, *The Reader and Shakespeare's Young Man Sonnets*, Shakespeare's poem "is a claim for the immortality of his subject." Rather than be placed in the tomb, or in "a common grave," the young man is placed within the poem, where he will be "entombèd in men's eyes." Alegría mimics this idea in her own poem when she disappears in the final line of her poem, into "a fleck of foam." Clearly Alegría is four-hundred years and far removed from Renaissance English poetry, and yet, the recognition by the poet that verse can give life to that which death has removed is a view that extends beyond time and space. Alegría might subvert classical English elegiac meter, but she still makes effective use of the traditional Shakespearean model.

There are importance distinctions between Shakespeare's recognition that poetry creates a lasting memory and Alegría's bid to compress her life into twenty-six lines of poetry. Shakespeare's Sonnet 55 and Sonnet 81 are not about the poet. There is no attempt by the poet to preserve his own life or to account for the events that have transformed or defined his life. There is no self-consciousness in these two poems, as there is in Alegría's poem. In his study of Shakespeare's sonnets, *Shakespeare and English Renaissance Sonnet*, author Paul Innes claims that "Sonnet 55 is the definitive enactment" of the poet's desire to "sustain for ever the truth and beauty of the friend." In contrast, Alegría makes no similar claim for her poetry. Her poem is meant to convey memories and not absolute truths. Another important difference between Alegría's poem and Shakespeare's sonnets is that the reader begins to know Alegría after reading her poem. This is not true for Shakespeare's sonnets 55 and 81, which contain no descriptions of the young man. He remains a mystery, whether one sonnet or the entire sequence is studied. While Shakespeare's sonnets claim to keep the young man's memory alive beyond the grave, as Hammond observes, the poems manage "to keep him entirely hidden" from the reader's view. The historical reality is that scholars are still uncertain who the young man was, while readers will have no difficulty in determining who Alegría was. Her life will remain in plain view for each generation of readers to understand.

Source: Sheri E. Metzger, Critical Essay on "Accounting," in *Poetry for Students*, Thomson Gale, 2005.

Mary Potter

Potter is a university writing instructor and fiction writer living in San Francisco. In this essay, Potter shows how Alegría adds up the significant moments in her life to transform her experiences into verse through a series of poetic turns.

Fugues (1993), Claribel Alegría's collection of elegies and love poems, contains the poem "Accounting," a tally of experiences singled out as "electrical instants" in the aging poet's life. As a reviewer commented in *Booklist*, the collection is "lyrical" and "speaks of the solitary self and the self that is lost and found in love." Likewise, in "Accounting" the poet draws on past experiences in order to gather this self back to the present moment of composition, through which she desires to be transformed. Alegría wants to transmogrify herself "into a verse," to change her form into something surprising and perhaps strange, like a "shout" and "a fleck of foam." In this poem, Alegría uses her craft to achieve a metamorphosis. Arranging sensory images in lines that create dramatic tension, the poet's goal is a complete change in appearance and character. Sixty-eight years old at the time of the poem's writing, Alegría faces her own mortality, so by the end of the poem, she releases herself into the poet's domain—the natural world of sound and images.

Born in Nicaragua in 1924, Alegría is the leading poetic spokesperson in support of the Sandanista movement (FSLN) to restore democracy to her homeland, which fought against and overthrew the U.S.-backed Somoza regime in 1979. Because of her

> *In this poem, Alegría uses her craft to achieve a metamorphosis. Arranging sensory images in lines that create dramatic tension, the poet's goal is a complete change in appearance and character.*

father's close alliance with Somoza himself, from early childhood on she was raised in exile in El Salvador. Educated in America, she met her husband in college, the journalist Darwin J. Flakoll, who also translated most of her works. For decades, they collaborated on numerous testimonies to revolutionary movements throughout Latin America. In an earlier collection of poetry, *Woman of the River*, Flakoll translates "Accounting" as "Summing Up." The poem's title in Spanish, "Contabilizando," means to "calculate, reckon, count up," and in these twenty-six lines the poet experiences a reckoning, adding up the "few" moments in her life that really count. While accounting is a mathematical process, logical and precise, she uses it to play against the mysterious and transformative power of the poetic process. In another poem in *Fugues*, "Ars Poetica," she celebrates the literary craft that draws her closer both to understanding the transformative power of commonplace objects or experiences and to political awakening. While one plus one equals two in ordinary accounting, the minutes and memories that Alegría adds up in her poetry do not yield a predictable result. By the poem's end, her accounting comes undone.

This mysterious process is fueled by her political consciousness as much as it is by her deliberate craft. Whereas her early collections, from 1948 to 1961, were more strictly literary, at times sentimental, introspective, and lyrical, after 1965 her work changes direction toward *letras de emergencia*, wherein the emerging spirit of her work is an urgent response to a crisis situation. In this way, "Accounting" embodies her political conviction as it satisfies her "urge to mould" herself "into a verse."

"Accounting" is also a poetic composition, an arrangement of sounds and images into lines that create a drama. The first fifteen lines alternate between precise memories of her life and sensory details. The poem's tension increases through a pattern of turns on these moments and images firmly fixed in her memory. It may look like a simple poem of casually recollected memories, but the arrangement of its lines is intentional and intricate. First, the "electrical instants" she quantifies are "six hours in Macchu Pichu," "ten minutes necessary / to lose my virginity," "fifteen minutes in Delft," and "this sultry hour" when she is writing the poem. Interspersed amid this chronology of her life are sounds like "the buzzing of the telephone / while awaiting the death of my mother," "the hoarse voice / announcing the death [assassination] / of Monsignor Romero," and, turning away from the theme of death to birth, "the first wail of my daughter." Then, in the sixteenth line, the poem takes its most unexpected turn, unfurling into "I don't know how many years / dreaming of my people's liberation." She defies time itself by framing these years as an "electrical instant" that encapsulates the Nicaraguan struggle and in the line that follows, the oxymoronic "certain immortal deaths." She has lost track of the time she has spent yearning for her people's freedom, and during these decades, the countless lives lost. Lives that were lost fighting injustice achieve immortality, Alegría believes, as in this poem and in her memory the significance of such lives cannot be touched by time or tallied like a body count. Just as the assassination of Archbishop Oscar Romero by a member of the Salvadoran death squads in 1980 was both another turning point for Alegría and the start of her political career, so his assassination in "Accounting" receives singular notice. After 1980, her works became mostly *testimonios* or testimonies of the traditionally voiceless, oppressed people, speaking out against government-sponsored terrorism in Central America and other regions.

In the first seventeen lines, the poet accounts for two "deaths" before turning to the "immortal deaths." In the next two lines, she takes another dramatic turn, moving from sound to sight, recreating "the eyes of that starving child" and "your eyes bathing me with love / one forget-me-not afternoon." She replaces the eyes of a dying child with the eyes of her lover as she once remarked that "mis poemas son poemas de amor a mis pueblos" (my poems are love poetry for my people). Death and love combined summon her back to her current "electrical instant," the present hour, when she sits yearning to change herself through verse into "the shout" and "a fleck of foam." As if she were carefully fording a stream, turning to find her next foothold stone by stone, in this poem she moves among the sounds and sights of her past to sum up her life and transform it. She is able to do this by establishing a pattern of moments alternating with sensory details, building dramatic tension, then breaking this pattern to achieve metamorphosis in the poem.

Critic Sandra Maria Boschetto-Sandoval writes in "Claribel Alegría: Overview," "As poet, essayist, journalist, novelist of fantastic fiction, and writer of *testimonio*, Alegría functions in a manner very similar to that of a cartographer. Tracing the heights, depths, and contours of her memory, Alegría charts the . . . regions of her psyche. The effect is not unlike that of a series of symmetrical mirrors, simultaneously reflecting inward and outward." She remarks further, "To situate Alegría's opus within its Latin American sociohistoric and political context is to . . . ground reality in a specific historic moment when subjects come to see themselves as integral parts of a collective process of intervention in history." Through poetry, poets attain immortality, and in "Accounting," Alegría reaches past the temporal limitations of her years on earth to place herself in history, among her generation of writers committed to artistic, political, and social engagement. By adding up all of the moments that have mattered, she finds that they are incalculable.

Source: Mary Potter, Critical Essay on "Accounting," in *Poetry for Students*, Thomson Gale, 2005.

Jo Anne Engelbert

In the following essay excerpt, Engelbert examines Alegría's unique approach in her elegiac poems.

In the post-Matanza era, elegiac poetry in Central America is eloquent through stark simplicity. The great cathedral organ of Hispanic tradition is sparingly intoned or renounced in favor of an unamplified voice that is at once personal and collective. Death in the Central American isthmus is not *cortés,* as elegized by Manrique; Death as personified by Alegría is the implacable god Tlaloc demanding blood; his victims are the dispossessed, stripped of land, customs, dress, language, and history. The language of elegy must faithfully reflect this; a lament for the children of the Woman of the River Sumpul must of necessity be as pure as water, uncompromised by reliance on the codes of power.

It is not merely the diction of elegy which is problematized by La Matanza, but the very function and nature of this poetry. In the very midst of chaos, who can pretend to comfort, to reconcile? Who perceives an order to be restored or a power capable of restoring it? Classical resignation and spiritual quietude are often replaced in this latitude by exhortation to action. Boccanera (1981, 15) observes, "En pueblos donde la represión y Muerte son ya una costumbre de la barbarie, la poesía pasa de la elegía a la denuncia, de la clandestinidad al exilio, y nada contra la corriente para no perecer ahogada en la sangre del pueblo agredido" (In countries where repression and death have become the praxis of barbarity, poetry moves from elegy to denunciation, from clandestinity to exile, and swims against the current in order not to drown in the blood of the oppressed). In Central America, Alegría and others are creating a new elegiac tradition that does not merely denounce but which essays a new response to the human needs of the bereaved. Its elements are a rigorous sobriety of expression, identification with the oppressed, a poetic persona that is collective rather than individual, and a sensibility that reflects New World beliefs and values. A fundamental departure from received tradition is the emergence of the female elegist.

> *"Using few of the resources of the traditional elegy, Alegría has created a poetry that approximates its weight and scope and resonance."*

Some religious communities, as a symbolic gesture, renounce the luxury of instrumental music. "For orthodox Jewry the absence of musical instruments is regarded as a symbol of the absence of the departed glory of the Temple and a reminder of the tragic history of a people scattered over the four quarters of the globe" (Tobin 1961, 166). Similarly, in Alegría's poetry the absence of verbal opulence signifies somber remembrance and complete identification with the subject.

The normal recourses of poetry fail under the weight of this subject matter. Manuel Sorto writes (quoted in Guillén 1985, 131),

El sangrerío es grande
demasiado grande

para medirlo con metáforas.
Ninguna alucinación se le parece.

(The river of blood is immense
too great
to be measured in metaphors.
No hallucination can equal it.)

The inadequacy of metaphor to the expression of horror is what Neruda alludes to when he writes, "The blood of the children / flowed out into the streets / . . . like the blood of the children" (Forché 1985, 257). No comparison, no simile, no linguistic elaboration can equal the efficacy of the poet's naked, unmediated voice recounting concrete experience. Alegría never speaks about death in the abstract, nor does she speak about "the dead." Rather she speaks, with maternal tenderness, of "mis muertos" (my dead). In her fictional autobiography *Luisa in Realityland*, she recounts the childhood ritual of nightly prayers for her dead and recalls her dread of omitting the name of a single individual whose soul, on her account, might fall into limbo. As she grew older she added name after name to her rosary of souls until the list threatened to become interminable (Alegría 1987, 13). Even now, she tells us (Alegría 1981, 91), her paradise in Mallorca fills with phantoms after dark, the ghosts of all her dead.

As in the indigenous tradition alluded to above in which "death was never a line of demarcation," Alegría blurs and dissolves boundaries. Her dead mingle promiscuously with the living; they come and go at will, appear in the street, vanish in the mist. But it is in life, not in death, that she wishes to remember her host of souls. "Tu muerte me cansa," she tells her father, "Quiero olvidarla ahora / y recordar lo otro" (I am weary of your death, / I want to forget it for a while and remember all the rest) (Alegría 1981, 95). The faces she holds in memory are vibrantly alive; her father's, for example (Alegría 1981, 96):

Tu vida y no tu muerte:
tu rostro aquella tarde
cuando llegaste humeando de alegría
y alzándola en vilo
le anunciaste a mi madre
que ahora sí,
que ya es seguro,
que le salvé la pierna
a Jorge Eduardo.

(Your life and not your death:
your face that afternoon
when you came in beaming with joy,
held it up for all to admire,
and announced to my mother
that yes, finally, it was certain
that you had saved Jorge Eduardo's leg.)

There are no panegyrics in this poetry. Alegría does not speak *about* the dead; rather, she speaks *to* them with the naturalness of everyday conversation. "Remember that hot day," she asks her father, "when we stole the only watermelon / and wolfed it down, just the two of us?" (Alegría 1981, 96). She imagines her mother at the age of twelve, face flushed, braids flying, performing a stunt on her roller skates. In the timeless zone of memory she asks her (Alegría 1981, 122),

¿ Cuándo perdiste
esa alegría?
¿ Cuándo te convertiste
en la muchacha cautelosa
que colgó los patines?

(When did you lose that joy?
When did you become
that cautious little girl
who put away her roller skates?)

The dead invoked by Alegría are disconcertingly active; they do not, cannot, rest. They rise and leave the cemeteries to seek justice; they mount guard, harass the living, lie in ambush, ready to accost the passerby. Gesticulating, winking, waving, they pursue the poet, desperate to tell their stories. Their rage is palpable:

nadie sabe decir
cómo murieron
sus voces perseguidas
se confunden
murieron en la cárcel
torturados
Se levantan mis muertos
tienen rabia

(no one can say
how they died.
Their persecuted voices are one voice
dying by torture in prison
My dead arise, they rage.)
(Forché 1982, 55)

They are legion; they form a solid wall that reaches from Aconcagua to Izalco. In desperation the poet struggles to hold them all, to retain them in memory lest they fall into the limbo of oblivion. But they are too many; she cannot contain them all: having described herself as a cemetery apátrida, she says that her dead "no caben," (they do not fit). *Presentes* (present in spirit), like the ghostly guerrilla fighters in poems by Roberto Obregón or Roberto Sosa who rise at night to fight alongside their companions, these dead in their anger "continue the struggle" (Alegría 1981, 157–58).

In her book *Poetry in the Wars* Edna Longley observes, "The 'I' of a lyric poem does not egocentrically claim any privilege as structuralists would have it. Strategically individualist, but truly collective, a poem suppresses self in being for and about everyone's humanity" (Longley 1987, 17). The particulars of Alegría's poetic persona—her loneliness, weariness, even the fungus between her toes—are often links to the collective subject (all of the lonely, weary, pauperized expatriates living in Madrid got fungus infections in the public baths where everyone went to "scrub off the stench exile" (Forché 1982, 28). Her poems do not so much suppress self as transform and transcend it; her progressive identification with those who have fallen in the struggle becomes more and more intense with the passage of time. In poem after poem she identifies herself with those who have suffered or died in the struggle. She submerges herself in the collective historical subject and her voice is one with the chorus, the river of voices raised in protest:

Ya no es una la voz
es un coro de voces
soy los otros
soy yo
es un río de voces
que se alza
que me habla de la cárcel
del adiós
del dolor
del hasta luego
se confunden las voces
y los rostros se apagan
quién le quitó a ese niño
su alegría?

(It is no longer a voice
it is a chorus of voices
I am the others
I am myself
it is a river of voices
that is rising
that speaks to me of prison
of goodbyes
of suffering
of so long for a while
the voices blend together
the faces dissolve
who snatched the smile
from that little boy?)
(Alegría 1981, 172)

"Sorrow," the longest and most powerful of Alegría's elegiac poems, actually takes the form of such a chorus or river of voices. Dedicated to Roque Dalton, "Sorrow" is one of the most original and profound elegies in Central American poetry. An entire poetics of solidarity could be extracted from its strategies for voicing a collective lament. The poem is an *arpillera* pieced of fragments, vivid scraps of personal experience commingled with verses by poets and artists who were witnesses to the common struggle.

"Voces que vienen / que van" (Voices that rise and are gone), the poem begins. We recognize them from familiar phrases—"cuando sepas que he muerto / no pronuncies mi nombre," "verde que," "puedo escribir los versos más tristes," "me moriré en París" (when you know that I have died / do not speak my name) (green, I want you green) (tonight I can write the saddest verses) (I will die in Paris) (Forché 1982, 18). Besides the fraternity of poets—Dalton, Lorca, Neruda, Vallejo, Antonio Machado, and Hernández—others identified with the cause are invoked as well. Victor Jara appears and Violeta Parra, Che Guevara, and Sandino. Their words are stitched together in a graphic representation of solidarity, appliquéed upon the strong fabric of the poem's personal statement. The poem's eight sections are eight stations of the course of mourning. The invocation of the voices is followed by the recollection of a dusty pilgrimage to the grave of Lorca ("no te pusieron lápida / no te hicieron el honor / de arrancar los olivos / combatientes / torcidos") (They didn't give you a grave marker / they did you the honor of tearing up / the twisted, the stubborn olive trees) (Forché 1982, 24). The third section evokes the sense of loss that is the experience of exile. The expatriates floating like wraiths along the cold boulevards of Madrid recognize each other by the mark on their foreheads, the hunted look in their eyes. The next three sections recount the poet's response to the "implacable news" of the death of Roque Dalton. She passes from stunned horror to an elevated experience of identification with all those who have suffered or died for the cause: in the seventh section she projects herself through prison walls to a narrow cell and lies on a cot listening in the darkness to the screams of the tortured. We recall the ritual of her childhood litanies, now become an exercise in horror: "empiezo a contar nombres / mi rosario de nombres / pienso en el otro / el próximo / que dormirá en mi catre / y escuchará el ruido de los goznes / y cagará aquí mismo en el cano / llevando a cuestas / su cuota de terror" (I begin counting the names / my rosary of names / I think about the other / the next one who will sleep here / on my cot and listen / to the groaning hinges / and shit right here in this open pipe / hunched beneath his quota of terror). The intensity of this emotion is the poem's climax:

Desde mi soledad
acompañada
alzo la voz y pregunto
y la respuesta es clara.

(from my solitude I raise my voice
I ask and the answer is clear.)

One by one, voices call out to her in the darkness: "Soy Georgina / soy Nelson / soy Raúl" (I am Georgina / I am Nelson / I am Raúl). The chorus of voices rises, growing more and more powerful, drowning out the voice of the jailer demanding silence. She rends the veil of time that separates her from herself, from the others. Suddenly there are wine and guitars and tobacco, and sorrow has become reunion. She takes a piece of coal and scrawls on the wall, "más solos están ellos / que nosotros" (they are more alone than we are), the only consolation this elegy can offer and the only consolation that it needs.

In this fraternity of suffering, the dispossessed have their homeland in each other. Salvadoran guerrillas often repeat, "we have our mountain [i.e., our refuge] in the people." The poets of this era find their mountain, their "habitat," in the consciousness of their counterparts in solidarity, regardless of era or place of birth.

"Sorrow"'s eighth section, an epilogue, parallels traditional elegiac form by referring confidently to the persistence of the poem itself, exactly as Salinas observed ("words are spoken here, precisely, in order that something not perish: words themselves"), with the enormous difference that the poem, in this tradition, is no longer the work of a single individual; this is its precise strength:

existen los barrotes
nos rodean
también existe el catre
y sus ángulos duros
y el poema río
que nos sostiene a todos
y es tan substantivo
como el catre
el poema que todos escribimos
con lágrimas
y uñas
y carbón.

(the bars do exist
they surround us
the cot also exists
with its hard sides
the river poem
that sustains us all
and is as substantial as the cot
the poem we are all writing
with tears, with fingernails and coal.)
(Forché 1982, 43)

The poem's final words are not a pious generality but a challenge, an incitement; the function of this poetry is not to reconcile but to engage:

y surge la pregunta
el desafío
decidme en el alma quién
quién levantó los barrotes?

(and the question arises, the challenge
tell, me, in spirit, who
who, raised up this prison's bars?)
(Forché 1982, 42)

Using few of the resources of the traditional elegy, Alegría has created a poetry that approximates its weight and scope and resonance. With others of her generation, she has helped define a New World elegiac tradition, individual and collective, unmediated and profound, a poetry "for and about everyone's humanity."

Source: Jo Anne Engelbert, "Claribel Alegría and the Elegiac Tradition," in *Claribel Alegría and Central American Literature*, edited by Sandra M. Boschetto-Sandoval and Marcia Phillips McGowan, Ohio University Center for International Studies, 1994, pp. 183–98.

Ana Patricia Rodríguez

In the following essay, Rodríguez discusses Alegría's career, her partnership with Darwin J. "Bud" Flakoll, and her support for her homeland.

Claribel Alegría is one of the most respected and prolific writers of Central America. Since the late 1940s she has written more than forty books across many literary genres, including novels, novellas, stories, essays, *testimonios* (testimonials), children's stories, and poetry. Her works have been published in more than fourteen languages throughout Europe, Latin America, and the United States. With Darwin J. "Bud" Flakoll, her husband and partner in writing, Alegría has translated and edited other writers' work, produced anthologies, and cowritten novels, *testimonios*, and journalistic exposés. She has lectured and read widely from her work in diverse international media and academic forums, especially during the 1980s, when she was recognized unofficially as cultural ambassador of El Salvador in exile. In "The Writer's Commitment" (which first appeared in the journal *Fiction International* in 1984) Alegría identified herself as a profoundly "committed writer," one who envisions social change, struggles for human rights, and produces a transformational "literature of emergency." Tracing her own political and literary transformations, she explains that, early in her life, she wrote poetry without knowing "what was happening in my country—El Salvador—or my region—Central America." The Cuban Revolution in 1959, the Sandinista Revolutionary Period in Nicaragua from 1979 to 1989, the Salvadoran Civil War from 1979 to 1991, and her own personal relationship to these historical events transformed her writing.

These social movements and historical moments indelibly marked both her prose and poetry.

Born in Estelí, Nicaragua, on 12 May 1924, Clara Isabel Alegría Vides was taken to live in El Salvador by her parents at the age of six months. A binational citizen and international traveler, she has claimed Nicaragua as her *matria* (motherland) and El Salvador as her *patria* (fatherland). Her father, Daniel Alegría, was a Nicaraguan citizen and medical doctor who was exiled from Nicaragua after expressing his discontent with the United States Marine occupation of Nicaragua, critiquing the Somocista repression of peasants and dissidents in his country, and voicing support for the revolutionary forces of Augusto César Sandino. Although he never returned to Nicaragua, Alegría's father remained a fervent supporter of Sandino's ideals in Central America. Upon being terrorized by the Nicaraguan National Guard, the Alegría family fled to the northwestern department of Santa Ana in El Salvador, the home of Alegría's mother, Ana María Vides. There, Alegría grew up as a member of the landed coffee oligarchy, to which her mother's family belonged.

Alegría was reared amid the privilege of her socio-economic class, although from an early age she demonstrated a sense of autonomy and free thought, electing to attend public schools rather than the private parochial schools preferred by her siblings. In a 2000 interview with Antonio Velásquez, Alegría explains that in Santa Ana she had access to good libraries, wherein she began to read at an early age. Her parents introduced her to the poetry of the Spanish Golden Age, including that of San Juan de la Cruz and Santa Teresa, and many Latin American writers, among them Rubén Darío, Gabriela Mistral, and Rómulo Gallegos. She learned at an early age that she wanted to be a poet, thereby challenging prescribed gender roles and traditions of Salvadoran elite society.

In 1943, perhaps seeking other directions for herself and her artistic production, Alegría moved to the United States to attend George Washington University in Washington, D.C., where she earned a bachelor's degree in philosophy and letters. In 1948 Alegría published her first book of poetry, *Anillo de silencio* (Ring of Silence), for which the Mexican philosopher and writer José Vasconcelos wrote the prologue. In his travels through Central America, Vasconcelos met the young Clara Isabel Alegría Vides. Vasconcelos, according to sources, suggested to her the pen name of Claribel Alegría. During her residence in Washington, D.C., in the late 1940s and early 1950s, Alegría met the Spanish poet Juan Ramón Jiménez, whom she called her mentor. In her interview with Velásquez, Alegría affirms that "Juan Ramón Jiménez fue, en ese sentido, muy estricto conmigo y me decía que había que tener oficio para ser poeta, para ser novelista, y yo nunca había tenido un oficio de narradora, solamente de poeta" (Juan Ramón Jiménez was, in a sense, very strict with me and he would tell me that one has to have vocation to be a poet, a novelist, and I only wanted to be a poet, not a prose writer). Despite her initiation in poetry, Alegría has been recognized both for her poetry and prose. In 1978 her book *Sobrevivo* (I Survive) received Cuba's Casa de las Américas prize for poetry, while her novel *Cenizas de Izalco* (1966; translated as *Ashes of Izalco*, 1989), cowritten with her husband, was the first Central American novel published by the prestigious Seix Barral of Barcelona.

> *"She learned at an early age that she wanted to be a poet, thereby challenging prescribed gender roles and traditions of Salvadoran elite society."*

While studying at George Washington University, Alegría met Flakoll, a student studying journalism and diplomacy, whom she married in 1947. Together they formed a deep partnership that lasted a lifetime of family commitments, worldwide travels, and writing projects. They lived in the United States, Mexico, Argentina, Chile, France, Spain, and Nicaragua, meeting many writers with whom they collaborated on various projects. During that period of living as expatriates, Alegría and Flakoll produced poetry anthologies, in which they compiled and translated the work of international writers. These anthologies include *New Voices of Hispanic America* (1962), *Unstill Life: An Introduction to the Spanish Poetry of Latin America* (1970), *Cien poemas de Robert Graves* (One Hundred Poems of Robert Graves, 1981), *Nuevas voces de Norteamérica* (New Voices of North America, 1981), and *On the Front Line: Guerrilla Poetry of El Salvador* (1989). While living in Paris from 1962 to 1966, Alegría and Flakoll met the writers of the Spanish American "Boom" who resided in that city. The couple became lifelong friends of the Argentine Julio Cortázar, who participated in their enthusiasm and support of the Sandinista Revolution until his death. Flakoll and Alegría lived for years in Deyá, on the island of Majorca in Spain, which serves as the setting for the novella *Pueblo de Dios y de Mandinga* (1985; translated as *Village of God and the Devil*, 1991).

In 1979 Alegría and Flakoll relocated to Nicaragua to join the Sandinista reconstruction efforts. They cowrote an historical text, *Nicaragua: La revolución sandinista—Una crónica política, 1855–1979* (Nicaragua: The Sandinista Revolution—A Political Chronicle, 1855–1979, 1982), and produced several anthologies of poetry and prose, published in solidarity with the revolutionary movement in El Salvador. During this period Alegría and Flakoll were prolific, publishing *La encrucijada salvadoreña* (The Salvadoran Crossroads, 1980), *Homenaje a El Salvador*, and *On the Front Line*. They also collaborated in the writing of testimonial and resistance texts such as *No me agarran viva: La mujer salvadoreña en la lucha* (1983; translated as *They Won't Take Me Alive: Salvadorean Women in Struggle for National Liberation*, 1987), *Fuga de Canto Grande* (1992; translated as *Tunnel to Canto Grande*, 1996), and *Somoza: Expediente cerrado: La historia de un ajusticiamiento* (1993; translated as *Death of Somoza*, 1996). Alegría explained to Velásquez that, in this testimonial production, it was Flakoll who took charge: "En los testimonios los dos escribimos todo, pero él sabía estructurarlos mejor porque era periodista" (We wrote everything in the testimonies, but he knew how to structure them better than I since he was a journalist).

Many critics have marveled at Alegría and Flakoll's personal and professional relationship, often asking them to explain the secret of their success. In a 1990 interview with David Volpendesta, Alegría explained that Flakoll "at the beginning of our marriage, was my critic in poetry." In his *Gestos ceremoniales: Narrativa centroamericana, 1960–1990* (Ceremonial Gestures: Central American Narrative, 1998), the critic Arturo Arias suggests that Alegría and Flakoll's collaboration manifests a new north-south sensibility in Alegría's work, which transgresses the stereotypes ascribed to both North Americans and Central Americans and facilitates a better understanding between both peoples. Married to a progressive North American man, Alegría, according to Arias, was forced to "confrontar esa otreadad que era constitutiva de su ser" (confront an otherness that was part of her being) and to adopt a "transformativa" (transformative) and transnational perspective.

Equally known for her poetry and prose innovations, Alegría describes her work as sui generis. Her first novel, *Cenizas de Izalco*, and her novellas—*Luisa en el país de la realidad* (1987; translated as *Luisa in Realityland*), *Despierta, mi bien, despierta* (Awaken, My Love, Awaken, 1986), *El detén* (1977; translated as *The Talisman*, 1991), *Album familiar* (1982; translated as *Family Album*, 1991), and *Pueblo de Dios y de Mandinga*, the last three of which are collected in an English translation titled *Family Album* (1991)—combine various literary genres in single texts. Alegría's novels and novellas incorporate literary forms such as poetry, diaries, and letters to produce the effect of a literary montage or collage. This interpolation and mixing of literary forms articulates, at times, multiple voices and perspectives. Alegría populates her texts with members of the aristocracy and exploited groups, foreign travelers, and subjects of all classes, genders, ages, and political positions. Converging in single texts, these voices represent the constructed nature of literature and the complex mosaic of Salvadoran society. Although appearing sometimes deceptively simple and written in girls' voices, Alegria's prose texts, especially *Cenizas de Izalco* and the novellas, question the foundations of Salvadoran traditional values, social hierarchies, and power structures, which are embedded in the ideals of family, home, nation, and reality. Sometimes possessing a poetic quality, as in the case of *Luisa en el país de la realidad*, Alegría's prose narratives are also highly lyrical and enigmatic. Her poetry and prose narrative, hence, cannot be separated, although in her interview with Velásquez, Alegría claimed, "En realidad creo que mi pasión es la poesía" (In reality, I think my passion is for poetry).

Alegría began her literary career writing poetry, which has remained a constant endeavor throughout her life. She has written many books of poetry, including *Anillo de silencio*, *Suite de amor, angustia y soledad* (The Suite of Love, Anxiety, and Solitude, 1950), *Vigilias* (Vigils, 1953), *Acuario* (Aquarius or Aquarium, 1955), *Huésped de mi tiempo* (Guest of My Time, 1961), *Vía única* (One Way, 1965), *Aprendizaje* (Learning, 1970), *Pagaré a cobrar y otros poemas* (Paid on Delivery and Other Poems, 1973), *Sobrevivo*, *Suma y sigue* (Sum Up and Continue, 1981), *Flores del volcán/Flowers from the Volcano* (1982), *Poesía viva* (Living Poetry, 1983), *Mujer del río* (1987; translated as *Woman of the River*, 1989), *Y este poema río* (And This River

Poem, 1988), *Fugues* (1993), *Variaciones en clave de mi* (Variations in the Key of Me, 1993), *Umbrales/Thresholds: Poems* (1996), and *Saudade/Sorrow* (1999). Flakoll and Carolyn Forché have faithfully translated many of Alegría's poems, although some of these books of poetry have not been translated into English, especially her earliest works. Throughout these works Alegría has produced poems that are lyrical, self-reflective, and intimate and that speak to the universal themes of joy, love, desire, anger, angst, sadness, loss, melancholy, and mourning. At the same time, her poetry has responded to the sociopolitical struggles in Central America, increasingly becoming self-referential and critical of power structures in the region. Poetry has remained a constant in Alegría's life, and with the passing of her husband in 1995 she has returned to poetry in her later projects.

According to Alegría, her poetry is not political but rather a "mis poemas son poemas de amor a mis pueblos" (love poetry for her people), an ideal that is most apparent in her poems such as "Tamalitos de Cambray" (Little Cambray Tamales), "Mujer del río" (Woman of the River), "Documental" (Documentary), all published in *Mujer del Río*, and other poems dedicated to the memory of fallen Central American writers and revolutionaries such as Roque Dalton. Along with the Salvadoran poet Dalton, who claimed in his 1977 poem "Como tú" (Like You) that "la poesía es como el pan, de todos" (poetry, like bread, is for everyone), Alegría produces literature that is accessible to a wide range of readers. In the field of contemporary poetry, she draws from the poetic traditions of Central American *exteriorismo* (exterior poetry), Latin American conversational political poetry, and the international decolonizing militancy of engaged poets of the mid to late twentieth century. Alegría's poems abound with concrete images, historical allusions, colloquialisms, and revolutionary themes. Her "Ars poética," from *Fugues*, celebrates the literary craft that brings her closer to political awakening and understanding of the transformational power of commonplace objects and experiences. In the images of the crow, sun, valleys, volcanoes, and debris of war the poet is able to "catch sight of the promised land."

Her book of poetry *Mujer del río* overflows with images of water, trees, and leaves, all intermingling in the poet's memory. In "Desde el puente" (From the Bridge) the poet recounts the passing of her life as "the water flows below," and she rushes to remember "la masacre / que dejó sin hombres" (the massacre / that left Izalco without men) that she witnessed at the age of seven. The adult poet asks herself, "cómo podré explicarte / que no cambiado nada / y que siguen matando diariamente?" (How can I explain to you / nothing has changed / they keep on killing people daily?). By the end of "Desde el puente" the committed poet questions an intellectualism masked in philosophy and a poetry detached from life, one that "cuidadsomente omitían / la inmundicia que nos rodea / desde siempre" (carefully omitted / the filth / that has always / surrounded all). With resolve, Alegría's committed poet grows claws and beaks in order to survive the "tufo a carroña" (stench of carrion) left behind by the destruction of El Salvador. In 2000, when interviewed by Velásquez, Alegría reconfirmed her lifelong endeavor to produce literature committed to universal themes, local struggles, and common people. She states that "Para mí el oficio de escribir es un oficio como tantos otros, y así como el zapatero tiene que hacer buenos zapatos, el escritor está llamado a comunicar, a comunicar ideas, sentimientos" (For me the craft of writing is a craft like many others. Like the shoemaker has to make good shoes, the writer is called to communicate, communicate ideas, feelings).

In "The Writer's Commitment" Alegría recognizes that with the wars in Central America, especially in El Salvador, her "poems took on an edge of protest." She also began to write more narrative texts that assumed marginal testimonial perspectives. She dedicated herself to developing parallel yet intertwined projects: the "literary-poetic" and "crisis journalism"—in other words, poetry and prose narrative. Many critics analyze Alegría's multifaceted literary production, paying particular attention to her representation of women, social movements, revolution, and history. They examine Alegría's early use of fantastic literature, feminist discourse, and *testimonios.* In 1994 Sandra M. Boschetto-Sandoval and Marcia Phillips McGowan published *Claribel Alegría and Central American Literature*, an anthology of critical essays on Alegría's work, in which critics such as Arias, Jorge Rufinelli, Ileana Rodríguez, Margaret Crosby, Boschetto-Sandoval, and Phillips McGowan discuss Alegría's lifelong commitment to producing socially, politically, and artistically engaged literature. Along these lines, the critic George Yúdice, in "Letras de emergencia: Claribel Alegría" (Literature of Emergency: Claribel Alegría, 1985), examines Alegría's production of "letras de emergencia," an emergent and urgent literature. Whether in poetic or prose form, Alegría's texts respond to particular historical conditions and represent distinct literary discourses and perspectives such as the testimonial voices of female revolutionary fighters and marginalized people.

According to Arias, Alegría is the initiator of a new wave of Central American poetic and prose narrative in the 1960s. Although living most of her adult life outside of Central America, Alegría is associated with a generation of committed writers in El Salvador such as Dalton, Manlio Argueta, and Matilde Elena López. Like these writers, Alegría addresses political, historical, and cultural issues and challenges power structures and hierarchies in El Salvador. She has pushed the limits of social realism and linear narrative, fusing poetry and prose in her experimental texts and crossing the lines between history and literature. Her poetry reconstructs historical events such as the conquest of El Salvador and "La Matanza" (The Massacre) in 1932, in which more than thirty thousand peasant and indigenous people were killed almost overnight in El Salvador by the military government of General Maximiliano Hernández Martínez. The dictator Martínez virtually erased this event from the public record by having all related documentation destroyed. Rectifying this act of "lobotomía cultural" (cultural lobotomy), as Alegría calls it in "Clash of Cultures," an essay for the September 1986 issue of *Index on Censorship*, Alegría's work preserves and retells the history of the massacre for generations of Salvadorans, who read her poetry and prose in school. In lieu of proper documentation, Alegría's personal memories and poetry restore the lost memory of the Salvadoran people. As she explains in "Clash of Cultures," she and Flakoll "had to reconstruct from my childhood memories when I was seven years old and what grown-ups had told me in hushed tones as I grew older."

Alegría and Flakoll's life of partnership and collaboration ended with his death on 15 April 1995, a loss so great that Alegría was moved to write a farewell book of poetry, *Saudade/Sorrow*. According to her, the Portuguese word *saudade* refers to the deep sense of loss and sadness experienced with the death of a loved one. Alegría has continued to live in Managua, Nicaragua, where her neighbors include the Nicaraguan writers Ernesto Cardenal and Sergio Ramírez.

Claribel Alegría's prose narrative and narrative poetry withstood one of the most repressive periods in Central American history. Writers such as Alegría sought a revolution in form and content, but always with the idea that literature belongs to people and might speak with them, not for them. Hence, *testimonio* and testimonial poetry has been a strong discursive current in Central America. Alegría's command of multiple literary genres, including prose and poetry, undoubtedly has placed her at the vanguard of political, solidarity, feminist, and third-world literary movements. During her lifetime she has worked tirelessly to put Central America on the literary map and to make literature, especially poetry, "a basic human right" within reach of all people.

Source: Ana Patricia Rodríguez, "Claribel Alegria," in *Dictionary of Literary Biography*, Vol. 283, *Modern Spanish American Poets, First Series*, edited by María A. Salgado, Gale, 2003, pp. 10–16.

Margaret B. Crosby

In the following essay, Crosby discusses the roles Alegría has fulfilled as both a human-rights activist and poet.

"My main concern, rather than to talk about me, is to talk about my countries," says Claribel Alegría in the Fall 1989 issue of *Curbstone Ink*. "To talk about what is happening in El Salvador and Nicaragua is important," she continues. "Just to let people know what is happening right there, right then: that's my main concern. Nicaragua and El Salvador. I consider them both my countries."

Alegría, who was born in Nicaragua on 12 May 1924 and grew up in El Salvador, is one of the major contemporary voices in the struggle for liberation in Central America. As a poet, novelist, essayist, storyteller, translator, and indefatigable human-rights activist, she combines both love and revolution, the personal and the political, in her work. It reflects not only a strong commitment to Latin-American social change, but also her concern for the status of Latin-American women. As Nancy Saporta Sternbach observes, "Women of all ages and stages of growth and personal evolution populate her work. Whether Alegría is writing testimony or fiction, poetry or essay, the voice, the heart, the mind of women—Latin American women—are central and omnipresent. From an early age, Alegría defined herself as a feminist, as her work amply demonstrates."

Alegría divides her work into two categories: literary-poetic and *letras de emergencia* (emergency letters). The first category refers to the sentimental, introspective, lyrical poetry that typifies her early collections published from 1948 to 1961. The second category describes her politically conscious poetry and prose, published from 1965 to the present. These works address the prevailing realities and problems in her Central American homeland. As she explains in her 1988 essay "The Writer's Commitment," *letras de emergencia* is a phrase that captures "the double meaning of urgency and the emerging spirit of her work" and is a response to a crisis situation. She further defines this concept in her essay "Our Little Region" (1991), where she says that it "is any book, poem, article or speech that openly defends a cause or situation in which [the writer] deeply believes, such as the Nicaraguan Sandinista revolution or the necessity for a thorough political revolution in El Salvador." Whether her reply to the political crisis in her countries is expressed by writing or by speaking at international symposia about Central America, it is a heartfelt response that characterizes all of her work.

Alegría believes it is crucial for artists to take sides and commit themselves to the struggle for liberation. In commenting on the role of the artist, she adamantly states in "Our Little Region" that "Any artist who avoids commitment in the struggle is guilty at least of ivory tower escapism and at worst of complicity with the Squadrons of Death and the total militarization of society." Furthermore, in "The Writer's Commitment" and also in an interview with American poet Carolyn Forché she admits that if she were to meet a Central American writer who sidestepped political commitment and favored the Latin-American Right, she would refuse to be his or her friend.

Born in Estelí, Nicaragua, Alegría is the daughter of a Salvadoran mother, Ana María Vides, and a Nicaraguan exile. Her father, Daniel Alegría, was a medical doctor and an anti-interventionist during the U.S. Marine occupation of Nicaragua in 1924. Since he openly opposed the marines' presence in his country, they terrorized him and his family by aiming and firing at his wife and six-month-old daughter. Three months later the family fled Nicaragua and settled in Santa Ana, El Salvador where Alegría was raised and educated. From El Salvador her father helped Augusto César Sandino, who initiated the Sandinista movement in 1927 and who led the peasant uprising against the U.S. occupation of Nicaragua. In 1934 Sandino was assassinated. After that there was a price on Daniel Alegría's head, and he could only return to Nicaragua clandestinely.

In 1943 Alegría came to the United States, where she received a bachelor of arts degree in philosophy and letters from George Washington University. During this time she was the protégée of Juan Ramón Jiménez, the renowned Spanish poet and recipient of the 1956 Nobel Prize for literature. Jiménez taught Alegría the rigor, discipline, and

"As a poet, novelist, essayist, storyteller, translator, and indefatigable human-rights activist, she combines both love and revolution, the personal and the political, in her work."

craft of writing, and his influence can be seen in her early volumes of poetry. In 1947 Alegría married Darwin J. ("Bud") Flakoll, a U.S.-born journalist she met at George Washington University.

Alegría published *Anillo de silencio* (Ring of Silence), her first collection of poems, in 1948. This book marked the beginning of several collections of subjective, lyrical, and somewhat introspective and self-searching poetry. Her first narrative piece was *Tres cuentos* (Three Stories, 1958), a collection of three short stories for children. In all three stories, according to Diane E. Marting in *Women Writers of Spanish America*, "flora and fauna communicate with children, revealing a special fantasy world. . . . [T]he impossible becomes the possible . . . and the fine line between dreams and reality is temporarily banished."

The Cuban revolution in 1959 represented a turning point in Alegría's life. To her the revolution demonstrated that social and political change in Latin America as well as an end to U.S. imperialism and oppression in Cuba were possible. The events of the revolution also raised her political consciousness and caused her to depart from what she calls the egotistical navel gazing and childhood nostalgia of her earlier works. As her global perspective expanded, her poetry began to change, focusing more on the misery, injustice, and brutal repression in El Salvador and Nicaragua.

During the course of their life together, Alegría and Flakoll have traveled, lived, and worked in the United States, Argentina, Chile, Mexico, Nicaragua, France, and Spain. In 1961 they lived in Uruguay, where he worked for the American embassy. During this time they befriended Uruguayan writers such as Mario Benedetti, Carlos Martínez

Moreno, Carlos Real de Azúa, Idea Vilariño, and Manolo Claps.

From 1962 to 1966 they lived in Paris, where they associated regularly with the Latin-American Boom novelists Julio Cortázar (Argentina), Carlos Fuentes (Mexico), and Mario Vargas Llosa (Peru)—all of whom were at that time committed political leftists. In addition, Alegría and her husband began a lifelong friendship with Cortázar and his two wives, first Aurora Bernárdez and later Carol Dunlop.

During this period Alegría became obsessed with Latin-American politics and literature as well as her childhood memories. Fuentes urged her to write a novel based on her memories of the 1932 peasant uprising at Izalco, El Salvador, where dictator Gen. Maximiliano Hernández Martínez and his army slaughtered thirty thousand peasants and Indians in the name of anticommunism. Since writing about the massacre was both painful and difficult for her, Flakoll suggested they write the novel together. The result was *Cenizas de Izalco* (1966; translated as *Ashes of Izalco*, 1989). Published by Seix Barral, a major Barcelona press, the novel was a finalist for the publisher's annual literary prize.

The novel anticipates Alegría's subsequent recurring themes: mother-daughter relationships, U.S. intervention in Central America, female/male relations, Third World—First World relations, political repression as reality and metaphor, and revolution as the eruption of a volcano. In addition, the *matanza* (massacre) of 1932, which forms the setting in this novel, appears as a regular motif in other works. As a historical novel, *Cenizas de Izalco* is one of the first El Salvadoran novels to deal with the horror of the 1932 insurrection.

The relationship between mother and daughter forms the nucleus around which all other conflicts in the novel revolve. The protagonist, Carmen, a bourgeois El Salvadoran woman who lives in Washington, D.C., returns to El Salvador for her mother's funeral. Married to a conservative gringo, Carmen experiences an identity crisis roused by her mother's death and her reading of the diary her mother left to her. The diary, which belongs to her mother's secret North American lover, "serves as a bridge between the cultural, social revolution (the political sphere) and the private, intimate one (the personal) of one woman's life," according to Sternbach. Carmen realizes that she has never known her mother and that they both have been stifled by the same cultural constraints. They have lived lonely and meaningless lives restricted by a lack of personal autonomy and intellectual freedom. The novel also critiques the sexist and racist social structure that subordinates women and peasants.

In order to write the novel, Alegría and Flakoll traveled to El Salvador in 1964 to do research on the massacre. There they discovered that General Hernández Martínez had performed what *Curbstone Ink* termed a "cultural lobotomy on the Salvadoran people." In a 1986 essay, "The Two Cultures of El Salvador," Alegría explains that in 1932 General Hernández Martínez "ordered the destruction of all newspaper files in the country that dealt with the bloody events of those days. Libraries were ransacked to make sure no documentation of the massacre remained ... the only documentation we could find consisted of three yellowed newspaper clippings a friend had hidden in his private library and a brief account in William Krehm's book *Democracies and Tyrannies in the Caribbean.* All the rest we had to reconstruct from my childhood memories of when I was seven years old and what grown-ups had told me in hushed tones as I grew older."

The events of 1932 have had a profound effect on Alegría. In talking with Forché she recalls, "I remember the Guardias Nacionales (National Guard) bringing dozens of prisoners into the fortress across the street from my home with their thumbs tied behind them with bits of cord, shoving them along with rifle butts. I remember the shots at night." "And then," she says in an excerpt from *Curbstone Ink*, "I started learning at a tender age about the terrible injustices."

When *Cenizas de Izalco* was first published, the Alegría family did not like its criticism of their upper-class standing and burned most of the first edition. Consequently, the novel did not reach El Salvador until ten years later. According to Alegría, Col. Arturo Armando Molina, the El Salvadoran dictator at the time, wanted to leave office as a great liberal. Shortly before the end of his term in 1976 he requested that all Salvadoran writers be included in the publications of the El Salvadoran ministry of culture. They published *Cenizas de Izalco* without reading it, classifying it as a high-school textbook because the title spoke of El Salvador. Alegría believes that since then the novel continues to be available in El Salvador because it has the seal of the ministry of culture. It has gone through twenty printings, and within El Salvador it is her best-known work.

In 1966 Alegría and her husband moved to the village of Deyá on the island of Majorca, Spain. There they spent twelve tranquil and productive years, resulting in the publication of several joint translations. In addition, Alegría published three volumes of poetry—*Aprendizaje* (Apprenticeship, 1970), *Pagaré a cobrar* (Installment Payments, 1973), and *Sobrevivo* (I Survive, 1978)—as well as a novella, *El detén* (1977; translated as "The Talisman" in *Family Album*, 1991). In this novella Alegría treats the shocking subject of a young woman's sexual abuse. Karen, the fifteen-year-old Central American protagonist, attends a Catholic boarding school in the United States, where she befriends the bitter and aloof Sister Mary Ann. Throughout their conversations, Karen shares her memories of her childhood friends as well as her sexual abuse by her mother's sadistic boyfriend. Karen learns that the nun is also a survivor of sexual abuse.

The novella is important for several reasons. First, Alegría makes central to the novel two themes that emerged in *Cenizas de Izalco*: the sexual oppression and powerlessness of women, and the relationship between mother and daughter. Second, she critiques Catholicism and its inherent condoning of physical abuse, personal suffering, and the denial of pain such as that experienced by the nuns and boarding school students who must prove their love for the Lord. Finally, by treating a rather taboo subject such as sexual abuse, she leads the El Salvadoran novel in a new direction: from an overt concern for linguistic experimentation, narrative technique, and social realism, all of which typified El Salvadoran fiction of the 1970s, to a preoccupation with feminist and women's issues.

The late 1970s represent a significant period in Alegría's life, characterized by a stronger political commitment on her part. In 1978 *Sobrevivo* won Cuba's prestigious Casa de las Américas prize for poetry. In this collection Alegría the "spokespoet" serves as an eyewitness to certain events. Through pre-Columbian myths and Central American history and geography Alegría addresses cultural imperialism, family relationships, exile, poverty, class differences, torture, disappearance, death, and the urgent need to change the political and social situation in her homeland. Electa Arenal contends that in *Sobrevivo* Alegría "asserts the strength of human life and mourns human suffering," adding that "the title refers both to the daily act of surviving and to the miracle and the guilt of surviving in our times."

In 1979, at age fifty-five, Alegría with her husband returned to Nicaragua for the first time since she fled the country as a small child. This visit represented another turning point in her life as she witnessed the triumph of the Sandinista movement and the end of Somocismo, the dictatorship of Anastasio Somoza and his two sons. As Arenal observes, "Alegría's [political] exile and return to Nicaragua run parallel to the history of the Sandinista [resistance] movement. This almost lifelong exile taught perseverance and gave perspective." For the next six months, Alegría and Flakoll traveled throughout Nicaragua gathering information and testimonies from people associated with the revolution for a five-hundred-page book of history and testimony entitled *Nicaragua: La revolución sandinista—Una crónica política*, 1855–1979 (Nicaragua: The Sandinista Revolution—A Political Chronicle, 1855–1979). They did the actual writing in Majorca and published the book in 1982.

In 1982 Alegría also published *Flores del volcán/Flowers from the Volcano*, a book of previously published poems translated into English by Forché, and a novella, *Album familiar* (translated in *Family Album*, 1991). In the latter she returns to the theme of political awakening that had emerged earlier in *Cenizas de Izalco* . While the main action takes place in Paris, where the protagonist Ximena lives, a subplot occurs in Managua, Nicaragua, in 1978, on the day Edén Pastora seizes the national palace in a concerted effort to overthrow the Somoza regime. Alegría shows how Ximena, an upper-middle-class El Salvadoran-Nicaraguan wife and teacher, explores her relationships with her French husband, other family members, and nanny. When her politically active cousin confronts her fears and indifference as well as the disparity between her familial values and the nature of Central American reality, her political and social consciousness is awakened, and she commits to helping the revolutionary cause and the construction of a new Nicaraguan society.

During the 1980s testimonies dominated both El Salvadoran poetry and prose. With Flakoll, Alegría published two testimonial works that echo the voices of marginalized and oppressed people. The first work, *No me agarran viva: La mujer salvadoreña en lucha* (1983; translated as *They Won't Take Me Alive: Salvadoran Women in Struggle for National Liberation*, 1987), is dedicated to the thousands of Salvadoran girls and women who continue to fight courageously in the struggle for liberation. The book charts the politicization and militarization of Eugenia, a young woman from a bourgeois background who joins the guerrilla forces, becomes a commanding officer, and later dies in the struggle. The reader learns about her through the testimonies of her sisters, friends, and other companions, at the same time learning about women of different social classes whose testimonies describe their experiences with war and their ability to survive hardship.

In addition, the book describes Eugenia's relationship with her politically active husband, outlines and discusses the problem of machismo within the revolutionary organizations, and explores the role of the children of revolutionaries and their participation in the struggle. Eugenia incarnates the "new Salvadoran woman" and the new revolutionary subject. Her story speaks collectively for countless other women who have valiantly risked their lives so that others may live a life of peace.

The second work, *Para romper el silencio: Resistencia y lucha en las cárceles salvadoreñas* (Breaking the Silence: Resistance and Struggle in Salvadoran Prisons, 1984), is the testimony of Toño, a politically aware student leader who spent two years incarcerated as a political prisoner. The book recounts his ordeal as well as the tribulations and testimonies of many other political prisoners. Covering a six-year period, the book describes in detail the prisoners' daily suffering and the methods of torture the authorities used on them. While the book is painful to read at times, it also conveys hope. When the prisoners organize to demand more food as well as improvements in sanitary facilities and general living conditions, each request granted represents a small triumph. By singing collectively and scratching messages in a communal cork cup passed around the prison, they restore and maintain a sense of self while giving voice and dignity to their struggle.

Between 1985 and 1987 Alegría stopped writing poetry and testimonies to create three novels. The first of these, *Pueblo de Dios y de Mandinga* (1985; translated as "Village of God and the Devil" in *Family Album,* 1991), depicts the life of Slim and Marcia, a married couple who have recently moved from Paris to Deyá, Majorca. Their relationship suggests an autobiographical parallel to that of Alegría and Flakoll. In this work Alegría radically departs from some of the recurring themes seen in her previous novels to delve into magic realism. The novel humorously treats the idiosyncrasies of the local people, whose traditions and behavior are steeped in legends, folklore, superstitions, and rituals. Everyday life is a bizarre mixture of the supernatural and natural worlds, including the creation of a black hole that escapes from a rusted old bird cage where it is stored.

One of the major themes of the novel is nostalgia for life before tourists began to invade the island every summer. The town of Deyá is in a transition period in which the traditional way of life is dying out due to rapid population growth and construction. Sensing that things will never be the same as they once were, Slim and Marcia decide to return to Central America, where Marcia finds comfort in her ceiba tree.

The second novel Alegría published during this period was *Despierta, mi bien, despierta* (Wake Up, My Love, Wake Up, 1986). As Sternbach notes, "The intersection of a feminist and political consciousness in her female protagonists" is a recurring theme in novels such as *Cenizas de Izalco* and *Album familiar. Despierta, mi bien, despierta* also exemplifies this theme. Sternbach explains, "Speakers in the poems and protagonists in her fiction are often Central American women who have chosen a comfortable, bourgeois life outside their country. Furthermore, these women are not in a state of political exile, but rather are complacently content with their washing machines and other technological comforts."

The novel takes place in 1980, a few months before the assassination of El Salvadoran archbishop Oscar Romero. The protagonist, Lorena, is an upper-middle-class El Salvadoran woman married to a member of the oligarchy. Although her social class affords her many privileges, her life is virtually meaningless. She is lonely and bored, and her marriage is dull. When she has an affair with a young guerrilla poet she meets at a writer's workshop, she becomes more attuned to the political and social situation in her country. As a result, her consciousness is raised and her dormant sexuality awakened. Furthermore, she volunteers to help Archbishop Romero and the revolutionary cause by doing clerical work at his office.

Despierta, mi bien, despierta adheres to a formula that Alegría began in *Cenizas de Izalco,* and like *Album familiar* it falls into the category of resistance narrative, a term that describes much El Salvadoran prose fiction during the 1980s. According to literary critic Barbara Harlow, resistance narratives "propose specific historical analyses of the ideological and material conditions out of which they are generated, in Nicaragua, . . . El Salvador . . . or elsewhere. . . . [Moreover, they] contribute to a larger narrative, that of the passage from genealogical or hereditary bonds of filiation to the collective bonds of affiliation." In both *Album familiar* and *Despierta, mi bien, despierta,* Alegría criticizes upper-class values and shows how the protagonists, by their own ignorance and indifference, are complicit in the oppression of rural working-class people. As each protagonist looks critically at the values her family and social class uphold, she decides to break the "hereditary bonds of filiation" and join the collective struggle to help her people effect social change in her country. Once her political and social consciousness is awakened, she is forever changed and can never go back to the way she once was.

Alegría's most recent novel is *Luisa en el país de la realidad* (1987; translated as *Luisa in Realityland*, 1987), which consists of alternating prose vignettes and poetry. The English translation, which includes two extra episodes and repeats seven key poems at the end, was published first because the Mexican publisher delayed production of the book.

Alegría gives a collagelike effect to the novel by weaving fiction, Central American history and folklore, Mayan mythology, testimony, and autobiographical memoir into the narrative structure. According to literary critics John Beverley and Marc Zimmerman, her objective is "to give some sense, through a montage of different literary forms, of the overall historical and political process Central America has gone through from the 1930s to the present, in her case presented, however, from within the intimate world of a particular woman's memories and experience."

Memories are central to this novel. Alegría uses the perspective of Luisa, the seven-year-old child protagonist, to reflect class struggle and keep alive the collective memory of the rural working people. Luisa learns her family history and the history of her country by observing what happens and by listening to the anecdotes, adventures, memories, and testimonies told by her parents, relatives, nanny, and others. One of the points Alegría makes in the novel is that without a sense of one's past, one cannot imagine a future. Furthermore, she ends the novel in the American edition with a long poem entitled "The Cartography of Memory," in which the poetic voice speaks from a position of exile. Lamenting her inability to return to El Salvador, the poetic voice remembers her country and its history and imagines a future of "rebellious, contagious peace." In short, as Sternbach contends, "more than any other aspect of Alegría's writing, the role and function of memory, especially that of female protagonists in fiction or speakers in poetry, serves as a powerful tool for self-realization, recognition, and determination."

Alegría's latest work is a bilingual collection of combat poetry she and Flakoll edited, *On the Front Line: Guerrilla Poems of El Salvador* (1989). The collection is comprised of poems by El Salvadoran revolutionaries on the different fighting fronts of the Farabundo Martí National Liberation front (FMLN) and includes poems by well-established poets as well as lesser-known poets. The poetry conveys the struggles, hopes, and dreams of writers whose greatest desire is the collective construction of a better future for El Salvador.

Despite Alegría's lengthy career and impressive list of publications, she has been until recently virtually unknown outside Latin America; criticism devoted to her work has been minimal. Her popularity is growing, however, as more of her work becomes available in translation and as more scholars study Central American literature. It is safe to project that within the next few years the critical attention paid her will steadily increase.

At present Alegría and her husband divide their time between their homes in Managua, Nicaragua, and Majorca, Spain. Since 1980 Alegría's commitment to social change and her opposition to successive regimes have kept her in exile from El Salvador, where she cannot safely reside. Once she is able to return, however, she hopes to promote a national literacy campaign.

Source: Margaret B. Crosby, "Claribel Alegria," in *Dictionary of Literary Biography*, Vol. 145, *Modern Latin-American Fiction Writers, Second Series*, edited by William Luis and Ann Gonzalez, Gale Research, 1994, pp. 25–32.

Sources

Agosín, Marjorie, "The Volcano's Flower," in *Americas*, Vol. 51, No. 1, January February 1999, pp. 48–53.

Alegría, Claribel, "Accounting," in *Fugues*, Curbstone Press, 1993, p. 31.

———, "Summing Up," in *La Mujer del Rio (Woman of the River)*, translated by D. J. Flakoll, University of Pittsburgh Press, 1989, p. 89.

Boschetto-Sandoval, Sandra Maria, "Alegría, Claribel," in *Contemporary World Writers*, 2d ed., edited by Tracy Chevalier, St. James Press, 1993, pp. 14–16.

Engelbert, Jo Anne, "Claribel Alegría and the Elegiac Tradition," in *Claribel Alegría and Central American Literature: Critical Essays*, edited by Sandra M. Boschetto-Sandoval and Marcia Phillips McGowan, Ohio University Center for International Studies, 1994, pp. 183–99.

Hammond, Gerald, *The Reader and Shakespeare's Young Man Sonnets*, Macmillan, 1981, pp. 71–72.

Innes, Paul, *Shakespeare and the English Renaissance Sonnet: Verses of Feigning Love*, St. Martins, 1997, pp. 125–26.

McGowan, Marcia Phillips, "Closing the Circle: An Interview with Claribel Alegrí," in *Claribel Alegría and Central American Literature: Critical Essays*, edited by Sandra M. Boschetto-Sandoval and Marcia Phillips McGowan, Ohio University Center for International Studies, 1994, pp. 228–45.

Moyers, Bill, "Claribel Alegría," in *The Language of Life: A Festival of Poets*, edited by James Haba, Doubleday, 1995, pp. 5–16.

Review of *Fugues*, in *Booklist*, Vol. 95, Issue 5, November 1, 1998, p. 483.

Review of *Fugues*, in *Publishers Weekly*, Vol. 240, No. 42, October 18, 1993, p. 69.

Shakespeare, William, "Sonnet 55," in *The Norton Shakespeare, Based on the Oxford Edition: Romances and Poems*, W. W. Norton, 1997, p. 587.

———, "Sonnet 81," in *The Norton Shakespeare, Based on the Oxford Edition: Romances and Poems*, W. W. Norton, 1997, p. 596.

Valenzuela, Luisa, Review of *Fugues*, at www.curbstone.org, (last accessed May 17, 2004).

Further Reading

Agosín, Marjorie, ed., *These Are Not Sweet Girls: Latin American Women Poets*, White Pine Press, 1995.

This anthology of Latin American poets includes poets from the beginning to the end of the twentieth century. The poems are arranged thematically, and the editor has included lesser-known poets to balance the inclusion of those who are well known.

Alegría, Claribel, *Death of Somoza*, Curbstone Press, 1996.

This is a nonfiction book that reads like a novel, as the author relates the attempts of Somoza's own self-appointed assassins to murder the dictator.

Heyck, Denis Lynn Daly, *Life Stories of the Nicaraguan Revolution*, Routledge, 1990.

This book contains the stories of twenty-four individuals. The book is divided into political lives, religious lives, and survivors' lives.

Kunzle, David, *The Murals of Revolutionary Nicaragua, 1979–1992*, University of California Press, 1995.

After the Sandinista revolution in 1979, more than 300 murals were created that depicted the issues that Nicaragua was facing at the time of the revolution. After the Sandinista government was voted out of office in 1990, many of the murals were destroyed. This book is one way to preserve them.

Ramirez, Sergio, and D. J. Flakoll, *Hatful of Tigers: Reflections on Art, Culture and Politics*, Curbstone Press, 1995.

This book is a collection of essays that explores the U.S. involvement in supporting the Somoza dictatorship in the 1960s and 1970s. It is very much an indictment of U.S. policy in Central America.

Randall, Margaret, and Floyce Alexander, eds., *Risking a Somersault in the Air: Conversations with Nicaraguan Writers*, Curbstone Press, 1990.

This book is a collection of interviews with fourteen Nicaraguan writers whose writings were important in the period leading up to and following Nicaragua's revolution.

Rushdie, Salman, *The Jaguar Smile: A Nicaraguan Journey*, Henry Holt, 1997.

This book was the result of Rushdie's 1986 visit, during which he witnessed events as diverse as political protests and poetry recitals. Rushdie also includes interviews with soldiers and observations about ordinary life in Nicaragua.

Answers to Letters

Tomas Tranströmer

1983

Most critics would agree that Tomas Tranströmer is Sweden's most important poet since World War II. He has been associated with a variety of literary movements, lived through periods of enormous change in the world of poetry, and published poems with great diversity in form and content. Throughout his life, however, Tranströmer has published elegant and thoughtful poetry that explores the unconscious and challenges the reader's conception of the world, such as "Svar på brev" ("Answers to Letters"), from the collection *Det Vilda Torget* (*The Wild Market-Square*). Beginning with the discovery of a letter that was delivered twenty-six years earlier, the poem is a journey through the labyrinth of time, memory, and the past. It uses striking, often dream-like, comparisons and a sophisticated prose style to dramatize a journey of self-discovery.

The "self," or the identity of the poem's speaker and the object of this journey, is an elusive element in "Answers to Letters," partly because it is tied to both unconscious and conscious worlds. Tranströmer, an eminent psychologist in Sweden, is as interested in the workings of the unconscious self as he is in the function and purpose of poetry. The mature and profound meditation on these ideas leaves the reader with a poem that is characteristic of the eminent international poet highly regarded in the United States since the American poet Robert Bly began translating his material in the 1960s. He is now commonly accepted as a master in his native Sweden. "Answers to Letters," which was originally published in Stockholm in 1983, is available in

Tomas Tranströmer

Robin Fulton's English translation, *New Collected Poems*, published by Bloodaxe Books in 1997.

Author Biography

Born in Stockholm, Sweden, on April 15, 1931, Tranströmer grew up with his mother, a primary school teacher, and his maternal grandfather, a ship's pilot. He attended high school during Sweden's postwar boom years, and after his obligatory military service, he spent eight years traveling and studying a variety of subjects at the University of Stockholm. In 1958, Tranströmer married Monica Blach and began working as a psychologist in Stockholm until, in 1960, he took a job as a psychologist in residence at an institution for juvenile delinquents near the city of Linköping.

By this time Tranströmer had published *17 dikter* (*17 Poems*, 1954), which anthologized a selection of poetry written in his late teens and early twenties, and *Hemligheter på vägen* (*Secrets on the Way*), which broadened Tranströmer's poetic style and revealed some of the experience he gathered while traveling in Europe and Africa. During the 1960s, the poet came under the attack of certain Swedish critics, but his reputation began to grow internationally. Tranströmer became particularly successful in the United States, partly due to his friendship and collaboration with the American poet Robert Bly, a relationship that has continued for over forty years. Bly has long been one of the most influential translators of Tranströmer's poems into English, although Robin Fulton's translation of the complete works has become a standard text.

While continuing to publish collections of poetry throughout the 1970s and 1980s, including *Östersjöar* (*Baltics*, 1974) and *Det Vilda Torget* (*The Wild Market-Square*, 1983), Tranströmer also furthered his career as a psychologist in Västerås, Sweden. He suffered a stroke resulting in an inability to talk in November of 1990, but he was writing again soon enough to publish his autobiography, *Minnena ser mig* (*Memories Look at Me*) in 1993. Since then he has published a book entitled *Sorgegondolen* (*The Sad Gondola*, 1997), his eleventh collection of poetry. Tranströmer has received numerous literary awards, including the Neustadt International Prize for Literature 1990.

Poem Text

In the bottom drawer of my desk I come across a letter that first arrived twenty-six years ago. A letter in panic, and it's still breathing when it arrives the second time.

A house has five windows: through four of them the day shines clear and still. The fifth faces a black sky, thunder and storm. I stand at the fifth window. The letter.

Sometimes an abyss opens between Tuesday and Wednesday but twenty-six years may be passed in a moment. Time is not a straight line, it's more of a labyrinth, and if you press close to the wall at the right place you can hear the hurrying steps and the voices, you can hear yourself walking past there on the other side.

Was the letter ever answered? I don't remember, it *was* long ago. The countless thresholds of the sea went on migrating. The heart went on leaping from second to second like the toad in the wet grass of an August night.

The unanswered letters pile up, like cirrostratus clouds promising bad weather. They make the sunbeams lusterless. One day I will answer. One day when I am dead and can at last concentrate. Or at least so far away from here that I can find myself again. When I'm walking, newly arrived, in the big city, on 125th Street, in the wind on the street of dancing garbage. I who love to stray off and vanish in the crowd, a capital T in the endless mass of the text.

Poem Summary

Stanza 1

Beginning directly on the left margin, without the indentations of the other five stanzas, stanza one is set apart from the rest of the poem. Tranströmer may be implying that the first lines are an introductory statement, or the subsequent indentations may be meant to underscore the fact that the letter the speaker finds at the bottom of his desk drawer is "breathing." In any case, the two sentences of the first stanza reveal a speaker, or a character that narrates the poem, who has "come across" a letter that arrived twenty-six years previously. The phrase "come across" does not imply any urgency or action; it is the letter itself that "arrives," "in panic" and still breathing after twenty-six years, like a ghost to haunt the speaker. The speaker's passivity, and his inability to respond to his past or to major questions that are breathing and panicking, will be an important theme in the following stanzas.

Stanza 2

The second stanza's description of a house with five windows, all of them looking out to a clear and still day except the one revealing a "black sky, thunder and storm," is a somewhat mysterious image, since this would never be the case in an actual house. In fact, Tranströmer seems to be implying that this house is an abstract metaphor as opposed to a real place; "a house" instead of "my house" or "the house" signifies that the speaker is speaking in a general or unspecific way. Also, a reader might at first picture a house with four windows, or at least four views, one on each side. A fifth window with a view that is entirely different from the others may signify something outside the normal area of perception.

The two-word sentence "The letter," which stands alone as if to emphasize its striking presence, connects the fifth window and the black storm to whatever it is that the letter represents. The fact that it is related to an obscure, stormy past may suggest that the letter contains questions that have haunted the speaker for a long time. And since the letter seems to represent some kind of living, breathing past, it may be that the letter has suddenly opened up a window to the past for the speaker and allowed him, or forced him, to confront something that he is unable to answer.

Stanza 3

Stanza three begins by discussing time, observing that an "abyss" can occur between two days, but many years can pass in a very short time. This "abyss" refers, in part, to sleep, which can be a dreamland of an undefined amount of time and occur on an entirely different plane of existence. The poem "Dream Seminar," which comes shortly after "Answers to Letters" in *The Wild Marketplace*, expands on the idea that dreams can inhabit a separate and timeless world related to the subconscious. This is one reason that time is like a "labyrinth"; the past, subconscious memories, and major unanswered questions about life continue to haunt and confuse people until it seems that they are struggling through a previous passage of the maze of life.

It is also significant that the speaker compares time to a labyrinth because it suggests that he desperately wants to find a way out of time and to escape. Death is the obvious way to fully escape from time, and Tranströmer will continue to be interested in the idea of death later in this poem, but there is also the possibility of escape from normality that was represented by the "fifth window" of stanza two. There is a sense in which the speaker might need to confront "the hurrying steps and the voices" of the past, which appear to be more like haunting ghosts than fond memories, but are nevertheless intriguing keys to the speaker's identity. The speaker may desire to find the other self that is "walking past there on the other side," and answer the letter that is haunting him.

Stanza 4

The speaker's question of whether he ever answered the letter, and the fact that he cannot remember, emphasizes the uncertainty and stormy panic of the past and suggests that the letter may even be unanswerable. As if to stress that this is a vast problem and confusion, Tranströmer then provides the somewhat confusing image, "The countless thresholds of the sea went on migrating." "Thresholds" denotes entrances to the sea, or perhaps beaches, but it is difficult to imagine how they might migrate; perhaps the poet intends to evoke an image of the seas changing shape over hundreds or thousands of years of geological time. In any case, this phrase also has a double meaning related to the fifth window of stanza two and the "abyss" of time in stanza three. The threshold of the sea is a repetition, in a different form, of the previous imagery of the window and the entrance into the abyss of the past, and it is important to note that the speaker's access into this world of unanswered questions is constantly "migrating" and changing.

Stanza four's final sentence is another image of the progression of time, and again the reader should notice that time is not a straight line. Like a toad on wet grass, each heartbeat and each second leaps in a haphazard and even impulsive path, without a clear direction. What does seem true about the pattern of time is that each second is tied exactly to each heartbeat, as if an individual person's experience of time determines the objective reality of seconds, days, and years. Tranströmer highlights this contradiction between objective time and the individual whim by combining the abstract and general image of "the heart," as opposed to "my heart," "leaping from second to second" with the very specific image of "the toad in the wet grass of an August night."

Stanza 5

By changing the image of one letter to "unanswered letters pil[ing] up," and associating them with stormy weather that takes the shine out of sunbeams, the poet reinforces the idea that the letters are somehow haunting him and reminding him of things that are unresolved. The third sentence, "One day I will answer," stands out as a declaration, but it is not an immediate resolution, and the idea that the speaker will not be able to do so until he dies reinforces the idea that he is unable to confront the memories and questions in the letter or letters.

However, the next sentence, which suggests that the speaker may be able to respond or confront his past once he is able to "find myself again," is more hopeful. Tranströmer is explicitly confronting his reader with the idea that the speaker must enter an obscure labyrinth of his time in order to find his identity. The speaker cannot "find [him]self," or know who he really is, while looking out one of the four windows from stanza two that reveal the "clear and still" daylight. He must enter the world of the panicked, breathing letter that is very far away from "here," by which the speaker presumably means his home and his everyday life.

The final two sentences of the poem visualize a specific image of the speaker "finding himself again" and answering the letters from his past. The speaker suddenly envisions the place where he can concentrate and find his identity: "newly arrived, in the big city, on 125th street" amongst garbage blowing around in the wind. This location, which is very specific in the sense that it is so carefully and precisely described but simultaneously quite formless since the speaker is walking "in the wind," is likely to refer to New York City. The 125th street of Harlem, New York, an area known in the twentieth century for its dominant African American population, is quite well known because it is the location of the Apollo Theater, where many African American celebrities have begun their careers.

The tension between specificity, or identity, and formlessness continues in the final sentence of the poem. Its emphasis, which Tranströmer underscores with diction, or word choices, like "stray off," "vanish," and "endless mass," seems to be on the speaker's disappearance into obscurity. The sense of formlessness is also emphasized by the use of sentence fragments in the last four sentences. Yet the phrase "capital T" is vital to the balance between formlessness and fixed identity in the closing line of the poem; it immediately connects the speaker to the poet's identity, since a "T" begins Tranströmer's first and last names, and it stands out strongly as a contradiction to the "endless mass." The reader is left unsure whether the process of answering letters, turning to the past, and entering the labyrinth of time, will allow the speaker to find his identity or wash him away into obscurity.

Themes

Time, Memory, and the Past

Many of Tranströmer's central thematic concerns in "Answers to Letters" are related to time. This is most explicit in the third stanza and its description of the speaker's experience of the labyrinth of time, but each stanza refers to time in some manner, often in connection to the speaker's memory and past represented by the rediscovered letter. Stanza one introduces the theme of an object representing something twenty-six years in the past that is still breathing and panicking; stanza two seems to refer to some obscure and cloudy version of time outside its "fifth window"; stanza four describes time in unique visual terms emphasizing that it does not run in a straight line; and stanza five envisions the speaker in a contradiction between a vague point in time in the future ("one day"), and the specific moment of walking in the wind of 125th street.

Like the speaker's letter, which can be a source of meaning and promise but also a cause for fear and panic, time plays a somewhat contradictory role in the poem. There is a strong sense throughout the

Topics For Further Study

- Tranströmer has had a lifelong interest in psychology, and he has worked for many years as a psychologist in Västerås, Sweden. How does "Answers to Letters" relate to the field of psychology? Can you find other examples of poems that reflect themes related to psychology in *The Wild Market-Square* in other collections of Tranströmer's poetry? How do these poems bring out psychological ideas and how do psychological theories improve or change your understanding of them? Do some research into the theories of famous twentieth-century psychologists such as Sigmund Freud or Carl Jung in order to construct your answer.
- Robert Bly is Tranströmer's friend and chief advocate in the United States. Read some of Bly's poetry, such as *This Tree Will Be Here for a Thousand Years* (1979), and discuss the similarities and differences between Bly's and Tranströmer's poetry. Choose a poem of Bly's to compare in depth with "Answers to Letters," taking into account poetic technique and approaches to similar themes. Or, after reading some of Bly's nonfiction essays and criticism in addition to selections of his poetry, explain why you think Bly might have developed such an interest in Tranströmer's work.
- One of the most important Swedish artists since World War II is the filmmaker Ingmar Bergman. Watch Bergman's film *Fanny and Alexander* (1982), as well as some of his earlier classics such as *The Seventh Seal* (1956). How do you think *Fanny and Alexander* relates to "Answers to Letters?" How does Bergman's style compare to Tranströmer's? How do you think each artist is suited to his medium? Compare the portrayal of Sweden in their works, as well as their common imagery and their explorations of psychology and the unconscious.
- Tranströmer has published numerous collections of poetry over the years. Read some of his early material, some of his work during the 1960s and 1970s, and some of the other poems in *The Wild Market-Square*. How has his style changed over time? How have his techniques, themes, and subject matter changed, and what are some of the key ways in which his recent poetry is unique, innovative, and different? Discuss what makes "Answers to Letters" distinctive, and compare it to another poem that you think addresses similar issues.

poem that time is haunting the speaker, and that time is an evil labyrinth or a black and cloudy storm from which he desperately wants to escape into the sunbeams and clear weather. Yet the speaker also seems to want to confront the strange phenomenon of time, to find the "self" walking past him on the other side of the wall in time's labyrinth. He wants to answer the unanswered letters from the past and face the questions they pose, and he insists that he will confront the stormy past when, in the last stanza, he says, "One day I will answer." Tranströmer seems to be commenting, therefore, on the nature of time itself; the speaker needs to escape from time in order to find himself, but he can only experience his "self" and find an identity within the structure of time.

Stanza five's solution to this problem, which consists of the speaker's proposal to answer the letters when he is dead "and can at last concentrate," or at least "far away from here so I can find myself again," is quite contradictory. This process seems to involve straying off and "vanish[ing] in the crowd," another example of escaping from time, while simultaneously requiring a specific point in time, when he is "newly arrived" in the big city. Concluding the poem with the image of a fixed point in an "endless mass," or capital "T" in an infinite amount of text, Tranströmer highlights the contradiction between being within and without time. Although one letter is, in a sense, meaningless in an endless string of letters, it is still a unique and individual point in time, even if the same letter will be repeated over and over again. The "answers to letters" are only possible at a particular point in time, but the answers are also only possible when the speaker has stepped outside of time and can see the whole picture.

Identity

"Answers to Letters" is, in part, a journey of self-discovery. This journey begins as soon as the letter arrives, but it is not explicit until, in the third stanza, the speaker discusses hearing "yourself" on the other side of a wall in time's labyrinth; here it becomes clear that the speaker is searching for his own identity, not for another person who wrote the letter. The journey to find the "self" then builds until it reaches the climax in the line: "Or at least so far away from here that I can find myself again." This sentence, which ties directly back to the initial image of a letter delivered twenty-six years ago yet "in panic" and "still breathing," suggests that Tranströmer sees a paradox in the search for the self. While the speaker needs to be close enough to understand the immediate and specific aspects of his identity, he also needs to remain far enough away to see the permanent and timeless essence of his selfhood. The poet may be suggesting that identity must always consist of a paradoxical combination of the timeless, permanent self, and the extremely specific, localized, and individual details that cannot describe anyone else.

The Unconscious

The search for identity (see above) is closely related, for Tranströmer, to the workings of the unconscious and conscious mind. The "fifth window" of stanza two, which is likely to be a reference to the unconscious mind, emphasizes that the unconscious self must relate and interact with the conscious self. While the unconscious self is a timeless and even vague or illogical phenomenon, the conscious self is located in a very specific timeframe and series of actions. A psychologist with a longstanding interest in the interaction between the unconscious and conscious worlds, Tranströmer is interested in expressing the ways in which these two worlds must combine, if their combination is possible, in order to form a whole and complete self, or an identity.

Style

Prose Poetry

"Answers to Letters" is a prose poem in five stanzas, which means that it consists of five sections, in this case much like paragraphs, with lines of text that are not intended to have specific line breaks. The poem, therefore, reads almost like a very short story; it does not require its reader to pause over each line or sound out a specific "meter," or sequence of stressed and unstressed syllables. Tranströmer maintains a careful rhythm of language, employs poetic techniques such as repetition, and balances each word carefully with those around it. But, because of the prose appearance of the text itself, each stanza appears to be a sort of independent thought written in the same prose style as one might use to answer a letter.

Metaphor and Simile

Tranströmer frequently uses the comparative devices of metaphor and simile, both of which are figures of speech that suggest a similarity between two objects or actions (although a simile is characterized by the use of the words "as" or "like"). As many critics have suggested, Tranströmer's metaphors and similes do not merely serve as descriptive tools; they are often used to transform the reader's experience of reality. They involve rapid shifts to ideas that may seem unrelated to the "tenor," or the original source of the comparison.

This technique of liberal association, which often seems illogical, is an element of Tranströmer's poetry that some critics have associated with Surrealism. Poets whom Tranströmer admired and by whom he was influenced, the French Surrealists placed a great deal of emphasis on the workings of unconscious thought, and the melding of conscious and unconscious worlds. Tranströmer, whose interest in the unconscious mind connects to his lifelong career as a psychologist, may have similar aims when he employs a unique spectrum of freely associated comparisons in "Answers to Letters."

Historical Context

Sweden in the Early 1980s

Swedish politics were preoccupied with questioning the policy of neutrality, which had been in place since World War II, after a Soviet submarine ran aground near a Swedish naval base in 1981. The early 1980s in Sweden were also marked by the reelection of the socialist Social Democratic Party, which had been in power for forty-four years when a coalition of non-socialist parties won the election of 1976. An economic downturn led to a Social Democrat victory in 1982, and a return to the policies of the Swedish "welfare" state, which

Compare & Contrast

- **1980s:** In Sweden, the environment and nuclear energy, along with questions over the Swedish policy of neutrality, are the major political issues of the day.

  Today: Sweden is a member of the European Union (since 1995), but Swedish voters decline to join the common European currency in 2003, a vote that went ahead just days after the shocking assassination of Sweden's foreign minister. Like the assassination of the Swedish Prime Minister in 1986, investigators are unable to determine the motive of the killer.

- **1980s:** In the United States, Ronald Reagan, a Republican and former actor, is president. The decade marks the advent of household computer technology and an atmosphere of economic conservatism.

  Today: Republican George W. Bush is president of the United States, and the social agenda of the government is more conservative since the terrorist attacks on the World Trade Center and the Pentagon in 2001.

- **1980s:** The Social Democratic Party regains control in Sweden, and the country recovers from the economic downturn that marked the late 1970s. Sweden has a reputation as a country with one of the most extensive social service networks in the world.

  Today: Sweden retains its extensive social service network and enjoys one of the highest standards of living in the world. The Swedish economy is growing faster than others in most of Western Europe.

places a large emphasis on redistribution of wealth and an extensive network of social services. Schools, universities, health care, pensions, and various economic support schemes in Sweden were funded entirely through taxation.

Swedish Poetry after World War II

Until the mid-1960s, Swedish poetry was predominantly associated with high modernism and "formalism," or poetry that placed an emphasis on structure and style as opposed to content. T. S. Eliot was one of the most influential critics and poets to espouse this view and, although it was rapidly going out of fashion in the years following World War II, it remained popular in Sweden for some years. By the 1960s, however, a younger generation of poets was emerging with a tendency to focus on political content and a directly engaging style. As Joanna Bankier writes in her literary biography of Tranströmer, "Swedish writers and poets coming of age in the 1960s began to feel that aesthetic form and aesthetic pleasure might be obstacles to empathy, hindrances evoking indecency in the face of human suffering."

These writers, as Bankier observes, disdained the distanced and measured tone, which they associated with writers of the previous generation. The divide between formalism and politicized or "raw" poetry grew less urgent during the 1970s, but traces of these two aesthetic approaches remained an important issue amongst Swedish poets. Tranströmer himself had been, perhaps unfairly, associated with the formalists and condemned by many in the younger generation. By the time *The Wild Market-Square* was published in 1983, however, it was generally acknowledged that he had been engaged in numerous experiments in form since the 1960s.

Surrealism

The artistic movement known as Surrealism was founded by the French poet and critic André Breton in the 1920s. Surrealism was heavily influenced by the preceding movement of Dadaism, which stressed irrationality and anarchy, and both movements were a reaction against the rationalistic European culture that, some artists believed, led to the horrors of World War I. But Surrealism is unique in its emphasis on positive expression, unconscious thought, and the melding of the unconscious and conscious worlds. Breton and other Surrealist poets became known for free-association and a startling psychological, illogical thought process.

Aside from the poets who were working directly under Breton's Surrealist manifesto, Surrealist thought had a wide-ranging influence in literature, art, theater, and film. It has been linked to Samuel Beckett and the Theater of the Absurd as well as with the stream-of-consciousness writing technique practiced by James Joyce and others. Although he has also been associated with "formalism," Tranströmer is known to have an interest in Surrealism and his poetry often exhibits some of the leaps of unconscious association for which Surrealists became known.

Critical Overview

Swedish critics initially associated Tranströmer with the high modernist "formalist" tradition characteristic of his generation. The poet never strictly conformed to this description; his work changed drastically over time, he engaged in numerous experiments in form, and many critics, including Urban Torhamn, have acknowledged his connection to the Surrealist movement. But Tranströmer was nevertheless associated with formalism, particularly when, in the 1960s, a young and radical generation were fiercely advocating a politicized and direct poetic style. As Joanna Bankier notes in her *Dictionary of Literary Biography* entry on the poet, during this time of change, "critics took issue with Tranströmer's craftsmanship and formal restraint."

This stigma remained with Tranströmer for many years, although in the United States, due particularly to Robert Bly's championing, he retained a prestigious reputation as an innovative and liberal poet. Describing why the younger Swedish generation disavowed Tranströmer's style, Bly writes in his 1990 article "Tomas Tranströmer and 'The Memory'":

> He likes this "suspension," where objects float in a point of view that cannot be identified as "Marxist" or "conservative," right or left. During the sixties many critics in Sweden demanded that each poet commit himself or herself to a Marxist view, or at least concede that documentaries are the only socially useful form of art.

As the trend that began with the generation of the 1960s grew less pronounced, however, Swedish critics began once again to consider Tranströmer a unique master. Bankier describes the recent criticism of the poet as wide-ranging, often treating his work as a "consideration of his language or an intertextual examination." "Answers to Letters" has received little individual critical attention, but the discussions of *The Wild Market-Square* or Tranströmer's work as a whole are often highly applicable, such as Gary Lenhart's description of how "Tomas Tranströmer's poems occupy 'the slot between waking and sleep,'" in his article "Hard Edge Fog."

Criticism

Scott Trudell

Trudell is a freelance writer with a bachelor's degree in English literature. In the following essay, Trudell discusses the journey of self-discovery in "Answers to Letters," arguing that the speaker uses the poem to answer the letters of his past and define who he is.

The central metaphors in Tranströmer's poem are the letters that the speaker desires to answer, from the initial letter that arrived twenty-six years before to the "unanswered letters" that "pile up" in the final stanza, but it is not entirely clear what these metaphors represent. They could, in part, be meant to signify a friend or lover, or the memory of such a person who has been lost or left behind. Or, given the fact that the initial letter is "in panic" and the speaker seems anxious to clear the clouds associated with the letters, Tranströmer may be implying that the letters signify unanswered questions about the world that have reemerged to haunt the speaker. Perhaps this is why they have become so pressing and confusing as to "make the sunbeams lusterless."

But there is also a sense in which the letters are representations of the speaker's very personal past, or artifacts of who he used to be. Particularly when he uses the phrase, "you can hear yourself walking past there," while discussing the "labyrinth" of time, Tranströmer appears to be implying that the letters should be understood as messages from himself, as if his past self is communicating with his present self. Indeed, it becomes particularly clear in the final sentences of the poem that the letters, which the speaker can only answer once he "can find [him]self again," are closely associated with his identity. The conflict for the speaker is one of answering who he is, and the phrase "Answers to Letters" may refer to his need to declare his selfhood and "answer" himself.

For the speaker, the two main aspects of this process are "find[ing] myself," and declaring this identity in the form of a poem. Neither of these goals are particularly easy, and it becomes clear in "Answers to Letters" that both are precarious and inexact processes. Nevertheless, the poem both acknowledges the complexity of such a journey of self-discovery and manages to formulate an answer to the speaker's persistent questions. By the end of the poem, it becomes clear that although his identity comes very close to vanishing altogether into something that he cannot understand, Tranströmer has accomplished this unique and individual journey, and left behind a poem that is itself a visionary declaration of his selfhood.

The first element of the poem's theme of identity is the speaker's search for the diverse elements of his "self." Tranströmer dramatizes this journey with a number of careful poetic techniques, but perhaps the most important of these is the way in which he weaves together the past and present, the specific and the general, in order to display the contradictory nature of identity and suit the imagery of the poem to the story it tells. "Answers to Letters" describes a series of events that move closer to a specific point, such as "125th Street" or "the toad in the wet grass of an August night," but simultaneously seem to move further away from anything specific, such as "countless thresholds of the sea" and "the endless mass of the text." This relationship between the focused, specific, and rational, and the general, timeless, and irrational, is the key stylistic feature the poet uses to visualize and express the process of introspection. Examining it closely reveals some of Tranströmer's most important ambitions in the poem.

The paradox between the specific and the timeless is so appropriate for representing the process of self-discovery because, as Tranströmer recognizes, identity is divided between these two extremes. Each person's "self" is comprised of the particular actions and events of a lifetime, or everything that might fit into a biography, as well as the unique and permanent world of inner thoughts that make up what some would call a "spirit." It is only in the combination of these two aspects that the speaker seems to have the chance to discover his identity, which is why Tranströmer insists on combining paradoxical images in order to envision the process of self-declaration. "Answers to Letters" does not simply point out that the self has these two elements; it probes the possibility of combining them into something coherent within the structure and limits of the discipline of psychology.

"This relationship between the focused, specific, and rational, and the general, timeless, and irrational, is the key stylistic feature the poet uses to visualize and express the process of introspection."

In his essay "Hard Edge Fog," Gary Lenhart describes the "vocabulary of contraries" in Tranströmer's poetry as a "landscape" that is "at once tangible and mysterious. Despite the recurring Baltic fog, the objects in his dreams have sharp edges and a particular insistence." Critics such as Lenhart and Robert Bly have connected this poetic style, which is readily apparent in "Answers to Letters," to Tranströmer's interest in the relationship between the unconscious and conscious worlds. When the "thunder and storm" of the fifth window occurs at the same time as the "day shines clear and still" in the other four windows, or the "countless thresholds of the sea" go on "migrating" at the same time as the location is fixed to the leaps of a toad on an August night, it is clear that the unfathomable, endless, and obscure world of the unconscious is closely intertwined with the clear, exact, and ordered world of the conscious.

The paradoxes of the final stanza make it particularly clear that these worlds need to combine in order for the speaker to find what he thinks of as his "self." His identity is incomplete without acknowledging the vast world of his unconscious, but as soon as he turns to face the fifth window and confront this part of his self, the speaker seems in danger of "vanish[ing] in the crowd" altogether. Because the unconscious world is timeless and unfixed, a limitless landscape of dreams, the brief meeting of unconscious and conscious selves threatens to result in an "endless mass of text," leaving the speaker without the coherent self-understanding he seeks. The idea that the speaker can only answer the letters when he is "dead and can at last concentrate" emphasizes this problem and highlights the additional paradox that the

What Do I Read Next?

- Tranströmer's *New Collected Poems* (1997), translated by Robin Fulton, contains all of the poet's major collections. From the elegant verse and striking imagery of *17 Poems* to the diverse and challenging meditations in *The Wild Market-Square* (1983) and *The Sad Gondola* (1996), this book is the definitive source to explore after "Answers to Letters."
- *This Tree Will Be Here for a Thousand Years* (1979) is a collection of poetry by Tranströmer's friend, translator, and enthusiast Robert Bly. Many of the poems in this volume, like "Answers to Letters," offer a visionary meditation on the duality of consciousness.
- *André Breton: Selected Works* (2003), edited by Mark Polizzotti, is an excellent introduction to the poetry of the famous surrealist author André Breton, including helpful biographical information and important selections from his prose.
- Robert Bly's *American Poetry: Wilderness and Domesticity* (1990) is a passionate work of nonfiction that articulates Bly's theory of poetry and justifies his long-standing attack on many of the poets popular with the university elite.
- *The Selected Poetry of Rainer Maria Rilke* (1989) provides an important body of work by the famous twentieth-century Austrian writer, whose brilliant poetry ranges from mystical to philosophical to historical.

speaker cannot genuinely find his identity until he no longer physically exists, when he is an entirely fixed and lifeless subject.

Nevertheless, the speaker qualifies this statement with the sentence, "Or at least so far away from here that I can find myself again," which suggests a more successful outcome in the struggle to reconcile his conscious and unconscious worlds. The sentences that follow this one form a more specific vision of this reconciliation, envisioning the very specific location of 125th Street's "wind on the street of dancing garbage" and the paradox of "a capital T in the endless mass of the text." The fact that this "endless mass of text" is the final image of the poem reinforces the possibility that the speaker has been lost in the faraway realm of the unconscious into which he has journeyed, but the capital "T" is a powerful balance to this threat. Since "T" is the first letter of Tranströmer's first and last names, it is a key sign of hope that the speaker, and the poet, have reached the essence of the self.

The merging of the narrative voice of the poem and the poet himself is not a subtle trick or quirky touch in the final line; it is central to the search for identity in "Answers to Letters." By claiming explicitly that he is the identity in question, Tranströmer is urging the reader to regard the poem as more than a mere dramatization of a fictional search for selfhood. The "capital T" is a sign that the poem is a self-conscious declaration that consists of, as its title suggests, "answers" to the poet's own "letters," or unanswered questions and memories from his past. In this sense, the entire prose poem, or the individual stanzas of indented prose themselves, might be considered "answers" to the past and declarations of identity.

Like much of the poetry in *The Wild Market-Square*, Tranströmer allows a vision or possibility such as this declaration of selfhood to remain floating in the reader's mind. He does not insist upon strictly fixing his meaning, but allows the stanzas to remain partly in his own very personal world of meaning and partly in the more general and understandable form of answers to the vague past. This allows the reader some access into Tranströmer's theories of the melding of unconscious and conscious worlds, and it establishes an important commentary on the ambiguous and contrary nature of identity. But, perhaps more importantly, it also offers a visionary glimpse into the poet's extremely unique and personal understanding of himself.

Source: Scott Trudell, Critical Essay on "Answers to Letters," in *Poetry for Students*, Thomson Gale, 2005.

Robert Bly

In the following essay, Bly provides an overview of Tranströmer's life and works and asserts that Tranströmer "leads a movement of poetry . . . toward a poetry of silence and depths."

1. Tomas Tranströmer seems to me the best poet to appear in Sweden for some years. He comes from a long line of ship pilots who worked in and around the Stockholm Archipelago. He is at home on islands. His face is thin and angular, and the swift, spare countenance reminds one of Hans Christian Andersen's or the young Kierkegaard's. He has a strange genius for the image—images come up almost effortlessly. The images flow upward like water rising in stone lonely place, in the swamps, or deep fir woods.

Tranströmer's poems, so vivid in English, show the ability of certain poetry to travel to another culture and actually arrive there. As Tranströmer said in a letter to the Hungarian poets, published in the magazine *Új Írás* in 1977: "Poetry has an advantage from the start. . . . Poetry requires no heavy, vulnerable apparatus that has to be lugged around; it isn't dependent on temperamental performers, dictatorial directors, bright producers with irresistible ideas." He also remarked, "Poems are active meditations; they want to wake us up, not put us to sleep." At many places I go in this country, I meet people for whom Tranströmer is an awakener. They receive the fragrance of the depth from him; they see the light suddenly released by one of his brief quatrains. His work has become a strong influence now on many younger American poets.

Swedish society is most famously a welfare society, *the* welfare society; it is perhaps the first society in history that has had the means to adopt as an ideal the abolition of poverty. But it is also a technological society like ours, and one given to secular solutions. Tranströmer reports how difficult it is in such a society to keep in touch with inner richness. What happens to the "vertical" longings, the longings for the divine? A poem called "Below Freezing" brings up this issue.

> We are at a party that doesn't love us. Finally the party lets its mask fall and shows what it is: a shunting station for freight cars. In the fog cold giants stand on their tracks. A scribble of chalk on cardoors.

> *"In Tranströmer's poems the link to the worldly occasion is stubbornly kept, yet the poems have a mystery and surprise that never fade, even on many readings."*

> One can't say it aloud, but there is a lot of repressed violence here. That is why the furnishings seem so heavy. And why is it so difficult to see the other thing present: a spot of sun that moves over the house walls and slips over the unaware forest of flickering faces, a biblical saying never set down: "Come unto me, for I am as full of contradictions as you."
>
> I work the next morning somewhere else. I drive there in a hum through the dawning hour which resembles a dark blue cylinder. Orion hangs over the frost. Children stand in a silent clump, waiting for the schoolbus, the children no one prays for. The light grows as gradually as our hair.

"The children no one prays for" is a painful line. Tranströmer is not coming down on the side of orthodox Christianity, yet a part of him is aware that children are deprived, even endangered, by not being prayed for. There is more light now than in primitive times, but it moves over "an unaware forest of flickering faces."

2. Tomas Tranströmer was born in Stockholm on 15 April 1931. He is an only child. His father and mother divorced when he was three; he and his mother lived after that in an apartment in the working-class district of Stockholm. He studied music and psychology and still plays the piano enthusiastically, as his recent poem on Schubert makes clear.

The early fifties were a rather formal time, both here and in Sweden, and Tranströmer began by writing highly formal poems, all elements measured. His first book, *17 dikter* (17 Poems), published in 1954, contains several poems written in classical meters adapted from the Latin. That collection includes many baroque elements in its language. Tranströmer's language has gradually evolved into a more spoken Swedish, and he has written both prose poetry and free verse; but, as he remarked during a recent interview published in

Poetry East: "Often there is a skeleton somewhere in the poem with a regular number of beats and so on in each line. You don't have to know that, but for me it's important."

Tranströmer's second book, *Hemligheter på vägen* (Secrets on the Road), contained fourteen poems and appeared four years later. In 1962, after another gap of four years, he published *Den halvfärdiga himlen* (Half-Finished Heaven), with twenty-one poems—fifty-two poems in all in about ten years. In 1966 came *Klanger och spår* (Resonance and Foot-Tracks) and in 1970 *Mörkerseende* (Eng. *Night Vision*). Three years later he published *Stigar* (Paths) and in 1974 a long poem, *Östersjöar* (Eng. *Baltics*), describing the island where his family on his father's side have lived for generations.

Tranströmer's early poetry could be described as baroque romantic, with elements visible from both the eighteenth and the nineteenth century. Like the romantics, Tranströmer loves to travel, and a chance encounter may evolve into a poem; but Göran Printz-Påhlson notes a crucial difference between Tranströmer's work and that of the romantics: "The traveler is brought to a halt, and the experience is imprinted with ferocious energy, but not interpreted." Tranströmer works slowly and steadily on poems and often writes only seven or eight a year. That may be one reason why his poems have so much weight.

Tranströmer worked for some years as a psychologist at the boys' prison in Linköping and then moved with his family to Västerås, about sixty miles west of Stockholm. There he works as a psychologist for a labor organization funded by the state. His responsibilities involve helping juvenile delinquents reenter society, assisting persons with physical disabilities in choosing a career, and work with parole offenders and drug rehabilitation. His family consists of two daughters, Paula and Emma, and his wife Monica, who finished her training as a nurse a few years ago and has worked from time to time with refugees who are resettling in Sweden.

Tranströmer's three most recent books have been *Sanningsbarriären* (Eng. *Truth Barriers*) in 1978, *Det vilda torget* (Eng. *The Wild Marketplace*) in 1983, and last year a fine new collection, including some of his strongest poems, *För levande och döda* (Eng. "For Living and Dead").

3. Tranströmer values his poems not so much as artifacts but rather as meeting places. Images from widely separated worlds meet in his verse. In the letter to the Hungarian poets he said, "My poems are meeting places. . . . What looks at first like a confrontation turns out to be connection." The poem "Street Crossing" describes an encounter between the ancient Swedish earth and a Stockholm street.

> The street's massive life swirls around me;
> it remembers nothing and desires nothing.
> Far under the traffic, deep in earth,
> the unborn forest awaits, still, for a thousand years.

He remains "suspended" so as to hear things.

> one evening in June: the transistor told me the
> latest on the Extra Session: Kosygin, Eban.
> One or two thoughts bored their way in
> despairingly. . . . I saw heard it from a suspension
> bridge together with a few boys. Their bicycles
> buried in the bushes—only the horns
> stood up.
> ("Going with the Current")

He likes this "suspension," where objects float in a point of view that cannot be identified as "Marxist" or "conservative," right or left. During the sixties many critics in Sweden demanded that each poet commit himself or herself to a Marxist view, or at least concede that documentaries are the only socially useful form of art. Tranströmer has received several attacks for resisting that doctrine. Art still needs the unconscious, he believes; that has not changed. He also believes that a poem needs a place for the private, the quirky, the religious, the unexplainable, the human detail that the collective cannot classify. "Out in the Open," for example, is neither a nature poem, nor a political poem, nor a religious poem. One of its purposes evidently is to draw from all these sections of psychic experience without choosing among them.

> Sun burning. The plane comes in low
> throwing a shadow shaped like a giant cross that
> rushes over the ground.
> A man is sitting in the field poking at something.
> The shadow arrives.
> For a fraction of a second he is right in the centre
> of the cross.
>
> I have seen the cross hanging in the cool church
> vaults. At times it resembles a split-second shot of
> something moving at tremendous speed.

One of the most beautiful qualities in Tranströmer's poems is the space we feel in them. I think one reason for this is that the four or five main images which appear in each of his poems come from widely separated sources in the psyche. His poems are a sort of railway station where trains that have come enormous distances stand briefly in the same building. One train may have some Russian snow still lying on the undercarriage, and another may have Mediterranean flowers still fresh in the compartments and Ruhr soot on the roofs.

The poems are mysterious because of the distance the images have come to get there. Mallarmé believed there should be mystery in poetry, and he urged poets to get it by removing the links that tie the poem to its occasion in the real world. In Tranströmer's poems the link to the worldly occasion is stubbornly kept, yet the poems have a mystery and surprise that never fade, even on many readings.

4. Tranströmer has said that when he first began to write, in the early fifties, it still seemed possible to compose a nature poem into which nothing technological entered. Now, he says, he feels that many objects created by technology have become almost parts of nature, and he makes sure in his poetry that technology and its products appear. Some sights brought about by technology help him see more vividly a countryside scene: "All at once I notice the hills on the other side of the lake: / their pine has been clear-cut. They resemble the shaved / skull-sections of a patient about to have a brain operation." Perhaps nature can help you see a semi: "The semi-trailer crawls through the fog. / It is the lengthened shadow of a dragonfly larva / crawling over the murky lakebottom." Man-made objects are not necessarily without life.

> I drive through a village at night, the houses step
> out into the headlights—they are awake now, they
> want a drink.
> Houses, barns, nameposts, deserted trailers—now
> they take on life. Human beings sleep:
> some can sleep peacefully, others have tense faces
> as though in hard training for eternity.
> They don't dare to let go even in deep sleep.
> They wait like lowered gates while the mystery
> rolls past.

5. Recent poems bring forward a fresh emphasis: the poems circle in an intense way around the experience of borders, boundaries of nations, the passage from one world to the next, the weighty instant as we wake up and step from the world of dream to this world, the corridors through which the dead invade our world, the intermediate place between life and art, the contrast between Schubert's music and Schubert, "a plump young man from Vienna" who sometimes "slept with his glasses on."

The title of a recent collection, *Sanningsbarriären*, translated as both *Truth Barriers* and *The Truth Barrier*, suggests a customs gate. Tranströmer remarked that truth exists only at the border between worlds. On this side of the border there is doctrine, and on the other side infinity, so that we experience truth only at the moment of crossing. But, alas, there are guards who do not want us to cross.

In "Start of a Late Autumn Novel" Tranströmer, inside an uninhabited island house, finds himself neither asleep nor awake: "A few books I've just read sail by like schooners on the way to the Bermuda Triangle, where they will disappear without a trace." This description is rueful and funny. He's right: sometimes we finish a book and can't remember a word. As the poem continues, he lies half asleep and hears a thumping sound outside. He listens to it—it is something being held down by earth. It beats like a heart under a stethoscope; it seems to vanish and return. Or perhaps there is some being inside the wall who is knocking, "someone who belongs to the other world, but got left here anyway, he thumps, wants to go back. Too late. Wasn't on time down here, wasn't on time up there, didn't make it on board in time." So apparently a successful passage to the other world and back has to do with timing: the Celtic fairy tales also emphasize that. The poem ends with his amazement the next morning when he sees an oak branch, a torn-up tree root, and a boulder. When, in solitude, we see certain objects, they seem to be "left behind when the ship sailed"; Tranströmer says they are monsters from the other world "whom I love."

A poem called "December Evening '72" begins: "Here I come the invisible man, perhaps in the employ / of some huge Memory that wants to live at this moment. And I drive by / the white church that's locked up. A saint made of wood is inside, / smiling helplessly, as if someone had taken his glasses." The first two lines suggest that Tranströmer as an artist believes himself to be a servant of the Memory. He writes a poem when some huge Memory wants to cross over into this world; and this view of art seems more European than American. Often in America the artist believes his or her job is to tell the truth about one's own life: confessional poetry certainly implies that. Following that concept of art, many workshop poets comb their personal memory and write poems about their childhood, filling the poems with a clutter of detail. This clutter sometimes ensures that the piece will remain "a piece of writing" and will not become "a work of art."

Tranströmer has the odd sense that the Great Memory can only come in when the artist is alert to it. While on guard duty in a defense unit a few years ago, he wrote:

> Task: to be where I am.
> Even when I'm in this solemn and absurd
> role: I am still the place
> where creation does some work on itself.
>
> Dawn comes, the sparse tree trunks
> take on color now, the frostbitten
> forest flowers form a silent search party
> after something that has disappeared in the dark.

But to be where I am . . . and to wait:
I am full of anxiety, obstinate, confused.
Things not yet happened are already here!
I feel that. They're just out there:

a murmuring mass outside the barrier.
They can only slip in one by one.
They want to slip in. Why? They do
one by one. I am the turnstile.
("Sentry Duty")

He experiences the Great Memory as "somebody who keeps pulling on my arm each time I try to write." Again we feel ourselves at a boundary, being influenced by something on the other side. In "From the Winter of 1947" the dead press through into our world, as the stains in wallpaper: "They want to have their portraits painted." And in "Street Crossing," for one second as he crosses a busy Stockholm street, the poet has the sensation that the street and the earth below it have eyes and can see him.

Tranströmer begins his Schubert poem by describing New York from an overlook, "where with one glance you take in the houses where eight million human beings live." He mentions subway cars, coffee cups, desks, elevator doors. Still, "I know also—statistics to the side—that at this moment in some room down there Schubert is being played, and for that person the notes are more real than all the rest." And what are notes? When sounds are absorbed and shaped by and inside, say, a string quartet, they contain vibrations that resonate somewhere inside us and awaken "feelings" that we seem not to have felt in daily life. There is evidently a layer of consciousness that runs alongside our life, above or below, but is not it. Perhaps it is older. Certain works of art make it their aim to rise up and pierce this layer, or layers. Or they open to allow in "memories" from this layer. Some artists—Tranströmer, Pasternak, and Akhmatova come especially to mind—keep the poem spare and clear so it can pierce the layers, or leave room for the Memory.

The art of Schubert puts Tranströmer at a boundary between worlds, and at such a boundary he sees astonishing truths.

The five instruments play. I go home through
warm woods
where the earth is springy under my feet
curl up like someone still unborn, sleep, roll on so
weightlessly
into the future, suddenly understand that plants are
thinking.

Art helps us, he says, as a banister helps the climber on a dark stairwell. The banister finds its own way in the dark. In certain pieces of music happiness and suffering weigh exactly the same. The depths are above us and below us at the same instant. The melody line is a stubborn "humming sound that this instant is with us / upward into / the depths."

Swedish magazines often fill themselves with abstract hallucinatory poetry, typewriter poetry, alphabet poetry—poems that are really the nightmares of overfed linguists, of logical positivists with a high fever. Tranströmer, simply by publishing his books, leads a movement of poetry in the opposite direction, toward a poetry of silence and depths.

Source: Robert Bly, "Tomas Tranströmer and 'The Memory,'" in *World Literature Today*, Vol. 64, No. 4, Autumn 1990, pp. 570–73.

Joanna Bankier

In the following essay, Bankier likens Tranströmer's poetry to surreal art and classical music in its approach to modern society.

In a poem entitled "Galleriet" (The Gallery) Tomas Tranströmer records how, staying overnight at a motel, he is haunted by faces appearing on the wall. They have a dreamlike quality and impose themselves on him, demanding attention and compassion.

Jag låg över på ett motell vid E3.
I mitt rum där fanns en lukt som jag känt förut
bland de asiatiska samlingarna på ett museum

masker tibetanska japanska mot en ljus vägg.

som tränger fram genom glömskans vita vägg

I stayed overnight at a motel by the E3.
In my room a smell I'd felt before
in the oriental halls of a museum:

masks Tibetan Japanese on a pale wall.

But it's not masks now, it's faces

forcing through the white wall of oblivion
(*TSP*, 140)

As in so many other poems, the poet has been following the flow of traffic, a figure he often uses to suggest socialization. When the flow is arrested, the realization erupts into consciousness that socialization imposes a role and makes life into a set of ritualized performances which allow only for a minimum of stylized movement.

I karriären rör vi oss stelt steg för steg
som i ett no-spel
med masker, skrikande sång: Jag, det är Jag!
Den som slogs ut
representeras av en hoprullad filt.

We move through our career stiffly, step by step,
it's like a No play
white masks, high-pitched song: It's me, it's me!
The one who's failed
is represented by a rolled-up blanket. (*TSP*, 142)

An inauthentic self masks the lack of true identity. This fabricated self is the individual's prime commodity in a society governed by the laws of the market. It must be vociferously displayed and aggressively defended in the struggle for survival, not so much biological survival as social, since the good life is identified with a successful career and a failure in this respect cannot be compensated; it is beyond redemption: "The one who's failed / is represented by a rolled-up blanket." To improve one's social status amounts to a "moral" obligation. It is as if, deprived of a spiritual dimension, we still strive to rise above ourselves and have replaced Plato's ladder with social climbing.

Ours is a world in which, quite literally, time is money. People who work in the industrial and commercial machinery become caught up in the profit-making and time-saving frenzy and come to regard others as well as themselves in terms borrowed from economics. The self is no longer endowed with intrinsic value and becomes purely instrumental. It is treated like any other commodity. It has been reduced to what it can produced, accomplish, and achieve and is subject to the usual advertising process: the mask makes itself known with a "high-pitched song: It's me, it's me!"

Neither is it easy to keep the social world at bay; it has a way of invading even our leisure. The habit of time saving will not let itself be confined to the hours between nine and five, Tranströmer writes in an earlier poem: "Fritidens måne kretsar kring planeten Arbete / med dess massa och tyngd.—Det är så de vill ha det"; "The moon of leisure circles the planet Work / with its mass and weight.—It's as they wish to have it." The social role cannot be thrown off. The mask adheres to the bearer's face; the professional persona invades all areas of life, narrowing our vision.

> En man känner på världen med yrket som en
> handske.
> Han vilar en stund mitt på dagen och har lagt ifrån
> sig handskarna på hyllan.
> Där växer de plötsligt, breder ut sig
> och mörklägger hela huset inifrån.

> A man feels the world with his work like a glove.
> He rests for a while at midday having laid aside the
> gloves on the shelf.
> There they suddenly grow, spread
> and black out the whole house from inside.
> (*TSP*, 78)

The negation of the intrinsic value of human life has brought about a state of affairs where everyone is in bondage: "Välkommen till de autentiska gallerierna! / Välkommen till de autentiska galärerna! / De autentiska gallren!" (*SD*, 146); "Welcome to the authentic galleries! / Welcome to the authentic galleys! / The authentic grilles!" (*TSP*, 140).

> *There is an anarchic, violent trait in the midst of the Tranströmeran mildness, a barely contained rage at what he considers a state of bondage."*

From time to time criticism of the social machinery is voiced and someone exposes the general state of misery. Someone writes a book, acquires followers; committees are set up to investigate, memorandums and reports are issued. For a while the surface of things is ruffled by agitation; debates around dinner tables grow more intense. Then things go back to normal.

> Hör samhällets mekaniska självförebråelser
> stora fläktens röst
> som den konstgjorda blåsten i gruvgångarna
> sexhundra meter nere. (*SD*, 149)

> Listen to society's mechanical self-reproaches
> the voice of the big fan
> like the artificial wind in mine tunnels
> six hundred meters down.

These self-reproaches must remain without effect, however, as every culture casts a spell in the shape of an ideology whose nature remains hidden from the insiders. Not only value but also perception is governed by a set of culturally shared conventional notions and ruling metaphors, and any change would require it change in vision: "Men vi ser de här händelserna från fel håll: ett stenröse istället för sfinxens ansikte" (*D*, 190); "But we see these events from the wrong angle; a heap of stones instead of the face of the sphinx."

Our passionate striving for knowledge cancels out the mystery at the heart of existence. Skepticism imposes limitations of its own kind, whereas Tranströmer would want us at least to entertain the notion that things are different from the way they appear. Above all he wants us to be able to "see things from a fresh angle where everything is not already set according to the usual stereotypes" (TT).

Of course, this is easier said than done, as any neurotic could testify. The insider is the last one to acknowledge his own blindness. Or, as Tranströmer writes in a poem from the early seventies:

Två sanningar närmar sig varann. En kommer
inifrån, en kommer utifrån
och där de möts har man en chans att få se sig
själv.
Den som märker vad som håller på att hända ropar
förtvivlat: "Stanna!
vad som helst, bara jag slipper känna mi själv."

Two truths approach each other, one comes from
the inside and one from outside
where they meet there is a chance to get to know
oneself.
The one who notices what is about to happen cries
out: "Stop!
anything but getting to know myself."

Common wisdom has it that poetry makes nothing happen. It does not send merchandise across the oceans, stop wars, or end poverty. Yet poetry can at times be efficacious in breaking spells and illusions. It can point to alternatives and illuminate spots of blindness. It can show the value of looking at an old problem from a new perspective. It can be a training ground for a flexible, playful, and, as far as it goes, unencumbered vision.

Such a motivation seems to underlie Tranströmer's delight in reversals of perspective, imaginative solutions, invitations to look at contemporary reality "through the inverted periscope." He loves to unsettle our conventional notions: set the static in violent motion, make what appears to be moving into something absolutely still.

Andas lugnt . . . En okänd blå materia är fastnaglad
vid stolarna.
Guldnitarna flög in med oerhörd hastighet
och tvärstannade
som om de aldrig varit annat än stillhet.

Breathe calmly . . . An unknown blue material is
nailed to the chair
The gold upholstery tacks flew in with unheard-of
speed
and stopped abruptly
as if they had never been anything but stillness.

Or he puts together images made up of incongruous elements: "the Ship, / like the cloud weightless hanging in its space / And the water round its prow is motionless, / dead calm. And yet it's storming!"

Where have we seen these incongruities before? Of course, the surrealists! The American poet Leslie Ullman once said that some of Tranströmer's poems remind her of René Magritte's paintings, and indeed they do. There is a similar clarity of vision and outline. There is a similar appearance of ordinariness in the details. There is the balanced composition. The greatest affinity, however, lies in the shuffling of conventional perceptions, the insistent breaking up of the automatism of associations. Where a bright blue sky makes us expect daytime, Magritte gives us lighted streetlamps in the lower part of the picture. Where "ship" makes us associate to weight and gravity, Tranströmer gives us levity and suspension in space, the incongruity of storm and dead calm in the same picture.

Surely these permutations must exercise our vision, flex the muscles of our imagination, make us more receptive to seeing "other things that also exist." This ambition is another, more general point of affinity between Tranströmer and the surrealists, especially Eluard, whom he read very early and of whom he wrote in 1966:

Gick länge längs den antipoetiska muren.
Die Mauer. Inte se över.
Den vill omge vårt vuxna liv
i rutinstaden, rutinlandskapet.

Eluard rörde vid någon knapp
och muren öppnade sig
och trädgården visade sig.

Walked for a long time along the anti-poetry wall.
Die Mauer. It's forbidden to look above it.
It wants to surround our adult lives
in the routine city, in the routine landscape.

Eluard touched some kind of button
and the wall opened
and the garden appeared.

"Life is occupied territory," Tranströmer says in an interview in 1982. "Existence is locked into other people's decisions . . . all those people who put words in your mouth, who decide what you are supposed to see, what you are supposed to say. It's quite visible in a totalitarian state, but in a democracy. . . . Yet there are tiny cracks of freedom, safety valves. The task of the poem is to tend to those cracks, to keep them open" (TT). There is an anarchic, violent trait in the midst of the Tranströmeran mildness, a barely contained rage at what he considers a state of bondage. It would be possible to pursue at great length the poetic strategies he uses to escape it, but there are also other ways of keeping the tiny cracks of freedom open.

Since much of the socialization people undergo takes place below the level of consciousness—we get caught up in it the way we naturally begin to march in step when we hear military music—Tranströmer suggests places of refuge and escape. In several poems classical music is made to stand for freedom and peace and resilience, as in "Allegro," which appeared in book form in 1962.

Jag spelar Haydn efter en svart dag
och känner en enkel värme i händerna.

Tangenterna vill. Milda hammare slår.
Klangen är grön, livlig och stilla.

Klangen säger att friheten finns
och att någon inte ger kejsaren skatt.

Jag kör ner händerna i mina haydnfickor
och härmar en som ser lugnt på världen.

Jag hissar haydnflaggan—det betyder:
"Vi ger oss inte. Men vill fred."

Musiken är ett glashus på sluttningen
där stenarna flyger, stenarna rullar.

Och stenarna rullar tvärs igenom
men varje ruta förblir hel.

I play Haydn after a black day
and feel a simple warmth in my hands.

The keys are willing. Soft hammers strike.
The resonance is green, lively and calm.

The music says freedom exists
and someone doesn't pay tax to Caesar.

I push down my hands into my Haydnpockets
and imitate a person looking at the world calmly.

I hoist the Haydnflag—it signifies:
"We don't give in. But we want peace."

The music is a glass-house on the slope
where the stones fly, the stones roll.

And the stones roll right through
but every pane stays whole. (*TSP*, 55)

After a day that has been more than usually trying, the poet plays Haydn on the piano. One imagines that if "the resonance is green, lively and calm," it must be because the outer world is dark and agitated. It is also a world of unfreedom, a material existence which must be given its due, a place where one must pay "tax to Caesar." Consciousness is beleaguered. The inner world is invaded by foreign patterns and rhythms.

It is not just that Haydn's music is a refuge. Tranströmer's stance in "Allegro" is one of heroic defiance. A similar stance of passive resistance, of heroism, is echoed in "Schubertiana," from *Sanningsbarriären* (1978; Eng. *The Truth Barrier*): "This music is so heroic, Annie says, and she is right." Although the tone is offhand and playfully ironic, the diction natural, and the occasion undramatic—the poet is playing the piano in a small circle of friends—the idea of heroism seems meant to be taken quite seriously. The music of Haydn and Schubert has a way of effecting a transformation of the temporal, rhythmic patterning of experience. Earlier in "Schubertiana" Tranströmer had been describing New York in images reminiscent of Eliot's "Unreal City."

I kvällsmörkret på en plats utanför New York, en
utsiktspunkt där man med en enda blick kan om-
fatta åtta miljoner människors hem.
Jättestaden där borta är en lång flimrande driva, en
spiralgalax från sidan.
Inne i galaxen skjuts kaffekoppar över disken,
skyltfönstren tigger av förbipasserande, ett vimmel
av skor som inte sätter några spår.
De klättrande brandstegarna, hissdörrarna som
glider ihop, bakom dörrar med polislås ett ständigt
svall av röster.
Hopsjunkna kroppar halvsover i tunnel-
banevagnarna, de framrusande katakomberna.

In evening darkness a place outside New York, an
outlook point where with one glance you can take
in the homes of eight million people.
The giant city over there is a long shimmering
drift, a spiral galaxy seen from the side.
Inside the galaxy coffee cups are pushed across the
counter, shop windows beg from passersby, a whirl
of shoes that leave no trace.
Climbing fire escapes, elevator doors that glide
shut, behind doors with police locks a steady swell
of voices.
Slumped over bodies doze in subway cars, the
hurtling catacombs. (*TSP*, 143)

In Tranströmer's description of the city a few significant details are set in relief, making New York into a figure for the fragmentation and dehumanization of modern life. The city is first seen from a point so distant and superior that it can be taken in "with one glance," in an attitude of condemnation, almost of outrage.

When the poet/observer moves closer, it becomes possible to discern, not people, but parts of people: hands, feet, "slumped over bodies," and the things that they manipulate and use. Coffee cups are being pushed across counters by invisible hands; a throng of feet is moving up and down the streets, up and down the elevators. An identical mechanical rhythm has taken possession of them. It is as if the mechanical rhythm of the machine were catching, imposing itself in many subtle ways on the men and women who live in big cities and who are in constant contact with clocks, schedules, and conveyor belts. Eight hours a day, forty hours a week, time is patterned on the reiterated appearance of the next item on the conveyor belt, the next train arriving at the station, or the next appointment to be met. The "slumped over bodies [that] doze in subway cars," which Tranströmer likens to catacombs in motion, are not people; they are zombies caught in the powerful machinery which regulates their movements and hurls them forward. All the while "a whirl of shoes that leave no trace behind" reminds us that the city is an image for time passing without leaving the slightest trace. Everything is ephemeral, lives and dies in time; no substance, no essence survives beyond the fleeting moment when the sole of the shoe touches the pavement.

"To live means to leave traces," Walter Benjamin says, echoing the Proustian notion that existence is possessed only in memory (*R*, 155). The present moment leaves no trace in consciousness; there is no experience, no sense of being until the moment is relived in memory. Tranströmer's living dead, however, have no time for remembering; their lives are wholly swallowed up by the hectic rhythm of the metropolis.

New York, then, is presented as pure negativity, an image of modern industrialized technological society, a peculiarly modern form of evil. As such it is more a fictional place than a real one, a place seen through the mediating prism of literature, a bleak vision we have inherited from the nineteenth century. Tranströmer's New York, like the London or Paris of other modern texts, is the embodiment of an idea, "one of the major forms in which we become conscious of a central part of our experience and of the crisis of our society," to borrow a formulation from Raymond Williams. For Williams, this vision of the city is, as he says, "in the end as relentless and conventional as pastoral" (*CC*, 240). Tranströmer is keenly aware of the conventional nature of this bleak vision, weighted with the authority of a powerful modernist literary tradition. To balance it—the poem is among other things about the balance of good and evil—Tranströmer offers, simply, the music of Schubert: "Jag vet också—utan all statistik—att just nu spelas Schubert i något rum därborta och att för någon är de tonerna verkligare än allt det andra"; "I also know—without statistics—that right now Schubert is being played in some room over there and that for someone these sounds are more real than all the other" (*TSP*, 143).

The terms in which the argument is couched are deliberately paradoxical: music, the most fugitive and immaterial among the arts, is for some people more "real" than the colossal agglomeration of steel and concrete, the vast spread of buildings, of institutions, and the ten million lives caught up in its dehumanizing rhythm. One individual, intuitively recognized and acknowledged without recourse to "statistics," to scientific measurements, who is playing Schubert's music, outweighs the formidable pressure of the metropolis. Speaking of the people who would be unable to understand the message of Schubert's music, those whom the music is not addressing, Tranströmer writes: "the many who buy and sell people and believe that everyone can / be bought, don't recognize themselves here. / It is not their music."

As it turns out, looking at music as a subversive activity has a tradition of its own. An impassioned argument in favor of music as the form in which inner time is mirrored can be found in the writings of the German philosopher Ludwig Feuerbach (*MT*, 247) and also in the texts of the neo-Marxist members of what is known as the Frankfurt School, in Ernst Bloch in particular, for whom music constituted a model for Utopia (*MF*, 143). How music can be the antidote to the metropolis is further developed in "Schubertiana:" "De fems stråkarna spelar. Jag går hem genom ljumma skogar med marken fjädrande under mig / kryper ihop som en ofödd, somnar, rullar viktlös in i framtiden, känner plåtslight att växterna har tankar" (*D*, 144); "The string quintet is playing. I go home through warm forests with the ground springy under me, / curl up like an embryo, fall asleep, roll weightless into the future, suddenly realize that plants have thoughts" (*TSP*, 144)

In the inner world—suggested by the childlike trust in "I go home"—time is elastic, stretches back to an existence before birth and forward into the yet-unformed future as well as down to a more archaic way of being where it becomes possible to perceive "that plants have thoughts." When one is listening to the string quintet, time becomes reversible and hence is transcended. There is the characteristic feeling of weightlessness associated with moments of transcendence, which in an earlier poem, "Balakirev's Dream," is explicitly associated with music: "I konsertsalen tonades fram ett land / där stenarna inte var tyngre än dagg"; "In the concert hall was conjured up a land / where the stones were not heavier than dew." At the same time, to "curl up like an embryo" suggests a blissful, unconscious participation in nature, a fusion of the inner and the outer world, of subject and object, that is often associated with music, as testified to by Jameson's reading of Ernst Bloch.

> The sonata itself is proof of a kind of dialectic inherent in the musical experience, whereby this ontological relationship to the tone finds its fulfillment in that unfolding in time, in that temporal process and movement toward a future plenitude, which we know as musical form. Thus music is profoundly Utopian, both in its form and in its content. . . . The transfigured time of Utopia offers a perpetual present in which there is a specific, yet total ontological satisfaction of every instant. Death in such a world has nothing left to take; it cannot damage a life already fully realized.

Bloch saw music as an antidote to alienation, a blueprint for a future Utopia, and he made music the foundation of his theoretical work *Das Prinzip Hoffnung* (The Principle Hope).

Seen in this light, music becomes one of the means by which the individual can still assert a precarious inwardness. In musical time the confusing mass of sensations and events in ordinary existence is reshaped, rhythmicized, as it were, and made to reflect a human order and a human time. Thus we would live twice: once in linear time, subject to decay and disintegration, harassed and confused by the welter of phenomena and sensations, carried along with the flux; and then again in a spacious musical time, which is an "interweaving not only of moment with moment, but of the transiency of moments with the permanence of that which sustains us in their passage" (*BF,* 11). Or, as Tranströmer himself has it, in the closing lines of "Schubertiana:"

> . . . Den långa melodin som är sig själv i alla förvandlingar, ibland glittrande och vek, ibland skrovlig och stark, snigelspår och stålwire.
>
> Det envisa gnolandet som följer oss just nu
> uppför
> djupen. (*D,* 145)
>
> ... The long melody that remains itself in all its transformation, sometimes glittering and pliant sometimes rugged and strong, snail-track and steel wire
>
> The perpetual humming that follows us-now-
> up
> the depths. (*TSP,* 144)

Source: Joanna Bankier, "Breaking the Spell: Subversion in the Poetry of Tomas Tranströmer," in *World Literature Today*, Vol. 64, No. 4, Autumn 1990, pp. 591–95.

Sources

Bankier, Joanna, "Tomas Tranströmer," in *Dictionary of Literary Biography*, Vol. 257, *Twentieth-Century Swedish Writers after World War II*, edited by Ann-Charlotte Gavel Adams, Gale, 2002, pp. 277–90.

Bly, Robert, "Tomas Tranströmer and 'The Memory,'" in *World Literature Today*, Vol. 64, No. 4, Autumn 1990, pp. 570–73.

Lenhart, Gary, "Hard Edge Fog," in the *American Book Review*, Vol. 9, No. 4, September–October 1987, p. 10.

Tranströmer, Tomas, "Answers to Letters," in *New Collected Poems*, translated by Robin Fulton, Bloodaxe Books, 1997, pp. 136–37.

Further Reading

Balakian, Anna, *Surrealism: The Road to the Absolute*, University of Chicago Press, 1986.

Balakian offers a rewarding insight into the movement that, many critics would argue, has significantly influenced Tranströmer's poetry.

Bly, Robert, *Leaping Poetry: An Idea with Poems and Translations*, Beacon, 1975.

Bly's theory of "leaping poetry" is a vital contribution to the critical understanding of Tranströmer and other post–World War II European poets popular in the United States.

Steene, Birgitta, "Vision and Reality in the Poetry of Tomas Tranströmer," in *Scandinavian Studies*, Vol. 37, 1965, pp. 236–44.

Steene offers a general analysis of Tranströmer's techniques and themes. Although it was written long before the publication of "Answers to Letters," her essay provides insights into some of the most important themes of the poem.

Tranströmer, Tomas, and Robert Bly, *Air Mail: Brev 1964–1990*, compiled by Torbjörn Schmidt, translated by Lars-Håkan Svensson, Bonnier, 2001.

This collection of letters charts the long-standing correspondence of Tranströmer and his friend, fellow poet, and advocate in the United States.

Fading Light

Robert Creeley

1988

Robert Creeley's poem "Fading Light," originally published in a 1988 collection of poems titled *Windows*, was republished in 2001 in *Just in Time*, which contains the entire contents of three of Creeley's earlier collections. These poems illustrate the themes and styles with which the poet engaged himself as he approached the age of seventy. Thus it represents a mature effort of a poet who has been writing since his late twenties. The poem is short, only twelve lines long, and its line length is somewhat more extended than in most of his poems. Many of Creeley's poems are short, sometimes so short that they achieve comprehensibility only as part of a longer cluster of poems. The typical Creeley poem tends to be a sinewy stream of words on a mostly white page. Indeed, for a poet who often places a single word, sometimes a word as simple as "the" to stand alone as a line, his lines in this poem mark a minor stylistic shift. "Fading Light" is a poem that begins with a very simple image—an image of dusk seen through an open window—a commonplace, almost impersonal image that is transformed from perception into reflection on time and memory, all in an austere, remote style, one in which the diction is kept spare and deliberately simple. Belying the simplicity of the diction, however, the poet uses a number of techniques to cause the work to be somewhat difficult to interpret in a first reading or hearing. The poem is punctuated as one sentence, but it is composed of fragments that are so deliberately, ambiguously constructed that the reader has to interpret where and how the different parts interact to create a meaningful whole. It is the difficulty in understanding what exactly is being said that causes a careful reader to attend to the diction, syntax, imagery, and sound of the poem.

Author Biography

Robert Creeley was born in Arlington, Massachusetts, on May 21, 1926, the son of a physician. In 1928, his left eye was injured in an accident, which resulted in blindness and eventual removal of the eye. His father died in 1932, leaving his mother overwhelmed with the responsibilities involved in liquidating his father's medical practice.

Creeley attended Harvard from 1943 to 1946, interrupted by a stint as an ambulance driver in India during World War II. He was not a diligent student and dropped out of Harvard during his senior year without receiving a degree. In 1950, he began a literary correspondence with Charles Olson, which proved beneficial to him. Creeley taught at Black Mountain College in North Carolina from 1954 to 1955, where he associated with a number of experimental poets and artists. Visiting San Francisco in 1956, he came to know a number of the Beat poets including Jack Kerouac, Gary Snyder, and Allen Ginsberg. During subsequent years Creeley taught at colleges in New Mexico, British Columbia, and California, before moving permanently to Buffalo, New York in 1966. His poems, however, do not show a sense of place, and critics have noticed that it is often very difficult to attach poems to biographical or geographical places in the poet's life.

In 1960, Creeley received the Levinson Prize for ten poems published in the May edition of *Poetry*. His work attracted critical acclaim and was anthologized in a number of influential collections such as A. Poulin's *Contemporary American Poetry* in 1980. From 1989 to 1991 he was the New York State Poet. Since 1989, he has taught poetry and humanities at the State University of New York, Buffalo. He won Yale's Bollingen Prize, one of America's most distinguished recognitions for poetry, in 1999. In September 2001, he was awarded the prestigious Lannan Lifetime Achievement Award for his works, a recognition that included a substantial financial reward. Creeley has published his work through major publishing houses, but much of it has also been issued in small editions by small presses and is difficult to locate. Fortunately, his works have been collected and reprinted in more extensive collections. "Fading Light" was reprinted in 2001 in the book *Just in Time*. He has given many interviews, some of which are reprinted in works by literary critics. Creeley has also issued recordings of himself reading his poetry and has influenced many poets who came of age in the 1970s.

Robert Creeley

Poem Text

Now one might catch it see it
shift almost substantial blue
white yellow light near roof's edge
become intense definition think
of the spinning world is it as
ever this plate of apparent life
makes all sit patient hold on
chute the sled plunges down ends
down the hill beyond sight down
into field's darkness as time for
supper here left years behind waits
patient in mind remembers the time.

Poem Summary

Lines 1–3

The very first line of "Fading Light" introduces several key aspects of the poem. The poem begins

Media Adaptations

- *Poetry in Motion*, directed by Ron Mann in 1982, was released on DVD by Public Media in 2002. It features performances by a number of the Beat poets, including Robert Creeley, in front of live audiences.
- A CD of Creeley reading poetry titled *Robert Creeley* (2001) was released on the Jagjaguwar label.
- Creeley reads his poetry with a jazz trio on a CD titled *The Way out Is Via the Door* (2002).
- The Electronic Poetry Center maintains a website on Robert Creeley at www.wings.buffalo.edu, which includes links and selected poems.
- The Academy of American Poets maintains a website on Creeley at www.poets.org, which includes numerous links.

with an immediate, emphatic "Now," followed by an impersonal "one" who could be the poet himself or, indeed, anyone, a pronoun that is followed by "might catch" in which the possibility of seizing a moment is at once asserted and then immediately questioned. Terry R. Bacon has remarked that "Creeley's poetry is expressed in the perpetual NOW. It is a 'real time' rendering, in a very solipsistic sense, of the universe he perceives." The title of poem has helped to establish that the poem is about dusk, and it is this moment of dusk to which the poet directs attention, as though perception could freeze the moment into something palpable. Creeley repeats verbs, as he will do throughout the poem—"catch it see it." His refusal to punctuate conventionally or to add connective words such as "and" begins a pattern of disjointed phrases marked by verbs that are connected elusively to their grammatical subject. The reader, indeed, must supply the subjects and make sense of the phrasing in order to make this poem meaningful.

The transition from the first line to the second line demonstrates that Creeley will use the poetic technique of enjambment in this poem. Enjambment occurs when a line's sense continues into the next line, with no pause. Commonly, lines that are not enjambed, which are called end-stopped lines, have some kind of punctuation, such as a comma, period, or dash, to show the reader that a pause is necessary. Enjambed lines, on the other hand, rush onward, usually to find a pause in the middle or end of a subsequent line. All the lines except the last one in this poem are enjambed. Interestingly, Creeley says in the interview included in *Just in Time*, "I read the breaks." Thus, in his own reading, the poet would pause at the end of lines, whereas the meaning of the lines clearly demands that one go on into the next line. While there may be other interpretations, there seems to be a pause after the first "it," in the first line, with a second pause after the word "shift." Thus, the natural reading of the first line seems to go over into the second, and would be punctuated thus: "Now one might catch it, see it shift . . ." That the poet does not write it as it would be spoken is a clue that his intent is to frustrate the reader's uncritical expectations.

The second line repeats the uncertainty of the first. The "it," which we infer to be the fading light of the title, is "almost substantial blue," teetering just outside the poet's certain grasp. The light is indeterminate, being "blue / white yellow light." The jumble of adjectives will be paralleled later in the poem by a heaping of verbs and adverbs. All of this is deliberately confusing, but the confusion in syntax is related to the confusion in perception. The light is fading, indeterminate, of changing color and quality, and the concepts and recollections about to occur in the poem are similar in their elusiveness.

Lines 4–6

The reader has to supply the connections between the subject and the various verbs of the poem. While one might fairly easily interpret that one might "see it shift . . . become intense definition," the word "think," which is characteristically poised at the end of a line, is a verb without a clear subject. Perhaps Creeley is telling readers that one might "catch it" and one might "think / of the spinning world." Here, there is a transition from object to concept. Creeley has steadfastly tried to eliminate concepts and abstractions from his poetry, following the advice of the American poet William Carlos Williams, with whom the young Creeley corresponded and who is credited with the poetic slogan "no concepts but in objects." The spinning world is something, however, that has to be thought about, not directly perceived. This shift starts to take the poem beyond sight into what lies beyond.

Readers see the abstractions and ambiguities become more apparent as the poem progresses. The "of the spinning world is it as" is very easy to stumble over when reading aloud. Perhaps Creeley wants readers to read his words as "think of the spinning world. Is it as ever?" The answer is not obvious, and in struggling for a resolution to the demands of the tortured syntax, perhaps the poet makes his point. The fading light is hard to catch, and the meaning is hard to catch, and it may be the reader who has to supply the meaning that the world and the poet fail to make clear. A striking image, "this plate of apparent life" contains both the abstract word "life" and the concrete word "plate" which will foreshadow "supper" in the penultimate line. By this point, the poem has gone beyond perception to asking questions about the world and about life. The world has changed, or why else would the poet seem to ask "is it as / ever?" Likewise "apparent" gives no clear direction to "life"; it merely seems to undercut the solidity of life. Everything Creeley says, he seems to contradict.

Lines 7–12

Suddenly there is a different kind of shift, occurring as usual right before the end of a line. The poet says "hold on / chute the sled plunges down ends / down the hill . . ." It is as though he puts some motion into the middle of a deliberately confused situation, and the reader speeds up and reads, right after the word "patient" about a chute and a sled plunging down. The word "down" is repeated three times in two lines. "Patient" is used twice, once in the middle of the poem and once in the last line. Additionally, Creeley uses "time" twice within three lines. This repetition and quickening pace push the poem to its conclusion. Memories, triggered by the fading light of the poem's title, start rushing out like objects down a chute, like a sled rushing down a snowy hill in winter. In keeping with the indeterminate, contradictory nature of this poem, this rush is juxtaposed with the repeated word "patient."

Thom Gunn has said that as Creeley has matured as a poet "the book rather than the individual poem becomes the meaningful unit." It might be useful to note at this point that this poem was placed near the end of a book titled *Windows* and is immediately adjacent to other poems that are clearly observations of the world through windows of various sorts. A poem on the facing page is titled "Echo" and talks of weather that is grey and cold. The darkness, the sled, the position next to other winter poems all make "Fading Light" a winter reverie. The fading light is a real event outside a literal window, and the poet observes the ways the colors shift at dusk, and he thinks of the passage of time and life, which seems like a plunging sled going downhill to the "field's darkness" but, back inside, "supper here left years behind waits." The vision of light fading into darkness triggers in the poet memories of suppers years before, and yet he does not act, but "patient in mind remembers the time."

In this poem, Creeley plays with language so that readers' observations of reality are brought into question, so that they can think mindfully about the things of the world. On the other hand, it is reasonable to notice that this is a poem written by a man who is entering old age, that the "fading light" may also be the fading energy and life force of the writer. It would be very much like Creeley to hide any personal reference in wordplay and tortured syntax. In this reading of the poem, Creeley recognizes that even the fading light is transitory and ephemeral, that the world continues to spin, and that what is ultimately left to him in the face of death is a patient holding on and a looking back as his life's story rushes on faster and faster.

Themes

Uncertainty

One of the significant themes of this poem is uncertainty. Just as the fading light of dusk makes clear vision impossible, the words of this poem emphasize the uncertainty of perception and memory. Starting with the first line's "one might catch it," the poem contains constant repeated references to uncertainty. The "almost substantial" light, which is "blue / white yellow" is of indeterminate color and materiality. Life itself is but "apparent" life, nothing palpable and direct, but vague and indeterminate. Near the end of the poem a sled goes "down the hill beyond sight down / into field's darkness." Nothing certain can be asserted about what happens in that darkness.

Impersonality

Creeley does not say that these events and perceptions occurred to him. Neither does he create a persona, a voice of another character, who tells his own story to a reader. Some of the most significant themes of impersonality occur at very strategic places in the poem, in the first and last lines. It is "one" who might perceive this light. The experience is a common one. Everyone, except for the blind, has experienced fading light at dusk. It is

Topics For Further Study

- In the 1950s a group of young poets became known as the Beat poets, the harbingers of the Beat Generation. Do research on this group, identify four key participants, and locate at least one characteristic poem from each writer. What do all these poets have in common, and how are their poetic voices distinctive?
- Two influential creative movements of the period from 1950 to 1965 were abstract expressionism and jazz. Locate an art print of an abstract expressionist such as Jackson Pollock or Mark Rothko and find a recording of jazz that you think complements the work of art. Then choose a poem by Creeley or Kerouac or Snyder, or another poet who was writing in that time, and perform the poem in front of the art, with jazz playing in the background.
- Poetry festivals are a relatively recent phenomenon. Using the Internet, try to locate as many poetry festivals as you can. Do not limit yourself to the United States; other festivals occur in Britain and Australia, for instance. Do these festivals identify featured poets? Who are the poets who are identified as special guests? Try to locate poems by these poets.
- Music and poetry have an ancient connection. The word "lyric," for example, is derived from the early musical instrument called the lyre. Make a personal compilation of songs whose words can stand alone as poetry. Write up the words and try to analyze them as poetry. What literary techniques can you find?
- Poetry readings occur frequently in many locations, including book stores, coffee houses, and other smoke- and alcohol- free environments. Try to attend at least four different readings at different venues if possible. Keep a record of the kinds of poems you hear. What are the subjects and techniques? Do any of them seem especially effective to you? Summarize your results in a brief written evaluation.
- One way to encounter poets for the first time is to read anthologies. Go to a library or a book store and spend some time looking through a collection of work by different poets. What poets appeal to you? Using reference works or the Internet, research their lives and careers.

quite significant that the poet does not say that "I" might have seen this light, but that "one," which represents the self as well as the universal consciousness, might have seen the light. Although Creeley does sometimes include himself in his own poems, he usually writes deliberately subdued poems in common diction, taking the focus off the poet and putting it into the words and images. In the middle of the poem he uses the phrase "makes all sit patient." This is an ambiguous and impersonal word, which can be interpreted as "it makes all persons patient" or, alternatively, "it makes me all patient." A less careful poet would probably give the reader one possible interpretation. Finally, at the end of the poem, "patient in mind remembers the time" does not say whose mind is doing the remembering. On the one hand, it can be the poet's own memory, but he does not say that it is his. On the other hand, while a memory must be someone's memory, the universality of the experience, indeed, its mundane character, suggest that it is someone's memory, and perhaps everyone's memory. It is through an impersonal description of optical and mental events that the poet tries to link his own perceptions with those of his audience.

Memory

This is a poem that ends up inside the poet's (or is it the reader's?) head. In the middle of the poem we find a shift from the immediate occasion of the work, which is a vision of dusk, presumably a winter dusk seen through a window, to a series of meditations and memories. At the end of the fifth line Creeley introduces an unpunctuated question: "is it as / ever this plate of apparent life / makes all sit patient . . ." Here he ties the present to the recurring past. He also seems to evoke a memory from childhood, sitting patient and waiting for supper to be served. This memory is more likely from childhood than from adulthood in that children are often hungry and impatient to be served, whereas adults are more in control of the food and the supper ritual. He also uses words such as "chute" and "sled," which seem to allude to a New England childhood. The chute is a coal chute, and coal was often burned to heat buildings seventy years ago, and of course the sled is only used in a snowy climate. The sled is an apparatus of childish pleasure, and Creeley most likely has a particular hill in mind and a particular dark field from his childhood, though he does not identify any of them for his readers. Finally comes supper, but this is not a supper awaiting the poet in the present; rather, it is a memory of "supper here left years behind." And by the last lines of his poem, the poet makes it extremely obvious that he has gone back into memory when he concludes by saying, "patient in mind remembers the time."

Mortality and Anxiety

It is important to remember that this is a poem by a man approaching old age. Like many modernist writers, Creeley does not take comfort in the promises of traditional religion; there is no hope of heaven or redemption in his work. Death induces anxiety and insecurity for him. Anxiety is not totally negative, however, if it sharpens perceptions and leads to a cherishing of all the mundane events of daily life. For a poet who abhors simile, this work nevertheless employs something similar, a metaphor, which is an implied comparison between two dissimilar things. The fading light of the title can be compared to the waning life force of any person. Always one to eschew melodrama, Creeley makes his poem impersonal and universal. Everyone is fated to die. Death is, simultaneously and paradoxically, both the most personal and the most impersonal of fates. The impersonality of this poem, its uncertainty, and its lapse into early memory all find a culmination in the poem's overriding existential concern, which is the poet's confrontation with anxiety and his own mortality.

Style

Diction

At first the diction of the poem seems unremarkable. There are no odd, unusual, or difficult words. A careless reader might not even think of noticing the diction, but that would be a mistake. Creeley has very consciously picked out words that do not call attention to themselves. There has long been a struggle in American writing between stylists who utilize uncommon diction and unusual imagery and those, like Creeley, who try to use common speech. This struggle goes back centuries, hearkening back to the English Civil War and the elaborate and erudite poetry of the cavaliers on the one hand, and the sturdy and direct Puritan texts on the other. Creeley has enlisted the banner of plain speech and straightforward expression.

Enjambment

The poet makes extensive use of the device of enjambment in this poem. Enjambment is the technique of continuing the sense of a line forward into the next one. It is to be contrasted with the end-stopped lines that are characteristic of much metered and formal poetry. In this poem the last word of every line, except for the last, leads the reader on into the subsequent line. There is no reason to pause at the end of each line, at least no reason that would lead to a comprehensible and natural reading of the poem. It is very apparent that Creeley deliberately enjambs each line in order to produce poetic effects. The first effect is that of a breathless tumbling into the images of the following lines. A second effect is to isolate subject from verb and to shatter phrases, isolating words in space at the end of the lines. In most enjambed poems, the technique makes for a more fluid and natural oral interpretation, but here the enjambment does just the opposite, calling attention to the artifice of the work.

Syntactic Suspension

Many poems do not resolve themselves until their concluding lines. This phenomenon is true of Shakespearean sonnets as well as this poem. What Creeley does that is distinctive here is to present a long "sentence" that is not a conventional sentence at all. Though expressed in common words, and containing elements of a sentence such as multiple verbs and associated phrases and clauses, and though it does hang together to make a comprehensible sequence of thoughts, it is not a prosaic expression, but a poem that uses the rules of language for an unconventional purpose. It is not until the very last phrase, "remembers the time," that the reader can see what the first line signifies, that the fading light of the title triggers a memory of supper years before. The poet suspends the syntax in several ways, using enjambment, lack of conventional punctuation, and omission of words that would help clarify the meaning, all to postpone the reader's comprehension of his poem until the very last line. This syntactic suspension makes the poem challenging to interpret.

Historical Context

When Creeley published "Fading Light" in 1988, he was entering a phase of his career as a distinguished elder statesman of American poetry. Having gone to India during the 1940s, he had been associated with important creative writers at Black Mountain College, and later with the Beat poets. By the time he published this poem he, along with other formerly radical members of his generation, had become converted into fixtures of the poetic establishment. It is a familiar progression, from radical to tenured and respected professor, but by the late 1980s he, along with such luminaries as his old friends Allen Ginsberg and Gary Snyder, had found themselves embraced by an establishment they had once opposed.

During the early days of Creeley's career, modernist formalism, epitomized by the work of W. H. Auden and T. S. Eliot, was at the center of American academic poetry. Things started changing rapidly during the late 1950s with the rise of confessional poets such as Robert Lowell, as well as the emergence of Creeley's Beat friends. The 1960s were anarchic in many ways. Frequently poets felt obliged to take political stances, but Creeley, though he sympathized with the anti–Vietnam War activists, did not employ his poetry as a political tool. By the 1980s, as this poem was written, the American poetry scene had fragmented into multiple segments, each with its own audience, purposes, publications, and venues.

One of the trends in American poetry when Creeley wrote this poem was the rise of a new type of academic poetry. It is true in some sense that much poetry has been academic, in that poets often are drawn to teaching, and good poets are sometimes rewarded with teaching positions at colleges, though William Carlos Williams was a practicing physician and Wallace Stevens had been a corporate attorney. But by the 1980s, the proliferation of creative writing programs in universities around the country had led to the rise of what poet Albert Goldbarth called "po-biz," in which recipients of graduate degrees in creative writing wrote books of poetry, reviewed the books of others in similar programs, and were rewarded with academic jobs and the occasional monetary prize. The increasingly academic direction of poetry coincided with a dramatic fall-off in the size of the poetry-reading public, as poets began to write primarily for small specialized audiences. Creeley had participated in the prototype of the master of fine arts programs back in his years at Black Mountain College. Though that school did not survive long, subsequent generations of aspiring poets went in the academic direction.

Another trend in the late 1980s was a countercurrent in poetry, the rise of a new formalism. Poetic tastes had veered from popular tastes; rhyme and meter seemed to have fallen out of favor sometime before the death of Robert Frost. Throughout the 1960s and 1970s free verse became the dominant form of poetry. Some of it could be superb, as Sylvia Plath at her best, but as poetry became easier to compose, it also could tend toward sentimentality, slackness, and narcissism. A number of poets returned to formal structures with new enthusiasm. Poets as different as Derek Walcott, Dana Gioia, Anne Stevenson, Donald Justice, and Seamus Heaney published new work in *The Formalist*, *The New Criterion*, and other places. A number of important anthologies of formalist verse were published, and displayed a far different aesthetic intent than does most of Creeley's work.

Finally, at the time "Fading Light" was published, other poets initiated still other movements in American poetry. The first slam poets came on the scene. Slam poetry is a competitive poetry event in which audience members judge poetic performances by assigning scores to them, and these scores are added and tabulated much like the scores in figure skating or Olympic diving. In a typical slam poetry night, several poets pay entry fees and some advance to second or third rounds, and at the end of an evening a winner is announced. Many of the successful performances turned out to be comic or dramatic, with expressions of outrage at sexual, racial, or social oppression a staple of the slam scene. Around the same time, poetry festivals sprang up. In 1986 the Geraldine R. Dodge Festival began. It is a juried festival, in which organizers invite distinguished poets to give readings and workshops in a festive environment of public performance. Other festivals, such as the Austin International Poetry Festival in Texas, are non-juried, and provide multiple stages and microphones to all participants. Both types of festivals try to return poetry to its origins in the spoken word and in performance. What all these movements try to do is to take poetry off the printed page and to showcase it for listeners.

Critical Overview

At the beginning of the twenty-first century, Creeley found himself securely placed among the grand elder statesmen of American poetry. His Bollingen and Lannan awards cemented his critical reception. Yet not all critics are impressed by the kind of poetry his career presents. Writing in an article on Creeley's mentor William Carlos Williams, Christopher MacGowan writes in *The Columbia History of American Poetry* that "The whole line of American poetry to which Williams is such an important figure, the line that includes such figures as Olson and Creeley, comes under similar attack from time to time." A great deal has been written about him in the last fifty years, both positive and negative. Carol Muske Dukes has said that "some critics find that he is occasionally hyper-oblique, self-consciously cute, and for all his brevity, overwrought." She quotes critic John Simon who said, "There are two things to be said about Creeley's poems: They are short; they are not short enough."

Other critics are more charitable. Don Byrd wrote that "When Creeley's poetry is dull, as it sometimes is, it is the dullness of the real, and when it is exciting, as it often is, it is the excitement of the real." Noting that Creeley began his career in rebellion against academic poets only to end up as an academic himself, Byrd distinguishes between academic and underground poets by their different approaches to poetry. "The academic poets, to paraphrase Gertrude Stein, write writing as it is prepared: Creeley writes writing as it is written." Writing in 1996, Bill Piper remarks on Creeley's ability to avoid self-repetition when he states that, "Unlike many artists who reach a stride and remain with it, often becoming stale, he seems to diversify, and his work gains in interest with his deepening experience."

In her review of *Windows*, the collection in which "Fading Light" was originally published, Penny Kaganoff relates the book's title to its contents: "these carefully honed poems themselves function as 'frames' through which Creeley measures with mature insight and inventiveness the limits of reality and existence." Numerous critics have remarked on the immediacy and directness of Creeley's poetry, as does Terry R. Bacon, who declares, "Creeley's perceptions are epiphanies: glimpses of moments in the life situation that are brought into sharp focus through the high energy transference that is presumed to occur." In a 2002 review of *Just in Time*, Stephen Whited says, "The author's comforting, bebop inner voice chatters away insistently, harmonizing and connecting moment with moment, like a Charlie Parker solo." Remarking on the development of themes in Creeley's work, Whited goes on to note, "Aging has changed the focus of the familiar subjects to whom the seventy-five-year-old Creeley continuously returns; the pleasant influence of narrative and memory has been more evident in his work since the mid-'80s." Regardless of their enjoyment of his austere and oblique poetry, critics agree that Creeley has been a major influence on many younger poets and a significant presence in late twentieth-century American poetry.

Criticism

Frank Pool

Pool is a published poet and reviewer and a teacher of high school English. In this essay, Pool discusses elements of formal structure in Creeley's poem.

A young or inexperienced reader of poetry might well be perplexed upon first encountering Robert Creeley's poem "Fading Light." The poem lacks many of the features that are prominent in other poems. There is no rhyme and no meter, as in traditional verse, and yet the poem also lacks the colloquial familiarity of much contemporary free verse. Instead, the poem is difficult to grasp upon first reading, and even in subsequent perusals does not easily yield up its meaning and structures. Still, Creeley is regarded as a major poet, and as with many works by major writers, this poem reveals a structure that, while not obvious or simple, nevertheless connects the apparently chaotic lines and imagery into a coherent whole.

Some critics believe that a poem can best be interpreted in isolation, that close reading of the words on the page will generate a sound understanding, that biography and literary history are extraneous to the comprehension of a poem. On the other hand, it seems undeniable that knowing about the history and circumstances of a poem's composition adds to our appreciation. Creeley began his writing shortly after World War II. He became associated in the early 1950s with a group of writers and artists at Black Mountain College in North Carolina, an avant-garde experimental school where Creeley worked with the man who most influenced his early work, Charles Olson. There he also met Jackson Pollock and other pioneers of abstract

> *"It is the counterpoint of end-stopped lines played off against the syntactic enjambment of the meaning that provides the most important structure of this challenging poem."*

expressionism in art. Like the abstract expressionists, Creeley faced the problem of form. He rejected the traditional verse forms that were the fashion of his time, striking out for a different modernist style. Serious art makes substantial demands on its creators; slackness and laziness are constant temptations when one has thrown over the old rules and old canons of style. Arthur Ford has stated that Creeley often quoted Pollock's proclamation: "When I am in my painting, I am not aware of what I am doing." As Ford also explains, "The form that a poem takes never precedes the poem itself but rather comes from the demands of the poem as it is in the process of being uttered." Given this aesthetic, what are the formal demands of "Fading Light," and how does Creeley meet them?

In striving for an alternative way of making poems, Creeley was influenced by Ezra Pound, William Carlos Williams, but most especially by Charles Olson. Olson devised a theory of "projective verse" in which the determining factor of line length is the poet's breath. Creeley was influenced by the way that Williams would sprinkle words vertically down the page in very short lines. He instinctively believed that the poet should pause momentarily at the end of each line, emphasizing and highlighting it. Ironically, in hearing recordings of Williams, Creeley was struck by the way the older poet did not read his work that way. Nevertheless, Creeley had picked up an important formal technique by his creative misreading. He always pauses a bit at the end of each line. As he said in an interview with Charles Bernstein, "I read the breaks. To me, like percussive or contrapuntal agencies, they give me a chance to get a syncopation into the classic emptiness. . . ." By "contrapuntal," he refers to the technique in music of having two independent but harmonically related melodies playing together. He further says, "I mean, it gives me, not drumming precisely, but it's a rhythm of that character." It is the counterpoint of end-stopped lines played off against the syntactic enjambment of the meaning that provides the most important structure of this challenging poem.

All the lines end without completing a thought; a reader cannot pause and make sense. The meaning of the lines compels the reader to keep on going until there is a comprehensible place to pause. Creeley makes the task more difficult by refusing to provide any punctuation except for a period at the very end, as though this poem were one coherent sentence. The pauses make the poem sound strange. Nobody talks that way; language is not being used for its accustomed purposes; what readers encounter is a poem with everyday words arranged in a puzzling rhythm and expressing thoughts that do not make immediate sense. Thom Gunn, the critic and poet, assures readers that Creeley always reads the line breaks as little silences. Creeley knows full well that he emphasizes words such as "it" and "as" and "on" and "for." None of these words allow the reader to pause, but since readers are expected to pause, readers experience the rhythm of voice and silence in counterpoint to the flow of phrases and images in the poem.

Besides setting up a contrapuntal struggle between sound and sense, Creeley's lines also echo and rhyme words in the lines. In the Bernstein interview, talking about poems from the same collection that includes "Fading Light," the poet says about his line breaks, "It's also an agency for a lot of half-rhyming or accidental echoing that I really enjoy. It's sort of like water sloshing into a pan . . . Lapping at the edges." As the poem concludes it accelerates almost like a sled reaching the bottom of a hill.

> chute the sled plunges down ends
> down the hill beyond sight down
> into field's darkness as time for
> supper here left years behind waits
> patient in mind remembers the time.

The repetition of "down" within, at the beginning, and at the end of only two lines emphasizes the motion of the poem and sets up a melody of repeated sounds. Likewise, "time," "behind," "mind," and "time" set up a repeated rhyming structure in an otherwise unrhymed poem. If these are what Creeley calls "accidental echoing," they are certainly improvised melodies that he sets up in counterpoint to his strange and halting rhythm. Ford has said about Creeley's poems that

> the poem must be free from a preconceived rhythmical structure, while at the same time adhering to

> certain rhythmical patterns within itself, which may involve in fact, similar and dissimilar sounds within and between lines, textures of words and sounds, indeed textures of ideas themselves.

While there is indeed a contrapuntal texture of rhyme and near rhyme in this poem, the most important structure is that provided by syntax. Due to the enjambed lines and the lack of punctuation, it is not immediately apparent where phrases and clauses begin and end, except that they evidently never end at the conclusion of a line. The reader has to determine where to pause within the lines to make the poem meaningful. If the poem were to prove meaningless after all the effort it demands, critical readers would react negatively. Fortunately, the poem can be read in ways in which there are meaningful images and ideas. The poem begins with a reference to a light that seems to shift as it fades. This image is followed by musing about the world, and an elliptical question, "is it as / ever . . ." Then halfway through the poem Creeley introduces imagery of sitting "patient" (not patiently) followed by the accelerating phrases and images of a sled plunging down "beyond sight." As Gunn remarks, "The result is a kind of eloquent stammering; there is a sense of small persistent difficulties all right, but of each being overcome in turn, while it occurs—the voice hesitates and then plunges forward." Far from being left beyond the poem's field of vision, however, readers are brought back to "supper here left years behind" and a repeated motif of "waits / patient in mind" and, in a parallel rhythmic vein, "remembers the time."

The key to the poem is its last word. Creeley has said about his work that, "Nothing is permitted to quite end, or stop, until the final word of the poem." The poem is a meditation on time, on time's passage, on the endurance of the world, and resolves with a memory of time gone by. In baroque contrapuntal music, the disparate yet harmonious melodies must resolve themselves in the concluding bars. In Creeley's poem, the syntactical problems and the eloquently stammering line breaks resolve themselves in the announcement of the poem's true theme: time. It is somewhat ironic that this poem should reflect a classical or baroque structure, given its deliberate understated diction and its refusal to fly away into theory or metaphor. The words are the most plainspoken imaginable, and the poet is one who early in his career turned away from verbal pyrotechnics, elevated diction, and erudite allusions. Indeed, as Tom Clark, writing in *Robert Creeley and the Genius of the American Common Place*, asserts "In the dialectical unfolding of literary history the moment of the common comes typically as an antidote to periods of over-refinement and baroque difficulty."

Creeley began his career writing poems that were significantly different from those of W. H. Auden, T. S. Eliot, and Robert Frost, only to find himself, late in life, perhaps without thinking about it, incorporating formal techniques akin to musical composition. Perhaps this reversion to formalism is less surprising than it might first appear. Ford notes that Creeley is more of a formalist than most readers realize.

> Creeley's poetry exhibits a much greater regularity and formalization than is usually assumed; and, what is even more significant, much of his poetry and prose, especially from the later years, can be understood best as products of the push toward form, of the classical need for preexistent form despite the modernist dismissal of it.

Ultimately there is something quite satisfying in finding form in a Creeley poem. A poet who wanted to make poetry new, a high modernist of the last half of the twentieth century, in his later years writes poetry that is formally challenging and

What Do I Read Next?

- Robert Creeley's book *Just in Time* (2001) consists of three shorter poetry collections written by Creeley between 1984 and 1994. It contains the poem "Fading Light," among others, as well as informative interviews with Charles Bernstein.
- Arthur Ford's *Robert Creeley*, though published in 1978 and therefore not including the poet's later work, is nevertheless a quite readable introduction to Creeley's life and the first half of his career.
- *Robert Creeley's Life and Work* (1987) contains a large number of short reviews and essays on Creeley's work. It also includes some of his early letters to other poets who were influential in his developing style.
- A. Poulin's *Contemporary American Poetry* (1980, 3d ed.) has a good selection of Creeley's poems along with many others by his contemporaries.

complex. The true artist must constantly deal with the opposing demands of freedom and formalism, and Creeley has demonstrated that the creative response to sterile formulaic formalism lies, not in ecstatic verbal excess, but in the creation of disciplined, controlled, and innovative structures of form and meaning.

Source: Frank Pool, Critical Essay on "Fading Light," in *Poetry for Students*, Thomson Gale, 2005.

Thom Gunn

In the following essay, Gunn explores the language of Creeley's poetry, including its movement, form, and tendency toward neutrality.

Popular though Robert Creeley's poetry has become in recent years, its language has never fitted in with the official current notions of the poetic. For example, the verbs do not work harder than, say, the adjectives; there is as little metaphor as in the most straightforward prose; and the diction throughout tends to be general, unsuited to the sensory effects we prize nowadays. So much for the orthodoxies of the twentieth century, Creeley might remark, but I am left trying to reconcile my conviction that poetry does work primarily through the vigour of its language with my experience that *his* poetry does speak to me, and to many others, in a way that is powerful and persuasive.

How does his language work, then? In commenting on the neutrality of Creeley's diction, one poet has evoked the name of Waller, and another has compared his pared-down antirhetorical flatness to the plain style of an early Elizabethan like Barnabe Googe. Nor do you have to go far to pick up Renaissance echoes: here is a poem from about 1960 called "For Friendship":

For friendship
make a chain that holds,
to be bound to
others, two by two,

a walk, a garland,
handed by hands
that cannot move
unless they hold.

Neither Waller nor Googe are inappropriate names to connect with this sweet-natured and sweet-sounding generalization, in which the complete neutrality of language exposes a density of definition, and if the sheer melody of Waller is not achieved (or even aimed at), it is in a sense glanced at by the tetrameters, which Creeley both creates and at the same time carefully rejects in the lineation of the first stanza. The rejection of regularity, minute though it is here, already points to a great difference between Creeley's and any Renaissance practice. The poem reminisces about iambs but it has its own slightly shifted rhythm, which is sustained not by a tradition but by the varying pace of the singular voice.

If Creeley has come to dislike simile, finally, as "always a displacement of what *is* happening," he has come also to dislike all regularization, because it does something like the same thing. In a recent interview he said about Charles Tomlinson's use of the triadic line, which was invented late in life by William Carlos Williams, that Tomlinson was "missing where the initiating impulse is in Williams." It is all-important for him then to be true to what *is* happening, to stick to the initiating impulse, to keep from what he sees as the dead predictabilities of a systematized rhythm or language. Throughout his career I notice the recurring term *stumbling* for his poetic procedure, most recently in the "Prayer to Hermes" (from *Later*, not included in *The Collected Poems*), in which he addresses the god,

My luck
is your gift,
my melodious
breath, my stumbling.

If one stumbles, led or pushed by impulse, one stumbles into the unforeseen, the accidental. Even so, the accidental may have its patterns. In a poem of more than twenty years ago, "For Love," he says:

Let me stumble into
not the confession but
the obsession I begin with
now. . .

A confession may be for once only, but an obsession recurs. However, it recurs as something felt afresh and with its original force: to adopt Lawrentian terms, you might say that it rises up again as a renewal and not a repetition. The poetics of impulse and renewed accident is closer to Lawrence's "poetry of the present" ("flexible to every breath," said Lawrence) than to the sententiae, or perhaps cynical epigrams, of Googe's beautiful poem "Of Money."

It was Creeley who made the famous remark that form is never more than an extension of content, and in so far as the accidents of composition are embodied in the surviving poem, his remark is constantly illustrated, for he apparently does not tidy up the odd, the peculiar, or the awkward. His suggestive or at times puzzling strangeness is directly opposed to the calculations behind those kinds of rhetoric of which he has so much dread. There is for example the disconcerting language of the last lines of "The Whip": "for which act //

I think to say this / wrongly," where because the reference of "this" is unclear and the locution "I think to" unusual, the whole poem is called in question: thus the characteristics of the style enter the content of the poem, as they always must.

Easy as Creeley's poetry looks at first glance, then, much of it is to be grasped only with the closest attention. *The Collected Poems* is a formidable volume to read straight through: even though it stops short at 1975, thus omitting two later books, it is 678 agreeably printed pages long. You are lucky in fact if you have had the opportunities to read most of the work as it came out in the original collections over the last thirty years.

But certain general impressions strike me at once about his career as a whole. The first is that the style goes through only quite minor changes from beginning to end. I find more of the wonderful comedy early on, and the most recent poetry of all (I am thinking of *Later*) has been hospitable to some dreadfully soft emotion about growing old, but essentially the poetry is still written with the same plain, terse language and the same sure command over the verse movement. The next general tendency is that there *are* changes in the organization of the poems volume by volume. The early poems are complete in themselves, independent of each other, however much they may share themes. In the collections of the 1970s, however—*Pieces* and *In London*, for example—poem leads into poem, group leads into group, and the book rather than the individual poem becomes the meaningful unit. There is also in these books far more fragmentary material included—what you might plausibly call notebook jottings, some of them interesting in connection with the rest of the work or with our thinking about Creeley, some of them less so. The poetics of accident may permit a stumble of this sort, entitled "Kid":

> "What are you doing?"
> Writing some stuff.
>
> "You a poet?"
> Now and then.

Form here is only too clearly an extension of content. I can afford to comment with a certain acerbity because my admiration is so great elsewhere: I want to warn the new reader who dips into the enormous book and pulls out this kind of thing before coming to the good writing. But it would be a mistake for any critic to train his big guns on such minimal poems; there are a large number of them, exercises, notations, experiments, jokes, but after all, there is a certain proportion of deadness present in the complete collected works of any poet.

> *"His suggestive or at times puzzling strangeness is directly opposed to the calculations behind those kinds of rhetoric of which he has so much dread."*

In one sense, though, "Kid" *is* a characteristic poem, for its very modesty. It is an epigram, of sorts. Creeley is at once to be differentiated from his old associates Olson and Duncan by the kind of poem he wants to write. Where their ambitions were epic, expansive, inclusive, drawing upon whole libraries of external material, his were doggedly narrower, drawing almost entirely on the irregular pulse of the personal. This is not to say that he aims at the "lyric," even though he has entitled many a poem "Song," for with him it is the speaking voice that matters, not singing or lyring but stumbling, with all the appearance of improvisation, tentatively and unevenly moving forward, but with a singular gift of "melodious breath," a gift for the true-sounding measure that Williams himself once praised. (Before you accuse Creeley of speaking in cliché about his lines taking "the beat from the breath," you should remember that it was he and Olson who originated the phrase; it is not their fault that others stiffened it into platitude.) And his narrow subject matter, that field of energy through which he stumbles, is the intensely apprehended detail of the heterosexual private life.

The feeling in his best poetry is fresh and clean; as though it is discovering itself just as it gets written. Creeley takes nothing for granted, and if his doing so makes for the wonderful unexpected funniness of "I Know a Man," and for the hilarious lines in his serious troubadour poem "The Door," and for the frankness of "Something," the poem about the pee-shy lover, it is also responsible for a depressed awareness of vulnerability like that illustrated in the note about going through New York in a taxi where he records his "continual sense of small . . . persistent difficulties." The vulnerability exposed in Creeley's poetry is almost constant. But nobody has ever pretended that stumbling was a fluid motion; it is, precisely, an encountering of small persistent difficulties in moving ahead, and if the phrase about New York describes one of the main subjects of his poetry it of course can be taken to refer to the style as well. Finally you could say that his strength arises from his constant perception of weakness. If he is the most heterosexual of poets he is also the least macho.

One situation you can find again and again in Creeley is that of the speaker in bed, either alone or not, uneasily lapsing in and out of sleep, in and out of dream. It occurs for example in a well-known poem, "The World," which starts:

I wanted so ably
to reassure you, I wanted
the man you took to be me,

to comfort you, and got
up, and went to the window,
pushed back, as you asked me to,

the curtain, to see
the outline of the trees
in the night outside.

To hear a reading by Creeley at his best is to be aware of the importance he gives to line-endings. He makes a point of pausing on them *always,* whether there is punctuation or not; his free verse line is thus always preserved as an audibly identified unit. The result is a kind of eloquent stammering; there is a sense of small persistent difficulties all right, but of each being overcome in turn, while it occurs—the voice hesitates, and then plunges forward. You can see how such a reading suits the above lines, with what kind of obstinate holding-on it must stumble forward, even past the interruption, the almost pushed-in qualification of "as you asked me to," and finally getting there, to the end of the sentence, having thus *felt* its way through the poem's opening. The movement forward in these lines is certainly as much part of the meaning as the language itself, which as usual is plain in the extreme. Plain yet not always obvious: "ably" makes a point of much subtlety about the kind of firm flexibility he would have if he were the man she took him to be. And that third line, a breath-unit in itself, implies a large and complicated statement about assumptions and appearances. I want to go on to quote the rest of the poem, taking it in two more parts, not only because it is one of Creeley's best but because once you have come to terms with it you have made an entry into all of his work by discovering the comprehensiveness of packed life beneath the apparently simple and prosaic surface. It is a bare scene indeed: nothing much, nothing physical anyway, has been seen with clarity, nothing much has been done. An outline of trees is visible, that is all, because a curtain has been pushed back. But an outline of certain feelings has also been suggested, and that gives us something to go on when we embark on the long second sentence:

The light, love,
the light we felt then,
greyly, was it, that

came in, on us, not
merely my hands or yours,
or a wetness so comfortable,

but in the dark then
as you slept, the grey
figure came so close

and leaned over,
between us, as you
slept, restless, and

my own face had to
see it, and be seen by it,
the man it was, your

grey lost tired bewildered
brother, unused, untaken—
hated by love, and dead,

but not dead, for an
instant, saw me, myself
the intruder, as he was not.

It is a sentence so thick with comma-enclosed qualifications, because so much is happening simultaneously, that you can easily lose yourself in it. But the remedy is in the voice: it is even truer of Creeley than of most poets that the way to understand him is to learn how to read him aloud. From testing one reading against another you can "feel out" what it is "we felt" that ties the first part of the sentence together. We felt not merely each other's hands, not merely the wetness (of orgasm, it must be), but the grey light which in dream vision congeals to the ghost of the dead brother. Such exploration of the voice shows the density of the sentence to be wonderfully justified: it is not sensory writing in the usual way, not like Tennyson or Hart Crane, but it is as if, rather, Creeley goes directly to the organs that do the sensing. Synaesthesia occurs casually and as a matter of course. And the greyness when it comes the third time has become a quality of being—for the grey brother who lived in some limbo, where he still momentarily persists, was "unused, untaken": his greyness, his indefiniteness was such that "the world" had no use for him at all, it did not even exploit him. The reading voice (mine, yours, not necessarily Creeley's) continues, interrupting itself, but resuming, into a further change. The ghost intruder for an instant looks on me, the speaker, as the intruder in the bed. That is the man *he* takes me to be. By comparison with him even I seem "able"—competent, fluent, potent—belonging as I do to the world of the living. The pathos is far-reaching.

I tried to say, it is
all right, she is
happy, you are no longer

needed. I said,
he is dead, and he
went as you shifted

and woke, at first afraid,
then knew by my own knowing
what had happened—

and the light then
of the sun coming
for another morning
in the world.

The last line would perhaps be weak if "the world," though not referred to as such before this, had not picked up so much weight of meaning during the poem as a whole. The world here is the real world with its common-sense light contrasting to the grey light of the love-making and the ghost: but wasn't it also the place that produced the brother, that rejected him so thoroughly before his death? The reassurance of the new day is tempered by the implication that we are creating our own ghosts of deprivation and despair as we go about our lives.

The poem is characteristic of Creeley at his best. He has gone beyond, or behind, the classic twentieth-century split between image and discourse: he does not attempt sharpness of physical image, and the discursive part of the poetry is more aptly termed "assertion" (the word used of it by Robert Pinsky, the poet who compared him to Googe). Though "The World" takes a narrative form it is like many of Creeley's nonnarrative poems, in that the real course it follows is that of the mind, wandering, but at the same time trying to focus in on its own wandering and to map a small part of its course accurately and honestly, however idiosyncratic that course may seem to be—idiosyncratic in its pace, in its syntax, even in its subject matter. In attuning our voices to that mind, in paying our full attention to the way it moves and shifts, we become part of its own attentiveness and can share in "the exactitude of his emotion."

It is by that sharing that the apparent idiosyncrasy ceases to be such, that is ceases to be special or unique. Creeley himself has the best comment here, on the opening page of the introduction to his Penguin selection from Whitman: "It is, paradoxically, the personal which makes the common in so far as it recognizes the existence of the many in the one. In my own joy or despair, I am brought to that which others have also experienced."

Source: Thom Gunn, "Small Persistent Difficulties," in *Robert Creeley's Life and Work*, edited by John Wilson, University of Michigan Press, 1987, pp. 401–09.

Arthur L. Ford

In the following essay, Ford discusses form in Creeley's poetry, arguing that Creeley is a classicist who has struggled, often successfully, with the projectivist inclination to disregard a priori form.

The tradition within which Creeley writes—the Williams, Olson, Projectivist tradition—insists that the poet be free to choose the form most suitable to the point being made; indeed, as seen in Chapter 2, Creeley maintains that the poem itself must be free to receive the form resulting from its own insistence. Since each utterance is unique, the syllables and lines must arrange themselves into a unique configuration. One observer of Creeley's poems, Robert F. Kaufman, has said flatly: "In fact, the whole idea of formal organization and measure is repugnant to him. . ." On the other hand, an equally perceptive observer, Carl Harrison-Ford, introduced Creeley to Australian readers by saying that Creeley is "a man who sees recurring patterns. . ." Both quotations are taken out of context, of course, but they do illustrate the nature of the debate—and for many the confusion—over the shape of Creeley's poetry and fiction. Is it possible to have in poetry both form and flux? Can one man see recurring patterns and yet reject the whole idea of formal organization? Williams is a poet closely associated in the mind of the reading public with "free verse," and yet he came near the end of his career to the "triadic line," a versatile variation of the terza rima, although still a formal construct; and Creeley is a poet whose best known statement may well be, "Form is never more than an extension of content," and yet his poems consistently arrange themselves in two, three, or four line stanzas, and his fiction, as seen in Chapter 5, exhibits a concern for form and recurring pattern. Any commentator on Creeley's work must decide for himself to what degree Creeley inclines to the formal, to the recurring and stable shape behind a poem or piece of fiction. Is Creeley repelled by formal organization, and if so, how to account for his quatrains? Does he see recurring patterns, and if so, how to account for the bits and fragments particularly of his later poems and for the difficulty of knowing how to read *A Day Book* and *Presences?* Or perhaps form is used by Creeley in the way he saw Whitman's form, while sitting beside the ocean in California: "The constantly recurring structures in Whitman's writing, the insistently parallel sound

"Creeley speaks often of the poem shaping itself while it is being formulated, of the poem assuming its own unique presence resulting from the pressure of the creative circumstance."

and rhythms, recall the patterns of waves as I now see them daily." The shape of the wave is always the same, but each wave is unique in its own composition.

I Creeley as Classicist

Again to begin simply: Creeley must be seen as a classicist who needs and in fact uses standard, a priori poetic forms and who more recently has been searching for usable external forms for his poetry, and yet who because of his time, his associations, and his own statements is best known among his contemporaries as a Projectivist poet. The irony upon which he relies so heavily in his poetry and fiction has its parallel here. Perhaps the tentative, probing, hovering rapier technique and the thematic concern with the search for but never attainment of form and self demand a substantial, external form. Whatever the cause, Creeley's poetry exhibits a much greater regularity and formalization than is usually assumed; and, what is even more significant, much of his poetry and prose, especially from the later years, can be understood best as products of the push toward form, of the classical need for preexistent form despite the modernist dismissal of it.

Creeley speaks often of the poem shaping itself while it is being formulated, of the poem assuming its own unique presence resulting from the pressure of the creative circumstance. In this sense, the poet cannot be consciously aware of the form of the poem until the words begin to appear, and for Creeley this apparently means before they begin to appear on the page. In a lecture delivered at the Literarisches Colloquium, Berlin, in 1967, he said. "What I have written I knew little of until I had written it," echoing a statement made three years earlier, "I have never explicitly known—before writing—what it was that I would say." But—and here is the crucial point—a poem created without conscious preplanning need not be formless. Another New Englander, Robert Frost, user of the stanza and the iamb, claimed for the poem: "It must be a revelation, or a series of revelations, as much for the poet as for the reader."

Creeley too recognizes that a mind can—and must—intuitively shape the poem that is being uttered, and can—and with Creeley almost always does—fall back upon certain recurrent forms for the outline or at least the skeleton of that shape. In an interview for the *Times Literary Supplement* in 1964, Creeley quoted E. R. Dodds' *The Greeks and the Irrational:* "Automatic or inspirational speech tends everywhere to fall into metrical patterns" and then, two years later, he stated more explicitly what these patterns tend to be for him: "Because I am the man I am, and think in the patterns I do, I tend to posit intuitively a balance of *four,* a foursquare circumstance, be it walls of a room or legs of a table, that reassures me in the movement otherwise to be dealt with." More recently, looking back on nearly three decades of productivity, Creeley acknowledged his predisposition toward patterns. "My tidinesses," he said, "are insistent. Thus the forms of things said moved through accumulated habits of order. . ." While asserting then, as seen in Chapter 2, that each poem must be true to its own insistence, Creeley quite clearly recognized at least by the mid-sixties that his poems tend to arrange themselves in certain recurrent patterns, reflecting order, balance, and symmetry. Furthermore, it is possible to follow the interplay between the projective line and rhythm (breath and syllable) and the persistence of pattern throughout the development of Creeley's poetry. Creeley's best poetry, then, does not so much reflect a conflict between Projective Verse and standard forms as a successful fusion of the two.

II The Earlier Poetry

In *For Love*, Creeley's first substantial volume, which covers the formative decade of the 1950s, we can see the poet working out an accommodation between the freedom resulting from his reaction against the fixed metrics of the 1940s and his own predisposition toward pattern. In the early poems such as "Hart Crane," "The Song," "The Crisis," and "Le Fou," Creeley spreads his lines across the page, arranging them in projectivist units. But even here, the pattern hovers in the background, as in "Le Fou." The "organic" quality of this poem has been discussed earlier; it is sufficient here to point out that the poem is based on a 4-2-4 line stanza arrangement once the lines set off from the lefthand margin are either raised to complete the preceding line or are brought back to the left-hand margin. The only exception is the final "good-bye," appropriately so. Such a rearrangement of the line, of course, destroys the poem—image, rhythm, and line are no longer working together—but it does reveal a more traditional pattern behind what appears to be projectivist lining.

Very early, however, Creeley shifted to more overt traditional stanza forms, usually composed of two or three units with an occasional four line unit and with frequent combinations. "The Rhyme" will serve as illustration.

> There is the sign of
> the flower—
> to borrow the theme.
>
> But what or where to recover
> what is not love
> too simply.
>
> I saw her
> and behind her there were
> flowers, and behind them
> nothing. (*For Love*)

Here the stanza is more than regular; each is grammatically complete in itself, a feature found frequently in Creeley's poems of the early fifties when the stanzas tend to fix themselves on the page with individual insistence.

In Section Two of *For Love*, the poems of 1956 to 1958, the quatrain becomes the predominant form, with most stanzas ending with periods, thus emphasizing again the auditory as well as visible presence of the stanza unit. Even a poem such as "The Invoice," which uses an unusually colloquial diction and syntax, is arranged in three logical and grammatical units.

> I once wrote a letter as follows:
> dear Jim, I would like to borrow
> 200 dollars from you
> to see me through.
>
> I also wrote another: dearest M /
> please come.
> There is no one
> here at all.
>
> I got word today,
> viz: hey
> sport, how are you making it?
> And, why don't you get with it. (*For Love*)

As discussed in Chapter 5, Creeley was going through an important period in his life while writing the poems roughly contained in the second half of *For Love*. His first marriage had ended in 1955; and early in 1957, he married his second wife, Bobbie. Again as discussed in Chapter 5, Creeley's poetry reflected this change as it moved through a bitter skepticism of marriage to a treatment of woman as mythic muse and, finally, to an acceptance of woman and the reconciliation of human relationships with poetic production represented in Bobbie. In a portion of an interview quoted in Chapter 5, Creeley observed that as he personally became more relaxed his lines became more lyrical; and part of the movement toward a more lyrical line involved an easing but not an elimination of the four line stanza. Now the lines lengthened and the syntax tended to run on from stanza to stanza, resulting in a greater flexibility and fluidity of line. The effect is not to eliminate the stanza as the controlling presence but rather to place it in the background, thereby allowing it to give shape to the poem without obtruding into it. As Creeley's attitude toward love relaxed, as his lines relaxed, so did his stanzas. Exceptions remain, of course, but now the stanza patterns tended to serve not as external skeletons but as internal skeletons, giving physical shape to the poems without making the reader so blatantly aware of the form.

The success of this more relaxed pattern can be seen in the poems, "The Rose" and, particularly, "For Love," discussed in the conclusion to Chapter 4, but it can be seen in other poems from this section as well, including "The Name," Creeley's poem to his daughter by his first marriage.

> Be natural,
> wise
> as you can be,
> my daughter,
>
> let my name
> be in you flesh
> I gave you
> in the act of
>
> loving your mother,
> all your days
> her ways,
> the woman in you
>
> brought from
> sensuality's measure,
> no other,
> there was no thought
>
> of it but such
> pleasure all women
> must be in her,
> as you. But not wiser,
>
> not more of nature
> than her hair,
> the eyes
> she gives you.

There will not be another
woman such as you
are. Remember
your mother,

the way you came,
the days of waiting.
Be natural,
daughter, wise

as you can be,
all my daughters,
be women,
for men

when that time comes,
Let the rhetoric
stay with me
your father. Let

me talk about it,
saving you such
vicious self-
exposure, let you

pass it on
in you. I cannot
be more than the man
who watches. (*For Love*)

Here as in most of Creeley's poetry the insistence is on physical reality—the name, the act of conception, the child—played off against the father's rhetoric, ironically, of course, the poem itself. He is asking that his daughter, "all my daughters," be natural, that is, complete the forms they are growing toward (as a poem grows toward its completedness and finally occupies its form), while he, the father, talks about it and watches. The irony of the poem results from the child's naturalness opposing the father's rhetoric; however, through this "rhetoric" the child receives her greatest gift, the father's love. Although lines are short, the first sentence stretches out over five quatrains, fifty-eight words followed by the three word switch, "But not wiser," at the end of stanza five.

As discussed in Chapter 4, Creeley achieved a level of personal ease during the composition of these late poems in *For Love* with his marriage to Bobbie, an ease reflected in the integration of myth and Creeley's own reaction to woman. To this integration must be added the successful combination of syllable and line on the one hand and a need for external form on the other. Perhaps this is why many readers find the poems in the last third of *For Love* among Creeley's most satisfying.

III The Later Poetry

Creeley's poetry changed during the sixties, of course, and an important aspect of this change can be seen graphically in a discussion between Creeley and Allan Ginsberg at the Vancouver Poetry Conference in 1963 and in an epilogue to the published transcript of that discussion in 1968. In a major section of that transcript Creeley discussed the literal physical requirement conducive to his act of composition, insisting that ideally he should have a typewriter (as opposed to pen or pencil), strong rhythmic music, and paper, usually an 8 ? 11 sheet.

> I best like, most like, the yellow copy paper that's not spongy, but has a softness to it, so that when you type, the letter goes in, embeds a little. I hate a hard paper. When you erase this paper you take a layer off. . . . So I got a legal size sheet. And it was suddenly a terror, because I would finish what was normally my habit of dealing with the paper and realize that I had about six inches left at the bottom that was blank. This set up a whole different feeling.

Creeley did not simply drop a casual remark in the midst of other ideas; this was the point he was making. He was and is acutely aware of the physical context of his own body, and it is not stretching the point to suggest that the same temperament that needs a prescribed physical surrounding for composition also composes poetry and fiction that need external forms.

At the time of this dialogue, however, Creeley's poetry—the poetry of the last part of *Words* and most of *Pieces*—was becoming more and more jagged and elliptical as he attempted to freeze a moment in the fixed frame of the poem. As discussed earlier, particularly in Chapter 2, such an attempt must fail, but the effort as a whole need not fail since each poem contributes to the perception of what is being attempted. In his epilogue to the discussion with Ginsberg, written in 1968, Creeley described how he consciously attempted to move away from those physical conditions described in the dialogue by writing in notebooks. He hoped to achieve a greater immediacy by having the poem come where and when it will. Ironically, perhaps this freedom from physical contexts that Creeley sought resulted in one more context that he found useful: the notebook or journal. Particularly in *Pieces*, and most obviously in two recent prose works, *A Day Book* and *Presences*, Creeley uses the form of the journal to give shape to his statements; and because the form is there, his statements are allowed to take on an even greater sense of formless immediacy. In the poems the two, three, or four line stanzas often remain, but now the moment is caught in the act of spontaneous notebook jotting.

The poems of *Words* and *Pieces* have been discussed in earlier chapters; perhaps it is best here to say simply that the journal entry provided an opening up of Creeley's poetry and a relaxation of the impression, if not always the line. Some poems are presented as off-hand remarks (again the fragment): "So tired / it falls / apart" (*Pieces*). Other lines suggest casual rumination as the mind wanders over interesting paradoxes:

Nowhere one
goes will
one ever
be away
enough from
wherever
one was.(*Pieces*)

Even longer, complete poems, however, often use the journal appearance to provide the form for a series of itemlike stanzas.

Kids walking beach,
minnow pools—
who knows which.

Nothing grand—
The scale is neither
big nor small.

Want to get the sense of "I" into Zukofsky's
"eye"—a
locus of experience, not a presumption of expected
value.

Here now—
begin!
. . . .(*Pieces*)

The movement is simple: from observation of an event in stanza one to an abstraction based on that event in stanza two to a relevant reference to an external source in stanza three and then to action resulting from the previous sequence in stanza four. Each item is placed carefully in its appropriate form: Stanzas one and two of equal bulk and shape, stanza three relaxing into longer lines, and stanza four blurting out its three words.

Pieces then is, as Denise Levertov suggested, best read as a journal. Although many of the poems were apparently written literally as journal entries, within the context of the present discussion it is the device of the journal that is important because it gave to many of the poems in this volume and, significantly, to the volume itself both the excitement and convincingness of immediate utterance and the fact of preexistent form. In other words, the sense of a physical journal and the literal act of writing in that journal gave to Creeley enough framework so that he could include anything in the volume—even items that appear formless. It is a mistake, therefore, to see Creeley's poetry moving from order to disorder; rather, it must be seen simply as moving to another kind of order.

IV Presences as Form

From early in his career Creeley published his poetry together with paintings or graphics; however, it must be said that the combination of graphic and poetry was more often sympathetic than illustrative; that is, his poems did not comment on or illustrate the paintings (as did Williams' *Pictures from Brueghel,* for instance) but rather paralleled, in tone perhaps, the paintings or graphics used. An early example is *The Immoral Proposition*, published in 1953 with seven drawings by his friend, René Laubrès; and more recent examples are *St. Martin's* (1971) and *Away* (1976), each with a series of monoprints by his wife Bobbie, and the poem "People," published in a separate volume in 1971 with a series of sketches by Arthur Okamura. In this volume, Okamura's sketches depict tiny human figures arranged together into various geometric shapes and patterns or into stylized shapes such as flowers, while the accompanying poem, in short three line stanzas, makes direct and indirect references to them.

In the examples cited, Creeley appears to be using the illustrative matter as a stabilizing element for his poetry, much as he might use a quatrain or any other external form within which and against which his lines work. More recently, however, Creeley has produced a curious piece of prose that mystified a number of people, but that can be understood to some extent at least within the context of this discussion of form. *Presences* was originally written as an accompanying text to a collection of paintings by Marisol, but the text apparently had so little to do with the paintings that the publisher at first refused to use it. In one sense the publisher was correct—the work is not a text for the paintings; in another and more important sense, however, the publisher was wrong, because Creeley is attempting in this prose work what he sees Marisol doing in her paintings—that is, to lock dreamlike experiences on the canvas through crystallized surreal devices. The fact that his images do not correspond to hers and, further, that his words to not gloss her paintings apparently caused confusion in the minds of some readers, but the work becomes accessible if seen from another angle—or perhaps more accurately from two other angles.

First, in regard to Creeley's need for a priori form. The work itself is divided into five sections with each section subsequently divided into three parts of approximately 500, 1000, and 1500 words each. Creeley was interested in a manuscript of approximately 15,000 words and normally thinks in terms of 500 words to the page; therefore, he needed thirty pages of material. Furthermore, he was intrigued with the mathematical symmetry of combining these into groups of a single page, a double page, and a triple page and then shifting them according to a simple formula as represented on his title page:

1. 2. 3.
2. 3. 1.
3. 1. 2.
1. 2. 3.
2. 3. 1.

Creeley was interested in the fact that a diagonal line could be drawn from right to left through the numbers. This therefore became the principle upon which *Presences* is organized. The form is blatantly exterior, even formularized; however, the effect is to free Creeley from form rather than to trap him in it because now that this need is fulfilled, he can roam where he will, where his mind and feelings take him.

And this brings us to the second necessary approach to *Presences*. Creeley's mind and feelings took him in this work back to a persistent preoccupation over the past twenty-five years—a preoccupation that he saw also in Marisol's paintings. Perhaps even more than before, the insistence in this work is, as he says here, "When I show myself as I am, I am, I return to reality." Even while moving through memories of his own past, through personal feelings, through reactions to ideas, none of which appear to follow a linear development, all of which appear as almost journallike entries (the dates of composition are included following various "entries" and again one is reminded of the journal aspects of *Pieces* and *A Day Book*), Creeley's thrust is toward the actuality on the page. He insists throughout on the fact, from the title *Presences* through a discussion in the work itself: "Human life he had begun to recognize as an accumulation of persistent, small gestures and acts, intensively recurrent in their need if not, finally, very much more than that. The *ideas* they delighted in, or suffered, however much they did affect the actuality of all, were nonetheless of a very small measure of possibility." He even attempts using words almost abstractly to suggest, but more than that, to *make real* a "presence": "The clock, on the wall, walks to the door. The door, in the wall, walks to the stair. The stair, up the wall, walks to the window, both ways." Creeley here and elsewhere in *Presences* uses the surreal technique of objects melting into other objects (like Dali's clocks) and the cubist device of seeing various planes of an object simultaneously ("both ways"); however—and this is a crucial qualification—Creeley can do this only because he has already established the form. Because the hole is clearly there to be filled and because it is filled with hard facts, "presences," Creeley is in his own mind free to move nonlinearly across the work. Ironically, the very arbitrariness of the form—geometrically arranged units of five hundred words each—releases Creeley to a freedom of movement and development.

The thesis of this chapter—that Creeley is a classicist who has struggled, often successfully, with the projectivist inclination to disregard a priori form—is seen most clearly in the epigraph to *Presences*. Creeley quotes the contemporary painter, Donald Sutherland: "Classicism is based on presence. It does not consider that it has come or that it will go away; it merely proposes to be there where it is." The fact of form is inextricably bound up with other facts of the poem or piece of fiction. Just as the emotion, the object, and the word must be substantial and able to exist as realities on the page, so must the form, the configuration, the field, the grid. Classicism for Creeley, as for Sutherland, is the insistence on the hard presence, one of which is the shape of the work itself. Creeley needs these "presences," which can be, finally, either fact as form or form as fact.

Source: Arthur L. Ford, "Form as Fact," in *Robert Creeley*, Twayne Publishers, 1978, pp. 116–27.

Loss Pequeño Glazier

In the following essay, Glazier discusses Creeley's talents as a writer, his connections to Black Mountain College, and his beliefs about the art of writing.

For the second half of this century, Robert Creeley's work as an innovative poet has occupied a singular place in postwar American letters. The contributions of Creeley, with Charles Olson, were instrumental, through Projective Verse, to the definition of emerging senses of poetic form in the 1950s. The *Black Mountain Review* (1954–1957), which Creeley edited, was a landmark literary journal of the period. Creeley's work, along with that of other poets connected with Black Mountain College, has also been a benchmark against which subsequent poetry has been measured. Perhaps most important, Creeley's career has placed him as immediately active in the record of the contemporary American "new poetries." Though known primarily as a poet, Creeley's poetry is intricately tied to other genres of writing, prose the most important among them. He has also made substantial contributions in essays, letters, editing, autobiography, collaborations with artists, the interview, and various forms of miscellaneous writing. The fact of literary engagement is crucial to Creeley's work; his sense of writing as a multifaceted engagement may well stand as a definition of the contemporary literary endeavor.

Known for the dictum, "form is never more than an extension of content," Creeley has largely been connected with Black Mountain College and with Projective Verse. The latter, developed primarily in the early 1950s, was not meant as a defining style for any poet but as a means of breaking from poets associated with the New Criticism and their insistence on form as extrinsic to the poem, dominant at the time. Creeley also had considerable interchange with other poetic alternatives, including the Beat poets. Further, he coedited the anthologies the *New American Story* (1965) and *The New Writing in the U.S.A.* (1967), which presented the work of divergent groups of writers. To date, Creeley has been mentor to or advocate of many American poetry movements including the Beats, Objectivists (retrospectively), the San Francisco Renaissance, poets of the New College of California and the Naropa Institute, writers associated with a multitude of small presses, and most recently, Language poets. Creeley's involvement with this last school includes his inclusion in *This 1* (1971), credited by Ron Silliman as being a harbinger of language-oriented poetry. In addition, two of Robert Grenier's five critical texts in the issue were about Creeley; one of these included the assertion, as related by Silliman in his introduction to *In the American Tree* (1986), that "Projective Verse is *Pieces* On," an acknowledgment of the importance of Projective Verse and Creeley's collection of poems *Pieces* (1968) to emerging poetries. Creeley's literary involvement and lasting contribution, more than with any single poetic idiom however, has been with the possibilities of new writing—and he has been a tireless campaigner for efforts exploring these engagements.

Though popularly considered a love poet, Creeley's poems are given to explore the incongruities of such relations, rather than allowing for their easy statement. Creeley has, especially in his early work, presented the persona of an "unsure egoist"; many of these poems carry a veneer of accessibility yet often befuddle the reader with senses of conflicting identity, shortfalls in the possibilities of interpersonal communication, and a persistent characterization of the self as isolated. He is also known for his formal investigations in the late 1960s; here his texts are multiform, stanzaic verse giving way to

"The fact of literary engagement is crucial to Creeley's work; his sense of writing as a multifaceted engagement may well stand as a definition of the contemporary literary endeavor."

brief epiphanies, observations, sketches, prose interruptions in the form of journal entries, personal reflections, and rhythmic notation reminiscent of the improvised jazz that was formative to his early creative development. This period was to prove the most rankling to literary critics representing conservative American poetic ideologies. Though the poetics of his recent work take a turn as yet unexplored to any depth by contemporary critics, Creeley's entire oeuvre stands as a monumental contribution to the realignment of poetic form in the second half of the twentieth century, and his poetic achievement renders, as Robert Hass suggests in *Twentieth-Century Pleasures* (1984), "what the mind must, slowly, in love and fear, perform to locate itself against, previous to any discourse."

Robert White Creeley was born in Arlington, Massachusetts, on 21 May 1926. His parents, Oscar Slate and Genevieve Jules Creeley, soon moved the household—Robert, his older sister, Helen, and Teresa Turner, the family housekeeper—to a farm in West Acton. In 1928 Robert Creeley suffered an injury that resulted in the loss of his left eye three years later. Oscar Creeley, a successful physician, died in 1930, and Robert Creeley found himself growing up in a household of women. He enjoyed a closeness to nature and in later years reflected on his youth in West Acton as essentially a small-town experience despite their geographic closeness to Boston. He considers himself to have been raised in "the New England manner, compact of puritanically deprived senses of speech and sensuality," an environment in which one did not feel encouraged to linger over words and in which the sentiment was that "life was real and life was earnest, and one had best get on with it."

At age fourteen he entered Holderness School, a boarding school for boys in Plymouth, New Hampshire. His early interest in writing was evidenced by the articles and stories he published in the Holderness School literary magazine, the *Dial*. In 1943 Creeley entered Harvard University, but his attendance was interrupted by service as an ambulance driver for the American Field Service in the India-Burma theater during World War II. In winter 1945 Creeley returned to Harvard and married Ann McKinnon the following spring. With Ann he would have three children, David, Thomas, and Charlotte, born in 1948, 1950, and 1952, respectively. He assisted in editing the special E. E. Cummings issue of the Harvard *Wake*, which included contributors such as William Carlos Williams, Marianne Moore, Allen Tate, Karl Shapiro, Wallace Stevens, and Mark Van Doren. The *Wake* also included Creeley's first published poem, "Return."

With its street ending in "darkened doors" (a "darkness" that recurs in subsequent work) and the disaffiliated sense of home evoked in the closing lines—"enough for now to be here, and / to know my door is one of these"—"Return" makes clear that Creeley's homecoming from war, as for many, was less than satisfying. As Creeley has noted, a new social perspective had to be found: "The value of one's life as a progression toward some attention was gone because the war demonstrated that no matter how much you tried, as Morganthau said: *facts have their own dynamic*."

The Creeleys lived in Truro, Massachusetts, with Robert Creeley commuting to Harvard until the summer of 1947, when in his last semester he withdrew from the university. The Creeleys then moved to Rock Pool Farm near Littleton, New Hampshire, and practiced subsistence farming while living on Ann Creeley's income from a trust fund. At Rock Pool Farm Creeley also bred pigeons and chickens, which he showed in Boston. During these years Creeley began to listen to jazz, especially Charlie Parker, Thelonious Monk, Max Roach, Jacky Byard, and Dick Twardzik. He was "fascinated with what these people did with *time*. Not to impose this kind of intellectual term upon it . . . this was where I was hearing 'things said' in terms of rhythmic and sound possibilities." Creeley credits Henry Miller, Kenneth Patchen, D. H. Lawrence, and Hart Crane with making clear to him the possibility that a writer has "access to your feelings and can really use them as a demonstration of your own reality." However, jazz took him further: besides the acoustic and improvisatory elements these musicians employed, Creeley credits them with extending the possibilities of his writing by making clear "how *subtle* and how sophisticated . . . how *refined* that expression might be."

In December 1949 Creeley heard Cid Corman's Boston radio program *This Is Poetry* and began a correspondence with Corman, which lasted for six years. In 1950 Creeley gave his first public poetry reading on Corman's program and became American editor for Rainer Gerhardt's German magazine *Fragmente*. During this period Creeley and Jacob Leed collected manuscripts for a proposed (but never published) experimental magazine, the "Lititz Review."

Meanwhile a friend had sent to Creeley two of Charles Olson's poems for the magazine. Creeley responded to Olson with some criticism, thus beginning an extraordinary correspondence that lasted until Olson's death in 1970. These literary exchanges produced more than a thousand pieces of correspondence; the "range and articulation" of the letters, Creeley has written, "took me into terms of writing and many other areas indeed which I otherwise might never have entered." The correspondence was vital to the developing interests of both writers and formed, as George F. Butterick noted, "a critical document for understanding the emerging poetics of a generation, as well, perhaps, of the poetries yet to come." One of the principles of these "emerging poetics" is Projective Verse, usually circumscribed by Creeley's declaration that "form is never more than an extension of content" and Olson's instruction in his essay "Projective Verse" (1950) that poems proceed from "the HEAD, by way of the EAR, to the SYLLABLE" and from "the HEART, by way of the BREATH, to the LINE." One of the motivations behind Projective Verse was to provide a means of breaking from poets associated with the New Criticism. As Creeley has subsequently explained, "The forties were a hostile time. . . . The colleges and universities were dominant in their insistence upon an *idea* of form extrinsic to the given instance." What was objectionable was the "assumption of a *mold*, of a means that could be gained beyond the literal fact of the writing *here and now*, that had authority." Projectivism was not meant as a defining style for any single poet but recognized "that writing could be an intensely specific revelation of one's own content, and of the world the fact of any life must engage." Creeley later reflected on Olson's "Projective Verse" essay and its subsequent "curiously mystic effect upon people." According to Creeley: "I took it to be a series of observations akin to Pound's rules of thumb, 'a few don'ts' for example, and used it in that sense. [Olson] showed me how the line might be organized in terms of the breath involved in it. [This approach] is a fairly practical application of emotion in terms of a given series of beats and is not at all a mystique."

In 1951, with children to support, the Creeleys moved to France, hoping to survive more economically on Ann Creeley's income. Much of the material gathered for the "Lititz Review" went into Corman's *Origin* I (1951), the Olson issue, in which Creeley's poem Hart Crane appeared. *Origin* II (1951) featured a special section of Creeley's work. Because of the inflation in France the Creeley family moved to Majorca, Spain. Creeley was briefly editor at Martin Seymour-Smith's Roebuck Press at Majorca, an experience that—along with the increasingly bitter tensions in his marriage—played a key role in his novel *The Island* (1963). In 1952 *Le Fou*, his first book of poems, was published by Golden Goose Press. On Majorca Creeley and his wife started the Divers Press, an independent press that focused on publishing experimental writers and was founded to create "a place defined by our own activity and accomplished altogether by ourselves—a *place* wherein we might make evident what we, as writers ... hoped our writing might enter." The press published Corman's *Origin* VIII (1953) as well as books by Olson, Paul Blackburn, Irving Layton, Douglas Woolf, Larry Eigner, Robert Duncan, and Katue Kitasono. Divers Press also published Creeley's second book of poems, *The Kind of Act Of* (1953), and a collection of Creeley's stories, *The Gold Diggers* (1954).

Through Ezra Pound, Creeley had met René Laubiès. Illustrations by Laubiès, with their simple yet bold brush strokes and emphasis on materiality, were published on the covers of Creeley's *The Kind of Act Of*, *The Gold Diggers*, and his later book *The Whip* (1957). *The Immoral Proposition* (1953), published by Jonathan Williams as *Jargon*8 and printed on long, folded pages loosely bound by string, comprises poems by Creeley, each accompanied by a drawing by Laubiès.

As a poet Creeley was intensely conscious of "elders" such as Pound, Williams, and Louis Zukofsky. Nevertheless he commented that "initially I had thought that my work as a writer would be primarily in prose." This is evidenced by his manifesto in *Origin* II, which discussed Projectivism and a possible new approach to prose. Any consideration of Creeley's poetry must include a reading of his prose. Visual art also opened up new avenues for Creeley. In 1953 at a gallery in Paris he was struck for the first time by Jackson Pollock's work, discovering in Abstract Expressionism specific approaches to writing.

A decisive opportunity arose when Olson proposed that Creeley edit the *Black Mountain Review*. Intended as a promotional vehicle for the college, the Black Mountain magazine had under Creeley's editorship some affinities to *Origin*. Creeley hoped to extend these interests and to explore "the *ground* that an active, ranging critical section might effect" by including "critical writing that would break down habits of 'subject' and gain a new experience of context generally," a vision that has stayed with Creeley to this day. In March 1954 the first issue of the *Black Mountain Review* came out just before Creeley left Majorca to teach at Black Mountain College, meeting Olson for the first time. At Black Mountain he was introduced to artists and writers with whom he would maintain lifelong contact and began his first, somewhat awkward, teaching experience. Black Mountain was an artistic community that included visual artists, musicians, and dancers as well as writers; it offered students a chance to develop their own approaches to creative work. Because of the journal the label "Black Mountain School" soon came into use to describe contemporary poets such as Olson, Duncan, Denise Levertov, Edward Dorn, and Blackburn—writers that, though sharing specific interests, vary in their writing styles.

In July Creeley returned to Majorca and unsuccessfully tried to repair his troubled marriage. He continued to edit the *Black Mountain Review*, publishing issues in the summer, fall, and winter of 1954. (Only three more issues of the magazine appeared, in 1955, 1956, and 1957—each with cover art by Laubiès.) Creeley's last Divers Press book was an anonymous pamphlet, *A Snarling Garland of Xmas Verses* (1954), "a wallet pocket-book" of five poems fashioned from one folded pullout strip of long paper. Distraught about the breakup of his marriage, he returned to Black Mountain College and resumed teaching.

At Black Mountain there was a great deal of interaction with painters known as Abstract Expressionists. Creeley formed close relationships with Pollock, Philip Guston, Jack Tworkov, Willem de Kooning, Esteban Vicente, John Chamberlain, Dan Rice, and John Altoon. Later, at the Cedar Bar in New York, Creeley came to know Franz Kline. With Guston and another painter, Ashley Bryant, Creeley "gradually ... began to come into the relationship to painters that does become decisive." (Bryant had contributed the frontispiece drawing to *Le Fou*.) Creeley considers Altoon extremely important because "the things he drew, made manifest in his work, were images in my own reality." Most important was the Abstract Expressionists' approach to art: "Their ways of experiencing activity, energy—that whole process, like Pollock's 'when I am in my painting'—that the whole condition of their way of moving and acting and being in this activity was so manifestly the thing we were trying to get with Olson's 'Projective Verse,' the open field." Painting, in the mid 1950s, Creeley felt, "was far more fresh as imagination of possibility than what was the case in writing, where everything was still argued with traditional or inherited attitudes and forms." The affinities between Projectionism and Abstract Expressionism are evident in Tworkov's statement in 1957: "My hope is to confront the picture without a ready technique or a prepared attitude, a condition which is nevertheless never completely attainable; to have no program and, necessarily then, no preconceived style." Creeley's *All That Is Lovely in Men* (1955), published by Jonathan Williams, includes drawings by Rice. These illustrations had "disposition toward, for, and of, SPACE," which Creeley liked tremendously. He insisted that "there is no matter more urgent, now, than how we occupy our space."

In 1956 Creeley resigned from Black Mountain College and headed for San Francisco "to see the Pacific Ocean, if nothing else." Creeley spent a remarkable three months in San Francisco, where he met Beat poets Allen Ginsberg, Jack Kerouac, Philip Whalen, Michael McClure, Gary Snyder, and other writers. San Francisco at the time, writes Creeley, was "an intensive meeting ground" full of "blasts of sound, and talk of Pollock, *energy*" and "packed with things *happening*." Creeley published poems by some of these writers in the seventh and final issue of *Black Mountain Review*. Through vital participants in the new poetries of the West Coast, Creeley also made lasting friendships.

The next few years would see several important events in Creeley's life. He received a B.A. from Black Mountain College in 1955 and married Bobbie Louise Hoeck two years later. Children in the Creeley household at the time included Kristen (stepdaughter), Leslie (stepdaughter), Sarah (born 1957), and Katherine (born 1959). In 1960 he completed an M.A. from the University of New Mexico; he lectured there periodically until 1966. His publications during this time included *If You* (1956), *The Whip*, and *A Form of Women* (1959). He was awarded the Levinson Prize for ten poems in *Poetry* and a D. H. Lawrence Fellowship, both in 1960. In addition he was included in Donald Allen's anthology *The New American Poetry: 1945–1960* (1960), the defining anthology of the decade.

For Love: Poems 1950–1960 , Creeley's first widely circulated book of selected poems, was published by Scribners in 1962. The collection was widely reviewed and nominated for a National Book Award, selling more than forty-seven thousand copies. Of Creeley's popularity at the time, Robert Hass remembers going into college lounges "jammed with people sitting on the floor, nodding their heads in profound sympathy and agreement with some [Creeley] poem they had heard only once."

Consisting of three chronological sections covering 1950 to 1960, *For Love* is best known for its presentation of the love lyric, in which, in Olson's words, "the intimate / is an exactitude." In his prefatory note to *For Love*, Creeley comments: "Insofar as these poems are such places, always they were ones stumbled into: warmth for a night perhaps, the misdirected intention come right; and too, a sudden instance of love, and the being loved, wherewith a man also contrives a world (of his own mind)." Though popularly considered a love poet, Creeley typically explored the incongruities of such relations. Especially in this early work, Creeley presents, as Charles Altieri has written, the persona of an "unsure egoist." Many of the poems have a veneer of accessibility yet befuddle the reader with varied senses of conflicting identity, shortfalls in the possibilities of interpersonal communication, and a persistent characterization of the self as isolated. Creeley has since commented that he had not expected a collection concerned with "marital confusion, loneliness, and isolation" to be so popular; that it struck such a chord in readers at the time was a significant statement about modern culture itself.

The poems in *For Love* tend to be compressed and urgent, focusing on a single event or fact of observation. One of the most often discussed of these poems is "The Warning," in which

For love—I would
split open your head and put
a candle in
behind the eyes.
Love is dead in us
if we forget
the virtues of an amulet
and quick surprise.

The phrase "for love" echoes the title of the collection. An immediate "quick surprise" for the reader is that "The Warning" is a warning; it is not about love's pleasantries but its limitations. The act proposed in the first stanza is immediate, ritualistic, and violent. (Creeley has suggested that this proposed act is rather "a true measure of an ability to love," a defining boundary in the possibility of the relation.) The poem clearly conveys to the reader pent-up energy and violent pressure, as illustrated by the phrase "split open your head."

A similar pressure is expressed in "The Whip." (Creeley has written about the idea of "the whip" as having to do with the conflict between the mind and the body: "It's a weird tension and the torque that's created by that systematization of experience is just awful . . . something was really, you know . . . slashing and cutting me.") In this poem the narrator is in bed. Two women are present: one "on / the roof," a troubling, dreamlike presence who is a "woman I / also loved"; and the other tangibly next to him and, by contrast, inert. His reaction to this crisis of values, "lonely," is to cry out. The woman next to him puts her hand on his back, and, paradoxically, this tender act "whips" the narrator. The message for the marital relationship then is doubt and misperception.

The narrative of this poem also has a parallel in Creeley's story "The Musicians." Here, there is also a woman on the roof, dressed in a housecoat, seemingly deranged because of a love gone wrong. The persistent presence of three characters—of whom one is always detached—typifies the relations of both the poem and the story. The title also proceeds from the jazz sense of "whip it" or "whip that thing," which serves as an exhortation for a musician to play an instrument. (This phrase can also refer to sexual activity.) There is music playing on a phonograph, and musical instruments are present, though unused. What the characters in the story "play" however, are proposed narratives, that is, other stories; hence the title might suggest "tell that story." "The Whip" also operates rhythmically. Observing the terminal junctures at the end of each line, one gets a clear sense of a rhythm that communicates "the bleak confusion from which [the poem] moves emotionally" in bursts of jazzlike phrasing. Creeley states that it is jazz "that informs the poem's manner in large part. Not that it's jazzy, or about jazz—rather, it's trying to use a rhythmic base much as jazz of this time would. . . . That is, the beat is used to delay, detail, prompt, define the content of the statement or, more aptly, the emotional field of the statement. It's trying to do this while moving in time to a set periodicity—durational units call them." The third sense of the title is "whipped up," meaning exhaustion of the characters. In this sense the narrator is recounting the poem's activity "wrongly," since the exacerbation of interpersonal situations really leads to emotional constriction.

Creeley taught at the University of British Columbia in 1962 and 1963, then returned to New Mexico as a lecturer until 1966. During this time he completed *The Island*, set on Majorca in the early 1950s. This novel, "a process of discovery," on one level discovers that "no wife—indeed no other person—can reify one's existence, that the 'love' that demands such reification is really a form of infantile dependency." But *The Island* involves discovery in other ways and is crucial to Creeley's poetry. Resonant in breadth to Olson's *Maximus Poems* (1953–1975), Duncan's *Passages* (1968–1987), Ginsberg's *Howl* (1956) and *Kaddish* (1960), Williams's *Paterson* (1946–1963), and Pound's *Cantos* (1917–1969), *The Island* was Creeley's "first 'long poem'; it was the first piece of serial writing that went on for many days, weeks, and so forth." As such, it opened up, as Creeley relates, "a great deal of possibility for me.... I think it permits poems like 'The Finger' to be written." In terms of structure, *The Island* follows a numeric procedure: "Each chapter is an economy of five pages in length, with five chapters to each of the four parts. And five times four is twenty, which is the number of chapters in the book." *The Island* , then, should be viewed as a formal investigation. In this way it shares more with poetry than fiction of the period. Creeley is insistent that *The Island* had no preexisting narrative plan or outline: "I did *not* 'work out the novel in my mind. . . . 'I 'worked it out' *literally* as I wrote it."

In 1963 Creeley read and lectured with Olson, Duncan, Ginsberg, Levertov, and others at the Vancouver Poetry Festival, another defining literary occasion. Creeley was a Guggenheim Fellow in 1964, the same year he won the Oscar Blumenthal Prize for thirteen poems in *Poetry* magazine. He also received a Rockefeller Foundation grant in 1965. That year the Scribners edition of *The Gold Diggers and Other Stories* was published, as was the *New American Story*, which he coedited with Donald Allen. In addition Creeley participated in the Berkeley Poetry Conference, another significant gathering of new poets. In 1966 he was visiting professor at the State University of New York at Buffalo. (Although he has had concurrent appointments, his affiliation with Buffalo has been continuous since he became professor of English there in 1967; he was appointed David Gray Professor of Poetry and Letters in 1978 and Samuel P. Capen Professor of Poetry and the Humanities in 1989.) He was the subject of the National Educational Television film *Poetry USA: Robert Creeley* (1966), and a British edition of collected poems, *Poems 1950–1965* (1966), was published. Creeley also edited *Selected Writings of*

Charles Olson (1966). This volume, introduced by Creeley, includes the *Mayan Letters* (1953), an extraordinary group of letters written to Creeley while Olson was in Mexico; a selection of Olson's essays and poems; and Olson's defining "Projective Verse" essay. The following year Creeley received the *Poetry* Magazine Union League Civic and Arts Foundation Prize, participated in the World Poetry Conference in Montreal, and, with Donald Allen, edited *The New Writing in the U.S.A.*

At a time when Creeley could have perpetuated the well-received forms of writing in *For Love*, he pushed forward, extending the writing process and his investigation of its materiality, moving from a "generative" to a "conjectural" mode. *Words* (1965) was an important advancement in Creeley's poetic project. In this work Creeley explores several aspects of the possibility of the poem. Adhering consistently to his idea of "measure," the poem emerges in Creeley's work as an active engagement with its own language. As he commented in Berkeley in 1965, "measure" is for Creeley "the actual measure of the speech, the way the words are going . . . the topography or actual ground, in no metaphoric sense, of where it is one is moving. . . . In other words, how does one gain a use of that place where he or she is, in no sentimental or enlarging way? How do you get to ground?" Words themselves are experienced as physical in relation to the poet's presence. In *Words* Creeley's work explores a literal physicality of subject matter. This is prefigured by the epigraph (a quote from Williams), which evokes "a counter stress, / born of the sexual shock, / which survives it." In addition to the clearly intended sense of the text as the body, poems such as "The Woman" ("you have left me / with, wetness, pools / of it, my skin / drips"), "The Dream," and "Distance" also graphically explore elements of the heterosexual experience. This is the element of Creeley's work to which M. L. Rosenthal reacted so vehemently in his well-known essay "Problems of Robert Creeley." (Sherman Paul's often cited response to Rosenthal's attack appeared in a 1975 issue of *Boundary 2*. These two essays provide opposing arguments in the reception of Creeley's work of this period.) The heterosexual experience is reiterated by the recurring image of "the hole," as illustrated in this section of "The Language":

I heard words
and words full
of holes
aching. Speech
is a mouth.

The image of "the hole" refers to both the incapacities of language and to sexuality from a male viewpoint. In these poems "the hole" is a site of incredible tension. The gendered view of sexuality in these poems may be the most difficult element of Creeley's work to reconcile. In this regard, Charles Bernstein remarks in *Contents Dream* (1986) that "Creeley's work attests to the experience of maleness as a social condition, replete with the troubling and problematic values that are so central a part of that role." Certainly "troubling" values are evoked in these poems. As the tension of gender escalates, *Words* leads to explicit gender-based violence. Wendy Brabner alludes to this mechanism as a tendency by the poet to "confront [his] fears and conquer them through some form of violent action." This brutality emerges most strikingly in "Enough" ("Your body is a garbage can") and "Hello" (where "he" caught "the edge of // her eye and / it tore, down, / ripping.")

Violence can also be seen as a statement of Creeley's poetics, "ripping" language to pieces. Part of this process involves discarding logical relations and embracing verbal positioning resembling Abstract Expressionism in image, representation, and arrangement of compositional elements, thus working to eschew traditional methods of knowing. In his essay "A Sense of Measure" Creeley rejects the assumption that order "can be either acknowledged or gained by intellectual assertion, or will, or some like intention to shape language to a purpose which the literal act of writing does not in itself discover." Early into *Words* logical associations begin to disintegrate as Creeley's writing pursues this course. In "I Keep to Myself Such Measures" the narrator asserts that "there is nothing / but what thinking makes / it less tangible." As the poem "The Window" declares, "I can / feel my eye breaking" or the proposal of "Intervals" that "*who / am I*—/ identity / singing."

Toward the end of *Words* short poems stand out, illustrating modes of abstraction in this collection and also substantially prefiguring work to be collected in *Pieces*. Among these are the four-line poem "The Farm" ("Tips of celery, / clouds of // grass—one / day I'll go away"), "Joy," "A Piece," and "The Box." The last is dedicated to the artist John Chamberlain and uses words as a material to create a work of sculpture:

Three sides,
four
windows. Four
doors, three
hands.

Like a work of sculpture, the poem has defined, solid parameters. Its construction is less than typical, a fact that the reader (who would expect four sides of a box) observes with the first line. As Creeley has noted about painting, "If no one sees a painter, or, rather, what he is doing—finally, not 'doing'—doesn't he still have *things*?" Creeley's poetics insist here on words as real and concrete components of the poem operating, as Joseph M. Conte has suggested, as "paradigmatic forms whose elements continually evaluate *their own* affinity and dissimilarity." The poem has "things" substance: it attempts to constitute an object with mass—one constructed of common objects—but pieced together the way an Abstract Expressionist sculpture might be. This constellation follows Creeley's account of Pound's instruction that "poetry is a form cut in time as sculpture is a form cut in space." Through this construction, Creeley shows his engagement with "making the world / tacit description / of what's taken / from it."

Creeley collaborated with R. B. Kitaj on *A Sight* in 1967, the same year *Robert Creeley Reads*, a recording of Creeley reading from *Words*, was released. It was followed by *The Finger* (1968), which was illustrated with collages by Bobbie Creeley. *Numbers* (1968), written at the suggestion of Robert Indiana, is a "sequence of poems involved with experiences of numbers," accompanied by ten strikingly colored folio serigraphs by Indiana. The subsequent publication of the sequence in *Pieces*, though textually accurate, cannot convey the visual dimension and graphic richness of this earlier presentation of the text.

Creeley's maturation as a poet is closely linked to *The Island*. According to Creeley, writing the novel "led me to feel through things in a more various way. . . . I'm more at ease with myself; I have much more very literal confidence." As a result Creeley has described the poems collected in *Pieces* as approaching "a far freer context of statement." Preceding the better-known 1969 Scribners collection *Pieces* was the 1968 Black Sparrow Press book of the same title, which has thirteen pages of poems with eight collages by Bobbie Creeley. These full-page collages are composed of fractured images that cohere through their dynamics on the page and are a significant element in the original edition of *Pieces*. The epigraph to *Pieces* is Ginsberg's statement "I always wanted, / to return / to the body / where I was born." Though one critic has contended that this epigraph evidences saturation "by a discourse on masculinity," Creeley has argued for a sense of the body as "the [poetic] 'field' and . . . equally the experience of it." As Creeley insists: "It is, then, to 'return' not to oneself as some egocentric center, but to experience oneself as in the world, thus, through this agency or fact we call, variously, 'poetry.'" *Pieces* explores this "field" through its engagement with form.

Creeley is direct about this project, opening the collection with an untitled poem:

As REAL as thinking
wonders created
by the possibility—
forms. A period
at the end of a sentence
which
began *it was*
into a present,
a presence
saying
something
as it goes.

Creeley's emphasis on form argues that the tangible presence of discrete words and phrases, freed from conventional syntactic relations, makes the text "real." According to Williams this freeing of words is comparable to what Gertrude Stein had accomplished in *Tender Buttons* (1914). Stein had "completely unlinked [words] . . . from their former relationships in the sentence." The goal of such unlinking is to present words as "things" that occupy relational space. These "things," Creeley has written, "are large or small objects, having the fact of space in whatever dimension becomes them." Thus *Pieces* is composed of many fragments of text, "pieces" of poems. "Sometime in the mid-sixties," Creeley later wrote, "I grew inexorably bored with the tidy containment of clusters of words on single pieces of paper called 'poems.' . . . My own life, I felt increasingly, was a *continuance* . . . and here were these quite small *things* I was tossing out from time to time, in the hope that they might survive my own being hauled on toward terminus." Breaks in poetic flow, uncertainty about exactly where a poem begins or ends, and the appearance of seemingly incongruent forms, such as journal entries and fragments of letters, contribute to the interruptive quality of *Pieces*. Some of these "pieces" have conventional titles, but more frequently the poems begin with a phrase in all capital letters, exist within a textual flow set off by bullets, or achieve a status of being curiously attached to titled poems, reflecting the chronological accumulation of this text. *Pieces* emphasizes the "fact of process" of composition in an effort to "trust writing." The proposal is to move the poem into the present; its "realness" will be qualified by "presence"—process being the route to the poem's realization. As to method, in "Here" it is proposed:

My plan is
these little boxes
make sequences . . . [.]

With the "plan" of the journal-like progression of these poems, the following consideration arises:

Lift me
from such I
makes such declaration.

"Such I" alludes to a primary dilemma in Pieces. The narrator of these poems, as he tries to be more and more immediate, suffers a consequent split in identity. Creeley has described this dilemma by writing that "As soon as / I speak, I / speaks." In "They" Creeley writes of the mind following what is "true" then adds "and *I* also," indicating the contrast between what is thought and the "I" of the poem. However, this is more than a contrast; it is a constant friction, "*a* 'poet' of such impossibilities 'I' makes up," as Creeley writes in "Echo." The instability of the "I" stands out in *Pieces* for the intensity of conflict; through his later poems and autobiography, Creeley will continue to explore the dimensions of the "I" positioning, in Creeley's words, "the sense of 'I' into poet Louis Zukofsky's 'eye'—a locus of experience, not a presumption of expected value."

Creeley was a visiting professor at the University of New Mexico when *Words* and *Pieces* were published. The retrospective collection *The Charm* (1969) was also published by the Four Seasons Foundation at this time, bringing back into print works that were long unavailable. These include "Return," poems from *The Kind of Act Of*, and parts of *Le Fou* not included in *For Love*. In 1970 Creeley participated in the International Poetry Festival at the University of Texas and the Neuvième Biennale Internationale de Poèsie at Knokke-le-Zoute, Belgium. His books, *A Quick Graph: Collected Notes and Essays* and *The Finger: Poems 1966–1969* were published in the same year. He moved his family to Bolinas, California, in order to serve as visiting professor at San Francisco State College in 1970–1971. This move provided an opportunity to meet various writers, including Joanne Kyger, Tom Clark, Aram Saroyan, Bill Berkson, Clark Coolidge, David Meltzer, and Philip Whalen, among others. Also in the community were musicians such as the Jefferson Airplane, the Rowan Brothers, and Steve Swallow (who would later compose music based on Creeley's poems) and artists such as Kitaj and Arthur Okamura (who Creeley knew from Majorca). Some of Creeley's poems and prose of this period directly draw on Bolinas experiences and persons. In 1972 his radio play, *Listen*, was produced in London. *Listen*, *A Sense of Measure* (essays and an interview), and *A Day Book* were all published the same year. *A Day Book* is composed of a series of journal entries and "In London," a selection of poems later printed in Creeley's *Collected Poems, 1945–1975* (1982). "In London" contains a substantial number of poems, similarly performing an act of "direct recording." Fragmentary poetic "pieces" dominate the first part of the collection with many references to "place." The original publication of *A Day Book* was a lavishly produced collaboration with Kitaj.

In 1973 Creeley's *Whitman: Selected Poems*, a tribute to Whitman's "instruction that one speak for oneself," was published. This same year he established residence in Buffalo, where he and his family maintain a permanent home. His next few collections of poetry, *His Idea* (1973), *Thirty Things* (1974), *Backwards* (1975), and *Away* (1976), are the only sections in the *Collected Poems* which appear as originally printed by small presses. These books record the "factual life" of the development of Creeley's poetics during this period and, as such, exemplify an insistence on the practice of writing. *His Idea* seems to stand as a continuation and denouement of his work in *Pieces*, a single series of individual fragmentary poetic pieces each beginning with a phrase or word in capital letters, in which "Days go by / uncounted." *Thirty Things* consists of thirty, mostly occasional, individually titled short poems maintaining, in Duncan's words, "a tension between resignation and resolution." Some of these poems are directed to individuals, sometimes evoking Bolinas by direct reference or facts of geography; other poems express a consciousness of time's passing such as "Still" ("Still the same / day? / Tomorrow") and "One Day" ("One day after another—/ perfect. / They all fit"). *Backwards* (the title suggesting direction, though regressive), is a short collection, similarly composed of discrete, titled poems showing a like discontent with time standing still, as in the two-line title poem of the collection: "Nowhere before you / any of this." *Away* consists of poems in a variety of formats, individually titled poems as well as sequences of poetic phrases separated by bullets. "For My Mother: Genevieve Jules Creeley" stands as an excursion into thematic material that emerges strongly in his later works. In this collection the idea of abstraction in poetry is again questioned. In "Berlin: First

Night & Early Morning," an interlocutor interrupts a flow of poetic phrases to say:

You: "too abstract,
try it,
all,
over again . . . [.]"

As Creeley moves forward in his career, it is evident that he will leave behind "exacerbated tension" and explore, as in the Williams epigraph to *In London*, "But what to do? and / What to do next?"

Creeley's prose works are also important in understanding his literary accomplishments. As Stephen Fredman relates, "Creeley [says] that not until toward the end of writing *Words* . . . did he begin to loosen his sense of formal necessity, to free ideas and expressions from the imperative of reaching a rested conclusion. He began then to write serial compositions, starting with *Pieces* . . . and continuing in the three prose books collected in 'Mabel.'" The three texts in "Mabel: A Story" as published in the *Collected Prose* (1984), are "A Day Book," "Presences," and "Mabel: A Story." *A Day Book*, writes Creeley, is "precisely what it says it is, thirty single-spaced pages of writing in thirty similarly spaced days of living." As such, it resonates with *Thirty Things* and its accompanying prose works. Written for a collaboration with Kitaj, "A Day Book" is direct, exploratory, and improvisatory; it is principally an investigation of the possibilities of form, particularly of writing within specified form. (As originally published, *A Day Book* is physically an experiment in form. In an oversized format, Creeley's writing appears "solid" because of its large font and is juxtaposed with striking large plates by Kitaj.) *Presences*, proposed because Marisol had seen *Numbers*, Creeley's collaboration with Robert Indiana, was originally published in the United States by Scribners as *Presences: A Text for Marisol* (1976). It was designed with large type and little gutter area and was accompanied by photographs of sculptures by Marisol. The text of *Presences* consists of "a series of improvisations upon Marisol's images, both sculptural and personal." Fredman has noted that in *Presences* "there is much for Creeley to identify with in Marisol's art: the isolation, the immensity of the heart, the repetition of frontality, and the constant use of the self." The text contains five sections of six single-spaced pages of text in permutations of 1-2-3, beginning and ending with 1. Of this numeric arrangement, Creeley writes, "I wanted a focus, or frame, with which to work, and *one, two, three* seemed an interesting periodicity of phrasing." "Mabel," "begun as an imagination of women" for a collaboration with Jim Dine, contains five sections of six single-spaced pages of text in permutations of the same 1-2-3 sequence.

Creeley's essay *Was That a Real Poem or Did You Just Make It Up Yourself* (1976) is an extraordinary statement of poetics; it has also served as an exemplar for the craft of the essay, influencing contemporary writers. A distinctly individual blend of autobiography and poetics, *Was That a Real Poem* presents to the reader an account of Creeley's development as a poet. Acknowledging that, "my thinking about poetry may or may not have anything actively to do with my actual work as a poet," he describes his work based on personal feelings, his past, and a resilient sense of poetry qua poetry. He believes that "what we call *poems* are an intrinsic fact in the human world whether or not there be poets at this moment capable of their creation." The matter of poetic creation is beyond him, and although at times a source of despair, it is somehow comfortingly *there* nonetheless. In a sense, this manifesto allows for personal involvement in writing while letting the process stand by itself, beyond the personal. Moreover, this statement is a definitive accomplishment, providing a locus of activity for the contemporary poem, "a *place*, in short, one has come to, where words dance truly in an information of one another, drawing in the attention, provoking feelings to participate."

Creeley divorced his second wife, Bobbie, in 1976 and, in the spring of the same year, embarked on an extensive reading tour of New Zealand, Australia, and Asia. In 1977 Creeley married Penelope Highton, whom he met in New Zealand. He would have two children with Penelope, William and Hanah, born in 1981 and 1983, respectively. The next year he accepted the position of David Gray Professor of Poetry and Letters at Buffalo and found a new publisher, New Directions. Creeley's first New Directions book was *Hello: A Journal, February 29–May 3, 1976* (1978), poems written in the form of journal entries from tours and readings Creeley had given in Fiji, New Zealand, Australia, Singapore, the Philippines, Malaysia, Hong Kong, Japan, and Korea. Creeley abandons the use of heterogeneous forms, structuring the poems as discrete units, often in stanzaic form or as poetic fragments under the aegis of a specific geographic location. The result is a reflective and consistent tone of voice in which a sense of hope emerges as a direct result of observations. For example, in "Soup (Palmerston North, New Zealand)":

Bye-bye, kid says,
girl, about five—

peering look,
digs my one eye.

A change of direction is indicated in "Out Here." The narrator of the poem sits in the corner of an airport bar. He relates how "a few minutes ago" he was thinking in a sexual mode characteristic of his earlier writing, but then retracts the thought, explaining that such an approach applies "not any more," because "it's later." The speaker finds himself "spooked, tired, and approaching / my fiftieth birthday" as he relates his in-transit status, surroundings, and thoughts. Then, finally:

I'll be a long way away
when you read this—and I won't
remember what I said.

Correspondingly, the text itself is "not any more, it's later," a direct invocation of the title of his following collection of poems. *Robert Creeley: A Gathering* (1978) seems to have marked a change in the direction of the author. This collection, a 570-page issue of *Boundary 2*, sought to present "critical orientations and disclosures . . . as diverse as the occasion of a first gathering demands," effectively constituting a forum on Creeley's innovations and assembling many important statements about his work. The following year, *Was That a Real Poem and Other Essays* was issued by the Four Seasons Foundation, making available, along with the title essay, some previously uncollected poetic statements, including his introduction to *Whitman: Selected Poems* and "The Creative," "On the Road," and "A Sense of Measure."

Even as these collections were published, Creeley was entering a completely different arena of poetic investigation, abandoning formal fragmentation. It might have been a disillusionment with such experiment, as he writes in "Still Too Young," "all I'd hoped for / is going up in abstract smoke" and "I'm too old to do it again / and still too young to die" or because simply that formal discontinuity does not suit the project at hand. As indicated in the poem "Age," the poet has accepted the altered situation or at least does not indicate he wishes to change it: "There's no surprise now, / not the unexpected / as it had been. He's agreed / to being more settled." The facts of Creeley's changed circumstances shift the "I" into a retrospective position, leading to reflection. The titles of Creeley's five later collections of poetry all consider various forms of reflection, whether relating to memory, in *Later* (1979) and *Memory Gardens* (1986), optics, in *Mirrors* (1983) and *Windows* (1990), or acoustics, in *Echoes* (1982).

Concomitant with this exploration, Creeley increasingly worked with different surface modes of the poem; the subject matter of his poems shifts to include natural phenomena, a more accepting gesture toward the marital relationship, a willed, though not always positive, sense of human endurance, and, as Fred Moramarco writes in an article collected in *Robert Creeley's Life and Work* (1988), content "characterized by a greater emphasis on memory, a new sense of life's discrete phases, and an intense preoccupation with aging." These facts of aging, significantly, are facts of human life and, like childhood ("When I was a kid, I / thought like a kid—// I *was* a kid, / you dig it"), are presented in an "angle of incidence" to the form of the poem. Age has many faces in these later poems, from simple facts of observation ("now my hands are // wrinkled and my hair / goes grey" or "I am no longer / one man—// but an old one") to a sense of despair, such as in "Prayer to Hermes," where "these days / of physical change" bring to the poet "a weakness, / a tormenting, relieving weakness." Here this reference is tied to the advent of winter, the season likened to the poet's body. Writing, as in earlier works, continues to be simultaneous with the body. Creeley insists on a "*physical* sentence." It is a sentence on the page; it is a "life" sentence (physical aging).And as a writer, his sentences also become "older." The poem's activity must similarly accommodate this "sentence," and the structure of the poem must respond to and feel "the meat contract, // or stretch, upon bones" with a sense of compacted attention and tightened poetics. With the contraction of subject matter in these poems comes a greater potency of the activity within the circumscribed area. His insistent return to the idea of "echoes" delineates a poetic form of his own making. (The idea is introduced early in his writing, evoked significantly in *Words* and *Pieces*, and brought to focus by the fact that an entire volume is titled Echoes.) The "echo," as investigated by Creeley, is expressed as something ultimately beyond grasp; what becomes foregrounded then is the act of *reaching* for the echo. In "My Own Stuff" Creeley expresses this idea: "It is a / flotsam I could / neither touch quite / nor get hold of . . . yet / insistent to touch / it . . . [I] kept poking, trying / with my stiffened / fingers to get hold of" and "its substance I had / even made to be / there its only / reality my own." Of course, grasping for echoes can only leave the hand empty. The place at which the poet has arrived seems an empty one because "there is / no one here but words, / nothing but echoes." Yet these poems are not empty. Creeley's later work is true to his long-standing commitment to the poem as direct observation and to textual elements of the poem constituting real objects.

The poem "Helsinki Window" in *Windows* is an example of a poem where words work in a circumscribed area. This poem is dedicated to the Finnish-born writer Anselm Hollo, whom Creeley has elsewhere described as "a man who lives daily, humanly, in the physical event of so-called existence." In "Helsinki Window" direct observation clings to Creeley's compositional urge, "daily" and "humanly" bounded in nine poems of roughly twelve lines each. Here, "at the edge of this / reflective echo," each rush of phrasing issues from what is immediate: the "same roof," "old sky," "windows now lit," "a bicycle / across the way," a "spare pool / of light." The elements of the poem are drawn from what may almost exclusively appear through a single window. The window's view is full of *things*; yet the things cohere only within the compacted structure of their frame. The window, as a frame, does not create a "picture," rather an area for the relations of "things." Creeley has pointed out that Abstract Expressionism "regains the canvas as surface—or literally imposes as significant surface anything on which the painting occurs" thereby causing painting to lose "its historical sense of *picture*, insofar as our sense of a picture seems to imply something which is referential." The same focus on surface applies to Creeley's poems and the result is "classic emptiness." Yet it is an emptiness which is full, the poem itself—"it / is *there* here *here*"—and it is concrete and immovable—"no / other thing can for a / moment distract it be / beyond its simple space."

"Sonnets," in *Echoes*, consisting of six twelve-line and one fourteen-line poem, also witnesses form compacting the information of the poem. The "window" of observation in this case is memory. Memory pushes "a twisting / away tormented unless" into the "presence" of writing. The rhythm of these poems arises from the regularity that the enclosure of form exerts on the text. This text can be highly rhythmic at times:

> teeth wearing hands wearing
> feet wearing head wearing
> clothes I put on take now
> off and sleep or not or sit . . . [.]

Of greatest importance is the density of the writing. This density, Creeley has stated, is "a situation in which each word becomes not so much singular as though its meaning were to be abstracted from its companies, but each word is a possible pivot or shift or relocation of what it is that I seem to be . . . trying to get said." In "Sonnets" there is the feature of past events (including literary precedent, as the use of the sonnet form suggests); there is the action of the poet's "I," bridging from these events to the present; but equally, there is the active sense of writing as an immediate and central "thing" operating to "get said" what is necessary. Despite the element of recollection, the focus of this work is not on what is reflected but on reflection itself, as in the collection's epigraph, "echo or mirror seeking of itself, / . . . makes a toy of Thought." Since thought has itself become a compositional element, "I is not / the simple / question // after all, / nor *you* / an interesting answer." What emerges in this collection is the interrogation of reflection, its circumscription by thought processes, and its condensation within formal frames. Thought itself becomes "consequential, / itself an act, a // walking round rim / to see what's within."

The first two volumes of *Charles Olson and Robert Creeley: The Complete Correspondence* were published by Black Sparrow Press in 1980, marking the first availability of this copious correspondence. Two major volumes of collected writings also appeared in the early 1980s. *The Collected Poems of Robert Creeley, 1945–1975*, including a section of "Uncollected Poems," works printed in magazines that never appeared in books, and *The Collected Prose of Robert Creeley*, reprinting Creeley's diverse excursions into the genre, including *The Gold Diggers*, *The Island*, *Listen*, and "Mabel: A Story." These were followed in 1989 by *The Collected Essays of Robert Creeley*, bringing together a diversely published body of critical writing that would be nearly impossible to assemble otherwise. The influences for these essays include Lawrence, Edward Dahlberg, Williams, and Olson, though Pound is also clearly in Creeley's mind. These writings manifest Creeley's agreement with Pound that critical writing should come "from those defined in the arts relating" and follow creative works as "the two feet of one biped" follow each other.

The same year Creeley's autobiography not only explored his personal past but extended the form of the autobiography itself. Much as Creeley's *Was That a Real Poem* offered an alternative vision of the literary essay, his autobiography, first published in the Contemporary Authors Autobiography Series (1989), reconsiders the narrative. (It was published separately as *Autobiography* in 1991 and republished in Tom Clark's *Robert Creeley and the Genius of the American Common Place* in 1993.) Though asserting that "there is an awful, self-consciously recognized limit to what may be called my sincerity," Creeley is perhaps unparalleled in making his feelings appear as facts. Thus, though this autobiography has facts necessary to its genre, Creeley's insistence that "we believe a world or have none" creates a narrative of a life lived inseparable from a writer's poetics. "It is the pleasure and authority of writing that it invents a life to live in the first place," Creeley maintains. His prose is an example of such writing. Focusing on his youth, family, and early adulthood, Creeley presents an account that is full of biographical facts and also argues for "a scale for [the] diverse presence" of humanness. As such, this very personal account presents the facts of his life as the facts argue a life. "What cannot be objectified is oneself," Creeley acknowledges, "Yet the fiction, finally for real, is attractive." In this way, the self is presented as only one possible version of lived selves. As Bernstein notes, "Amidst the onslaught of events, the self provides only an *apparent* centering or agency, always subject to readjustments and recentering." What the autobiography manifests is "fictions" made fact in the literal act of writing.

The Essential Burns was also published in 1989 and offered selections, in Creeley's words, among his "first delights in hearing and reading poetry as a boy." The appearance of Creeley's correspondence with Irving Layton made available documents covering, "perhaps the most seminal period in recent Canadian and American literary history" and showing the rich transnational communication that influenced the literature of both countries. Creeley's *Selected Poems* (1991) was compiled by the poet from his vast output. Creeley's choice of the contents was guided by his feelings about the place of poetry: "Why poetry? Its materials are so constant, simple, elusive, specific. It costs so little and so much. It preoccupies a life, yet can only find one in living. It is a music, a playful construct of feeling, a last word and communion." Standing by his earlier work, he drew heavily on *The Charm* and *For Love*, with an even but sparser inclusion of his subsequent writings. The last poem in the book, "Body," is set off as if making a statement, concentrating on the presence of the body and the physical circularity of human experience, suggesting themes from *Pieces*, though this poem is from *Echoes*. In 1993 Olson's *Selected Poems* was edited by Creeley, and it offered him the opportunity of presenting his personal selection of the works of the poet who was "the first practical influence upon me of a contemporary." Accordingly, Creeley acknowledges the selections as "unavoidably [his] own" and proposes that they be read keeping in mind that their relationship provided "a measure, an unabashed response to what either might write or say." Creeley points to the precedent of their collected correspondence to suggest that this collection stands as Creeley reading Olson, certainly true to their writing relationship.

Creeley has unarguably attained and has accepted the status of an elder statesman of poetry. His recognition during the 1980s and 1990s has been impressive. His works have been translated and published in the Netherlands, Germany, Austria, Spain, Mexico, Italy, Denmark, Norway, Czechoslovakia, and France, among other countries. His many awards have included the Shelley Memorial Award from the Poetry Society of America (1981), a National Endowment for the Arts grant (1982), two DAAD Fellowships in Berlin (1983 and 1987), the Leone d'Oro Premio Speziale, Venice (1985), the Poetry Society of America Frost Medal (1987), a Distinguished Fulbright Award as Bicentennial Chair in American Studies, Helsinki University, Finland (1988), distinguished professor rank at the State University of New York (1989), the Walt Whitman Citation, which included service as New York State Poet (1989–1991), and an honorary doctor of letters granted by the University of New Mexico (1993). He also received the Horst Bienek Lyrikpreis from the Bavarian Academy of Fine Arts in Munich (1993), Germany's highest honor to a living foreign poet and an award that few other American authors have received. Perhaps most significantly Creeley enjoys the distinction of having been elected to the American Academy of Arts and Letters.

Though the physical presentation of Creeley's poems has changed considerably through his career, Creeley's attention has remained focused on writing as determined by the facts of experience, rather than by preconceived forms. This attention has advanced a sense of writing that, in addition to having roots in what is intensely familiar (the "common place" of his later lectures), also has no determined limit of genre. Some of his most notable later literary accomplishments include his autobiography, the occasional prose essay, interviews, orally presented poetry, and lectures. Aside from teaching he makes literary tours of the United States and the world. In addition to these genres of "writing," Creeley's commitment to discourse between the arts and technology have witnessed his poems being set to jazz (Steve Swallow's *Home*, appearing in 1980, and Steve Lacy in the 1985 release *Futurities*) and his participation in films (*Creeley*, produced by Documentary Research in 1988 and *Robert Creeley*, released as part of the Lannan Literary Series in 1990), CD-ROM (*Poetry in Motion*), and recently, the Internet. He has, however, expressed caution about this latest medium, suggesting that one must be conscious of "what happens to knowledge when its traditional relation to ordering and retrieval (memory) is intensively mediated by instrumentation exterior to its own function."

Of great significance have been his contributions to gallery and public art (such as his eight poems engraved on the bollards at Seventh and Figueroa Streets in Los Angeles) and his collaborations with visual artists. Creeley's engagement with the visual arts has been a consistent factor in his writing. His recent collaborators include Susan Barnes, John Chamberlain, Francesco Clemente, Cletus Johnson, Susan Rothenberg, Robert Therrien, and Martha Visser't Hooft. His collaborations with Johnson, in which Creeley provided texts for "visual transformation" by Johnson, were exhibited at galleries in Buffalo and in New York. Creeley's work with Clemente has been significant. *It* (1989), published by Bruno Bischofberger in Zurich, is a substantial volume containing sixty-four pastels by Clemente and twelve poems by Creeley. In *7 & 6* (1988) Creeley provides poems for seven of Therrien's works. (The collaboration also includes prose by Michel Butor.) Creeley's responses to the works are factual, sometimes humorous, and address the image (presented on the facing page) with a "literalism [that] twists into pleasurable knottiness." Creeley's collaborations are "wholly in keeping with Therrien's own no-nonsense approach." *Life & Death* (1993) is particularly illustrative of the intensity with which Creeley approaches such collaborations. Creeley viewed Clemente's series *The Black Paintings* (1991–1993) on a bright Sunday morning in the artist's studio. He relates that the light made the paintings "tangible" to him and that "for me they tell a story, a very old one, of how humanly we live both as one and as many, in a world particular to our lives but also far vaster and more communal than such personal limits can ever acknowledge." Creeley wrote a poem for each image but returning home realized he wished to say more and so wrote a second half to each poem. True to the spirit of this collaboration, the paintings are reproduced in *Life & Death* with the poems in the order Creeley viewed them and with bullets separating the pair of textual creations for each painting.

Creeley remains a popular poet, though recent critical attention to his work has varied in frequency. Two recent critical "gatherings" in *Poetics Journal* (1991) and *Sagetrieb* (1991) include several articles on Creeley's work. A special issue of *The Review of Contemporary Fiction* recently appeared, focusing on Creeley's prose and offering contemporary evaluations of *The Gold Diggers*, *The Island*, Creeley's autobiography, and his experimental texts. Two new books have appeared: *Tales Out of School: Selected Interviews* (1993), which has five lengthy interviews (four from *Contexts of Poetry*), and *Robert Creeley and the Genius of the American Common Place* by Clark. In this hybrid critical and biographical work Clark focuses on Creeley's view of the "common-place" through interviews with Creeley, a transcript of "Some Senses of the Commonplace" (a talk Creeley gave at the New College of California in 1991), and Creeley's "Autobiography." The most important form of recognition, however, has been the very real and lasting changes Creeley's work has effected in postmodern poetry. Clark, in *The Poetry Beat*, credits Creeley with "creating a mass-democratic cottage verse that ushered postwar American poetry outside the halls of fading ivy, and in turn made possible a whole new generation of 'post modern' academicism." Thus, the visibility of the tradition for which Creeley speaks, as Bernstein points out, is substantially greater than it was thirty years ago, and "while this tradition and its current manifestations are hardly in the mainstream of official culture, the magnitude of related subterranean, ground level, and occasionally above-ground anthologies, presses, magazines, and public readings is incomparably greater, and far more entrenched—a circumstance that Creeley has significantly helped to bring about."

Source: Loss Pequeño Glazier, "Robert Creeley," in *Dictionary of Literary Biography*, Vol. 169, *American Poets Since World War II, Fifth Series*, edited by Joseph Conte, Gale, 1996, pp. 78–97

Ekbert Faas

In the following essay, Faas discusses Creeley's friendship with Allen Ginsberg, the various roles he has played in the literary world, and his turbulent path to success.

"None of the so-called Black Mountain Writers wrote in a literally similar manner. That is, Olson's modes of statement are certainly not mine, nor are they Duncan's, nor Denise Levertov's—and so on. What was, then, the basis for our company? I think, simply the insistent feeling we were *given* something to write, that it was an obedience we were undertaking to an actual possibility of revelation." Creeley's statement in an interview stresses the openness of the very "school" he helped found and promote. At the same time, its main tenor recalls similar statements by the Beat poets such as, say, Ginsberg's account of the genesis of *Howl*: "I suddenly turned aside in San Francisco," Ginsberg recalls, "... to follow my romantic inspiration—Hebraic-Melvillian bardic breath. I thought I wouldn't write a poem, but

> *"In addition to being a poet, Creeley, throughout his life, has fulfilled multiple other roles as teacher, publisher, editor, and organizer of various literary movements."*

just write what I wanted to without fear, let my imagination go, open secrecy, and scribble magic lines from my real mind." No wonder that Creeley, in *A Quick Graph* (1970), quotes these words as a further, non-Black Mountain instance of the new poetry of revelation.

Creeley and Ginsberg first met in 1956 just when Black Mountain College had been shut down and *Howl* was completed in manuscript. Whatever sense of a common creative impulse they then discovered had thus been reached independently. On the other hand, both poets shared a common background which Creeley is clearly aware of—the disorientation of their childhood, school, and university years during the time of the Depression, of World War II, and of its aftermath: "it's the background for Allen Ginsberg, myself and many of our contemporaries. The disturbance of these years came at the end of the Depression and the chaos of values and assumption of values, the definition of values was very insistent. For example, although we had no knowledge literally of one another, Allen and I had many friends in common at that time. William Cannister was perhaps the most painfully vivid instance of one of 'the best minds of [our] generation' that one saw 'destroyed by madness.' Bill had the compulsive need to kill himself and this need was almost a societal condition, I mean it was almost the actual situation of feeling in those years: a sort of terrifying need to demonstrate the valuelessness of one's own life."

In fact, Creeley's early life resembles Ginsberg's to the point where circumstances seem interchangeable except for their specific denominations. Creeley was born on 21 May 1926 in Arlington, Massachusetts (Ginsberg a few weeks later, on 3 June of the same year in Newark, New Jersey); after attending Holderness School, Plymouth, New Hampshire, Creeley entered Harvard in 1943 (Ginsberg entered Columbia in the same year). Creeley studied under such luminaries as F. O. Matthiessen, Harry Levin, and Delmore Schwartz (Ginsberg studied under equally well-known academics: Meyer Schapiro, Mark Van Doren, and Lionel Trilling); helped edit an issue of the Harvard *Wake* (Ginsberg edited the *Columbia Review*); was temporarily suspended from the university for carrying out of Lowell House an unhinged door which was about to be painted (Ginsberg was dismissed from Columbia for his unflattering remarks about the university president and for tracing a skull and crossbones plus an anti-Semitic inscription into the dust of a dormitory window); and finally dropped out of Harvard during the last semester of his senior year (Ginsberg received a bachelor of arts degree in 1948). More seminal than what Creeley and Ginsberg were taught at the university was what they learned from association with nonacademic friends. While driving a truck for the American Field Service in the India-Burma theater during 1945 and 1946, Creeley was initiated into drugs, an area Ginsberg discovered under the guidance of two older mentors hanging out around Columbia, Jack Kerouac and William S. Burroughs. Kerouac and Burroughs also gave Ginsberg the modernist education in literature and the arts which Creeley, during 1946 and 1947, explored by frequenting a bohemian circle in Provincetown, Massachusetts—particularly through his acquaintance with Slater Brown, friend of both E. E. Cummings and Hart Crane. A major part of this education was in jazz, whose rhythms were to exert a great impact on Creeley's and Kerouac's writings. "This is what I was doing from 1946 to 1950," Creeley remembers. "I was frankly doing almost nothing else but sitting around listening to records."

The post-university years for both Ginsberg and Creeley were marked by similar restlessness and ferment. After a series of visions in which he heard a voice reciting from Blake, Ginsberg underwent four sessions of psychiatric counseling followed by an eight-month stay in a hospital for psychoanalysis and therapy; he subsequently worked as a book reviewer for *Newsweek* magazine, was a market research consultant in New York and San Francisco, traveled to Mexico, and finally returned to the Bay Area where he helped organize the second San Francisco renaissance, launched by the famous reading at the Six Gallery. Creeley, married since 1946 to Ann McKinnon, tried subsistence farming near Littleton, New Hampshire, defaulted on his mortgage, moved to Fontrousse outside Aix-en-Province and later to Lambesc in France, then spent two years in Mallorca, taught at Black Mountain College from March to July 1954 and again during 1954 and 1955, divorced his wife with whom he had had three children, left Black Mountain, and traveled to San Francisco via Albuquerque. For all their turmoil, it was these half dozen years or so before they met in which Creeley and Ginsberg developed their distinct poetic idiom and poetics.

In Creeley's, rather than Ginsberg's, case this also was a period of intensive and widespread literary enterprise. In addition to being a poet, Creeley, throughout his life, has fulfilled multiple other roles as teacher, publisher, editor, and organizer of various literary movements. While at Harvard he helped edit the E.E. Cummings issue (Spring 1946) of the Harvard *Wake*. Early in 1950 he and a friend, Jacob Leed, decided to publish their own magazine but failed due to problems with Leed's handpress. Yet much of the material they had collected was incorporated into the first issue of Cid Corman's *Origin*. Contact with Corman also led to Creeley's correspondence with Olson, who exerted a major influence on the younger poet. As a result, Creeley became editor of the *Black Mountain Review* and finally a teacher at Black Mountain College. Before that, while living in France and Mallorca, Creeley acted as American editor for Rainer Gerhardt's short-lived magazine *Fragmente* and as editor-publisher at his own Divers Press. In October 1952, Richard Emerson and Frederick Eckman published Creeley's first volume of poems, *Le Fou*, as a chapbook in the Golden Goose series. Two other collections of poems, *The Kind of Act Of* (1953) and *A Snarling Garland of Xmas Verses* (1954), as well as *The Gold Diggers* (1954), a collection of eleven short stories, appeared under Creeley's own imprint.

A source common to both Creeley's and Ginsberg's literary pursuits before 1956 was the work of William Carlos Williams, whose book four of *Paterson* includes a 1949 letter by Allen Ginsberg. Two years earlier, Ginsberg, at age twenty-one, had already interviewed the older poet for a local Paterson newspaper. What he learned from Williams was close indeed to the earlier breath-rhythm experiments à la Charles Olson and Creeley. By 1955, Ginsberg recalls, "I wrote poetry . . . arranged by phrasing or breath groups into little short-line patterns according to ideas of measure of American speech I'd picked up from W. C. Williams' imagist preoccupations." Creeley himself discovered Williams through *The Wedge* when that volume of poems first appeared in 1944. The book to him was a godsend, and Williams's introductory remarks about a poetry revealed in the process of writing have stayed with him as a formula to describe the verse of both Black Mountain and Beat poets: "When a man makes a poem, makes it, mind you, he takes words as he finds them interrelated about him and composes them—without distortion which would mar their exact significances—into an intense expression of his perceptions and ardors that they may constitute a revelation in the speech that he uses." Another influence on both poets came from the work of Ezra Pound whose *Make it New* was a present for Creeley's twentieth birthday. Like *The Wedge*, that book was "a revelation" to him "insofar as Pound there spoke of writing from the point of view of what writing itself was engaged with, not what it was 'about.'"

The words highlight Creeley's insistent concern with language which, at least theoretically speaking, differs from Ginsberg's more vision-oriented creativity. Both tendencies emerged before the poets first met in San Francisco. Crucial here was the involvement with their separate circles of artistic associates. In Ginsberg's case, there was a strengthening of his ties with Burroughs and Kerouac as well as new friendships with Gregory Corso, Peter Orlovsky, Gary Snyder, Lawrence Ferlinghetti, and others in San Francisco. In Creeley's, there was a series of new contacts with Cid Corman, Charles Olson, Denise Levertov, Larry Eigner, Robert Duncan, and others, many of them conducted through correspondence before the poets finally met in person. In December 1949, Creeley by chance heard Cid Corman's radio program "This Is Poetry," wrote to him, and as a result found himself reading soon after on the same station. This was followed by further readings of his own works as well as those of Joyce and Williams on station WTWN, St. Johnsbury, Vermont. The subsequent attempt in 1950 to launch his own magazine in collaboration with Jacob Leed made Creeley write to Williams and Pound, which led to many important new contacts including Paul Blackburn, Jacques Prevert, and Denise Levertov.

Most crucial among all these was Charles Olson, some of whose poems had reached Creeley via Vincent Ferrini. At first Creeley was "rather put off" by Olson's verse, feeling that this poet was simply "looking around for a language" with the result of "a loss of force" in his poetry. But Olson's response ("i says, creeley, you're / off yr trolley: a man / god damn well has to come up with his own lang., syntax and song both, / but also each poem under hand has its own language, which is variant / of same") quickly made him reverse his verdict and initiated the most influential friendship in Creeley's life. Their correspondence of nearly one thousand letters which lasted till Olson's death in 1970 provided "a practical 'college' of stimulus and information" to the younger poet long before he began teaching at Black Mountain College in 1954.

Teaching at Black Mountain at first meant a whole new fulfillment which, however, turned to misery over the breakup with his wife, Ann, who had stayed behind in Mallorca. Another mishap was a car accident which left the driver with a broken leg, Creeley with a severely wrenched shoulder, and another friend with a broken back. A few months later, just at the turn of 1955–1956, Creeley left the college "in real despair, with a marriage finally ended, separated from [his] three children, [and] very confused as to how to support [himself]." One hope in traveling west was that he might manage to shed "Easternism," which Ginsberg, then living in the Bay Area, had been trying to do for some months now. A brief sojourn in New Mexico, where Creeley had plans of settling down, brought little fulfillment in this quest. Staying with friends only made him feel more dependent and restless, and after about a month or so he continued toward San Francisco—"to see the Pacific Ocean, if nothing else."

But San Francisco had a lot more to offer than that. Meeting the Beat writers particularly gave Creeley some of the self-liberation he had yearned for. Most of his later comments on the Beats share the same tenor. Burroughs and Kerouac, he suggested in 1965, had helped free literature from the imposition of "story," "plot," and "continuity" by making the writer a mere recording instrument of what, in Burroughs's phrase, "*is in front of his senses at the moment of writing*." Gary Snyder with his Zen Buddhist transluminations of reality had opened a whole new "successful relation of hope" in his poetry. Most important, Ginsberg assured Creeley, as Williams had, that his emotions were not insignificant. In doing so, he also helped him open up toward a more expansive way of writing. Until 1956, Creeley had been "habituated to the use of poetry as compact, epiphanal instance of emotion or insight. I valued its intensive compression, its ability to 'get through' a maze of conflict and confusion to some center of clear 'point.' But what did one do if the emotion or terms of thought could not be so focused upon or isolated in such singularity?" Here Ginsberg, in the way he had revitalized Whitman's prosody in *Howl*, provided Creeley with an example of what was possible. He also helped him recognize *Leaves of Grass* as the perhaps unsurpassed force behind the major open-form long poems of this century, such as Pound's *Cantos* , Williams's *Paterson*, and Louis Zukofsky's A. Creeley's later attempts "to deal with reality over a man's life" in his poems since *Pieces* (1968) follow the same tradition.

When Creeley first met Ginsberg and his Beat friends in March 1956, he was instantly invaded by their whole new sense of freedom. Within hours of his arrival in San Francisco, he was swept up in a curiously unprecedented whirligig of activities. "Great parties at Locke McCorkle's house out in Mill Valley—Allen [Ginsberg] and Peter [Orlovsky] charmingly dancing naked among a dense pack of clothed bodies, flowers at the prom! Jack [Kerouac] and I sitting on the sidelines, shy, banging on up-ended pots and pans, 'keeping the beat.' Gary Snyder's wise old-young eyes, his centeredness and shyness also. Phil Whalen's, 'Well, Creeley, I *hope* you know what you're doing. . . . '" Neither Creeley nor his new friends knew too much about one anothers' writing. But whatever they shared during the first few days of their meeting was taken on trust on the level of immediate sympathy and understanding. Walking through the city, Ginsberg would read *Howl* from his big black binder notebook each time they would stop in a cafe or just at a curb or on a park bench. A little later, Creeley typed the stencils for a small "edition" of the yet unpublished poem on a typewriter he had borrowed from Kenneth Rexroth's wife, Marthe. In turn, Creeley was asked eager questions about Olson and "Projective Verse"—"was it just more razzle-dazzle intellectualism? McClure and Whalen were particularly intrigued, and were at this time already in correspondence with [Olson]. Allen, as always, was alert to any information of *process* that might be of use."

A concrete result of Creeley's three-month visit to San Francisco was the historic seventh issue of *Black Mountain Review* in which Kerouac, Burroughs, Ginsberg, McClure, Whalen, and Snyder appear side by side with Black Mountain poets such as Jonathan Williams, Joel Oppenheimer, Denise Levertov, Charles Olson, and Creeley himself. With Allen Ginsberg as a contributing editor, the journal, just before its decease in 1957, managed to bring together the two perhaps most influential movements in post-World War II American literary history. To Creeley himself, there was "unequivocally a shift and opening of the previous center." Yet the welcome given to the new poetic associates was far from uncritical. True enough, editor Robert Creeley, under "Books and Comments," published Kerouac's "Essentials of Spontaneous

Prose" as well as Williams's preface to Ginsberg's yet unpublished *Empty Mirror*, which credits the author with Dantean insights into the terrors of this century. But he also published a long review of *Howl* by former Black Mountain student Michael Rumaker, who comes close to rivaling Norman Podhoretz's later put-down of the Beats in "The Know-Nothing Bohemians." The reviewer found *Howl* deficient in precision of both feeling and language which strikes him as "cumbrous and hysterical." Whatever anger may have inspired the poet is corrupted with "sentimentality, bathos, Buddha and hollow talk of eternity." To Rumaker, a "listing of horrors described with inaccurate adjectives sheared would have produced greater shock—the cumulative adjectives exhaust whatever fine tension of feeling the poet may have had in the concept—but it is reduced to hysteria and the force of the poem loses by way-wardness, thrashing about.... It's sparseness that's needed here, to let the poem emerge from its adjectival obfuscation."

Such critical strictures may well have been prompted by Creeley's teaching at Black Mountain. Cut out "any too repetitive detail, or bunch of adjectives, etc." and altogether try to be more terse, he had advised Rumaker in an earlier letter from Mallorca. But as editor of the *Black Mountain Review* Creeley remained impartial. A footnote calls Rumaker's and Williams's comments evidence "of a concern with 'poetic means' more generally. It is certainly not a question of 'right & wrong,' but of the size of an image, and of its containment in form. In this respect Allen Ginsberg's work is an excellent occasion, and he himself is an active man." But whatever his initial response to *Howl*, Creeley was quick to realize that all the publicity given the Beats and their attitudes would damage their reputation, perhaps even their achievement as writers. Remembering the early days of *Origin*, he somewhat ruefully observed how now, in 1960, almost everyone was "getting into the so-called act," with journalists throwing around "crazy block-buster" slogans like the "beat generation." "I hate to see," he wrote Cid Corman on 17 December 1960, "the loss of attention to writing as writing, that has come of all the excitement about the social attitudes of the 'beat' or its contrary, the politically intellectual etc.—I much admire a good deal of Ginsberg's work, for example the beginning sections now to KADDISH—but would really best like reading them in a context that insisted on their quality as writing." In retrospect, Creeley understood that a poem like *Howl* makes real Pound's claim that artists are the antennae of the race by drawing our attention to crises that might otherwise go unattended. But where others looked for strange philosophies, he kept drawing attention to Ginsberg's poetic experiments with the formal organization of the long line.

In turn, Ginsberg was slow to appreciate fully the peculiar complexities of Creeley's poetry. For some reason or another, he confessed in 1956, he could not understand his poems "for at leastaways a half year, then they make sense." Creeley's verse was "hard," but at the same time "how spare and tender." Still more difficult to Ginsberg were Creeley's short stories which even after two years remained "confusing" to him. He was all the more surprised by the German editors of *Akzente* who "really broke up" over Creeley's works and thought them great. "Your laconism or purity or whatever seems to fit German present psyche perfectly," he reported back to Creeley in New Mexico. Always eager to publicize his friend's writings, Ginsberg elicited similar reactions from quarters which to a large extent stay closed to his own poetry even today. "Yalies buy your style," he wrote Creeley after a reading in New Haven; "amazing what quick reactions. Popular favorite. I wind up reading for laffs, i.e. overstate or over-racily read, rather than understate as your own style of reading them." So Ginsberg continued to read his friend's works along with his own even though some poems in *The Whip* (1957) added new problems just at the point when he thought to have cracked Creeley's secret. "It usually takes me time to understand how simple you are, or straight. Anyway it's a heavy thick long eggy book," he wrote Creeley on 4 January 1959.

Ginsberg's and Creeley's personal contacts since 1956 have been few and far between—for instance, at the Vancouver and Berkeley poetry conferences of 1963 and 1965 or on the occasion of sporadic private encounters. One reason for this was the rapid consolidation of the poets' respective styles and reputations after 1956. By the time of their first meeting, Ginsberg's first collection of poetry was still in manuscript while Creeley had already published several smaller collections of his poems and a volume of short stories. Inversely, Ginsberg was the first to gain international fame with *Howl and Other Poems* (1956) and the obscenity trial following its publication. Obviously, his was a poetry of apocalyptic vision and Whitmanesque vatic gestures. Creeley's reputation, first realized with *For Love, Poems 1950–1960* (1962), was of an altogether different kind. The poet, wrote Peter Davison in *Atlantic*, "has a subtle, almost feminine sensibility, and the best of his poems are those dealing with the intricacies that exist between men and women." Creeley, Frederick Eckman had written earlier, is "the most *conserving* poet I know; he wastes nothing—in fact, at times, rather too little. Creeley's poems are characterized by constriction, the partially revealed vision, economy of utterance. . . . Creeley is a desperate man, artistically speaking, a purist's purist who utters not one grunt more than he actually knows." Creeley's tendency since then, in his novel *The Island* (1963) and more recent collections of poetry like *Pieces* (1968), has been toward linguistic relaxation and daybooklike expansiveness. But the hallmark of his poetic style and vision as a poet (to quote Arthur L. Ford)—"of the fragile point of contact between people" and exploring his feelings "with disarming understatement and precise perception"—has remained consistent throughout.

Despite their obvious temperamental differences, Ginsberg and Creeley have steadily deepened their friendship and mutual respect for each other over the years. This is particularly true of Creeley who jokingly admits to his filial dependence on Ginsberg ("I need you, dad") and straightforwardly states his affection for the other poet: "I have great love for you, and faith likewise." In turn, Ginsberg's recent poem "After *Later*" pays homage to a poetic mode which the author has wrestled with over the years.

I am, finally
no one—
to be a Ginsberg,
Ridiculous,
yet I am
That and
no one.
Creeley
There is
no identity
Point fixe
"Everything is
water
if you look
long enough."

More successful is Creeley's "The Messengers" for Allen Ginsberg, which invokes the smile of his friend's quick eyes lighting a kind world as well as his voice rising "on the sound of feeling."

Aie! It raises the world, lifts,
falls, like a sudden sunlight, like
that edge of the black night sweeps
the low lying fields, of soft grasses,
bodies, fills them with quiet longing.

There is genuine love for the fellow poet, and an admiration for his work, greater perhaps than that which Creeley feels for any other living poet. Such, at least, is the verdict in a reference he wrote for Ginsberg in November 1964. "He is, for me," it reads, "the most accomplished of my contemporaries, and he has opened up possibilities for the craft of poetry which inform the whole art. I am speaking of the ground of feeling which he has managed to articulate, of the prosody required to manage this, and of the qualifications of the concept of literal *person* equally involved. . . . I learn from his example daily."

Source: Ekbert Faas, "Robert Creeley," in *Dictionary of Literary Biography*, Vol. 16, *The Beats: Literary Bohemians in Postwar America*, edited by Ann Charters, Gale, 1983, pp. 141–148.

Sources

Bacon, Terry R., "Closure in Robert Creeley's Poetry," in *Modern Poetry Studies*, Winter 1977, pp. 227–47.

Bernstein, Charles, Interview in *Just in Time*, New Directions, 2001.

Byrd, Don, "Creeley, Robert," in *Contemporary Poets*, 6th ed., edited by Thomas Riggs, St. James Press, 1996.

Clark, Tom, *Robert Creeley and the Genius of the American Common Place*, New Directions, 1993, p. 82.

Creeley, Robert, *Just in Time: Poems, 1984–1994*, New Directions, 2001, pp. 7, 8, 30, 201.

Dukes, Carol Muske, "Straight from the Hearth," in *Los Angeles Times Book Review*, June 23, 1991, p. 8.

Ford, Arthur L., *Robert Creeley*, Twayne Publishers, 1978, pp. 24, 36, 117.

Gunn, Thom, "Small Persistent Difficulties," in *Robert Creeley's Life and Work*, edited by John Wilson, University of Michigan Press, 1987, p. 406.

Kaganoff, Penny, Review of *Windows*, in *Publishers Weekly*, Vol. 237, No. 15, April 13, 1990, p. 59.

MacGowan, Christopher, "William Carlos Williams," in *The Columbia History of American Poetry*, edited by Jay Parini, MJF Books, 1993, p. 416.

Piper, Bill, "Robert Creeley," in *American Writers*, Suppl. 4, Charles Scribner's Sons, 1996, pp. 139–61.

Whited, Stephen, Review of *Just in Time: Poems, 1984–1994*, in *Book*, March–April 2002, p. 78.

Further Reading

Campbell, James, *This Is the Beat Generation: New York—San Francisco—Paris*, University of California Press, 2001.

This book introduces readers to the major poets and writers of the Beat Generation, among whom are Allen Ginsberg, Gary Snyder, Jack Kerouac, and

Robert Creeley. It provides cultural and historical background for this literary movement.

Clark, Tom, *Robert Creeley and the Genius of the American Common Place*, New Directions, 1993.
Clark's slim book contains a great deal of biographical material and the poet's "Autobiography." It also has many photographs and some poems, and includes transcripts of Creeley's interviews.

Creeley, Robert, *The Collected Essays of Robert Creeley*, University of California Press, 1989.
This is a collection of essays, reviews, and miscellaneous literary correspondence edited by the poet. Although these writings seem disconnected at first glance, they provide an insight into Creeley's aesthetic sensibility.

Edelberg, Cynthia Dubin, *Robert Creeley's Poetry: A Critical Introduction*, University of New Mexico Press, 1978.
This book covers Creeley's early poetry, and it contains a large number of commentaries on individual poems.

Ghazal

Elizabeth Spires

2002

The title of Elizabeth Spires's poem "Ghazal" does not indicate anything about its subject but describes the style in which it was written. A ghazal is a form of poetry that originated in Iran many centuries ago and made its way throughout the Middle East and Asia primarily through the extension of the Muslim influence in that part of the world. Over the years, people of other cultures and geographies began to experiment with ghazals, and today they may be found in the United States and many other western countries. The basic structure of a ghazal is generally retained by contemporary poets, although not many adhere strictly to the ancient rules of the original Persian poets.

Spires's "Ghazal," which appears in her most recent volume of poetry called *Now the Green Blade Rises* (2002), is a reflection on the death of her mother, as well as a contemplation on the inevitability of the poet's own aging and eventual death. It is elegiac in tone and filled with quiet solitude, recalling specific moments of the tragic event: the phone call informing her of the news, the airplane flight to her mother's town, the funeral, the jewelry she inherited, snippets of pleasant childhood memories. All of these thoughts are conveyed in brief images presented in couplets and maintaining some of the formal structure of a traditional ghazal.

Author Biography

Elizabeth Spires was born in 1952 in Lancaster, Ohio. She grew up in a Catholic home, attending both parochial and public schools, and developed a love of reading early on. Her parents were very supportive of her ambition to be a writer and when it came time for college, Spires left her small hometown and headed east to New York where she enrolled as an English major at Vassar College. Her initial intent was to be a short story writer, as she had been reading primarily stories, novels, and biographies since childhood. But at Vassar, Spires began taking poetry workshops and before long decided to try her hand at writing and publishing poems.

Spires received her bachelor's degree from Vassar in 1974 and returned to Ohio where she worked as an editor for a textbook publisher in Columbus, as well as a freelance writer of children's books. Her talent as a young poet is evidenced in the prestigious journals that published her early work—the *American Poetry Review*, the *New Yorker*, *Poetry*, and the *Partisan Review*, among others. In 1978, she moved to Baltimore to pursue a master's degree at Johns Hopkins University. The collection of poems she presented as her thesis in the master's program turned into her first published book in 1981, called *Globe*.

Since then, Spires has published four additional collections of poems, including *Now the Green Blade Rises* in 2002. This is her first volume of work written after her mother's death in 1998, and many of the poems in it reflect feelings of loss, mourning, and aging. "Ghazal" originally published in the Fall 2001 edition of *Ploughshares*—is one such poem from the collection. In addition to poetry, Spires has also published six books for children, most recently *The Big Meow* in 2002. Her awards include the Academy of American Poets Prize (1974), National Endowment for the Arts fellowships (1981, 1992), the Pushcart Prize (1981, 1995), and a Guggenheim Fellowship in Poetry (1992), among others.

In 1985, Spires married the novelist Madison Smartt Bell, and the two had a daughter in 1991.

Elizabeth Spires

Poem Summary

Lines 1–2

The structure of Spires's "Ghazal" will be addressed later in detail, but one cannot analyze the poem's meaning without acknowledging the importance of its style. Contemporary writers of ghazals take some liberties with the original standard form but leave enough intact to make the framework recognizable. In this poem, Spires uses a pair of homonyms instead of rhyming words in the couplets, and the like-sounding terms she has selected greatly strengthen the work's message and tone. "Morning" and "mourning" produce an intriguing play off of one another throughout, and the controlled shift from one to the other conveys the overall somber mood of both words.

In the first two lines, the setting is doleful, with the speaker hearing her "name in the black air," or the darkness of "early morning." She claims it is "called out," but it is ambiguous as to whether her name is actually spoken by someone in the room or on the telephone or she has only dreamed she hears it. Line 2 suggests the latter, and it sets the tone of the remainder of the poem: "a future of mourning" brought on by a foreboding "premonition" of death and sorrow. These lines also mark the first use of the word "black," which will appear twice more in keeping with the general melancholy of the work.

Lines 3–4

These lines introduce a second person into the poem, later disclosed as the speaker's mother. Line

Media Adaptations

- A videotape of Spires's interview with Michael Collier in 2003 is part of *The Writing Life Videos* series produced by HoCoPoLitSo at Howard Community College in Maryland. Spires discusses the poems from *Now the Green Blade Rises*.

3 implies that every time a mother and daughter meet over the course of their lives and say their usual goodbyes, they are actually "rehears[ing]" for the final time they will utter the words. Line 4 describes the last time the speaker sees her mother alive. They are "in a desert . . . on a white September morning," apparently before the daughter is leaving to go home. Note the description of the morning spent with her mother as *white*—completely opposite the *black* morning air that surrounds her upon her mother's death. This is the first juxtaposition of black and white in the poem. It will occur again, but with an interesting shift in context.

Lines 5–6

The gist of these lines is that the speaker has been informed of her mother's passing, and she must fly out West for the funeral. But the images are more intriguing than that. The "call" in line 5 refers back to the speaker's name "called out" in line 1 and adds to the ambiguity of whether the latter is an actual word spoken or simply part of a bad dream. In literal terms, it makes no difference; but, poetically, the effect is intriguing, even enigmatic. To retain the ghazal style, the word "morning" (or "mourning," in this case) needs to appear in the second line of the couplet. Here, Spires works it aptly into a scenario about flying west through time zones and finding the time of day upon arrival the same as it was at departure.

Lines 7–8

In lines 7 and 8, the juxtaposition of black and white returns, but this time the distinction between black as *negative* and white as *positive* is not apparent. In fact, the "blank whiteness" that "outlines / everything" connotes as much sorrow, grief, and foreboding as "black air" does in line 1. The speaker says she has "always worn black," which may mean, of course, a simple preference in fashion, but the implication here is more profound. Her confession of always wearing black indicates a longtime sense of dread and a fear of death—her own or a loved one's. The "white" of a sunny September morning in line 4 has become hollow, empty, and blank on the morning of her mother's funeral.

Lines 9–10

This poem is not only about sorrow and grief but inheritance and family bonds as well. Lines 9 and 10 describe a pair of pearl earrings—note that they are *black* pearls—that the deceased mother has left to her daughter. The jewelry has been passed down from grandmother to daughter to granddaughter, symbolizing the importance of a direct link between the generations of women in the family. The mother's simple note that they are the grandmother's "*Good*" earrings suggests not only the jewelry's own value, but also the value of bloodlines and family heritage. The doleful tone of "Ghazal" is sustained with the mention of the ink in which the mother wrote her note—it, too, is black, the "color of mourning."

Lines 11–12

On the surface, these lines appear to be the only ones in the poem containing joyful, positive images, yet the descriptions include language that suggests otherwise. The speaker's memory of the songs her mother "used to sing" evokes a contemplative sadness over the fact that she will no longer hear them. The "morning glories" are "Blue," and one imagines that their spelling could just as easily be *mourning* glories. An image of death is intrinsic in the "tree of heaven," and even the "owl" that sits there implies a lonely, mournful existence. The "sacred mornings" of the speaker's childhood suggests not only an upbringing in a religious home, but also a reverence for those times long ago when death and grief were not prevalent.

Line 13

Line 13 returns to the idea of family bonds and inheritance but, here, what is passed down from generation to generation is death. This time, the speaker adds a fourth generation to the line—her own daughter, before whom she herself will die. The repetition of the word "before" adds a dirge-like quality to line 13, sounding out the dull dreariness of inescapable fate: "Your mother before you. Her mother before her. I, before my daughter."

Line 14

Line 14 is a quote attributed to the speaker's mother, though whether they are words she actually ever spoke or a remark the daughter can imagine her making is irrelevant. Its importance lies in the plain, direct resignation of the message: each generation experiences the same pain of inevitable loss as the ones before and the ones after it. In this sense, all of a family's women are at one time or another "*daughters in mourning*."

Line 15

This line defines the speaker while at the same time employs a rule of traditional ghazal structure. The poet identifies herself as the "firstborn" daughter of a mother whose name is also "*Elizabeth*." Calling herself a "namesake" serves to strengthen the ties between parent and child that have already been well established in the poem. A typical traditional ghazal requires the use of the poet's name or pen-name in the first line of the final couplet. Spires manages this technique flawlessly here in both structure and in keeping with the overall message of the work.

Line 16

The last line of the poem again resorts to repetition of the main homonym to express the somber resignation to life's unavoidable outcome. The poet, born "on a May morning," cannot ever return to the innocent, unknowing comfort and warmth of that day. Instead, she recognizes that time and loss take their toll on the human spirit and eventually one accepts that what used to be can never be the same again.

Topics for Further Study

- Try to write a ghazal in strict traditional form. What is the greatest challenge with this style? How does it manipulate the subject of the poem?
- Research several traditional ghazals translated into English from their original language(s). Are their subjects similar to one another? Discuss their similarities and differences, specifically addressing the couplets as they stand on their own and how they form the poems as a whole.
- In Spires's poem, the speaker's mother says, "*We are all daughters in mourning*." If a father tells his son, "We are all sons in mourning," is there a difference in connotation? If so, what role does gender play in the message of this poem?
- Discuss Spires's use of colors in "Ghazal." What do black, white, and blue have in common? What other colors may have worked as well and why? If no others would work, why not?

Themes

Mortality and Grief

"Ghazal" is a poem of grieving. Its central focus is on the overwhelming sorrow of a daughter recalling the death of her mother, but there is an undercurrent of *generalized* sadness at work too. While the main human subject appears to be the mother, the speaker's presence in every line is heavy and foreboding. Her grief stems not only from her parent's death but from recognition of her own mortality as well.

Losing a loved one naturally brings about suffering and bereavement in those left behind. The speaker is pained by the memories of her mother's songs and flowers and the "sacred" times they had together when she was a child. She feels deep sorrow in recalling the last time she saw her mother, apparently saying their usual goodbyes after a visit at the parent's home out in the West. Neither, of course, knows that it is the final time they will see one another, yet the daughter claims that *all* their previous "partings were rehearsals for the final scene." This rather ominous assertion implies an ever-present sense of mortality—a nagging thought of death in the back of the mind even when one is very much alive and healthy.

Throughout "Ghazal," the speaker mixes the grief over losing her mother with disturbing allusions to the inevitability of her own dying. In a dream, she experiences a premonition of death, supposedly her mother's, yet perhaps the vision is of her personal "future of mourning" rather than the parent's demise in particular. She makes a point of noting that she has "always worn black," suggesting a resignation to her own mortality as well as to that of others. In the end, her grief also becomes a resignation, as she accepts that she "cannot go back" to the morning of her birth, which represents a time before there is an awareness of sorrow and death. It is common for one who is middle-aged—as Spires was at the time she wrote this poem—to begin to think more about mortality and to dread what the future will surely bring, especially as the signs of aging force the issue. But those thoughts are intensified even more when one experiences the death of a parent. In a sense, the poet has lost not only her mother but a vital part of her own being that has died with her.

Love, Loss, and Family Ties

It is easy to see "Ghazal" as a poem whose main theme focuses on doom and gloom with no signs of a positive outcome whatsoever. Yet, it is a poem that needs to be read in context with the overall theme of the work in which it is included. *Now the Green Blade Rises* derives its title from the lyrics of a song by the same name written by John MacLeod Campbell Crum in 1928. Part of the lyrics preface Spires's book and suggest a theme of hope and redemption rising from the ashes of despair:

Now the green blade rises from the buried grain,
Wheat that in the dark earth many days has lain;
Love lives again, that with the dead has been;
Love is come again like wheat arising green.

While Crum wrote the entire lyric as an Easter poem commemorating the death and resurrection of Jesus, Spires uses the first stanza to imply that ties among loved ones may indeed live on even after the physical being is gone. In "Ghazal," she establishes the presence of the mother-daughter bond in the first line of the poem with the phrase, "My name in the black air." It seems obvious that she refers to her own name, but at the end of the poem one learns that "*Elizabeth*" is also her mother's name. The ambiguity serves to blend the bloodline into a continuous flow, stressing the importance of strong family ties, among both the living and the dead.

Loss of life is undeniably a major factor in the poem, but even such morbidity ties generations together. The mother is attributed with explaining that "*We are all daughters in mourning*," and the speaker confirms that notion with, "Your mother before you. Her mother before her. I, before my daughter." Despite the overwhelming sorrow imparted in these statements by both mother and daughter, there is also an unmistakable softness and genuine love portrayed as well. The fact that such a doleful, melancholy poem can reverberate with love beyond loss, and family ties beyond death suggests that the poet's experience may not be as hopeless as it seems.

Style

The Ghazal

The ghazal (pronounced "guzzle,") originated in Iran in the tenth century, growing out of an earlier, lengthier Arabic form of poetry. The brevity of traditional ghazals—usually no more than twelve couplets—and their rich, concentrated imagery eventually made them the most popular style of poetry in Iran. As the Muslim influence spread throughout the Middle East and Asia, ghazals grew in popularity throughout the region, especially in India and Pakistan. In more recent years, European and American poets have experimented with this form, though usually not in keeping with the precise pattern of the original ghazals from Iran.

Spires's poem follows enough of the ghazal style to make its construction recognizable, though it by no means adheres to it strictly. Each couplet of a traditional ghazal is written as a self-sustained unit that expresses a complete thought and could stand alone as a poem if extracted from the ghazal. The lines are composed in the same meter and always open with a rhyming couplet. The rhyme of the first couplet is then repeated in the second line of each succeeding couplet, making the typical rhyming pattern AA, BA, CA, DA, and so forth. In "Ghazal," the meter fluctuates, and the lines of the opening couplet do not end with rhyming words but with homonyms: "morning" and "mourning." Instead of ending succeeding couplets with words that rhyme with "morning," Spires simply repeats the homonyms at the end of each couplet's second line.

Traditional ghazals also require that the two or three words preceding the last word of the first line rhyme with their counterparts in the second line of the opening couplet and then in alternate lines throughout the poem. Obviously, this rule is particularly challenging and one that many western poets do not follow. In "Ghazal," it means that the words "the early" from the opening line would have to rhyme with "future of" in the second line, "white September" in the fourth, "was still" in the sixth, and so on.

The final couplet of an original ghazal often includes the name or penname of the poet, and Spires does conform to this tradition. The intriguing twist in this case, however, is that her first name, Elizabeth, is also her mother's, so she essentially includes her own name and the name of the poem's subject at the same time. The reason for this inclusion is to allow the poet an opportunity to express his or her state of mind and to become a personal part of the poem. Spires accomplishes this in her final couplet, but one may argue that she does so in all the preceding couplets as well.

Historical Context

The subject of Spires's poem "Ghazal" is extremely personal and unlikely to be influenced by cultural or political events of the time it was written. Its title, however, is apparently disconnected from what the work is about, identifying only the structure and perhaps implying that such a subjective poem is better served with a simple and benign name. But the ghazal form of poetry itself embodies a long history in parts of the world largely unknown or misunderstood by many contemporary westerners. In recent years—during the period after Spires's mother's death in 1998 and the subsequent publication of her book based on it in 2002—the area where ghazals began has had a profound impact on events and people all across the globe.

Tension between Iran and the United States has been escalating over the past two decades, leading to the U.S. suspension of all trade with the Middle Eastern nation in 1995. This move came about amid accusations that Iran was a state supporter of terrorist groups and was also attempting to develop nuclear weapons. Despite the election of Mohammed Khatami, a moderately liberal Muslim cleric, to the presidency in the late 1990s, no relations with the U.S. government were established.

Within Iran, civil turmoil has also been escalating since 1999 when conservative, hard-line members of the government placed new restrictions on the free press. Pro-democracy students held mass demonstrations to protest the move at Tehran University in the capital and at other major colleges across the country. The hard-liners reacted with demonstrations in favor of fundamental Islamic laws, and the new president, who remains in power as of this writing, was ineffective in resolving the conflict. Instead, Khatami's progressive political views have been harshly criticized and all but squelched by the conservative Guardian Council in association with the fundamentalist Ayatollah Khamenei. In 2002, Khatami called for legislation to limit the powers of the Guardian Council and restore presidential powers to enforce the constitution, but the council has not relented thus far. Student demonstrations for social and political reforms continue, and relations with the United States remain nonexistent.

Pakistan and India also figure heavily into world events of the past few years, stemming from a long history of tension and violence between the two nations, primarily caused by a land dispute in the region of Kashmir. In 1998, the United States placed sanctions against both countries after India detonated underground nuclear devices in a seeming show of might, and Pakistan retaliated with its own series of nuclear tests. In 1999, Pakistani troops entered Indian territory in Kashmir and weeks of intense fighting ensued before Pakistan withdrew. The two nations were on the brink of war again in 2002, spurred mainly by escalating attacks by Muslim militants in India purportedly crossing over from Pakistan. The crisis ended only after Pakistani president General Pervez Musharraf aided in stopping state-sponsored guerrilla infiltration into Indian-controlled Kashmir.

Musharraf's relationship with the United States has come full circle since the 1998 U.S. sanctions on Pakistan. After the terrorist attacks of September 11, 2001, were linked to Osama bin Laden, the United States lifted the sanctions and asked for Pakistan's help in securing bin Laden from the Taliban government in Afghanistan. Musharraf's efforts to persuade the Taliban to cooperate were fruitless, but Pakistan agreed to allow U.S. fighter planes to cross its airspace and U.S. troops to have bases there when the American military action in Afghanistan began in late 2001. Over time, Musharraf proved to be a welcomed ally of the Bush administration despite fierce opposition from many fundamentalist Pakistani leaders and citizens. In early 2002, Musharraf made a public denouncement of religious extremism, citing its detrimental effect on Pakistani society, and vowed that no terrorist groups would be tolerated in his country.

Musharraf's condemnation of Islamic extremism is a major controversy in some areas of the Middle East and western Asia, but much of the world views it as a progressive step forward in the war on terror. The fact remains, however, that in lands where everyday living is dominated by violence, hatred, and economic suffering, the rich cultural heritages of people—including their literature, art, poetry, and history—are often overshadowed simply by the struggle to survive.

Critical Overview

Spires's work in both poetry and children's books has been well received and admired since she first began publishing it. Her poems are most often praised for the simplicity of their style and richness of their imagery. Her tone is recognized as soft and contemplative, and she is noted for choosing words that connect to the reader's own experiences. Some critics have suggested that her latest collection, *Now the Green Blade Rises*, is more melancholy and spiritual than previous books, as its inspiration was the death of her mother. In a book review for *The Antioch Review*, critic Ned Balbo states, "Spires's book of growth and mourning . . . explores the twinned impulse to sing and to lament with poems as thoughtfully lyrical as any she has written." In regard to a poem from the collection about parents and children, Balbo claims, "This understanding of opposing forces—toward life and death, future and past—provides the underlying tension of Spires's work: she remains a poet for whom Metaphysical is both a living tradition and a subtly shaded intellectual stance." Balbo's final assertion that "her sacramental eye remains that of one of our best, and most distinctive, poets" is evidence of Spires's achievement in contemporary American poetry.

If any negative comments crop up in critical reviews of *Now the Green Blade Rises*, they are generally benign and mixed with positive statements. For instance, a review in *Publishers Weekly* says that "The death of the poet's mother occasions this fifth collection's opening sequence, a mixture of narrative pieces and sentimental lyrics, which generally depict a world flattened and bleached by grief." Accusing Spires of writing *sentimental* poems is not the harshest of criticism and this reviewer seems to allow for it based on their sorrowful inspiration. Overall, the reviews have been good, and Spires continues to be recognized as a twenty-first-century poet worth reading.

Criticism

Pamela Steed Hill

Hill is the author of a poetry collection, has published widely in literary journals, and is an editor for a university publications department. In the following essay, Hill examines "Ghazal" as a part of Spires's overall theme of a continuous life/death cycle, notes its similarity to her other poems, and suggests a preoccupation with melancholia in middle age.

An individual poem pulled from a collection in which a recurring theme runs through most of the works may be read, enjoyed, analyzed, and understood on its own; however, reading it in context with its partner poems contributes to a deeper, well-rounded comprehension of its message and inspiration. "Ghazal" is one poem in a volume of many poems about the inevitable passing of time and what it means to the human being—aging, sadness, loss, fear, and death. But it does more than share an overall theme with other poems in the volume. It also shares images, subject matter, tone, even specific descriptions with some of them, and not just those in *Now the Green Blade Rises*. In Spires's previous collection, *Worldling*, many of the concepts bear an unmistakable resemblance to the melancholia that pervades the poet's latest book.

The preface to *Now the Green Blade Rises* includes an inscription to Spires's mother, commemorating her birth and death dates, and four lines from John MacLeod Campbell Crum's Easter lyric, of the same name, commemorating the death and resurrection of Jesus Christ. Crum's message is intended to inspire hope and renewed spirit, and one would like to think that Spires's purpose is the same. And perhaps it is. Yet, there is a conspicuous gloom that hangs over her use of the lines, "Love lives again that with the dead has been; / Love is come again like wheat arising green." If the dolor is not apparent from the book's preface, it is more evident in a poem from the collection also bearing the name "Now the Green Blade Rises" and including the same four lines from Crum's lyric.

In "Ghazal," one of the early images is of a haunting "premonition dreamed" that the speaker experiences prior to learning of her mother's death. She claims to hear her "name in the black air, called out in the early morning," but it is unclear at this point whether someone is actually calling to wake her up or if someone in her dream is speaking her name. In "Now the Green Blade Rises," the image is the same, only less ambiguous: "I had a dream, black and pictureless. / You were calling my name / over a great distance. It hung / suspended in the dark air." The "you" is conclusively the speaker's mother in this poem, and the general pall that overshadows the mood is conveyed in the color black as it is in "Ghazal." Both poems use connotations of darkness and emptiness to portray the speaker's mindset: "black air," "blank whiteness," and "ink the color of mourning" in "Ghazal" and "the world is ash," "black and pictureless," and "dark air" in "Now the Green Blade Rises."

Toward the end of the collection's title poem, the lines from Crum appear, followed by Spires's three closing lines: "There, soul to soul, / we would have forever / to finally speak again." Unlike the old Easter lyric's attempt to inspire the joy of renewed life, Spires's end-thought suggests that only after her own death will the speaker be able to talk with her mother again. The same fatalism is evoked in the speaker's final statement in "Ghazal": "I cannot go back to that morning." Both works close with a sad, resigned melancholy—that of a middle-aged daughter coming to terms with a parent's death, as well as with dread and recognition of her own death.

It is not surprising nor even remarkable that a collection of poems stemming from the loss of a loved one would concentrate on themes of grief and depression. In "Ghazal," one can understand—and forgive—the fact that the speaker brings other generations into her morbid world, including her own daughter. The line, "Your mother before you. Her mother before her. I, before my daughter" speaks to the ominous connection between mothers and daughters, a link that translates into an inheritance of death in the poem. This grim message, wrapped in its sorrowful tone, is acceptable, if not expected, considering the inspiration for it is a profound loss. But why would the same despairing sentiment apply to a wonderful *gain*—that is, to the birth of a child and a new life just beginning?

The impetus for Spires's second-most recent volume of poems, *Worldling*, was the birth of her daughter. Obviously, not every aspect of having a baby, raising a child, and dealing with all the issues of new motherhood is sheer bliss. There are undoubtedly problems—moments of fear and self-doubt, anger and frustration when routines are drastically altered, possibly even flickers of regret or dread. But one may safely assume that these thoughts are fairly common and will come and go in the normal course of strengthening the bonds between mother and child. What, though, can one assume about a mother's overwhelming sense of pending loss, even as her new life arrives? If one line from one poem expresses this unusual and distressing mindset, it is the final line of "The First Day," from *Worldling*: "*I have had a child. Now I must live with death.*"

The message here is both remarkable and provocative—and perhaps it helps explain the speaker's inclusion of her daughter in the chain of dying mothers and daughters mentioned in "Ghazal." The claim from this poem that "*We are all daughters in mourning*" rings a mournful bell indeed, but, apparently, its inspiration does not lie only in the death of the speaker's mother. Instead, it goes backwards, at least to the birth of her own daughter, several years before her mother even died.

> "*The message here is both remarkable and provocative—and perhaps it helps explain the speaker's inclusion of her daughter in the chain of dying mothers and daughters mentioned in 'Ghazal.'*"

In "Ghazal," Spires uses a matter-of-fact listing of how generations pass away—grandmother before mother, mother before daughter, etc.—to depict a quiet surrender to time's passing. In "The First Day," these lines describe the same resignation: "That's how it is in this world, birth, death, / matter-of-fact, happening like that." The difference, of course, is that the former poem is inspired by death and the latter by birth. It is as though no distinction can be made between beginnings and endings because a beginning always leads to an ending, so why separate them? In various interviews, Spires has been known to lament the coming of middle age, seeing it more as the beginning of the end instead of the middle of anything. Her poems from the volumes produced during this time in her life reflect heavily this melancholy and fatalistic point of view.

The lines borrowed from Crum's Easter lyric, which make up the preface to *Now the Green Blade Rises*, play an ambiguous role in Spires's message, as one is not really *sure* that the words are meant to imply hope and rebirth or simply bemoan the fact of inevitable death. In *Worldling*, the preface to a poem called "Easter Sunday 1955"—comprised of lines written by nineteenth-century British novelist Anthony Trollope in a letter—leaves no room for doubt: "*Why should anything go wrong in our bodies? / Why should we not all be beautiful? Why should there be decay?—why death? /—and, oh, why, damnation?*"

In short, this poem details a memory of the speaker in which she was a child visiting her grandmother along with her parents. The setting then

What Do I Read Next?

- To understand and appreciate the development and mainstays of a poet over time, one should read both the latest and the earliest of the poet's material. Spires's first volume is *Globe* (1981), collected from poems she composed as a master's student. Though she was a very young writer at the time, these poems show the maturity and insight of one much more experienced. They make for an interesting comparison to the poems in her later books.
- *Rooms Are Never Finished* (2003), by renowned Indian poet Agha Shahid Ali, is a striking collection of ghazals inspired by the recent death of his mother. Like Spires's book based on her own mother's death, Ali's poems explore loss and family bonds, as well as the journey back to his homeland of Kashmir to lay his mother to rest.
- There are thousands of websites about ghazals, many offering helpful insights into the history, form, and current application of this style of poetry. One of the best is the *AHA! Poetry* site at http://www.ahapoetry.com/ghazal.htm featuring easily understandable commentary on ghazals, the rules of their form, and a nice selection of sample poems. This site is an online branch of AHA Books of Gualala, California.
- The award-winning author of *A Wrinkle in Time*, Madeline L'Engle collaborates with her photographer daughter, Maria Rooney, in a wonderful collection of both prose and photos called simply *Mothers and Daughters*. L'Engle's stirring text about family bonds among women is woven through Rooney's beautiful black and white photography of mothers and daughters from all races and ethnic backgrounds.

moves forward to the present as she watches her own daughter gather Easter eggs and mournfully admits that she finds herself "too quickly, / in the here-and-now moment of my fortieth year." The poem ends with the lines: "Beautiful child, / how thoughtlessly we enter the world! / How free we are, how bound, put here in love's name /—death's, too—to be happy if we can." Once again, the positive is counteracted by the negative. A child may be "free" but also "bound"; she may be born in "love's name," but in "death's too."

Reading Spires's work created prior to *Now the Green Blade Rises* and reading the poems that surround "Ghazal" in this latest collection give one a profound sense of *knowing* where this particular work comes from. The reader knows why it begins with a "premonition dreamed"—a preoccupation with death is generally ominous. The reader understands why the speaker has "always worn black" and why the dark color blends so easily into "a blank whiteness"—there is no difference between beginnings and endings, no distinction between black and white. And, perhaps most telling, the reader knows why the poet chose to create her ghazal using two homonyms as opposed to two rhyming words. She was born on "a May morning" and took her place in the long line of "*daughters in mourning*." One need not look for any division between the two.

Source: Pamela Steed Hill, Critical Essay on "Ghazal," in *Poetry for Students*, Thomson Gale, 2005.

Kate Covintree

Covintree is a graduate student and expository writing instructor in the Writing, Literature, and Publishing department at Emerson College. In this essay, Covintree explores Spires's poem in terms of formal elements of structure as well as how structure creates poetic tension.

Following in the footsteps of the ancient Turks and Persians, Spires includes a poem titled "Ghazal" in her fifth book of poems, *Now the Green Blade Rises*. In Spires's case, this poem is a direct elegy for her mother, who died in 1998, and to whom the collection is dedicated. The first section of this book is filled with poems of loss and grief, and Spires uses this specific poem to move the reader through the initial days after her mother's death. In a 1995 interview for the *Southwest Review*, Spires told A.V. Christie that she believes "everything is connected and that we go on in some form or fashion and possibly that form or fashion leads us back into physical existence." Based on this quote and the title of her poem, it is apparent that Spires is aware of how important structure is to a poem. Spires chooses the ghazal form to echo her obsession and meditation surrounding her mother's death.

In his essay "Writing the Reader's Life," which is found in the collection *Poets Teaching Poets*, Dobyns qualifies the type of structure necessary for poetry: "[i]t is the formal elements of language, texture, pacing, and tone imposed upon the informal elements." Spires uses the formal elements of the ghazal to organize the informal emotion of her grief. This form has certain specifications and rules. A traditional ghazal is written in couplets with a rhyme scheme of *aa*, *ba*, *ca* etc. Not only are demands of language within this form, but there is also a demand on the theme of the poem. According to the *New Princeton Handbook of Poetic Terms*, "the principal subject of the ghazal is earthly or mystical love, and the mood is melancholy, expressing sadness over separation from the beloved." Such a practice of governing a theme with a form recognizes the role formal elements can play in expressing the informal elements that Stephen Dobyns defines as "action, emotion, setting, and idea."

The primary informal elements Spires wrestles with are action and emotion. As stated earlier, her poem begins with the late night call telling of her mother's death and moves from there. For this ghazal, the poet's mother is the lost beloved, which moves the love out of mysticism or romance and allows it to enter a type of unconditional existence. As Spires explains in the interview with Christie

> [t]he 'big' poems in our lives are about our doubts, fears, conflicts, and passions—all the emotions we spend so much time and energy trying to ignore and repress so that we can get through day-to-day life. But sooner or later, . . . the 'dragon' has to be dealt with.

By this time in her own life, Spires was a mother herself. While this shift in her own life influenced her understanding of the world, her mother's death is indeed a very "big" moment in the poet's life. The speaker of this poem must deal with her own dragons and travel across the country to wrestle with memory and mortality.

The reader can assume that the poet and speaker are the same and not simply an anonymous speaker because this follows in the tradition of the

"She has brought the reader into the darkest moments of night and throws the reader into the immediacy of her experience."

ghazal form. Since the twelfth century, writers of ghazals have been incorporating their name, or some variation of it, at the end of the poem. What is especially effective about this structural element in terms of this poem is that the author's name is the same as her mother's. In a sense, this poem is about the author's own death not simply because she is also named Elizabeth but because a mother is the life-bringer. The "Elizabeth" spoken of at the end of the poem is representative of more than one thing: the writer, the ghost, and the mother.

Within the form of a ghazal, each stanza is supposed to stand alone so that the final result is more an accumulation of related but separate thoughts than a logical progression. In Spires's case, it is an accumulation of events surrounding her mother's death, an accretion of minutiae that when taken together form an imperfect portrait of her emotional self.

This poem's mood is somber and is expressed well through the tone of the poem. Though her lines are long, the length allows the reader to absorb each line before moving to the next. If the line length does not make the reader pause, every line is stopped at least once by a comma, period, or other type of punctuation, with the intent to slow the reader down and give greater weight to each sentence. Spires moves the reader carefully through each line, building into her ideas little by little. As her poem progresses, the sentences become more distorted and shift into phrases and ideas: "Your mother before you. Her mother before her." Spires has removed verbs and replaced them with the ideas that swell together as memories of her mother. Like the stillness of her mother, many of her sentences no longer contain an action. These sentences reinforce the meditative and melancholy tone brought on by the loss of the beloved.

Spires's use of language also helps create the mood of her poem. In following the ghazal's form, the word she chooses to repeat is "morning." From the first stanza, she uses morning's homonym, "mourning." There is a softness and a settled-ness in her word choice and repetition that pacifies the reader into a ruminative reflection on loss. When the poem moves away from such soothing language it is to add to the tension of the poem and the involvement of the reader. Along with formal elements, Dobyns lists a second part of structure in his essay. The second part of poetic structure, according to Dobyns, is "the creation of tension to make the reader want to know what is going to happen: the making and controlling of anticipation." From the first line, Spires works with this kind of structure.

Since Spires begins the poem with the speaker asleep in bed, Spires immediately pushes the reader into an intimate and personal scene. She has brought the reader into the darkest moments of night and throws the reader into the immediacy of her experience. It is an intimacy literally revealed through sound, by a call. Sonically, the line moves smoothly until the cacophonous fifth word "black" is used to describe "air." The lightness and ethereal elements of air are broken by the heavy sharpness of the preceding word. After the pause of air, the sharpness of "black" returns with "called." The word "called" almost mirrors the earlier word with the repetition of the sharp *k* sound and the *l* sound as well. The words even have a reflexive effect with the *b* and *d* looking in to the most intense moment of that line, the call of her mother's death. Her late night phone call that tells of an ending is now the catalyst for this reflective poem.

Starting a poem with an ending, the poem continues to move out of any chronological order. From the pronouncement of death, the poem moves back and forth between traveling to the funeral and memories of the mother. Even the moments happening in the present are blurred in terms of the sequence of events. Are the "black pearl earrings" found before or after the speaker decides what to wear. The actual details of this sequence are trivial, and so Spires works in terms of the poem's pattern and moves from questions of clothes to an item of clothing. In addition, while the poem begins "on a white September morning," it ends with a reference to a "May morning." In the final line, the poet writes "I cannot go back to that morning," and it is both of those mornings that have become inaccessible.

At one point, Spires even appears to stop time when she writes "impossible, but the sun / didn't move." This moment of stasis echoes her emotional numbness. By the end of the poem, the structure of time is completely blurred. Spires is writing to a ghost (her mother), and simple chronological time is no longer important. Instead, a larger scale of time reveals itself, one of generations. In this poem, it is the generations that are essential in coping with death. It is her mother's words that make this clear near the end of the poem: "we are all daughters in mourning." The inevitability acts as a type of salve. Even her own name, the same as her mother's, demonstrates the impact of generations. Though one Elizabeth is dead, another is still alive and still a mother. Like the generations, this name stretches beyond the poet, beyond motherhood, beyond the reader, and beyond the poem.

Source: Kate Covintree, Critical Essay on "Ghazal," in *Poetry for Students*, Thomson Gale, 2005.

Elizabeth Spires and A. V. Christie

In the following interview, Christie provides background on Spires's life and career, and Spires comments on how her subject matter is evolving as she reaches middle age.

Think of the word "spires" or the word "aspires," and you see ascendance, a reaching, a rising up, a breathing upon, a breathing into life—you hear the word "spirit." Elizabeth Spires's work seems deeply linked with all the facets and motives of these words associated with her name. Even in her first book of poems, *Globe*, published in 1981, one senses a poet of deeply metaphysical and transcendentalist leanings, its first poem "Tequila" already interested in "taking the only road / out of the valley, / the one that leads everywhere."

Born in 1952 in Lancaster, Ohio, Spires avidly read her way through the Children's Room of the Circleville Public Library. Her choices in books were particularly indiscriminate, "including about three hundred sappy biographies," she says. She then moved on to the O. Henry Awards volumes in another part of the library and remembers distinctly, when she was twelve, reading Flannery O'Connor's "Everything That Rises Must Converge." It was then that she decided she would be a writer. In retrospect Spires feels that probably one of the most defining gifts her parents gave her was the unspoken assumption "that girls could do anything that boys did . . . and that they had a perfect right to. I read any book that I wanted to, went to any movie that I wanted to, and had no curfew as a teenager. This in a fairly conservative small town where many parents were overprotective of their children." Though neither of Spires's parents went to college, it was assumed she would. She attended both parochial and public school, and although she never felt pushed, Spires pushed herself (she admits she was an overly serious child). Her decisions about going to the East for school, majoring in English, and becoming a writer met consistently with her parents' approval. "I guess they had faith that I would figure out some way to support myself as I pursued my goals," she says.

Although she thought she would write short stories, at Vassar College she started taking poetry workshops, studying first with Judith Kroll, then with William Gifford (he continues to be a crucial friend and discerning voice). She decided that if, five years out of Vassar, she had not had some "positive response" to her work, she would give up poetry altogether. Until that time, she would devote all her time and energy to it.

After she graduated, Spires worked in Columbus, Ohio, for an educational publisher as an editor and freelance writer of children's reading texts. Her poems began to appear in *The New Yorker, Poetry, The American Poetry Review,* and *The Partisan Review,* among other prestigious magazines. (Of course, this period was not without its sting: Spires recalls receiving, in a one-year span, fifty rejection slips in a row.) In 1977, Spires also approached Elizabeth Bishop, a long-standing influence, to ask for an interview; it was subsequently published in *The Paris Review,* and, as Bishop's last full-length interview, remains a vital literary record.

Spires moved to Baltimore in 1978 to pursue her M.A. at the Johns Hopkins University Writing Seminars. Her master's thesis eventually became the book *Globe*, described by Norman Dubie as "wonderfully born of metaphor . . . almost like a dream [these poems] reproach us, and still we wake refreshed."

Since that time Spires has followed with three more volumes of poems: *Swan's Island*, *Annonciade*, and *Worldling*, and several children's books—three published relatively recently. She's won grants from the Guggenheim and Whiting foundations, had poems appear in dozens of anthologies, and edited *The Instant of Knowing,* a collection of occasional prose pieces by Josephine Jacobsen.

Spires met her husband, Madison Smartt Bell, just as *Globe* was being published. She was giving a reading at a summer writers' conference in Maine where Bell was staff assistant to George Garrett. They were married in 1985 at the Ladew Topiary Gardens just outside Baltimore, and, except for a year here or there in London or Iowa, they have continued to live in Baltimore, both teaching at Goucher College, writing, and raising their eight-year-old daughter, Celia.

"At middle age, she's realizing more than ever how important relationships are to parents, mentors, close friends—'those who have died, are dying, or are going to die'—and what's received from this older generation."

And now here Spires is at mid-career, a time she's looked closely at in other poets, such as Robert Lowell and John Berryman, for what can be learned from their shifts of approach. "I don't think it's some sort of phoenix-like redefinition for me," she says, "so much as a new stage or chapter that grows out of whatever was there before; there's no part of a life that springs out of nothing. I am still just writing poems about what is directly in front of me that's all-engrossing, trying to write really directly. I've never been prolific; for me poems are like major events. Even if they're about something small—that something may seem small to other people, but it doesn't feel small to me."

At middle age, she's realizing more than ever how important relationships are to parents, mentors, close friends—"those who have died, are dying, or are going to die"—and what's received from this older generation. "I don't think I realized. I thought middle age was about life, not death. If you're lucky, you're still far from your own death or halfway, but not all the way." Her poems now are exploring such losses and relationships, the ways one unwillingly advances into a void that is made up of loss, where, as she writes in a new poem, "soul to soul, / we would have forever / never to speak again."

"I see where the next book is heading; it is preoccupied with these losses," she says. "Middle age is about beginnings and ends. For me, at least. Especially if you become a parent in middle age." In her fourth book of poems, *Worldling* (Norton, 1995), Spires focused with a pressing intelligence on conception, pregnancy, and motherhood, on the exact ways in which these are transformative experiences. Her meditations on the subjects are immaculate and lyrical. In her poem "The First Day," she writes, "I have had a child. Now I must live with death."

"I know that that's a line that makes some readers cringe, but to me that's the way it was. You have to say it, but then you realize that the way you said it is probably not good enough. Maybe the line doesn't achieve it in language. I wasn't striving to be ultrapoetic. That line connects to what I'm still thinking about: my own mortality and the mortality of those close to me. And, too, there's the actual physical end: you start to wonder what happens after death, what shape and form are we in after we die? There's a subject for poetry!"

Spires says she's never thought in terms of giving herself formal writing projects. "When I was working on my second book, the one thing I thought about was that I had more of a sense of a line. I thought the syntax of my sentences was becoming more complicated and emphatic. I like writing poems with long lines the best, but I don't have ideas for them very often. You feel like you've got all the power in the universe behind you—you're in charge of the waves of the ocean: here I am making it all go and happen."

Some of the poems she's working on now are "shadowed by myths"—a poem, for example, about Robert Frost in which he compares himself and his wife, Elinor, to Cadmus and Harmonia. "These characters in myth are archetypal figures. Trying to see deeply into your life, you may, sooner or later, see it clearly in archetypal terms. There's nothing we can live through or experience that doesn't already exist as an archetype." Almost in one breath she has at the ready Philip Larkin's disparaging and snide corrective about poets' use of "the universal myth kitty." But, too, there is Allen Grossman's expansive and inspiring lecture on Orpheus, a piece she theorizes has resoundingly informed contemporary poets' uses of myth. Spires keeps "searching and scouring" for writing to excite her, for poets that she's not read at all. May Swenson and the Australian poet Gwen Harwood are her current amazements, just to name two.

A sense of her deepest writerly passions and resolve comes clear, though, as she discusses her writing for children. She is particularly taken with the phrase "a word-inspired world," used in one critic's review of her recent children's book *The Mouse of Amherst*. The mouse in question, Emmaline, becomes diligent wainscot apprentice to Emily Dickinson. Emmaline laments, "There was an emptiness in my life that nothing seemed to fill." Her longing to "touch something untouchable" leads her to poetry and to, as a *New York Times* critic notes, "the nourishing power of words." To Spires, this "word-inspired world," this world of reverie and imagination, is what completes one's existence, makes it feel full and whole. "Without it," she says, "the physical world seems impoverished. But with it, day-to-day life feels endless and infinite."

"Children who like to read, and who grow up with books in the house, easily enter the world I'm talking about," says Spires. "I'm concerned, though, at the number of children who don't know this world of words exists. The way a story or poem is written, as well as what it's about, can pull children into thinking about this whole business of language. It can make them think about the power of words and imagination and, possibly, how they can use that power themselves."

"For most adults, the relevance of poetry to their lives is even less than I would have believed it was in my twenties and thirties, and I didn't think then that I had any illusions. Most people appear to be living without poetry quite nicely. They may turn to poetry at some terribly critical moment—a birth or wedding or funeral. But how can anyone possibly commit to a life of words and not be concerned about what poetry has come to mean, what place it occupies in the present time and culture?" Her comments call to mind the fevered work of anthropologists trying to keep a foundering language alive. "You feel this force against you if you write serious fiction or poetry; you're trying to do your part. You hold on—blown horizontal—and just try to not let go of the tree."

Spires is thinking of a new poetry assignment for her students at Goucher College, based on May Swenson's poem "Too Big for Words." She'll ask her students to place themselves at that border between language and the ineffable, the very place from which Spires has so compellingly spoken throughout her career. Just as she says in her own introduction here, with "the edge of time so close," she continues to stand at each and every threshold resolutely, looks with directness as she is "lived by events." She attends to them, giving keen attention to everything from workmen raking seaweed into piles at the empty governor's mansion to how a white curtain on a fall afternoon can suggest the soul or time's continuum, its lifting a figure for the present's fluid move into the past.

Source: Elizabeth Spires and A. V. Christie, "About Elizabeth Spires," in *Ploughshares*, Vol. 25, No. 4, 1999, pp. 210–15.

William V. Davis

In the following essay, Davis discusses Spires's strengths and weaknesses and the themes and tones common to her work.

Elizabeth Spires's themes, she says, "draw on many sources: childhood, memories, places, and visual images such as paintings and photographs, illuminated manuscripts, and medieval books of hours." The poet she most admires, and with whom she shares themes and forms, is Elizabeth Bishop.

Spires was born in Lancaster, Ohio, on 28 May 1952 to Richard C. and Sue Wagner Spires. Her father worked in grounds maintenance; her mother was a real-estate broker. Elizabeth Spires was educated at Vassar College (B.A., 1974) and Johns Hopkins University (M.A., 1979). She is married to Madison Smartt Bell, a fiction writer. Spires currently teaches creative writing at Goucher College and at Johns Hopkins.

Globe (1981), her first full-length collection, contains twenty-two poems divided into three sections, preceded by a one-poem prelude, "Tequila," which sets the direction the book will take; the speaker leaves on a road "that leads / everywhere." The three sections of the book, each one longer than the last, "lead" out from the childhood world of home and family in the first section, through a series of character sketches (most of them dealing with women in historical settings), to the tone poems at the end of the book. Both structurally and thematically *Globe* moves to increasingly wider explorations of the world.

The first six poems of the first section are the strongest poems in the book. The speaker's parents, described as somewhat shadowy or dreamlike and "dark" (the father "dark and immediate," the mother's "face in darkness"), brood over the child, who is "falling toward the future," reaching "across the dark," singing through "the nights of my childhood," even though, caught up in and revolving through her "reveries," she knows she has forgotten "what the world meant to me then," but believes, as the first, title poem, has it, that false memories are "better than forgetting."

The other two sections of *Globe* are much more objective, at times even mechanical, and suggest the inevitable movement out into a wider world than that of childhood. The character sketches are set in several early American places ("Widow's Walk," "Salem, Massachusetts: 1692"), in literary history (Dante Gabriel Rossetti), and in other cultures ("Courtesan With Fan," "After Three Japanese Drawings"), most of them focused on women and their difficult lives. Structurally these poems seem transitional, a necessary stage Spires needed to work through. Although they are at the center of the book, they are not central to it.

"Elizabeth Spires is one of the most important young poets in America. The auspicious beginning represented by her first books suggests that she will find a secure place in the world of contemporary poetry."

The final section of *Globe* contains the most diffuse, amorphous poems, a "negative music of silence." These are self-indulgent, precious, private, "poetic" tone poems. In several of the poems ("Snowfall" and "Blue Nude," the first two in the section, are good examples) Spires weaves words and images together into a kind of fugue of meaning and emotion in which "each page [is] only / part of a larger story," even if this "story" remains at one remove.

Although the poems in *Swan's Island* (1985) are drawn from various times (the six "Storyville Portraits," for instance, are based on E.J. Bellocq's photographs of the New Orleans redlight district of 1912), places, and sources, Spires has made them her own. There is an evenness of tone to this book that *Globe* lacks, but most of these poems, although often they are more proficient than the earlier ones, are not more memorable than the best poems in *Globe*.

The most powerful, fully realized poems in *Swan's Island* are short (several are sonnet length), compact, intense, and fully under control. Spires is a lyric poet and her longer poems, those not broken down in parts, tend to get away from her at this stage of her career. The best poem in *Swan's Island* is "Two Shadows." It begins:

When we are shadows watching over shadows,
when years have passed, enough to live

two lives, when we have passed
through love and come out speechless
on the other side, I will remember
how we spent a night, walking the streets
in August, side by side . . . .

In Spires's next book, *Annonciade* (1989), the second, central section is a prose interlude titled "Falling Away," in which she documents in a short autobiographical "history" the dominant themes of the book:

> Memory: I am sitting at my desk in sixth grade at St. Joseph's Elementary in Circleville, Ohio. It is a winter morning in 1964, and we are in the middle of catechism. The classroom is old-fashioned, with high ceilings and wood floors, the crucifix above the front blackboard in a face-off with the big round clock on the back wall.

This prose meditation mixes memory, imagination, and time, the three touchstones of Spires's work from the beginning, which are brought to climax and most fully detailed in this, her most accomplished book.

The theme of time runs throughout the book. There is hardly a page without some reference to it. "My birth," Spires says, is "a tear in time's fabric." And even if this "everlasting present" in which "there will always / be, for us, a tomorrow tomorrow," is simultaneously seen and recognized as a "past preserved and persevering," a "sentimental past," it is celebrated as it is announced—it is, indeed, that which Spires's *Annonciade* is all about.

Annonciade is, therefore, Spires's most definitive exploration of the world. There are poems set throughout America and in England, France, and Switzerland. There are poems focusing on earlier ages, on Spires's obsession with travel, and on her exploration of the psyche (particularly the female psyche).

There is an apocalyptic theme running through *Annonciade*. In "Sunday Afternoon at Fulham Palace" one reads, "It is easy, too easy, to imagine the world ending / on a day like today . . . ." In "Thanksgiving Night: St. Michael's" Spires writes: "we walk out, out on a finger of land / that points like a sign to World's End," where "the dead, living, and not-yet-born" are "gathered / around the great table." Even with this apocalyptic mood, Spires's title poem ends with "strange intimations of happiness," reminding one of William Wordsworth's "Intimations Ode" (1807), but Spires's poem, which combines allusions to Thomas Mann as well as to Wordsworth, is firmly contemporary, as she finds "intimations of happiness" even in the face of possible annihilation. An *annonciade* is an acknowledgment, like poetry itself, of the possibility of life in the face of death. In "The Celestial," the last poem in the book, fish in a Buddhist temple pond gaze "upward and forever."

Elizabeth Spires is one of the most important young poets in America. The auspicious beginning represented by her first books suggests that she will find a secure place in the world of contemporary poetry.

Source: William V. Davis, "Elizabeth Spires," in *Dictionary of Literary Biography*, Vol 120, *American Poets Since World War II, Third Series*, edited by R. S. Gwynn, Gale Research, 1992, pp. 291–292.

Sources

Balbo, Ned, Review of *Now the Green Blade Rises*, in the *Antioch Review*, Vol. 61, No. 4, Fall 2003, pp. 786–87.

Christie, A. V., "'The Power of the Visible Is the Invisible': An Interview with Elizabeth Spires," in *Southwest Review*, Vol. 80, No. 1, Winter 1995, p. 35.

Dobyns, Stephen, "Writing the Reader's Life," in *Poets Teaching Poets: Self and the World*, edited by Gregory Orr and Ellen Bryant Voigt, University of Michigan Press, 1996, pp. 240–53.

Review of *Now the Green Blade Rises*, in *Publishers Weekly*, Vol. 249, No. 33, August 19, 2002, p. 82.

Spires, Elizabeth, *Now the Green Blade Rises*, W. W. Norton, 2002, pp. 25, 33–34.

———, *Worldling*, W. W. Norton, 1995, pp. 11, 33–34.

Further Reading

Ali, Agha Shahid, ed., *Ravishing Disunities: Real Ghazals in English*, Wesleyan University Press, 2000.

This is a collection of over one hundred modern and contemporary poets, including Diane Ackerman, W. S. Merwin, William Matthews, and John Hollander, writing ghazals in their native English language. The introduction and afterward by editor Agha Shahid Ali provides excellent details on what a ghazal is, how challenging it is to write ghazals in English, and how the process differs from writing ghazals in their original Middle Eastern languages.

Christie, A. V., "The Power of the Visible Is the Invisible: An Interview with Elizabeth Spires," in *Southwest Review*, Vol. 80, No. 1, Winter 1995, pp. 35–57.

This lengthy interview with Spires provides excellent insight into the way the poet feels about her own work and that of others, what has inspired her to write, how she selects topics, the importance of form in writing, and a host of personal opinions on a variety of topics. Although the interview took place several years before the poems of *Now the Green Blade Rises* were composed, she explores many of the same themes that appear in her latest collection.

Spires, Elizabeth, *Worldling*, W. W. Norton, 1995.
This collection by Spires is the one preceding *Now the Green Blade Rises*, and the similarities in themes are remarkable. *Worldling* explores the subjects of birth, death, change, and immortality, specifically the birth of her own daughter and the subsequent struggle of the poet to come to terms with aging, family, and pending loss.

Taylor, Henry, "In the Everlasting Present: The Poetry of Elizabeth Spires," in the *Hollins Critic*, Vol. 39, No. 2, April 2002, pp. 1–19.
Taylor writes in depth about Spires's themes and style in this substantial article. Written several months before the release of *Now the Green Blade Rises*, Taylor's review of her work is thorough, insightful, and appealing throughout.

Hymn to Beauty

Charles Baudelaire

1857

"Hymn to Beauty" comes from the "Spleen and Ideal" section of Charles Baudelaire's book *Les Fleurs du Mal* (which translates into English as *Flowers of Evil* or *Flowers of Suffering*). First published in 1857, it has become one of the most widely read and influential collections of poetry ever to come out of France. Like Edgar Allan Poe, whose works Baudelaire was instrumental in introducing to French audiences through extensive translations and critical works, Baudelaire viewed the universe with acute sensuality that leaned toward a fascination with the supernatural and the macabre. At the same time, his own aesthetic theories led him to the conclusion that beauty, mysterious and unknowable as it was, was the artist's main concern. Baudelaire is considered to be a precursor to the French symbolist movement that developed decades later, at the end of the nineteenth century, and included Stéphane Mallarmé, Arthur Rimbaud, and Paul Verlaine. Most modern and postmodern poetry was influenced in one way or another by symbolism.

Baudelaire's book *Les Fleurs du Mal* was subject to government censorship when it was published. Both Baudelaire and his publisher were forced to pay hefty fines for poems that were deemed indecent. In addition, six poems were removed from the second edition, published in 1861. After the poet's death, several editions were published with different configurations of his poems. "Hymn to Beauty" is included in the recent compilation *Charles Baudelaire: Complete Poems* by Routeledge, translated from the French by Walter Martin.

Author Biography

Charles Pierre Baudelaire was born on April 9, 1821, in Paris, France. His father, Joseph-François Baudelaire, had been ordained as a priest, but left the priesthood during the French Revolution (1789–1799) and worked as a tutor, giving him connections with high levels of French aristocracy. He was sixty years old when he met and married Baudelaire's mother, Caroline Archimbaut-Dufays, who was twenty-six. Baudelaire was six when his father died. For a short time, his mother showered him with affection, but the following year she married Jacques Aupick, a military man who eventually rose through the ranks of the military to become an ambassador and then a senator. Aupick was strict with his stepson, sending him away to military school, where Baudelaire began a lifelong struggle against authority.

Baudelaire was expelled from high school in 1839, though he received his degree later that year. He soon decided that he would be a writer, although his parents pressured him to study law. He enrolled in a law school in Paris, but while there he spent his time with artists and bohemians. He developed an addiction to opium and contracted syphilis, of which he was to die years later.

When he turned twenty-one, Baudelaire inherited a large sum from his father's estate, but went through it quickly, immersing himself in a bizarre, satanic lifestyle until his mother had to step in and have a guardian appointed for his money. He wrote sporadically. His first major sweep of fame came in 1856, when he translated a book of Edgar Allan Poe's verse. His introductions to the two volumes of Poe's work he translated are still considered among the best Poe studies published.

In 1857, Baudelaire published *Les Fleurs du Mal*, a book of poems considered so shocking that he was tried and found guilty of obscenity, ordered to pay a fine, and to remove six of the poems from the second edition in 1861. The obscenity charge made it difficult for him to find a publisher, and his failing health made his writing difficult and infrequent. He moved to Brussels in 1863 and, in 1866, suffered a stroke that paralyzed him and made him unable to talk. He was returned to his family home and, on August 31, 1867, at the age of forty-six, Baudelaire died in his mother's arms.

Charles Baudelaire

Poem Summary

Lines 1–4

"Hymn to Beauty" begins with a question that might seem strange to readers who only think of beauty as a pleasant experience. Baudelaire asks Beauty (which is capitalized, as a proper name) whether it is demonic or divine, whether it comes from heaven or hell. The poem is unique in showing that Beauty is as likely to be horrifying as it is to be wonderful. This ambiguous relationship is one that continues throughout the entire poem. In the last two lines of the first stanza, the way that Beauty can hold conflicting ideas together is compared to the effect of wine, because, like inebriation, beauty throws all things, including good and evil, together at random. Wine has been considered since antiquity to raise the animalistic, instinctual side of human nature, and the poem points out that, under the influence of Beauty, even the most severe moral opposites are hard to discern.

Lines 5–8

The personification of Beauty is continued in the second stanza with a mention of Beauty's eyes. Though Baudelaire may have had someone in particular in mind when he wrote this poem, most

Media Adaptations

- A website dedicated to the works of Charles Baudelaire, and in particular to the various editions of his collection *Les Fleurs du Mal*, is located at www.FleursDuMal.org with links to other websites of interest regarding the poet.

likely his mistress, Jean Duval, the image of Beauty here is described as an idea that has been imbued with human traits. Traditionally, beauty is linked with serenity and self-contentedness, but the Beauty that Baudelaire imagines in line 5 is closer to the "demonic" image of the first stanza, with flaring suns and burning sunsets that suggest the fires of hell. This fiery imagery is balanced, however, by the calm image in line 6 of "phantom fragrance"—not only is its source so subtle that it cannot be identified, which is what makes it a "phantom," but the use of the pleasant word "fragrance" contradicts the harshness of the demon imagery that precedes it. Line 7 recalls the intoxicating effect of wine with its mention of drugs, while line 8 continues the idea of Beauty turning natural order around, as the social roles played by men and boys are reversed.

Lines 9–12

The poem's original question, from lines 1–2, is repeated in line 9. As a twist on the poem's constant personification of Beauty, Fate is introduced. Instead of being talked about as a person, though, Fate is presented as a dog that follows after Beauty, "faithfully." It is rare that a poet would consider Fate weaker than anyone or anything, and the fact that Baudelaire shows Fate as Beauty's faithful pet is a clear indication of how powerful he thinks Beauty to be.

In the second half of this stanza, the poet expresses fear for Beauty's great power. That power is not used wisely. It could lead to ruin, but then again, the poem also admits that it could lead to love. The one constant that the poet identifies in Beauty's use of power is that it is always going to be used erratically. As line 12 tells readers, Beauty rules, but does so without responsibility.

Lines 13–16

Once again, the poem returns to the idea of Beauty as a frightening creature. Its personification in the form of a beautiful woman is retained in line 13, where it is presented as someone whom the poem's speaker has watched dancing. The dancing referred to, however, is perversely on a grave, where more solemn behavior is expected. In line 14, at the very center of the poem, Baudelaire states clearly one of the poem's main points, about the relationship between Beauty and Horror, calling Horror a "dazzling jewel," implying that it is used to make Beauty even more appealing than it naturally is. If Horror is a decoration, though, Beauty also uses Murder like a move in a game, a stratagem. In this case, the game pits Beauty against "useful fools," who presumably would not appreciate Beauty's charms without the presence of danger.

Lines 17–20

The "man-fly" referred to in line 17 is a moth, which is attracted to a candle or other source of heat and light, flying toward it and then burning up as a result. In the same way, the poem implies, men are drawn to beauty, knowing that it will end in their own destruction. As it is presented here, men do not merely accept their destruction by Beauty, but actually welcome it, thinking of it as martyrdom, as if they are dying for an important, noble cause. Lines 19 and 20 draw a direct comparison between a lover giving in to desire and a person who knows that he is destined to die and so goes to his grave eagerly. The center of this connection between love and death is that Beauty is the motive for both.

Lines 21–24

Baudelaire makes it clear in this stanza that this poem is not a philosophical reflection on all aspects of Beauty, such as where it comes from, but is only concerned with the practical effects of Beauty as he experiences it. He says that he is not at all interested in its origins, but only with the thrill that he draws from contact with it. The images that the poem uses in line 23 show how desperate its speaker feels for any slight glimpse of Beauty, longing for a glance at her eyes or even just her feet. At the end of this stanza, Beauty is referred to as a Goddess, which is a concept that runs through all of Western civilization, one familiar to the mythologies of ancient Greeks and Egyptians.

Lines 25–28

The first line of the last stanza serves as a sort of summary of the poem, restating the most significant ideas about Beauty that have been raised. It reminds readers of the senses that one can use to experience Beauty, and of the poem's uncertainty about whether it is good or evil. Baudelaire goes on to ignore the question of good or evil, though, saying that he does not care about morality, that Beauty is so important to him that it does not matter whether it is "a blessing or a curse." The reason for this, which has not been brought up earlier, is the despair that he feels toward life in general, which he characterizes as "the dead hours of this grim universe." He expresses his willingness to accept whatever Beauty has to offer, whether it is heavenly or hellish, as long as he can experience Beauty's light within the darkness of his existence.

Themes

Sensuality

The word "sensual" refers to works that evoke the five senses in order to make their audience *feel* the experience that is being described, as Baudelaire does in "Hymn to Beauty." While the narrow sense of the word "sensuality" only implies a reference to the senses, there is also a common association of the word with sexuality. In this poem, Baudelaire uses physical images to give an erotic allure to Beauty, whom he has presented as a particular person. The poem is particularly focused on the mystery and attraction of the eyes. Beauty is said early on to have eyes in which "suns flare and sunsets burn," in stanza 6 she is said to have "smiling eyes," while in stanza 7 he calls her "my dark-eyed queen."

The poem also mentions things such as fragrance, dancing, and jewels, which are all associated with sexual attraction. Overall, the image of Beauty as personified here is not that of a passive, spiritual or innocent beauty, but of a worldly woman who uses her sexual prowess to lure men into doing her bidding.

Nihilism

This poem projects a philosophical stance that rejects moral and religious values. That stance is referred to as "nihilism."

If the poem showed no understanding of the traditional values at all, then it could be said to be building its own moral vision of the world afresh. As it is, though, it shows a great deal of awareness of the ordinary concepts of heaven and hell, good and evil. It asks Beauty in the first line whether it is demonic or divine, and then repeats that question several times throughout. It is the poet who is making the distinction between what is good and what is bad, and therefore the poet must have some sort of system in mind that recognizes different levels of morality.

In the end, though, Baudelaire says that he does not care whether Beauty is "a blessing" or "a curse." He is willing to accept Beauty under any conditions. This rejection of traditional values, with full awareness of what they are, is what makes the poem nihilistic. The speaker of the poem seems conscious of the fact that his worship of Beauty may drive him toward destruction—not necessarily a physical destruction, but the destruction of his soul. Still, he stands by his belief that Beauty is worth more than good or evil, heaven or hell. He recognizes traditional values, but does not accept them; instead, he finds Beauty to be more important than even the most important aspects of traditional moral systems.

Redemption

At the end of the poem, Baudelaire identifies Beauty as a source of redemption in his life. After openly rejecting traditional values in line 26, when he asks, "Who cares if you're a blessing or a curse?" he goes on to explain life as being bleak and empty, describing everyday existence as "the dead hours of this grim universe." In this void, there is only one thing that gives him "light," and that is Beauty.

Even while he is identifying Beauty as a source of light, he also calls it his "dark-eyed queen." The contrast between light and darkness in this image gathers together all of the poem's themes in just a few words. The dark eyes are used to signal the attractiveness of Beauty, and are also used to show Beauty as a mysterious presence, with a depth that cannot be readily understood. At the same time, the world is mysterious, but in a frightening, dead way. Paradoxically, the dark eyes of Beauty are able to generate a light that cuts through the darkness of life and makes it bearable. At the same time that he is rejecting the universe as being grim and dead, Baudelaire finds the horrors of life redeemed by the negative powers of Beauty. He does not find the darkness of Beauty's eyes grim at all, but instead finds them enlightening.

Topics For Further Study

- Interview members of the local government where you live, and report on their thoughts about what sort of literature they think they would prosecute for being obscene.
- Many of Baudelaire's poems have been put to music, often by classical musicians. Adapt "Hymn to Beauty" to the type of music that you like best, and record your composition.
- "Hymn to Beauty" is about a beautiful woman who is considered a "sacred monster." Research popular women who are famous for their "bad girl" images. Try to determine what behavior is considered to be too shocking for the American public.
- "Hymn to Beauty" ends up with its speaker saying, "Who cares if you're a blessing or a curse." Do you think that is really the way that he feels? Explain your answer with direct quotations from the poem.

Style

Iambic Pentameter

This translation of "Hymn to Beauty" follows an iambic pentameter rhythm structure. This means that the basic rhythm is iambic. An *iamb* is a two-syllable segment of poetry, with one unstressed syllable followed by a stressed syllable, as in "di-VINE" or "with-OUT." This unstressed-stressed pattern is the general rhythm followed throughout the poem, as in the line "like STU-pe-FY-ing DRUGS your KISS-es TURN." The translator takes liberties with this basic pattern often, in lines like "WHO CARES if YOU'RE a BLESS-ing OR a CURSE?" This is sometimes necessary to maintain the integrity of the poem's language in its original French.

Pentameter means that the poem has five iambs in each line, for a total of ten syllables per line. This poem maintains the syllabic count quite strictly.

Iambic pentameter is the most common metrical pattern in English, because it follows the natural rhythm of the way that English is spoken. The original French version of "Hymn to Beauty" is measured, but it is not as strict about the number of syllables per line or the patterns of stresses in the words.

Quatrain

This poem is written in *quatrains*, or four-line stanzas. This pattern gives poems a balanced, logical, symmetrical feel. Quatrains frequently employ a rhyme scheme of *ABAB*, which means that the first and third lines (the *A* lines) rhyme with each other and the second and fourth lines (the *B* lines) rhyme with each other. This is the rhyming pattern used in "Hymn to Beauty." Other common rhyme schemes for quatrains are *AABB* and *ABCB*, in which only the even-numbered lines end with similar sounds. The geometric versatility of having two pairs of lines per stanza is what makes the quatrain a popular form.

Historical Context

Charles Baudelaire is associated with the intellectual and artistic scene in Paris in the 1850s, which is where he wrote his most significant poetry. Paris has long been considered one of the great centers for artists, with a tight-knit, thriving community of poets, novelists, and painters who were willing to starve for the sake of their passionate commitment to their arts. The city has existed for centuries, since it was founded as a fishing village by the Romans in 52 B.C., and it has been the capital of France since the fifth century. In Baudelaire's time, though, Paris was in the process of becoming the cosmopolitan city that it is known as today.

At the beginning of the nineteenth century, Paris was still organized like a small medieval town. It only contained about a third of the land of

Compare & Contrast

- **1850s:** Louis Napoleon, a nephew of Napoleon Bonaparte who conquered Europe in the early years of the century, rules France as a dictator, taking for himself the name Napoleon III.

  Today: France is a democracy, with an elected parliament and president.

- **1850s:** Paris is considered one of the cultural centers of the Western world, and artists flock there to be part of its thriving artistic scene.

  Today: Paris is still considered one of the world's great cultural centers. Because of improvements in travel and communication, its appeal is not just limited to people from Europe and America, but from all over the globe.

- **1850s:** One characteristic of the romantic age, which dominates art during the first half of the century, is a fascination with the occult or supernatural.

  Today: Very few poets concern themselves with issues like the supernatural power of beauty, focusing instead on how beauty can be found in the commonplace.

- **1850s:** The French government suppresses poetry that it finds "obscene," as it does with several of the poems in Baudelaire's collection *Les Fleurs du Mal.*

  Today: Printed materials, such as poems and novels, are rarely if ever prosecuted for obscenity.

contemporary Paris, and was surrounded by walls with gates to let traffic in and out. Only twelve of the current twenty municipal subdivisions, or *arrondissements*, made up the city.

When Napoleon Bonaparte became emperor of France in 1804, he modernized the town by building bridges, streets, and massive monuments, with the aim of making Paris one of the grandest capital cities in the world. The Industrial Revolution, which affected urban areas around the globe, did even more to change the city's character. Farming gave way to factory work as the mainstay of the country's economy by mid-century, bringing people from all over rural France to the city in search of employment. The population doubled between 1836 and 1866, from one to two million people, then up to three million in 1886, and reaching a peak of four million by 1904 (today the population stands at just over two million).

The growing urban population brought with it the usual problems that plagued ancient cities all over the world trying to cope with major population shifts. Slums grew up, crime thrived, the streets became congested and disease spread. For artists like Baudelaire, the burgeoning town offered an inexpensive place to live and to commune with others of similar interests. His most fertile period of work was spent in the Latin Quarter, which is the area around the Sorbonne, a famous art school, where he lived as part of the "bohemian" subculture that has been traditionally associated with Paris for centuries.

When Napoleon III proclaimed himself Emperor of France in 1853, he set about instituting a project of urban renewal for Paris. Major thoroughfares were widened and straightened, and the city annexed a large area called "La Petite Banlieue" ("The Little Suburbs"). Its population immediately grew by 400,000, but the annexation also allowed planners to chart out a more reasonable scope for the city, which had become cramped within the same perimeters that had confined it for hundreds of years.

The expansion and modernization of the city were finished by the 1870s, when Napoleon III was ousted from office after losing the Franco-Prussian War. There were detractors who thought that the changes had ruined the character of a traditionally simple, classically organized city, but the vast majority agreed that Paris would have suffered even more from the changes that industrialization brought if it had not been modernized to address the future.

Critical Overview

The collection that "Hymn to Beauty" comes from, *Les Fleurs du Mal*, overcame a rocky start to become one of the most recognized and influential books of poetry ever written. When it was first published in 1857, Baudelaire and his publisher were sued for indecency. Each had to pay fines. Worse, however, was the fact that reviewers were frightened away from offering positive reviews. As A. E. Carter explained it, this was a catastrophe that can hardly be understood in the modern age of marketing. "In 1857 the uses of publicity were not properly understood: instead of profiting by the lawsuit, Baudelaire's career suffered an undeniable setback. Poetry is seldom an easy article to market, especially poetry like his, and now publishers had a sound excuse for turning down his manuscripts. Not until twenty or thirty years later did the 1857 stigma prove negotiable. It has paid off pretty well since; *Les Fleurs du Mal* have always smelled of forbidden fruit." The second edition of the book, in 1861, is the one on which Baudelaire's considerable reputation is built—the six poems deemed to be indecent were removed, and roughly a hundred new poems were added.

Baudelaire was considered a breakthrough poet, at least by other poets. His reputation was discussed, but his works were not widely available until after 1917, when the copyright ran out and his works fell into public domain. Baudelaire was a powerful influence on the French symbolists, who gained international acclaim in the late 1800s. He was also a strong influence on T. S. Eliot, whose artistic theories were central to the development of the Modernism movement from the 1920s forward.

Contemporary critics are able to see the influence that Baudelaire's poetry has exerted on the literary world over time. Most literary analyses focus on his fascinations with Satan and beauty, such as when Lewis Piaget Shanks noted, in 1974, that "Baudelaire could never shake off the Catholic dualism, that consciousness of our warring flesh and spirit." It is this dualism that has made him a model poet—his poetry is intellectually challenging, but still based in the experiences of the senses.

Criticism

David Kelly

Kelly is an instructor of creative writing and literature. In this essay, Kelly examines the ways in which Baudelaire's poetry fits into the literary categories of romanticism and symbolism, while actually being a part of neither movement.

Depending on which critics you read, the poetry of nineteenth-century French writer Charles Baudelaire might be fitted into several different places in literary history. Some place him as a late member of the romantic movement; others as a precursor, by several decades, of the French symbolists. Still others will resist putting him into any category, and will explain the illogic of doing so by saying that his work was just too unique to force into a grouping with any others. All of these assertions have been made by intelligent, thoughtful critics, and each is right in its own way (and therefore, of course, wrong in its own way as well). In a poem like Baudelaire's "Hymn to Beauty" readers can see the elements of several different literary schools, as well as elements that defy any attempt to narrow the scope of his achievement. While it is good to avoid insisting that the poet is anything that he is not, there are even more compelling reasons for taking a look at possible schools of thought that he could be affiliated with, if only to better understand how literary style evolves over the course of generations.

To start with, the last claim is the most obviously true: that Baudelaire wrote from such an original perspective that his talent cannot entirely be claimed by any larger movement. This is actually true of any artist, no matter how much teachers try to use them as examples of what was going on in their societies. Technically, a writer who does not "make it new," to use Ezra Pound's brief and eloquent description of the artist's goal, would not be worth talking about, and therefore would never even have the chance to stand for her or his crowd. But it should only be after we accept the fact that all artists have individual styles that we start grouping them into general categories. It takes nothing from Baudelaire's accomplishment to take note of the ways in which his writing is similar to that of others with whom he had things in common. The only reason to steadfastly refuse to categorize him would be if someone insisted that he could have no other identity than that of his grouping: if forced to reduce his work to "nothing more than" an example of romanticism or symbolism, then a good idea might be to say that he was too original to give an honest answer. As it is, though, the most honest intellectual thing to do is to at least *try* different modes on his poetry, to see what might be relevant.

If one is to look for the closest literary movement to Baudelaire, it is natural to look at the one that came before him. Rare is the writer who shows no trace of the sensibilities that shaped his or her world. In the case of a poem like "Hymn to Beauty," there are quite a few traits linking the work to romanticism. By the 1850s, when the first edition of Baudelaire's book *Les Fleurs du Mal* went to press, romanticism had been around for over a half a century, an exhaustively long stretch for a movement based on spontaneity. His work could be considered romantic if one focuses on its antecedents, although, like almost all poetry from that time that was worth reading, it was bursting out of the romantic's norms.

A brief history of romanticism shows that a poem like "Hymn to Beauty" would not have been possible without it. Most critics, though hesitant to claim any definitive moment that a literary movement came to life, would be comfortable with accepting the date 1800 as literary romanticism's start. It was then that, in the introduction to the second edition of their poetry collection *Lyrical Ballads*, William Wordsworth and Samuel Taylor Coleridge lambasted the intellectual approach to art, asserting that beauty was to be found in the ordinary elements of everyday life. Clearly, their approach was a product of the same sensibilities that had given rise to the American Revolution in 1776 and the French Revolution in 1789, with all of them stressing that individuals know what is best for themselves and are not bound to follow the rule of "experts" in order to determine right from wrong or, in the case of artists, in order to know beauty.

It is the second generation of British romantics that we generally associate with the romantic movement. These writers, most notably John Keats, Lord Byron, and Percy Bysshe Shelley, lived to pursue beauty and individuality. Their lives exemplified the melancholy and self-destructive commitment to love that is evident in "Hymn to Beauty" as well as in much romantic poetry. Beside the gloom and emphasis on individual experience that most people think of when they think of romantic poetry in its prime, there is one more relevant element, that of a fascination with the supernatural and the macabre. One sees this in the masterpiece of Shelley's wife, Mary Wollstonecraft Shelley, who, at age twenty, published *Frankenstein*, a tale that has been constantly revived through the ages to warn of the dangers that can occur when the scientific, rational world crosses over into the territory of the supernatural. The supernatural also plays a strong role in the short stories and poems of American author Edgar Allan Poe, who Baudelaire wrote extensively about and admired. It is easy to see the romantic

"Rather than being viewed as one who offers more of the same, most artists would probably hope that the public will start seeing all art in an entirely new way just as they themselves are becoming known."

themes that run through Baudelaire's work in general, and especially through a poem like "Hymn to Beauty," in which he expresses the willingness to consort with demons, if necessary, if that is what it would take to call upon beauty to quell his worldly sorrow.

But there are so many ways that Baudelaire differs from the romantic tradition that it is clear that, if he can only be put in one category, this is not it. If romanticism developed in literature as a rejection of classical rules, such as strict form and regular meter, then the poetry that Baudelaire produced is far from the romantic tradition. Before he arrived, French poetry was dominated by writers who one would have no trouble whatsoever categorizing as romantics: writers like Alfred de Musset, Alphonse Lamartine, and especially Victor Hugo, whose career preceded Baudelaire's by decades and whose life continued long after the author of *Les Fleurs du Mal* was in his grave. While these traditionally romantic poets, the masters of French poetry, considered the role of the poet as being the expression of individuality, Baudelaire objected to verse that had not been carefully crafted. There are two obvious explanations for this. First, there is the natural inclination of the rising young artist to reject the works that are currently being celebrated, thus to make more room in the public consciousness for himself or herself. Rather than being viewed as one who offers more of the same, most artists would probably hope that the public will start seeing all art in an entirely new way just as they themselves are becoming known.

In Baudelaire's case, this self-serving drive coincided with a genuine aesthetic drive to restore the

What Do I Read Next?

- Jean-Paul Sartre, one of the most famous names in twentieth-century philosophy, published a book-length examination of Baudelaire in 1950, commenting on the complexity of the poet's vision. Titled *Baudelaire*, it is available from New Directions Press.
- Before the publication of *Les Fleurs du Mal*, Charles Baudelaire was already famous for his translations of the poetry and prose of American writer Edgar Allan Poe, for whom he had great empathy. A good source for Poe's poetry is *Edgar Allan Poe: Poetry and Tales*, edited by Patrick F. Quinn and published by Viking Press in 1984.
- Though he wrote decades before the writers usually grouped together as French symbolists, Baudelaire is sometimes talked about as the earliest writer of that movement. Examples of the most significant poets of French symbolism are gathered in *Four French Symbolist Poets: Baudelaire, Rimbaud, Verlaine and Mallarmé*. It was translated with an introduction by Enid Rhodes Peschel and published by Ohio University Press in 1981.
- Though they did not write in the same style, Victor Hugo was Baudelaire's acquaintance and closest peer in French poetry of the 1850s. *Selected Poems of Victor Hugo: A Bilingual Edition*, translated by E. H. Blackmore and A. M. Blackmore and published by the University of Chicago Press in 2001, gives a good sampling of Hugo's poetic output.
- One of the truest ways to gain a sense of a writer is to see what they had to say informally to their friends. Baudelaire comes across as a mass of uncertainty and conflicting desires in *Selected Letters of Charles Baudelaire: The Conquest of Solitude*, translated and edited by Rosemary Lloyd and published by the University of Chicago Press in 1986.
- Baudelaire's influence on the British and American poets of the twentieth century cannot be overstated. Lachlan Mackinnon dedicated an entire book to this subject: *Eliot, Auden and Lowell: Aspects of the Baudelarean Inheritance*. It was published in 1983 by the Macmillan Press.

craft aspect to poetry that the romantics, in their emphasis on the individual's self-importance, ignored. As Paul Valéry, one of France's leading poets and critics of the twentieth century, put it in his essay "The Position of Baudelaire," "The romantics had neglected practically everything demanding concentrated thought. They sought the effect of shock, enthusiasm, and contrast. Neither measure nor rigor nor depth tormented them excessively. They were averse to abstract thinking and to reasoning—and not only in their works, but also in the preparation of their works, which is infinitely more serious. The French seemed to have forgotten their analytical talents." Though he shared the romantics' sensibilities, Baudelaire brought to poetry a new concern for craft that romanticism specifically disdained.

Though he is generally considered a great influence on the symbolist movement, critics seldom categorize Baudelaire as a symbolist himself. The term "symbolist" is generally associated with the poetry and poetic theory of Stéphane Mallarmé, who gathered an actual literary movement around himself in his home, outlining his theories (with frequent nods to Baudelaire). For the symbolists, poetry should be wild in spirit, but structurally it should be made of carefully chosen symbols that can explain themselves. The best symbolist writing reaches beyond the writer's personal experience and also transcends intellectualism. Admirers of symbolist poetry note the skill with which it is constructed; detractors note that when it is poorly done, it ends up dense and obscure. By symbolist standards, Baudelaire's poetry, such as "Hymn to Beauty," might seem over explained; he tells his ideas to the reader, rather than making them arrive at their own conclusions.

Baudelaire was neither a romantic poet nor a symbolist, and yet he was both. Such is the nature of literary movements. He is evenly divided between different strategies that have polarized poetry throughout its history and that will continue to be open matters for debate for the rest of eternity: the question of form versus spontaneity, of tradition versus individual vision, and of skill versus inspiration. What makes his position in the center between these two movements even more important is that, end to end, they dominated more than a century of the modern world. That both romantics and symbolists should claim Baudelaire as their own should not be considered a contradiction, but instead should serve as a reminder of just how important one individual can be in changing the current of thought.

Source: David Kelly, Critical Essay on "Hymn to Beauty," in *Poetry for Students*, Thomson Gale, 2005.

Kathryn Oliver Mills

In the following essay, Mills discusses Baudelaire's wide body of work and the impact he has made on later writers.

Charles Baudelaire is one of the most compelling poets of the nineteenth century. While Baudelaire's contemporary Victor Hugo is generally—and sometimes regretfully—acknowledged as the greatest of nineteenth-century French poets, Baudelaire excels in his unprecedented expression of a complex sensibility and of modern themes within structures of classical rigor and technical artistry. Baudelaire is distinctive in French literature also in that his skills as a prose writer virtually equal his ability as a poet. His body of work includes a novella, influential translations of the American writer Edgar Allan Poe, highly perceptive criticism of contemporary art, provocative journal entries, and critical essays on a variety of subjects. Baudelaire's work has had a tremendous influence on modernism, and his relatively slim production of poetry in particular has had a significant impact on later poets. More than a talent of nineteenth-century France, Baudelaire is one of the major figures in the literary history of the world.

The extent of the influence of Baudelaire's family background on his life and work has been the subject of some interest to critics. In his life-story there are classic ingredients for neurosis, and his adult life was shaped by a triangle of family relations that some believe explains his complicated psyche. Baudelaire's father, François Baudelaire (1759–1827), came from a family of woodworkers, winegrowers, farm laborers, and craftsmen who had lived near the Argonne forest since the seventeenth

"More than a talent of nineteenth-century France, Baudelaire is one of the major figures in the literary history of the world."

century. He went to Paris on a scholarship and in the course of a long career there became a priest; worked as a tutor for the children of Count Antoine de Choiseul-Praslin, even composing a manual to teach Latin; resigned his priesthood during the Reign of Terror; married Rosalie Janin, a painter, and had a son, Alphonse Baudelaire (1805–1862); earned a living as a painter; and from the age of thirty-eight until retirement worked his way up the ranks of the civil service.

François Baudelaire was sixty when he married the twenty-six-year-old Caroline Dufayis (1793–1871) in 1819; Charles was their only child, born in Paris on 9 April 1821. Caroline was an orphan: her mother, who came from a family of solicitors from the same part of France as the Baudelaires, died in England, where she had emigrated for unknown reasons; little is known about Caroline's father except that his name was Charles Dufayis and that he was supposed to have died in July 1795 at Quiberon Bay in southern Brittany when Revolutionary forces put down a peasant revolt aided by émigrés. It is not known whether or not the difference in his parents' ages affected their son, but Baudelaire was just six when his father died, so he had no opportunity to know his father well. The death of François Baudelaire, though, set the scene for several major dramas in Baudelaire's life: his inheritance at twenty-one of a respectable fortune; the establishment of a board of guardians that was to control Baudelaire's financial fortunes for most of his adult life; and the remarriage of his mother to Jacques Aupick, a man with whom Baudelaire could not get along.

Aupick (1779?–1857), like Caroline Dufayis, was an orphan. His father was an Irishman who died in the military service in France; his mother, who might or might not have been his father's legal wife, died shortly afterward. The young Aupick made his way successfully in the military: with no real family advantages, he was a general by the end of his life, and he had served as the head of the Ecole Polytechnique (Polytechnic School) in Paris, as ambassador to Constantinople as well as to Spain, and as a senator. Caroline Dufayis Baudelaire met Aupick at the beginning of 1828, a year into her widowhood, and they were married rather precipitously on 8 November 1828, probably because of the stillborn child born a month later. Aupick was transferred to Lyon in December 1831, and in January 1836 he was transferred back to Paris, where he stayed until 1848, when he was sent as a diplomat to Constantinople.

It is understandable that Baudelaire might be jealous of his mother's new husband, as he was deeply attached to his mother both materially and emotionally. Their close relationship was of enduring significance, for during the course of his life he borrowed from his mother an estimated total of 20,473 francs and much of what is known of his later life comes from his extended correspondence with her. Although quite possibly Baudelaire's attachment to his mother did lead to his resentment and dislike of his stepfather, it is interesting to note that he did not manifest resentment early on. As a schoolboy in Lyons from 1832 to 1836 Baudelaire's letters to his parents were mostly affectionate and he referred to Aupick as his father. Easy relations within the family persisted through Baudelaire's high-school years at Louis-le-Grand in Paris, where Colonel Aupick had been transferred. Far from being "maudit" (cursed) in the tradition of his later legend, Baudelaire was actually a prize student of whom both parents were proud. Even when he was expelled from Louis-le-Grand in 1839 for refusing to give up a note passed him by a classmate, stepfather and stepson appeared to be on good terms.

Baudelaire began referring to his stepfather as "the General" (Aupick had been promoted in 1839) in 1841, around the time his family contrived to send the young man on a voyage to the Indian Ocean. After passing the "bac," or *baccalauréat* (high-school degree), in 1839, several months after his expulsion from the lycée, Baudelaire spent two years in the Latin Quarter pursuing a literary career and, of particular concern to Aupick, accumulating debts. To save Baudelaire from his debts, a family council was called in which it was decided to send him on a long voyage in June of 1841, paid for from his future inheritance (the parents later agreed to pay for it themselves as a gesture of goodwill). Baudelaire did not want to go, and in fact he jumped ship at the Ile Bourbon, returning to Paris in February of 1842. If the stiff forms of address in his letters of this time are any indication, Baudelaire resented his family's intervention in his way of life and held his stepfather responsible for it.

Familial censure only became more institutionalized. By June of 1844 Baudelaire had spent nearly half of the capital of the 99,568 francs he had inherited two years before. The family decided that it was necessary to seek a *conseil judiciaire* (legal adviser) to protect the capital from Baudelaire, and on 21 September 1844 the court made Narcisse Désirée Ancelle, a lawyer, legally responsible for managing Baudelaire's fortune and for paying him his "allowance." The sum paid him was enough for a single young man to live on comfortably, but Baudelaire had expensive tastes and he was bitter about this intervention for the rest of his life. Relations among family members soured. Baudelaire could no longer bear to be around "the General" and there were long periods of time when Mme Aupick was not permitted to see her son. For the next fifteen years Baudelaire's letters to his mother are laced with reproach, affection, and requests for money, and it was only after her husband's death—in 1857, the year of the publication of *Les Fleurs du mal* (The Flowers of Evil)—that relations between mother and son began to improve.

Financial constraint, alienation, and complex emotions defined Baudelaire's life, and it is against this backdrop of complicated family relations that some of the best poetry in the French language was written. Though Baudelaire's interest in verse was manifest as early as his days in the lycée, his public emergence as a poet was slow and complicated by many sideline activities through the early 1850s.

Baudelaire began making literary connections as soon as he passed the bac, at the same time that he was amassing debts. From 1839 to 1841, while he was living in the Latin Quarter, he became associated with the École Normande (Norman School), a group of student-poets centered around Gustave Levavasseur, Philippe de Chennevières, and Ernest Prarond. None of these people became major poets, but they were involved in Baudelaire's first ventures with poetry. Prarond claims to have heard Baudelaire recite as early as 1842 some of the poems that were later published in *Les Fleurs du mal.* Baudelaire considered participating in a collective publication with Levavasseur, Prarond, and another person named Dozon. He withdrew his contribution, however, because Levavasseur wanted to correct the "idiosyncrasies" in his work. Baudelaire was never without literary acquaintances. His professional social activity continued throughout his life, and in the course of his literary career he became acquainted with writers such as Victor Hugo, Charles-Augustin Sainte-Beuve, and Théophile Gautier. As his rejection of Levavasseur's corrections suggested, though, Baudelaire—like the speakers in his poetry—was always an individual within the crowd.

Baudelaire's first publications of poetry were probably disguised, for reasons known only to himself. Eleven poems published between 1844 and 1847 in *L'Artiste* under the name of Privat d'Anglemont—another friend in Baudelaire's literary circle—have been attributed to Baudelaire, and in fact nine of these poems have been included in the definitive Pléiade edition of Baudelaire's collected works published 1975–1979. The first poem published under Baudelaire's own name appeared in *L'Artiste* on 25 May 1845; Baudelaire probably wrote the sonnet "A Une Dame Créole" (To a Creole Lady), which celebrates the "pale" and "hot" coloring of the lovely Mme Autard de Bragard, on his trip to the Indian Ocean. The poem is not a prodigious showing for someone who was already establishing a reputation for himself in Parisian circles as a poet, and Baudelaire's next official publication of verse did not take place until a full six years later, in 1851.

In *De quelques écrivains nouveaux* (On Some New Writers, 1852) Prarond described Baudelaire as a poet who had achieved a certain reputation without having published a verse. Although the statement was not technically accurate in 1852, it illustrates a facet of Baudelaire's reputation. Even though he had no record of solid achievements, Baudelaire, with his compelling personality, had the ability to impress others, and he was already deliberately cultivating his image with eccentric stories designed to shock and test his acquaintances. For example, he liked to recite to friends his poem "Nightmare," which features a man who witnesses the rape of his mistress by an entire army.

Early in his career Baudelaire's reputation was more solidly based on his nonpoetic publications. In 1847 he published his only novella, *La Fanfarlo*, an autobiographically based work that features a tortured hero named Samuel Cramer. He wrote a handful of essays and reviews for various journals, notably *Le Corsaire Satan*; these works including *Le Musée classique du bazar Bonne-Nouvelle* (The Classical Museum of the Bonne-Nouvelle Bazaar) and *Comment on paie ses dettes quand on du génie* (How to Pay Your Debts When You're a Genius)—were collected in *Curiosités esthétiques* (Esthetic Curiosities, 1868) as well as *L'Art romantique* (Romantic Art, 1868), the second and third volumes in the posthumously published *Oeuvres complètes* (Complete Works, 1868–1873). Baudelaire also wrote two of the *Salons* that contribute to his reputation as a discerning, sometimes prophetic, and often amusing critic. Although *Salon de 1845* (1845) went unnoticed by critics, the next year his *Salon de 1846* made a good impression on a small circle.

Although he does not develop an aesthetic theory in *Salon de 1845*, Baudelaire does launch his idea that heroism can exist in life's ordinary details. The essay notably displays a particularly charming feature of Baudelaire's critical writing: the sharp and colorful illustration of points. The works of one painter, for example, are witheringly dismissed: "chaque année les ramène avec leurs mêmes désespérantes perfections" (each year brings them back with the same depressing perfections); another painter's works, writes Baudelaire, recall the pictures of travel brochures and evoke a China "où le vent lui-même, dit H. Heine, prend un son comique en passant par les clochettes;—et où la nature et l'homme ne peuvent pas se regarder sans rire" (where the wind itself, says H. Heine, sounds comical as it blows through bells; and where nature and man cannot look at each other without laughing).

In the important *Salon de 1846* Baudelaire critiques particular artists and in a more general way lays the groundwork for the ideas about art that he continued to develop in his "Salon de 1859," first published in *Revue française* in June and July of that year, and up until his essay "Le Peintre de la vie moderne" (The Painter of Modern Life), which appeared in *Le Figaro* in November and December of 1863. As Baudelaire defines it in *Salon de 1846*, art represents an ideal for Baudelaire: "L'art est un bien infiniment précieux, un breuvage rafraîchissant et réchauffant, qui rétablit l'estomac et l'esprit dans l'équilibre naturel de l'idéal" (Art is an infinitely precious thing, a warming and refreshing drink which reestablishes stomach and spirit in the natural equilibrium of the ideal). Although art leads to an abstraction, "l'idéal," the references to stomach and drink indicate that for Baudelaire the ideal is built on concrete particulars. Indeed, as he goes on to explain in *Salon de 1846* "Ainsi l'idéal n'est pas cette chose vague, ce rêve ennuyeux et impalpable qui nage au plafond des académies; un idéal, c'est l'individu redressé par l'individu, reconstruit et rendu par le pinceau ou le ciseau à l'éclatante vérité de son harmonie native" (Thus the ideal is not the vague thing, that boring and intangible dream which swims on the ceilings of academies; an ideal is the individual taken up by the individual, reconstructed and returned by brush or scissors to the brilliant truth of its native harmony).

At the time he wrote *Salon de 1846* Baudelaire believed that romanticism represented the ideal, and he presents the painter Eugène Delacroix as the best artist in that tradition. Baudelaire, though, also articulates principles that later took him beyond romanticism to a more radical view of art. He propounds that beauty must contain the absolute and the particular, the eternal and the transitory, and in a section of *Salon de 1846* titled "De l'Héroïsme de la Vie Moderne," (The Heroism of Modern Life) he elaborates that the "particulier" can be found in contemporary and ordinary urban life: "Le spectacle de la vie élégante et des milliers d'existences flottantes qui circulent dans les souterrains d'une grande ville, —criminels et filles entretenues, —la *Gazette des Tribuneaux* et le *Moniteur* nous prouvent que nous n'avons qu'à ouvrir les yeux pour connaître notre héroïsme" (The spectacle of elegant life and of the thousands of existences which float in the underground of a big city—criminals and kept women—the *Gazette des Tribuneaux* and the *Moniteur* prove that we have only to open our eyes in order to recognize our heroism). Modern life as inspiration for art is an idea that Baudelaire develops in "Le Peintre de la vie moderne" with reference to the artist Constantin Guys. As Baudelaire observes in 1846, Delacroix works in the grand tradition, and a new tradition has not yet come into being.

Despite several halfhearted attempts to indulge his parents' desire for his settled employment, throughout the 1840s Baudelaire was committed to his vocation as a poet, and as an artist he did his best to absorb the "spectacle" of Parisian life by living the life of a bohemian and a dandy. After the naming of the *conseil judiciaire* he affirmed a new identity by changing his name to Baudelaire-Dufayis, adding his mother's maiden name to his father's family name (this gesture lasted until the Revolution of 1848). He was particular about his dress, and virtually every contemporary description of him describes his changing hairstyles, from flowing locks to a shaved head to short, clipped hair. Early in the decade he took up with Jeanne Duval, the mulatto mistress with whom he had a long and complicated affair; in the late 1840s he met Marie Daubrun, the second inspiration for the three love cycles of his poetry. He had already had a bout with gonorrhea by this time and had picked up syphilis, the disease that was probably the cause of his death. Baudelaire attempted suicide once, on 30 June 1845. He cultivated an interest in art and painting, which fueled his continued accumulation of debts—he was a generally unlucky but enthusiastic collector. He began a pattern of moving from hotel to hotel to escape creditors and was well acquainted with the seamy side of Paris, a familiarity that is evident in his poems.

The year 1848 marked the beginning of a strange period in Baudelaire's life, one that does not quite fit with his life as a dandy, and which he himself later labeled "Mon ivresse de 1848" (My frenzy in 1848) in his *Journaux intimes* (Intimate Journals, 1909). Baudelaire—the product of a bourgeois household, the elitist poet of refined and elegant dress, the man who in the 1850s embraced Count Joseph de Maistre, an ultra-royalist aristocrat, and who had already expressed admiration for the aristocratic views of Edgar Allan Poe—participated in the French Revolution of 1848 that lead to the overthrow of the constitutional monarchy.

As Richard Burton documents extensively in *Baudelaire and the Second Republic: Writing and Revolution* (1988), Baudelaire did have strong revolutionary sympathies during this period. He was influenced by thinkers such as François Marie Charles Fourier, Félicité Lamennais, and Emanuel Swedenborg. His dedication of *Salon de 1846* to the "bourgeois" may well have been intended as ironic. Baudelaire wrote a positive and approving preface for Pierre Dupont's *Chant des ouvriers* (Song of the Workers, 1851), which praises the working man. He sought out Pierre-Joseph Prudhon, one of the great writers and thinkers of the 1848 revolution. With Champfleury, a journalist, novelist, and theoretician of the realist movement, he started a short-lived revolutionary newspaper after the provisional government was established. Most dramatically, he physically participated in the revolutions of February and June, actually fighting on a barricade and, according to some contemporaries' accounts, apparently shouting, "Il faut aller fusiller le général Aupick" (We must go shoot General Aupick").

Although a school of criticism has grown up in which Baudelaire is labeled a revolutionary, it would be a mistake to reduce the life and thought of this complex man to political dogma. Baudelaire was undeniably fervent, but this fervor must be seen in the spirit of the times: the nineteenth-century romantic leaned toward social justice because of the ideal of universal harmony but was not driven by the same impulse that fires the Marxist egalitarian. It is also possible, given Baudelaire's relationship with his stepfather and his famous cry on the barricades, that at least part of his zeal was motivated by personal feelings. Furthermore, even during this heady period Baudelaire never lost his critical acumen and spirit of contradiction. He rose repeatedly during speeches for the May 4 elections to interrupt idealistic speakers with pointed, embarrassing questions. In *Mon coeur mis à nu et Fusées; journaux intimes* (My Heart Laid Bare and Fusées; Intimate Journals, 1909) he elaborates on the "ivresse de 1848": "De quelle nature était cette ivresse? Goût de la vengeance. Plaisir *naturel* de la démolition (What was the nature of this drunkenness? A desire for vengeance. A *natural* pleasure in destruction).

After Louis-Napoleon Bonaparte's *coup d'état* in 1851, Baudelaire ceased all political activity. To the extent that he considered politics in his later years, his outlook was anti-egalitarian and anti-activist—reminiscent of the aristrocratic conservatism represented by Poe and de Maistre, in other words: "There is no form of rational and assured government save an aristocracy.... A monarchy or a republic based upon democracy are equally absurd and feeble." For the most part, though, Baudelaire's *Intimate Journals* reveal his relative lack of interest in politics, his disillusionment with mankind and all of its institutions, and his ultimate faith in the classless aristocracy of the "Dandy."

After a long period of incubation, of familial reproaches that he had wasted his life, and of a reputation based on potential, a few publications, and force of personality, Baudelaire came into his own as a literary personage in the 1850s. On 9 April 1851 eleven poems were published in the *Messager de l'Assemblée* under the title "Les Limbes" (Limbo); these poems were later included in *Les Fleurs du mal.* In March and April 1852 Baudelaire's first major study of Poe was published in *Revue de Paris.* In "Edgar Allan Poe, sa vie et ses ouvrages" (Edgar Allan Poe, His Life and His Works) Baudelaire notes views that were probably influenced by de Maistre as well as brought out by Poe: belief in original sin; faith in the imagination, which Baudelaire called "la reine des facultés" (the queen of faculties); approval of the cult of Beauty and of poetry for its own sake; and hatred for progress and nature.

In 1854 and 1855 Baudelaire's first translations of Poe's writings were published in *Le Pays.* A meticulous translator, Baudelaire was known to hunt down English-speaking sailors for maritime vocabulary. His translations of Poe culminated in *Histoires extraordinaires* (1856; Tales of Mystery and Imagination), which included "Edgar Allan Poe, sa vie et ses ouvrages" as a preface; *Nouvelles Histoires extraordinaires* (1856; New Tales of Mystery and Imagination); *Aventures d'Arthur Gordon Pym* (1858; originally published as *The Narrative of Arthur Gordon Pym*, 1838); *Eureka* (1863; originally published 1848); and *Histoires grotesques et sérieuses* (1865; originally published as *Tales of Grotesque and Arabesque*, 1840).

Also in 1855 the *Revue des deux mondes* published eighteen poems with the title of *Les Fleurs du mal.* Two of Baudelaire's prose poems were published for the first time that same year in a festschrift, "Hommage à C. F. Denecourt." The festschrift publication is particularly interesting because the prose poems were published alongside two poems in verse, so that "Crépuscule du Soir" (Dusk) appeared in verse and in prose.

In June of 1857 the first edition of *Les Fleurs du mal* was published by the fine letter press of Auguste Poulet-Malassis. Although Baudelaire considered publishing *Les Fleurs du mal* with the large printing house of Michel Lévy, which published his translations of Poe, he chose the smaller press of Poulet-Malassis out of a concern for quality. A tyrannical author, Baudelaire took rooms near the offices of his publishers so that he could better supervise the placement of every comma. The press was solicitous of Baudelaire's corrections, and Poulet-Malassis became a devoted friend: he lent Baudelaire large sums of money though he himself eventually went bankrupt and to debtor's prison for his own debts; he tended to Baudelaire during his last days in Brussels, though the writer had signed over Poulet-Malassis's legal rights on some works to the publisher Hetzel; and when on his deathbed Baudelaire chose Lévy to publish his *Oeuvres complètes*, Poulet-Malassis loyally rallied to the cause, ceding his legally exclusive rights to Baudelaire's works and doing what he could to help produce a satisfactory edition.

About one month after *Les Fleurs du mal* went on sale in July 1857, a report was drawn up by the Sûreté Publique (Public Safety) section of the Ministry of the Interior stating that the collection was in contempt of the laws that safeguard religion and morality. Thirteen poems were singled out and put on trial. In contrast with the last time he went to court, when he acquiesced to the imposition of a *conseil judiciaire*, Baudelaire fought this battle to the last. The proceeding betrays some of the misunderstandings that have infected views of his poetry ever since.

To intercede with the government on his behalf Baudelaire made the unfortunate choice of Aglaé

Sabatier, "la Présidente," a woman to whom he had been sending anonymous and admiring poems since 1852. The third muse for the trilogy of love cycles in *Les Fleurs du mal*, "Apollonie" (as she was also known) was without great political influence, and her dubious social standing probably did not lend credibility to Baudelaire's claims for morality. Baudelaire's defense at the trial was threefold: that he had presented vice in such a way as to render it repellent to the reader; that if the poems are read as part of the larger collection, in a certain order, their moral context is revealed; and that his predecessors—Alfred de Musset, Pierre-Jean Béranger, George Sand, Honoré de Balzac—had written far more scandalously and gotten away with it. Baudelaire's lawyer unwisely emphasized the last point, which was easily dismissed: that others have gotten away with transgression does not justify one's own. Six of the poems were condemned—the ban on them was not lifted until after World War II, on 31 May 1949—and both Baudelaire and his editors were fined.

Though the trial was an ordeal and certainly did not help improve the poet's relations with his mother (General Aupick was dead by this time), the trial was not ultimately detrimental to Baudelaire. The condemned poems were excised, and the book went back on sale. Baudelaire subsequently achieved a certain notoriety, for better and for worse. For the better, *Les Fleurs du mal* got good reviews from critics that counted. Emile Deschamps, a founding father of 1830s romanticism, published a poem in praise of the collection in *Le Présent*. Gustave Flaubert, who had endured a similar trial for *Madame Bovary* (1857), wrote to Baudelaire on 13 July 1858 that "Vous avez trouvé moyen de rajeunir le romantisme. Vous ne ressemblez à personne (ce qui est la première de toutes les qualités). . . . Vous êtes résistant comme le marbre et pénétrant comme un brouillard d'Angleterre" (You have found a way to inject new life into Romanticism. You are unlike anyone else [which is the most important quality]. . . . You are as resistant as marble and as penetrating as an English fog). On 30 August 1887 Hugo wrote to Baudelaire that his flowers of evil were as "radiant" and "dazzling" as stars. In contrast, the influential Sainte-Beuve maintained a significant silence. There were many negative reviews by lesser critics, but none that affected Baudelaire's reputation.

For the worse, Baudelaire's legend as a *poète maudit* (cursed poet) exploded at this time, and Baudelaire, as always, contributed to this reputation by shocking people with elaborate eccentricities. He invited people over to see riding breeches supposedly cut from his father's hide, for example, or in the middle of a conversation casually asked a friend, "Wouldn't it be agreeable to take a bath with me?" It is difficult to sort out which stories about Baudelaire are true and which are fictive—later on someone apparently thought that Baudelaire had actually gotten unreasonably angry with a poor window-glazier, misconstruing the prose poem "Le Mauvais Vitrier" (The Bad Glazier) as reality. Baudelaire's legend as a *poète maudit* obscured his profound complexity, and Charles Asselineau's preface to *Charles Baudelaire, sa vie et son oeuvre* (Charles Baudelaire, His Life and Work, 1869), the first biography of the poet, only sealed his notorious image by passing on the more infamous anecdotes.

Another effect of the condemnation of *Les Fleurs du mal* is that the excision of six poems probably prompted Baudelaire to write the new and wonderful poems published in the collection's second edition of 1861. After the trial he experienced a surge of creative activity. In *Baudelaire in 1859* (1988) Burton posits that this rebirth of energy had to do with a reconciliation with his mother. General Aupick had died in April of 1857, and in 1858 Baudelaire switched from the formal *vous* to the more intimate *tu* in addressing his mother. He wrote several of the important poems in the second edition—including "Le Voyage" (The Voyage) and "La Chevelure" (The Head of Hair)—in 1859, during a long stay at Honfleur in the "Maison Joujou" (Playhouse) of his mother. Whatever the reason for this literary activity, Baudelaire wrote thirty-five new poems between 1857 and 1861, adding "Tableaux Parisiens" to the already existing sections of *Les Fleurs du mal* and creating more or less the definitive version of the collection.

Baudelaire's only collection of verse is composed of six sections: "Spleen et Idéal" (Spleen and the Ideal), "Tableaux Parisiens" (Parisian Tableaus), "Le Vin" (Wine), "Fleurs du mal" (Flowers of Evil), "Révolte" (Revolt), and "La Mort" (Death). In the trial of his poems Baudelaire had argued that there was an "architecture" that organized the meaning of his work, and this organizing principle has been the subject of debate among critics. There is certainly a progression from "Au lecteur" (To the Reader), the poem that serves as the frontispiece, to "Le Voyage," the final poem.

"Au lecteur" invites the reader into the collection by portraying regretful yet irresistible corruption and ennui while forcing the reader into complicity with its well-known conclusion: "—Hypocrite lecteur, —mon semblable, —mon frère!" (Hypocritical reader, my mirror-image, my brother!). Intervening poems explore various facets of the poet's experience, many of which represent struggles with what Blaise Pascal called the "gouffre" (the abyss). "Le Voyage" surveys the disappointed hopes of speakers who have traveled far and wide only to find what "Au lecteur" had promised, "Une oasis d'horreur dans un désert d'ennui" (An oasis of horror in a desert of tedium). The final cry of this poem, "Nous voulons . . . / Plonger . . . / Au fond de l'Inconnu pour trouver du *nouveau*" (We want . . . / To plunge . . . / To the bottom of the Unknown in order to find *something new*), is addressed to death and is ambiguous: it either launches the collection's journey on a new course from that set in "Au lecteur," thus possibly concluding *Les Fleurs du mal* on a note of optimism, or it ends the poem's quest in death. In either case, there is clearly a movement toward closure, and perhaps resolution, in *Les Fleurs du mal.* Reading the poems by following too rigorous a system would do injustice to them, however. Although there is a general sense of progression in *Les Fleurs du mal*, individual works do not always fit the pattern assigned to their part in the collection.

In similar fashion, though Baudelaire's legend glossed him as the satanic poet of ennui, sordid details, and forbidden sensuality, in fact his poetry treats a variety of themes with a range of perspectives. He does deal with topics that fueled his scandalous reputation. As "Au lecteur" promised, the collection is dominated by the poet's Catholic sense of original sin. "Le Mauvais Moine" (The Bad Monk), in the section "Spleen et Idéal," describes the poet as a "mauvais cénobite" (a bad monk) who is trapped in the "odious" grave of his soul. Redemption, given this situation, appears hopeless: "Ô moine fainéant! Quand saurai-je donc faire / Du spectacle vivant de ma triste misère / Le travail de mes mains et l'amour de mes yeux? (O lazy monk! When will I ever know how to turn / the living spectacle of my sad misery / into the work of my hands and love of my eyes?) Many poems echo this expression of futility for man's spiritual condition, especially in "Spleen et Idéal" and notably in the four "Spleen" poems (LXXV, LXXVI, LXXVII, LXXVIII) within that section. While some poems end without hope, however—"Spleen LXXVIII" concludes with "atrocious" Anxiety staking the poet's skull with a black flag—others betray the desire to break out of imprisonment in sin. "Le Mauvais Moine" concludes by expressing that wish ("When will I ever know how . . . ?"), though it is in the tenuous form of a question.

For Baudelaire, the love of Beauty and sensual love are two specific examples of man's capacity for original sin. In *Les Fleurs du mal* Beauty is a compelling but often terrible phenomenon described in terms of hard, lifeless matter. Even the woman of "Le Serpent qui danse" (The Snake Which Dances), a poem about movement, has eyes that are "deux bijoux froids où se mêle / L'or avec le fer" (two cold jewels where / Gold mixes with iron), and Beauty of "La Beauté" (Beauty) is like "un rêve de pierre" (a dream of stone) that inspires love "éternel et muet ainsi que la matière" (as eternal and mute as matter). The power of this inhuman Beauty is terrible. "La Beauté" reduces the poet to a "docile" lover who is virtually chained to his idol. "Hymne à la Beauté" (Hymn to Beauty) concludes with the same helpless devotion to Beauty's powers of distraction and more explicitly articulates Beauty's dual nature: her look is "infernal et divin" (infernal and divine), and the poet is so addicted that he does not care whether She comes from Heaven, Hell, or both.

Baudelaire does not just treat Beauty as an abstract phenomenon; he also writes about individual women. Baudelaire's three love cycles reflect his experiences with three different women—Duval, Daubrun, and Mme Sabatier—and discussions of his love poems are often organized around the poems associated with each woman. It is not always clear, however, which poems are associated with whom.

Jeanne Duval was a mulatto and a sometime actress who, according to Baudelaire, did not understand and in fact undermined his poetry and whose attraction was powerfully physical. Baudelaire met Duval in the early 1840s and lived with her periodically, but by the late 1840s he was writing to his mother that life with her had become a duty and a torment. Nonetheless, it was not until 1856 that they broke up; the rupture was at her instigation, and even afterward Baudelaire continued to support her financially: as usual, his was not the conventional response to a situation.

Baudelaire's relations with Marie Daubrun were less extended. She was a blonde, Rubenesque actress who seems never seriously to have reciprocated Baudelaire's fascination for her. Baudelaire had met her in the late 1840s or early 1850s but probably did not become intimately involved with her until around 1854. Their sporadic connection ended when Marie left Baudelaire to go back to Théodore de Banville.

Apollonie Sabatier represented a different sort of attraction from that of Jeanne and Marie.

"La Présidente" had been a model and the mistress of various men, one of whom left her a stipend that secured her independence. Her position as an independent woman who had a history with men placed her in the demimonde, the "half-world" that is neither part of "le monde," the world of social acceptability and prominence, nor part of the underworld of prostitutes. She was much admired as a tasteful, witty, intelligent woman, and her social evenings were attended by artists such as Théophile Gautier, Maxime Du Camp, Ernest Feydeau, and Flaubert. Baudelaire's feelings for Mme Sabatier started as admiration from afar: he sent her anonymous letters accompanied by poems. Eventually he revealed his identity to her. When she finally responded to him, however, he dropped her with a letter in which he tells her that her capitulation, whether it was physical or emotional, had turned her from a Goddess into "a mere woman." Despite the direct stares of Nadar's famous photographs, Baudelaire's was a complex personality. On the one hand he experienced animal love and a sense of duty with Jeanne; on the other hand he felt platonic love for Mme Sabatier and yet he betrayed her. His relations with women were far from entirely pleasant.

Baudelaire's complicated experiences with these women and with others undoubtedly shaped his poetry about them. Some readers view Baudelaire as a mere sensualist and in some poems he certainly does celebrate the sensuality of women, of scent, and of sensation, but it is important to note that his poetic descriptions of women are multidimensional. Although there are extremely sensual poems, such as "Parfum Exotique" (Exotic Perfume), "La Chevelure" (The Head of Hair), and "L'Invitation au Voyage" (Invitation to a Voyage), Baudelaire also wrote poems, such as those dedicated to Beauty, in which a woman is admired as a hopelessly unattainable object of art—"Je t'adore à l'égal de la voûte nocturne" (I Adore You as the Vaulted Night Is High), for example, or "Avec ses vêtements ondoyants et nacrés" (With Her Undulating and Pearly Garments).

Indeed, contrary to the stereotype of Baudelaire as a lustful idolater, in many of his sensual poems he alchemizes the physical elements of the woman into an ethereal substance. The ultimate importance of "la chevelure" is as a source of memories, and in "Parfum Exotique" the initial scent of the woman's breast becomes the exotic perfume of an imaginary island. When Baudelaire idolizes the woman as a form of art, similarly, by the end of most poems the woman's body is conspicuous by its removal. In "Je t'adore à l'égal de la voûte nocturne" the speaker tells the woman that he loves her "d'autant plus, belle, que tu me fuis" (all the more, beautiful one, when you flee me). The image of "la froide majesté d'une femme stérile" (the cold majesty of a sterile woman) in "Avec ses vêtements ondoyants et nacrés" does not invite embraces.

For Baudelaire, as for the English metaphysical poets, the human struggle starts with the flesh but ultimately takes place on the metaphysical plane. Woman, on this level, represents good or evil. Some poems portray the woman as demonic, in the tradition of "Hymne à la Beauté." In "Sed non Satiata" (But she is Not Satisfied), the speaker cries to the woman: "Ô démon sans pitié! verse-moi moins de flamme" (O pitiless demon! Throw me less fire). "Le Vampire" (The Vampire) is about the symbiosis of the vampire woman and the enslaved poet. Other poems—these are usually the ones associated with Mme Sabatier—represent the woman as a redemptive angel against a somber background. The play between light and dark in these poems ranges from the simple to the complex. In "Reversibilité" (Reversibility) there is a simple counterpoint between the "Ange plein de bonheur, de joie et de lumières" (Angel full of happiness, of joy, and of lights) and the tortured speaker. A more complex interplay between light and dark occurs in "Aube Spirituelle" (Spiritual Dawn) when the monstrance-like memory of the woman shines against a backdrop of the sun drowning in its congealing blood. Such complexity is again evident in "Confession," when the "aimable et douce femme" (amiable and sweet woman) confesses her "horrible" lack of faith in humanity.

Behind Baudelaire's struggles with sin and ennui is an articulated awareness of Satan, notably in the section "Révolte." "Le Reniement de Saint Pierre" (St. Peter's Denial) concludes with the speaker congratulating Peter for denying Jesus. In "Abel et Caïn" the narrative voice urges Cain to ascend to heaven and throw God to earth. "Les Litanies de Satan" (The Litanies of Satan) is addressed to Satan and has the refrain "Ô Satan, prends pitié de ma triste misère!" (O Satan, have pity on my sad misery!). These are strong poems, understandably shocking to the readers of his day, but Baudelaire's struggles with evil do not ally him with Satan. In his poetry Baudelaire represents himself as trapped and cries out in a despair that suggests his awareness of sin as a burden. Baudelaire is not a diabolic preacher; with C. S. Lewis, he would point out that Satan is part of the Christian cosmology.

Baudelaire's "Doctrine of Correspondences" suggests a belief of sorts in a pattern for the world and in relationships between the physical world and a spiritual one. This view, probably influenced by Emanuel Swedenborg and viewed as an antecedent to symbolism, is presented in the poem "Correspondances." Nature is presented as a "temple" whose living pillars speak to man and whose "forest of symbols" (forêt de symboles) observe him. Baudelaire writes that "Les parfums, les couleurs, et les sons se répondent" (Perfumes, colors, and sounds interact with each other) like echoes in a "ténébreuse et profonde unité" (dark and deep unity). Although he does not include a direct expression of faith in God or gods in the poem, Baudelaire's profoundly mystical belief in the world's fundamental unity is clear. "Correspondances" epitomizes Baudelaire's complicated spirituality.

Indeed, the subject of Baudelaire's faith has been much debated. The references to God and to Satan in his poems, letters, and intimate journals have been counted; the validity of his last rites has been weighed; his confession of faith to Nadar has been examined. Most critics agree that Baudelaire's preoccupations are fundamentally Christian but that in *Les Fleurs du mal* he fails to embrace entirely Jesus Christ and his power of redemption. Debates about Baudelaire's Christianity have not resolved the matter, though, nor is a label for Baudelaire's faith necessarily desirable for reading his poetry. *Les Fleurs du mal* is best read on its own terms, with a respect for its complexity. The constant thrust of the collection is to impart to the reader an awareness of tension between the physically real and the spiritually ideal, of a hopeless but ever-renewed aspiration toward the infinite from an existence mired in sin on earth. This thrust is evident in poems in which the speaker bemoans enslavement to the soul's "gouffre" (abyss) or to Beauty's fascinations, in which he cries out to Satan in rage, in which he delves into the sensual to escape the physical world, and in which he articulates a feeble hope in love's redemptive capacity and the possibility of unity.

Baudelaire's ambiguous relationship with the material world and his desire for another world are evident in his poems about the city of Paris. While some critics, notably Edward Kaplan, have argued that "Tableaux Parisiens," the section added to the edition of 1861, shows a "conversion to the real world as it exists," critics such as F. W. Leakey have pointed out that in these poems Baudelaire treats the city the way he treats the female body in "Je t'adore à l'égal de la voûte nocturne," that is, by moving away from it as a physical presence. "Paysage" (Landscape) invokes concrete details of Paris—"Les tuyaux, les clochers, ces mâts de la cité" (the pipes, the bells, the masts of the city)—but the poem concludes with the poet behind closed shutters, his head on his desk, resolving to make "de mes pensers brûlants une tiède atmosphère" (a warm atmosphere from my burning thoughts).

In "Le Soleil" (The Sun) the poet walks the streets of Paris, but he appears to see the city as a literary text rather than on its physical terms. He goes "Flairant dans tous les coins les hasards de la rime, / Trébuchant sur les mots comme sur les pavés" (Seeking out the hazards of rhyme in all corners / Stumbling on words as on cobblestones). "Le Cygne" (The Swan) is a magnificent poem that records the changes wrought in Paris by the Baron Georges-Eugène Haussmann. Although he accumulates concrete details, Baudelaire again removes himself from the physical presence he is recording by recasting what he sees: "Je ne vois qu'en esprit tout ce camp de baraques . . ." (I see all these barracks . . . only in spirit) and "tout pour moi devient allégorie" (everything becomes an allegory for me). Baudelaire's reputation as the father of modern poetry about cities is largely based on the "Tableaux Parisiens," which describe the streets of Paris in such gritty detail; the importance of these street scenes for the poet, though, is that he usually plunges into them with the desire to transcend them.

Baudelaire's theory of correspondences and his introduction of such topics as the city and the ugly side of man's nature to poetry in verse are responsible for the modern quality of *Les Fleurs du mal*. Baudelaire also deals with a variety of themes in the Romantic tradition, however, including solitude; the *mal de siècle*, which in Baudelaire's terms becomes ennui; the special plight of the poet; introspection; yearnings for the infinite; and romance. Furthermore, Baudelaire's prosody is traditional: his alexandrines are no more loosened than those of the Romantics, and he uses a wide variety of classical forms.

Even in his treatment of Romantic themes, however, Baudelaire is radical for his time. He imagines solitude not as a state of nature but as it happens in cities, presenting it in counterpoint to city crowds. The person who experiences ennui, as opposed to *mal de siècle*, is mercilessly self-aware and is troubled by original sin and a divided self. For Baudelaire the poet is endowed with special powers but is also a clumsy albatross ("L'Albatros") or slothful sinner ("Le Mauvais Moine"). No longer mournful meditation in picturesque settings, introspection turns ugly with Baudelaire, a guilty pleasure to be squeezed like "une vieille orange" (an old orange), as Baudelaire asserts in "Au Lecteur." The infinite is no longer the divine perceived in stars; it is found in the expansiveness of scents, in the imagination, in poetry, in cold-hearted Beauty, in the desire to escape.

To traditional forms and traditional themes Baudelaire brought imagery and situations that had never before existed in French poetry. "Une Charogne" (A Cadaver) provides an excellent example of how Baudelaire uses Romantic and even classical themes to go beyond them. The poet takes a walk with his beloved and concludes that, although time passes, his poetry will immortalize her. Unlike Pierre de Ronsard's poem on that classical theme, "Quand tu seras bien vielle" (When You Are Very Old), however, Baudelaire's meditation is prompted by a human cadaver whose guts spill across the page, the poem graphically detailing the flies, vermin, and stink. The speaker instructs his beloved that when she, too, is a rotting corpse, she should tell the vermin—who will eat her with kisses—that "j'ai gardé la forme et l'essence divine / De mes amours décomposés!" (I have maintained the form and divine essence / Of my decomposed loves!). Just as he exploits grotesque physical details only to extract from them an "essence divine," so Baudelaire uses poetic convention while transforming it.

Similarly, Baudelaire's use and mastery of traditional technique revolutionized French poetry by so clearly representing a unique sensibility. In "Le Cygne," a poem detailing the poet's thoughts as he walks through a changing Paris, Baudelaire sensitively communicates modern anxiety and a modern sense of displacement. The poem begins with an abrupt exclamation, "Andromaque, je pense à vous!" (Andromache, I am thinking of you!). A series of repetitions compounds the initial sense of urgency. The frequent recurrence of the verb *je pense à* (I am thinking about), though, also indicates the meditative nature of the poem; the repetition of words such as *là* (there)—along with a myriad of sharp descriptions—show that meditation interacts with the speaker's close observations. Syntax broken across stanzas conveys the reach of the poet's thoughts and observations as well as a sense of breathless haste.

The speaker returns to the same thoughts—notably, a swan escaped from a zoo and Andromache, the wife of the Trojan hero Hector—and the use of exclamation points is heavy: he is obsessed and slightly frantic. The gist of the speaker's meditations is that he is haunted by absences: by Paris as it is no longer, by the swan who has lost his native soil, by Andromache's losses. Those absences are present in this poem by virtue of Baudelaire's prosody. Andromache's fall into destitution is represented in the space caused by the enjambment between stanzas: "... et puis [je pense] à vous / Andromaque, des bras d'un grand époux tombée" (And I think of you, / Andromache, fallen from the arms of a great husband). The lament of all who have suffered losses is emphasized by an enjambment that forces a quick draw of breath right before the end of the sentence and that accents the finality of "jamais" (never) at the beginning of the next sentence:

> "Je pense . . .
> . . . .
> À quiconque a perdu ce qui ne se retrouve
> Jamais, jamais!"
> (I think . . .
> . . . .
> Of whomever has lost that which can
> Never, never be found again!).

In *Les Fleurs du mal* traditional prosody and themes combine with novel thoughts and inspiration to create works of supreme originality.

Although there were not many reviews of the second edition of *Les Fleurs du mal* and not all of those published were favorable, Baudelaire became an established poet with its publication. Saint-Beuve—though he never did review *Les Fleurs du mal*—ranked him grudgingly among the leaders of a new generation of poets as he remarked that poets coming along seemed to be in the style of Hugo, Gautier, Banville, and "even Baudelaire." Younger poets started to dedicate poems to Baudelaire. Charles Asselineau in *Charles Baudelaire: Sa vie et son oeuvre* (1869) describes Baudelaire as accepted and blossoming with success after 1861. On the strength of that success, in fact, Baudelaire attempted an application to the Académie Française in 1861, seeking—many thought ironically—the place of Henri Lacordaire, a Roman Catholic priest. The taint of the trial and of his reputation was too strong, though, and Baudelaire thought it prudent to let his candidacy drop before he met with certain failure.

In the 1860s Baudelaire diversified from poetry in verse to literary activity in several different spheres. He wrote *Les Paradis artificiels, Opium et Haschisch* (The Artificial Paradise, Opium and Hashish, 1860), in which he resumes the interest in drugs that he had first explored in 1851 with *Du Vin et du haschisch* (On Wine and Hashish), an article published in *Le Messager del'Assemblée*. He also wrote seven articles for Jacques Crépet's *Les*

Poètes Français (French Poets, 1862), including pieces on Hugo, Gautier, and Marceline Desbordes-Valmore. These essays were published later along with others in *Curiosités esthétiques* . The note on Baudelaire in Crépet's volume, written by Gautier, was fairly positive. This anthology established contact between Baudelaire and his first major biographer, Crépet.

Baudelaire also continued with essay projects on topics of miscellaneous artistic interest, for example, the expression of his admiration for Wagner in 1861, *Richard Wagner et "Tannhäuser" à Paris*, and a valedictory tribute to Delacroix in 1863. The most significant of these essays was his definitive article on modern art. Around 1859 Baudelaire met the sketch artist Constantin Guys and began writing "Le Peintre de la vie moderne" (The Painter of Modern Life). This essay, ultimately published in *Le Figaro* in 1863, brings to fruition his ideas about "l'héroïsme de la vie moderne" (the heroism of modern life) first expressed in *Salon de 1845* and *Salon de 1846*. Where in the *Salon de 1846* Baudelaire discusses the duality of art in general terms, in "Le Peintre de la vie moderne" that duality specifically defines art's modernity: "La modernité, c'est le transitoire, le fugitif, le contingent, la moitié de l'art, dont l'autre moitié est l'éternel et l'immuable" (Modernity is the transitory, the fugitive, the contingent, half of art, the other half of which is eternal and immutable). Art is composed of the eternal and the contingent; modernity which can occur in every historic era—is a function of finite particulars "qui sera, si l'on veut, tour à tour ou tout ensemble, l'époque, la mode, la morale, la passion" (which, if you like, will be one by one or simultaneously the era, fashion, morals, passion). Baudelaire illustrates these principles by discussing in detail the interests and techniques of "CG," his designation for the artist who wished to remain anonymous, from his brush stroke to his Crimean War drawings for the *Illustrated London News*.

Central to Baudelaire's estimation of Guys is that Guys is not an artist but is, rather, a man of the world. For Baudelaire, a broad interest in the world as opposed to the restricted perspective that he associates with most "artistes" is crucial to interesting art. Along with this line of thought Baudelaire elaborates his notion of the dandy, who is not only the elegant dresser of usual associations but also a man of the world who lives according to the highest aesthetic principles. Baudelaire also develops his ideas about "la foule," the crowd, which is the solitary artist's domain "as water is for the fish." He devotes an entire section to the aspects of modern life that the true artist must absorb: military life, the dandy, cars, women, prostitutes, and even makeup.

In that last section, "Eloge du Maquillage" (In Praise of Makeup), Baudelaire makes explicit two more concepts that are important to his ethos. First, true to the metaphysical import of flesh already described in his poetry, Baudelaire makes it clear that for him there is a spiritual dimension to physical rituals: he speaks of "la haute spiritualité de la toilette" (the high spirituality of the toilet) and states that fashion must be considered "un symptôme du goût de l'idéal" (a symptom of a taste for the ideal). Second, as a corollary to the importance he attaches to fashion, makeup, and the codes of the dandy, Baudelaire touches on his unromantic distaste for the natural. Everything beautiful is beautiful by calculation, he opines. Art is necessary to correct the natural state of man, which on the physical level is unattractive and on the spiritual level is a state of original sin. By the early 1860s Baudelaire had found a model for his ideals in the person of Guys, and he gave full expression to his artistic aesthetic in "Le Peintre de la vie moderne."

Baudelaire continued with scattered publications of poetry in the 1860s. In 1862 he published twenty prose poems in *La Presse*. This landmark year marks a shift in his creative endeavors from poetry in verse to poetry in prose: thereafter most of his creative publications are prose poems. Baudelaire managed to write only fifty of the one hundred prose poems he had projected. These poems were posthumously collected in 1869 as *Petits poèmes en prose* (Little Poems in Prose) and published with *Les Paradis artificiels*; later they were published by the better known title *Le Spleen de Paris, petits poèmes en prose* (The Spleen of Paris, Little Poems in Prose, 1917). *Le Spleen de Paris* is, as Baudelaire would say, a "singular" assemblage of works that represents an extremely ambitious literary project. In his correspondence he refers to the prose poems as a "pendant" (a completion of) to *Les Fleurs du mal*. He explains in what senses *Le Spleen de Paris* completes *Les Fleurs du mal* when he articulates his ambitions for the prose poems in "A Arsène Houssaye," a letter that became the preface to the collection. Houssaye was the editor of *L'Artiste* and *La Presse*, which published some of the prose poems individually.

In "A Arsène Houssaye" Baudelaire is careful to point out that the main predecessor for the genre of prose poetry was Aloysius Bertrand's *Gaspard de la Nuit* (Gaspard of the Night, 1842), a relatively little-known work about gothic scenes in Paris. Bertrand did not label his short pieces "prose poems," though: Baudelaire is the first poet to make a radical break with the form of verse by identifying nonmetrical compositions as poetry. Baudelaire offered a tantalizing statement about his goals for the new form: "Quel est celui de nous qui n'a pas, dans ses jours d'ambition, rêvé le miracle d'une prose poétique, musicale sans rythme et sans rime, assez souple et assez heurtée pour s'adapter aux mouvements lyriques de l'âme, aux ondulations de la rêverie, aux soubresauts de la conscience?" (Who among us has not, in his days of ambition, dreamed the miracle of a poetic prose, musical without rhythm or rhyme, supple and agile enough to adapt to the lyrical movements of the soul, to the undulations of daydreams, to the leaps of consciousness?).

Having mastered the forms of traditional verse, Baudelaire wanted to do nothing less than create a new language. Unlike Bertrand's "picturesque" topics, Baudelaire associates his new language with the modern topic of the city. In "A Arsène Houssaye" he states that the ideal that obsesses him is born "surtout de la fréquentation des villes énormes, . . . du croisement de leurs innombrables rapports" (especially from frequenting large cities, . . . from the interconnection of their innumerable points of relationship). In contrast with the "architecture" of *Les Fleurs du mal*, these interconnections are presented without order. The work has "ni queue ni tête, puisque tout, au contraire, y est à la fois tête et queue, alternativement et réciproquement" (neither tail nor head because, on the contrary, everything is at once head and tail, alternately and reciprocally). *Le Spleen de Paris* is modern in that it represents a break with traditional form, is about urban life, and is consciously without order.

It is worth noting that in his preface Baudelaire refers to the form of the work as "prose lyrique." He does not in the collection refer to the works as poems in prose, and the title, *Le Spleen de Paris, petits poèmes en prose* was chosen after Baudelaire's death by editors and critics. It is true that critics chose this title from titles that Baudelaire considered in his correspondence, and that in his correspondence Baudelaire most often refers to his endeavours as "poèmes en prose." Among the most significant challenges posed by *Le Spleen de Paris*, though, are the questions surrounding its form: is this poetry? Did Baudelaire succeed in his ambition to forge a new poetic language? In her classic tome on prose poetry *Le Poème en prose du Baudelaire jusqu'à nos jours* (The Prose Poem from Baudelaire to the Present, 1959) Suzanne Bernard defined the important characteristics of the genre: "l'unité, la gratuité, la brièveté (unity, gratuitousness, and brevity). Most critics have tended to discuss the themes of the poems rather than their form, however, accepting poetry in Baudelaire's wake as an attitude rather than a set of rules. This collection, which has been growing in popularity among critics, still contains much to be explored.

Baudelaire's poems in prose are short anecdotes, bitter satires, and reveries about unusual topics, including dogs, mud, aged tumblers, windows, widows, and poor people standing outside fancy eating establishments. Several critics, notably Pierre Emmanuel, have noted that there is more compassion in these works than in Baudelaire's poetry in verse. This compassion can take strange forms—the speaker of "Les Yeux des pauvres" (The Eyes of the Poor) is so moved by a family of poor people that he hates the companion he had loved for her lack of sympathy. "Assommons les Pauvres" (Let's Knock Out the Poor) concludes with the speaker sharing his purse with a beggar, but it is after having beaten him like "cooks who want to tenderize a steak."

It is true, though, that whereas Baudelaire most often offers visions of beauty in *Les Fleurs du mal*, he commonly and sympathetically treats the poor in *Le Spleen de Paris*. In fact, the speaker in "Mademoiselle Bistouri" concludes by praying to God—as opposed to the devil—to have pity on crazy people. Furthermore, while many of the prose poems are about ugliness, they often accept and possibly even transcend ugliness. "Un cheval de race" (A Thoroughbred) is about a woman well past her prime who is "bien laide" (very ugly) but "délicieuse pourtant" (nonetheless beautiful). In "Perte d'auréole" (The Lost Halo) the speaker loses his "halo" in the mud, but concludes that he is better off without it and that the halo is actually much better suited to "some bad poet."

While the speaker in the poems of *Les Fleurs du mal* sought escape, in the prose poem "Déjà!" Baudelaire describes a speaker who had escaped on a boat which then returned to shore. At first he alone among the passengers is regretful, but in the last paragraph of the poem he celebrates "la terre avec ses bruits, ses passions, ses commodités, ses fêtes;" (earth with its sounds, its passions, its conveniences, its celebrations). As with *Les Fleurs du mal*, it would be a mistake to pigeonhole the poems in this collection, which unlike his first has no headings. There are some harsh, disturbing poems in *Le Spleen de Paris*—"Le Gâteau" (The Cake), for example, which is about a fratricidal war between two natives over a piece of cake. As critics have noticed from the very beginning, however, the prose poems address banalities and travails of life quite differently from *Les Fleurs du mal.*

It is not coincidental that Baudelaire's departure from traditional form and his exploring new themes occurred in chronological conjunction with "Le Peintre de la vie moderne." Certainly, Baudelaire's break with traditional notions of poetry had a far-reaching effect on subsequent poetry, from Authur Rimbaud's *Les Illuminations* (1886) to modernist experimentation with form. In fact, Henri Peyre, an eminent scholar of French poetry, argues in *Connaissance de Baudelaire* (1951) that *Le Spleen de Paris* has had a greater influence on poetry than *Les Fleurs du mal.* This conclusion is surprising because it is only relatively recently that Baudelaire's prose poetry has attracted critical attention, but few critics have disagreed with Peyre. *Le Spleen de Paris* undoubtedly has had a significant influence on modern poetry.

During the period in which he was seriously exploring prose poetry, Baudelaire experienced a series of financial disasters. He had sold his writings to Poulet-Malassis, who had gone bankrupt in 1862. *La Presse* stopped publishing his poetry in prose. He had signed over to Michel Lévy sole ownership for his translations of Poe for 2,000 francs, so he lost a regular income; furthermore, he could not get Lacroix and Verboeckhoven, another printing house based in Brussels, interested in his work. These circumstances led Baudelaire to travel to Brussels, where he hoped to earn money with a lecture series and to make contact with Victor Hugo's publisher, Lacroix et Verboeckhoven.

Baudelaire arrived in Brussels on 24 April 1864 and checked into the Hotel du Grand Miroir, where he stayed, enduring a miserable sojourn, until his stroke in 1866. His lecture series was a failure: he got less money for the lectures than he was expecting, and though his first lecture got a good review, the rest were described by those who attended as disasters because of Baudelaire's stage fright. Baudelaire describes his last attempt to lecture in excruciating terms: there were three enormous drawing rooms, lit with chandeliers and candelabras, decorated with superb paintings, a "profusion" of cake and wine—and all for ten or twelve people. He did not even bother to deliver the entire talk. In addition to the disappointment of the lecture series, Baudelaire did not make contact with Lacroix, who never accepted his invitations. Also, Baudelaire found the culture and climate of Belgium stifling, so stifling that while there he began writing a vitriolic indictment of the country titled "Pauvre Belgique!," which was published in *Oeuvres posthumes et correspondances inédites* (1887).

Despite his unhappy situation, Baudelaire stayed on in Belgium, perhaps because he was hoping for a satirical book to come out of the stay, perhaps because he did not want to return to France without something to show for the trip, or perhaps because he could not pay his hotel bill. His time in Belgium was not in fact wasted: Poulet-Malassis had emigrated there to escape creditors in France, and with his help Baudelaire published *Les Épaves* (The Wreckage, 1866), in which he assembled the condemned poems and other pieces left out of the French edition of *Les Fleurs du mal.* Baudelaire also became acquainted with Mme Hugo, even becoming a regular visitor at her home, and made contacts with local artists, notably with the engraver Félicien Rops.

While visiting the Rops family, Baudelaire collapsed during a trip to the Eglise Saint-Loup on 15 March 1866. Baudelaire's health had been deteriorating for some time. There was no effective cure for syphilis in his day, and so although he thought he was cured of it in the early 1840s, his disease erupted in 1849, and again in the spring of 1861. In letters from January 1862 he describes recurrent and distressing symptoms. The doctors never mentioned syphilis in connection with his final illness, but it seems very likely that the cerebral hemorrhage of 15 March was caused by the debilitating effects of the disease.

The Rops took Baudelaire back to Brussels, and by 31 March paralysis had set in. He was transported to the Clinique Saint-Jean et Sainte Elisabeth on 3 April. By 4 April, Baudelaire was incapable of speaking coherently. Madame Aupick arrived in Brussels on 14 April and returned with Baudelaire to Paris at the end of June. Baudelaire was eventually moved into a hydrotherapeutic establishment, and it was there that he died on 31 August 1867.

The terrible irony of Baudelaire's story is that this supremely articulate man spent the last seventeen months of his life reduced to incoherent monosyllables. This aphasic state was special torture for him because he seemed to understand what was going on around him but was unable to express himself. A particularly sad example of this situation touches on the publication of Baudelaire's complete works. He had wanted to find a publisher for them before his stroke, and his friends organized themselves to bring about what had become a last wish. Baudelaire conveyed with signs that he wanted Lévy as publisher, and this request was arranged. Ever the perfectionist, Baudelaire wanted to oversee the production of the manuscript. He knew, however, that he was in no condition to do so. In the hopes that he would eventually recover, Baudelaire used a calendar and a book published by Lévy to indicate that he wanted the process to wait until 31 March. This date came with no improvement in Baudelaire's health, and his collected works had to be prepared without his supervision; the seven-volume *Oeuvres complètes* (Complete Works) were not published until after his death, between 1868 and 1873. Biographies were also quickly available: Asselineau's anecdotal *Charles Baudelaire, sa vie et son oeuvre* was published two years after the poet's death; the first scholarly biography of Baudelaire was written by Jacques Crépet in 1887 and completed by his son Eugène in 1907: *Baudelaire. Étude biographique revue et complétée par Jacques Crépet.*

Baudelaire had achieved an important reputation in the literary world by the time of his death; writers such as Stéphane Mallarmé, Paul Verlaine, and Rimbaud openly sang his praises. In his correspondence Rimbaud called him a "génie, un voyant" (genius, a visionary). In articles written for the journal *L'Art* in November and December 1865 Verlaine credited Baudelaire with writing poetry about modern man. Mallarmé celebrated Baudelaire in essays and took up many of his themes (Poe, escape from the physical world, and desire for the infinite). Baudelaire's influence has carried over into the twentieth century and to other countries in the work of such writers as Pierre-Jean Jouve, Pierre Emmanuel, and T. S. Eliot.

Though Baudelaire was accepted as a poet during his lifetime, his status with nineteenth-century critics was tenuous. Of 1500 books, 700 copies of Crépet's biographical study remained in 1892. Lurid articles that exaggerated Baudelaire's legendary eccentricities attended his death. Important scholars such as Ferdinand Brunetière and Gustave Lanson remained relatively ignorant of Baudelaire's achievements.

Toward the end of the nineteenth century small magazines began to perceive Baudelaire's work more clearly and to free him of the myth of decadence that had grown up around him. Baudelaire's importance was not fully recognized by the world of criticism until the twentieth century, though. In 1926 Paul Valéry's "Situation de Baudelaire" (The Situation of Baudelaire) was published as an introduction to *Les Fleurs du mal*; in 1927 Marcel Proust published the influential "A propos de Baudelaire" (On the Subject of Baudelaire). These essays and others brought about a renaissance for Baudelaire's fortunes in France, and by World War II his work was regularly anthologized and used in schools.

Baudelaire's writings have also come to be greatly appreciated abroad, notably in England, where he was introduced by the critic Arthur Symons and where the American poet Eliot subsequently introduced him to American and English modernist poetry. Baudelaire is now an important figure in the literary canon. Critical articles and books about him abound; the W. T. Bandy Center for Baudelaire Studies at Vanderbilt University is devoted to recording all major publications on the author and his work. In the 1980s and 1990s the prose poems seem to have become a particularly appealing topic for scholars of Baudelaire.

Baudelaire's poetry has gone beyond what was once selective appreciation on the one hand and widespread notoriety on the other to general acclaim. Unlike Hugo, who cultivated his relationship with the public, Baudelaire in his career set himself apart by cultivating an eccentric image, by living an unconventional life, by writing poetry in verse that used romantic topoi to upset them, and by launching a new form. While he did seek recognition, Baudelaire and his poetry are defined by their distinct individuality.

In *Mon coeur mis à nu*, Baudelaire described a dynamic—"De la vaporisation et de la centralisation du moi. Tout est là." (The dispersion and the focusing of the self: those two movements are of the essence)—that strongly characterizes his life as well as his work. Willing to outrage public opinion and yet desirous of popular acclaim, he spoke penetratingly on the human condition. From Baudelaire's personal, dark ruminations come epiphanies that illuminate even the twentieth century. His poetry is read for those moments when, as Baudelaire wrote in his notebook, "la profonder de la vie se révèle tout entière dans le spectacle, si ordinaire qu'il soit, qu'on a sous les yeux. Il en devient le symbole" (the depth of life reveals itself in all its profundity in whatever one is looking at, however ordinary that spectacle might be. That vision becomes the symbol of life's depth).

Source: Kathryn Oliver Mills, "Charles Baudelaire," in *Dictionary of Literary Biography*, Vol. 217, *Nineteenth-Century French Poets*, edited by Robert Beum, Gale, 1999, pp. 27–46.

Sources

Baudelaire, Charles, *Complete Poems*, translated by Walter Martin, Routledge, 2002, p. 59.

Carter, A. E., "Chapter Four: *Les Fleurs du Mal*," in *Charles Baudelaire*, Twayne's World Authors Series, No. 429, Twayne Publishers, p. 83.

Shanks, Lewis Piaget, *Baudelaire: Flesh and Spirit*, Haskell House Publishers, 1974, p. 47.

Valéry, Paul, "The Position of Baudelaire," in *Baudelaire: A Collection of Critical Essays*, edited by Henri Peyre, Prentice-Hall, 1962, p. 13.

Further Reading

Emmanuel, Pierre, "Erotic Religion," in *Baudelaire: The Paradox of Redemptive Satanism*, translated by Robert T. Cargo, University of Alabama Press, 1967.

The author, a renowned French Catholic poet and literary critic, examines Baudelaire's mixture of religion, beauty, and death.

Hamburger, Michael, *The Truth of Poetry: Tensions in Modernist Poetry since Baudelaire*, Anvil Press Poetry, 2002.

Hamburger's book has been praised for clarifying the issues that make twentieth-century poetry vague and confusing to readers, tracing its roots to changes brought about by Baudelaire.

Lloyd, Rosemary, *Baudelaire's World*, Cornell University Press, 2002.

Lloyd's book is part biography, with the most recent research available, and part sociological examination of nineteenth-century France.

Poulet, Georges, and Robert Kopp, *Who Was Baudelaire?* World Publishing, 1969.

This book is interesting because it blends biography, critical examination, examples of Baudelaire's work, and prints of artwork from the poet's time. Poulet wrote the long critical essay; Kopp wrote the biographical segments.

Richardson, Joanna, "The Author of *Les Fleurs du Mal*," in *Baudelaire*, John Murray Publishers, 1994, pp. 221–50.

This biography of Baudelaire, published in Great Britain, is arranged by periods in the poet's life. There is a detailed description of the controversy and legal battle surrounding his book's publication.

Late and Deep

Paul Celan

1952

Paul Celan's poem "Late and Deep" has been translated into English by John Felstiner and included in the collection *Selected Poems and Prose of Paul Celan*. It is a relatively early work from the poet's career, originally published in 1952 in *Poppy and Memory*, as it was called in English. This poem is a disturbing one, dealing as it does with the recent memory of the Holocaust, of Jewish history through the ages, and of the constant pressure for conversion to Christianity that Jews have faced from ancient and medieval times up until the present. It is a poem that seems to affirm an oath or prayer but that ultimately undercuts its own promises. The poem is characterized by allusions to Christian and Jewish scripture and history, and it seems to beckon forward and backward, from the time of the Exodus from Egypt, up to the Holocaust, in a never-ending saga of oppression, faith, and the futility and the barrenness of that faith. Celan is a Jew, writing in the German language of his people's oppressors, but he is a Jew who has lost faith in a personal God, making this poem bitter in its renunciation of hope.

Author Biography

On November 23, 1920, Paul Antschel was born in Czernowitz, Romania, which at that time was the easternmost province of the Austro-Hungarian Empire. He was the only son of Leo and Friederike Antschel, a Jewish couple. After high school he studied medicine briefly in Tours, France, and returned to Czernowitz in 1939, where he studied romance languages and literature. In 1940, the Soviet Union annexed his hometown, and the following year the Germans invaded. His parents were deported in 1942 to a concentration camp, where his father died of disease and his mother was executed by a shot to the back of the head. Celan later wrote many poems that seem to refer to his mother; he only mentions his father once in all his work.

Antschel was not deported, though he was sent to a forced labor camp. In 1943, he returned to Czernowitz, which had been captured and occupied by the Russians. Toward the end of the war, he worked in Bucharest as a translator and editor. By 1947, he had taken his pen name, Paul Celan, which contained the letters of the Romanian version of his name, Ancel. He used the name Celan exclusively for the rest of his life.

In 1948, Celan moved to Paris, where he would live the rest of his life. He wrote poems in German and occasionally in French. The book that first gained him attention was his second collection, *Poppy and Memory*, in which "Late and Deep" appears. His reputation as a poet continued to grow, and he was awarded a number of literary prizes for his work in the German language, though he remained relatively unknown in France. In 1969, he visited Israel, years later than other men of his generation and stature usually did. Filled with despair and guilt, in April 1970 he apparently drowned himself in the Seine in Paris. A posthumous collection of poetry was published in 1971. His work has continued to attract critical attention in Germany, France, and the United States.

Poem Summary

Lines 1–2

This poem contains some rhythms in the original German, but it is not highly metered. It is, instead, an example of modernist, free-verse poetry that does away with rhyme and meter. The lines are as long or short as the phrases they convey, rather than being of a unified length. Many of the lines are relatively long, and in both the German original and in the English translation are end-stopped, which means that a reader should pause after each line, except for the one line ending with "dreamless sleep," which should be read continuously into the following line "and flourish the white hair of time." The end-stopped lines provide a choppiness to the poem and also serve to foreground the poem's images.

The images themselves are striking, almost surrealistic. Speech appears both spiteful and golden, and "the apples of the mute" makes an inability to speak palpable as a fruit. Celan is noted for the care with which he picks words, as well as for the ambiguity of his allusions. In the opening two lines, which comprise two complete sentences, speech is contrasted with non-speech. A night begins, and this night seems to be the darkness descending on the Jewish people. Apples are traditionally associated with Adam and Eve and their fall from grace, which in Christian theology is the root of original sin. Though Jewish, Celan alludes frequently to Christian ideas and beliefs.

Lines 3–12

In the next few lines, the English translation reads, "we do a thing." The original German for "thing" is *Werk*, a word that also can mean "the workings of God." This "thing" is "gladly left to one's star." In a poem such as this, a word like "gladly," when applied to the speakers, is bitter. As gladness is far from the emotion of this poem, one must assume the word is used either with irony or as a desperate and deliberate falsehood. The "we," representing the Jewish people of Europe, are standing in "our lindens' autumn." The linden is a characteristic European tree, and the Jews, the "ardent guests from the South," are in the autumn of their time in Europe, and facing the winter of sacrifice.

The word "swear" is used four times before the end of the stanza. Whatever the difficult ambiguities of the poem, it is clear that some kind of ritual oath is in progress. It is an oath to "Christ the New," to the New Testament whose proponents the Jewish people have resisted for centuries. Now, inexplicably, the speakers, presumably the Jews, are willing to swear by Christ, to swear to the world, and to swear aloud. Furthermore, these oaths are taken "gladly," a word that occurs twice in the first stanza.

Lines 13–18

No Jew can swear such oaths and remain Jewish. Hence the short line, "They cry: Blasphemy!" To swear by Christ is to blaspheme the God of Moses. The German text may also be translated "They cry: you (plural) blaspheme!" This second-person plural is the counterpoint of the "we" in the first stanza. The speakers are blasphemers. Who, then, is the "They" who cry? Although there is no definite referent, it is possible that Celan is talking about Jewish monotheism and the cultural and religious history that has manifested itself in the "white hair of time." It is a specific kind of guilt that afflicts the speakers of the poem. They have sworn a blasphemous oath and, as Celan will say at the end of the poem, for nothing. Their culture calls them to account.

Or are they speaking to the Germans? Or, in a surreal nightmare where identities shift, is he speaking simultaneously to Jews and Germans, to anyone who might listen? Though it seems that Jews would be more likely than Germans to accuse the speakers of blasphemy, subsequent lines indicate a shift of attention toward the speakers' German oppressors. Amy Colin, writing in *Paul Celan: Holograms of Darkness*, has said that "Celan hides both 'I' and 'You' behind various masks, destabilizing the harmonious unity within a lyric voice and within consciousness." At the center of the poem, the speakers acknowledge their guilt, but ask "who cares?" Then comes a long line in which the white meal (or flour) of the Promise has been ground "in the mills of death." That industrialized imagery depicts the routine technological and bureaucratic machinery of the Holocaust. The mills of death grind up human bones in violation of every Promise (significantly capitalized here) and "you" present the unholy offering to the brothers and sisters, the closest and dearest, of the Jewish speakers. This is a hideous parody of the Jewish Passover or the Christian communion, perhaps of both at once.

Then, in a single line, Celan repeats the strange, haunting image. "We flourish the white hair of time." Like a flag brandished in defiance, this dreamlike and disturbing image of age and time evokes the ancient history of the Jewish people, a people who are heirs to a long tradition, and who are also running out of time.

Lines 19–26

In the penultimate stanza, the poet acknowledges the warning of blasphemy and employs repetition to restate that the oath-takers "know it full well." There is a conscious resignation and desperation in this poem, and an acceptance of guilt. The Jews were infamously accused of guilt in the death of Christ, and seem to be accepting a similar kind of guilt in swearing to "Christ the New." The poem builds to a crescendo of imagery and rhetoric. Ominous signs are invoked, for they are accepted along with guilt. The "gurgling" sea makes the sound of a slit throat, and the "armored windblast of conversion" is militaristic and religious at the same time. A day of midnights is an oxymoron, but darkness falls upon the earth as the speakers pray for something that "never yet was."

Here, Celan turns the thrust of the poem against itself, and denies the possibility of redemption even through desperate, blasphemous oaths and the acceptance of guilt. For the image of what "never yet was" is a man who comes forth from the grave. In other words, there is no hope for the Jews, not even in Christ, because a man coming forth from the grave "never yet was." It is futile to convert. In any event, during the Holocaust the Jews were not given the option of converting to Christianity, though in other ages this act had sometimes prevented their murder. The speakers of this ironic and bitter oath call upon signs and portents, and especially they call upon the central mystery of Christianity, the resurrection of Christ, but they cannot believe a man has ever come forth from his death.

Line 27

Last words of poems are often significant. Celan ends his impassioned oath or prayer with the word "grave." It is with that word, which names the destination of all men, of all speakers, of the martyred and murdered Jews, that Celan falls silent.

Themes

Conversion

One of the important themes in this poem is the desperate resort to conversion by the Jews. Many times over the centuries, Jews have been forced to choose between betraying their faith and losing their lives, as well as the lives of their families. Sometimes they choose death, and at other times they convert externally, hoping to keep their faith alive in secret. It was often the function of the Inquisition to ferret out these secret Jews. Whatever choice they made, the Jews faced anguish, and their forced conversions were always suspect, just as they cut Jews off from their own co-religionists. This poem deals with a defiant and doomed choice to convert. Conversion is thus a more painful and serious matter to Jews than it might be to members of some other religions.

Guilt

Celan's life and work show the influence of guilt. Perhaps this experience is an example of "survivor's guilt," which may have led to his suicide, like that of his contemporary Primo Levi. There are several levels of guilt in this poem. First, the poet himself may feel guilt that he has survived the Holocaust when so many, including his parents, have

Topics For Further Study

- Do research on some of the main writers on the Holocaust, paying special attention to Paul Celan, Primo Levi, and Elie Wiesel. What sorts of writing did they produce, and what are the parallels in their biographies?
- Locate and listen to a recording of Henryk Gorecki's *Third Symphony*, which is a lament for the atrocities committed against the Polish people by the Nazis. What emotional effects are conveyed by his music, and how do they compare to the emotions expressed by Paul Celan?
- Locate and watch two or more videos or DVDs dealing with the Holocaust, such as *Schindler's List*, *Shoah*, or *Anne Frank, The Whole Story*. How do different directors approach the topic in different ways?
- The crimes of the Holocaust can be compared to several other genocides. Do research into the genocide against the Armenians during World War I, against the Rwandans in the 1990s, and compare them both to the crimes of the African diaspora and to the depopulation of many parts of the Americas. Make a chart listing significant similarities and the most important differences between these events.

perished. Second, the speakers, those who swear a blasphemous oath, revel in their guilt, saying that they do not care about it. They challenge the elements, the moral and physical order of the universe, challenging the sea and the "armored windblast of conversion," even the fundamental basis of time with a "day of midnights." Third, there is a collective guilt that was attributed to the Jews by Christians, who blamed them for the death of Christ. This guilt has a long and sordid history, and has endured from early Christian times up to the present. In Celan's poem, the guilt is accepted, along with the guilt of the apostasy of the oath-takers. It is not absolutely clear whether the guilt is personal, internalized, or external, but in any event it is pervasive, and a central theme of the poem.

Irony

Irony can mean many things. Fundamentally, irony is a recognition of the difference between reality and our expectations. Three major types of irony are situational irony, dramatic irony, and verbal irony. In the first type, we find that an action leads to a result contrary to what we can foresee. In the second type, we observe others and watch how they misunderstand the world and each other. In verbal irony, we recognize that what people say is not what they mean, and yet they are not lying or trying to deceive us. Celan uses a special kind of irony in this poem. He sets his reader up to expect that the speakers of the poem are taking some sort of conversion oath, or are in some way praying to Christ and violating their Jewish faith. He moves from simple promises to grander and more portentous speech, invoking awesome miracles until he gets to the miracle that undercuts all previous speech. His assertion that no man has "come forth from the grave" lets careful readers know that all the previous language was not meant in the way it has seemed. If he swears on behalf of what he knows has never come, he cannot have meant his oath in the way it first seemed.

Despair

How does one write poetry after the Holocaust? How can a man see the mass murder of his people, endure the death of his mother and father, and continue to be a sensitive human being who continues to write? How does one write in German, the language of the murders? All these are existential questions a poet such as Celan has to face. There is no escape from a deep sense of despair, mixed with guilt. All of Celan's work is shaped by the sense of despair. He seems sometimes to hold out the promises of religion—in this poem, of the promise that the Jews can convert themselves into something that they are not. Whenever he offers hope, though, he immediately refutes it. Celan's poetry is a testament to deep despair.

Style

Repetition

One of the chief characteristics of poetry is its repetition. This poem repeats several phrases and elements. "We swear" is repeated four times. This repetition emphasizes the ritualized and formal nature of the oath being taken. All these examples are from the first stanza. The swearing is consecutive and repetitive. In the middle of the poem are several acknowledgments of "We've known it," and "Known it long since." In this sequence, however, the repetition is interrupted by other imagery, until it occurs one more time, in the penultimate stanza, "We know it full well," which provides a transition to the repeated guilt motif, which in turn transforms itself from "let the guilt come" to "let come what never yet was" to the ultimate line, "Let a man come forth from the grave." Thus, Celan uses at least three distinctive methods of repetition. He repeats "swear" in a compact section of his poem; he repeats "known" twice in one stanza, then comes back to it in another stanza. Finally, he links the repetition of "guilt" with "let come" in his powerful concluding lines.

Surrealism

Surrealism is a twentieth-century movement in art and literature that tried to express the operation of the subconscious mind. Surrealism uses dreamlike imagery and often juxtaposes harshly jarring, disturbing, or incongruous imagery. In art, Salvador Dali is often associated with this movement. Paul Celan wrote an early essay on the surrealist Edgar Jené, indicating his interest in the movement. Several aspects of "Late and Deep" show surrealistic influences. Most prominent is the perplexing and dreamlike "we flourish the white hair of time." The German verb means "to brandish" in English. The image is nightmarish, as human hair functions as an object, a totem, or a flag. Similarly, the stair in the water, birds to a shoe, and the white meal "You grind in the mills of death" all have a surrealistic and nightmarish quality.

Allusion

In general, an allusion is an indirect reference or hint to something outside the work in which it occurs. It can be a reference to history, to events surrounding the composition of a poem, to a song or cultural practice, to another work of literature, or, indeed, to almost anything else. Many students have problems catching allusions, and those problems are magnified by the work of a poet such as Celan. Even academic critics find themselves unsure of the meaning of Celan's allusions. Some things, however, are clear enough. Celan was well-read in both Jewish and Christian tradition, and he alludes to them both in his poetry. This poem seems to allude to the parting of the Red Sea or perhaps even the Great Flood, and to the condemnation of Christ when, according to the New Testament, the Jewish mob took responsibility for Christ's execution on themselves and their children, and also to the darkness during the daytime that accompanied Christ's death on the cross. Additionally, "Spiteful like golden speech" might be an allusion to Hitler. It must be remembered that some allusions can be precisely attributed to the poet, and others are suggestive and indirect. This poem has some very clear allusions and some that are less certain.

Historical Context

"Late and Deep" is, very clearly, a poem that is a response to the Holocaust, or as many Jewish scholars have come to call it, *Shoah*, which is Hebrew for "catastrophe." It is difficult to grasp the enormity of this crime against humanity. Tens of millions of human beings died during World War II, some by disease and hunger, others by bombing, shooting, and other acts of warfare, but the Holocaust refers to the intentional, deliberate, and systematic deportation and murder of European Jews under the control of Nazi Germany and its puppet states. There are many resources for learning about the Holocaust; historical documentation is plentiful, the account of this period is presented in schools, and in some communities survivors of the Holocaust are still alive to tell their stories. In all the history of human evil, the Holocaust is different from other wicked events in that the Jews were singled out for their racial characteristics, which meant that there was no way for them to submit or cooperate with their conquerors, options that most other people have used, even in defeat. Instead, there was a conscious effort to exterminate the entire Jewish race. The methods used by the Nazis were thorough, routine, and bureaucratic. Approximately six million Jews were killed during the Holocaust. Other populations besides Jews, including Gypsies, homosexuals, and communists, were targeted, but the racial violence against the Jews was central to the Nazi regime's ideology and purpose.

After the fall of the Third Reich in 1945, the evidence of the Nazi crimes became public. Almost no Jews remained in countries such as Germany,

Compare & Contrast

- **1940s–1950s:** Paul Celan's parents are deported from Czernowitz, Romania, to a concentration camp, where they die.

  Today: Only a few regimes in the world, such as North Korea, incarcerate large numbers of people in concentration camps.

- **1940s–1950s:** Existentialism and surrealism are important political and artistic movements in Paris, influencing artists, writers, and thinkers throughout the world.

  Today: Postmodernism dominates critically acclaimed culture and thought.

- **1940s–1950s:** The free world is locked in a struggle against Nazi fascism, followed by a confrontation with Soviet communism.

  Today: With the collapse of communism, the free world confronts the challenge of international terrorism.

- **1940s–1950s:** Poets and writers use books and magazines to disseminate their stories, essays, and novels to a text-centered audience.

  Today: In addition to books and magazines, poets, writers, and musicians use Internet weblogs, websites, and file-swapping to get their ideas and writings out to multiple audiences.

Poland, and Romania. Celan, like so many people of his time, became a displaced person. He moved between the Soviet Union, Romania, and Austria before settling in Paris. This poem was published within seven years after the end of the war. Many European Jews abandoned the lands of their birth and took up new lives in the state of Israel, founded in 1948. Others made their lives in nations such as France, Australia, or the United States.

Dealing with the Holocaust as a literary matter was very difficult. It has been famously remarked that after Auschwitz, writing poetry is barbaric. Paul Celan, on the other hand, used all the tools of modernist literature to write poetry that did not succumb to sensationalism or emotionalism. In his own way, Celan offered his readers a kind of verse that was daunting and haunting, allusive and elusive. His postwar years were spent in an era in which many thinkers and artists abandoned the certainties of previous generations and committed themselves to philosophies such as existentialism, which was particularly influential in France as Celan began his poetic career. Clarise Samuels, in the conclusion to her book *Holocaust Visions: Surrealism and Existentialism in the Poetry of Paul Celan* says that, "Celan has depicted an existentialist universe described artistically in surrealist terms. The purpose of this vision is to shock and destroy so that society can renegotiate its structures, its values, and basic social relationships." As other Jewish writers looked with hope at the birth of the state of Israel, Celan and others, such as the Italian Jewish writer Primo Levi, remained in Europe and wrote at the behest of their own dark muses.

Critical Overview

The poetry of Paul Celan has generated intense critical interest for over fifty years. Writing in 1972, Jerry Glenn begins his book on Celan by stating, "Paul Celan is generally considered to be the most accomplished German-speaking lyric poet to emerge in recent decades." Even the most cursory examination of bibliographies in books about the poet reveals a rich secondary literature. Much of this literature is in German, but a substantial portion is in English, and some of it is in French. In her book *Pathways to Paul Celan: A History of Critical Responses as a Chorus of Discordant Voices*, Bianca Rosenthal declares that the beginning of Celan's critical reception was 1953, the year after *Poppy and*

Lodz ghetto Jews boarding the train to Auschwitz

Memory was published. She states that he "stepped into the literary scene with this volume and immediately attracted attention." Several critics pointed out, either positively or negatively, the surrealistic aspects of Celan's work. Rosenthal quotes an anonymous reviewer in Stuttgart who said "Celan was able to name that which cannot be expressed and to transform it through complex imagery into comprehensible reality." She also quotes another German critic, Wieland Schmied, who compared Celan to Shakespeare and denied the poet was a surrealist, claiming that Celan's tightly controlled composition puts him far outside the surrealist camp.

As all major poets must do, Celan progressed stylistically and thematically as he matured. As Rosenthal said, "After the mid-1950s his poetry became more reticent and hermetic. The sounding voice changes into word artistry on the way to becoming the absolute poem." Celan's book *Sprachgitter* was, as Glenn says, "greeted by almost unanimous critical acclaim, and the book quickly solidified Celan's claim to a position as one of the leading German-speaking poets of the postwar era." Many critics have noted the turning in his poetry. Glenn explains: "The language continues to grow harder and colder, and the words sparser." The title itself, like much of the poet's work, is highly ambiguous, and is based on a medieval window containing a grill that allowed cloistered nuns to speak to the world.

Many critics have emphasized the care with which Celan chose his words. There is speculation about his allusions, about the influence of the German language and Hebrew. Amy Colin believes that "It is Celan's love for both his German mother tongue and for the language of the Jewish people that inspires his acrobatic language act over the abyss." It is striking how very detailed many of the critical works are, going down to the level of the significance of a single word, or even a single vowel. At the roots of his poetry is language in search of itself, a complex interplay between disparate linguistic and cultural traditions and, most profoundly, the response to the great tragedy of the Holocaust. Critical attention to Celan is still lively, and the 1997 publication of John Felstiner's *Paul Celan: Poet, Survivor, Jew* has contributed a full-length biography against which the many private allusions can be measured.

Criticism

Frank Pool

Pool is a published poet and reviewer and a teacher of high school English. In this essay, Pool deals with problems of interpretation in Celan's poem by discussing allusion and ironic reversal.

Paul Celan's poem "Late and Deep" poses many problems for interpretation. His work is compact and allusive, and contains a multiplicity of possible meanings. A reader cannot always be certain of the meaning of terms and imagery, but given the respect accorded to the poet, perhaps it is best to say that one gets out of the poem what one can bring to it, based on knowledge of Celan's other work, and upon the typical themes, concerns, and motifs he uses. Celan often uses private symbols, and as his career progressed, his work became more and more spare and allusive. Some critics have accused him of hermeticism—of writing verse that is deliberately obscure and closed to interpretation by anyone but the poet himself. "Late and Deep," however, was included in his first widely-published collection, *Poppy and Memory*, and while it is difficult to understand in many places, Celan's meanings and intent may be discerned through a careful reading.

Celan frequently uses both Jewish and Christian imagery. He remains a Jew, and a Jew who writes in German, the language of his parents' murderers, when he could have also written in French, or Romanian, or Ukrainian, or Russian. He is deeply read in Jewish thought and literature, as well as in Martin Luther's German translation of the Christian Bible. Celan's concern with religion is quite apparent in his word choice, in his allusions, and in his subject matter. For all his urbane European sophistication, he remains at his core a Jew whose parents died in the Holocaust, and who can never escape the history of his people. Yet he is a nonbelieving Jew who, like fellow Romanian Jewish writer Elie Wiesel, has lost whatever religious faith he once may have held.

One of his most characteristic techniques is to work with religious allusions, which are often uplifting and hopeful, but which the poet undercuts, denies, or refutes. Jerry Glenn, in his book *Paul Celan,* reports on the German critic Wienold's identification of this technique by the term *Widerruf,* which means, in effect, "poetic refutation." This refutation is a darkly ironic commentary on the hopes and promises offered by religion in its scriptures, prayers, and songs. For Celan, God's blessings are illusions, God is absent or nonexistent, and the futile cries for deliverance for his oppressed and slaughtered people are overwhelmingly, unbearably, poignant.

"Late and Deep" is a thorough example of the *Widerruf* technique, in that it seems to hold the promise of salvation through conversion from Judaism to Christianity, but in the end, not only the Second Coming, but also the First Coming of the Messiah is refuted and denied. Glenn quotes the German critic Weinold who has said that this poem "proclaims the impossibility of the Resurrection." Because the Resurrection is not possible, the hope it offers to Christians, or even to Christian converts, is no longer possible either. Therefore, it "accordingly reverses the Biblical quotation and suspends the effect of the Christian symbolism."

The poem is clearly about the Jews, the "ardent guests from the South," who swear an oath to "Christ the New." This conversion may be one more instance of forced conversion, which Jews have been subjected to over the centuries, or it may be in some sense free, but it is in every way unsatisfactory, because it blasphemes Jewish values, and perhaps, Christian ones as well. The poem begins with the image of "golden speech," which may allude to the oratory of Hitler or perhaps to the centuries of eloquent rhetoric employed by Christian bishops and preachers to persuade the Jews to abandon their faith and convert. The Jews are from the South, and are

> *"For Celan, God's blessings are illusions, God is absent or non-existent, and the futile cries for deliverance for his oppressed and slaughtered people are overwhelmingly, unbearably, poignant."*

now in the land of the linden, which is a very typical European tree, much beloved by the Germans. "Autumn," several critics relate, is a word Celan associates with his mother, who was sent to a concentration camp during the Holocaust and was executed by being shot in the back of the head.

Images of sterility and futility abound. The speakers "swear to wed dust to dust." The last phrase is redolent of Christian burial prayers and images of death juxtaposed with wedding vows. The "birds to a wandering shoe" alludes to the medieval image of the Wandering Jew, outcast and moving eternally across the world. Glenn, in his book on Celan, quotes from the *Encylopaedia Judaica* that Ahasver, the "Wandering Jew, is not a single person, but is rather the entire Jewish people, which has been scattered throughout the world since the crucifixion of Christ and . . . will remain homeless until the end of the world." Clearly, there is no rest, there is no permanent home for the speakers of this poem. When the poet says that the speakers will swear to wed "our hearts to a stair in the water" the image is two-fold. First, in Celan's early poetry, water is a positive image. (It is thus darkly ironic that his death in 1970 was to be an apparent suicide by drowning in the Seine in Paris.) In this poem, however, regardless of its positive aspects, a stair in the water is unstable and shifting, fruitless, much like "sacred oaths of the sand," which in ironic reversal, parallel and mock Christ's saying, "upon this rock I will build my church."

There are biblical allusions in the poem. The rooftops may allude to the Jewish scripture of Isaiah 15:3, which warns of catastrophe. "In the streets they wear sackcloth; on the roofs and in the public squares they all wail, prostrate with weeping."

What Do I Read Next?

- *Selected Poems and Prose of Paul Celan* (2001), translated by John Felstiner, includes "Late and Deep" as well as other representative poems by Celan. Both German and English texts of the poem are presented.
- *Night* (1960), by Elie Wiesel, is a very personal account of the Holocaust by a man who was approximately the same age as Celan and came from the same part of Europe.
- *The Holocaust: The Fate of European Jewry* (1990), by Leni Yahil, is a dense volume that might be better sampled than read cover to cover. Nevertheless, it is a valuable detailed account of the *Shoah*.
- John Felstiner's *Paul Celan: Poet, Survivor, Jew* (1997) is the first full-length biography of the poet in English. It includes details of Celan's personal life as well as the sources and methods of his poetry.
- Jerry Glenn's *Paul Celan* (1972) is a good introduction to the criticism of specific Celan poems. The text is well written and accessible.

Celan was quite familiar with Christian literature, and may be alluding to Luke 12:3. "What you have said in the dark will be heard in the daylight, and what you have whispered in the ear in the inner rooms will be proclaimed from the roofs." These apparent allusions are succeeded by images of "dreamless sleep," which hint simultaneously at either peaceful sleep, or death, or even both at once.

The German language provides overtones of additional meaning. In such a line as "You grind in the mills of death the white meal of Promise," the word "meal" is unambiguously milled grain, such as corn meal. An observant reader who did not know German might be tempted to think of a meal such as the Last Supper, but the German does not have the same ambiguity as the English. The capitalized "Promise" in German is the word used in the phrase, "The Promised Land." This promise is nothing but the promise of death, the ground-up white bones of the slaughtered and crushed Jews whose promise comes to naught.

The whole poem seems to represent a religious person speaking an oath, but who is the speaker and who is being addressed? As we have seen, it is apparently a poem spoken by or on behalf of the Jews. The "you" that is being addressed, however, is a bit more problematic. Although it might seem to be God, who "grinds in the mills of death," and the one addressed in the line "You warn us: Blasphemy!" the German original dispels such a supposition. The word "ihr" in German is the second person plural familiar, which is something that English does not make unambiguously clear. The "you" could address the Germans or other Christians who want to convert the Jews, but it is not a reference to God.

A major image is the Jewish acceptance of the blasphemous attribution of guilt for the death of Christ, a blood-libel that has haunted the Jewish people throughout the weary centuries of Christian dominance. This alleged guilt is based on Matthew 27:25 in which Pontius Pilate tries to talk the Jewish crowds out of executing Christ, and they replied "His blood be on us, and on our children." Celan seems to suggest that even an acceptance of such guilt, blasphemous to any believing Jew, will not bring forth redemption. To accept that Jesus Christ was the Messiah or to proclaim belief in a Trinity is contrary to Jewish scripture. Yet, in the desperation of this poem, the speakers are willing to embrace such views, with a catch. The "gurgling sea" and the "armored windblast of conversion" allude both to Pharaoh pursuing the fleeing Hebrews across the Red Sea, and perhaps to the armored divisions of the German military. Celan asks that these things come once again, but he is deeply ironic and deeply pessimistic in this prayer.

In his final twist, Celan says, "let come what never yet was!" After all the signs and portents, in a world gone mad with killing, the invocation is to something that has not ever been—"a man come forth from the grave." With this touch, the poet denies the hope of a Second Coming by denying that there was ever a man, Jesus Christ, who came to earth, died, and then came forth from the grave. The poem, in all its bitterness, says that the Jews, even if they accept conversion, would find no refuge in a religion founded on a belief in something that "never yet was."

Source: Frank Pool, Critical Essay on "Late and Deep," in *Poetry for Students*, Thomson Gale, 2005.

Laura Carter

Carter is currently employed as a freelance writer. In this essay, Carter considers how both the events of the Holocaust and the struggle for identity inform Celan's work.

In the poem "Late and Deep," Celan relies chiefly on historical and theological themes to reach his audience. The work, rife with both Christian and Jewish terms, images, and themes, provides a window into the internal struggles of the author. To classify Celan's effort as simply "Holocaust poetry" is to dismiss the complexities of the work itself. It is a poem informed not only by Celan's anguish and grief over the events of the Holocaust, but also through the struggle to embrace his own Jewishness in a hostile postwar climate.

The duality of Celan's poetic imagery sets up a theological tension within the work. Consider the Creation imagery within the very first few lines of the poem—the speaker declaring "we eat the apples of the mute." The apples could be seen as one of many pivotal symbols within the context of the entire work. An ancient Jewish allegory of Cant. 2:3, 5 and 8:5 (quoted in David Lyle Jeffrey's "A Dictionary of Biblical Tradition in English Literature") identifies the "fair apple tree" as Israel, fairest among nations for its passion for the Law (Shab. 88, Tg. Ket. Cant. 2:3 in Jeffrey), or as the Lord, shading Israel from harm (Midr. Rab. Cant. 2:3 in Jeffrey). In direct contrast, Christian allegorists associate the apple (Cant. 2:5 in Jeffrey) with the fruits of Christ's sacrifice, particularly the Eucharist. Identification of the apple tree with the cross on which Christ was crucified was constant and inevitably associated with the tree of the original Garden of Eden. Christ is often identified as the second Adam, reversing the fall of mankind into sin as suffered by the first Adam.

Immediately in line 3, the reader is left with another image, Celan's star, but as to the meaning of what "thing" or intent the speaker assigns the symbol is another matter altogether. Of course, there is the immediate association with the Star of David or the Star of Bethlehem and the tension those elements together create. Taken in another context, the Star of David was worn by the Jews during the Holocaust as a means of identification. Thus, Celan comments with biting and almost painful sarcasm on the way the Star—a symbol of sacredness for both Christianity and Judaism—was used to single out, define, and ultimately mark the destruction of the European Jew.

> *"As symbols shift and change from traditional meanings, so too the emotional tenor of the work is transformed from hope to despair."*

As symbols shift and change from traditional meanings, so too the emotional tenor of the work is transformed from hope to despair. On the powerful use of religious imagery in Celan's poetry, John Felstiner's work "The Strain of Jewishness" comments on poems that he claims "build their energy by oscillating between prayer and revolt: Blessed art thou, No One." Felstiner characterizes this as the "strain of Jewishness" in Paul Celan's work. According to Felstiner, Celan "knew well enough the burden of being Jewish, and avoided any religiosity, but a Jew he had to be and chose to be." It was a tenuous, attenuated strain, says Felstiner, "yet a tough one: sometimes it was all [Celan] felt he had." Celan lived under the specter of the Holocaust, haunted by the loss of his parents and his own eighteen-month internment at a Nazi labor camp, and it is this personal history that informs the author's work.

According to Raul Hilberg's "The Destruction of the European Jew," the picture of the Jew the Nazis relied so heavily upon to fuel propaganda is part of a tradition of hatred that originated in Germany several hundred years ago. Martin Luther had already created the framework on which a disparaging stereotype of Jewish people was built, namely that Jewish people are bent on world domination, referring to them maliciously as the "killers of Christ and all of Christendom" and as "a plague, pestilence and pure misfortune." In a speech delivered in 1935 to the Hitler Youth, Gauleiter Julius Streicher mirrored this sentiment—spinning hatred in the context of religion—by reducing the Jewish people to little more than "that organized body of world criminals, against whom already Christ had fought, the greatest Anti-Semite of all times" (quoted in Hilberg). Celan was a direct target of this intense hatred, one that did not immediately evaporate at the end of the war. It would be the late 1950s before Germany began to prosecute war criminals. Of 1950s Germany, Felstiner says "there was numbness, repression, denial, apathy, or expedient forgetfulness of the European Jewish catastrophe." To reenter Europe in the 1950s as a German and contemplate what would later be labeled the Holocaust was very difficult for many Germans and involved either coming to terms with military defeat and mass murder in Germany or a regression into denial and resentment.

The movement within "Late and Deep" indicates Celan's misgivings about hope, faith, and salvation after enduring in such a hostile environment. In light of his personal history, such movement illuminates the author's psychic struggle with the Holocaust and his attempts to reconcile his Jewishness. At the outset of the poem, the speaker swears allegiance "by Christ the New to wed dust to dust," with unusual zeal, raising the question of the speaker's conversion. But the tone immediately shifts to a rather strong objection or cry of "blasphemy." At this point comes an acknowledgement of the reality of the speaker's fate, as dictated by the "mills of death," rather than God's "Promise" of redemption for his chosen people. Celan calls on the gruesome images of the Holocaust to amplify a feeling of abandonment and alienation. In the midst of his personal dilemma and abandoned by God, the speaker abandons all hope, all faith, defying all prospects of a miraculous salvation with the challenge, "Let come what never yet was!"

In an attempt to reinvent his own existence, the speaker first embraces a dogma completely contrary to his own beliefs, without effect. His declaration or oath to "Christ the New" is indicative of a movement toward repentance and humility before God, often followed by an acknowledgement of the Resurrection in the Christian tradition. It appears the speaker is cornered by despair and his words, at first, might be construed as a plea for forgiveness. However, Abraham in Genesis 18:27 uses dust as a metonym or figure of speech for human mortality. The irony of the situation is that the author cannot escape his anguish, whether he chooses to take an oath to devote or "wed" himself to the blasphemous promises of Christ or embrace his own heritage of ashes. The speaker cannot reinvent nor save himself.

Remorse, not repentance, does indeed come midway through the poem for the speaker. A charge of "Blasphemy!" brings with it a sense of resignation. "We've known it long since," repeats the speaker, "but who cares?" The history informing Celan's work explains the underlying tension in his poetic voice, brought to life in the passionately charged words of the speaker who, faced with the horrible reality of the Holocaust, reaches out in vain to find some answers. The atrocities of the Holocaust seem irreconcilable. During this incredibly dark time in history, no one in Germany seemed to be listening. Thousands of Jews were led to their death without protest, as thousands of Germans turned a blind eye to the fate of their neighbors. That denial of something so terribly real could run so deep in a culture is captured in the poem's frenzied tone. Intense, rife with emotion, the work is erratic and even at many points absurd. The speaker's sense of hope and solidarity has been shattered by a paradoxical guilt for simply being Jewish, for being the object of such inhumane malice, and for blaspheming his people's beliefs in the struggle for hope and survival. Feelings of alienation and of abandonment are echoed in verse.

Theologically conflicting religious symbols used throughout Paul Celan's "Late and Deep," shifting in meaning, transmuting in form, suggest that for Celan, peace of mind is elusive at best. The speaker's increasing agitation crescendos into his last words of desperate challenge, daring or beseeching God to materialize in some form, any form, to make sense of it all. The irony of the speaker's bitter soliloquy is that no one seems to be listening.

Source: Laura Carter, Critical Essay on "Late and Deep," in *Poetry for Students*, Thomson Gale, 2005.

James K. Lyon

In the following essay, Lyon discusses Celan's influential work about the Holocaust, the flexibility he possessed speaking four languages, and his talents as a writer of both prose and lyric poetry.

Paul Celan (pronounced say-*lahn*), whom George Steiner has called "almost certainly the major European poet of the period after 1945," is known primarily for his verse. Yet his reputation as a lyric poet overshadows a small but significant body of prose works that deserve attention both for their close links to his poetry and as independent creations.

Paul Antschel, the only child of Jewish parents, Leo Antschel-Teitler and Friederike Schrager, was born in Czernovitz (now Cherniutsi, Ukraine), capital of the Romanian province of Bukovina, on 23 November 1920. He grew up in a multilingual environment. German, the language spoken at home and in some of the schools he attended, remained his mother tongue throughout his life, and Vienna was the cultural lodestar of his youth; but his language of daily speech was Romanian. Before his bar mitzvah he studied Hebrew for three years, and by the time he began a year of premedical studies at the École préparatoire de Médecine in Tours, France, in 1938, he was also fluent in French. Returning to Czernovitz shortly before the outbreak of World War II, he learned Russian at the university and, after Soviet troops occupied Bukovina in 1940, in the streets. When German troops captured the city in 1941 his parents were deported and shot, but he survived. After eighteen months at forced labor for the Germans, he escaped to the Red Army and returned to Czernovitz, which was again under Russian control. There, sometime in late 1944, he wrote the remarkable "Todesfuge" (Death Fugue), perhaps the most powerful poem ever written on the Holocaust. It was included in his first two collections of poems, *Der Sand aus den Urnen* (The Sand from the Urns, 1948) and *Mohn und Gedächtnis* (Poppy and Memory, 1952).

Leaving Czernovitz in 1945 for Bucharest, Antschel joined a surrealist circle, became friends with leading Romanian writers, and worked as a translator and reader in a publishing house. For his prose translations from Russian into Romanian—primarily of Mikhail Lermontov, Konstantin Simonov, and Anton Chekhov—and for publication of his own poems, he used several pseudonyms before transmuting Ancel, the Romanian form of his surname, into Celan in 1947.

Sometime between 1945 and 1947 he wrote a two-page prose fragment that has survived under the title" Geräuschlos hüpft ein Griffel ... "(A Stylus Noiselessly Hops. . ., 1980). This work reveals his indebtedness to surrealism. In it a noiseless slate pencil or stylus writes under its own power, first on a slate tablet, which is the earth, and then on a "Blatt" (leaf or page) in a tree-top. Further surrealistic sequences show a man in a room who finds that the window has been locked by a powerful, unseen external hand, and the same man looking into a mirror, only to see his coat buttons and the carpet transformed into mirrors. At this point the series of dreamlike scenes breaks off.

"Creative extensions and elaborations of his poetry, Celan's prose works express the strain of being Jewish, the struggle to reclaim language in a nonpoetic age, and the need for dialogue as a means of connecting oneself with and orienting oneself in the modern world."

Late in 1947 Celan went to Vienna, where he joined a circle of leading avant-garde painters, writers, and publishers. His friendship with the painter Edgar Jené gave rise to a brief prose piece, "Die Lanze" (The Lance), which he and Jené wrote jointly early in 1948 and circulated on mimeographed sheets to announce a reading of surrealist texts as part of an exhibition of surrealist painters in Vienna. Like "Geräuschlos hüpft ein Griffel...," "Die Lanze" consists of typical surrealist images: "rainbowfish" flying through the sky, a giant hammer in the air, and waves beating against treetops. It ends with speakers casting nets into the water—an image also found in Celan's early poems. The work contains a dialogue, a format that became a hallmark of his later prose works.

A second prose piece, *Edgar Jené und der Traum vom Traume* (Edgar Jené and the Dream of the Dream, 1948), written at about the same time as "Die Lanze," purports to be a discussion of Jené's paintings but quickly becomes a confessional essay on what happens in the "Tiefsee" (deep sea) of the writer's mind, the "große Kristall der Innenwelt" (huge crystal of the internal world) into which he follows Jené and where he explores his paintings. Aware that language has become false and debased, he seeks to regain a naive view of the world and to recover pristine speech or "truth" that cannot be restored by reason, but only by venturing into the depths of the mind and engaging in dialogue with its "finstere Quellen" (dark sources). With this newfound freedom, he engages Jené's paintings in a dialogue. In the process Celan sketches the contours of "die schöne Wildnis auf der anderen, tieferen Seite des Seins" (the beautiful wilderness on the other, more profound side of existence), the internal world in which most of his poetry takes place, a world of "true" language obscured by lies, an internal darkness that is dispelled only by the light of "true" language. In prose marked by unusual new compound nouns, Celan's many interrogative sentences give one the sense that he wishes to engage his reader in a direct dialogue.

Leaving Vienna in July 1948, he settled in Paris and began studies in German philology and literature. In March 1949 the Swiss journal *Die Tat* published a collection of his brilliant but enigmati aphorisms titled" Gegenlicht" (Counter-Light). These aphorisms appear surrealistic in their subversion of conventional time and of space and object relationships—trees fly to birds, hours jump out of the clock, a woman hates a mirror's vanity. Behind them lies a Kafkaesque awareness that the world makes no sense. For Celan it seems that only in the paradox of new language combinations can the world be made coherent, and only in a dialectic of contradictions can truth be rendered. Hence, an aphorism that juxtaposes a battleship and a drowned man might be read as a pacifist statement: "Man redet umsonst von Gerechtigkeit, solange das größte der Schlachtschiffe nicht an der Stirn eines Ertrunkenen zerschellt ist" (One speaks in vain of justice as long as the largest battleship has not been smashed to pieces on a drowned man's brow).

Celan took his Licence des Lettres in 1950. In 1952 he married the graphic artist Gisèle de Lestrange, with whom he had a son, Eric, who was born in 1955. Though he wrote no original prose for almost ten years, the works Celan chose to translate into German were usually prose. For him each translation was a new linguistic creation, a means of establishing his identity and verifying his existence within language. He never gave up German as his mother tongue, telling a friend, "Only in one's mother tongue can one express one's own truth. In a foreign language, the poet lies." Though all of these translations reflect his unique prose style, one reveals almost more of himself than of the original—his rendering of Jean Cayrol's prose narration for Alain Resnais's *Nuit et Brouillard* (Night and Fog, 1956), a film on the Holocaust that Celan endowed with an authentic Jewish voice for German-speaking viewers.

The address he delivered upon receiving the Bremen Literary Prize in 1958 (translated, 1969) is Celan's most personal prose work. After referring to the Bukovinian landscape of his youth and his acquaintance with Martin Buber's Hasidic tales in this world "in der Menschen und Bücher lebten" (where humans and books lived), the address becomes a discussion of his relationship to the German language, one of the few elements of his spiritual existence he did not lose under the Nazis. This language, he says, "mußte nun hindurchgehen . . . durch furchtbares Verstummen, hindurchgehen durch die tausend Finsternisse todbringender Rede" (had to pass . . . through a frightful muting, pass through the thousand darknesses of death-bringing speech). From its miraculous survival, he now attempts to write "um zu sprechen, um mich zu orientieren . . . um mir Wirklichkeit zu entwerfen" (in order to speak, to orient myself . . . to outline reality). He states his views on poetry as dialogue, as a "Flaschenpost" (message in a bottle) cast out and addressed to "etwas Offenstehendes, auf ein ansprechbares Du vielleicht, auf eine ansprechbare Wirklichkeit" (something that stands open, perhaps an addressable Thou, an addressable reality). But he accomplishes this painful task as one who "mit seinem Dasein zur Sprache geht, wirklichkeitswund und Wirklichkeit suchend" (goes to language with his very being, stricken by and seeking reality). Besides being a statement of personal poetics, this piece stands, like Buber's *Ich und Du* (1923; translated as *I and Thou*, 1937), as an expression of man's need for a relation to an "Other."

In 1959 Celan became a reader in German Language and Literature at L'École Normale Superieure, a position he held until his death. While in the Swiss Alps in July 1959 he was to meet Theodor Adorno at Sils-Maria. Forced to return to Paris before they met, Celan composed "Gespräch im Gebirg" (1960; translated as "Conversation in the Mountains," 1972) the following month; it was a reflection on this missed encounter; he later called it a "Mauscheln" (jabber, schmooze) between himself and Adorno. This most distinctly Jewish of his prose works portrays a meeting in the mountains between "Jud-Klein" (Jew-Small) and "Jud-Groß" (Jew-Big). It opens with involved sentences punctuated with dashes, thought fragments, and repetitions as Jew-Small walks through the Alps reflecting on the landscape, his own Jewishness with which he does not feel at ease, the nature of silence, and, finally, the nature of speech. After meeting Jew-Big, he admits that he came there to talk with someone, and immediately they make a distinction between "Reden" (talk) and "Sprechen" (speech) as they reflect on hearing, remembering, and language. Jew-Small, who dominates the conversation, delivers a long reverie on the Jewish dead and on his love for an ancestral candle as it symbolically burns toward extinction: "Auf dem Stein bin ich gelegen, damals, du weißt, auf den Steinfliesen; und neben mir, da sind sie gelegen, die andern, die wie ich waren, die anders, die anders waren als ich und genauso, die Geschwisterkinder; und sie lagen da und schliefen, schliefen und schliefen nicht, und sie träumten und träumten nicht . . ." (On the stone is where I lay, back then, you know, the flagstones; and near me, that's where they were lying, the others, who were different from me and the same, the cousins; and they lay there and slept, sleeping and not sleeping, dreaming and not dreaming . . .). Gradually he realizes that in the dialogue with Jew-Big he is meeting himself, that is, encountering and beginning to accept his people, his heritage, and his Jewish identity.

In 1960 Celan traveled to Darmstadt to receive the Georg Büchner Prize from the German Academy of Language and Literature. His acceptance speech, *Der Meridian* (1961; translated as "The Meridian," 1977), is viewed by critics as a statement of poetic theory, but it is also a literary expression of how Celan attempts to make sense of the world. Written as a dialogue with his listeners, it is punctuated by reservations or uncertainties about the poet's craft, leading the listener/reader through a labyrinth of images relating to the poet's quest for speech in an age when speech has become nearly impossible. After an exposition of Büchner's tragedy *Dantons Tod* (1835) and his short story "Lenz" (1839), both of which for Celan pay homage to the "Majestät des Absurden" (Majesty of the Absurd) characteristic of our era, he expresses doubts about the existence of literary "art"; before anything else, the contemporary writer must radically question the existence of such art. Writing a poem is a search for an "Ort" (place), perhaps a place that does not exist, a "u-topia." Poetic creations do not enjoy universal, a priori existence but arise only through encounters, through the meeting of a voice with an Other, through dialogue that allows an "I" to orient itself through speech and understand itself through contact with a Thou, an act that enables this "I" to discover the "meridian" that connects it through language to the rest of the world.

Before his suicide sometime in April 1970—he had been missing since the middle of April and his body was found in early May—Celan produced only one more prose work, a brief address delivered to the Hebrew Writers' Association on 14 October 1969 during a trip to Israel; it was published in the Tel Aviv magazine *Die Stimme* in August 1970. In the address Celan expresses gratitude for discovering in Israel an "äußere und innere Landschaft" (external and internal landscape) conducive to creating great poetry. He draws an analogy between these two landscapes: "Ich verstehe . . . den dankbaren Stolz auf jedes selbstgepflanzte Grün, das bereitsteht, jeden der hier vorbeikommt zu erfrischen; wie ich die Freude begreife über jedes neuerworbene, selbsterfühlte Wort, das herbeieilt, den ihm Zugewandeten zu stärken" (I understand . . . the grateful pride in every homegrown green thing that stands ready to refresh anyone who comes by; just as I comprehend the joy in every newly won, self-felt word that rushes up to strengthen him who is receptive to it).

Under the heading "Prose," the 1983 edition of Celan's collected works includes three letters he wrote in response to survey questions. Celan wrote brilliant letters; like Rainer Maria Rilke's, they could almost qualify as a separate genre. But so few of them have been published that it is not yet possible to give a general analysis of their style and content.

Creative extensions and elaborations of his poetry, Celan's prose works express the strain of being Jewish, the struggle to reclaim language in a nonpoetic age, and the need for dialogue as a means of connecting oneself with and orienting oneself in the modern world.

Source: James K. Lyon, "Paul Celan," in *Dictionary of Literary Biography*, Vol. 69, *Contemporary German Fiction Writers, First Series*, edited by Wolfgang D. Elfe, and James Hardin, Gale, 1988, pp. 55–60.

Sources

Celan, Paul, "Late and Deep," in *Selected Poems and Prose of Paul Celan*, translated by John Felstiner, W. W. Norton, 2001.

Colin, Amy, "Innovation and Repetition," in *Paul Celan: Holograms of Darkness*, Indiana University Press, 1991, p. 107.

Felstiner, John, *Paul Celan: Poet, Survivor, Jew*, Yale University Press, 1995.

———, "Paul Celan: The Strain of Jewishness," in *Commentary*, Vol. 79, No. 4, April 1985, pp. 44–49.

Glenn, Jerry, "Early Poems and *Mohn und Gedächtnis*," in *Paul Celan*, Twayne Publishers, 1973, pp. 62–63.

———, "*Sprachgitter*," in *Paul Celan*, Twayne Publishers, 1973, p. 91.

Hilberg, Raul, *The Destruction of the European Jews*, Holmes & Meier, 1985, pp. 13–20.

Jeffrey, David Lyle, ed., *A Dictionary of Biblical Tradition in English Literature*, William B. Eerdmans, 1992.

Rosenthal, Bianca, *Pathways to Paul Celan: A History of Critical Responses as a Chorus of Discordant Voices*, Peter Lang Publishing, 1995, pp. 6–7, 91.

Samuels, Clarise, *Holocaust Visions: Surrealism and Existentialism in the Poetry of Paul Celan*, Camden House, 1993, p. 124.

Further Reading

Chalfen, Israel, *Paul Celan: A Biography of His Youth*, Persea Books, 1991.

This short book traces Celan's life up to the point where he moves to Vienna in 1947 and contains a number of poems that can be linked with specific instances in his life.

Hoffman, Eva, *After Such Knowledge: Where Memory of the Holocaust Ends and History Begins*, Public Affairs, 2004.

As the survivors of the Holocaust die of old age sixty years after the event, how does the memory of this event affect subsequent generations? This book of essays deals with the personal reactions of the second generation, the children of the survivors, and takes up issues of personal and collective responsibility.

Levi, Primo, *Survival in Auschwitz*, Touchstone Books, 1995.

This book is an account of Levi's ten months in the infamous death camp. It is remarkable for its restraint and close observation of life and death.

Wiesel, Elie, *The Night Trilogy: Night, Dawn, The Accident*, Noonday Press, 1987.

These three short novels deal with young men surviving the Holocaust, victims becoming executioners, and trying to make a new life with the memories.

Maternity

Anna Swir

1970

"Maternity" by Anna Swir has appeared in two of the English translations of her works: *Talking to My Body* and *Happy as a Dog's Tail*. The title of the poem is appropriate to its content since the poem is about a woman facing her newborn child for the first time and trying to come to terms with this new situation. While the publication date of the poem is not mentioned in the English translations, it is known that Anna Swir had a daughter who is the likely subject of the poem. This daughter would have been born sometime in the 1930s or 1940s, but the poem was probably written a long time afterward. Its first appearance was in the 1970 Polish publication of a collection called *Wind*. *Happy as a Dog's Tail* was published in Poland in 1978 and published in the United States in 1985. *Talking to My Body* was published in the United States in 1996.

In the first publication of "Maternity," the poem had two additional stanzas that were removed for *Talking to My Body*. These two stanzas seem only to repeat the already established message and do little to add to the poem. Furthermore, the additional two stanzas spell out a conclusion rather than allowing the readers to figure it out on their own. Consequently, the shortened version seems to have a more dramatic ending and more impact on the reader's imagination. Perhaps for these reasons, the two stanzas were dropped in the second English collection of Swir's poems. "Maternity" fits into Swir's central theme in these two collections, which is referencing the body, but it also inludes themes of motherhood, love, and independence.

Anna Swir

Author Biography

Anna Swir (actual name Swirszczyńska) was born in Warsaw, Poland, on February 7, 1909. Her father, an artist, was unable to keep his family out of dire poverty. Swir grew up doing her schoolwork and sleeping in her father's workshop. Nonetheless, in a group of poems that she wrote years later about her mother and father, she expressed a close bond and sincere gratitude. Swir managed to put herself through college where she studied medieval and baroque Polish literature. A poem of hers was published in a popular magazine in 1930 when she was only 21 years old. Swir's first book of poetry and drama was published in 1936, the same year she went to work for an association for teachers, where she stayed until 1939. At the same time, she was the chief editor of a very famous magazine that was read by most of the children of Poland during that period.

When the Nazis invaded in 1939, she became a member of the Polish Resistance, writing for underground publications as well as helping to maintain the intellectual life of Poles through secret poetry readings and other literary meetings. During the Warsaw uprising in 1944, she helped to nurse the soldiers at a makeshift military hospital. After the destruction of Warsaw, she moved to Krakow where she lived from 1945 until her death in 1984. Although the war was a pivotal point in Swir's life, she waited almost thirty years before she wrote about it. The result was a collection of poetry published in 1974 entitled *Building the Barricade*.

As her pre-war activities indicate, for a number of years Swir was best known for her many poems and stories for children. After the war, from 1946–1950, she was the director of a theatre for children. Her second book of poetry was published in 1958, followed by other collections in 1967 and 1970. Continuing her work as a playwright, too, Swir wrote an opera for young people in 1963, and a play in 1976 set in World War II that won a special award from the Polish Prime Minister.

In her sixties, Swir began to write about the female experience in love, desire, motherhood, fate, old age, disease, and rejection. In 1972, she published *I'm a Woman*, and in 1978 *Happy as a Dog's Tail*—both collections of poetry that emphasized feminism and eroticism. This was followed posthumously in 1985 by *Suffering and Joy*, a collection of poems about her parents. Perhaps because of her war experiences, Swir replaced her religious faith with a belief in only the realities of the flesh. Her prime devotion seems to have been to her country. However, when Swir died of cancer in 1984, her daughter reported that Swir had reconciled with the Catholic Church. In that same year, Nobel Laureate Czeslaw Milosz and Leonard Nathan translated into English the poems in *Happy as a Dog's Tail*. In 1996, they would publish a revised collection of Swir's poetry in *Talking to My Body*. In both books, they provided a lengthy and excellent analysis of Swir's life's work.

Poem Text

I gave birth to life.
It went out of my entrails
and asks for the sacrifice of my life
as does an Aztec deity.
I lean over a little puppet,
we look at each other
with four eyes.

"You are not going to defeat me," I say
"I won't be an egg which you would crack
in a hurry for the world,
a footbridge that you would take on the way to
    your life.
I will defend myself."

I lean over a little puppet,
I notice

a tiny movement of a tiny finger
which a little while ago was still in me,
in which, under a thin skin,
my own blood flows.
And suddenly I am flooded
by a high, luminous wave
of humility.
Powerless, I drown.

Poem Summary

The Event

The first four lines of "Maternity" deal with the obvious topic of life. However, Swir looks at birth in terms of both a new life, the baby, and a sacrificed life, that of the mother. Using the first person, Swir says "I gave birth to life," not "I gave birth to a baby" or "a child" or anything yet connected to her as a human. Rather, Swir is focused on the product of birth as a living creature that not only has a birth, but also will have a death and a life in between. This perspective is extended in the second sentence (lines 2–4) with the use of what appears to be an odd word choice: "entrails." When discussing birth, one usually uses terms such as "womb" or "uterus" or even "belly." Entrails has the meaning of guts or intestines. Unless Swir's biology is faulty, she chose "entrails" to associate the product of her body with other eliminations to emphasize that what came out this time was something living. This unique turn of events demands something from her life in turn. Swir likens the demands of motherhood to the human sacrifice once made to the gods by the Aztecs, perhaps because the commitment is so total and all-consuming.

The Confrontation

In the next three lines, Swir starts to focus in on the baby, whom she calls "a little puppet." This mother seems still not to be sure of what she has gotten herself into. What is this little creature she has been given? It is too hard to believe that it is a real living human, so is it a toy? But the toy is looking at her just as she is looking at it. "With four eyes" is dropped into the next line to heighten the impact of the two staring at each other. One wonders if Swir wrote "four eyes" because the mother recognizes a similarity between her own eyes and that of the child.

The Defiant Statement

In a pique of independence, the mother tells the baby that she is not going to "defeat" her mother. The word choice indicates that the mother views the existence of this child as a conflict in her life and the baby as someone engaged in a power struggle with her. The mother wants to get it straight from the beginning that the mother was not just the shell to this egg, not just a vessel that carried the child only to be cast aside. The mother declares that she will defend herself from being used, from being walked on like "a footbridge," by the child. The message is made clear as Swir separates out "I will defend myself." The notion that a mother would need to defend herself against her child is contrary to the traditional picture of a mother willingly giving of herself in every possible way to provide for her child's needs.

The Realization

The mother's defiance ends in the third stanza as she once again leans over the "little puppet" and makes a discovery. Drawing the reader's attention to her revelation, Swir puts "I notice" by itself on the second line. What she notices is the "tiny movement of a tiny finger." This baby is becoming more real by the minute. That finger was just "a little while ago" still inside the mother, waiting to be born. The baby was just under her mother's skin, where the mother's own blood flows. Swir may have chosen this way to describe the previous physical relationship to connect to the universal saying about "my own flesh and blood." In fact, Swir uses "my own blood." These lines are a re-crafting of an old expression to explain the mother's steps toward the realization of the closeness and uniqueness of her relationship with this child.

The Surrender

When "suddenly" the light goes on and the connection is made in the mother's mind, she is "flooded" with emotion. Surprisingly, the emotion named is not that of love, but of "humility." Swir dramatizes her choice of humility over love by placing "of love" on a separate line. The reader knows that the mother has been overwhelmed with love for the child, but Swir probably chose "humility" as the descriptive word in order to emphasize her feelings as being the same as one experiences when in the awesome presence of a wonder of nature or a miracle of God. The final line, "Powerless, I drown," indicates a total surrender to motherly love. Consequently, the poem has moved from a first stanza that sets the scene and expresses assessment, to a second stanza that is a declaration of defiant independence, to the third and final stanza that is a capitulation to maternal instinct and attachment as natural and inevitable as an ocean wave or the life cycle itself.

Topics For Further Study

- Explore the relationship between Czeslaw Milosz and Anna Swir. How has Milosz been important to the development of an American audience for Swir?
- Consult some of the English-language anthologies that contain poems by Swir and comment on the anthologist's reasons for choosing to include this Polish poet.
- Swir was involved in the Polish underground during World War II. Research the Polish underground and describe the work that she and other notables, such as Pope John Paul II and Czeslaw Milosz, did to resist Nazi occupation.
- Swir is considered a feminist poet. Who are some other feminist writers and what traits do they have in common?
- Do a search for poems about motherhood from other writers in other eras. How does the attitude toward motherhood change or stay the same through the years? How do the poems differ if the author is male instead of female?

Themes

Maternal Love

The title of the poem makes it obvious that maternity is the subject that Swir wishes to explore. Her description of that first private meeting between mother and child is one to which any mother could relate. This event is an important transition in a woman's life. She is no longer just herself because there is now an extension of herself. That extension may be very much like the mother, or very different. Either way, the new person is an enormous responsibility for the mother. Panic is a common reaction as the reality of the 24-hours-a-day, 7-days-a-week, 18-years-or-longer commitment sinks in. The mother cannot help but wonder how she is going to keep this tiny creature alive and take care of it. There is also the very natural reaction of concern on the mother's part about what is going to happen to her own life in terms of personal time and space. How is she going to fit this child into her life? How will she be able to meet the demands of motherhood? The answer, for Swir, is to humbly submit to the power of maternal love and let its great force carry her through all that will come.

Independence

As a feminist, Swir advocated a woman's independence and a freedom from stereotypical roles. In the feminist debate, motherhood has sometimes been blamed for trapping women into a dependent housewife status. Feminism has worked to prove that having children does not mean that a woman cannot continue a career or continue to have roles other than solely that of mother. Therefore, the mother in "Maternity" is quick to try to set limits on her relationship with her child. She makes it clear that becoming a mother does not mean that she is now going to sacrifice her whole life for that of her child. The child may have already been given life by her mother, but she is not going to be allowed to suck the life out of her mother. The child must make her own way without using her mother as a vehicle on the path of life just as she was the vehicle of birth. By the end of the poem, though, the narrator realizes that providing sustenance and guidance is not something the child will take from the mother, but is something that the mother will lovingly give as a natural part of her life. Her independence as a woman is not being taken away; rather, a new dimension is being added to her humanity.

Flesh

Czeslaw Milosz, Swir's best-known critic, says that the central theme to all of Swir's later works is flesh. Certainly, in "Maternity" there are many references to the flesh of the human body. There is nothing more "flesh of my flesh" than giving birth. Swir includes "entrails" and "eyes" in her description of the contact that the mother and child have made. It is a body part, a tiny finger, that catches the mother's notice and causes her to remember that a short time before that finger was under her flesh, her skin. In the end, just as her blood once flowed past the child in her womb, now a flow of emotion envelops her. Thus, the theme of flesh is continued in this poem about giving birth and all the non-physical elements that are involved in this physical process.

Style

Free Verse

Free verse does not use the fixed line lengths nor the strict metrical and rhyme patterns characteristic of formal poetry such as a sonnet or haiku. Instead, free verse varies line length to aid in achieving a desired impact. In "Maternity," Swir uses line length to feed the reader only one bite of thought at a time. She waits from one line to the next to drop the other shoe, so to speak. For example, the line "and asks for the sacrifice of my life" is stopped to let the reader wonder about or assume the meaning of "sacrifice." Then the next line "as does the Aztec deity" explains the kind of sacrifice with a comparison that is probably much more harsh than the reader expected.

Rhythm and sound patterns in free verse are created by the use of assonance, alliteration, internal rhyme, and the like. Swir uses short, choppy lines in the first stanza, perhaps as an indication of reticence. However, when the narrator talks to the child in the second stanza, the lines are longer to resemble speech. The third stanza is a mix of short and long lines as the narrator struggles with feelings of wonder and understanding. Rhythm is also created within lines by designing phrases of about equal length and by repeating phrases that have the same syntactical structure. The result is a cadence similar to the balance of phrases in a musical composition. In 1855, Walt Whitman was the first major poet to use free verse; today, it is the most popular form of poetry.

Narrative Poetry

Some poems, like prose, have a story, a setting of time and place, a specific point of view, and characters dramatizing the message. The main character, perhaps the only one, will be the "I" in the poem. The speaker may be the poet or a fictional character and may be speaking to another character, perhaps in a dialogue. Usually, however, the speaker in a narrative poem is a lone character speaking about a deep and personal concern. In "Maternity," Swir gives the reader the story of a new mother greeting her baby. The time is soon after the birth ("a little while ago was still in me"), but the place is not mentioned. One can imagine the place to be in a hospital. Swir opens with "I," thus immediately establishing the point of view. The speaker is the poet, but presented as if she were any new mother. The other character to whom she speaks is the baby. Undoubtedly, the speaker is talking about a deep and personal concern at a moment like this one between mother and child. Consequently, "Maternity" fits all the characteristics of a narrative poem.

Visual Imagery

Visual imagery, the most frequently used type of imagery in poetry, is a mental picture, or image, created by words. The image can be a symbolic interpretation or a metaphor providing a description. In "Maternity," Swir brings to mind the Aztec practice of human sacrifice to express the totality of a child's demands on its mother. She compares the baby to a "little puppet" and uses the images of a cracked egg and a footbridge to describe the use a child might make of a parent. At the end of the poem, Swir creates a picture of a wave of water drowning the mother to express the overwhelming feeling of humility that consumes her as she is overawed by the miracle of life and accepts the inevitability of maternal love. All these images help to establish the complexity and conflict of the relationship between mother and child.

Historical Context

Twentieth Century Poland

Anna Swir lived from 1909 to 1984, a time period that saw a multitude of changes in the country of Poland. The dominant power in eastern Europe from the fourteenth to the seventeenth centuries, Poland did not even exist as a separate country when Swir was born. From 1772 to 1918, the Polish territory was divided among Russia, Austria, and Prussia. However, at the end of World War I, the state of Poland was restored as a consequence of the dissolution of the Russian, Austrian, and German empires. Heavily dependent on agriculture, the Polish economy was reformed and modernized in the 1920s, but suffered from the Great Depression of the 1930s along with the rest of the world. A leader of the Polish workers' movement, Jozef

Compare & Contrast

- **1930s and 1940s:** Between the World Wars, literature in independent Poland flourishes. After the Nazi invasion, cultural and intellectual pursuits are forbidden, thus forcing the literary community to work underground.

  1980: Anna Swir copyrights the poems published in 1978 as *Happy as a Dog's Tail*, including the poem "Maternity." 1980 is the last year that Polish writers enjoy a freedom unknown in other Eastern bloc countries. In 1981, the government ends its liberal publication policy. As a result, a large underground press develops.

  Today: After the 1989 defeat of communism, censorship ends. Polish literature again becomes a vital part of the culture and is now available to the rest of the world.

- **1930s and 1940s:** The spectre of Hitler looms over all of Europe, especially in neighboring Poland. During the invasion of Poland, millions of Poles die in the effort to defeat Germany. Poland is then enslaved after World War I by a Soviet takeover.

  1980: Because of the Gdansk shipyard strike, the government is forced to reach an accord with the 10-million member trade union Solidarity.

  Today: Poland is no longer a Soviet satellite state but a vibrant independent democracy whose gross national product is the highest in Europe by the mid-1990s.

- **1930s and 1940s:** In 1933, Czeslaw Milosz's first book of verse, *Poem of Frozen Time*, expresses fears of an impending war and worldwide disaster. During the war, he publishes three anti-Nazi books through the underground literary community. After the war, Milosz works in the diplomatic service.

  1980: Milosz wins the Nobel Prize for Literature for his body of work in poetry and essays. He retires from his job as a professor of Slavic Languages and Literatures at the University of California at Berkeley.

  Today: Milosz, an American citizen since 1970, remains in the United States and translates two books of Swir's poetry.

Pilsudski, gained control of the government in 1926 and stayed in power until his death in 1935. The military regime that followed was ineffectual and unable to defend itself against the invasion, in September of 1939, by Nazi Germany on the western border and the Soviet Union on the eastern border of Poland.

Nonetheless, the 20 years of independence between the wars had fostered a richness of intellectual, artistic, and scholarly life. By 1939, Swir was 30 years old, had published a book of poems, and was working as an editor. After the invasion, the Nazi suppression of most literary activities drove Swir and others to meet secretly. She helped with underground publications and the perpetuation of intellectual pursuits. This effort was diminished by the exodus and death of many of Poland's writers and artists whom the Nazis deported and executed in an attempt to destroy the intellectual culture of Poland.

The Germans virtually exterminated the Jewish population of Poland at Auschwitz and other camps, as well as in the infamous Warsaw Ghetto Uprising in 1943 that Swir witnessed and wrote about in a later collection of war poems. The Nazis killed three million ethnic Poles as well. Meanwhile, the Soviets forced two million Poles into eastern labor camps where many died. However, after Germany declared war on the Soviets in 1941, Stalin organized Polish armies to fight the Germans and both Poland and the U. S. S. R. raised flags over the German capitol when the Nazis were defeated.

After World War II, Poland became a Soviet satellite country and a rigid police state. Particularly in the 1950s and 1960s, intellectuals were subject to government pressures. As a result, students demonstrated for intellectual freedom in 1968 but were met with harsh reprisals and the isolation of the intelligentsia. Finally, after Polish cardinal Karol Wojtyla became Pope John Paul II in 1978, and made an inspirational trip to Poland in 1979, the intelligentsia and the labor movement formed a coalition under the protection of the church, and began to build a countersociety.

In 1980, the Solidarity labor union, under the leadership of an electrician named Lech Walesa, initiated strikes in the shipyards of Gdansk. Thus began the first independent social and political movement in postwar eastern Europe. However, the government reaction to the strikes was to impose martial law and force Solidarity underground until 1989. With the liberalized policies of Mikhail Gorbachev in the U. S. S. R., Solidarity was able to force the Polish communists to grant concessions that eventually led to the demise of communism in Poland and the establishment of a democratic society. Unfortunately, Swir died in 1984, five years before the new freedoms were established.

A wave symbolizes the mother's feelings in Swir's poem

Critical Overview

If imitation is the sincerest form of flattery, then perhaps being anthologized is the sincerest form of critical acclaim that an author can merit. While access to literary criticism concerning Anna Swir is limited in English, many of her works are available in anthologies. People who are experts in poetry know the craft well and know who the best poets are, wherever they are. Consequently, there are a number of English language anthologies containing poems by Swir, and amazingly, three of them were published in 2003.

Kiss Off: Poems to Set You Free, published in January of 2003 by Mary D. Esselman and Elizabeth Ash Velez, includes Swir's Poem "She Does Not Remember." Also in January of 2003, Roger Housden published *Ten Poems to Open Your Heart.* Although none of the ten poems chosen for this book is by Anna Swir, Housden uses an excerpt from Swir's poem "The Same Inside" as part of his discussion of poems that illustrate kindness. He calls "The Same Inside" "a remarkable love poem" that shows Swir capable of "the great beating heart of compassion that the Buddhists say exists naturally in all beings." Later in 2003, Roger Housden published another book about love. The description on the book flap says that *Risking Everything: 110 Poems of Love and Revelation* is an anthology that

> brings together great poets from around the world whose work transcends culture and time. Their words reach past the outer division to the universal currents of love and revelation that move and inspire us all. These poems urge us to wake up and love. They also call on us to relinquish our grip on ideas and opinions that confine us and, instead, to risk moving forward into the life that is truly ours.

Since four of Swir's poems are included in this collection, this description then applies to her work as well. Furthermore, the biographical piece on Swir included in this book provides the following criticism:

> A militant feminist and author of uninhibited love poems, her work conveys an erotic intensity and warmth, along with an empathy and compassion for those who suffer. Her poems on war and the Nazi occupation of Poland were among the finest of her generation.

Another form of flattery for an author is for a doctoral student to write about that person's work. In 2002, a dissertation was approved at the University of Michigan entitled: "Bodies in Search of Self: Body and Identity in the Poetic Works of Audre Lorde, Anna Swirszczynska and Marina Tsvetaeva." The author, Laura Ann Miller-Purrenhage, says that these authors are "well-known for their sometimes shocking use of the body in their poetry and prose." She adds that:

> the confluence of historical and personal trauma, modernity and postmodernity and the strain of racist, sexist and heterosexist marginalization spurred these authors toward the body as a site where they could explore their views of identity and, simultaneously, taught them that the body is an integral part of the self.

Miller-Purrenhage claims that Swir and the other two authors "create a poetics of identity that embraces the fragmentation, fluctuation, multiplicity and embodied nature of the self" and mirror the "poetics of identity" in their "stylistics."

There were English-language reviews of Swir's poetry collections when they were translated for publication. Writing for *Magill Book Reviews*, Eric Howard says that: "Swir's great excellence as a poet is that she communicates profound sentiments in language that, even in translation, is simple, direct, and unforced."

Seamus Heaney, winner of the Nobel Prize in Literature in 1995 and one of Northern Ireland's most notable contemporary poets, refers to Swir in his writings about literature. *Finders Keepers: Selected Prose 1971–2001* is a collection, not of Heaney's poetry, but of selected prose works that include memoirs, lecture transcripts, and literary criticism, among other topics. Heaney twice quotes Swir: once when discussing inspiration, and once when discussing the poetry of Robert Lowell.

Another Nobel laureate, Czeslaw Milosz, provides extensive insight into the creativity of Swir in his introduction to the two collections of her poetry that he translated and published in the United States: *Happy as a Dog's Tail* and *Talking to My Body*. In these two books, Milosz added a transcript of a conversation that he and his co-translator, Leonard Nathan, had about Swir that discusses her style, motivation, topics, and quality. Further, Milosz included several of Swir's poems in his anthology of poetry from around the world, *A Book of Luminous Things*. All of this attention from anthologists, students, and Nobel poets constitutes impressive critical acknowledgment of Swir's talent and insight.

Criticism

Lois Kerschen

Kerschen is a freelance writer and part-time English instructor. In this essay, Kerschen discusses two of the most notable characteristics of Swir's poetry: the brevity of her style and the dualism of her subject matter, both of which are evident in "Maternity."

The brevity of Anna Swir's poetry is deeply rooted in the history of the Polish language. The written form of the Polish vernacular originated in monasteries and religious chapters in the eleventh century, where the important historic and dynastic events were recorded according to their dates. These calendar notes were necessarily brief, using a minimum of words. In addition, the early secular literature of Poland from the Middle Ages could be intensely personal. Swir studied medieval literature in college and was, therefore, familiar with these elements from that period. As a poet, Swir achieves both this brevity and intensity of emotion in her work, thus creating a form that is as simple and direct as possible, as evidenced in "Maternity."

Medieval poetry included "miniatures" or very short poems that were highly stylized, but gave only a cameo expression to an idea. Swir took this miniature form, stripped it bare, and created a message bearer as quick as a lightning bolt. Her poems have more content than a haiku, and do not use a set form like a haiku, but the intent of a sharp point made quickly is the same. Swir believed that a poet should forego style and use only the most necessary and useful words. The result is uniquely intense poetry. Leonard Nathan, a co-translator with Milosz for Swir's books, notes that, in Swir's poetry, "the situations are filled out with a few strokes, the characters are nameless, the locale anywhere. It's almost geometrical, a matter of line more than color, of form more than substance." In "Maternity," it is true that the characters are nameless and the locale anywhere, even though we suspect that the scene described is autobiographical. However, the anonymity of characters and locale are what make the message universal.

There is also a history in European poetry of a dialogue between the body and the soul. Certainly, Swir continues this tradition of detachment in her book *Talking to My Body*, although Swir may not have considered the "self" that talks to the body to be a soul. In "Maternity," she is not talking to her own body, but to this strange product of her body that she attempts to keep separate from her self. Czeslaw Milosz, Swir's chief critic and translator, says that the theme of Swir's poetry is flesh: "Flesh in love and ecstasy, in pain, in terror, flesh afraid of loneliness, giving birth, [as in "Maternity"] resting, feeling the flow of time or reducing time to one instant." Bogdana Carpenter, a critic for *World Literature Today*, agrees that the body is the center of Swir's poetry. Further, it is the gate to knowledge of the self and the world. Carpenter adds, "In the dichotomy between the abstract and the physical, between philosophy and experience, ideas and sensations, Swir emphatically opts each time for the second term of the opposition."

But is the dichotomy not reconciled every time a poet puts pen to paper? Is not the expression of the abstract in printed, physical form, a meeting of these two opposites? Does the poet not bring her sensations, experience, ideas, and sensations all together in a poem? Swir certainly seems to do so, but perhaps that is why her poems are so brief. Perhaps she believes that the chance to reconcile these opposites is so fleeting that it can be captured for only a moment in a poem. "Maternity" succeeds in capturing this fleeting connection: the physical aspect of giving birth leads to the abstract emotion of love; the experience of giving birth leads to the philosophy of humble acceptance; the sensation of giving birth leads to new concepts about motherhood.

"'Maternity' succeeds in capturing this fleeting connection: the physical aspect of giving birth leads to the abstract emotion of love, the experience of giving birth leads to the philosophy of humble acceptance, the sensation of giving birth leads to new concepts about motherhood."

Leonard Nathan says, in the dialogue between himself and Milosz about the Swir poems they translated, "The voice of these poems is that of a woman seemingly isolated from or indifferent to moral and social concerns." However, a woman who participated in the Polish resistance could not possibly be indifferent to moral and social concerns. It is possible, though, that she set those concerns aside for a while or gave them expression in a different reality. The trauma of the war most likely is the reason for her belief in the reality of the flesh to the exclusion of other realities. Carpenter suspects that it is because of Swir's war experiences with death, physical suffering, and wounds that she has such an interest in the flesh, "For the experience of war is not so much a spiritual as a physical and biological experience, and it most often brings a realization that very little matters beyond flesh."

Swir did not write about the war in her poetry until thirty years after the end of the conflict. Perhaps that part of her was hidden away. Such a reaction is fairly common among survivors of trauma—i.e., a separation of the bad experiences from the rest of one's life, as if the trauma were in another life, another world. Such a reaction allows the victim to feel that the same bad experiences could not happen in the present life because they belong to an old place and time that no longer exists. The memories are locked away in a trunk in the mind's attic and never allowed out again. Nonetheless, the person has been changed. Swir exchanged religious belief for a belief in the flesh, and proceeded to struggle with the conflict of body and soul through her poetry.

This struggle is discussed at length in the dialogue between Milosz and Nathan. They conclude that one of the results of her materialism is a mortality of human relationships. If every encounter is strictly physical, then a deeper relationship that is warm, ongoing and sympathetic does not seem possible. However, this theory does not hold true in "Maternity," because the initial distance that the mother tries to establish between herself and her child—a distance that is typical of Swir—is cast aside in the bonding that is too strong to resist.

John Carpenter, in a review for the *Kenyon Review*, connects the poems about the Warsaw Uprising with powerful statements about the defense of life, "about the life-affirming instincts and reactions of the human body when it finds itself menaced by danger. She [Swir] describes these reactions as having a power that often took her by surprise." Another explanation for the duality in Swir's poetry is offered by Eric Howard, in an article for Magill Book Reviews. He says that the mixture of fleshly realism and ecstasy is one of frailty and power. "A key to Swir's poetic technique is to move from the mundane to the transcendent, often by paying proper attention to the

What Do I Read Next?

- *Happy as a Dog's Tail* is another translation of Swir's poetry by Czeslaw Milosz and Leonard Nathan. It was published in the United States in 1985. It contains virtually the same Introduction and Dialogue as *Talking to My Body* and has many of the same poems.
- *New and Collected Poems: 1931–2001* is a collection of poetry by Czeslaw Milosz, winner of the Nobel Prize in Literature in 1980 and translator of Swir's poetry. Received with rave reviews, the poetry reflects his realm of worldly experience from his twentieth to his ninetieth birthday.
- *A Book of Luminous Things: An International Anthology of Poetry* (1998) is a collection that was personally chosen by Czeslaw Milosz. Prefaces to most of the poems, written by Milosz, greatly enhance the reader's understanding and enjoyment. The collection, which includes Chinese, American and European poetry, includes several selections from Swir's works.
- *Risking Everything: 110 Poems of Love and Revelation* (2003), by Roger Housden, is an anthology of poems that urges us to wake up and risk moving forward into life and love. Four of the poems are by Anna Swir: "The Greatest Love," "Dithyramb of a Happy Woman," "The Same Inside," and "Thank You, My Fate."
- Czeslaw Milosz is one of Swir's biggest fans, yet she is not included in his anthology *Postwar Polish Poetry*. The reason is probably that this book was published in 1965 and Swir did not begin publishing the feminist and erotic poetry for which she gained attention until a few years later. Nonetheless, this book is a good look at her peers.

human, specifically the woman's, body." This latter idea seems to fit "Maternity" in that Swir moves from the physical experience of giving birth, an everyday occurrence in the world, to the transcendent epiphany of maternal love.

Howard also says that in Swir's poem "What is a Pineal Gland" the poet muses on how much, if at all, one person can belong to another. Swir concludes in this poem that the bodies of the two lovers are apart, with the implication, Howard says, that they are apart even from those who live in them. In "Maternity," Swir answers that question differently: a mother and child belong to each other, with the emphasis it seems on the mother being possessed by the child. Although Swir tries to explain to the child that they are separate bodies, the fact that the child's body came out of her own is too overwhelming a connection to win the argument. She has to concede to their bond.

Swir's feminism also contributes to her duality, at least in the expectations of others. She writes about a woman's life in the twentieth century when the perceptions of a woman's role are so much in flux that emancipation sometimes means loneliness. For Swir, the isolation extends to her separation from her religion and her alienation from her own body. It does not, however, separate her from her country. It might be expected that someone as skeptical and removed from idealism as Swir would not be patriotic, but the Polish experience has resulted in a country where patriotism is in the very marrow of the culture and even Swir could not escape from that. On the contrary, she embraced her loyalty with a devotion as religious as any faith. She may have been a liberated woman, but she yearned for the liberation of her country as well. Once again, the expectation that Swir was too hedonistic to care about politics is as misplaced as the mother's expectation in "Maternity" that she can escape her loyalties to her child.

A review of "Maternity" shows that this poem is indeed another of Swir's poems that approaches a subject from the viewpoint of flesh. This poem also continues the dialogue between body and soul, but for once the soul looks back at her with a baby's eyes. Whereas Felicity Rosslyn, a critic for the

PN Review found that Swir's poetry describes an involvement with the flesh that removes the person from consciousness, responsibility, and memory, in this poem, the mother can no longer escape reality through physical ecstasy. Her body has produced something else physical that has sufficient power to "flood" and "drown" her defiant detachment, making her submit to the "wave" of emotion that will make her answer to and be responsible for this child. As a result, the poet known for shockingly erotic poetry, her worship of the flesh, her independence, has created a mother's poem that is a traditional sentiment written in Swir's unique brevity and style.

Source: Lois Kerschen, Critical Essay on "Maternity," in *Poetry for Students*, Thomson Gale, 2005.

Laura Carter

Carter is currently employed as a freelance writer. In this essay, Carter examines the role of both flesh and feminism plays in shaping the poet's work.

Swir's "Maternity" is part of a poetry collection that mirrors the poet's feminist leanings and her attempts to come to terms with eroticism. Critic and poet Czeslaw Milosz, in the introduction to *Talking to My Body*, writes of the central theme of Swir's poetry: flesh. Milosz describes her work as an expression of the flesh, "flesh in love—ecstasy, flesh in terror, flesh afraid of loneliness, exuberant, running, lazy, flesh of a woman giving birth, resting . . . feeling the flow of time or reducing time to one instant." Maternity relies on this theme, working as one of the many of the poetic snapshots of Swir's that delve into the human condition, that of the flesh.

Characteristic of Swir's poetry is a marked separation of the speaker from her body. The poem opens with the speaker having given birth to new life, a life that "came out of [her] entrails." Instead of being a cause for celebration, the birth is equated to an expulsion from the body, followed by "viscera," or internal organs. The words give a somewhat gruesome depiction, equally sterile and scientific in their assessment. Moving on to the next line, the poem speaks of the baby not as joy anticipated, but rather as the "sacrifice of" the speaker's life.

Rather than relief after the birth, a psychic struggle ensues. As the work moves forward, the speaker defies the new life, exclaiming "You are not going to defeat me." The speaker is not an egg waiting to be cracked; she will not be taken off guard. She is not someone to be walked over. Instead of pulling the baby to her or shielding it in her nurturing arms, she is poised and ready to defend herself against this alien entity whom minutes ago emerged from her very flesh. The speaker's reaction is very hostile, which is not at all what one might expect from a new mother.

> *"Tiny movements give way to a flood of humility, and the speaker drowns in emotion."*

There is a shifting at the end of the poem when "the little puppet" becomes the flesh of her flesh. Tiny movements, the wave of a tiny finger, give way to a flood of humility, and the speaker drowns in emotion. The defiance and bravado the speaker displays earlier in the work betrays her own vulnerability. The image of the cracked shell is really a metaphor for her emotional vulnerability. She is more fragile and sensitive than she lets on. She acknowledges this life as a part of herself. Realizing the ramifications of motherhood, the responsibility is almost too much for the speaker to bear. She is overcome by the connection. The sacrifice of the speaker's life, the reader concludes, is really her heart.

Swir's poetry is informed by her life experience as a woman but also as a survivor of the Nazi occupation of Poland during World War II. In the introduction to *Talking to My Body*, Milosz quotes the poet who once waited an hour to be executed. She was radically changed by the experience. To this end, Swir claims "War made me another person. Only then did my own life and the life of my contemporaries enter my poems." But, according to Milosz, Swir had an equally difficult time finding the proper form for what she had seen and lived through. "Maternity" is a reflection of this deeper struggle, one Milosz says is rooted in what he coins a "paradoxical duality." The personae of Swir's poems is "trapped by their flesh, but also distinct from it." He concludes that Swir's poetry "is about not being identical with one's body, about sharing its joys and pains and still rebelling against its laws."

In "Maternity" there is a huge shift in voice, from one of complete disconnect to the reality or deeper consciousness of a tie that cannot be broken. The line "I lean over a little puppet" is repeated twice, part of a distinct movement of the flesh. The birth of the baby is recounted as if a vital part of her body has been lost. There is an alienation of the flesh after exiting the speaker's body. Four eyes meet, yet there is no soulful connection. The form the baby's flesh has taken is different; it is not recognized by the speaker. Then, suddenly, eyes meet once more, the biological connection is recognized, and there is a uniting of the flesh once again, between mother and child. The puppet is an appropriate metaphor; it mirrors the same duality of which Milosz speaks. At one point, it is a lifeless form; at another, an impressionable life force.

A violent shift in imagery mirrors a violence of shifting emotions, from one of detached observation, to one of defiance, and finally complete surrender. There is a rebellion occurring against what the speaker should feel. She is distinct from her own flesh, yet hopelessly trapped in it. The speaker has become engulfed by the natural bond that occurs between mother and child, as the tiny life in front of her tugs at her heartstrings. Sweet release does not come with the speaker's acceptance; rather, she is drowning rather than languishing in love. These final words mirror doubt, incredible fear, and a sense of loss, reasonably shaped by the poet's own life experiences. Swir's rebellion within involved justifying the atrocities, or the seeming inhumanity of the war with the realities of the flesh, of all that is human, of joy, of passion, and particularly, of love. It is quite possible that in the hope of the flesh, she saw an inevitable hopelessness in the human condition, a vulnerability in being human.

During the 1950s and 1960s, women in ever-increasing numbers began to question their roles in society. According to Ruth Rosen, author of *The World Split Open*, women saw their role models, their mothers, "thwarted in their efforts toward self-realization and expression." For many, it was "a deep and bitter lesson." There was a strong resolve by many not to let this happen again. In a discussion of Betty Friedan's *The Feminine Mystique*, Rosen mentions the educated women whose interviews formed the basis of Friedan's work. "Many of these educated women, Friedan discovered, had nurtured dreams that were never realized, but also never forgotten." Rosen then concludes that the postwar conviction that women should limit their lives to the role of wife and homemaker "had tied them to the family, closed opportunities, and crushed many spirits."

There is no male figure in Swir's poem; the events are described from the perspective of someone who is completely and utterly alone, isolated in her motherhood, and, as the poem reaches its ultimate conclusion, her overwhelming passion. The initial description of the birth process is taken from a feminist perspective and opens the poem up to a slightly different interpretation. The baby of Swir's work becomes the speaker's undoing. In the beginning, the speaker mentions the birth of her child as if it were a human sacrifice. She looks into her own child's eyes without feeling. The poem then moves forward in protest rather than appreciation. This new relationship is a threat, marked by defiant declaration: "I won't be / a footbridge that you would take on the way to your life / I will defend myself." Within the passage, the speaker initially likens herself to a cracked egg, a metaphor for her own vulnerability. The fear of motherhood is not necessarily one of responsibility a new parent faces in shaping the future of a child, but of the speaker's own future, evoking her strong battle cry.

The depiction of motherhood in Swir's "Maternity" mirrors the author's amazing ability to speak to the unspoken, of capturing the true essence of an event riddled with feeling. Moving in and out of the realms of the flesh, Swir captures with complete candor and intensity the anticipation of motherhood and all that it implies. Swir's raw, honest assessment is a bridge to understanding fears and emotions lurking within the maternal conscience. Her impressions of motherhood affirm its undeniable role in defining and shaping the lives of women.

Source: Laura Carter, Critical Essay on "Maternity," in *Poetry for Students*, Thomson Gale, 2005.

Bogdana Carpenter

In the following review, Carpenter compares the themes of the body and love in the poems in "Talking to My Body" to Swir's earlier war poems.

Talking to My Body is the third volume of poetry in English by Anna Swir (her real name was Anna Swirszczy—ska); *Happy as a Dog's Tail* appeared in a translation by Czeslaw Milosz and Leonard Nathan in 1985, and *Building the Barricade*, a volume of poems about the 1944 Warsaw Uprising, translated by Magnus J. Kry—ski and Robert A. Maguire, was published in Poland in 1979. Almost simultaneous with this latest superb translation of her poetry in English, Milosz—who has been Swir's enthusiastic promoter on both sides of the Atlantic—published a brilliant analysis of her poetry in Poland.

The title of the English volume captures well what is at the center of Swir's poetry: the body. Even if metaphysical questions lurk behind a number of her poems, it is the body for this poet that is the gate to knowledge: knowledge of the self and knowledge of the world, "a gate / through which I will leave myself / and a gate / through which I will enter myself." In the dichotomy between the abstract and the physical, between philosophy and experience, ideas and sensations, Swir emphatically opts each time for the second term of the opposition.

In the dialogue between the two translators which forms a postscript to the volume, Leonard Nathan wonders how Swir, an author of deeply tragic poems about war and death, could write erotic poems celebrating the ecstasies of the flesh. Where Nathan sees an incongruity, there exists in fact a close connection, and one is tempted to answer by asking whether Swir would ever write her poems of "flesh" without the war experience of death, physical suffering, and wounds. For the experience of war is not so much a spiritual as a physical and biological experience, and it most often brings a realization that very tittle matters beyond flesh.

Although most of the poems in the present selection are contained within the thematics of the body, the volume includes a striking group of poems entitled "Poems About My Father and My Mother" that reveals a new face of the poet: one of love and tenderness. Short and terse, these snapshots of scenes and episodes from the past are formally akin to her war poems, but what is new and different is their warm and affectionate tone. They communicate a sense of continuity between the two generations, of harmony and deep identity between parents and daughter. Stemming from a double impulse, a desire to leave a record and a need to give expression to the feeling of gratitude, they pay back with love for the love once received: "Twenty-four hours / I was dying of fever. // Twenty-four hours / mother knelt / and prayed by my bed. // Twenty-four hours / father lay, face down / on the floor. // They saved me."

Source: Bogdana Carpenter, Review of *Talking to My Body*, in *World Literature Today*, Vol. 71, No. 3, Summer 1997, pp. 616–17.

"In the dichotomy between the abstract and the physical, between philosophy and experience, ideas and sensations, Swir emphatically opts each time for the second term of the opposition."

Eric Howard

In the following review, Howard calls the poems in "Talking to My Body" quite simple and accessible but profound.

Anna Swir's *Talking to My Body*, as the title implies, concentrates on the body. This work may receive more attention than it might have otherwise as a result of another Polish woman, Wislawa Szymborska, who won the Nobel Prize in Literature for 1990. *Talking to My Body* is a large collection, with approximately 150 pages of poetry, a dialogue between translators Czeslaw Milosz and Leonard Nathan, and an introduction. The poems typically are quite simple and accessible but profound. Swir's poems are also short. Milosz notes in the dialogue that "There has been a tendency in Polish poetry of the last decades to search for expression in as few words as possible."

A key to Swir's poetic technique is to move from the mundane to the transcendent, often by paying proper attention to the human, specifically the woman's, body. Her feminism is expressed in such poems as "Goddess of Matriarchy," which contains a characteristically earthly simile, in which the goddess' fingers are like "superhuman fiery carrots."

In "What Is a Pineal Gland," the poet muses on how much, if at all, one person (one body) can belong to another. Watching a lover sleep, she notes that "the body performs its work / with which I am not acquainted," such as the action of the lungs, the viscera, and the pineal gland, of whose activity she admits she is largely ignorant. These reflections lead to the "cold" conclusion that "our two bodies" are "apart," even implying that they are apart from those who live in them as much as they are apart from one's lover.

The first section of the book pays tribute to her parents and their suffering. Her father was a painter; the family went hungry. When World War II came to his studio and destroyed forty year's worth of his work in one bombing raid, he started over again in the morning. He was, as the poems in the section note, crazy. Swir's admiration and comparison for the strength of those who suffer is moving. It seems clear that she has learned her compassion from her own experiences. Swir's great excellence

"Swir's great excellence as a poet is that she communicates profound sentiments in language that, even it translation, is simple, direct, and unforced."

as a poet is that she communicates profound sentiments in language that, even it translation, is simple, direct, and unforced.

Source: Eric Howard, Review of *Talking to My Body*, in *Magill Book Reviews*, June 1, 1997.

Sources

Carpenter, Bogdana, "*Talking to My Body*," in *World Literature Today*, Vol. 71, Summer 1997, p. 616.

Carpenter, John R., "Three Polish Poets, Two Nobel Prizes," in *Kenyon Review*, Vol. 20, No. 1, Winter 1998, p. 148.

Esselman, Mary D., and Elizabeth Ash Velez, *Kiss Off: Poems to Set You Free*, Warner Books, 2003, p. 114.

Heaney, Seamus, "The Government of the Tongue," in *Finders Keepers: Selected Prose 1971–2001*, Farrar Straus & Giroux, 2003, pp. 197, 206.

———, "Lowell's Command," in *Finders Keepers: Selected Prose 1971–2001*, Farrar Straus & Giroux, 2003, pp. 228–29.

Housden, Roger, *Risking Everything: 110 Poems of Love and Revelation*, Harmony Books, 2003, front jacket flap and p. 162.

———, *Ten Poems to Open Your Heart*, Harmony Books, 2003, pp. 72–73.

Howard, Eric, "*Talking to My Body*, Anna Swir, translated by Czeslaw Milosz and Leonard Nathan: 1997 Poetry," in *Magill Book Reviews*, Copper Canyon Press, 1996.

Miller-Purrenhage, Laura Ann, "Bodies in Search of Self: Body and Identity in the Poetic Works of Audre Lorde, Anna Swirszczyńska and Marina Tsvetaeva," Ph.D. diss., University of Michigan, Abstract, in *Dissertation Abstracts International*, Vol. 63, No. 10A, 2002, p. 3543.

Milosz, Czeslaw, ed., *A Book of Luminous Things: An International Anthology of Poetry*, Harvest Books, 1998, pp. 200, 204, 219–20, 233–35, 296.

Nathan, Leonard, in *Talking to My Body*, translated by Czeslaw Milosz and Leonard Nathan, Copper Canyon Press, 1996.

Rosen, Ruth, *The World Split Open: How the Modern Women's Movement Changed America*, Penguin, 2000, pp. 3–15.

Rosslyn, Felicity, "Miraculously Normal: Wislawa Szymborska," in *PN Review*, Vol. 20, No. 5, May–June 1994, p. 14.

Swir, Anna, "Maternity," in *Talking to My Body*, translated by Czeslaw Milosz and Leonard Nathan, Copper Canyon Press, 1996.

Further Reading

Kridl, Manfred, *A Survey of Polish Literature and Culture*, Columbia University Press, 1967.

This book presents a general picture of the development of Polish literature from the Middle Ages to 1945. Included is information about the cultural background and social movements of the literary works. The section on pre–World War II Polish literature gives a good backdrop to the time when Swir was beginning her career.

Krzyzanowski, Julian, *A History of Polish Literature*, translated by Doris Ronowicz, rev. and enl. by Maria Bokszczanin and Halina Geber, Polish Scientific Publishers, 1978.

This book is a translation of a famous work by Krzyzanowski, who is considered one of the greatest historians of Polish literature. While multiple editions of this book have made it familiar to the Polish reader, it was actually written with foreign readers in mind so that they might have a guide to Polish literature along with its historical and cultural background.

Milosz, Czeslaw, *The History of Polish Literature*, Macmillan, 1969.

Considered the standard in English for information about the literary tradition in Poland, this volume is written by a Nobel prize–winning Polish author who lives in the United States and is responsible for a number of translations of Polish literature, including Swir's *Talking to My Body*.

Spearing, A. C., *Readings in Medieval Poetry*, Cambridge University Press, 1987.

Anna Swir was greatly interested in and influenced by the poetry of medieval times. This book is a collection of essays on some of the most famous poems of that period.

Memory

Sarah Arvio

2002

Sarah Arvio's poem "Memory" is one of forty-nine poems collected in her first book, *Visits to the Seventh*, published in June 2003 by Alfred A. Knopf in New York. Poems in this collection capture traces of dialogue between a woman and several ethereal presences; they talk about the break-up of the woman's love affair and the death of her mother. In "Memory," which first appeared in *Raritan Quarterly*, the poet examines remembrances of the lovers' quarrel that lead to the break-up. *Visits to the Seventh* marks Arvio's literary debut, accomplished by Arvio in her forties after publishing poetry in several literary journals such as *Poetry*, *The Paris Review*, and *Best American Poetry 1998*. The poet's dialogues with these visitors—either ghosts of the dead, the voice of Arvio's inner life or a chorus of her poetic muses—speak to the meaning of life and the sense of longing created by the insufficiency of memory. "Memory," like most of Arvio's poems in this collection, is written in free verse, the term typically used to describe non-metrical and unrhymed poetry, common among contemporary poets. Metrical verse derives its structure from a set of formal rules for the length and arrangement of each line. Arvio groups her poems in stanzas often linked together by lines that continue a thought, a piece of dialogue or an action into the following stanza.

Sarah Arvio

Author Biography

Sarah Arvio, author of "Memory" and other poems collected in her first volume of poetry, *Visits from the Seventh*, was born in 1954 in Philadelphia, Pennsylvania, and grew up near New York City among radical Quakers. She was educated at schools abroad and later attended Columbia University, where she studied writing. Arvio could not envision herself as a creative writer, she told *Borzoi Reader* for its website, until she began undergoing psychoanalysis and studying her dreams. "When I thought about writing my own words, I imagined pressing down so hard on the pen that I broke the nib," Arvio said. "When I looked inward I saw nothing but turmoil and grief. I couldn't realize my thoughts; I had a voice but couldn't use it." Soon after turning forty, Arvio found her poetic voice, the product of an "open, amazed mood" that allowed her to listen to her thoughts. She told *Borzoi Reader*: "I found my own thoughts intriguing and even beautiful."

It was not until she was in her forties that Arvio was able to publish her first collection of poems, which critics have hailed as a highly original debut. Arvio has supported herself as a translator for the United Nations in New York and Switzerland. *Visits from the Seventh* was published in June 2002 by Alfred A. Knopf. The first eleven poems in this collection won *The Paris Review*'s Bernard F. Conners Prize and were reprinted in *The Best American Poetry 1998*. Other poems from her first book won *Poetry*'s Frederick Bock Prize. In 2003, Arvio was awarded the Rome Prize of the American Academy of Arts and Letters. "Memory" was first published in *Raritan Quarterly*, a humanities journal published by Rutgers University. Arvio has published poetry in literary magazines such as *The Paris Review*, *Poetry*, *Southwest Review*, and *Literary Imagination*. She also has translated literary works, such as Fray Ramôn Panâe's short story, "How the Men Were Parted from the Women," which appeared in the anthology *The Oxford Book of Latin American Short Stories*.

Poem Text

"And do we remember our living lives?"
Did I remember the clock or the door,
or the words "I love you" or the word "why";
did he recall the blue vein in my wrist
or only the ice-blue burn in my eye?

What remained of the room and of the night,
the kiss or the argument that ensued?
"You see, our memories are much like yours,
here a shadow, a sound, a shred, a wisp . . ."
"And do we want to remember?" one said.

"Never never Oh give me the blurred wish
or the dream or the fact half-forgotten,
the leaf in the book but not the read page,
not what I saw but what I felt I saw,
not what I felt but how I wished to feel,

give me what I can bear to know I felt."
I choose to recall only the blue dusk.
"Do you think you choose? If only you could
determine your secret determinants."
Did I recall the cocktail as it smashed

against the wall there, so close to my eye,
did I forget why I left my home, why?
The full events of that terrible time
dissolving into the deep hues of dusk
and leaving essence to the inner eye.

Poem Summary

Stanza 1

In "Memory," a woman still suffering from the break-up with her lover is addressed by the invisible "visitors" who inhabit a "seventh" dimension, the "sixth" being sex, which they have explained in poems that precede this one in the collection. The first line begins with their question: "And do we remember our living lives?"—our lives as they were lived without the revision of memory? In the first, five-line stanza, the woman in the poem recalls the details of a daily life in which strife and death are temporarily absent—details such as the clock measuring seemingly endless time or the door in which a lover enters. Near the end of this stanza, however, the reader becomes unable to deny what is coming, tipped off by language escalating in emotion from the almost quotidian though tender "I love you" to an urgent and anguished "why?" What caused the argument, which the poet does not actually discuss in detail in the poem. What was its now elusive trigger? What did the speaker mean to the lover who broke from her?

Stanza 2

In the second stanza, lines 6 through 10, the poet's unseen visitors reveal to her that death does not take the sting out of memory, improve the quality of its ability to record events, or resolve its conundrums. "You see," the visitors say, "our memories are much like yours, / here a shadow, a sound, a shred, a wisp." But they also frame for her the choice that she has, which will allow her to put aside memory's puzzle. "And what do we want to remember?" one said.

Stanzas 3 and 4

The third and fourth stanzas describe the poet's immediate rebellion. She believes she can improve her memories by summoning the courage to relive the terribly painful emotions this catastrophic lover's quarrel provoked. The third stanza begins, in the first three of five lines, as the poet's prayer: "Never never Oh give me the blurred wish / or the dream or the fact half-forgotten, the leaf in the book but not the read page." She asks for even more, not merely the facts but what they meant, what she can bear to know.

Stubbornly, perhaps, the woman in the poem tells her visitors in the next stanza that she has made a choice. "I recall only the blue dusk," the aftermath of dissolution in its sad and non-negotiable finality, and not the climactic pain of her last argument. But her visitors, made wise by the transformation of death and the realities of life in the untouchable seventh dimension, attempt to be instructive about the inevitable nature of memory. "Do you think you choose?" they say. "If only you could determine your secret determinates." The last line of this penultimate stanza reveals the poet's immediate reconsideration of her desire to overrule memory as it leads us to the poem's end. Her anguish is once again poignantly apparent.

Stanza 5

In lines 23 to 25 of the last stanza, the narrator's acknowledgement of "that terrible time" recedes, yielding again to the blue transition of dusk and leaving only the essence of catastrophe to the realm of "the inner eye."

Themes

Longing for Life

"Memory" continues to look at the paradox these invisible visitors present to the woman in the poem—her inability to fully examine and appreciate life while she is in the middle of living it, and the visitors' urge to go back to resolve their own issues now that they have the benefit of a perspective earned through death. Other poems in the collection delicately examine the visitors' state of being and their desire to use the woman in these poems vicariously. In this poem, the visitors serve as psychological mentors attempting to instruct her in how to manage the same things they do, such as the pain of loss, while grasping at the straws of memory to make sense of it all.

The Unreliability of Memory

"Memory" examines the distortion of the memory, making it impossible to reassess or sort out events and how they affected not only self-perception but also perceptions of an important, once-loving relationship. The visitors may identify with the woman in the poem, but they are also critical that she does not understand the futility of what she is doing.

Unresolved Issues

The woman in "Memory" longs to know if the last argument she had with her lover killed not only the relationship but also the attraction they once had for each other. She combs her memories, hunting for clues, but can only relive the emotions—regret, anger and fear—that she felt during the argument.

Style

Contemporary Poem

The internal structure of Arvio's poem "Memory" is, unlike a galloping, faithfully iambic Victorian epic, informal and therefore unobtrusive. This allows the poet to construct lines that sound

Topics For Further Study

- Read the rest of the poems collected in Arvio's first volume of poetry, *Visits from the Seventh.* Compare Arvio's poems with the poetry of other American women such as Sylvia Plath, Maxine Kumin, Anne Sexton, Denise Levertov and Rita Dove. What makes these poems uniquely feminine?
- What elements of poetic structure does Arvio employ in "Memory" and other poems in *Visits from the Seventh*? What might their function be? Compare the structure of this poem with the structure of a poem by a modern formalist poet such as Robert Frost, Richard Wilbur or Anthony Hecht as well as neo-formalists such as Rhina P. Espaillat, Dick Davis and Dana Giola.
- What might the color blue represent in the poem "Memory?" Compare the use of blue in this poem to the use of pink, yellow, white, green and aqua in other poems in this collection. How does color allow the poet to create not only a picture in the mind's eye, but also a mood?
- Compare the supernatural voices captured by Ephraim and the others in James Merrill's *The Changing Light at Sandover.* What relationship do they have with their human medium? How do these supernatural conversations differ from those that spring from the relationship Arvio's unseen visitors have with the woman in Arvio's poetry?

like conversation to the reader. The flexibility of free verse allows the poet a series of stressed syllables, which give the lines a special poetic weight. For example, in the lines "did he recall the blue vein in my wrist / or only the ice-blue burn in my eye?" the poet uses the pounding cadence of "ice-blue burn" to emphasize the anger the argument elicited. Though the poem is relatively informal, Arvio uses sonic devices to emphasize other elements in the poem. The word "why" is rhymed at the end of a line with the word "eye" in the first stanza and again in the final stanza. The structure of the poem may not be guided by the rules of formal convention, but the poem does have symmetry. The poem is composed of five stanzas of five lines each, a neatness that echoes the suggestion of acceptance at the end. The third, fourth and fifth stanzas are each linked by a line that continues a thought introduced in the stanza above it, which reflects the poet's evolving perspective. A dramatic unity is suggested by the rhyming pattern established in the first stanza and repeated in the last. The poem makes maximum use of the word "blue"—a blue vein, ice-blue anger, blue dusk. The opposite of blue, the warmer shades of yellow that Arvio examines in other poems in this collection, is absent, as is red—the color typically associated with both passion and rage. In this poem, memory has rendered all facets of a lover's quarrel and its aftermath in monochromatic hues.

Historical Context

Contemporary Poetry

"Memory" is part of a collection of poems that reflect contemporary life in New York City, a city familiar to many Americans, even those who only know the city through movies or the pages of the *New Yorker.* These sometimes funny and erotic poems reflect the world view of a highly educated woman, one who laces her lines with French phrases, references to other poets and classic Hitchcock movies. The woman in these poems is the perfect audience for the aristocratic ramblings of the chorus of invisible visitors that people her work. In contemporary, post-feminist poetry, women writers can enjoy the fruits of liberation from the mandatory roles of child-rearing and housewifery. Their bold, witty work shows how able they are to avoid the self-destructive impulses evident in the poetry of some women writing a generation before, such as Sylvia Plath and Anne Sexton. Poet Mark

Strand, writing for the back of the book, asserts that these poems are neither sad nor confessional. Simply put, a confessional poem is one in which the poet speaks to the reader.

But Rob Neufeld, writing for the Asheville Citizen-Times and once a friend of Arvio's, disagrees. "The poems are, in good measure, confessional and we'd be cheated if they weren't," Neufeld writes, describing the glimpse of the poet taking a contemplative walk down Park Avenue in one poem. Other admirers of Arvio's work, such as New York poet Richard Howard, find links to Arvio's work to that of earlier women writers, such as Christina Rosetti and Virginia Woolf, because of its attentive interest in internal rather than external voices. "The whole series is an articulation of what we used to call 'the inner life': one woman's passionate questioning of her sources," he said. "Memory" is feminine in its self-conscious reflection on lost love and its ear to internal voices, but it is especially contemporary in its un-self-conscious ownership of anger, eroticism and humor. With this freedom, perhaps, comes the insistent flowering of a strong and compelling poetic voice at an age—past forty—that publishers apparently consider to be rare. Contemporary poetry has further pushed the boundaries of language, image, form and voice. Part of Arvio's cultural contribution might be helping to break through another artistic barrier that has constrained and discouraged writers, male and female alike.

Critical Overview

"Memory" is one of forty-nine poems in an award-winning collection hailed as a highly original debut, admired as "a splendidly odd and compelling first book" by the *Washington Post*. *Post* critic Edward Hirsch enjoys Arvio's "nervy, fanciful and unified" poetry and commends her attentiveness to her supernatural guests by calling her a "spiritual apprentice." Roy Olson, writing in *Booklist*, notes that the "poems sparkle with worldly wise wit." Critics and fellow poets enjoy the uniqueness of Arvio's dialogue with the supernatural visitors, and her ability to be both simultaneously funny and erotic in these contemporary odes to life. "Sarah Arvio's poems engage in an agitated description of the inner life," said poet Mark Strand, quoted on the back of Arvio's book. "The voices drop in and out like a beautiful quixotic chorus." Judy Clarence of the *Library Journal* commends Arvio's competence as a poet in avoiding the pitfalls of engaging the supernatural, which she calls "dangerous ground." "Writers who venture in the realm of the occult risk banality," Clarence says, adding that "Arvio's prodigious talent saves her."

Criticism

Lisa Trow

Trow is a published poet and writer. In this essay, Trow considers the value of employing supernatural voices as a poetic conceit.

"Memory" and other poems in Sarah Arvio's *Visits from the Seventh* give scant, if any, evidence of how the poet's upbringing in a strict Quaker household, and her subsequent psychoanalysis, affected her poetic voice. These poems are not unique because of their singular cultural references. The only archaisms in speech are the quirky and affected terms of endearment used by the poet's aristocratic invisible visitors. The anger and eroticism of this and other poems are not overblown in the rebellion of an unusually chaste or strict religious environment. "Memory" is not steeped in the self-conscious or hypercritical assessments of the heavily psychoanalyzed. Instead, this poem is open to any woman who experiences the shock of losing a love that had, before the unexpected catastrophe of argument, become a beloved fixture of life.

The origin of the poetry's wry and New York-worldly sense of humor that critics embrace when discussing this unusual collection of poems is not a surprise. Arvio is an educated, already well-decorated poet of diverse professional skills who knows New York City well. But what is unusual is the conceit on which the entire book is founded, a group of visitors—unseen, even to the poet—and their supernatural origin. They are souls who derive their sense of humor and the influence of their commentary from the vantage point of death. While other poets, such as Nobel Prize winner Wistawa Szymborska, unifies the poems of one collection with observations on the human callousness inherent in acts such as terrorism, Arvio constructs an interactive Greek chorus of dead souls and builds a book around their conversations with her.

The chorus seemingly understands its role before the poet does. She is instructed later in the collection, after having become aware of them through the exercise of a post-sexual seventh sense. "'It might / be best," one said, 'to call us a conceit.'"

> *"Longing and regret commingle here with the erotic charge that survives death."*

But what purpose does this conceit serve? The voices move in and out of these poems and sometimes require pointed invitations to appear. When they do appear, they cajole and tease, filling in for missing human equivalents, such as a mother who has died, or a lover who has left. To accentuate their elusiveness, these visitors require, like supernatural beings in any genre, that the woman in these poems keep quiet about them or risk losing contact. In "Memory," which appears more than half way into the collection, their capricious playfulness is absent. It is replaced by a more sober consciousness in possession of a secret that has eluded their human companion, who is now preoccupied with the violent quarrel that ended an important romance.

"Memory" is not a fun poem or one of the more lyrical in the collection. This is a pre-memorial poem, written after the death of love but before it is buried. The distance between the poet and her unseen muses is close, more personal and less transcendent. They sit on her shoulder, looking into her past without enjoying the view, something they take particular pleasure in doing in other poems in the collection, such as "Park Avenue." Here the ghostly visitors seem to want to assuage their host's pain by offering unflinching acceptance—even though they share Arvio's preoccupation with unsettled human relationships and the psychic unrest they have assured her follows lovers to the grave. Longing and regret commingle here with the erotic charge that survives death.

The rift between the lovers in this poem is swift and violent and the memory of love in the face of subsequent loss deteriorates quickly. "What remained of the room and of the night, / the kiss or the argument that ensued." An anguished respect for the danger of uncontrolled emotion remains, too. "Why," the poet asks twice. "Did I forget why I left my home why?" The stylistics of the poem emphasize the question and the role memory plays in the mutability of perception. "Why" is rhymed twice with "eye" in this otherwise informally structured poem. At its first mention, "eye" is literal and specific. It refers to the eye of the narrator and its ice-blue reflection of the cold, hard anger she feels for her lover. At the second mention, the narrator's eye is vulnerable to the violence of a cocktail smashing the wall close by. By the last line, the "eye" becomes realized as a symbol for memory and its abstract function of capturing the time as it passes and before it completely dissolves. This cold anger has frozen memory until it is warmed by the poet's reflection, perhaps making it even more elusive until it is only a stain on the mind's eye.

Looking into her past, the spirits are voyeurs to this anguish and to the narrator's insecurities. "Did he recall the blue veins in my wrist / or only the ice-blue burn in my eye?" The poet wonders, in the end, what she was to her lover. Was she attractive, warm, sensual and beloved? Or will he only remember her as the angry shrew she was when he saw her last? The visitors are consoling, saying she is not different from them, even as they watch her from their supernatural perch. Her memories are inexact, the same as theirs. The narrator remains conflicted, but the voices continue to console, now with condescension. "'And do we want to remember?' one said."

One cannot really chose how to remember one's life, how to set it in the proper context based on externals. The quality of memory does not allow such assurances. "'Do you think you chose?'" the voices say. "'If only you could / determine your secret determinants.'" The narrator's sense of resignation that follows is the product of impasse. With supernatural authority, the voices have contributed to the narrator's understanding of two key points about the nature of memory—its resiliency, invulnerable even to death, and its deeply occult nature, unknowable even to the dead.

For the wisdom of these visitors to resonate, one must accept the use of metaphor with proper respect and recognize its descent from an honorable literary tradition. Critics view *Visits from the Seventh* and its supernatural conceit variously as the foundation of an odd and fanciful collection, an important advance in the poetics of transcendence, or a dangerous flirtation with banality. Judy Clarence of *Library Journal* makes almost deprecating note of Arvio's "flair for the supernatural" and credits her "prodigious talent" for rescuing her from the pitfalls of literary gimmick. Ray Olson, writing in *Booklist,* recognizes Arvio's sagely and sometimes wisecracking visitors as less magic and more the voices of "unuttered thoughts most of us have." Other publications give

What Do I Read Next?

- In "Park Avenue," which also appears in *Visits from the Seventh* (2002), the poet describes a walk along the streets of New York, giving her invisible visitors the "intimate view" of the city they crave, and writing bits of their commentary down on scraps of paper.
- In her poem, "Motherlessness," also from *Visits from the Seventh* (2002), Arvio describes "the hole in the skin of her soul" left by the loss of her mother.
- Ezra Pound uses foreign words in *The Cantos (1–109)* (1964), a technique employed by Arvio in *Visits from the Seventh.*
- "Ode to a Nightingale," by John Keats, from *The Complete Poems* (1988), offers a vehicle for poetic transcendence in the form of an unreachable bird.
- Arvio's work has been compared to James Merrill's *The Changing Light at Sandover* (1982), which is based on extensive transcriptions Merrill and his housemate David Jackson took from a Ouija board. *The Changing Light at Sandover* reports the messages of Merrill's deceased friends as well as mythic, historical, and literary figures such as Gertrude Stein, William Butler Yeats, Richard Wagner, Homer, Jesus, Mohammed and the angels Michael and Gabriel, as well as the nine muses.

Visits from the Seventh a lineage with more gravitas. A critic from the *New Yorker*, who is quoted in the paperback publication of Arvio's collection writes "This extraordinary first book of poems takes its place in an authentic line of descent from such landmarks as Yeats's *A Vision* and James Merrill's *The Changing Light at Sandover*," an epic trilogy based on Merrill's transcriptions of Ouija board conversations with the poet's deceased friends, as well as Jesus, Plato, Nefertiti, Mercury, the nine muses and Michael the Archangel.

New York poet Richard Howard, quoted in the hardcover publication of Arvio's collection, seems to understand Arvio best, admiring the poems as "the most 'convincing' visitations since Merrill's Ouija-board transcriptions," but noting her possession by personal voices. "The whole series is an articulation of what we used to call 'the inner life': one woman's passionate questioning of her sources and their equally passionate (if often derisive) answers," says Howard, writing for the hardcover edition book jacket. "She has forged her own dialogue of the dead.... I love hearing her persuasive voices; they are the woman herself."

Perhaps such a manifestation of Quaker Inner Light and psychoanalysis is a chorus of spiritual advisers, in place to speak to the mysteries of life that can be explained and to identify the ones that cannot. Arvio's invisible visitors are a conceit. The visitors admit as much in "Three Green Stars," which appears in the last few poems of *Visits from the Seventh.* "We were driving in the Jersey meadows / a gray purple sky, roving orange spots, / white clouds lit miasmic yellow. 'It might / be best,' one said, 'to call us a conceit.'" But their voices spring from Arvio's imagination, tilled by years of self-examination, and a cultivated receptivity to self revelation. Their inspired speech has been hidden until Arvio gave them form, like a costume to put on and take off. "Memory" is a poem about a woman talking to her wiser self.

Source: Lisa Trow, Critical Essay on "Memory," in *Poetry for Students*, Thomson Gale, 2005.

Pamela Steed Hill

Hill is the author of a poetry collection, has published widely in literary journals, and is an editor for a university publications department. In the following essay, Hill examines Arvio's poem as a mental battleground on which the speaker's desire to remember and desire to forget wage a war that neither can win.

Arvio's "Memory" is one of those poems that is better served by reading it within the context of

> *"While it is arguable that she may feel less emotional turmoil with a few less voices popping in and out of her head, the questions, proclamations, and quirky suggestions made by the visitors prod her into staying focused."*

the collection that includes it. The purpose of the visitors that come to Arvio as she writes is more substantiated when one can hear the full range of the strange little spirits' admonishments, encouragements, playful quips, and philosophizing in a variety of situations. That said, however, there is enough ammunition in this single poem to lay open the age-old struggle between one's inner-self and one's *other* inner-self, exposing the hapless attempts of an individual to recall the good and forget the bad.

In an interview by poetry editor Deborah Garrison for *The Borzoi Reader Online*, Arvio calls the poems in *Visits from the Seventh* "love poems to life; poems of longing for life." Growing up Quaker, she was taught not to "glorify an afterlife" but to "long for this life." Perhaps these revelations help clarify the opening line of "Memory": "'And do we remember our living lives?'" This line is supposedly spoken by one of the ghostly visitors, but the curious phrase "living lives" is the thing to note, no matter who says it.

While the noun "lives" may invoke countless adjectives to describe it, the word "living" is not typically one of them. It seems redundant. Her use of "lives" implies living. The need to define lives as living suggests that there are other types of lives, lives that may be forgotten or repressed. The latter is most poignantly addressed in this poem.

Each stanza presents a back-and-forth, tit-for-tat banter about fond memories and not-so-fond memories. In the first, the question regarding living lives establishes the central inquiry that the remainder of the poem tries to answer. The speaker is not sure whether she can recall the specific tangibles—"the clock or the door—"or intangibles—"the words 'I love you' or the word 'why'"—of a personal event in her life. One must assume that the episode involves a romantic relationship in trouble, since someone is leaving and someone is asking why. Memory is tricky here. The speaker may not remember an important declaration of love, but she does recall a "blue vein" in her wrist. She does not know, however, whether her lover recalls that part of her or "only the ice-blue burn" in her eye.

Each of these snippets of thought is a part of the living life of the speaker, but she cannot fully accept that they reflect her actual past. The implication is that they are factual recollections because there would be no reason to question the memory of a clock, a door, or a conversation if those things never existed. Even the slightest bit of doubt allows one to repress thoughts that are too painful to accept as fact. The battleground is established between what the speaker thinks she remembers and what she would prefer to question.

In the second stanza, the "room" and the "night" appear to be accepted, if not desired, memories, but then there is a quick switch to ambiguity when the speaker tries to decide whether "the kiss or the argument"—or both—occurred next. Kissing and arguing obviously connote two very different events in a relationship, although they may both certainly happen in the same setting. But juxtaposing a pleasant moment with an unpleasant one suggests an unsettling battle between good recollections and bad.

In *The Borzoi Reader Online* interview, Arvio says this about the imaginary beings that visit her when she writes "Their memory is stronger than mine, and their associative powers are stranger and more vivid." Interestingly, in the poem "Memory," one of her visitors remarks, "'You see, our memories are much like yours, / here a shadow, a sound, a shred, a wisp.'" The point is not so much the contradictory opinions about the speaker's versus the visitors' recall ability, but the fact that the idea of memory is an important presence in the struggle of the inner-selves.

Just as important are the words used to describe the memories of both the human and the spiritual visitors—shadowy, shredded, wispy. The uncertainty and incompleteness of memories make them easier to repress at will. However, as is clear in the poem, even those intentionally stifled have a way of creeping into an individual's mind when least expected or least desired. The italicized lines provide the best defense for the repression side. They answer the question, "'And do we want to remember?'" with a resounding, "'*Never never*'" and then proceed with an explanatory list: a "*blurred wish*" is better than a "*fact half-forgotten*," what people think they see is better than what they actually see, what people wish to feel is better than what they really feel, and so on.

The fourth stanza of "Memory" reveals a rather desperate attempt by the speaker to simplify the battle going on in her head. She confidently uses the phrase, "I choose to recall" only to be immediately admonished by a visitor who asks sarcastically, "'Do you think you choose?'" This is perhaps the most poignant indication that the war on her mental battleground is one that cannot be won. She is not in control of her "secret determinants," and if not she, then who?

The latter part of the poem provides the greatest evidence of why the speaker wages such a frustrating war of emotions within herself. Again, she asks a question that implies an irony—if she does not really "recall the cocktail as it smashed / against the wall there, so close to [her] eye," then why ask the question? The details are too specific to be a total figment of her imagination. On the one hand, she longs to forget that such a violent event ever occurred in her life and on the other hand she cannot help but remember it.

In the final stanza of "Memory," Arvio makes a subtle connection to the first stanza, in which the word "why" is suggestive of something bad about a relationship but not conclusive. It is not clear who is asking why in the first stanza, the speaker or her lover, but in the final one, it is clearly the speaker who ponders the question. Again, the query is rhetorical at best. Is it likely that one who leaves her home, her lover, and life as she knows it would actually forget why? No, but the implication is that her mind would like to forget. In reality, she cannot, and so the struggle continues in its back-and-forth cycle.

In spite of the confusion, the speaker cannot be blamed for wanting to forget the "full events" of what she calls "that terrible time." Attempting to repress the memory of unfortunate or tragic moments in one's life is a fairly common human endeavor. With the passage of time, the speaker believes her memory of the events surrounding the break-up of her relationship is "dissolving into the deep hues of dusk," but dissolving does not necessarily mean going away. It may mean simply changing form. In this case, the "essence" of past events are now left to the "inner eye," but is the inner eye still not a part of the person who is trying to forget?

Arvio ends the poem here, without fully disclosing what the speaker's "inner eye" really is. Most likely, it is that part of the human psyche that accepts the truth no matter how painful it may be. Think of it as a kind of receptor that keeps its feelers out for the true "essence" of all the events that happen in a human's lifetime. The inner eye never turns away sad or bitter memories of the worst events in spite of attempts by the rest of the mind to do just that. This inescapable dichotomy is the main fuel for the battle of emotions that rages within the speaker. She may placate one side for a while, but the other side always chimes in with thoughts she would prefer not to entertain.

Perhaps this is the reason for the visitors. They not only act as little alter egos of the speaker but also allow her to carry on mental conversations with herself when plain, simple thinking is not enough or when it provides undesirable results. Thoughts or memories of certain events in her "living" life lead only to despondency, so handing that chore off to imaginary friends alleviates the pain of a direct confrontation. In "Memory," the visitors admit that they "*never*" really want to remember, that they much prefer wishes to facts or what they long to see instead of what they really see. Yet they are able at least to address the painful truth when they must. This is not always the case for the speaker.

The speaker tends to use the visitors to keep a foothold in reality even though it is not a pleasant thing to do. While it is arguable that she may feel less emotional turmoil with a few less voices popping in and out of her head, the questions, proclamations, and quirky suggestions made by the visitors prod her into staying focused. If she gave in wholly to her desire to forget, allowing this side of the inner-self war to win, one would have to consider what has really been won. Repression and avoidance will take their toll somewhere down the line. Let the battle continue, however, and the speaker herself endures.

Source: Pamela Steed Hill, Critical Essay on "Memory," in *Poetry for Students*, Thomson Gale, 2005.

Ray Olson

In the following review, Olson praises Arvio's edgy sophistication.

Arvio's debut collection extrapolates entirely on a single conceit—that voices from a seventh sensual dimension counsel the poet in the wake of a long love affair. Like the unuttered thoughts most of us have, the voices remonstrate, sagely advise, philosophically expatiate, pooh-pooh, and wisecrack, but seemingly with greater objectivity than one's own thoughts could achieve. Perhaps the distress of falling out of love has clouded the poet's self-consciousness. Certainly, the first poem's first stanza bespeaks confusion about identity: "'but we're your one design,'" the voices say, "or 'you're our one design'—which was it?" As the poet recalls scenes from the affair and adjusts to her new reality, the poems sparkle with worldly-wise wit, including droll observations about sex, defensive rationalizing about abortion, recriminations against Mom for not comforting her lovelorn daughter, and considerations of the many ways that love relates to death. If Arvio's book lacks the brutal impact of Margaret Atwood's cycle of poems on a love affair, *Power Politics* (1971), it compensates gratifyingly with edgy sophistication.

Source: Ray Olson, Review of "Visits from the Seventh," in *Booklist,* Vol. 98, No. 11, February 1, 2002, p. 917.

Rob Neufeld

In the following review, Neufeld recalls being in high school with Arvio and calls the poems in "Visits from the Seventh" masterful.

Spring calls forth the following review of new poems. Bird song makes us wonder if poets are feeling as lyrical as their avian models. Sarah Arvio, in *Visits from the Seventh* (Knopf), finds her muse, not in a bird or a bard, but in immaterial presences, who describe their location as

> the pang of once-had, a maybe-again,
> the shifting half-light, our home and habitat,
> those hours, soft-toned, windless, that favor passage,
> the usual relay of twilights.

Common experiences such as "shifting half-light" harbor vehicles for transcendence, which are parked somewhere between the mind's wishes and sensual details. With Arvio, we are in the territory of John Keats' "Ode to a Nightingale," except that we have given up the unreachable bird for a nuclear-age reality—unseen forces.

Once Arvio contacts her spirits, she faces a dilemma. The spirits instruct her to keep mum or imperil the process of revelation—for example, their hours:

> at work before dawn in the north country,
> the briny, eye-blue Baltic blustering
> hard by, the sun rising to never more
> than low in the sky, a cold yellow blur
> gleaming dull in the iced fourchettes of trees.

"Fourchettes" is a French word roughly meaning brackets or forks. Its use involves another poetic tradition. Ezra Pound in his "Cantos" repeatedly employed foreign terms to try to get words to do justice to his vision. For some poets, English isn't enough; speech is hardly enough.

In the poem, "Death," Arvio imagines that on the other side of death, bereft of tongue, she'll discover "a power almost to speak—although speak may not be the term. to say." It's a poet's challenge: Words can kill an experience. They are not as pure as sensation or thought.

I shared high school classes with Arvio in Rockland County, N.Y.; and talked with her about her poetry after college. I remember the time in high school that I'd challenged a stuffy classroom by asking students if they'd seen an unusually sunlit sky the day before. Arvio, who was often not in class, told me afterward she had, and I felt sheepish and brash. I'd killed the sunset experience with my declaration.

So, it's good to see Arvio creating this masterful book—masterful not only because of its bursts of song, but also because of its ongoing dialogue with higher beings. It's like a Walt Whitman poem in which the poet starts off in a searching mode and, through a process of questioning, reaches an understanding that carries the reader along with him or her. Like Whitman, Arvio takes a while to get to the point of redemption or resolution. In her 16th poem, as the spirits ask Arvio why she thinks she'd been chosen by them, she writes, "I barely recall the beginning now." The beginning had been lost love on a cosmic scale: the loss of her mother and the suicide of a lover.

Mark Strand, one of our most honored contemporary poets, is quoted on the back of the book: "These poems are not confessional or sad; rather, they are an extended hymn to the assuaging power of the imagination."

I disagree.

The poems are, in good measure, confessional and we'd be cheated if they weren't. In the poem "Park Avenue," we glimpse Arvio walking the streets of New York, gazing at reflective windows, leaning against caf walls, writing on available scraps of paper. She has dedicated her life to her suffering and to distilled poetic expression.

In her 26th poem, "Motherlessness," Arvio talks about the "hole in the skin of her soul," left unsutured by her separation from maternal love, "so even the sparest nuance of wind / is a feeling, and in cases like those, / can you conceive of a sexual touch?" Sex is the sixth sense, a spirit told her early on, and the seventh, referred to in the book's title, is the one that she and the spirits share.

Talking with Arvio about her poems more than 20 years ago now, I had put aside what were then her less-controlled cries to celebrate her writing's greatest strength: powerfully sound-rich lines. Lines such as these two in the poem "Library": "I was gunning down the road, wild with grief / after they told me he had shot himself."

In defense of the sometimes over-polemic feminist literature of the time, Arvio had, in 1980 counseled that all new literature needed time to grow. *Visits from the Seventh* demonstrates long and hard-earned growth—yet I see the effects of the ruling school of modernism as much as that of Arvio's personal muses. I long for more of her great lines.

Source: Rob Neufeld, "A Glimpse into the Making of a Poet," in *Asheville Citizen-Times*, March 22, 2002.

Sources

"Arvio, Sarah," in *Contemporary Authors Online*, Gale, September 11, 2003.

Arvio, Sarah, *Visits from the Seventh: Poems*, Alfred A. Knopf, 2003.

Clarence, Judy, Review of *Visits from the Seventh*, in *Library Journal*, Vol. 127, No. 5, March 15, 2002, p. 85.

Garrison, Deborah, Interview with Sarah Arvio, in *The Borzoi Reader Online*, at www.randomhouse.com (last accessed March 18, 2004).

Hirsch, Edward, "Poet's Choice," Review of *Visits from the Seventh*, in *Washington Post Book World*, June 9, 2002, p. 12.

Howard, Richard, in *Visits from the Seventh*, Alfred A. Knopf, 2002.

Nadel, Alan, "Replacing the *Waste Land*—James Merrill's Quest for Transcendent Authority," in *Modern American Poetry*, at http://www.english.uiuc.edu/maps/poets/m_r/merrill/nadel.htm, (last accessed May 17, 2004).

Neufeld, Rob, "A Glimpse into the Making of a Poet," in the *Asheville Citizen-Times*, March 22, 2002, at cgi.citizen-times.com/cgi-bin/story/arts/9595 (last accessed May 18, 2004).

Olson, Ray, Review of *Visits from the Seventh*, in *Booklist*, Vol. 98, No. 11, February 1, 2002, p. 917.

Review of *Visits from the Seventh*, in *Random House Online Catalog*, at http://www.randomhouse.com/catalog/display.pperl?0375709789 (last accessed May 17, 2004).

Strand, Mark, in *Visits from the Seventh*, Alfred A. Knopf, 2002, back cover.

Further Reading

Graham, David, and Kate Sontag, eds., *After Confession: Poetry as Autobiography*, Graywolf Press, 2001.

After Confession: Poetry as Autobiography is a compilation of twenty-eight essays by poets Billy Collins, Yusef Komunyakaa, Louise Glück, and others examining the persistent influence of confessional poetry on contemporary verse.

Komunyakaa, Yusef, and David Lehman, eds., *Best American Poetry 2003*, Charles Scribner's Sons, 2003.

Best American Poetry 2003 is one in a series of eagerly-awaited annual collections of contemporary poetry. This issue, by decorated Vietnam veteran Komunyakaa—an African American poet from the South, includes the work of well-established poets such as Rita Dove and Billy Collins as well as emerging talent such as Natasha Trethewey.

Schmidt, Elizabeth, ed., *Poems of New York*, Alfred A. Knopf, 2002.

Poems of New York is an anthology of poetry by poets who have made New York City their subject, beginning with Walt Whitman. Schmidt began collecting poems to celebrate New York City's unique character and vitality after the September 11, 2001 terrorist attacks.

Strand, Mark, ed., *The Contemporary American Poets*, Signet Classics, 2000.

The Contemporary American Poets is an anthology for the poetry beginner. It includes seminal poetry from the contemporary movement in the United States, written by poets such as A. R. Ammons, Sylvia Plath, Richard Howard, Charles Simic, and James Merrill.

Morning Walk

Claire Malroux

1996

Claire Malroux's "Morning Walk" was first published in French in her poetry collection *Aires*. Translated by American poet Marilyn Hacker, the English version of "Morning Walk" appears as the first poem in the collection *Edge* published by Wake Forest University Press.

Like many poems in *Edge*, "Morning Walk" addresses the themes of aging and the inevitable progression of time, as it explores the porous boundaries between different realms: life and death, the natural and the human, and the actual and the spiritual. The poem evokes both a physical and a psychological landscape, as the speaker observes elements in the world while taking a morning walk through her environs. The place she walks through is not specified—the poem could take place anywhere where there are buildings and trees. It seems to be an urban neighborhood, although it is filled with grassy spots, indicating parks or lawns. The poem moves through several tonal shifts, swinging between reticent pessimism and admiration, but concludes on an optimistic note celebrating the spiritual authority of nature. Malroux uses metaphor, simile, and personification to convey the ideas and images in the poem. These devices serve to underscore her ideas about the inter-relatedness of different worlds.

Author Biography

Claire Malroux was born September 3, 1935 in the small, rural town of Albi in southwestern France. The daughter of two elementary school teachers, Augustin and Paule Malroux, she grew up in Albi and in Paris. Malroux's book-length lyric narrative poem *A Long-Gone Sun* (France, 1998; New York, 2000) recollects her childhood during World War II, including her father's involvement with the French Resistance, which led in 1945 to his incarceration and death in the Nazi concentration camp Bergen-Belsen.

Malroux is the author of seven collections of poetry in French. (Her works in French have been published under the name Claire Sara Roux.) "Morning Walk" is from *Edge*, her first poetry book translated into English. *Edge* (1996) comprises poems from two of Malroux's collections in French, *Aire* and *Entre nous et la lumière*, as well as a number of previously uncollected poems. *Edge*, *A Long-Gone Sun*, and Malroux's forthcoming poetry collection *Birds and Bison* were translated into English by American poet Marilyn Hacker, who has been translating Malroux's work since meeting Malroux in 1989 at a conference in Grenoble. Hacker, who lives in Paris for part of each year, has also translated the poetry of other contemporary French poets, including Vénus Khoury-Ghata, Guy Goffette, Hédi Kaddour, and Marie Etienne.

In addition to her own poetry, Malroux is acclaimed for her translations of poetry and prose from English into French, including the writings of Emily Dickinson, Derek Walcott, Elizabeth Bishop, Emily Brontë, Edith Wharton, and Joyce Carol Oates. She has been awarded the French Legion of Honor for her translations of Dickinson's writings, as well as the Grand Prix National de la Traduction in 1995, and the Prix Maurice Edgar Coindreau in 1990.

Claire Malroux

Poem Text

I

The white ocean in which birds swim
Between the chimneys
Is it a dream
Beginning over again, or is it
The antiseptic other side of death?

2

The sun displays its face-paints
On a pallid stone wall
Bedecks the buildings
For luminous tournaments

It takes so few hours
To smooth away the night
While our wrinkles are
Irreversible

3

Watchful, the windows
Open their eyelids
The grass sleeps profoundly
Like an old child
Sucking the earth

4

The trees, chasubled in sparrows
Will always be ready to bless the day

Poem Summary

Stanza 1

In "Morning Walk," an unnamed speaker describes her observations of the natural and human-made world as she takes a morning stroll. Throughout the poem, the speaker's observations of the awakening world inspire her thoughts on subjects such as death and time. The poem opens with a metaphor comparing the sky, glimpsed between buildings, to the ocean: "The white ocean in which birds swim / Between the chimneys." The whiteness of the sky may be due to clouds, smoke, or the early morning light, but the lack of color creates a mood of stillness and quietude.

The opening image leads directly to the strange question in lines 3–5: "Is it a dream / Beginning over again, or is it / The antiseptic other side of death?" The first part of the question leads the reader to believe that the speaker will question whether what she sees (the sky) is dream or reality, but instead she introduces a different idea by wondering whether what she sees is something from the realm of the non-living. By posing this question, the poet conflates the observable world of sky, buildings, and birds with an imagined afterlife, which like the white sky is antiseptic or overly clean and blank. The first section concludes with this somewhat pessimistic image.

Stanza 2

In the first stanza of the second section, the speaker describes the effects of the rising morning sun. The sun transforms the pale human-made world by adding color and vitality to it: "The sun displays its face-paints / On a pallid stone wall / Bedecks the buildings / For luminous tournaments." Malroux uses personification to portray the sun, which gaily exhibits its hues and dresses the world in preparation for daily activities. The speaker's tone in this stanza is optimistic as she expresses admiration for the sun's power.

In the next stanza, however, the speaker returns to a more melancholic tone, as she observes that it takes very little time to erase the darkness of night but that the effects of aging persist: "It takes so few hours / To smooth away the night / While our wrinkles are / Irreversible." The speaker's admiration for the sun's energy has given way to her concerns about aging and time's inevitable progress. She implies that with each turning of night and day, human beings are marked by time in an unflattering way. In line 12, Malroux implicates the reader by stating "our wrinkles." All of humanity is affected by time's daily march, not just the speaker or the poet.

Stanza 3

The tone shifts again in stanza 3, as the speaker observes other daily events while she continues her morning walk. In lines 14–15, she imagines the windows alert and awakening as the morning unfolds, "Watchful, the windows / Open their eyelids." Using personification throughout this stanza, she then describes the grass continuing to slumber in line 16. In lines 17–18, Malroux uses a simile to further portray the grass, "Like an old child / sucking the earth." The simile is paradoxical, since infants are not old. In this simile the natural and human worlds are blended, as the grass is likened to a baby and the earth to its mother. The tone in this stanza is contemplative, neither particularly sad nor exuberant.

Stanza 4

In this short final stanza, Malroux again uses personification, as the speaker describes the trees she sees: "The trees, chasubled in sparrows / Will always be ready to bless the day." A chasuble is a sleeveless outer garment worn by priests during mass. The sparrows in this stanza cover the trees like an official robe, and the trees act like priests by being willing to bless each day. In this section as in the previous one, Malroux conflates the natural and the human worlds. She also ascribes spiritual authority to the natural world, as the trees have the power to bless the day. After several tone shifts, the poem concludes on an optimistic note, with the speaker observing how nature presides over each successive day.

Themes

Morning/The Sun

As the title indicates, the poem takes place in the morning, as the speaker walks through her environs. In the poem, morning is a time of change, when night's darkness is smoothed away by the mighty sun. In the second stanza, the speaker observes the effects of the sun's rising and how the light transforms the "pallid stone wall" and buildings into colorful and vital beings prepared "For luminous tournaments." Morning is also the time of the world's awakening as in lines 14–15 when "windows / open their eyelids." The sun is a symbol of transformative power; however, its daily rising also signals the passage of time, another theme of the poem.

Aging/Wisdom

The speaker laments the inevitable progress of time and its aging effects on human beings in lines 10–13 when she says, "It takes so few hours / To smooth away the night / While our wrinkles are / Irreversible." The sun's daily appearance and its energizing effects on the environment come at a price, as this very sun also fosters and illuminates the unappealing markers of time. The speaker's

Topics For Further Study

- Research the sun's role in the solar system, noting what kind of star the sun is and how it compares with other stars in the universe. Present your findings, using drawings, charts, photographs, and other graphics to convey the information.
- Imagine that you are a very old person, perhaps 100 years old. Write a letter to yourself, describing how it feels to be old and giving yourself advice about how to live your life. Include details about your daily rituals and habits.
- Research the geography and history of Paris or another city—perhaps your hometown—and create a walking map of the city. The map should show key sites with information explaining each site's significance. You may want to create your maps using large pieces of craft paper and paints or markers, or using a computerized drawing program.
- Research and discuss the health benefits of walking as a recreational sport. Consult health magazines and newspaper articles as well as encyclopedia entries. Interview the director of a walking club such as the American Volkssport Federation to find out more about why walking is a popular pastime in North America and Europe. List the health benefits on the board as you present your findings to your class.
- Research how the concept of time has been viewed in different cultures and in different eras. After conducting your research, present your findings to the class. Using a two-columned chart, discuss and list ways in which time is linear or progressive versus cyclical or repeating.
- Find a short story, song, or essay on the topic of walking. Play, perform, or read the piece to your class, and then discuss what role walking plays in the character's or author's life.

anxiety about aging is introduced in the first stanza of the poem when she wonders if the sky she sees between chimneys is "a dream / Beginning over again, or is it / The antiseptic other side of death?" Aging entails moving closer to death, and these lines express the speaker's fear of the non-existence following death, toward which the aging process draws her. However, aging also seems to entail peacefulness in the poem, as the speaker describes the grass as it "sleeps profoundly / Like an old child / Sucking the earth." This paradoxical simile—infants are typically very young—conveys the image of a wise baby unaffected by the comings and goings of the sun (unlike the alertly "watchful" windows). In the poem, the passage of time is cyclical as well as linear, as day repeatedly follows night, and in this image the old and the very young are blended together.

Mutability

The blending of seemingly opposing elements or characteristics occurs throughout the poem, supporting the theme of mutability or the interrelatedness of different worlds. In this poem as in other poems in *Edge*, the borders between realms are quite porous, and images frequently slip from old to young, inanimate to human, living to nonexistent, and earthly to spiritual. For example, Malroux frequently mixes together the human and the natural, often employing personification to do so, as in lines 19–20: "The trees, chasubled in sparrows / Will always be ready to bless the day." The trees act like priests, and the image moves from the natural earthly world to the spiritual realm of blessing. In the poem's first stanza, Malroux begins with a description of physical reality, which involves two different elements, the sea and the sky, which then become the psychological phenomenon of the dream, only to mutate once again into another realm altogether, the imagined "other side of death." The poem's shifting descriptions express the idea that things are interconnected in mysterious and intrinsic ways.

Nature

The natural world, including the planets, embodies power in the poem. The sun has the power to make the formerly drab earth vital and vigorous. While humans and human-made objects such as windows are subject to the sun's power, the natural elements such as the grass remain unaffected by the sun's rising, profoundly slumbering on. In the last stanza, Malroux ascribes spiritual authority to other natural elements, the trees, which have the ability to give benediction to each day. The speaker seems to take comfort in nature's steady capacities.

Style

Personification

Personification is a technique by which the poet ascribes human qualities to non-human objects or ideas. Malroux uses personification throughout the poem to describe what the speaker sees. In the second section of the poem, the sun is personified as it shows its "face-paints" like a person at a carnival and "bedecks the buildings" as if dressing the buildings for lively events. The sun is further personified in the next stanza, as it "smoothes away the night," as if it were a person smoothing out a piece of cloth. In the third section, both the windows opening "their eyelids" and the grass, which "sleeps profoundly," are given the qualities of a person in the morning, awakening or continuing to sleep. In line 18 of that stanza, the earth is ascribed the characteristics of a mother. In the final section, Malroux personifies the trees as priestly beings, wearing priestly garments (the chasubles) and "ready to bless the day."

By personifying the inanimate objects in the poem, Malroux establishes fluid connections between the human world and the natural and human-made worlds. In the poem, the sun, the earth, windows, grass, trees, and buildings behave like people getting ready for the day. The descriptions of the human-made and natural elements mirror the speaker's actions as she readies herself for the day, enjoying her morning stroll. By using personification, Malroux reinforces the theme of mutability, or the idea that the boundaries between different realms are not as solid as we might think they are. In the world of the poem, objects acquire human characteristics with ease and consistency.

Visual Imagery

Malroux also uses powerful visual images to express her ideas. She sets up a contrast between colorless images conveying lifelessness and colorful images embodying vitality. The colorless images appear in the first two stanzas, beginning with the "white ocean" in the first line. The ocean is a metaphor for the sky, but its whiteness suggests a sight drained of its usual hue and vigor. By the end of the stanza, this ocean/sky has become a reminder of the "antiseptic other side of death." The whiteness of the image becomes associated with nonexistence and a medicinally clean blankness. Malroux also uses colorlessness to describe the "pallid stone wall." Again, in this image, colorlessness is used to express a state of stillness or nonactivity. The pale images contrast with the sun's "face-paints," which imply bright, garish colors. The sun also "bedecks the buildings," presumably in vivid hues expressing vitality and playfulness. Malroux's use of colorlessness and color reinforces her portrayal of the sun as a powerful force as well as the poem's theme of the enduring strength of nature.

Historical Context

Although the poem was written in France during the 1990s, this context has little direct bearing on the poem itself, as it is set in an indeterminate place and time. The details of "Morning Walk" seem to be deliberately universalized: the unnamed speaker takes a morning stroll through a place with trees, grass, the sun, and buildings, and muses about issues such as aging and death. The speaker could be taking a walk anywhere where there are buildings and a few natural elements, and we do not know if she is even in a city, a suburb, or a small village.

It is possible that Malroux constructed the poem in this way to emphasize the universality of the poem's themes. By keeping the details nonspecific, Malroux makes the poem readily accessible to readers everywhere. Most people can relate to the activity of taking a morning walk, and most people have seen the sun rising and have strolled among buildings, trees, and grass. These familiar experiences draw readers into the poem and also reinforce the commonality of the speaker's reflections on aging and facing death. The physical landscape of the poem serves to illustrate the speaker's interior thoughts and feelings, which form the crux of the poem. By making the cultural and geographical context very general, Malroux highlights the meditative, philosophical aspect of the poem, rather than exploring particular contemporary issues. As Marilyn Hacker states in her preface to

Edge, "Claire Malroux's poems have no political agenda. But, often enough, they subvert expectations by simply using undramatic womanly quotidian gestures to signify the human universal."

Critical Overview

Although *Edge* has only been reviewed by a handful of American critics, this collection in which "Morning Walk" appears has been favorably received. Reviewers have praised the economy and force of Malroux's images as well as her philosophical insights and deployment of poetic structure. Writing in the *Boston Review*, Timothy Donnelly notes that the poems' "bristling intensity, clipped phrasing, and brilliant flashes of imagery are apt to remind many readers of Dickinson, whose work Malroux has translated." In his review in *World Literature Today*, Bruce King lauds Malroux's collection, stating, "Her poetry is unusual in its literary sophistication: it is very structured, yet highly elliptical; it is quiet, reticent, almost anonymous, at times even abstract and generalizing while treating of intense desires."

Reviewers have also praised Hacker's translation of the poems. Writing in *Prairie Schooner*, Eleanor Hamilton concludes, "Marilyn Hacker's choices for English words to correspond to the French are perfectly chosen. Or perhaps it just seems that way, the way great poems seem to set themselves upright on the page because we recognize their truth."

Criticism

Anna Maria Hong

Hong earned her master of fine arts degree in creative writing from the University of Texas's Michener Center for Writers. Her poems have appeared in several literary journals. In the following essay, Hong discusses Malroux's use of metaphor and personification to support the theme of porous boundaries in "Morning Walk."

Like many poems in *Edge*, "Morning Walk" explores the boundaries between different realms: night and day, the natural and the human, life and death, and the actual and the spiritual. For Malroux, these boundaries are highly permeable, and movement between apparently distinct worlds occurs frequently in the poem. In virtually every image, Malroux blends elements from disparate realms, shifting from one aspect to another.

> *"In Malroux's conception, the reader is also part of the mutable world of the poem, in which the boundaries between things are disregarded, and one moves easily from the human to the natural to the human-made and from dreaming to imagined afterlife to reality again."*

The poem opens with a typically slippery image: "The white ocean in which birds swim / Between the chimneys." In this metaphor, or comparison suggesting likeness between two things, the sky is likened to the sea, but the comparison is so complete that it is as if the sky and the sea—usually distinct elements of the earth—are one. As the stanza continues, other separate realms blur into each other, as the speaker wonders whether what she sees is "a dream / Beginning over again, or is it / The antiseptic other side of death?" The movement in these lines is from the concrete reality of the sky/ocean to the realm of dream to a third realm of nonexistence following death. In the speaker's mind, elements of the earth may be strange reverie or a kind of blank afterlife, and she does not seem to recognize divisions among these usually distinct states. Already, in this opening stanza, Malroux establishes the idea of quick and seamless movement between and among different aspects. One could say that in the mutable world of Malroux's poem, everything morphs and nothing stays in the realm it initially belongs to.

Throughout "Morning Walk," Malroux reinforces this theme of porous boundaries by describing objects in human terms. Using the device of personification, she ascribes human qualities to both natural and human-made things. In the second stanza, the sun acts like an optimistic and jubilant person displaying "its face-paints" as it "Bedecks the buildings." In the fourth stanza, the windows are described as wary people just waking up, "watchful" as they "open their eyelids." In contrast, the relaxed and also personified "grass sleeps profoundly / Like an old child / Sucking the earth." In the final stanza, the "trees, chasubled in sparrows" dress and act like priests always "ready to bless the day." In all these descriptions, there is movement from the inanimate world of nature or buildings to the human world. The description of the trees also establishes connections between the plant world and the animal world of the sparrows. In all the images, Malroux uses personification to shift fluidly from one realm to another, as if there were no boundaries between the human, the natural, and the human-made.

The temporal setting of the poem also emphasizes the theme of permeable boundaries. The poem takes place in the morning, as the strolling speaker notices the world awakening, shifting from night to day. However, this shift takes place gradually as the poem progresses. Malroux also conveys the sense of early morning almost entirely through her descriptions of the objects, which wake up, slumber on, or initiate the day with their blessings or energy.

The objects' actions, in fact, supplant those of the speaker, who remains noticeably in the background of the action. Malroux never uses the word "I" in the poem to indicate the speaker's actions or thoughts. From the poem's title, we can assume that the speaker is walking through the neighborhood, but in the poem itself, attention is shifted away from the speaker onto the things she sees. Emphasizing the objects in this way, again, reinforces Malroux's blending of the human and the inanimate—it is as if the objects were doing what the speaker would be doing instead of her. This expression of the speaker's presence through the description of objects conveys the idea that the speaker and the objects are one and the same and that the assumed boundaries between human beings and things do not actually exist.

Malroux's de-emphasis of the self in favor of objects is typical of many contemporary French poets. As John Taylor notes in his essay "From Intimism to the Poetics of 'Presence': Reading Contemporary French Poetry," which appears in *Poetry*, a number of French poets including Malroux have a bias toward things, and in crafting their poems, these poets attempt to illuminate and highlight the presence of objects. Unlike American poets, who often focus on the individual's perspective and stress the importance of human consciousness and experience, French poets such as Malroux do not necessarily elevate the human position in that way. These French poets ascribe as much importance to the existence of everyday objects such as trees, cups, and chairs as they do to human beings.

Like many of her contemporaries, Malroux underemphasizes the role of the speaker in her poem, placing the person on the same level as other elements in the poem. The speaker is not portrayed in any detail. We do not know what she looks like, nor do we know where she lives. She could be strolling through any place where there are buildings, grass, and trees. We do not even know if she is a she, since the gender is not specified. As mentioned, the speaker's thoughts, feelings, and actions are conveyed through the depiction of things. From these descriptions, however, we can surmise that the speaker is concerned with the progress of time, the movement toward death, and the process of aging.

In the third stanza, the speaker laments that "It takes so few hours / To smooth away the night / While our wrinkles are / Irreversible." These lines convey the speaker's anxieties about aging and moving closer to the nonexistence of death, as each day progresses. However, even in these lines where the speaker's emotions are conveyed, the speaker's singularity is erased. As Bruce King notes in his review of *Edge* in *World Literature Today*, "These are not poems of the subjective 'I' complaining or making a statement, but rather constructions through which an inner reality is found, articulated, and shaped."

Malroux's use of "our" in line 12 of the poem is significant, as the pronoun involves the reader and perhaps all humanity. In using the plural pronoun rather than the singular "my," Malroux again de-emphasizes the individuality of the speaker and instead directs attention to the general human condition. Like the other assumed boundaries, the lines between individuals melt away in the world of the poem.

The speaker's concerns about death, aging, and time are universal concerns that all human beings face. Although aging is a central theme that recurs throughout *Edge*, Malroux takes pains to highlight the generalized nature of the theme. Rather than emphasizing her own fears about these processes, the poet stresses the universality of these issues and makes the details in the poem universal as well. Most readers will be familiar with details such as chimneys, the sky, the sea, stone walls, wrinkles, grass, birds, and windows. Most people too have experienced taking a walk through their neighborhood or a city. For French readers in particular, this

What Do I Read Next?

- Malroux's book-length lyric narrative poem *A Long-Gone Sun* (2000), translated by Marilyn Hacker, recollects Malroux's childhood during World War II, including her father's involvement with the French Resistance, which led to his 1945 incarceration and death in the Nazi concentration camp Bergen-Belsen.
- Adam Gopnik's collection of twenty-three essays and journal entries about living in Paris in the late 1990s, *Paris to the Moon* (2001), examines national and local events from the point of view of a relocated New Yorker, covering topics as diverse as global capitalism, the decline of French cultural power, haute couture, cooking, sports, and Thanksgiving turkey.
- Ernest Hemingway's *A Moveable Feast,* first published in 1964 after the author's death, is his memoir of living in Paris during the 1920s. The book explores the vitality of the city as well as Hemingway's interactions with other expatriate writers, including Gertrude Stein and F. Scott Fitzgerald.
- In his essay "Mosaic on Walking," which was first published in the journal *Boulevard* in 1990, poet Mark Rudman ruminates on the solaces and pleasures of walking in New York City. The essay can also be found in *The Best American Essays 1991*, edited by Joyce Carol Oates and Robert Atwan.
- Marilyn Hacker's eighth poetry collection, *Squares and Courtyards* (2001), consists of lyric poems revolving around the themes of friendship, travel, cancer, illness, and time.
- Venus Khoury-Ghata's *Here There Was Once a Country* (2001) is another poetry collection Hacker translated from French into English. In the collection Khoury-Ghata, a Lebanese writer who has lived in France since 1973, relates events from her childhood in Paris and in Lebanon, where she witnessed a war that killed hundreds of thousands of Lebanese.

---

is a well-known scenario, and as Taylor points out in his essay in *Poetry*, poems in which the speaker takes a meditative stroll through the countryside or Paris occur frequently in contemporary French literature.

Malroux also employs universal symbols such as the sun and the earth, depicting them in familiar ways. The sun symbolizes power, energizing the waking world and pushing out the night, while the earth is depicted as a mother supporting the grass. Regardless of their individual experiences, virtually all readers can recognize these symbols functioning in these ways. By using such familiar details and symbols, Malroux removes barriers between the reader and the poet, enabling the reader to enter the poem's landscape easily and to identify with the issues and situation in the poem. In her preface to the collection, Hacker notes that Malroux is not a feminist or political writer. "Morning Walk" is a meditative poem, employing precise but common images to convey philosophical ideas. Rather than exploring current issues, Malroux elucidates enduring universal themes upon which poets in different time periods and in different cultures have ruminated.

However, Malroux's poem differs from other poetry on these subjects in her unique emphasis on the porosity of boundaries. In Malroux's conception, the reader is also part of the mutable world of the poem, in which the boundaries between things are disregarded, and one moves easily from the human to the natural to the human-made and from dreaming to imagined afterlife to reality again. It is a comforting notion that we too are part of the continuous fabric Malroux depicts, in which borders are illusory and in which the universe is populated with energizing stars, peaceful grass, and beneficent trees.

Source: Anna Maria Hong, Critical Essay on "Morning Walk," in *Poetry for Students*, Thomson Gale, 2005.

"A related characteristic of French poetry is the poet's relationship to 'things.'"

John Taylor

In the following essay excerpt, Taylor examines themes and approaches in contemporary French poetry, including that of Malroux.

Although emanating from sundry backgrounds, the poets who have adopted French as their poetic language agree in their insistence on the fruitfulness of overcoming linguistic difficulty. Beckett once remarked that he avoided English because "you couldn't help writing poetry in it." In a conversation with a friend, Lawrence Harvey, the Irishman added (as recorded in Anthony Cronin's *Samuel Beckett: The Last Modernist,* 1996) that "English because of its very richness holds out the temptation to rhetoric and virtuosity, words mirroring themselves complacently, Narcissus-like. The relative asceticism [of French] seemed more appropriate to the expression of being, undeveloped, unsupported, somewhere in the depths of the microcosm." When reading French poetry against a backdrop of ontology and metaphysics, it is crucial to keep in mind this "relative asceticism."

Although Beckett has few French "heirs," at least to date, much of the best contemporary poetry produced by the generation immediately following his own demands to be interpreted within an ontological framework—one, however, usually broader than that incarnated in the Irishman's verse and prose. A neo-Romantic search for a fleeting "apperception" of—or even a more prolonged "communion" with—Being distinctly motivates, in various ways, such poets as Bonnefoy, Jaccottet, du Bouchet, Dohollau, Baron Supervielle, Michel de Smet (b. 1912), Robert Marteau (b. 1925), Jacques Dupin (b. 1927), and Pierre-Albert Jourdan (1924–1981).

This orientation, sometimes accompanied by a quasi-scientific knowledge of natural things (one thinks of Marteau's admirably precise, yet also philosophically resonant, sonnets about various birds and trees), can be linked implicitly with some of Martin Heidegger's ideas. In France, Heidegger's thought was first popularized (with notorious misreadings) by Jean-Paul Sartre and then, more arrestingly, through commentary surrounding the short, oracular poems and prose poems of René Char (1907–1988), who was much admired by the German philosopher.

The point is not that this or that French poet, before writing, worked his way through *Being and Time* (1927), which, strangely enough, became available in French only in 1985. (Translations of other books by Heidegger were available earlier, of course.) The point is, rather, that key Heideggerean notions concerning death, man's separation from Nature and especially from Being, or man's use of reason, crop up in post-war poetry. The idea of a *logos* swelling upwards from the depths of Nature and potentially "hearkened to"—as Heidegger puts it—by the attentive poet also informs French poetics, as well as the corollary position—not far removed from Beckett's, after all—that what one intends to express lies beyond words yet must somehow be evoked, *with* words. The "abstractness" or "abstruseness" of which contemporary French poetry is sometimes accused often derives from the (foreign) critic's misprision of this philosophical framework. It is necessary to discern the nature-oriented, "earth-grounded," means mustered by poets struggling with exact perceptions that lead, however, to the ineffable. In *Une apparence de soupirail* (1982), Dupin summarizes this dilemma (and his own austere poetics) by avowing his desire to "write as if I had not been born. Anterior words: half-ruined, stripped, sucked into the abyss. Writing *without words,* as if I were being born." Similarly, on the other side of our existence lies another "wordlessness," the "silence" of death; and this "lack of words," as Marie-Claire Bancquart (b. 1932) phrases it in *Sans lieu sinon l'attente* (1991)—one could almost say this "want" of words—is "all we know about entering death." A poet, too, may project him- or herself into this absence-of-all-utterance, attempting, with analogous paradox, to capture a few "posterior" words.

At any rate, language, by its very essence, is considered to be ontologically problematic even by French poets who are not as explicit in their self-conscious linguistic cogitation as Michel Deguy (b. 1930) or Anne-Marie Albiach (b. 1937). For this same reason, when a poet like du Bouchet spreads words and phrases all over the page, these "layouts" bear only superficial formal resemblance to, say, similar verse-scatterings composed by Ezra Pound or Charles Olson. As du Bouchet scrutinizes a wind-swept mountain-scape, an extraordinary tension inhabits the blank spaces in his poem, while his lapidary, taut, syntactically wrenched utterances correspondingly seem to derive from a sort of "pre-historic"—even, paradoxically, "pre-linguistic"—cosmos, one in which the poet must (as he insists) "push down with all [his] weight on the weakest word so that it will burst and deliver its sky." Du Bouchet's poetry has been characterized as a *poésie blanche,* the term "blanche" here referring literally to "whiteness" or "blankness," and metaphorically to a hard-earned "purification," a "stripping-down to bare essentials." The artfully halting, doubting, inconclusive effects in many of Jaccottet's poems similarly mirror (are not just "about") the poet's grappling with the possibilities of getting "beyond" material facts and reaching out for elusive spiritual mysteries. His life-work charts his attempts (and, poignantly, his failures) to create in himself a readiness for—an acute receptivity to—an unpredictable, hypothetical, transitory instant in which an *ailleurs* or "elsewhere" becomes perceptible and thus almost reachable. Qualifiers like "perhaps" and "probably," as well as disaffirming adverbs and adjectives, not to forget conspicuous conditional verb tenses, masterfully evoke the hesitations and second thoughts preventing him from "arriving" at the envisioned *lieu.* For Bonnefoy, who has devoted perceptive essays to this linguistic paradox haunting him and so many of his *confrères,* the experience of what he calls "presence"—the reunion, however ephemeral, with plenitude; the apperception of transcendence, in the here and now—presumably must take place, if not exactly beyond words, then at least beyond the obfuscating conceptual connotations that usage has attached to them.

These poetic and philosophical ideas (necessarily simplified here) must also be juxtaposed with Cartesian notions concerning the centrality of the self. A substantial amount of contemporary French poetry and prose indeed revolves around the question of the self, to the extent that a given poet's implicit position *vis-à-vis* the Cartesian "I think, therefore I am" enables his output to be classified. With respect to the metaphysically- or ontologically-oriented poets mentioned above, for instance, a *sine qua non* condition for experiencing Being involves what might be christened "de-selfing": the self, the locus of language, is considered to be the fundamental barrier that must be pulled down, displaced, at least disaggrandized, or even—in some poets—bitterly dismissed, if they are to escape "outwards" from the imprisoning qualities of the human condition. Several poets indeed aim at transforming the enclosing "high stone walls" of the monadic self into—if nothing more transparent can be achieved—at least a thin, opaque veil. If successful, then a little *lumière*—a keyword in contemporary poetry and much more richly connoted than its English cognate—becomes visible, if not quite tangible. In *La Part des mots* (1983), de Smet notably observes that "a door kept open / to the light / nourishes the waiting / across from / the shattered words / of shadow." Du Bouchet graphically defines this necessary self-effacement as "writ[ing] as far as possible from myself," adding that he aspires to remain "farther from [himself] than from the horizon."

The short poems that Guillevic (1907–1997) devoted to the Atlantic (*Carnac,* 1961) delve into this *seminal* contradiction haunting him and his poetic kin: the writing self, writing its way to selflessness—an irresolvable contradiction, evidently; an unending quest. A human being cannot break out of his inherent ephemerality, his mortality; what the poet may initially perceive as "eternal," an authentic manifestation of Being, must soon thereafter be re-named as "no more than" (as Guillevic qualifies it) a mere thought or feeling enveloped by his own perishable self. He, moreover, cannot get "inside the stone," he laments in *Sphère* (1963); a poet is fated to deal with a mere mirage-like "trembling"—a recurrent word in Jaccottet's nature poetry as well. This persistent ambiguity—this perpetual struggle to overcome an inherent, inevitable "failure"—characterizes the work of several other poets. Surpassing Existentialism, such poetry, evoking the mind's *élan* towards Being and its corresponding inability to arrive fully, represents a new, more spiritual, attempt to define *la condition humaine.* In Jaccottet, this wavering between the positive and the negative is particularly gripping. Ever wrestling with the overwhelmingly pessimistic evidence of a materialism whose only horizon is death and annihilation, he nonetheless pursues his troubling "positive" intuition that there might nevertheless be, as he posits, "something between things, / like the space between the lime-tree and the laurel." He wonders recurrently how he might cross the "threshold," accede to this promising "space." "Threshold," too, is a key French poetic term.

A poet like Charles Juliet (b. 1934) takes a different angle on these problematics. Juliet's limpid poems explore existential distress, the daily discouragements of life, solitude, and fear. His successive poetry volumes thus trace, in almost diary-like fashion, the itinerary of a man perpetually struggling to get beyond despair and to attain inner peace. Intimately self-referential (all while remaining abstract enough, in symbolism, to create an immediate universality), his poems, set against a backdrop of metaphysical anguish and a loss of religious faith, appeal to the need for individuation, for self-fulfillment. It is the duty of poetry, he maintains, to teach him how to "adhere / to what I am"—an echo of Goethe's "become what you are." Similarly, Louis-René des Forêts (b. 1918), especially in his profound and troubling *Poèmes de Samuel Wood* (1988), attempts to come to terms with himself in the face of approaching death. Samuel Wood is a fictional construct, a poetic "voice" who expounds a philosophy of living (and writing) with respect to the certainty of his demise. In the final poem, des Forêts unmasks Wood—a mere "invented shade" not at all like himself—and admits that "this voice from elsewhere / inaccessible to time and wear / is no less illusory than a dream." He can only hope that something in this voice "nevertheless" persists, endures, "its timbre still vibrating in the distance like a storm / of which one cannot tell if it is coming near or going away."

A related characteristic of French poetry is the poet's relationship to "things." Because of the natural empiricism of most English-language poets, it is hard to imagine an exact equivalent of Francis Ponge (1899–1988), the French "thing-poet" *par excellence.* His prose poems—devoted to objects such as magnolia trees, potatoes, olives, lilacs, oysters, snails, pebbles, plates, fruit crates, water jugs, candles or bread—have proved to be stimulating exercises in perception and description. Significantly, these texts chronicle the "approach" toward these things—with which he cannot otherwise consort easily. Ponge, more than anyone else before him (except Rilke, the pioneer), poetically depicts the steep, uneven, even treacherous trail that language must climb before attaining a "thing," an "object." In contrast, William Carlos Williams's oft-cited "no ideas but in things" argues for a different teleology of the material world. Roughly speaking, the American poet begins with a fact and works toward an idea, while his French counterpart begins with an idea and works to the fact—as Ponge himself strikingly confesses at the end of his "preamble" to his famous text, "The Mimosa." "All these preliminaries," he concludes, "should be entitled: *The Mimosa and I.* But it's to the mimosa itself—oh sweet illusion!—that I now need to come . . . to the mimosa without me." For Ponge, in other words, the objectifying poetic process, aiming at grasping the "thing-in-itself," must necessarily take into account the Cartesian *cogito ergo sum* as well as its logical consequence: "Because I am, the outside world also exists." Tellingly, the ultimate rejection of the self-referential Cartesian axiom—in the name of what Ponge terms his "bias" or "prejudice" (*parti pris*) in favor of things—implies an initial acceptance of its validity. It is impossible to think of a French poet who has ignored its primacy. In a poem from *Edge* (1996), Claire Malroux (b. 1935) writes, for example: "I can't get too far in. The wall stops me / Where the spider of my shadow crouches / . . . I will stay on this side / . . . Without trying to find out what that sun / Might be."

Even in a man as capable of Ponge-like "down-to-thingness" as Jacques Réda (b. 1929), nearly every detail in his poems seems accompanied by bewilderment, stupefaction, admiration, joy, even occasional grumpiness—emotions all illustrating how uneasily or anxiously separated from the material world a French poet can be. In *La Liberté des rues* (1997), Réda refers to those "modest yet incontestable marvels" that he chances upon during his aimless wanderings (by foot or on his antiquated Vélo-Solex moped), especially through Parisian streets, but also as far as the headwaters of the Seine or even Dublin. In *Les Ruines de Paris* (1977), his serendipitous findings include acacias blossoming fragrantly in drab Parisian side-streets, shops selling cheap delicious wine, rare jazz recordings, carefully painted lead soldiers, and obscure cigarette brands. (Smoking strange tobacco mixtures, he avows, is his "way of seeking for the Absolute.") The "idea" inciting him to seek out, to ready himself for, such unpredictable "miracles" thus entails ever "going out"—the verb *sortir* and its synonyms occur emphatically in many a contemporary poet of like sensibility. In brief, he hopes to find "what [he] isn't looking for." Beginning with these odd, usually jubilant happenstances, Réda often spins off on one of those half-fanciful, half-serious metaphysical tangents that make his books so delightful and thought-provoking. Although quite different in tone, the increasingly aphoristic poetry of Christian Hubin (b. 1941) likewise struggles to reconcile the microcosmic with the macrocosmic, the brute physical detail with its potential metaphysical resonance.

Inversely, some French poets celebrate what is closest to home. Taking their example from the great, still insufficiently-acknowledged precursor in this domain, Jean Follain (1903–1971), poets such as François de Cornière (b. 1950) and Gil Jouanard (b. 1937) often devote their attention to "humble" everyday objects, landscapes and localities, as well as (in the former's case) family life. Moving from the particular to the general, or vice versa, their poems and prose poems meditate on the sense and the respect that one should give to the quotidian and to a "full instant" of being alive. Yet their vantage point on dailiness is not fully informed by an uncompromising realism; an attempt is made to get beyond facts to ideas (particularly in Jouanard's case) or to an oft-melancholy emotion associated with the fragility of human life and love, with the radiant "presence" of certain simple things, with the richness of "privileged moments," or with the perennial mysteries concealed in the most routine events. Often, what most intrigues is not what the poet relates, but rather what he intentionally omits. The outstanding lessons taught by Follain to his "intimist" descendants are how to look around, wherever one is, and to place the enigma between the lines.

Source: John Taylor, "From Intimism to the Poetics of Presence: Reading Contemporary French Poetry," in *Poetry*, Vol. 177, No. 1, October–November 2000, pp. 147–61.

Eleanor M. Hamilton

In the following review, Hamilton finds Malroux's poems stimulating and freeing and asserts that her work serves to explore the earth beyond the earth, truth beyond the truth.

As an American being introduced to the poetry of Claire Malroux, I am aware of the differences between French literary traditions and my own. There is a down-to-earth quality to American poetry, an urge to get to the truth physically as well as intellectually. In these poems by Claire Malroux, translated by Marilyn Hacker, there is no down-to-earth, and truth, as we know it, is illusory. Malroux's work serves to explore the earth beyond the earth, truth beyond the truth.

This collection includes poems selected from two books, *Aires* and *Entre nous et la lumière*, along with eleven evocative and haunting new poems. The bilingual collection begins with "Morning Walk." On the surface the images are exact, like those in a painting. The sky is "The white ocean in which birds swim / Between the chimneys." However, below the surface there is less tranquillity and little or no certainty: "Without a harbor / A single / Boat / Heads out to sea." From this point on, the poems examine the world the way "Fingers probe / The desert of a face."

Malroux's poetry is a mirror she reaches through in search of what lies behind it. As with Jean Cocteau's Orphè, the mirror often turns to water and forms only a thin surface between the poet and the underworld. "Basic Truths" begins with a daring first line: "Water is sobbing." In this poem, as well as in many of her poems, there is an almost unrelenting sense of mourning. As human life becomes more and more detached from its natural origins, the earth

> *"In these poems by Claire Malroux, translated by Marilyn Hacker, there is no down-to-earth, and truth, as we know it, is illusory."*

itself feels abandoned: "That's why it exhausts itself / Erecting secret / Catafalques / Such Gothic stalagmites / Of Grief."

Even the ground we walk on is a construction to be reclaimed by the sea. The human world is trapped by its limited vision of the land, which makes the human psyche all the more constrained. In contrast, the bird's life is regulated by the forces of the natural world, forces with the power to generate life out of death.

I don't want to give the mistaken impression that Malroux's poems are depressing to read, or that there is a heaviness and burden of responsibility to her work. Quite the opposite: I find her poems stimulating and freeing.

The poems from *Entre nous et la lumière* begin with a sequence of complex poems without titles. I read them as a successful effort to work through the importance of poetry to her life. In youth, her poetry was a means of coping with tragedy when "struggling skin on skin against the specter / of the wind life always grew green again / tangled in death's curls." Poetry made it possible for her to engage her spirit with the unfathomable.

The poet sees darkness within herself as well as darkness within darkness. Between the internal and the external lie the possibilities for poetry. For this reason, and for others, Malroux distrusts psychoanalysis because she believes there are areas of the human experience that can't be qualified, explained, or labeled, and shouldn't be.

Malroux does not try to provide answers beyond a spiritual probing of the mysteries inherent in nature. The series ends with the knowledge that whatever we produce is reclaimed by forces beyond ourselves. The "madman" in the poem steals what he can and sees the intuitive nature of the female as sexual energy that serves him:

In the body that female tree
On her back amidst her shuddering leaves

> *"Whether set in the suburbs or country, Malroux's poems could have been written in a city apartment."*

He watches for a climax
A revelation.

These lines bring to mind Marge Piercy's sequence of poems, "Laying Down The Tower" where the images of the Tarot deck are used to explore abuses of the male power structure. In Malroux's vision, the madman represents the desire to control what is beyond control. He lives on the outside and the female lives on the inside "in the digestive tract / of the earth."

The poems in *Entre nous et la lumière* and the new poems at the end of this collection, explore the poet's sense of her own mortality. She's not concerned with a loss of beauty, or loss of prowess, but with a lack of time. In the second series of untitled poems she writes, "Time has doors has windows / it is not this corridor of anguish / Whose long brevity we measure / Breathless."

Malroux is brilliant in her observations on the ways in which "Time inhabits us." Poem by poem she introduces new ways of viewing the inexorable realities of aging: "The diminishing number of lines / to be spoken on this stage, set for how long / The shadow grows, flesh hollows itself out, another / Takes your place. Step by step you leave yourself."

"Last Truths," the poem that concludes *Entre nous et la lumière*, envisions a future where humans become "Coiled fossils in the shallows / Without denying earth / Or its imprints." What awaits us is not judgment, but the reflection of what we failed to learn.

The collection ends with "Octet Before Winter," a poem that could very well serve as a later counterpart to T. S. Eliot's "The Love Song of J. Alfred Prufrock." Eliot's poem defined a modern sensibility early in this century. Malroux's poem comes to terms with the end of the century. Her poem is filled with cogent images, humor, and ironic pathos. There isn't a breathless anxiety so much as a deep breath. The women "who come and go / Talking of Michelangelo" are now "pregnant and slightly weary."

"Octet Before Winter" is not a collage of poignant observations. It's more a montage of cruel disappointments. Eliot wrote, "In a minute there is time / For decisions and revisions which a minute will reverse." Malroux concludes that "Today / Once again, nothing will be decided." In her view, the patient is not "etherised upon a table," instead "every sentence / unwinds the shroud, exposes / A lunar landscape of wounds." Her poem ends with an entreaty to look at life beyond the objectified self: "The gaze is everything in this blind room, / death to those who let themselves drown in it."

Marilyn Hacker's choices for English words to correspond to the French are perfectly chosen. Or perhaps it just seems that way, the way great poems seem to set themselves upright on the page because we recognize their truth.

Source: Eleanor M. Hamilton, Review of *Edge*, in *Prairie Schooner*, Winter 1998, pp. 193–95.

Bruce King, Review of Edge

In the following review, King identifies the poems in "Edge" as being constructions through which an inner reality is found, articulated, and shaped.

It is unlikely that readers of this review are familiar with the poetry of Claire Malroux, if only because her work is published in France under the name Claire Sara Roux. Her poetry is unusual in its literally sophistication: it is very structured, yet highly elliptical; it is quiet, reticent, almost anonymous, at times even abstract and generalizing while treating of intense desires. Malroux works within a poetic tradition in which the subject is unnamed and often found in the act of making and shaping. These are not poems of the subjective "I" complaining or making a statement, but rather constructions through which an inner reality is found, articulated, and shaped. The stanzas are brief images complete to themselves. There are literary echoes. A meditative mind is also a rational mind; it finds and controls the expression of its intensities of feelings.

Although most of the poems have images and settings alluding to the outside, their drama belongs to an interior world and concerns commonplace events and situations which give significance to a day. Whether set in the suburbs or country, Malroux's poems could have been written in a city apartment. Marilyn Hacker avoids describing the poems as feminist but notes that they at times allude to or make use of typical female situations or gestures such as using lipstick. Subtle changes, such as the solitariness of the speaker and her companion being transformed at night in bed, provide what little story there is.

Malroux is a prizewinning translator of American poetry into French, and at times her puns and wordplays feel Anglo-Saxon; some poems seem in the manner of Emily Dickinson, whom she has translated. While Hacker has found equivalents of Malroux's puns and unusual word choices, as much care has gone into the nuanced and exact translation of poetic technique. Hacker, who has been publishing translations of Malroux in American journals for a decade, has worked closely with the author to bring into English the rhymes and other patterns of sound that make these poems impressively musical. French is more sonorous than English, and its grammatical structures more self-reflective; the purposeful ambiguities that are part of modern French verse become concretized or vague in English. There can be no solutions to such problems, only attempted solutions.

Edge consists of selections from two of Malroux's books and some new poems, including "Gaudebo," dedicated to Derek Walcott, whom she has translated. The three groups of poems are different from one another; the recent ones use a longer line and are less fragmented and elliptic. *Edge* is published in Germaine Brée's Contemporary French Poetry in Translation series, which includes *Selected Poems* of Pierre Reverdy and Francis Ponge and such translators as Derek Mahon, John Ashbery, Paul Auster, John Montague, and C. K. Williams. The Malroux-Hacker volume easily belongs in such distinguished company.

Source: Bruce King, Review of *Edge*, in *World Literature Today*, Vol. 71, No. 1, Winter 1997, p. 114.

Sources

Donnelly, Timothy, Review of *Edge*, in *Boston Review*, Vol. 21, No. 5, October–November 1996, p. 46.

Hacker, Marilyn, "Translator's Preface," in *Edge*, by Claire Malroux, Wake Forest University Press, 1996, p. ix.

Hamilton, Eleanor M., Review of *Edge*, in *Prairie Schooner*, Vol. 72, No. 4, Winter 1998, pp. 193–95.

King, Bruce, Review of *Edge*, in *World Literature Today*, Vol. 71, No. 1, Winter 1997, p. 114.

Malroux, Claire, "Morning Walk," in *Edge*, Wake Forest University Press, 1996, p. 3.

Taylor, John, "From Intimism to the Poetics of 'Presence': Reading Contemporary French Poetry," in *Poetry*, Vol. 177, No. 1, October–November 2000, pp. 147–61.

Further Reading

Barzun, Jacques, *An Essay on French Verse: For Readers of English Poetry*, New Directions Publishing, 1991.

In this book, Barzun analyzes the verse of French poets from the neoclassicists writing in the seventeenth century onward through the contemporary period. He argues for the merits of French poetry, as he explains aspects of the French language and poetic forms.

Drake, David, *Intellectuals and Politics in Post-War France*, Palgrave Macmillan, 2002.

Drake elucidates the political thoughts of French intellectuals during the latter half of the twentieth century.

Kelly, Michael, and Margaret Atack, eds., *French Culture and Society: The Essentials*, Edward Arnold, 2001.

Designed for students, this reference book contains concise explanations and entries on individuals, issues, events, and ideas in France since 1918.

Shaw, Mary Lewis, *The Cambridge Introduction to French Poetry*, Cambridge University Press, 2003.

Shaw illuminates French poetry written from the Middle Ages through the present, discussing a wide range of topics, such as genres, politics, and philosophy. The book also contains a glossary of poetic terms.

White, Edmund, *The Flaneur: A Stroll through the Paradoxes of Paris*, Bloomsbury USA, 2001.

In this nonfiction book, White, who lived in Paris for sixteen years, guides readers through and around Paris's bookshops, boutiques, monuments, palaces, and other city sites, recounting each site's history and stories.

Rapture

Joelle Biele

2001

Joelle Biele's poem "Rapture" appears in her first collection, *White Summer*, published in 2002. The poem first appeared in print in the *Iowa Review* in 2001. This poem is representative of Biele's creative ability to turn the commonplace into something marvelous, to select the precise words that describe an emotion or a moment or all of nature in ways that the reader may not have previously considered.

"Rapture" is made up of thirty lines, each attempting to express or personify an example of the poem's title. While many people may reserve this word to describe something incredibly rare or even sacred, Biele here shows that sheer bliss can be found in virtually every minute of daily life, every sound, every taste, every *thing* within both the natural and not-so-natural worlds. Biele seeks to reveal the potential for ecstasy in things that are often overlooked or disregarded. Rapture, she suggests, is everywhere—but human beings must learn to recognize it.

While Biele's name is still relatively new and perhaps not widely known among contemporary American poetry readers, a poem such as "Rapture" provides a good introduction to the full body of her early work. Its energy, insight, and exquisite details demonstrate Biele's simple love for language—and a raw talent for using it.

Author Biography

Poet Joelle Biele was born in 1969, in the Bronx, New York. In 1991, she received a bachelor's degree in English from Tufts University in Boston, and she earned her master of fine arts and Ph.D. degrees from the University of Maryland, College Park, in 1993 and 1998, respectively. Even as a young poet, Biele was recognized as a strong talent in making language come alive in her work. The rich imagery and precise descriptions that comprise her poems earned her early recognition throughout contemporary literary circles. She was the winner of both the Ruth Lake Award and the Cecil Hemley Memorial Award from the Poetry Society of America. She received a 1998–1999 Fulbright fellowship to Germany, where she taught American literature, and she has served as a lecturer in the English department at the University of Maryland.

Biele's first full-length collection of poems, *White Summer*, won a First Book Award from the Crab Orchard Review Series in Poetry and was published in 2002. Her poem "Rapture" is included in this collection, but first appeared in the Winter 2001 edition of the *Iowa Review*.

Joelle Biele

Poem Text

It starts with a low rumbling, white static,
a broken shell to the ear. It starts with water,

tide pulling. It starts with the cold kiss of the sun.
It's hands clapping, birds clamoring,

and laughter coming through the walls.
It starts with snow breathing,

bottles falling, the night hum of a road.
It's a bus shifting gears.

It's the flower inside the tree, the song
inside the wood. It's a mouthpiece buzzing,

the *psh-psh* of a Bach cantata.
It's walking through a pile of leaves.

It starts with wet legs and poppies.
It starts with bitter chicory.

It's diked fields, the suck under your shoe.
It starts with an idling motor. It's horses in fog.

It starts with spilt sugar. It's sizzle and spatter.
It's your voice under water. It's a bell buoy's sway.

It starts with a sail luffing, whispering
in the wings. It starts with a policeman walking,

a rosy ear, a dog barking, honey and flies.
It starts with a knife sharpening

and plates smashing against the door.
It starts deep in the belly, the back of the throat.

It's need like salt, crackle and flame.
It starts with sounds you've never made.

It's not your voice in your mouth.
Your words are not your own.

It's the body breaking into islands.
It's the fall through wind lifting white leaves.

Poem Summary

Line 1

The word "it" appears twenty-seven times in the thirty lines of "Rapture," beginning with the first word. While this abundant use of a single word may not be remarkable, the manner in which it serves as the *gel* of the work is certainly worth considering. Throughout the poem "it" refers to one thing: rapture. The suggestion is that extreme joy originates in a variety of forms, especially in sounds. In the first line, it begins as a "low rumbling, white static," perhaps a likeness to white *noise*—the combination of all sound frequencies that creates a din. Line 1 serves not only as a first example of where rapture may begin, but it also introduces the importance of paying attention to sound, which the poem emphasizes throughout.

Line 2

This line alludes to the common belief that one can hear the ocean roaring in a seashell and also implies that the "low rumbling" in line 1 may indeed be the roar of the ocean. To maintain the image, Biele bluntly states that rapture also "starts with water," and the poem returns to water imagery several more times.

Line 3

The first two words of line 3 continue the ocean allusion begun in the previous line, but then the imagery takes an abrupt turn—from the ebb and flow of a sea tide to "the cold kiss of the sun." By juxtaposing these opposing images, Biele suggests the infinite possibilities of where rapture may be found. Playing opposites against each other to imply limitless options is also found in the contradictory description of the sun's "kiss" as "cold."

Lines 4–5

These two lines take rapture to yet another level but still allude to different sounds. Hands clapping, birds clamoring, and laughter so loud it is "coming through the walls" all infer a cacophony of sounds that are, if not pleasant, at least fun and generally upbeat. And any one of these sounds—no matter how loud or cacophonous—might contain the ingredients for creating rapture.

Lines 6–7

In these lines, rapture is likened to three distinct circumstances, though all have to do with things one can hear. The idea of "snow breathing" suggests a quiet, tranquil sound, barely audible, like soft human breathing. But this peaceful scenario is quickly contrasted with the loud, sharp clatter of "bottles falling." The "night hum of the road" is somewhere between quiet and loud sounds, as one can certainly hear cars and trucks traveling down the highway, but the "hum" of the passing vehicles is not generally considered annoying or clamorous.

Line 8

Until line 8, the sounds and images that represent rapture are highly illustrious and inventive. Now the switch is to the mundane, largely overlooked noise of "a bus shifting gears." The speaker's point, however, is well made with this unembellished, commonplace description: whether the sun is offering a cold kiss or a city bus is starting its route, rapture can be found in both.

Lines 9–11

Line 9 and the first part of line 10 return to a more creative, metaphoric language for the images they describe, incorporating nature in its simplest form as a symbol of rapture. The "flower inside the tree" and the "song / inside the wood" imply a serene harmony among these natural elements. The imagery in the latter part of line 10 again seems to take an abrupt turn, but perhaps there is a subtle connection among the tree, the "mouthpiece buzzing," and a "Bach cantata." Note that the wood of the tree has a *song* within it. This musical metaphor leads to the feel of a musical instrument's mouthpiece humming against a musician's lips. And this, in turn, leads to the "*psh-psh*" tone of a full-fledged religious choral by Bach. Whether the source of sheer joy is the very audible cantata or the imaginary song of a tree, rapture resides in either.

Lines 12–13

Line 12 claims that rapture may stem from the common autumn activity of "walking through a pile of leaves," and line 13 suggests that the season has changed—"wet legs and poppies" imply a walk through a colorful, damp field after a spring or summer shower—but the "it" remains the same. Rapture can be found during any season of the year.

Lines 14–15

Chicory is a perennial herb and leafy plant that is edible but often considered "bitter" in its raw form. Perhaps its purpose here is simply to play off the *seasonal* dried leaves and poppies mentioned in the previous lines. The "diked fields" and "the suck under your shoe" are surely connected to taking a walk, as well as to rain or dew or other watery imagery. Dikes are ditches or embankments created to help control water flow, and the "suck" is the squishing sound made by shoes when one walks across damp grounds. Considering such a noise *rapturous* is not likely for many people, but Biele infers that human beings need to find more pleasure in simple, uneventful things.

Line 15 includes the first address in second-person—it is the suck under *your* shoe. Until now, Biele has used only the generic third-person, as in line 2: a broken shell to *the* ear. The more personal "your" becomes more prevalent at the end of the poem, though it is not necessarily an address to any particular individual. It is more likely a universal *you* or even the poet speaking to herself in second-person.

Line 16

Compare the first image in line 16 to that in line 8. The sound of "an idling motor" is as ordinary as a "bus shifting gears," and both are of little significance in the average person's daily life. When a car motor *stops* working, however, an angry driver will pay very keen attention to it. The poet's approach is to find joy in a good engine instead of frustration in a bad one. The second image in line 16 appears to have nothing to do with the first unless the reader considers that both motors and horses have something to do with transportation. Aside from this dubious connection, "horses in fog" simply presents an intriguing visual image and is worthy of being called blissful.

Line 17

Like line 14, line 17 employs food imagery to describe rapture, though here it is sweet and oily instead of bitter. The "spilt sugar" is an obvious reference to sweetness, and "sizzle and spatter" are reminiscent of hot oil in a pan reacting to the heat beneath it.

Lines 18–19

These lines rely heavily again on water imagery. Line 18 also includes the second reference to "your": "your voice under water." The three distinct images in these lines are connected by their relationship to motion. When someone dives under water and attempts to speak, the result is mostly bubbles and ripples. The image then shifts to the "bell buoy's sway," which leads to swaying on a grander scale, "a sail luffing, whispering" ("luffing" means flapping).

Lines 20–21

In these two lines, rapture originates in a variety of disparate beings and things. Two of them—the policeman and the dog—are *doing* something: walking and barking. The other three are simply identified: "a rosy ear, . . . honey and flies." With these images, the poet nearly dares the reader to find a connection, but perhaps the point is not to look too hard. The central idea of the poem, after all, is that rapture can come from anybody and anything at any time.

Lines 22–23

If the reader is a bit befuddled by the hodgepodge items in the previous two lines, these two lines may seem even more odd in their unmistakable *violent* details. Until now, Biele's images have been pleasant, funny, upbeat, happy, peaceful, or simply mundane. But here rapture "starts with a knife sharpening / and plates smashing against the door." In keeping with the original notion that extreme joy is found in a variety of noises, a knife sharpening and plates breaking certainly fit the bill. But these are not generally considered *good* sounds. They do, however, suggest a sudden urgency, a compelling attempt to include *everything* in a virtual list of places where rapture may start. If this poem has a climax, these two lines are likely it. The work draws to a quick close after line 23 but not before describing the urgency in more detail and then letting the falling action bring it to an end.

Lines 24–25

Lines 24 and 25 portray the human element with more fervor than earlier parts of the poem. Previously, human needs seem fulfilled with simple pleasures—holding a shell to the ear, clapping hands, listening to music, walking through leaves. Now happiness comes from "deep in the belly, the back of the throat," as though the fulfillment level has grown more guttural, more imperative. The "need" is now "like salt, crackle and flame," a far cry from flowers, trees, wet legs, and poppies. Like the images themselves, the tone of "Rapture" has greatly sharpened toward the end.

Lines 26–28

These three lines help to *resolve* the poem, bringing it full circle in its myriad list of joys. All the sounds mentioned throughout the work contain the origin of rapture, many of them stemming from the actions of human beings. Here the human appears to have no control over pinpointing rapture—it just happens beyond his or her grasp. The use of second-person makes the address more immediate and personal, which is ironic considering the descriptions are much less concrete and vivid. The "sounds you've never made" may contain rapture, but what are they? If it is not "your voice in your mouth," whose is it? And if "Your words are not your own," whose are they? These questions are merely rhetorical and have no specific answers. The resolution, however, is that rapture originates in both the known and the unknown. "Your" job is to accept that.

Lines 29–30

The two highly metaphoric lines that end the poem rely solely on creative imagery to describe rapture instead of the more visible, objective depictions that permeate the rest of the work. The joyful feeling of the "body breaking into islands" implies a letting-go of the *whole* in order to experience the bliss derived from the *parts*. Note also that this metaphor employs yet another water image. Finally,

Topics for Further Study

- Write a poem using the word "it" fifteen times in twenty lines. To what does your "it" refer? Is it difficult or easy to describe the same thing fifteen different ways? How does the large number of uses in a short poem influence what "it" references?
- Do some research on the debate over the Christian belief in the "rapture." What does it entail and what are the basic arguments for and against it? What other religions, if any, have a doctrine similar to this one?
- Of all the classical music composers, why might Biele have mentioned Bach in particular in this poem? Why a "cantata" specifically and what is the "*psh-psh*" of one?
- Discuss the significance of the poem's title. Would calling it "Joy" or "Happiness" work just as well? Why or why not?

the imagery shifts again from the sea to the air, as in lines 2 and 3. Leaves falling and lifting through wind also imply a letting-go, emphasizing the origin of rapture in both the abstract and the concrete.

Themes

Joy in the Commonplace

The straightforward title of Biele's poem makes its central theme appear obvious: here is a work about what rapture is, at least in the poet's opinion. But perhaps it is not as simple as that. In parts of the world where fundamental Christianity is predominant—and in the United States particularly—*rapture* takes on a significantly religious meaning, referring to the period of time when Christians, both dead and alive, will ascend to heaven prior to the final war between good and evil, marking the end of time as humans know it. As dramatic as this scenario may seem, none of it is mentioned in Biele's poem "Rapture." Instead, this work concentrates on the less lofty ideals of what bliss really is, centering on the commonplace, minute, and often disregarded things and events that make up daily life. Most of these "rapturous" things do not even leave a distinct impression in people's minds.

Something as ordinary as clapping hands or laughing is rarely seen as a source of great joy. While both acts suggest a happy moment or occasion, neither is generally described in terms of ecstasy and euphoria. The same may be said for listening to a favorite piece of music or walking through a pile of leaves on a crisp autumn day. Again, the events are pleasant enough but *rapturous* seems a bit exaggerated. And if these cheerful, comforting times in one's life go largely overlooked for their bliss value, consider how much less attention is paid to "a bus shifting gears" and "an idling motor." Yet these innocuous, if not boring, everyday events also make Biele's rapture list.

To say the poem radiates a positive attitude is an obvious understatement, but perhaps the reason is not so conspicuous. If one's definition of rapture—aside from the end-of-time religious reference—is so narrow that it allows for only the rarest, most spectacular, glorious moments and events, then how often does a person actually get to experience it? For some people, perhaps a few times; for others, never. The point then is to find rapture in the places and times that one can experience every day. The old adage about taking time to stop and smell the roses is a simple way to explain this theme in "Rapture." But Biele would argue that there is a lot more to stop for than sweetly scented flowers—seashells, dogs, honey, and buses, to name a few.

Joy in Nature

A theme closely related to finding joy in the commonplace is finding it in nature, whether it is in everyday natural occurrences or more infrequent phenomena. Water imagery is important in the poem, appearing as an ocean and seashells, wet legs and diked fields, a buoy and a sailboat, and a human body "breaking into islands." A human's relationship with water is as common as enjoying the dew beneath one's feet and as sublime as feeling one's self actually become a part of the ocean.

Other areas of nature in which rapture may be found include sunshine and snow; flowers and trees; poppies and chicory; and birds, horses, dogs, and flies. The list is intentionally disparate to emphasize the notion of looking *everywhere* for joy.

A variety of tastes are also included—the sweetness of sugar, the "sizzle and spatter" of oil, the longing for salt. In these items, rapture is likened to the basest human need: food. Food is thrown into the mix of natural phenomena as easily as "the flower inside the tree, the song / inside the wood."

Finding various aspects of nature in a poem about joyful things should not be surprising, but "Rapture" offers an intriguing twist. Although a person may thematically separate finding bliss in commonplace items and finding it in nature, they are one and the same according to the poem. Biele moves flawlessly from water to clapping hands to snow to a bus to a tree and so forth. The point, again, is simple: look for joy in everyday things, and you are likely to find it.

Style

Free Verse

Free verse is the term applied to rhymed or unrhymed poetry that is *free* of the conventional or traditional restrictions on metrical structure that nearly always apply in formal poetry. Adding the word contemporary to the description simply means that the poetic language reflects the actual language of the poet's place and time, as well as the subject matter of the same. Instead of composing a poem that is limited to a specific meter or meters, free verse poets place more emphasis on cadence—or rhythm and flow of the language—especially in the form of common speech. Free verse poems tend to carry more relaxed tones and sound more like conversation than highly structured works. Biele takes even greater liberty in "Rapture" in that she not only foregoes metrical structure but also places little or no emphasis on cadence.

The two elements that immediately stand out when looking at this poem on the page are Biele's use of couplets and her use of the word "It." While couplets are usually two lines of poetry sharing a common meter or rhythm and expressing a complete, self-contained thought, neither is true of this poem. Since there is no rhyme scheme or particular meter used, the unifying factor in "Rapture" is the repetition of the word "It."

What "It" refers to, of course, is rapture, but that word is never mentioned except in the title. When a single word appears twenty-seven times in a thirty-line poem, it must hold special significance and yet the little pronoun "it" seems hardly worthy of such importance. Most likely, the opposite is intended. This small word does not get in the way, and, therefore, it is perfect to act as the bond holding together a string of crisp, detailed images, which are the actual highlights of the work.

Consider what the poem would look and read like if the word "It" were replaced in several instances with words like rapture or joy or bliss. The immediate recognition of a repeated word would be gone, but something more important would happen, too. The message would likely seem contrived and overworked. The poet's voice would appear decidedly lofty, if not didactic. Putting the humble pronoun to work instead allows the reader to be taken in by the rich imagery and intriguing items on the list, instead of wading through a dull recital of *Rapture is* . . . and *Joy is* . . . and so on.

Historical Context

The political and social events that made news in the early part of the twenty-first century left little about which to feel rapturous. Perhaps, however, these events lend an even greater urgency to the message in Biele's poem. A person needs diligently to seek out joy in the microcosm of everyday life because the world at large is a difficult place in which to find it.

In America and across the globe, the dominant stories of 2002 were the ongoing war against terror in Afghanistan and elsewhere following the devastating events of September 11, 2001, and the build-up of tensions between the United States and Iraq over the possibility of Saddam Hussein's possession of weapons of mass destruction. Heavy bombing raids eventually crumbled the Taliban in Afghanistan and flushed out al Qaeda terrorists hiding in the region, but their leader Osama Bin Laden was nowhere to be found. In Iraq, U.N. weapons inspectors, the United States, and Hussein were enmeshed in a seesaw battle over when and where inspections would take place, how they would be conducted, who would be interviewed, and what restrictions, if any, should be allowed. By the end of the year, no resolution had been found, and the two nations moved closer to war.

In January 2002, the year in America started with the scare of a copycat September-11 attack when a light airplane crashed into a high-rise building in Tampa, Florida. The pilot, fifteen-year-old Charles Bishop, was later determined not to be a terrorist and no one was killed other than him. Also in January, a disgruntled student at the Appalachian

A sail blowing in the wind off the San Blas Archipelago

School of Law in Grundy, Virginia, shot six people, killing three. In March, Andrea Yates was found guilty of drowning her five children the previous year; she was later sentenced to life in prison.

Other sensational stories that dominated the news included the May 2002 discovery of intern Chandra Levy's remains in Rock Creek Park in Washington, DC. Levy had disappeared in 2001. And in June 2002, Elizabeth Smart was kidnapped from her home in Utah, and was found alive nine months later, after being held by a fanatically religious man and woman who claimed she was part of their "family." Perhaps the most shocking event of 2002, however, came in October when for three weeks two elusive snipers roamed the roadways around Washington, DC, randomly gunning down men, women, and at least one child. Ten of their thirteen victims died. The pair were caught sleeping in their car at a rest stop on October 24.

Although the main news stories of the early twenty-first century were filled with violence, sadness, and shock, much of the media hype that surrounded them is simply a reflection of the human desire for sensationalism. Biele's poem reflects the other side of the coin. The simple joys of "listening" to a seashell, walking through leaves, or even noticing the sound of a bus shifting gears will never make the evening news, but they do make for a comforting *reprieve* from the evening news. A person needs only to choose a year and read its timeline of events to understand why.

Critical Overview

Because Biele's first collection is such a recent publication, sparse criticism is available. However, *White Summer* won a First Book Award from the Crab Orchard Review Series in Poetry, and poet and critic Allison Joseph, commenting why she selected *White Summer* for the award, notes, "Biele's poems, which range from short lyrics to longer meditations, are startling in their clarity, precise in their diction, and deft in their craft. . . . This book is alive in the world, not just merely of it." In a review of *White Summer* for the *Antioch Review*, poet and critic Jane Satterfield writes, "Biele's poems are perfectly pitched; oracular but not vatic, inviting and often arresting in their cinematic intensity and musicality." On the poem "Rapture" specifically, Satterfield comments, "Rapture, for this poet, then, is engagement, not escape."

Criticism

Pamela Steed Hill

Hill is the author of a poetry collection, has published widely in literary journals, and is an editor for a university publications department. In the following essay, Hill examines the religious aspects of "Rapture" and suggests that its message about divinity relies on images of movement in a secular world.

A poem titled "Rapture" apparently begs to be read as commentary on religious experience or religious belief, but readers need to be aware of various readers' perspectives before making such an assumption. The concept of a divine rapture—when only believing-Christians will be literally taken up into the heavens by Jesus Christ and saved from Armageddon—is obviously not a theory shared by all people around the world who consider themselves religious. Many people have never heard of it. Ideas of rapture, tribulation, and a final war between good and evil are most closely associated with the fundamental, evangelical branches of Christianity found in the United States, particularly in the rural South. Given this, the audience for Biele's poem narrows considerably, if, in fact, this poem is about that kind of rapture.

Perhaps the ambiguity is intentional. People who believe in a spiritual rapture—or at least those who are aware of the concept—can read the poem within the context of their own beliefs. Readers who understand the word "rapture" to mean only great joy may view it as an exploration of where happiness originates. Here, the intent is to look at it as *both*, suggesting the poem's secular images combine in an urgent movement toward religious bliss.

Most of the images in "Rapture" infer movement in one form or another, jittery, tense, pleasant, and agitating all at once. Movement is portrayed not only in the physical action of someone or something, but also in the *motion of sound*. The first declaration of where rapture begins is with noise: "a low rumbling." If the rumbling is the roar of an ocean, oceans move, and so do the sounds they make. If the rumbling is distant thunder, thunder *rolls* across the sky, starting low, becoming louder, then dissipating. The "night hum of a road" implies motion too, for the source of the hum is the movement of vehicles up and down the highway. The same may be said for "the suck under your shoe," which happens when one walks across a watery field, and for the "sizzle and spatter" of oil in a hot skillet, which not only makes the sounds described but also pops and jumps about in the pan. Noises, then, are on the move too.

Other images of movement in the poem are more obvious—hands clapping, birds clamoring, bottles falling, someone walking through leaves, a dog barking, plates smashing, and so on. These are actions that one can see happening, but they are also actions that can be *heard* just as readily. The point of interest is that most of the motions describing what rapture is or where it begins possess an undercurrent of tension or unease about them. The birds are not sitting on a tree branch or gliding through the air, but are *clamoring* in swift, frenzied movement. The laughter is not the simple sound of someone chuckling at a funny incident but is so hysterical that it seems to be "coming through the walls." The knife is not just lying on a counter or already in use cutting something; rather, it is "sharpening," suggesting a *preparation* for what is to come.

Nervous anticipation also provides the framework for the final four stanzas of the poem. Here rapture "starts deep in the belly, the back of the throat" where it is not yet completely recognizable,

"The only way the physical body can respond is to break down the very fabric of its being and let the spirit take over. The only way the human mind can relate is through metaphor."

but readers have the impression it will be soon. The "sounds you've never made" and the voice that is "not your voice in your mouth" imply a strange, transcendental experience that is both pleasant and frightening at once. And, finally, the ultimate human movement occurs in the last stanza with the body "breaking into islands," insinuating a complete loss of control of one's *common* self. So if the idea of motion is established as a dominant force in "Rapture," what does this have to do with religion?

Many fundamental Christian religious practices involve highly animated physical activity during services. Members of a congregation who are spiritually "moved" may jump up and down, clap their hands, wave their arms, shout, cry, or suddenly begin talking in a language that is not their own, called "speaking in tongues." But these actions do not generally occur as soon as the pews are filled. Rather, there is a gradual build-up, typically guided by a pastor who may begin a sermon slowly and softly, then speak louder and with more intensity, and then return to a whisper before shouting again until the congregation is stimulated to respond, physically as well as emotionally. In other words, he or she may start the service with "a low rumbling" and culminate it when listeners are so caught up in the fervor of the moment that their bodies seem to "[break] into islands," abruptly freed of physical—and worldly—restraints.

What if one reads Biele's poem the way an evangelist may present a sermon? Keeping in mind that too much embellishment renders an analysis futile, consider the *presentation* of the message in "Rapture." The initial images are soft, gentle, unassuming. The rumbling is low but it is only beginning. A

What Do I Read Next?

- Poet and writing professor Allison Joseph was on the committee that selected Biele's *White Summer* for the First Book Award from the Crab Orchard Review Series in Poetry. A noted poet in her own right, Joseph is the author of several collections of poems, most notably *In Every Seam* (1997). In this collection, Joseph writes about her childhood experience growing up black and female in New York City, combining stark personal reflection and powerful social commentary into a strong and accessible volume of poetry.

- Elizabeth Spires, a contemporary of Biele's, is a poet whose work also highlights the wonder of ordinary moments and events. Her collection *Worldling* (1995) explores such common topics as childhood, a beach, and old bottles, and does so with intimate details and images that make one think about them in new ways.

- Biele has authored articles on the work of some of America's most prominent poets, including Emily Dickinson and Adrienne Rich. In particular, Rich's intensely committed and risk-taking work seems to be a draw for many current, young women writers. Her collection *Diving into the Wreck* (1973) is an excellent introduction to her work and helped make her a distinct voice in modern American poetry as she writes of poverty, racism, sexism, violence, love between women, and human isolation.

- Contemporary poet Christine Hume's *Musca Domestica* won a first-book award upon its release in 2000. The title of the book is the Latin name for the common housefly, and Hume's work takes a humorous, inventive, and highly detailed look at the life of an ordinary fly—actually, a very imaginative metaphor for the life of an ordinary housewife. Much like Biele, Hume finds fascinating moments in a humdrum world.

"tide pulling" signifies movement, still gentle, but anticipatory. Suddenly the placid scene is shattered by loud noises: clapping, clamoring, hysterical laughter. And just as suddenly, the whisper of "snow breathing." Opposing images are juxtaposed throughout the poem, from snow breathing to bottles falling, from horses standing in fog to the sizzle of hot oil in a pan, from honey and flies to a knife sharpening and plates smashing. All these disparate descriptions lend a frenetic quality to the poem, keeping it in a constant flux of up and down, loud and quiet, agitated and calm. And all seem to be *leading* somewhere.

Movement is not always linear. Some things go in circles or with a series of stops and starts. The poem suggests the move toward rapture is a mixture of it all, but *progression* is the bottom line. Three references to normal, earthly transportation are mentioned in "Rapture"—a bus shifting gears, a motor idling, and a sailboat with "luffing" sails. Each one represents a different step along the way but all infer a type of motion. The bus may be either downshifting to come to a stop or shifting into a higher gear to get going somewhere. In keeping with the poem's message, the latter is most likely. An idling motor is a sure sign of anticipated movement, and the boat's luffing sail is already in motion—flapping erratically, but on the move nonetheless.

The only actual reference to religion in the poem is a subtle one at that. Bach cantatas are religious chorals, but Biele seems more interested in the *sound* of the music—the "*psh-psh*" it makes—than in the fact that it was written as a church piece. Still, this and the other musical allusions maintain the overall concept of sound and movement. The "wood" has a "song" inside it and the "mouthpiece" is "buzzing." Both suggest a cheeriness already present, but they also imply something even better to come.

What is yet to come is revealed toward the end of the poem, and there is a remarkable contrast between the style of the first twenty-three lines and that of the final seven. Most of "Rapture" is comprised of concrete, easily recognizable images of everyday objects and events. Each one is very audible and/or visible, and some are things one can taste or smell. But such sensory images give way to more metaphoric, transcendental, perhaps *spiritual* notions in the last few stanzas. Here, the ideas are more abstract and mysterious. Instead of telling the reader what a thing *is*, the poet tells us what it is *not*. "It," meaning rapture, "starts with sounds you've never made." It is "not your voice in your mouth," and the words you speak "are not your own." Whose voice is it? Whose words are they?

The suggestion is not that the voice is God's or the words are those of someone speaking in tongues—such a leap would reek of the forewarned embellishment. But it is reasonable to conclude that what all the motion and agitation and noises have been leading up to cannot be expressed in explicit, concrete terms. It is too grand, too monumental. In short, it is rapture. The only way the physical body can respond is to break down the very fabric of its being and let the spirit take over. The only way the human mind can relate is through metaphor. Whether the final description of rapture—a "fall through wind lifting white leaves"—implies an evangelical religious experience or not, at least the emotional high is unmistakable. And if Biele has written a poem about religion without ever mentioning the word, what a testament to the power of language.

Source: Pamela Steed Hill, Critical Essay on "Rapture," in *Poetry for Students*, Thomson Gale, 2005.

Laura Carter

Carter is currently employed as a freelance writer. In this essay, Carter considers the poet's use of imagery and its parallels to Eastern thought.

"Rapture" is a poem of beginnings. Biele's word play gives just a taste of a moment, scene, or situation. The line "It starts" is repeated frequently through the poem as words to usher in the early morning ocean tide, to an idling motor in the early morning fog, to a knife sharpening in anticipation of use. These images are not random but are carefully arranged elements that give the work its energetic flow, or life force. What one would consider innocuous or seemingly bland details encountered in everyday life are the fodder of life, and of living, for Biele.

Biele bombards the reader with sensory images or miniature life portraits, yet these pictures are not quite complete. At the poem's outset, Biele uses imagery to evoke the dawning day on the beach, as suggested by a "low white rumbling," "a broken shell to the ear," and a "cold kiss of the sun." At another point in the work, she mentions "diked fields," an "idling motor," and "horses in the fog," which is a scenic shift that takes the imagination to a morning on the farm. This series of associations runs a twisting path along the roadside, through the woods on a fall day, or in a sail boat, rhythmically moving to an ocean's sway. The sensory clues Biele uses to set the stage for her poem are transient; they are dissections of human experience working to evoke an image that is fleshed out by association rather than description. They are also suggestive in their nature. These images alone could not paint a picture, yet together they provide a frame of reference for the reader.

> *"Through her intricate, calculated, and careful word play, Biele takes readers for ride on a wave of emotion without boundry."*

John Tribble, series editor for the Southern Illinois University Press, comments on Biele's work in an online review of *White Summer*. Tribble says that "Biele investigates the problems of personal and cultural memory. Rich with images of flight and displacement, Biele's poems show a love for words, their music and physicality." He later asserts that the poet "reveals and revels in the power of language to shape and create experience."

Certainly, the sudden elation one feels stepping out onto a sunlit walk is fleeting and momentary. Biele brings readers to the edge of these moments. She defines them by texture, taste, and scent but they take no real shape. It is the harmonious union of images that reach the reader. These images are simply the beginnings of associations, of memories, making them all the more precious. These images all suggest something, and in their power to suggest, they belie that rapture is a pleasurable response beyond words, a sensation that begins and sometimes ends before one can even put pen to paper. This response to the everyday manages to transcend the everyday, transporting readers from one emotional state to another. Through her intricate, calculated, and careful word play, Biele takes readers for a ride on a wave of emotion without boundry.

Biele's poetics closely parallel Eastern thoughts on nature or the nature of things. Feng Shui is a search for balance and harmony with nature. Nature, in this instance, is not just a collection of natural objects. In Biele's work, images of nature sidle right up next to the everyday. She carefully weaves the sensations, the beauty, the sounds of nature with man-made rhythms, of bottles falling, of shattering of glass or of the steady hum of traffic. For example, the "psh-psh of a Bach cantata" is followed by the sound one makes walking through a pile of leaves. Both have an identical pattern of sound with a succinct nature that intrinsically links one to the other.

Shan-Tung Hsu, writing in his *Fundamentals of Feng Shui*, describes these patterns as being a part of natural law, patterns existing not only in nature but in human life. "It means patterns emerging from the inner nature of things." The entire poem is essentially a consideration of the inner nature of things. Each image has a succinct nature or pattern. Hsu explains, "The way that water moves on a surface, the way that veins form in marble, the way knots form on a tree trunk: these things have patterns that one can come to understand, that emerge spontaneously, without being forced or enforced." In Biele's work, images like "spilt sugar, a rosy ear, or birds clamoring," for example, have a succinct nature. Pour sugar from a spouted container in such a way and the granules form a soft, white pyramid. A rosy red ear has a certain fresh tint to it, whether burned by the sun or the cold. Birds clamoring make a boisterous or energetic sound.

The symbolic use of wind and water also give Biele's poem an Eastern harmony or unity. Feng Shui literally means "wind and water," the two fundamental elements of life in Eastern thought. Hsu explains that in one important Feng Shui classic called *The Book of Burials*, the nature of ch'i, the origin of all manifestations of form, is defined by wind and water. According to this important Eastern work, "Ch'i rides with the wind, is dissipated by wind and is confined by water." Consequently, says Hsu, on a metaphysical level wind and water give name to Earth's energy and represent the most dynamic and changeable forces in the world: the "ever-changing flow of manifestation, searching for dynamic balance." Ch'i is essentially "vital energy" or "life breath" in Eastern thought. The art of Feng Shui is to create a dynamic balance where ch'i, or life energy, can manifest.

Water and wind imagery give Biele's poem its dynamic balance. In the opening lines of the poem, the speaker asserts that rapture starts with "low rumbling, white static, a broken shell to the ear," following this immediately with "It starts with water, / tide pulling." Images of wind and water work together to define the ocean's tide, one of rumbling water whose sound is captured by the flow of wind through a conch shell and whose shape is dictated by the pull of tidal waters. The poem proceeds with a number of images describing rapture's inherent nature or ch'i, smatterings of water and wind imagery including wet legs, a bell buoy's sway, or a sail luffing. At the poem's end, rapture is "the body breaking into islands," then "the fall through wind lifting white leaves." A natural flow of imagery exists in Biele's poetry, one symbolically shaped by water and wind. The elements frame the poem, creating a natural flow or energy that gives life breath to delightful visual, olfactory, and tactile associations.

Biele has been compared to Theodore Roethke, a poet who reveled in nature, the nature of things, and elemental processes. Like Biele, Roethke saw parallels in nature, in its ability to represent or expand consciousness. Similarly, Biele's images of "wet legs and poppies" and a "flower inside a tree" are reminiscent of the work of William Carlos Williams. In one of his most notable poems, Williams took an image of a red wheelbarrow to demonstrate the power a simple image can project onto the page based on its inherent nature alone. Like Biele, both Roethke and Williams advocated or supported the fundamental notion of capturing the nature of existence in the essence of things in their work.

So, too, does Eastern thought. Behind the principle of Feng Shui is an insistence on the acknowledgement of and movement with patterns that emerge from and define the world to reach a higher level of awareness. From a metaphysical perspective, Taoist teaching dictates that the highest goal is to seek balance and harmony with nature. Like Roethke and Williams, Biele achieves this goal not only by presenting a series of powerful imagery but also by pairing seemingly random images to expose an interconnectedness resonating through the entire work.

It would be a mistake to gloss over Joelle Biele's poem "Rapture" as nothing more than a collection of images. The poet's selection of elements is carefully calculated, dictated by natural law. Her poetry follows a distinctive life rhythm and is a celebration not just of nature, but of life, of the ecstasy of everyday experience one so often forgets. In these breathless thoughts and images, one discovers an energy or ch'i that transcends the everyday.

Source: Laura Carter, Critical Essay on "Rapture," in *Poetry for Students*, Thomson Gale, 2005.

Sources

Biele, Joelle, *White Summer*, Southern Illinois University Press, 2002.

Hsu, Shang-Tung, *Tao of Feng Shui, Book One: Fundamentals of Feng Shui*, Blue Mountain Feng Shui Institute, 1999, pp. 9–17, 59–61.

Joseph, Allison, Jacket cover of *White Summer*, Southern Illinois University Press, 2002.

Satterfield, Jane, Review of *White Summer*, in *Antioch Review*, Vol. 61, Issue 3, Summer 2003, p. 587.

Tribble, John, Review of *White Summer*, at www.siu.edu, May 5, 2004.

Further Reading

Boller, Diane, Don Selby, and Chryss Yost, eds., *Poetry Daily: 366 Poems from the World's Most Popular Website*, Sourcebooks Trade, 2003.

As the title makes clear, this book is based on the Poetry Daily Website (www.poems.com), which posts a new "Today's Poem" every day of the year. The concept behind the book is that readers will read one poem a day throughout 2004—a leap year, and therefore 366 days long—and by the end of the year will have read more poetry than most people read in a lifetime. The poems selected are from the web site's first five years, and it is an admirable, eclectic collection well worth reading.

Chafe, Eric, *Analyzing Bach Cantatas*, Oxford University Press, 2003.

Classical music experts and novices alike will appreciate this insightful look at what are considered some of Western music's highest accomplishments. In clear, straightforward language, Chafe examines Bach's cantatas individually by combining theological, historical, and analytical approaches to help the reader gain the fullest experience from the music and words.

Holm, Bill, *Boxelder Bug Variations: A Meditation on an Idea in Language and Music*, Milkweed Editions, 1985.

This thin, unique compilation of poems, meditations, and essays bears a striking resemblance in its overall message to that of Biele's "Rapture." Holm uses the humble boxelder bug to comment on the importance of finding joy and beauty in the most unlikely, overlooked places and things.

Young, John E., *The Rapture Examined*, WinePress Publishing, 2003.

There are hundreds of books debating the reality, timing, and actual meaning of the Christian belief known as the "rapture." Young's book is not necessarily the best on the subject, but he attempts to offer fresh insights that aid the reader in making up his or her own mind. Young's opinion is decidedly that of a believer, but his argument is more intellectual than didactic.

A Rebirth

Faroogh Farrokhzaad

1964

The strength of Faroogh Farrokhzaad's "A Rebirth" comes not only from the words and images portrayed in her poem but also from the free-flowing meter and lack of rhyme. The free verse form sharply contrasts the style of her earlier poetry and reflects the dramatic transitions the poet was experiencing in her life. As she struggled to find a new definition of self, one that could rise above the oppressive female role set upon her by her Iranian culture, she simultaneously broke through the formal structure of the traditional Iranian poetry that had previously influenced her writing. Another Iranian poet, Farzaneh Milani, writes in a critical essay published in the poetry collection *A Rebirth*, from which the poem is taken, that Farrokhzaad's newfound voice and poetic form "attest to long years of formal confrontation with language, a diligent practice of the craft coupled with years of reflection and inner unfolding." In this fourth collection of Farrokhzaad's poetic works, and especially in the title poem, she demonstrates that in her life and in her writing, she has been reborn.

"Rebirth" was first published in Iran in 1964, just a few years before the poet's death. The entire collection of poems (and specifically the title poem) was dedicated to her lover of many years, Ibrahim Golestan, an Iranian short story writer and cinematographer. Golestan was reportedly the biggest influence in helping Farrokhzaad reach this dramatic transformation in her life and in her writing style. In turn, Farrokhzaad influenced a whole generation of Iranian women, who traveled with her through her poetry in her struggle to find freedom and a new definition of life.

Author Biography

Foroogh (also spelled Forough) Farrokhzaad was born January 5, 1935, into a middle-class family in Tehran, Iran, many decades before women experienced social liberation in the United States, let alone in Iran. Some Iranian women believe Farrokhzaad was the woman who began the movement for them. Had she been an American woman, Farrokhzaad's painfully personal poems might have been startling in her time, but to have written them as an Iranian woman was absolutely unthinkable. She was the first Iranian poet to ever write about a woman's perspective of life in Iran.

Farrokhzaad was born to a family of seven children, and by the age of sixteen she was married to her cousin, Parviz Shapur, a marriage her family did not approve of. The marriage ended in 1954, and Farrokhzaad lost custody of her son, Kamyar, who was given to her husband's family. These events stigmatized her socially, leading her into an ever-narrowing sense of isolation.

From this isolation came Farrokhzaad's first set of poems, published in 1955 as *Asir* ("the captive" or "the prisoner"), when she was only twenty years old. The book was heavily criticized by the patriarchal society that surrounded her. However, women rushed to read it. In the same year, unfortunately, Farrokhzaad also experienced a mental breakdown. In an effort to fully regain her psychological strength, she spent nine months traveling through Europe, which gave her a dramatically different perspective on life, especially as seen through the eyes of European women. It was during this time that Farrokhzaad wrote the poems that were collected in 1956 in *Divaar* ("the wall"), which was dedicated to her ex-husband. Through these poems Farrokhzaad exposes the restraints she experienced while trying to play out the traditional role of an Iranian woman and wife.

Many critics of Farrokhzaad's writing have commented on a reoccurring theme that runs through her work—that of a longing for love. Some critics believe she at least partially fulfilled that need in the relationship that developed between her and Iranian short story writer and cinematographer Ibrahim Golestan, whom Farrokhzaad met in 1958. Their love affair would last until her death, despite the fact that Golestan was already married. This same affair, and several more that Farrokhzaad experienced, further alienated her from the socially respectable standards of Iranian culture. However, her poetry, which reflected the changes she was going through, became even more popular.

In 1958, Farrokhzaad published her third collection, *Esian* ("rebellion"). That same year she also worked with Golestan on several movie and documentary projects. One of those movies was *The House is Black*, which was adapted from a prize-winning story about a leper colony. During the filming, Farrokhzaad adopted a child named Hassan from the leper colony and took him back to Iran. After Farrokhzaad's death, Hassan's biological father released correspondence from Farrokhzaad, letters from which he concluded that Farrokhzaad was a very good mother.

Farrokhzaad's fourth collection of poetry, *A Rebirth*, published in the United States in 1985, was first published in 1964 in Iran under the title *Tavallodi Digar*. Critics have commented that with this collection, Farrokhzaad finally discovered her voice. As David Martin, the English translator of Farrokhzaad's collection *A Rebirth*, writes in the introduction, her untimely death at the age of thirty-two "left much of her life's work undone."

On February 14, 1967, Farrokhzaad was in a hurry, leaving her mother's home. She swerved her jeep to miss an oncoming bus and was thrown into an embankment. She died from a concussion. Her voice was silenced on that day not only for Iranian women but, as Martin writes, for "all Iranis struggling to enter, and to come to grips with, the modern world."

Poem Text

i

All my existence is a dark sign a dark
                                        verse
that will take you by itself
again and again
through incantation of itself
over and over
to eternal dawn
                    bloomings and eternal growth
in this verse, in this sign
I sighed for you, sighed
in this verse, in this sign, I versified
you, I joined you
to tree and water and fire

ii

perhaps life
is a long avenue through

which a woman passes each day
with a basket
perhaps life is a rope
with which a man hangs
himself from a branch
perhaps life is a kid who
returns from school
life could be lighting up
a cigarette in the relaxing interval
between two
love-makings
or life
could be could be some confused
transit of a passerby
who takes
off his hat and to another passerby says
"good morning" with
a mean
-ingless smile

perhaps life is thatstopped instant in which
my gaze lays waste to itself,
my gaze into the no-no of your eyes
self-destructs
and there is a sense in this
which I shall mix in with
comprehension of the moon
and with perception of the pitch dark.

in a room as large as one loneliness
my heart, as large as one love, beholds
the simple subterfuges of its happiness
in the beautiful way the flowers in the vase
fade
in the sapling which you planted in our garden
and in the song of canaries, which
song is only as large as a window
. . .ah, this
is my share
this is my share
my share is a sky, which sky
will be taken form me by
hanging
a curtain over it
my share is to descend by
an abandoned stairwell and come together
with something in rottenness and exile
my share is a grief-stained stroll in memory lane
and giving up the ghost
in the sorrow of a voice
which calls to me, saying:
"I love
your hands."

I plant my hands in the garden
I shall grow green, I know I know I know
and swallows'll lay eggs
in deep cracks around my ink-
stained fingernails

I suspend earrings from my two
ears—earrings of two twin dark red cherries
and I'll paste dahlia leaves
on my fingernails
there is an alley where boys
who were in love with me—boys
with the same disheveled hair,
scrawny necks and stick-legs—
they dream of
a girl's innocent smiles
a girl who was carried away
one night by the wind

there is an alley
that my heart has stolen away
from my childhood's neighborhoods

the trip of a blob down the line of time
and said blob impregnating the dry line
of time
the blob of a conscious image which image
is reflected back from a party mirror
and it's this way
that somebody dies,
that somebody remains

iii
no hunting or fishing worth mentioning
in a piddling little old crick
which flows into a ditch
no pearls there for a fisherman to catch
I know a small sad mermaid
who lives
in an ocean and she
plays her heart
gently, gently
on a wooden lip flute—list! . . .
a small sad mermaid
who dies in the night from one kiss
and she
will be born at daybreak
from one kiss

Poem Summary

Section 1

In the first short section of "A Rebirth," the speaker sets up the theme of her poem, that of rebirth. She first describes the general emotion that weaves through her many births and deaths. Then she defines the power of the residue of those changes that affects the people who become involved in her many transformations.

She states that her life is a dark sign, or a foreboding message, almost as if she is warning the reader or anyone who becomes involved in her life that her sadness will sweep over them; and they may suffer as she has suffered. This sign will take you, she writes, "again and again," referring to the cycle of death and birth, death and reawakening to a new life form. Her life, she insinuates, has been filled with sorrow, no matter how many times it has been transformed. And the sadness of her life will influence the "you" she addresses in the first stanza. The speaker then states that the dark sign of her life will take the person addressed "to eternal dawn / bloomings and eternal growth." It will do so through an "incantation of itself," a phrase that could denote a prayer, a chant, or even a spell that might curse the person who becomes involved in her life. "I joined you," the speaker states, "to tree and water and fire." Note that the speaker did not say that she had "joined *with* "you," but rather she merely "joined you." The speaker might be returning to the statements in the first lines of the poem and is insinuating that through association with her (because she is a dark sign) this "you" is joined to the traumatic incidents in her life, which have transformed her. She may be referring to the tree as life itself. Water might be a form of nourishment or could also reflect tears. Fire might refer to the so-called hotter emotions of anger or passion. The "you" is joined to these elements because the speaker has "versified" him or her, placed the "you" there through the poetry of her transitions.

Section 2

Section two is the longest part of the poem. In it, the speaker attempts to define life, her need for love, and the weight of her art and her loneliness.

With the word "perhaps," the speaker begins several lines in which she tries to define life. Maybe life is the everyday occurrence of a woman passing through a market. Maybe life is the tragedy of a man who hangs himself. She then mentions the ordinary action of a child coming home from school and the emotional release of "lighting up / a cigarette" after lovemaking. But then she changes her mood. She seems to lose her confidence in defining life as the speaker throws in the word "confused." Two strangers pass one another on the street and exchange a greeting. The words of this greeting, "Good morning," appear to be friendly, but the words are empty, she writes. The smile of one of the passersby is "mean / -ingless." The word "meaningless," at least in translation, is hyphenated, so at first it reads that the smile is "mean." Only as the reader continues down to the next line is the interpretation changed from "mean" to "meaningless," which is still a little disturbing but not as intense.

In the above lines, the speaker tries to define life objectively, through observation of others. But in the next set of lines, the speaker turns to perceptions of herself. In doing so, her definition of life becomes even vaguer, more abstract, more elusive. Life becomes a "stopped instant." It becomes a gaze that "self-destructs." She compares life to her attempt to look into someone's eyes. But her gaze is stopped by the "no-no" of that person's eyes. She wants to know that person, but she cannot penetrate that person's soul any more than she can understand the moon or see in the "pitch dark." Life is not to be comprehended in this way.

The speaker next turns to her emotions. Maybe it is through her emotions that she can define life. Her heart, she writes, has been broken many times. Through her loneliness she has witnessed the "subterfuges" of her heart's "happiness." She has found and lost that happiness many times, and she compares that journey of love found and lost to the withering of a beautiful flower, to the planting of a young tree, to the "song of canaries," which might be beautiful, but the song is so small, "only as large as a window." The love she has experienced is transient. It fades; it is a mere sapling; it is a very small song. She wants a love as big as the sky, but her share of that sky "will be taken" from her as if someone had hung "a curtain over it." She knows it is there, but it is veiled, covered up, and she cannot see it.

Not only is her share of happiness veiled, it also descends "an abandoned stairwell." Whereas the sky should be overhead, implying something positive, hers descends a stairwell that no one uses any more. Her share not only descends, it rots in a place of exile. Her only remembrance of her share is in "a grief-stained stroll in memory lane." It not only is in the past, it exists in sadness. "In the sorrow of a voice," she hears it calling to her by stating, "I love / your hands." This is the poet referring to her art. It is with her hands that she creates her poetry, and it is through her poetry that she remembers her share of love, that she remembers her life. When she "plants" her "hands in the garden," she becomes alive. She grows "green," a sign of creativity, of life. She then repeats the phrase, "I know," as if someone were reminding her that it is through her poetry, through her art that she feels life most intensely. "I know I know I know," she writes, like someone who really did not have to be told; like someone who already knows but maybe does not want to hear it, or does not want it to sink in.

There are two images in the next section, "two twin dark red cherries" and "dahlia leaves / on my fingernails" that refer to the first cosmetics that a young Iranian girl can use. The red cherries are the fruit, freshly taken off a tree and dangled over the ear by its twin stems, as a sort of earring. The dahlia leaves are a substitute for fingernail polish. These images represent the coming-of-age transition when a young girl wants to attract attention from the opposite sex. Then the speaker refers to the young boys who paid attention to her, boys who "dream of / a girl's innocent smiles," or in other words, dream of a young girl's innocence. In that innocence, the speaker proclaims, a girl "was carried away / one night by the wind." This phrase implies something somewhat negative, as if the girl were taken away against her will. Or maybe taken away without her realizing the full consequences.

Then the speaker distances herself again. She writes of a "blob impregnating the dry line / of time." A blob is amorphous, formless, and unstructured. This could mean that the person to whom the speaker refers as a blob has fallen apart. Since all of Farrokhzaad's poetry is personal, this could refer to her mental breakdown or her loss of identity she suffered as a traditional Iranian wife. It might also refer to the Iranian dress code that requires all women to drape themselves in formless clothing and veils. But it could also be an allusion to her loss of her child. The next set of lines seems to imply that it might be a little of all these things.

"The blob of a conscious image which image / is reflected back from a party mirror." With these lines, the speaker could be talking about the "self" she sees only in reflection. And that reflection is distorted. There is nothing else in this poem that refers to something as happy as a party. From everything else that has been written before this line, the speaker does not convey a spirited personality—someone who would have fun at a party. But that is how the "blob" sees herself—in a "party mirror." And through this reflection, the speaker states this is the "way / that somebody dies." And yet somebody also "remains." In looking at herself through this mirror, the speaker might be saying, a part of her dies. It is not the real her. She cannot fully see herself. She sees only a shadow of herself—the part that remains.

Section 3

The third section, like the first, is very short. The speaker makes reference to water in the last stanza, another form of reflection. She begins by describing a "piddling little old crick," a small rivulet that "flows into a ditch." This is not a nourishing source of water, for nothing grows there. There are no oyster pearls to be found, no jewels. Nothing worthwhile. This might be the speaker still searching for a definition of herself. She does not feel confident that she has any depth or any treasure "for a fisherman to catch," but she does have dreams. She knows of a mermaid, a mythical creature. That mermaid is sad, though. The mermaid lives in the ocean, a very fertile and exciting place to live. And she is an artist too, who "plays her heart" on a "wooden lip flute." She is "small," the speaker states, implying that the speaker's dream is small too. There is, however, hope. The mermaid represents the commencement of rebirth. There are possibilities here, for "she dies in the night" and "will be born at daybreak / from one kiss." The speaker returns to the concept of rebirth here. However, the transformation of the mermaid remains dependent on a kiss.

Themes

Transformation

From the title of Farrokhzaad's poem "A Rebirth," it is easy to assume that this poem will focus on transformation. The words are present in the poem to suggest a rebirth. She uses phrases like "again and again" and "over and over" suggesting the cyclical motion of death and rebirth. She also closes her poem with the description of a mermaid who "dies in the night" and is "born at daybreak." But it is possible that the theme of rebirth is misleading, or not as complete as the word and the images suggest. There is transformation occurring, at least in an abstract way, but there are also many elements that seem to linger unchanged. The speaker is constantly sad and appears unsure of her identity. It could be possible that the real transformation occurs not on a deep psychological or spiritual level but rather on a more superficial level. The speaker is searching for her identity, which definitely changes. First she is all-powerful but in a sad way, inflicting her sadness on anyone who becomes involved with her. Later, she exists only as a "blob," an undefined mass of nothingness. Sometimes she sees herself as an artist, while at other times she dreams of herself as a mermaid. The strength of this poem might not so much be in a true transformation from a lost soul to someone who is fully realized, but rather in the fact that the speaker is able to finally see all the small changes she has gone through in trying to identify herself, in trying to find a sense of happiness, and in trying to define her life. In the recognition of those changes, maybe there will be a final reckoning and more complete understanding that will create a true transformation—the full realization of the mermaid awakening to a kiss.

Search for Love

A theme that runs through most of Farrokhzaad's poetry is the search for love. Farrokhzaad is a woman who believes she is not complete unless she finds

Topics For Further Study

- Select another Middle Eastern country, such as Saudi Arabia or Jordan, and compare the contemporary women's rights movement there to that in Iran. Do women have the right to vote? What are their roles in government, education, and science? Are there women in positions of power?
- Farrokhzaad published her poetry between the 1950s and the 1960s. What other female writers were being published in Iran at that time? What female poets have been published since the 1960s? How do their works compare to Farrokhzaad's? Do they lean toward the traditional or are they looking for change? Are their subjects personal or do they speak in abstractions?
- In the 1950s, the United States and Great Britain were involved in the affairs of Iran. Trace the relationship between Iran and the United States from the 1950s to the present day. Include information about the 1953 coup and how that affected Iran. Also research the American hostage-taking that occurred in 1979. Other topics you might explore include the Iran-Contra Affair and early-twenty-first-century fears that Iran might be developing nuclear weapons.
- Read the poetry of Sylvia Plath and compare her work to that of Farrokhzaad. Do you find similarities in their depression? How did each poet deal with her depression? What common themes do you find in their work?

the love of a man. She is searching not for the kind of love that a young boy with a "scrawny" neck and "disheveled hair" might give her. That young boy is merely attracted to her innocence. She wants much more than that. She wants a love as immense as the sky. Something so big she will never run out of it. She wants a love that will not wither like a flower or that is as small as a canary's song. Nothing will satisfy her less than love as big as the space in which the earth is suspended. She believes that if she finds that love, she will be transformed. She will be more creative. She will become a mythical being and will die from that love but will also be reawakened. She knows about love, and she dreams about love, but she never finds it. Love is hidden from her. She knows it exists but she cannot find it. The love that she dreams of is rotting and locked away in exile. But it is this search for love that drives her. Love is the nourishment that her life needs.

Meaning of Life

As the speaker of the poem searches for love, she also tries to define life, which becomes one of the themes in this poem. What is life all about? Is life only a collection of meaningless and ordinary gestures such as shopping for food or coming home from school? Or is there more to it than that? The speaker watches strangers passing on the street and hears their empty words. She implies that most social conversation is a waste of time. Words are exchanged but they have little meaning. But then when she tries to find meaning in a more intimate relationship, she finds that her efforts are stopped. There are no answers there. Then she tries to understand life by contemplating the moon. The moon is removed from the earth and might offer her a more objective point of view. It might offer her some answers. She finally concludes that this exercise is futile, and life can no more be understood than it is possible to see in the dark. Life cannot be comprehended. A person lives it but may never know or understand it.

Depression

Another major theme in this poem is that of depressed emotions. Loneliness and sadness permeate the text, as do negative images. For example, the speaker opens the poem by referring to herself as a "dark sign," a symbol or warning of something depressing about to happen. Those who gather around her, she warns, will be affected by her depression. In the second section of the poem, the speaker offers an image of a hanged man, which she presents as a possible meaning of life. She also refers to herself as a "blob," a nothing. Even when she hints that there might be a possibility of happiness, she states that things she loves are taken from her or hidden from her. She is tricked out of her happiness. She uses the belittling metaphor of a "piddling little old crick" to describe herself. Then she states that the waters of this "crick" support no life; and no treasure is found there.

Loneliness

Loneliness is the basis for most of the sadness in this poem. The speaker searches for love because she wants to rid herself of loneliness, which is dark and fathomless. Loneliness feeds the poet's art, giving her deep emotions to explore. In order to explore them and write about them, the poet needs to be alone. The poet also creates very lonely landscapes where everyone appears alone. When she hints of two people being together, the reader is assured that there is no union created. For example, the strangers who pass one another on the street may share the stage momentarily, but they do not share warmth or companionship. They exchange only meaningless words.

There is a "you" who the speaker addresses, but there is no sense that the speaker and this unnamed character disclose anything to one another. Even in the passage "I joined you to tree and water and fire" there is a separation between the speaker and the "you," as if the speaker is watching from a distance. The word *joined* does not convey the sense of two people coming together but rather one person (the speaker) joining another person (the "you") to the tree, as if she has glued that person there. There is also a single woman in the market without mention of any other people there, as if she is strolling by empty stalls and vacated streets. A single "kid" returns from school without mention of classmates, playmates, or family. A lonely man with a rope is about to hang himself without anyone around him persuading him to do otherwise. Even in the phrase "lighting up / a cigarette in the relaxing interval / between two / love-makings," there are no bodies, no two people coming together. There is only the cigarette and the objective act of making love. The people have been removed from this image, as if the act of love could be performed without anyone being there. Even at the end of the poem when a mermaid is introduced, she is alone. She receives a kiss before dying and another kiss at daybreak, but there is no one mentioned or identified as the giver of that kiss.

Style

Free Verse

"A Rebirth" is written in free verse, a nontraditional form of writing poetry. In free verse, there may be rhymed or unrhymed verse that is not limited to a regular metrical structure. In other words, instead of having to conform to a prescribed meter, free verse usually follows a cadence that mimics common speech. Another liberty in free verse is the line length, which may vary and may be used to heighten the emotional effect or to emphasize a particular meaning. These effects may be used to provide visual images other than just the words themselves. Although "A Rebirth" has been translated from Persian, the reader should assume that the translator attempted to mimic the effects of language use and line structure from the original poem.

In the second line of "A Rebirth," the reader may notice that the word "verse" appears on a line all by itself and is aligned flush right, thus making it stand out. In the fourth and sixth lines, the phrases "again and again" and "over and over" mirror one another, promoting a sense of repetition, such as one finds in the cyclical motion inherent in the concept of rebirth—born over and over again.

The poet also uses a break in lines 33 and 34, which causes a swift change in meaning. Line 33 is very short. There are only the words "a mean." It is not until the reader reaches the next line that the true definition of this word is completely understood. There is no hint of this switch because the hyphen that should have been attached to the end of "mean" does not appear until the next line. The hyphen is attached to the suffix "-ingless," and its appearance alters the understanding of the poet's intended meaning.

In line 35 the poet uses a space in the middle of a line to offer a visual expression of what she is trying to say. After the phrase "perhaps life is that" and before the next word "stopped," there is a gap, so that the reader can feel the "stopped instant" rather than just reading the words. In lines 70 and 74, the poet leaves the phrases "stained fingernails" and "on my fingernails" on lines by themselves and again places them flush right. They stand out because of their position and because of the repetition of the same word, "fingernails." The poet is tying them together visually in order to tie them together in meaning. The first fingernails are stained with ink, a visual image of the speaker as an experienced writer. The second set of fingernails is that of a young pubescent girl who has decorated her nails in an attempt to attract attention. By stressing and contrasting these two sets of fingernails, the poet emphasizes the passing of time and thus the transformation of the young girl to woman.

Metaphor

Another device used in "A Rebirth" is that of metaphor. A metaphor is a figure of speech in which one kind of object or idea is used in place of another to propose a likeness between them. Instead of the speaker stating in the first line that her life is filled with sadness, she states that "her existence is a dark sign." Many other metaphors are used, such as "life / is a long avenue," giving the reader the visual image of life being a road upon which one travels. The speaker also states, "life is a rope / with which a man hangs / himself." This is a very strong and depressing image, much more depressing than just stating that life can be difficult. Later the speaker states that her share of love "is a sky." The sky is huge, maybe even infinite. Instead of merely stating that her love is big, the speaker offers a metaphor that says more than the words she uses. Metaphors expand the meaning of words. By stating that her share of love "is a grief-stained stroll in memory lane," the speaker uses only eight words and yet gives the reader the great sense of sadness and maybe even regret that she feels for all the love she once found and then lost. She is haunted by those painful memories. The grief clings to her through her memories of them.

In lines 66 through 70, the author uses an extended metaphor, giving the reader a full image of how she feels about her art. She "plants her hands" in the earth, where they eventually will turn green and become the home for swallows. In using this garden and planting metaphor, the poet explains how fruitful she becomes when she writes. It is through her hands that she experiences her creativity. In digging down into her psyche, she is able to grow, able to produce. The "swallows'll lay eggs / in deep cracks" around her fingers. Through the use of metaphor, readers can take this image and come up with their own interpretations of what the poet is trying to say. Depending on the reader's experience with gardens, different emotions and different understandings will be reached, maybe even different from those the author intended. However, if the poet had only written that she feels very good when she writes poems, the reader may have come away with only a fraction of the meaning and the emotion that the full metaphor inspires.

Historical Context

Although the time of Farrokhzaad's writing is not mentioned in her poetry, the historical events that were unfolding around her heavily influenced her emotions and thoughts and should be understood in order to fully appreciate her themes and topics. "A Rebirth" was first published in the early 1960s in Iran. By this time, Farrokhzaad had witnessed war and foreign occupation of her country. She had lived under a fearful political regime that imprisoned intellectuals and artists to muffle voices of dissent. Nationalism was the political cry during the 1950s, as Iran attempted to break free of American and British involvement in their country. Political assassinations, exiles, and finally a major coup backed by the United States and Britain followed, all of which eventually toppled the nationalist movement and gave full power to a puppet monarchy, extinguishing the hopes of many Iranian citizens who were once inspired to create a modern definition of themselves. Western culture infiltrated Iran, some aspects of which were happily accepted. Other changes were not met with much enthusiasm, and stronger enforcement was needed. New laws were proclaimed. For example, a law was passed that made it illegal for women to wear any traditional Iranian head cover. The only apparel a woman could wear to cover her head was a Westernized hat.

Modernization was superficial in terms of actual benefits to the common people. Some women, who had been raised to believe that the only proper public attire was the chador (a long, draped cape that covered the body from head to toe), gave up their jobs and even refused to go shopping, preferring to stay home rather than to be exposed in public in Western-style clothing. Poverty also rose to incredible heights, further depressing the common people.

Although the world around them was changing, Iranian women were not always included in the best benefits. For example, in 1953 Tunisian and Lebanese women gained the right to vote, and in 1956 Egyptian woman were allowed to go to the polls. Iranian women were not allowed to vote until 1980. Also, traditional marriages were still honored, in which women were often married to men whom their parents had chosen for them.

Without an outlet for their voices, women felt isolated, as if they were alone in their suffering. It was in this atmosphere that Farrokhzaad's poems were published. Hers was the singular female voice

Compare & Contrast

- **1950s:** American and British intelligence agencies help to overthrow Iranian Prime Minister Mohammed Mossadegh, who wants to nationalize Iran's oil companies. The overthrow consolidates the power of Shah Mohammad Pahlavi, who favors foreign involvement in Iran's oil production.

  1970s: The Iranian revolution, lead by Ayatollah Ruhollah Khomeini, a religious leader, forces the shah out of power.

  Today: Madeline Albright acknowledges the United States's involvement in the 1953 coup, coming closer to apologizing to the Iranian people than any other U.S. official.

- **1950s:** Iranian women wear Western-style clothing and cosmetics in public.

  1970s: Miss Iran beauty pageants are held in Iran. The winner goes to the Miss Universe contest, which includes a bathing-suit competition.

  Today: Women are forced to wear *chadors* (long capes, dark in color, which cover women from head to toe) and *hejabs* (head coverings) whenever they appear in public.

- **1950s:** The Iranian film industry is dominated by melodramatic movies and comedies, commercial projects with no political statement and little literary merit.

  1970s: In the years preceding the 1979 Iranian revolution, a group of artists and intellectuals enjoy a new wave of cinematography. Movies of social consciousness are produced, such as the Dariush Mehrjui's film *The Cow*, about the affects of poverty.

  Today: Under strict governmental grading systems, Iranian movie production is heavily censored, but the industry is growing not only in numbers but also in international praise. Abbas Kiarostami and Mohsen Makhmalbaf are two of Iran's most famous directors.

that refused to be silenced. She wrote from the personal realm, something never done before, exposing her feelings and her discontent. As some of the titles of her books (*The Captive*, *The Wall*, *The Rebellion*) signify, she was fighting for her release. Other people, both male and female, afraid to speak out, listened to her.

Critical Overview

Farrokhzaad's collection *A Rebirth* has not received a lot of critical attention in the United States. However, her impact on Iran and especially on Iranian women cannot be overstated. *A Rebirth* has been widely recognized as a major work, and Farrokhzaad herself has been recognized as a major Iranian poet.

In his introductory remarks in *A Rebirth*, translator David Martin calls this collection a "masterpiece." He continues, "Her voice was already the most significant voice in women's poetry in this century in Iran—some say she was the greatest poetess in the long history of Persian poetry." Martin's remarks are repeated by many literary critics and academics familiar with Farrokhzaad's body of work and with the influence her poetry has had on Iranians. Although, due to the nature of her topics, Farrokhzaad's poetry strongly appeals to women, Martin argues it is not only Iranian women who benefit from her work, but "all Iranis struggling to enter, and to come to grips with, the modern world."

In a critical essay published in *A Rebirth*, Farzaneh Milani relates the long history of poetry in Iran, a history that tends to ignore female writers. It was more difficult for the male-dominated cast of literary critics to ignore Farrokhzaad's work, because, according to Milani, she tended not only "to express explicitly her unorthodox convictions in poetry, but also [had] the tenacity to act them out in life." Milani writes that Farrokhzaad "challenged and rejected accepted mores and assumptions" about the traditional role of women, and she journeyed into "forbidden fields in both life and literature." Milani further states that the appeal of Farrokhzaad's poetry might lie in the fact that her writing, which is filled with "rewoven webs of passion and love," might act as a "cathartic release for what voluptuousness offers and puritanical morality withholds from many of her readers."

Criticism

Joyce Hart

Hart has degrees in English and creative writing and is a freelance writer and author of several books. In this essay, Hart studies Farrokhzaad's poem from a feminist standpoint and questions the premise that this poem is about transformation.

Most literary critics praise Farrokhzaad for her bravery in writing, in a very personal and often painful way, about her emotions, frustrations, and fears. Hers was a singular voice heard in the midst of a very dark silence. Although her life's work encompasses only a relatively small collection of poems, she was able to catalog the major challenges she had to face as a woman living in a society that for the most part did not want her voice to be heard. She was strong enough to stand up for her rights when she became distraught over her marriage. Although she was ridiculed and socially exiled as a divorced woman, she was not afraid to explore her sexuality in a series of love affairs. But even if one acknowledges Farrokhzaad's courage and declares her as one of the first persons in Iran to cry out for women's rights, one has to question, when reading her poem "A Rebirth," to what kind of transformations does her poem refer?

If one were to focus only on the simplest definition of feminist theory, it might be to evaluate a piece of literature in terms of equal rights and a lack of male dominance. The premise behind feminism might be referred to as encouraging the self-actualization of women—fostering women to independently define themselves. This is a difficult challenge for women who live in a male-dominated society. Farrokhzaad fought against this dominance in her life and against the traditional laws of her society. But did she also fight against her own personal limitations in dealing with men in a one-on-one situation? Were her relationships with men on an equal standing? And if they were, how does her poem "A Rebirth" express this? What are her victories? How did she change?

Veiled Iranian women gather in Hamadan's central square

Farrokhzaad dedicated the collection of poems in which "A Rebirth" is contained to her lover, Ibrahim Golestan. Her dedication to him includes the first stanza of "A Rebirth," making it very clear that this poem in particular was written for him. And it is in this first stanza that the poet's voice exhibits its most strength. This strength, however, comes from a point of weakness. The speaker begins by declaring that all her "existence is a dark sign." And this negativity will affect anyone who becomes involved with her. In their coming together, both he and she will be cursed. So in some ways, she is exerting strength, like a wizard who places a spell. But where is the real power if both she and he are affected by the "dark sign?" She may be strong in that she is at least warning him of her effects, but from where are these effects coming? Surely they are not really coming from her. Who would wish negativity upon herself? In stating "all my existence is a dark sign" is she not implying that she is a victim of her circumstances? There is no empowerment in that sentiment. Victimization is antithetical to feminism. To fight for one's rights, one has to act. Victims, on the other hand, are passive.

In the second section of "A Rebirth," the speaker turns to the task of defining life. One way she does this is to recall moments when she has

> *"She is not gaining strength from within, but rather she waits for someone to bring it to her."*

gazed into her lover's eyes. When she does this, she is stopped and her "gaze lays waste to itself." She has tried to see into her lover's soul, but the door is slammed in her face by the "no-no" of his eyes. Her gaze then "self-destructs." She has tried to visually crawl into her lover, trying to find a definition of her life in him. When he does not allow this, is it just her gaze or is it her "self" that falls apart? The reason this question arises is because of the way she words this phrase. It is not her lover who makes her gaze disintegrate. Rather her gaze "self-destructs." She has diminished her own gaze. Should the reader then assume that she can create an image of herself only through the man? Does she feel incomplete without him? Can she not create a complete self on her own? Does this mean that she is dependent on man? If so, how will she ever be self-actualized? How can she ever expect to stand up on her own? The speaker might answer these questions in the next lines, in which she concludes that she can no more make sense of her own self-destruction (or her own life, for that matter) than she can make sense of the moon.

With this thought the speaker appears to disintegrate even further. She looks at flowers in a vase and instead of appreciating their beauty, she sees only the sadness in their wilting. Instead of enjoying the young tree planted in her garden by her lover, she sees only the weakness of the sapling. And in the simple enjoyment of the song of a canary, she hears only how small the sound is. These are the things, the "simple subterfuges" of her happiness. Her happiness, thus, is also dependent on outer things. She is not gaining strength from within, but rather she waits for someone to bring it to her. But even when they do, she cannot draw energy from it. She is, after all, a dark sign, which pollutes anyone's attempt to give her pleasure.

There is one image in this poem, however, that is strong and positive. But the speaker spoils the image. The metaphor begins with the statement "I love your hands." Then it moves into a reflection of her hands planting themselves in the garden. Here is strength. Not only does the speaker acknowledge her skill as a writer, she also takes action. She does not say that someone else takes her out to the garden and sticks her hands into the soil. Instead, she plants her own hands, and she knows they "shall grow green." These lines are vibrant, as if the dark sign has finally disappeared. Her hands are filled with power and creativity. And there is also another ingredient in this section that does not appear in the rest of the poem. Here there is peace. She is so content with her hands in the soil, she is sure that swallows will come and "lay eggs / in deep cracks" around her "ink- / stained fingernails." Although "ink-stained fingernails" in any other sense might conjure a negative image, here they bespeak her productivity as an artist. But even here, there is one flaw, although slight. The speaker plants her hands on the impetus of "the sorrow of a voice," a voice that tells her it loves her hands. For this image to be more complete, more full of energy and a sense of self, it would have been better if the speaker had supplied her own inspiration for going to the garden.

The weakest image in this poem is the speaker referring to herself as a "blob." In her favor, however, she does state that this image comes from her past: "my heart has stolen away / from my childhood's neighborhoods." So if there is any transformation, any rebirth symbol in this poem, here it is. Although she may still rely on a man to define her, that certainly is stronger than seeing oneself as a blob, a nothing.

But even by the end of the poem, even if she has transformed herself from a blob, she has changed into a form that is not much more elevated. In the last section of this poem, the image she uses is a "piddling little old crick / which flows into a ditch / no pearls there for a fisherman to catch." This metaphor does not conjure up greatness. Rather, it entails little more than the runoff from a quick rain. There is a trickle of water but no life is sustained by it. The product of its short-lived efforts is to fall into a ditch, not a stream. It gathers nothing and then disappears. No one bothers with it because there is nothing to be gained in it.

And finally, the last image is that of a "small sad mermaid." Here is Farrokhzaad's chance to celebrate rebirth. She hints at it, but the effort falls short. She summons a mythological creature, half woman, half fish, maybe much like Farrokhzaad herself, caught between two worlds. She cannot fully enter either one because she is not equipped to breathe on the land and yet she is lost without companionship in the

What Do I Read Next?

- *Veils and Words: The Emerging Voices of Iranian Women Writers* (1992) contains works by Farrokhzaad, Tahereh Saffarzadeh, Parvin E'tessami, and Tahereh Qorratol'Ayn. The book covers 150 years of the tradition of women writing in Iran. This book was written by Iranian poet Farzaneh Milani, who teaches literature in the United States.
- In *A Feast in the Mirror: Stories by Contemporary Iranian Women* (2001), edited by Mohammad Mehdi Khorrami, modern Iranian women writers demonstrate that their world is both distant and yet not too dissimilar from the Western world.
- Nahid Rachlin's book *Veils: Short Stories* (1992) was listed as one of the 500 best books written by women. Her collection portrays stories of Iranians living in their homeland and abroad, and covers topics such as family and friends, love, and war. Most of the focal characters are women who explore the effects of their culture on their lives.
- For a study of classical Persian poetry, *The Hand of Poetry: Five Mystic Poets of Persia* (2000) is a good place to start. Included in this book are poems of Sanai, Attar, Rumi, Saadi, and Hafiz, some of Persia's best male poets.
- *Wounded Rose: Three Iranian Poets* (1980) is a collection of some of Iran's best modern poetry. Poets in this collection are contemporaries of Farrokhzaad and include Simin Behbahani, Nader Naderpour, and Yadollah Royai.
- Susan Atefat Peckam was born to Iranian immigrant parents, and her award-winning poetry is filled with images of women affected by both American and Iranian cultures. Her poems have been collected in *That Kind of Sleep* (2001).

water. The speaker repeats herself, emphasizing the smallness and the sadness of this little mermaid, who is dependent on a kiss. One kiss places her in the dark sleep of the dead each night. The other kiss awakens her in the morning. Or in the speaker's words, "she will be born at daybreak / from one kiss." And here, in the final lines of this poem, the concept of rebirth is presented. But the concept is not concluded. Does the sad little mermaid die each night? And is she reborn every morning? Does anything change? Does she grow? Does she find happiness? And even if she does, even in the last line of this poem, the mermaid is dependent on that kiss. Someone has to come, someone has to plant his lips on her cheek. Someone has to feel sorry for her and ultimately revive her.

Source: Joyce Hart, Critical Essay on "A Rebirth," in *Poetry for Students*, Thomson Gale, 2005.

Sources

Martin, David, "Introduction," in *A Rebirth*, Mazda Publishers, 1997, pp. ix–xiii.

Milani, Farzaneh, "Formation, Confrontation, and Emancipation in the Poetry of Foroogh Farrakhzaad," in *A Rebirth*, Mazda Publishers, 1997, pp. 123–33.

Farrokhzaad, Foroogh, *A Rebirth*, translated by David Martin, Mazda Publishers, 1997.

Further Reading

Dumas, Firoozeh, *Funny in Farsi: A Memoir of Growing Up Iranian in America*, Villard, 2003.

Dumas relates the story of her family coming to the United States from Iran when she was only seven years old. With lighthearted humor, she points out the challenges of living in a country whose culture is dramatically different from her own.

Farmaian, Sattareh Farman, and Dona Munker, *Daughter of Persia: A Woman's Journey from Her Father's Harem through the Islamic Revolution*, Anchor, 1993.

Farmaian was the child of an Iranian Prince and the fifteenth of his thirty-six children. She lived a somewhat protected life in Iran until she became too politically involved and was sentenced to death. She escaped Iran and moved to the United States, where she wrote her memoir.

Hillmann, Michael C., *A Lonely Woman: Forugh Farrokhzad and Her Poetry*, Lynne Rienner Publishers, 1987.
This is the only biography and study of Farrokhzad that has been published in English.

Nafisi, Azar, *Reading "Lolita" in Tehran: A Memoir in Books*, Random House, 2003.
An Iranian professor, tired of the restrictions placed on the books she and her students were allowed to read, organized a small group of women to secretly read Western literature. This is a highly praised memoir of how Western literature changed these women's lives.

Reed, Betsy, ed., *Nothing Sacred: Women Respond to Religious Fundamentalism and Terror*, Nation Books, 2002.
In Reed's collection, such important writers and feminists as Arundhati Roy, Barbara Ehrenreich, Karen Armstrong, Gloria Steinem, Eve Ensler, Susan Sontag, Ellen Willis, and Laura Flanders discuss the oppression of women in the name of religious fundamentalism.

The Reverse Side

Stephen Dunn

2000

Stephen Dunn's poem "The Reverse Side" appears in his collection *Different Hours* (2000). Before *Different Hours* won the 2001 Pulitzer Prize, Dunn was already an established poet with ten books of poetry to his credit and numerous publications in prestigious periodicals. The Pulitzer brought his work to the attention of the general public, however, broadening his readership. "Dunn doesn't belong to a particular school of poets," writes Kevin C. Shelly in the magazine *Philadelphia*, "but the influences of William Carlos Williams, Wallace Stevens and Robert Frost are sometimes evident in his work."

"The Reverse Side" is a short philosophical meditation that explores the conflict between so-called fundamentalist and open-minded attitudes of living and is ultimately critical of those who choose moral certainty over tolerance of uncertainty. The poem suggests that a worthwhile way to live is to attempt to be as comfortable as possible with moral ambiguity. It is perhaps easiest to understand the poem when it is read in the context of the whole book, *Different Hours*, in which many other poems attempt to discern whether there are essential organizing principles in disorderly human lives.

Author Biography

Stephen Dunn was born June 24, 1939, in the Forest Hills section of New York City. As of 2004, he was the author of twelve books of poetry, including

Stephen Dunn

Different Hours (2000), which won the 2001 Pulitzer Prize for poetry. Other books include *New & Selected Poems: 1974–1994* (1994), *Loosestrife* (1996), and *Local Visitations* (2003). He has also written two books of prose: *Walking Light: Memoirs and Essays on Poetry* (1993) and *Riffs and Reciprocities: Prose Pairs* (1998). In addition to a Pulitzer, Dunn has been awarded many honors and prizes, including the Academy Award in literature from the American Academy of Arts and Letters, fellowships from the Guggenheim and Rockefeller foundations, and three National Endowment for the Arts creative writing fellowships.

As a young man, Dunn seemed destined for a very different kind of life. He was a valued basketball player for Hofstra University (where he majored in history), played basketball professionally for the Williamsport Billies from 19962 to 1963, and did a stint in the army as a sports writer for a regimental newspaper. Soon after, he landed a job as an advertising copywriter for Nabisco, a decision he explores in the poem "The Last Hours" in *Different Hours*. From 1964 to 1966, Dunn studied creative writing at the New School of Social Research. In 1966, he took a savings of $2,200 and went to Spain with his then wife (Lois Ann Kelly, whom he married in 1964) to test whether he might become a serious writer. From 1967 to 1968, Dunn worked as an assistant editor at Ziff-Davis Publishing Company in New York City.

Dunn describes his first novel in a 1996 radio interview with Angela Elam for *New Letters on the Air* as "a poor novel . . . deficient in plot and character but lots of liveliness in the language, and by doing that it instructed me that I should be writing poetry." Encouraged to pursue poetry by his friend, novelist Sam Toperoff, in 1970 Dunn earned his master of arts in creative writing from Syracuse University, where he studied with Philip Booth, Donald Justice, George P. Elliott, and W. D. Snodgrass. Dunn went on to work as a writer, editor, and teacher, and his poetry has been published in such prestigious periodicals as the *Nation*, *New Republic*, *New Yorker*, and *American Poetry Review*. Dunn has been Distinguished Professor of Creative Writing at Richard Stockton College of New Jersey, where he has taught since 1974.

Poem Summary

Epigraph

Dunn begins "The Reverse Side" with an epigraph, which is a short quotation used to introduce a literary piece. When a poem begins with an epigraph, the author typically intends the reader to read everything that follows in reference to that quotation. An epigraph usually provides a clue about a theme or situation in the poem or about the identity of the poem's speaker.

In the case of "The Reverse Side," the epigraph "The reverse side also has a reverse side" is an English translation of a Japanese proverb and serves as the source of the title of the poem. In the original Japanese, this proverb *Monogoto niwa taitei ura no ura ga aru mono da* literally means "in most things generally there is a reverse to the reverse." The Japanese word *ura* can mean "the reverse" as well as "a place which cannot be seen" or "a hidden implication," according to *Kenkyusha's New Japanese-English Dictionary*. This proverb seems to encourage a curious and investigative attitude towards life, a willingness to look behind the obvious "front" that things present to the world, perhaps similar in meaning to the English proverb "there are wheels within wheels."

But the epigraph has a little mystery about it too. It invites readers to imagine an object with more than one side, and of course everything that has a front usually has a back. But is "the reverse of the reverse" the same as "the front?" Or is it an aspect slightly different from the front, which in turn has its own "reverse side?" If this is the meaning, the proverb seems to indicate that there are infinitely possible "reverse sides" of any object or subject, like what happens when a mirror reflects a mirror. By using this cryptic quotation which itself proves to have some mystery and many possible meanings, Dunn may have intended to send the reader into the poem already in a questioning or investigative mode.

Lines 1–5

The point of view of "The Reverse Side" is first person plural, which seems to indicate that the speaker feels confident enough, perhaps based on life experience, to speak for or about a group of people. It also focuses the poem on general statements rather than on specific things having only to do with the speaker as an individual. The first line of the poem provides one other strong signal that the speaker means to focus on generalizations: it speaks about an abstract concept, "a truth."

The reader will not find any definite clues in "The Reverse Side" about the speaker's sex, age, or the place from which he or she is speaking. But the reader who experiences "The Reverse Side" in the context of all the other poems in *Different Hours*, or who is acquainted with Dunn's other books, may have good reason to suspect that behind the "we" of this poem is some version of Dunn—that is, the version of Dunn that his writings present to the world. This would be a fair conclusion because Dunn has expressed thoughts and feelings similar to those in this poem in many other poems and prose essays.

The first line of the poem, which begins "It's why," shows that the person speaking is already referring the reader back to the epigraph. Beginning with "It's why" also gives the reader the experience of dropping into the middle of the thoughts of a person, a little like coming into a movie after it has already begun. The indefinite pronoun "it" may cause the reader to scramble a little to catch up, maybe asking "What's why?" before referring back to the epigraph.

The first five lines present the idea of a deck of cards shuffled "inside" a person as an analogy. That is, these lines find similarity between how shuffling a deck of cards will produce a different deal each time, with how human beings can have contradictory thoughts or feelings, seemingly almost at random. It is also important to notice that the speaker says "some of us" experience thoughts and feelings this way. The speaker uses the pronoun "we" but is not speaking for everybody in the world. With this qualification the speaker lays the groundwork for points that will be made later in the poem, about other people who may not like to admit that they have contradictory thoughts and feelings.

Poems often operate as much by what they do not say, as by what they do. The end of the first five lines of Dunn's poem provides a good example. The speaker begins by saying "when we speak a truth," then provides an image of how some people immediately sense inside themselves a contradiction of something they just said. But the speaker does not finish the fifth line of the poem by saying "then we speak the opposite of what we said." The speaker only says "there it is." Presumably "there" means "inside us," where the deck of contradictory feelings is shuffled. By demonstrating—by omission—that contradictory feelings sometimes or often go unspoken, the speaker adds more information about what it is like to experience feelings this way.

Lines 6–7

Though lines 6 and 7 follow the period at the end of the poem's first sentence and come after the white space following the first stanza, they are a continuation of the thought of the first sentence. "And perhaps why" in line 6 refers to the same "why" as the first two words of the poem. In lines 6 and 7 the speaker provides an example of contradictory feelings: "as we fall in love / we're already falling out of it." The example is still given in general terms—no individual people falling in and out of love are specified. But this example is more specific than the extremely generalized "truth" of the first stanza, which shows that the speaker is starting to support and refine the points that were made in the first stanza.

Lines 6 and 7 also add an important aspect to what the reader is learning about the speaker's view of the world. He or she regards love—the subject of so many passionate poems and other proclamations throughout history—as an impermanent state. Almost at the same moment we fall into it, the speaker says, we begin to fall out of it. The speaker qualifies this statement in a subtle way, using "perhaps," just as in the first stanza the statement about contradictory feelings is qualified by "some of us." The way the speaker shows humility about making these assertions may earn the reader's trust and agreement more than if the statements were absolute in their claims. By these small qualifications, the speaker, who seems to be working out these thoughts as the poem progresses, allows for the possibility of error or for another point of view—for "the reverse side."

Lines 8–10

The third stanza begins as the first stanza did with "It's why," signaling that the speaker is continuing to work through thoughts on the same subject. The statements of the first two stanzas are carefully qualified. But in the third stanza the speaker makes a more assertive statement, indicating there is a group of people who react to the complexity of life differently than the "some of us" of the first stanza. This statement manages to be both sympathetic and critical toward people who insist there is only one way of looking at things, no "reverse side." The speaker suggests these people act this way either because they are "terrified" (in which case it is easy to have sympathy for them) or because they are "simple."

"Simple," unlike "terrified," is a word with multiple meanings, some of which imply sympathy on the speaker's part and some of which imply judgment or criticism. When the adjective "simple" is applied to people, it can have the positive meanings of unaffected, natural, or straightforward, but it can also have the negative connotations of ignorant, intellectually weak or silly. Because Dunn's speaker has expressed opinions to this point with some humility, the reader may feel that both positive and negative meanings are intended. That is, the speaker means to be both understanding and critical about an aspect of human nature. The speaker's complex attitude, as evidenced by his using the words "terrified" and "simple" together, is in itself an illustration of the point that the speaker is making: that every subject has multiple, sometimes contradictory, characteristics. Another meaning of "simple," not usually applied to people but also pertinent to Dunn's poem, is something that is not complex or intricate. By using the short but complicated word "simple" this way, Dunn's speaker expresses the opinion that nothing, if we allow ourselves to look closely enough, is free from complexity.

Each reader may have different ideas about "the great mystery" to which Dunn's speaker refers in line 10. The phrase brings to mind the language that philosophers and theologians have used for centuries to inquire into the nature of life and death, concepts of good and evil, the question of whether there is a God, and the purpose of the whole of existence itself. At this point in the poem, Dunn's speaker seems to feel that the reader has been carried along enough by the humble tone of the previous two stanzas that the statement about "the great mystery" may be made as though the existence of this mystery is a matter of mutual agreement and is self-evident.

Likewise, readers may come up with different answers for who the people are that "latch onto one story, / just one version." In attempting to answer this question, the reader steps into the very moral complexity about which the poem is speaking, because every word one might think of to characterize such people has a "charged" positive or negative connotation. Depending on who is doing the speaking, and who is being spoken about, one person's "fundamentalist" or "terrorist" may be another's "saint" or "freedom fighter," just as one person's "tolerance" may be another's "permissiveness."

Lines 11–14

The poem's fourth stanza begins to clarify who the people are who "latch onto one story." The speaker does this by contrasting these people with people who hold different attitudes, that is, the "some of us" of the first stanza. Whoever the "terrified and the simple" are, they are the opposite of who the speaker calls "the open-minded" in line 12, so we can assume that the speaker considers the "terrified and the simple" closed-minded.

But the fourth stanza does more than clarify who the speaker considers closed-minded. It also begins to express how difficult it is to keep an attitude of open-mindedness, even for people who believe it is the best way to live. "Image & afterimage," the speaker says, cause "even / the open-minded" to "yearn for a fiction / to rein things in." "Image & afterimage" refers back to the possible ways of looking at everything that the epigraph evokes. Without the responsibility to evaluate and understand these multiple aspects, the speaker acknowledges, life would be easier, implying a kind of sympathy for people who are not strong enough to meet the challenge. But the speaker clearly intends "a fiction," used the way it is in line 12, to mean "an untruth," to be a criticism of people who can persuade themselves to live with a lie. The examples the speaker gives in line 14 confirm this: "the snapshot, the lie of a frame." That is, a small photograph and a picture frame crop an enormous world to a manageable size. A picture frame is intended to focus the viewer on what is inside the frame, and to concentrate the attention by temporarily omitting other information. But the frame turns into a "lie" if the maker or viewer of the picture or the frame forgets, or denies, that the world extends in all its bewildering complexity beyond the frame.

There is another important "poetic event" in the fourth stanza, but it is small and easy to miss: the little word "oh" in line 11. "Oh" used in this way is a part of speech called an "interjection" or an "exclamation," and these are often found in what are called "lyric" poems. The lyric poem, rather than focusing primarily on telling a story, puts emphasis on expressing feeling through "musical language." That is, the lyric relies on the pure sounds that poetry can make to appeal to a reader's feelings, on a level different from literal, intellectual understanding. Until line 11 "The Reverse Side" uses fairly plain, conversational language characteristic of a "meditative" poem. But with the appearance of that little word "oh," the poem begins to shift into lyric territory. Human beings say "oh" or "ah" in this way when we want to emphasize how deeply we feel. It is a word without particular meaning in itself, one that resorts to pure sound to convey emotion. In using it here, Dunn's speaker makes a shift from merely *thinking* about how complex the world is to *feeling* how difficult that fact sometimes makes human life.

Lines 15–18

One characteristic of a poem that combines lyric and meditative elements is that once the leap is made from "thinking" into the lyric territory of "expressing feeling," the poem usually does not return to pure thinking about the subject. "The Reverse Side" conforms to this pattern: the final stanza asks a question that is at least partly unanswerable. The speaker's purpose, then, in asking such a question is to express emotion about the difficult predicament in which people find themselves when allowing themselves to investigate "the reverse side." By asking the question "how do we not go crazy," the speaker suggests that the very act of asking questions may support the sanity of people "compelled / to live with the circle, the ellipsis, the word / not yet written."

The images or ideas with which the speaker finishes the poem—"the circle, the ellipsis, the word / not yet written"—return the reader to the mysterious and ambiguous quality of the epigraph that begins the poem. Each of these images has multiple associations that apply to the speaker's thoughts and feelings about the morally complex nature of human life.

The circle has been used for centuries in human design to symbolize inclusiveness, unity, equality, emptiness, and eternity. The table at which King Arthur's knights sat was circular (round), as was the table at which the participants sat at the 1973 Paris peace talks that eventually concluded the U. S. involvement in the Vietnam War. The round table—Dunn's circle "we are compelled / to live with"—equalizes the status of all people who sit there and gives priority to no particular point of view. As such it is a symbol of an attempt at open-mindedness, a willingness to entertain opposing points of view.

An ellipsis is a punctuation mark used to indicate that letters or words have been omitted in written or printed language to focus the reader's attention on the words that remain. For Dunn's speaker, the ellipsis may represent thoughts or feelings that are difficult to formulate and, once formulated, are difficult to express or to live with.

The "word / not yet written" may be unwritten for a multitude of reasons. The word may be, as the previous image of the ellipsis hints, difficult to write because it might offend others or put the writer in danger. Writing the word may be beyond the writer's emotional, intellectual, or spiritual capacity. The word may not yet exist; it may need to be discovered or invented.

Taken together, "the circle, the ellipsis, the word / not yet written" represent the pressures of the real world on the sanity of people who want to remain open to the confusing complexity of that world. The speaker asks, on behalf of this group of people (the "some of us" of the first stanza), "how do we not go crazy." The question may be understood as a cry, a lament, a kind of groan that builds on the "oh" of line 11, and the question is in itself an attempt to relieve the pressure of the predicament the question describes.

Themes

Negative Capability

Dunn does not refer in "The Reverse Side" to the English poet John Keats (1795–1821) or Keats's concept of "Negative Capability," which Keats outlined in a famous 1817 letter to his brothers. But Dunn's poem is unquestionably concerned with the idea of Negative Capability, and Dunn proved he was well acquainted with the concept when, in a 1996 *New Letters on the Air* radio interview with Angela Elam, he said

> [W]hen I was younger, as most people are when they're younger, I needed certainties, or I craved certainties, maybe because you just live a life that's full of ambivalences, which I still do. But now I'm much more happy in the "Negative Capability" sense. . . . Keats praised Shakespeare for his "Negative Capability," that he was at home with doubts and uncertainties, and I'm increasingly at home with doubts and uncertainties.

The passage in Keats's letter that Dunn refers to is

> [A]t once it struck me, what quality went to form a Man of Achievement, especially in Literature and

Topics For Further Study

- Dunn's poem uses the circle as a symbol of open-mindedness, inclusiveness, and willingness to entertain opposite points of view. The table at which King Arthur's knights sat was circular (round), as was the table at which the participants sat at the 1973 Paris peace talks that eventually concluded the U.S. involvement in the Vietnam War. Research the long process that led to the choice of the round table at the Paris peace talks. What shapes for the table were proposed first, and why did the parties involved reject them? Draw up diagrams depicting each proposed shape. Next to them, list the pros and cons that were put forth for each suggestion.
- Search a major U.S. newspaper for a story about groups or individuals in conflict over religious or cultural issues. Examine your own thoughts or beliefs about the two sides of the issue. Then do enough research about the side of the conflict opposite from your own opinion to enable you to write a brief, persuasive summary of this point of view in unbiased language. How, if at all, did researching the opposing viewpoints affect your own?
- The publications of Italian astronomer Galileo Galilei (1564–1642) brought him in conflict with Roman Catholic Church authorities. What theory about the way the solar system is organized did Galileo's publications dispute, and why did the church see Galileo's theories as threatening? How long did it take the church to admit that errors had been made by the theological advisors in Galileo's case? What is the meaning of the statement *Eppur si muove* ("Nevertheless it does move"), attributed to Galileo after his trial for heresy?
- What two plays written by Pierre de Beaumarchais (1732–1799) showed sympathy for underprivileged people and the lower classes? Who regarded these plays as threatening, and why? Which violent political upheaval did the plays foreshadow? Which composers were inspired to turn these plays into operas, and how, in turn, were those operas regarded by the authorities in the countries where they were originally performed?
- What novel written by Harriet Beecher Stowe (1811–1896) is thought to have been influential in ending slavery in the United States, and how was it received when it first appeared? How did pro-slavery advocates draw upon the Bible to support the practice of slavery? How, in contrast, did anti-slavery advocates use Christian beliefs to call for an end to slavery? What is Abraham Lincoln supposed to have said to Mrs. Stowe when they met?
- What novel by Indian-born author Salman Rushdie (born 1947) caused Iranian spiritual leader Ayatollah Ruhollah Khomeini to issue a *fatwa* (death sentence) on Rushdie? What was it about the novel that upset many Muslims, and how did they show their anger? Which people connected with the publication of the novel were harmed?

> which Shakespeare possessed so enormously—I mean *Negative Capability*, that is when a man is capable of being in uncertainties, Mysteries, doubts, without any irritable reaching after fact and reason.

Keats's letter and Dunn's poem both suggest that a worthwhile way to live is to attempt to be as comfortable as possible with the moral complexity of the world, rather than to cling to any simplified "fiction" (as line 12 of "The Reverse Side" puts it) that misrepresents how ambiguous life can be. But though Dunn's poem presents as brave the choice to live with "Negative Capability," it does not say that it is an easy or comfortable choice. To the contrary, the poem's last sentence is a lament about how difficult a choice it is.

Fundamentalism

"The Reverse Side" never speaks of "fundamentalism," a word loaded with the judgment of a particular point of view. People who hold points of view labeled as "fundamentalist" by others do not often use that label to refer to themselves. But Dunn's poem is critical of the "terrified and the simple" who "latch onto just one story." For some, this is an apt definition of "fundamentalist." Racial, religious, and cultural groups have for centuries engaged in sometimes violent conflict to define or enforce who is inside and who is outside their group. This struggle may involve an attempt to decide which beliefs are "orthodox," a word *The New Oxford American Dictionary* defines as "conforming to what is generally or traditionally accepted as true; established and approved" and also "not independent-minded; conventional and unoriginal." Ideas that do not conform to orthodox beliefs or standards might be labeled "heresy." Throughout history, in parts of the world where groups with conservative religious ideologies have come to power, people with beliefs outside the norm have been in danger of being severely punished or even killed. In the last decade of the twentieth century, various media have often applied the word "fundamentalist" to religious and cultural groups that cling to conservative values, such as strict and literal interpretation of religious scripture, inflexible ideas about the roles of men and women in society, and opposition to Darwin's theory of evolution. For their part, people labeled "fundamentalist" often insist they are merely trying to maintain ancient religious or human values against what they view as immoral developments in the modern world.

Oppression

For the most part, "The Reverse Side" focuses on the personal difficulty of living in a morally ambiguous world, rather than on larger political considerations. But the point of view expressed in the poem does have implications that extend into the political arena. Following the poem's logic, it can be argued that dangerous political and cultural consequences result from *not* living with tolerance. When powerful people insist on conformity in ideas or beliefs, the result may be oppression and persecution of certain classes of people. Methods that have been used to enforce conformity have ranged from suppressing the ways ideas are shared (such as the Nazis burning books during World War II) to genocide (the deliberate killing of a racial, political, or cultural group, such as the massacre of the Tutsi minority by Hutu extremists in Rwanda). The individuals or groups who have used such tactics to enforce orthodoxy have often justified their actions as necessary to preserve important values or traditions. The modern era has been characterized by struggle between the idea that some values are important enough that almost any forceful action is justified in protecting them and the opposing notion that human disagreements can and should be worked out by peaceful negotiation in the political arena. Though "The Reverse Side" keeps its focus narrowed on the personal challenge of living with moral complexity, it participates in the same philosophical discussion as these larger considerations, and is influenced by them.

Style

Free Verse

"The Reverse Side" is written in "free verse," which may be simply defined as poetry without a regular pattern of rhyme or meter. In many languages when words are arranged in sentences, some words or syllables (parts of words) are stressed more than others. For instance, in the English word "before," the second syllable is emphasized more than the first. "Meter" in poetry is the organization of stressed and unstressed syllables into regular patterns. In casual speech people do not make an effort to organize stressed and unstressed syllables into patterns, but for much of history, poetry was expected to have an arrangement of a certain number of stressed and unstressed syllables in each line of the poem. The rhyming of certain words in poetry—a regular arrangement of words that sound alike—is a poetic device completely separate from meter, but rhyme and meter went hand in hand for many centuries as the two main formal characteristics of poetry. Many poetic forms were developed, such as the sonnet and the villanelle, which prescribed both rhyme and metrical patterns.

During the long period after ancient Hebrew and Egyptian poetry and before the seventeenth century, some individual poems were written without using meter and rhyme. But these exceptions were few and far between. In the seventeenth century a few poets began to feel hemmed-in by the demands of meter and rhyme and started to experiment with freer forms. By the nineteenth century, this became a major trend. In the late twentieth century, free verse gradually became the dominant style in which poetry was written in English, and poetry with traditional formal characteristics had to struggle against a reputation of being old fashioned. In "The Reverse Side," Dunn demonstrates the freedom of free verse when he breaks the uneven lines of his text to emphasize certain points. Line 13, for instance, ends with a dash. This punctuation momentarily "reins in" the progress of the sentence and the poem, a gesture that enacts or mimics the emotional meaning of this passage.

Repetition

American poet Robert Frost (1874–1963) famously criticized free verse as "playing tennis without a net." But free verse uses devices other than meter and rhyme to give shape and structure to a poem. Some of these techniques, especially repetition and parallelism, are the same devices that ancient Egyptian, Hebrew, Sanskrit, and Sumerian poets used. In "The Reverse Side," Dunn uses both devices. "Anaphora" is the technical word for repetition of a word or words at the beginning of two or more successive sentences or parts of sentences. Dunn's speaker begins several stanzas of "The Reverse Side" with "It's why," or "And perhaps why," and this use of anaphora ties the separate thoughts and examples together.

Meditative and Lyric Modes

Poetry has several distinct modes, each with its own defining characteristics and uses. Three of these commonly used in the twenty-first century are the "lyric," "narrative," and "meditative" modes. Many poems written in the late twentieth and early twenty-first centuries are a hybrid (mix) of one or more of these modes.

The narrative mode is the one that "The Reverse Side" uses least, as the poem does not focus primarily on telling a story. Instead, the poem is best read as a hybrid of the lyric and meditative modes. Ancient lyric poems were originally sung (with a "lyre," a kind of harp). The modern lyric poem can be characterized as a songlike outpouring of the speaker's thoughts and feelings, a poetic mode that usually excludes material that distracts such a focus. "The Reverse Side" sketches a moral predicament with a few economical strokes (compression and brevity being important characteristics of the lyric poem), then expresses how difficult that predicament is to live with.

The meditative mode is less focused on expressing feeling than it is on working out an idea or a philosophical argument. The lyric can sometimes be quite dramatic in expression or the way it makes emotional leaps. In contrast, the meditative poem usually explores its thoughts in a more plainspoken, subdued manner, and this is the way "The Reverse Side" begins. Emotion is hinted at, but thought and analysis are predominant in lines like "And perhaps why as we fall in love / we're already falling out of it." The meditative mode has been used for centuries to explore religious, philosophical, or political questions that impact on everyday life, and Dunn's poetry may be said to fall primarily into the meditative category. "The Reverse Side" is a good example of a poem that begins by meditating on concerns with both personal and cultural implications, then makes a leap to stronger feeling, based on that exploration. As was discussed above, the poem makes a clear leap into lyric territory with the question "How do we not go crazy" in line 15. Fear—in this case the fear of going mad—is exactly the kind of strong emotion the lyric poem specializes in expressing. And true to lyric strategy, once this strong feeling has been articulated, the poem ends quickly rather than introducing new elements.

Historical Context

"The Reverse Side" was written in the mid-1990s and published in 2000. In the poem the speaker's attitude toward "the terrified and the simple" who "latch onto one story, / just one version of the great mystery" is a mixture of sympathy and criticism. But in his essay "The Hand Reaching into the Crowd" from his prose collection *Walking Light*, Dunn (speaking on his own behalf) expresses an opinion that is more openly critical of those he regards as closed-minded. Echoing "The Reverse Side" almost exactly, he writes "We *are* our stories, which is why it is useful to know many. The scariest people I know are the ones who avidly subscribe to one story, one version of the world." In the essay he does not say explicitly what reason he has to fear such people. But one may suppose that what frightens Dunn is the kind of violent conflict that has often erupted in human history when one group has tried to enforce belief in their "story" at the expense of other people's stories, or even other people. The mid-1990s saw many examples of such conflict, including "ethnic cleansing" (persecution and murder for racial or cultural reasons) in Bosnia and Rwanda that took the lives of hundreds of thousands of people; the bombing by Timothy McVeigh of a U.S. federal building in Oklahoma City, which killed 168 people and injured more than 500; and the burning of more than 100 predominately black churches in the southern United States. Each of these events was apparently motivated by conflict between individuals or groups seeking dominance over another individual or group with opposing racial, religious, or political views. In the political arenas of many nations, the same kind of conflict played out in a less violent way, between rival groups who wished to limit the actions or privileges of groups with whom they disagreed. One example from the mid-1990s is the continuing conflict in the United States between those who want prayer and other religious expression to be allowed in the public schools and those who oppose that development based on the belief that prayer in public schools violates the principle of the separation of church and state.

There is another historical context for the writing of "The Reverse Side," a context personal to Dunn. While it is risky to draw literal associations between a work of literature and events of an author's own life, Dunn himself has connected (in an online interview with Philip Dacey for the *Cortland Review*) the tolerance for moral ambiguity to events from his childhood associated with the relationship between his father and mother. In this interview, Dunn said about his father that "he lived a noble lie. . ., a lie that I alone was privy to. He was my introduction to ambivalence and moral complexity." In his essay "A History of My Silence" from *Walking Light*, Dunn explains that his father gave all the family's financial savings to Dunn's grandfather to help pay hospital bills for the grandfather's mistress. When Dunn's mother confronted his father about the missing money, Dunn's father said he lost it at the racetrack, and he stuck to that story (except with Dunn, who later found out the truth). Carlin Romano, commenting in the *Philadelphia Inquirer* on how Dunn's childhood may have influenced Dunn's view of the world, writes "There were 'no orthodoxies possible' in that house, Dunn recalls."

Poetry, in general, is meant to be read without reference to the biography of the poet, and "The Reverse Side" can certainly be understood and enjoyed without knowing anything about Dunn. But poetry is not read in a vacuum, either, so a reader may be justified in finding clues in Dunn's own other writings and recorded statements that point to a particular interpretation of "The Reverse Side."

Critical Overview

Very few books of poetry caused much of a stir in the general culture at the beginning of the twenty-first century, the period when "The Reverse Side" appeared in Dunn's book *Different Hours*. But *Different Hours* did earn praise for Dunn from a small set of critics, and the book was awarded the 2001 Pulitzer Prize, one of the highest honors given for poetry.

A review of *Different Hours* by Bill Christophersen in *Poetry* refers to "The Reverse Side" specifically, commenting that the poem, among others in the book, conveys "the sense that truth is a chameleon." Several other critics comment on the tolerance or appetite for moral complexity strongly evident in "The Reverse Side," which is a feature of Dunn's poetry in general. Andrea Hollander Budy writes in her *Arkansas Democrat-Gazette* review of *Different Hours*:

> Dunn's speaker is a man who occupies the territory of the 'in-between,' staking claim to a place without definite answers to the philosophical questions posed throughout the book—and throughout Dunn's oeuvre. . . . He is one who defies labels and who is unafraid of admitting this.

Emily Nussbaum, in a review of *Different Hours* for the *New York Times Book Review*, remarks, "Dunn's poetry is strangely easy to like: philosophical but not arid, lyrical but rarely glib, his storytelling balanced effortlessly between the casual and the vivid." Several reviewers comment on the clear, simple diction (style of speech) of the poems in *Different Hours*. James Lawless, writing in the *Cleveland Plain Dealer*, notes, "These poems reinforce [Dunn's] reputation as a plainspoken man, whose sentences are easy but not simplistic." Joyce S. Brown, reviewing *Different Hours* for the Baltimore *City Paper*, similarly states

> These poems, although thoughtful, require no hard work to grasp. Even their form is uncomplicated: free verse, short lines, often with stanzas lasting only two or three lines. The tone is above all honest, unadorned, in some cases as harshly critical of human turpitude as the prophet Jeremiah.

Most reviews of *Different Hours* were positive, but Kevin C. Shelly in an article in the magazine *Philadelphia* quotes an unnamed fellow poet as saying of Dunn: "His poems now are too intellectualized and removed. . . . He's trapped by becoming successful. He's full of himself. His poetry now is very introspective. . . . The more intellectualized poetry becomes, the less successful it is."

Criticism

Patrick Donnelly

Donnelly is a poet, editor, and teacher. His first book of poems titled The Charge was published

> *"The last words of the poem—'the word / not yet written'—summarize the speaker's belief that not everything can or should be written or spoken, because it is impossible to do justice to the world's complexity with mere words."*

by the Ausable Press in 2003. In this essay, Donnelly demonstrates that Dunn's poem is a mix of two distinct modes of poetry.

In a March 2000 interview with Philip Dacey for the online journal the *Cortland Review*, Dunn said: "I've been refining how to write the poem of mind. I've tried for a poem of clear surfaces in service, I hope, of the elusive, the difficult to say." The poem "The Reverse Side" seems to be the perfect illustration of the goals Dunn describes in this statement. That is, it can be demonstrated that "The Reverse Side" is (primarily) a "poem of mind" with "clear surfaces" which takes up as one of its main subjects the "difficult to say." It is helpful to examine each of these three qualities in turn, to try to decide if Dunn has been successful in meeting the goals he set for himself and if meeting those goals is enough to produce a completely satisfying poem.

It may be assumed that Dunn meant by "poem of mind" a poem in the meditative mode, in contrast with a lyric or narrative poem. The main focus of a meditative poem (the mode toward which Dunn moved increasingly in the late 1990s) is the working out of an idea, or a philosophical argument, whereas the lyric puts emphasis on expressing feeling (usually strong feeling) and the narrative on telling a story. It can be argued that most poems of the late twentieth and early twenty-first century are a hybrid (mix) of two or more of these modes. Poets combine the modes because each mode provides a kind of poetic communication for which the others are not as well suited.

A poem of mind is one written from the "mind part" of the poet to the "mind part" of the reader; that is, from and to the intellectual aspect of human beings, the part that thinks, evaluates, deliberates, argues, etc. What other kinds of poems may there be? To continue the logic of Dunn's phrase, if there is a poem of mind, there are also poems of heart, gut, or sex organs, those parts of human beings that represent deep feelings, unconscious instincts, and uncontrollable passions. And there are poems of soul or spirit, which attempt to address whether there is any part of the human being that is eternal rather than mortal, and if so what that part is like and with what it is concerned. Of course human beings' thinking, feeling, instinctual, and spiritual capacities are not easily separated from one another, in art or in life—though at different periods of human history some people have tried, for aesthetic, religious, or philosophical reasons. In resistance to this attempt to divide human nature, it may be asserted that one definition of poetic success or greatness is the poem that speaks equally well to mind, heart, and spirit.

American poet Emily Dickinson (1830–1886) famously praised the kind of poems that "take the top of your head off" when you read them. It is instructive to interpret this comment almost literally; that is, she appreciated poems that put the "head" to one side, at least temporarily, to speak directly to heart, gut, and spirit. Even Dunn might concede that "The Reverse Side" is not such a poem. This poem seemingly wants to leave the head firmly *on*, because that is the part it is primarily speaking from and to. The poem's ambition is modest; it does not want to shake the earth. It is satisfied to delve a little into a difficult philosophical problem without solving that problem—or even completely stating every aspect of it—then to shift to the lyric mode to give the poem a satisfying close.

About that shift to the lyric, the poetic mode that emphasizes an outpouring of feeling: when Dunn said that he had "been refining how to write the poem of mind," he implicitly acknowledged that this is not such an easy task. The pure poem of mind may not be completely satisfying because human beings are not pure minded. So Dunn borrows from the lyric mode, beginning with the exclamation "oh" in line 11—that little word without particular meaning in itself which resorts to pure sound to convey emotion. Then the poem expands in the lyric-emotional direction with its question "How do we not go crazy" in line 15. The fear at the root of this question is the poem's primary emotional gesture, the moment with the potential to

What Do I Read Next?

- *Walking Light: Memoirs and Essays on Poetry* (2001) is a collection of Dunn's prose about his life and his thoughts on poetry. In several of the essays, including "The Hand Reaching into the Crowd" and "A History of My Silence," Dunn connects his views on moral complexity to events in his own life.
- *New and Selected Poems, 1974–1994* (1994) is Dunn's selection of poems that he considered his best from his first eight collections as well as poems that were new in 1994.
- Dunn has said in an interview with Philip Dacey for the online journal the *Cortland Review* that Fyodor Dostoevsky, author of the novel *The Brothers Karamazov* (1879), was the "first writer to wholly take over my consciousness." *The Brothers Karamazov* demonstrates—in its examination of mid-nineteenth century Russian religion, politics, and ethics—the kind of tolerance for moral complexity that Dunn admired and brought to his own poems.
- *The Trouble with Islam: A Muslim's Call for Reform in Her Faith* (2003) is a critique of fundamentalist Islam by Irshad Manji and a call for a return to the spirit of openness and independent reasoning that she asserts was a feature of the religion in its early years.
- Religious Movements maintains a web site at http://religiousmovements.lib.virginia.edu that explores the concept and history of fundamentalism in the Christian churches. The site includes external links and a bibliography.
- *Against Forgetting: Twentieth-Century Poetry of Witness* (1993), edited by Carolyn Forché, is an anthology of poetry that collects the work of poets such as Anna Akhmatova, Federíco Garcia Lorca, and Nazim Hikmet, who lived in violent times or who struggled against regimes with repressive ideologies.
- Alice Walker's *Possessing the Secret of Joy* (1992) is a novel with the political mission to educate readers about the culture and religious pressures that force some young women in parts of Africa, the Middle East, and Asia to undergo genital circumcision.
- Religious Tolerance maintains a web site at http://www.religioustolerance.org with information about the history of conflict between groups that want more religious expression allowed in the public sphere (schools, municipal buildings, etc.) and groups that want to keep religion strictly separate from the state.

create the most disorder, and it provides depth of feeling to a poem that otherwise has a fairly clear, unruffled surface.

It can be argued that the poem makes a retreat from the lyric mode with the examples the speaker gives (in lines 17 and 18) that symbolize the difficulty of living with an open mind: "the circle, the ellipsis, the word / not yet spoken." On the one (lyric) hand, these examples are mysterious; they do not spell out everything they may mean. They are content to gesture in the direction of meaning, and brevity and economy are quintessentially lyric characteristics. On the other (meditative) hand, these examples speak from and to the mind, rather than heart or gut. They are abstract, literary images, not easy to visualize, because they are mental rather than physical. "The Reverse Side" ends rather quickly after it reaches the outpouring of feeling in line 15—another characteristic of the lyric mode, which considers its goal accomplished when it has expressed strong emotion. But by illustrating its final point with mental images, the poem seems to retreat somewhat from the emotion that surfaced in line 15, back to the calmer meditative mode with which the poem began. *Except*—and here is an example of how small details in a short poem can have a large impact—the shortness of the poem's last line (with its implication of insufficiency), in combination with the line break that separates and disturbs the poem's final clause ("the word / not yet written"), may convey to the reader exactly the feeling of emptiness, unsupportedness, and insecurity the speaker is talking about in line 15. By these small devices, the poet infuses those abstract last images with a subtle undercurrent of anxiety.

One of the strongest clues that Dunn intended "The Reverse Side" to be read primarily as a poem of mind is the poem's plainspoken, conversational diction (way of speaking). The poem's modesty of ambition, and the qualified nature of the claims it makes, are reflected in its mild tone of voice. There is nothing fancy or distracting going on with the words in this poem that points to an overwhelming torrent of emotion, and no line of the poem would seem terribly out of place in a normal conversation. There are no "sound effects," like rhyme or meter, that call attention to themselves or try to appeal to a faculty other than the mind. The few examples of alliteration (repetition of consonants) such as "feel foolish," or of assonance (repetition of vowel sounds), such as "truth/foolish," "circle/word," receive so little emphasis as to seem accidental, as in conversational speech. This pared-down approach puts the focus squarely on the poem's philosophical debate and on the one emotional gesture. The relatively mild language of the poem is a signal that nothing specific seems to be hugely at risk during the moment the poem is spoken. Though the speaker's predicament is difficult, there is time to work it out in this philosophical way—or there is not, and the speaker accepts that. The poem does not solve the problem it describes, and it does not make any enormous, unexpected discovery. Even when Dunn makes his shift to the lyric mode, it is not accompanied by a shift in diction; there is no verbal earthquake to mimic the speaker's distress.

"The Reverse Side" employs one poetic tactic that tilts it, in spite of the meditative subject matter and tone, in the direction of a lyric poem: it does not spell out everything. Beginning with the epigraph (the Japanese proverb that is quoted at the beginning of the poem), the poem is open to multiple interpretations. The last words of the poem—"the word / not yet written"—summarize the speaker's belief that not everything can or should be written or spoken, because it is impossible to do justice to the world's complexity with mere words. The unspoken, the hinted at, is the territory of the lyric, in contrast to the pure poem of mind which usually wants to set out its ideas with much less room for conjecture. The pure poem of mind makes its case clearly—maybe too clearly to be satisfying as a poem—because it values scoring points and winning its argument over doing justice to any gray areas and ambiguities. But "The Reverse Side" is not a pure poem of mind: by including mystery as well as clarity, it frustrates any attempt at a single interpretation and instead encourages speculation. In poetic terms, this strategy is always risky, because a reader can go astray and the poem can fail. But in this case the risk was worth taking, because the poem's gestures toward what cannot be spoken give it a depth it might not otherwise have had.

"The Reverse Side" has mystery, but it does not have drama—it retreated from the emotional language that might have taken it in a dramatic direction. So, for most readers, it will not be a "take the top of the head off" poem. It is more likely to be a "nod of the head" poem, in which the reader acknowledges that the world is morally complex and that this can be frightening. It is interesting to speculate what a person belonging to the category the speaker characterizes as "the terrified and the simple"—a closed-minded person, in other words—might think or feel as a result of reading this poem. A truly closed-minded person probably would not read the poem at all, or any poem, because such people avoid challenges to their "one version of the great mystery." They avoid them for good reason—because most good poems do resist one story about the world, and every great poem does. But in a sense *all* readers are closed-minded to some extent, because every person has some subject about which they feel extremely vulnerable, some topic under which it feels dangerous to dig lest a fact difficult to face be uncovered. "The Reverse Side" has succeeded if it causes the reader to wonder if there is in fact any cultural or personal story in his or her own life that is off-limits to examination or questioning.

A reader who hungers for greater drama, more musical or complex language, or who longs to have the top of the head taken off, may not be fully satisfied by "The Reverse Side." But the poem has its place in *Different Hours*, where it works as an intriguing gateway to the third section of the book and provides a moment of satisfying speculation and mystery among other poems that are more straightforward. The "house" of poetry is big: there is room for this relatively quiet, restrained poem that combines aspects of the meditative and lyric modes. In other corners of the house of poetry is the gorgeous musical language of William Shakespeare and John Keats; the long, extravagant, "disorderly" odes of Walt Whitman, Federíco Garcia Lorca, and Alan Ginsberg; and the dark, intense, strange lyrics of Martha Rhodes and Louise Glück, to name just a few poets who might be contrasted with Dunn. The house of poetry as a whole, and even the work of these poets with far different temperaments, benefit from the presence of Dunn's modest voice, which attempts to speak in a way that is clear but never simplistic.

Source: Patrick Donnelly, Critical Essay on "The Reverse Side," in *Poetry for Students*, Thomson Gale, 2005.

C. E. Murray

In the following review excerpt, Murray praises Dunn's conversational style and delightfully taut lyricism in Different Hours.

The sampling of voices and poetic values in the five collections gathered here may serve to illustrate the scope, depth, and dimension of current American poetry, which seems to me based on a kind of collective unconscious. That is, the amazing expansive range of poetic styles and aesthetics that we label American has developed over three-quarters of a century of argument and innovation and counter-argument and counterinnovation, and the traces of that ferment show themselves in rich and varied ways: While Stephen Dunn offers a profound and unadorned vision of American middle-class life during middle age, Laurence Lieberman's latest immersion into Carribean island myths and misty realities provides revelations about survival on the edges of existence. David Bottoms's renderings of the South are deeply entangled with personal histories and mysteries, and Lynn Emanuel lyrically explores themes of self-consciousness, curious relationships, and literary obsessions. Lynne McMahon's jump-cut observations of self and her fresh guidance on intellectual resurrections are an altogether different treat.

Stephen Dunn's eleventh collection speaks volumes about the prominent place he has earned in American poetry. First, there is the consistent quality of his production at the far edge of mid-career. Then there are his graceful, fearless insights into the riches and ravages of middle age—whether basic conflicts of memory and desire, or related conditions of heightening mind and declining body, or the dailiness of life slowly draining of time. Last, and perhaps most remarkably, there is Dunn's conversational style, no doubt hard-earned but in its effect so casual, apropos, and compelling that it quietly surrounds the reader with recognitions that both inform and surprise.

> *"Balancing a wry and altogether individual sensibility with and against an unobtrusive technical control, his latest collection is full of cautious smiles, acquaintance with disappointment, and, as always, a delightfully taut lyricism."*

The opening poem of *Different Hours*, "Before the Sky Darkens," establishes Dunn's tone and temperament as he acknowledges advancing meanings of time past and time left:

More and more you learn to live
with the unacceptable.
You sense the ever-hidden God
retreating even farther,
terrified or embarrassed.
You might as well be a clown,
big silly clothes, no evidence of desire.

That's how you feel, say, on a Tuesday.
Then out of the daily wreckage
comes an invitation
with your name on it. Or more likely,
that best girl of yours offers you,
once again, a small local kindness.

These are splendid stanzas. In the first few lines, Dunn lets us know that by his estimation things aren't great—even your hard-to-find God figure is having second thoughts as you play the emasculated fool. Yet there's hope—the possibility of getting lucky with the current love of your life. All this may leave readers wondering whether existence at this juncture is merely dreary or really dreadful. Are we talking the price of salvation, or just another good time before it's finally over?

Dunn's apparent resignation to dwindling expectations is, in effect, his way of focusing on mortality. He says, "I like the intelligibility of old songs, / I prefer yesterday." This sense of diminishment seems only half-hearted, though, and it's certainly ironic. Dunn is well-known for turning the mildly uncomfortable or even absurd situation to poetic advantage—and bravo for him. In "At the Restaurant," he again strives for two pounds of meaning in a one-pound bag, allowing how protocol and manners are fine but far from enough for any life that is passionately experienced:

Certainly you believe a part of decency
is to overlook, to let pass?
Praise the Caesar salad. Praise Susan's

black dress, Paul's promotion and raise.
Inexcusable, the slaughter in this world.
Insufficient, the merely decent man.

Whatever happened to courage and outspokenness? Who can still connect brains with guts in a world given to easy compromise, indulgence, and caveat?

The methodical, IV-dripping sense of demise extends to one of Dunn's favorite pastimes—pickup basketball. Indeed, Dunn—who played for Hofstra University—may be America's number-one poet when it comes to draining a twenty-foot jump shot. Here he stares down a full-court press with his ego exposed like a blown-out shoe, in "Losing Steps":

Suddenly you're fifty;
if you know anything about steps
you're playing chess
with an old, complicated friend.

But you're walking to a schoolyard
where kids are playing full-court,
telling yourself
the value of experience, a worn down

basketball under your arm,
your legs hanging from your waist
like misplaced sloths in a country
known for its cheetahs and its sunsets.

Despite his protests, Dunn the poet remains quick, funny, and fit, ever seeking that "wild incipience in the air," or better and "Simpler Times":

I wanted to be a regular guy,
she a popular girl.
That night she baby-sat, oh
a breast never again would be
that sufficient or that bare.
I stopped right there.

This isn't merely a clichéd longing for when the baby-boom generation "ran in from the clean, safe streets / to laugh at Milton Berle." The memory is downloaded with its accuracy and feeling complete, a resonating moral certainty. For all that appears to be complaint and disappointment, the net effect of Dunn's writing is one of fundamental encounter with what is best about being alive: love, art, interesting work, self-discovery.

It should be noted that Dunn uses as an epigraph the famous line of the Portuguese poet Fernando Pessoa that "Life would be unbearable / if we made ourselves conscious of it." He also quotes Reynolds Price: "I regret only my economies." These thoughts anchor the continuing tensions that make Dunn's insights so viable. When he complains about "chronic emptiness" or suggests that "It's time to give up the search for the invisible," he also argues on behalf of "the fundamental business / of making do with what's been left us." To be sure, he reveals a joy in despair, high hopes in the face of defeat. This is a poet who exudes the demeanor to handle crisis with unusual grace.

Dunn also is firmly grounded in good sense, wisdom, and honest-to-God fears. The title poem opens with the poet surviving the kind of small-plane turbulence that leaves one prepared to kiss the good earth and thankful to have a future. Forget the diet; I'm alive and still able to enjoy that "dreamy life of uncommitted crimes." But as the dust of this life-or-death brush settles, existence returns to its limitations, intuitions, reciprocities, poor timing, occasional luck, and temporary respite from what inevitably ails you—as in the title poem:

No doubt, too, at this very moment
a snake is sunning itself in Calcutta.
And somewhere a philosopher is erasing
"time's empty passing" because he's seen
a woman in a ravishing dress.
In a different hour he'll put it back.

"Make it simple and sad" serves as mantra and motto here. Balancing a wry and altogether individual sensibility with and against an unobtrusive technical control, his latest collection is full of cautious smiles, acquaintance with disappointment, and, as always, a delightfully taut lyricism. Dunn is a force to be embraced.

Source: C. E. Murray, "The Collective Unconscious," in *Southern Review*, Winter 2001, pp. 404–08.

Judith Kitchen

In the following review, Kitchen praises Dunn's poetry for being the surprise that keeps on surprising and identifies Different Hours *as being less about the self and more about the realm of ideas.*

The difference between the elegant and the satisfying may be relevant to poetry. If a mathematical proof can be recognized for *what* it accomplishes, then some poems might be termed satisfying for their significance, their orchestration of meaning.

In Stephen Dunn's latest book, several poems fit that description. That is, they manage to become more of an already good thing. *Different Hours* has a lot of what we've come to expect from Dunn: wit and wisdom in equal measure, playful banter between epigraph and poem, serious dialogue between epigraph and poem, serious encounter with idea and concept, love of life. But there's a newfound sense of mortality that governs its message. On the back cover, Dunn states, "I am interested in exploring the 'different' hours, not only of one's life, but also of the larger historical and philosophical life beyond the personal."

Yet Dunn has made his trademark the idiosyncrasies of the personal. A few years ago, in a review of one of his books (see *The Georgia Review,* Winter 1996), I said, "My suspicion is that Dunn's inner landscape is even darker and more honest than his guileless speaker is willing to reveal—an idealess, imageless, almost wordless space in which he knows that the fragile body prays to an absent God and goes unheard." As if in answer, *Different Hours* admits some of that terrain—one poem is entitled "The Death of God"—and then explores it.

Dunn's poems never call attention to their craft, but he combines an ease of grace and wit, a simplicity of diction, and a rhythmical flow so that, neither image-ridden nor highly metaphorical, still his poems manage to mean more than they say. They reverberate with a kind of "aftershock," the surprise that keeps surprising. This is true for this collection as well, so the difference here is one of degree: the poems have become a fraction more serious, a smidgen more contemplative, a speck more solemn. And there is a slight shift in emphasis—*Different Hours* is not quite as interested in self, or others, as it is in the realm of ideas. He alerts us to this with certain gestures, as at the end of "Irresistible," where the simple description of the events in a movie gives way to his own interpretation:

That would have been understandable

and simply moral, and I wouldn't
have walked out into the welter
of the night, into the fraught air,
so happily implicated and encumbered.

Diction dictates stance, and the elevated language alerts the reader to the fact that something is at stake (although how many times can a word like *fraught* appear in one book?). The speaker is encumbered—happily so—by the complex, even perverse, ways of the heart. Never willing to settle for the "simply moral," for what Dunn later calls the "virtue" of the seldom-tempted, he is happy in his implication.

So this time I select a poem that ostensibly conforms to Dunn's own directive. Certainly its title announces something beyond the personal. In fact, its title raises—before the fact—all the red flags: of

"Dunn's poems never call attention to their craft, but he combines an ease of grace and wit, a simplicity of diction, and a rhythmical flow so that, neither image-ridden nor highly metaphorical, still his poems manage to mean more than they say."

exploitation, of the possibilities for expected response or false insight, and of the poet's appropriation of the subject matter.

Oklahoma City

The accused chose to plead innocent
because he was guilty. We allowed such a thing;
it was one of our greatnesses, nutty, protective.
On the car radio a survivor's ordeal, her leg
amputated without anesthesia while trapped

under a steel girder. Simply, no big words—
that's how people tell their horror stories.
I was elsewhere, on my way to a party.
On arrival, everyone was sure to be carrying
a piece of the awful world with him.

Not one of us wouldn't be smiling.
There'd be drinks, irony, hidden animosities.
Something large would be missing.
But most of us would understand
something large always would be missing.

Oklahoma City was America reduced
to McVeigh's half-thought-out thoughts.
Did he know anything about suffering?
It's the naïve among us who are guilty
of wondering if we're moral agents or madmen

or merely, as one scientist said,
a fortuitous collocation of atoms.
Some mysteries can be solved by ampersands.
Ands not *ors;* that was my latest answer.
At the party two women were talking

about how strange it is that they still like men.
They were young and unavailable, and their lovely
faces
evoked a world not wholly incongruent
with the world I know. I had no illusions, not even
hopes,
that their beauty had anything to do with goodness.

Dunn manages to avoid the pitfalls precisely because this poem *is* personal. The speaker is on his way to a party. Life goes on and, in this case, its banality accentuates the import of the larger issues. So the difference here is in the *way* Dunn is personal. He has always wryly pointed the finger at himself, but now he seems a bit more willing to implicate others as well. The poem circles and circles, moving from the inconceivable event to the all-too-conceivable self and back, as though trying to find the "something large" that it admits outright will always be missing. And still the poem itself probes for an answer.

At work here is what I would call a deliberate deflation. The event in all its horror is undercut by the fact that it is being reported, then re-reported at the party, reduced to small talk even as it occupies the center of attention. The speaker, rather than imagining the victims, the devastation, the aftermath, simply recounts the words of the one who experienced its reality. "Simply, no big words—" a prescription for poetry, for how to make it real. Poetry, then, might be able to do justice to the rippling implications of Oklahoma City. The echo of Auden in stanza four at least suggests that the masters know more about suffering than does McVeigh; poetry is, after all, thought-out thoughts. But that would be far too obvious for a poem by Stephen Dunn, and so we are forced to turn to the last stanza, to the way "the world I know" occupies the same line as the lack of illusions or hopes. Although the poet describes his own lack of hope, the "I" becomes generic as we face our own dark honesties. Under Dunn's subtle direction, we implicate ourselves.

How has he accomplished this? With orchestral legerdemain, the poem alternates between the world of the party (which ironically contains the world of ideas) and the world of half-thought thoughts (which overlaps with the physical world of pain). We are never in one place for long. Instead, we are forced to see the event in a context—and it happens to be the context in which most of us find ourselves most of the time: we participate peripherally, as observers, and we try to make sense of it. We want to know *why.* Rights and wrongs eddy in these stanzas. They mix with each other until they solidify: an alloy of competing loyalties and conflicting ideas. The hole at the center of rationality is set against the very rationalism of the Constitution. Science, religion, politics—nothing will serve up an answer. Nothing is transformed.

We're happy enough to watch someone implicate himself, but less willing to walk out of a poem fully encumbered. Yet, under the right circumstances, we appreciate the weight of obligation—and that is precisely what gives Dunn's poems their satisfying quality. The significance here is the mesh in which we see our lives and their often-unacted-upon insights so deftly reproduced.

I think I am still holding in my mind some sense of the *form* of elegance. The poetry of poetry. On the radio, the sportscaster calls the plays. In my mind's eye, I see the game unfold. Players I have come to know move on an imaginary plane. The ball laces the field. The team has found its form, the announcer says. For a moment, the game is beautiful.

Source: Judith Kitchen, "In Pursuit of Elegance," in *Georgia Review*, Vol. 54, No. 4, Winter 2000, pp. 763–80.

SuAnne Doak

In the following essay, Doak discusses Dunn's education, career, and major works.

On the back of the book jacket of Stephen Dunn's 1989 collection of poems, *Between Angels*, Philip Booth states, "To read Stephen Dunn . . . is to see the complexities of one's own dailiness brought to light . . . One starts to see the flower on the kitchen table." It is this ability to bring to light both the ordinary, expected, nonthreatening aspects of life and the inexplicable, startling, even subversive elements of human existence that has made Dunn one of the best poetic voices of the late twentieth century.

Stephen Dunn was born on 24 June 1939 in Forest Hills, New York, to a salesman, Charles F. Dunn, and his wife, Ellen Fleishman Dunn. He received a degree in history from Hofstra University (B.A., 1962), played pro basketball for the Williamsport (Pennsylvania) Billies from 1962 to 1963, and afterward worked a few years as an advertising copywriter in New York City. In 1966 Dunn went to Spain, as he says, "to try to change my life and see if I could write poetry, which I had started to write after a failed attempt at a novel." He was encouraged by friend and novelist Sam Toperoff, and two years later he enrolled in the creative-writing program at Syracuse University, studying with Philip Booth, Donald Justice, George P. Elliott, and W. D. Snodgrass.

After graduating from Syracuse (M.A., 1970), Dunn taught fiction at Southwest Minnesota State (1970–1973) and was a visiting lecturer in poetry at Syracuse (1973–1974). Since 1974 he has been a professor of creative writing at Stockton State College in Pomona, New Jersey, while residing in Port Republic with his wife Lois Kelly—a chef he married on 26 September 1964—and their two daughters, Andrea and Susanne.

He has also been adjunct professor of poetry at Columbia University (1983–1987), visiting poet at the University of Washington (1980), and has conducted poetry workshops at Bennington Writers Workshop (1983–1987) and Aspen Writers Conference (1977, 1987), among other places. He has served as director of the Associated Writing Programs' Poetry Series (1980–1982) and has given poetry readings at Yale University, the University of Texas, and the University of Utah, to name a few.

A partial list of Dunn's awards includes the Academy of American Poets Award (Syracuse University, 1970), the Theodore Roethke Prize (*Poetry Northwest*, 1977), a Guggenheim Fellowship (1984–1985), Writing Fellowships to Yaddo (1979–1989), National Endowment for the Arts Creative Writing Fellowships (1973, 1983, 1989), the Helen Bullis Prize (*Poetry Northwest*, 1983), and the Levinson Prize (*Poetry*, 1987). In addition to nine poetry collections (including one chapbook), Dunn has published reviews, essays, and interviews, and his work has appeared in many magazines and anthologies.

Looking for Holes in the Ceiling (1974), his first full-length book, which he considers "poetry that arose from my imagist education," is a strong collection, exhibiting a deft, spare style and evocative imagery. In "The Loss" he writes, "Even the tips of their fingers seem to be retreating," and in "Day and Night Handball" the ball is "hitting and dying like a butterfly / on a windshield."

The speaker in some of the poems is more distant than in Dunn's later work. "An Ambulance is Coming" describes how "a glove is lying on the curb. / There is a hand in it." But other poems have the ability to involve readers more; in them appears his distinctive, conversational voice, his ease of expression that contains depth of meaning. "The Rider" confides, "It is with me, that falling star," asking:

> Who will believe me
> if I insist
> that a large man was riding it,
> and the shell of a body
> drove my car home into the vacancies
> of garage and self,
> without mishap, or a single regret?

Present in many of the poems is an implied violation of benign-appearing situations that Dunn uses with great effect here and in subsequent books. The title character in "Fat Man, Floating" "would like to follow [the fish] / to the bottom . . . and live without the kind of breath / people shape into knives." Moving from the imagined into the real world, Dunn presages another cachet in his mature work: the ability to offer insights without didacticism.

> *"It is this ability to bring to light both the ordinary, expected, nonthreatening aspects of life and the inexplicable, startling, even subversive elements of human existence that has made Dunn one of the best poetic voices of the late twentieth century."*

Full of Lust and Good Usage (1976) manifests his further turn to the personal and the direct, containing sharply drawn imagery and free verse that balances musicality with plain speech. In "In the Room," for example, Dunn writes, "He lets the laugh / bubble up from the webs / of his chest . . . . / He could have lava on his shoulders, / he is that weighted down."

Familial relationships, which Dunn examines with compassion and sensitivity, comprise one motif. Uncloying affection is shown in "Grandfather," in which the title character's "fingers were a cage / and I the bird / he wanted to burst / unharmed into the world." In "Waiting with Two Members of a Motorcycle Gang for My Child to be Born," the gang members shake the speaker's hand, but "it might / have been my head," and he concludes with a wish that his daughter "make men better than they are."

"One Side of the Story" describes a woman who "had the black dress on." The narrator is "thinking of ways to keep the light going." As in succeeding books, Dunn explores in this poem the theme of a relationship's difficult mutuality with eloquent articulation, ending: "The lights go out when we blow them out / or turn them off. It would be lovely, / wouldn't it? to think only what's been felt / remains: that black dress on the floor, / your skin and the drift of my hands."

At times in *Full of Lust* Dunn inserts extraneous images, such as that of "Sophia Loren . . .

plac[ing] her / finger on a knot you are tying" ("Small Town: Cracks & Departures"), but most of the metaphors are relevant and incisive without histrionics. "Truck Stop: Minnesota" begins, "The waitress looks at my face / as if it were a small tip," and "For the Sleepless" focuses on "the dead, frozen bird / I stuffed in the garbage / [that] appears before my eyes."

A Circus of Needs (1978) completes what Dunn calls his "preparation for writing poetry." The strength of the collection lies in his increased ability to offer introspections about everyday life without succumbing to banality. "Essay on Sanity" cogently rejects veneration of the psychotic in poetry, arguing that even if those who are suicidal do "get to the reddest heart of things / it's because they can't see / the world of appearances." Insanity is an intrusion upon "the calm small ordinary / exchanges between people / who know knives / every once in a while are *not* / the silvercoated castrati of their worst dreams."

He injects wry humor into poems such as "Modern Dance Class," where an instructor considers the speaker a "toad among butterflies / he can't bear to look." Dunn returns to erotic discourse with "Scenario," which describes a romantic assignation at "Cafe del Amor," where the speaker says, "when sex intrudes / let no more than a gesture / end the tension." In "Belly Dancer at the Hotel Jerome," Dunn observes that "Fatima" is "blonde, midwestern," but her skill "danced the mockery out / of [her] wrong name."

By the time of his 1981 collection, *Work and Love*, Dunn was writing what he terms "poems in his own voice," initiating "a continuum on man/woman relationships," but touching upon other concerns as well. "Late Summer"—with its powerful contrast of "the magnificance, the variety, of animals . . . / "which is a sensible man's proof / that God exists," to Dachau, "a sensible man's proof of the opposite"—is only one instance where he broadens his scope from an inward-looking cosmology.

On occasion he risks glibness, but unlike lesser poets, he is able to pivot from levity to profoundness, first startling, then pleasing readers with his virtuosity. "Poems for People Who Are Understandably too Busy to Read Poetry" opens with this line: "Relax. This won't last long," but ends with "what poetry can do. / Imagine yourself a caterpillar. / *There's an awful shrug and, suddenly, / you're beautiful for as long as you live.*"

At other times Dunn evokes a more poignant mood. In "At the Film Society" a man/woman interlude occurs after a couple has watched a film in which "Liv Ullman touches . . . with a lust so deepened by grief / the rest of us feel our miseries / are amateurish," and "the best sex rises / like a trapped beast from our vacancies," compelling language that does not need embellishment.

The poem "Essay on the Personal" sets the tone of *Not Dancing* (1984): "finally the personal / is all that matters." In this book, Dunn hones both his subject matter and style, exploring new avenues to familiar topics and, from this point on, relying less on concrete imagery. In "Sick Days" he writes, "To stay at home is to believe too much / in the cycle of the water pump, / the ritual of cleanliness and food," and the abstractions "cycle" and "ritual" form a congruence with his lack of belief in the safety such terms promulgate.

Just when his analysis of everyday life strikes one as restrictive, he turns to universalities, grounding them in experience. Death, in "Wavelengths," is "a music . . . both popular and private," and fear is known by those "who've had experience with the dark / and know how it speaks." Loneliness is contemplated in "Atlantic City" while the narrator watches "the ocean in winter," which is "repetition's secret / link with solace."

"The Routine Things Around the House" describes a twelve-year-old boy's awakening sexuality:

I had asked my mother (I was trembling)
if I could see her breasts
and she took me into her room
without embarrassment or coyness
and I started at them,
afraid to ask for more.

Jonathan Holden commends Dunn's ability to achieve "aesthetic distance" and find "where the violence within meets, on equal terms, the violence without . . . ." Dunn considers the poem less about an event than "a legacy of limits." Because the boy's mother did not refuse his request or step beyond that disclosure, he is later able "to love women easily." And because Dunn does not cross the line between revelation and exposure, he is able to share that discovery with readers.

Local Time (1986), chosen for the National Poetry Series, exemplifies Dunn's definition of poetry as "an act of coherence amidst the fragmentation of modern life." In "Round Trip," after the speaker is mugged and has "closed the door and [given] whatever in [him] wanted to be alone and pitied / its hard uncomfortable chair," the speaker is once again a sane man grappling with the world's madness, yet still able to hope.

The long, meditative title poem, "Local Time," also ponders outside menaces to a safe domestic world: "The house had double locks / but in the dark a wrong person / would understand: the windows / were made of glass . . . ." Jennifer Krauss comments that it is "between the well-lit front porch and what's 'out there' in the dark that . . . Dunn's poetry dwells."

An element of this apprehension is evident in "Letter Home," in which the narrator admits his inherent, but often inadmissible, fear and need to the woman he addresses: "Last night during a thunderstorm, / awakened and half-awake, / I wanted to climb into bed / on my mother's side, be told / everything's all right—."

In "Parable of the Fictionist" the speaker confesses that he "sometimes longed / for what he'd dare not alter . . . something immutable or so lovely he might be changed by it." Dunn defines the term *fictionist* as "essentially someone who makes things up so that they will be true." This definition is important when applied to his work, because he states: "Though my poems apparently and often do draw from experience, I insist for myself that my poems go beyond their original intent. I feel that I'm in a poem with the first moment I startle myself. That moment usually creates an imaginative imperative that I try to extend and be equal to."

Between Angels continues Dunn's evolution into a poet whose concerns, according to Gregory Djanikian, represent a balance "between personal event and a broader historical perspective, between specific emotional upheavals and general categories of feeling and being" (*Philadelphia Inquirer*, 30 July 1989). The title of the poem "Sweetness" is an abstraction Dunn makes tangible by his inclusion of a discussion of the death of a friend's lover: the speaker offers "the one or two words we have for such grief / until we were speaking only in tones."

Tonal shading is what Dunn explores in "Tenderness": "Oh abstractions are just abstract / until they have an ache in them." He displays both subtlety and explicitness, as in "Clarities," dealing with a Chilean girl tortured to death:

> Sometimes there's a pity
> only the self can give, amniotic,
> a total curling in.
> I wish
> they had killed him, the father,
> allowed some end to what he saw.

"Forgiveness" offers initial tolerance for the "terrorist [who] pulls a pin: / Forgive the desperate, the homeless, / the crazed," but the speaker gives way to blunt anger: "No, no more good reasons." Poems such as "To A Terrorist" attempt to reach some understanding of people who perpetrate violence, "knowing there's nothing, / not even revenge, which alleviates / a life like yours," but to whom the narrator finally must say: "I hate the hatefulness that makes you fall / in love with death, your own included."

The title poem, "Between Angels," returns to the complex frustrations of "the bluesy middle ground / of desire and withdrawal . . . among the bittersweet / efforts of people to connect," asking, "The angels out there, / what are they?" The ambiguous boundaries of contemporary life cause Dunn to muse, "Oh, everything's true / at different times / in the capacious day," ruefully admitting the triviality of middle-class vicissitudes compared to those of "half the people in the world / [who] are dispossessed."

It is this duality of internal and exterior considerations that makes Dunn an extraordinary poet. Not only is he capable of investigating the personal without becoming confessional or mundane, he augments his range with external issues. In an age of prosaic diction, he imbues discursive language with lyric intensity, yet does not bombard readers with hyperbole. He maintains an impeccable balance between clarity and concealment, and he remains one of the best practitioners of a realistic and compassionate approach to relationships between men and women. Dunn's latest collection is *Landscape at the End of the Century* (1991).

Source: SuAnne Doak, "Stephen Dunn," in *Dictionary of Literary Biography*, Vol. 105, *American Poets Since World War II, Second Series*, edited by R. S. Gwynn, Gale Research, 1991, pp. 80–86.

Sources

Brown, Joyce S., "The *Hours* and the Times," in *City Paper* (Baltimore), June 13, 2001.

Budy, Andrea Hollander, "Finding the Hidden Darkness Everywhere," in *Arkansas Democrat-Gazette*, December 24, 2000.

Christophersen, Bill, "Down from the Tower: Poetry as Confabulation," in *Poetry*, Vol. 179, No. 4, January 2002, pp. 219–20.

Dostoevsky, Fyodor, *The Brothers Karamazov*, translated by Constance Garnett, 1879, reprint, Barnes & Noble Books, 1995.

Dunn, Stephen, *Different Hours*, W. W. Norton, 2000.

———, *New and Selected Poems, 1974–1994*, W. W. Norton, 1994.

———, *Walking Light: Memoirs and Essays on Poetry*, revised edition, Boa Editions Limited, 2001.

Dunn, Stephen, and Angela Elam, Interview, in *New Letters on the Air*, http://www.newletters.org, 1996.

Dunn, Stephen, and Philip Dacey, Interview with Stephen Dunn, in *Cortland Review*, at http://www.cortlandreview.com/features/00/03/index.html, March 2000 (last accessed May 17, 2004).

Keats, John, "To George and Tom Keats," in *Selected Letters of John Keats*, rev. ed., edited by Grant F. Scott, Harvard University Press, 2002, pp. 59–61.

Kenkyusha's New Japanese-English Dictionary, edited by Koh Masada, Kenkyusha, 1974, pp. 1921–22.

Lawless, James, "Pulitzer Prize Winner's Collection Has an Easy, Conversational Air," in *Cleveland Plain Dealer*, July 15, 2001.

The New Oxford American Dictionary, edited by Elizabeth J. Jewell and Frank R. Abate, Oxford University Press, 2001.

Nussbaum, Emily, "Poetry in Brief," in *New York Times Book Review*, August 19, 2001, p. 25.

Romano, Carlin, "From Snack Sonnets to Pulitzer Poetry," in *Philadelphia Inquirer*, April 29, 2001.

Shelly, Kevin C., "Poetic Injustice," in *Philadelphia*, May 2002.

Further Reading

Hirsch, Edward, *How to Read a Poem and Fall in Love with Poetry*, Harcourt, 1999.

This book is a collection of essays about poems from all over the world and from many different eras and includes a glossary of poetic terms and a bibliography.

Morris, John Graves, "Imaginative Imperatives and Intimate Ruminations: An Interview with Stephen Dunn," in *Hayden's Ferry Review*, Issue 28, Spring–Summer 2001.

In this interview, which took place in 2000, Dunn discusses the writers and life events that influenced his own writing.

Nims, John Frederick, and David Mason, eds., *Western Wind: An Introduction to Poetry*, 4th ed., McGraw Hill, 2000.

This book provides a guide to the different forms of poetry, including free verse, and an anthology of poetry in English.

Young, Dean, *Skid*, University of Pittsburgh Press, 2002.

To understand the wide variety of tone of early twenty-first-century American poetry, it is instructive to read Dean Young's poems in contrast with Dunn's. Dunn and Young share an obsession with mortality and have the same appetite for moral complexity. Wit is characteristic of both poets. But while Dunn's poems are plainspoken, Young's are wildly surreal; while Dunn is relatively well-behaved and restrained, Young is extravagant and mischievous.

Station

Eamon Grennan

1991

"Station" is a poem written in free verse by Eamon Grennan, an Irish poet who has spent most of his adult life in the United States. It was first published in 1991 in Grennan's collection *As If It Matters* (Dublin, Ireland, 1991; St. Paul, MN, 1992). It is also available in Grennan's *Relations: New and Selected Poems* (1998).

In "Station," the speaker and his young son are at the Hudson Valley train station in upstate New York. The boy's parents are divorced, and he is about to leave his father and go to visit his mother. The poem describes the scene at the train station and the thoughts of the boy's father, who knows this is a turning point in his relationship with his son; not only is the boy going away, he is also about to enter adolescence. This is a stage, a "station," along the boy's path to adulthood, and the father knows that things will never again be the same between them. He also realizes that he cannot find the right words to say to his son on this occasion.

One of a number of prominent Irish poets who live in America and teach at American universities, Grennan has written nine books of poetry. He has a growing reputation as one of Ireland's most accomplished contemporary poets. Grennan's work is notable for its concern with personal relationships, particularly within the family. His poems often describe the small details of domestic life, and a number of them explore the poet's relationship with his three children.

Eamon Grennan

Author Biography

Eamon Grennan was born November 13, 1941, in Dublin, Ireland, the son of Thomas P. (an educational administrator) and Evelyn (Yourell) Grennan and was raised in middle-class suburban Dublin. Grennan's interest in literature was first awakened by a young teacher named Gus Martin, at a boarding school run by Cistercian monks that Grennan attended. Martin managed to communicate to the adolescent Grennan his own enthusiasm for Shakespeare and other writers.

Grennan studied literature at University College, Dublin, where, as Grennan later wrote, he was fortunate to have teachers who nurtured his literary interests. Grennan was awarded a bachelor of arts degree in 1963 and a master of arts degree in 1964.

In the late 1960s, Grennan attended graduate school at Harvard University, where he continued to be inspired by what he described in the preface to *Facing the Music: Irish Poetry in the Twentieth Century* (1999), quoting Edmund Spenser, as "the brightness of brave and glorious words." He had a particular interest in Shakespeare and wrote his dissertation on Shakespeare's history plays. He earned a Ph.D. from Harvard University in 1973. The following year, Grennan became a member of the English faculty at Vassar College in Poughkeepsie, New York. Grennan went on to become the Dexter M. Ferry Jr. Professor of English at Vassar. He also taught Irish Studies at Villanova University.

In 1972, Grennan married Joan Perkins. They were divorced in 1986. Grennan's subsequent partner was Rachel Kitzinger, a college teacher. He has three children, Kate, Conor, and Kira.

Grennan's first three collections of poetry were all published in Ireland: *Wildly for Days* (1983), *What Light There Is* (1987), and *Twelve Poems, Occasional Works* (1988). With the publication in the United States of his fourth collection, *What Light There Is and Other Poems* (1989), Grennan began to gain a reputation among American as well as Irish readers. This collection was followed by *As If It Matters*, published in Ireland in 1991 and the United States in 1992, which includes the poem "Station." *So It Goes* was published in both countries simultaneously in 1995. *Relations: New and Selected Poems* followed in 1998.

Grennan received a National Endowment for the Arts award in 1991 and a Guggenheim fellowship in 1995. He won the James Boatwright Poetry Prize from *Shenandoah* magazine in 1995.

Other publications by Grennan are his translation of *Selected Poems of Giacomo Leopardi* (Dublin, 1995; Princeton, NJ, 1997). This book won the PEN Award for Poetry in Translation. *Facing the Music* is a collection of Grennan's previously published essays, spanning the years 1977 to 1997. His other works include *Selected and New Poems* (2000) and *Still Life with Waterfall* (2002). The latter was awarded the 2003 Lenore Marshall Poetry Prize, which annually honors the most outstanding book of poems published in the United States.

Poem Text

We are saying goodbye
on the platform. In silence
the huge train waits, crowding the station
with aftermath and longing
and all we've never said
to one another. He shoulders
his black dufflebag and shifts
from foot to foot, restless to be off, his eyes
wandering over tinted windows where he'll sit
staring out at the Hudson's platinum dazzle.

I want to tell him he's entering into the light
of the world, but it feels like a long tunnel
as he leaves one home, one parent

for another, and we both
know in our bones it won't ever
be the same again. What is the air at,
heaping between us then
thinning to nothing? Or those slategrey birds
that croon to themselves in an iron angle
and then take flight—inscribing
huge loops of effortless grace
between this station of shade and the shining water?

When our cheeks rest glancing against each other,
I feel mine scratchy with beard and stubble, his
not quite smooth as a girl's, harder, a faint fuzz
starting—those silken beginnings I can see
when the light is right, his next life
in bright first touches. What ails our hearts? Mine
aching in vain for the words
to make sense of our life together; his
fluttering in dread
of my finding the words, feathered syllables
fidgeting in his throat.

In a sudden rush of bodies
and announcements out of the air, he says
he's got to be going. One quick touch
and he's gone. In a minute
the train—ghostly faces behind smoked glass—
groans away on wheels and shackles, a slow glide
I walk beside, waving
at what I can see no longer. Later,
on his own in the city, he'll enter the underground
and cross the river, going home
to his mother's house. And I imagine
that pale face of his
carried along in the dark glass, shining
through shadows that fill the window
and fall away again
before we're even able to name them.

Poem Summary

"Station" begins with a simple sentence announcing "we" are on a railway station platform and are about to say goodbye to each other. The train is waiting, ready to depart, and the speaker is already imagining how he might feel when his son is gone. He is aware, in a regretful sense, of all the things he and his son have never said to each other. The implication is that there may be no more time or no other opportunity to say such things.

The boy puts "his black dufflebag" on his shoulder and shifts his weight "from foot to foot," perhaps indicating his discomfort with the prospect of saying goodbye to his father. The son is impatient to be on his way, and he looks not at his father but at the windows of the train. His father imagines him sitting in the train and staring out of the window at the play of light ("platinum dazzle") on the water of the Hudson River.

The father wants to give his son some encouraging, uplifting words before he leaves, but he is also conscious of his own mixed feelings. Although his son is about to enter the big, wide world, it seems to the father that the boy is about to go into a "long tunnel." The boy is leaving one parent for another, and father and son both know their relationship, as well as the boy's life, will never be the same again. The air between them seems thick with thoughts that ought to be expressed but then suddenly thin again, as if the moment has passed. The father's attention goes to the birds that "croon to themselves" in the angles between the iron girders at the top of the building ("iron angles") and then fly off gracefully over the river.

In the third stanza, the moment of farewell comes. Father and son embrace, their cheeks resting against each other. The father is conscious of the difference in their skin, his unshaven and bristly, his son's smooth but also showing the first signs of growing hair ("faint fuzz"), which reminds the father that his son is on the verge of puberty and adolescence. The father also realizes neither he nor his son is happy at this moment. His heart aches because he cannot find the right words to say to his son at this moment of departure, and he knows his son dreads an emotional scene in which his father *does* find the right words.

A sudden rush of people moving around them and announcements over the loudspeakers indicate that the train is about to depart. The boy says he has to be going. He and his father touch quickly, and then the boy gets in the train and vanishes from the father's sight. A minute later the train departs, and the father walks alongside it, waving, even though he cannot see where his son is sitting. He imagines his son's journey to his mother's house. The train will go underground to cross the river, and the father imagines the boy's face visible through the reflections that fill the window and disappear before they can even be identified.

Themes

Life Journey and Transition

At the literal level of the poem, the journey the boy takes is from his father's home to his mother's home. But this journey also symbolizes the boy's journey in life, from childhood to adolescence and beyond, which is clear from the father's reference to the "faint fuzz" growing on the boy's face. The father sees this first sign of adolescence as a

Topics For Further Study

- Divorce is common today. Research and report on how children are affected by divorce. What factors should be considered in deciding with which parent a child lives after a divorce? Why?
- How does a free-verse poem differ from prose? Is free verse more effective than rhymed verse? Why or why not? Why are most modern poems written in free verse?
- Why do parents and adolescent children sometimes find it hard to communicate with one another? Do parents often want to know too much about their children's lives? How do good parents strike the right balance between guiding their children in the right direction and letting them go their own way to learn from their own mistakes?
- Compose your own free-verse poem about an incident in which you and one or both of your parents were unable to communicate something important to each other, something that really needed to be said. How did this incident affect your relationship with your parent(s)? What did it tell you about yourself or about your parent(s)?

"beginning," the visible evidence that the boy is about to leave childhood behind. The significance of this beginning is conveyed by the father's use of the phrase "his next life." In other words, the coming change is so radical it will seem as if the boy is living a different, entirely new life, not merely an extension of the life he is now living, such is the gulf between childhood and adolescence. The images in the poem reinforce this meaning of a journey to maturity. The boy is like a young bird preparing to fly from its nest, and the train is a symbol for the process of life that carries him inevitably into adolescence and adulthood, and away from his father.

Communication

Each stanza emphasizes that this scene is an awkward goodbye between father and son. Much is felt but little is said. The father is keenly aware of all the things that should be said now, in this moment of parting, and of all the things that, when opportunity was there in the past, were never said. He may be referring to words of love or appreciation or understanding. It is a common experience in human relationships: when the time comes to part from a loved one, either for a short while or permanently, words fail. Feelings are deep and words cannot rise to the occasion.

The second stanza further emphasizes this fact. Father and son are both aware of the significance of the occasion, that things will never again be the same between them. The air is thick ("heaping between them"), which suggests it is full of unexpressed thoughts, but then the air goes thin again ("thinning to nothing") as the thoughts disperse. There is a sharp contrast between this scene and the actions of the birds that croon to themselves contentedly, unconcerned with things unsaid and able to fly at will, making effortless loops in the air. The father's growing confusion in this moment is suggested by the fact that he frames his thoughts not as statements but as questions, as if he has suddenly found himself in a situation in which nothing really makes sense anymore.

The third stanza is even more explicit about this gap of silence. In the case of the boy, there is only a fluttering of "feathered syllables" in his throat; actual words are a long way off. The word "fluttering" suggests the ineffective struggles of a young bird trying to fly from its nest and reflects the previous stanza's image of crooning, effortlessly soaring birds. The father feels only confusion; he is unable to find the right words to say in the present moment, and he can no longer understand the nature of his relationship with his son. It is as if in this moment of departure everything is falling apart.

The fourth stanza brings further attention to the inadequacy of the farewell between father and son: "One quick touch / and he's gone." In spite of the awareness on both sides of the need for words, it appears that nothing at all is said. Instead one quick touch—not even a hug—is left to carry all the weight of meaning that cannot be summoned in words.

Style

Imagery

The poem has many contrasts between light and dark. These contrasts suggest the mixed feelings the father has about his son's departure. Light is first suggested by the phrase "platinum dazzle" and the phrase "he's entering into the light / of the world." This imagery continues when the father feels the first growth of down on the boy's face, which he knows he can see "when the light is right." He refers to it as the boy's "next life / in bright first touches."

These images of light are opposed by images of darkness, like the "long tunnel," which implies darkness and enclosure. The phrase "long tunnel" expresses the father's gloomy thoughts about his son's departure. Also the railway station is a "station of shade" (contrasted with the "shining water" on the river). "Shade" can also mean "ghost," which would link it to the line "ghostly faces behind smoked glass" (referring to the passengers in the train), as well as to the insubstantial, fleeting shadows evoked at the end of the poem.

Alliteration

The poetic device used most frequently in the poem is alliteration, which is the repetition of initial consonant sounds. The most sustained example is stretched over three lines at the end of the third stanza, when the father imagines what is going on in his son's mind, as he, the father, tries to find the right things to say: "fluttering in dread / of my finding the words, feathered syllables / fidgeting in his throat." The repetition of the "f" sound gives the impression of a stutter, of words about to come out but not finding a way. The image of a young bird about to fly from its nest is appropriate, since it suggests the boy who is on the verge of a new stage in his life, on the way to adulthood. Another example of the sustained use of alliteration comes in the final stanza, with the repetition of the "g" sound: "ghostly faces behind smoked glass—/ groans away on wheels and shackles, a slow glide."

Assonance

The lines quoted above also show the use of assonance, the repetition of vowel sounds occurring in nearby words. This can be heard in the long "o" sound in "ghostly," "smoked," "groans," and "slow," which emphasizes the slowness with which the train begins to pull away. Another example of assonance, again with the long "o" sound, comes in the second stanza in the lines "and we both / know in our bones it won't ever / be the same again." The identical vowel sounds in the words "both," "know," "bones," and "won't" give way sharply to the vowel "e" in "ever"; the sudden change in the vowel sound is in keeping with the sense that something will not "be the same again."

A further example of assonance is the long "i" sound in the lines "when the light is right, his next life / in bright first touches." The sequence "light," "right," "life," and "bright" brings out the positive nature of the father's thought at this point. These lines are also notable for the internal rhyme (a rhyme that occurs within a verse-line rather than at the end) in "light," "right," and "bright."

Historical Context

Divorce in America

The experience of the boy in "Station" dividing time between divorced parents has become increasingly familiar to American children during the last quarter of the twentieth century. The divorce level first began to rise in the 1960s and continued to rise even more sharply in the 1970s. In 1975 projections from statistics supplied by the Current Population Survey suggested that about one-third of married people between the ages of twenty-five and thirty-five would end their first marriage in divorce. By 1996 this figure had in fact been exceeded, with 40 percent of people in that category then divorced. The divorce rate peaked in 1979 and 1981, when 5.3 per every 1,000 couples were divorced. The figure dropped somewhat to 4.7 per every 1,000 couples in 1989 and 1990. In 1990, 16.8 per every 1,000 children under the age of eighteen were affected by divorce.

The rising divorce rate produced new challenges for the courts, which had to decide which parent was to be awarded custody. According to a report prepared by the National Center for Health Statistics, in 1990 the mother was awarded custody of the children 72 percent of the time, in divorces in which custody was awarded. Joint custody was the second most common arrangement (16 percent), while fathers were awarded custody in only 9 percent of divorces.

The increase in the number of divorces also steadily changed the nature of the American family. The number of single-parent families increased, as did the number of "blended" families, in which divorced parents remarried and created a new family unit with children from their previous marriages.

Many research studies in the 1980s examined the effects of divorce on children. The studies showed that effects varied according to the age of the child and that there were short-term as well as long-term effects. In the case of teenagers, research showed that parental divorce was correlated with lower academic performance, dropping out of high school, use of alcohol and drugs, and aggressive or promiscuous behavior.

Contemporary Irish Literature

Grennan is a notable contemporary voice in a long line of distinguished twentieth-century Irish poets. The most prominent of all was W. B. Yeats (1865–1939), who was awarded the Nobel Prize for literature in 1923. After Yeats, the best known poet in Ireland was Patrick Kavanagh, although two Irish poets in exile in England, Louis MacNeice and John Hewitt, also produced notable work.

Around the time of Kavanagh's death in 1967, a new generation of Irish poets began to make their mark. The most renowned of these poets is Seamus Heaney (born 1939), who was awarded the Nobel Prize for literature in 1995 and who is widely considered the greatest Irish poet since Yeats. Heaney was raised in Northern Ireland, and like most Irish poets of the time, his work was affected by the social unrest and violence that began in that province in 1969. From 1969 until the late-1990s, the Irish Republican Army fought a terrorist campaign to end British rule over Northern Ireland. Over 3,500 people were killed in the conflict, which pitted Protestants against Catholics. Heaney's volume *North* (1975) directly confronts the issue of sectarian violence in Northern Ireland. Other Irish poets whose work was influenced by what were called the "Troubles" are Michael Longley, Derek Mahon, Seamus Deane, and John Montague. Montague's epic poem *The Rough Field* (1972) explores Ireland's past and incorporates material drawn from the "Troubles."

Heaney is one of several Irish poets (including Grennan) who have spent at least part of their careers living and working in the United States. Although Heaney is a resident of Dublin, Ireland, he also teaches at Harvard University. Thomas Kinsella, who was born in Dublin in 1928, went on to a teaching career in the United States. His *Collected Poems* appeared in 2001. Since 1989 John Montague has regularly taught fiction workshops at the State University of New York at Albany. Eavan Boland, whose *Collected Poems* appeared in 1995, taught at Stanford University. Another leading voice in contemporary Irish poetry, Paul Muldoon, has lived in the United States since 1987; he is a professor at Princeton University, and in 1999 he was elected Professor of Poetry at the University of Oxford.

The dispersal of Irish poets over a wide geographical area has stimulated a debate about how to define Irish literature. In the case of Grennan, the fact that he was living in the United States when the "Troubles" first broke out may explain why his work, unusual amongst his generation of Irish poets, is apolitical. Reviewers have suggested that his work is less easily identifiable as Irish than the work of some of his contemporaries.

Critical Overview

Although "Station" has not attracted specific comment from reviewers, the poem exhibits many of the qualities that typify Grennan's work and have won praise from critics. As Ben Howard writes in a review of *As If It Matters* for *Poetry*: "Grennan examines the tensions and banalities of middle-class life, the dynamics of marriage and parenthood, the trauma of divorce, the pain of separation from a son and daughter." Howard notes the influence on Grennan's work of Seamus Heaney and concludes that "his poems reflect a sensibility tempered by experience but ready for the next uncommon moment."

In an appreciative review of *As If It Matters* for *Hudson Review*, James Finn Cotter observes that Grennan "seeks for order in the ordinary world," and finds "Grennan's poems at their best possess . . . [a] sense of permanence and serious purpose. Here is poetry that will last, that will be read long after the present shadows have passed."

In a review in *America* of Grennan's *Relations: New and Selected Poems*, Robert E. Hosmer Jr. describes Grennan as a "master in his prime." He also makes a comment that could be directly applied to "Station": "Grennan's poems maintain a delicate balance of line and tone, filled with tender feeling, but never lapsing into embarrassing sentimentality or unbecoming bitterness, as he catalogues events in an ordinary life."

Criticism

Bryan Aubrey

Aubrey holds a Ph.D. in English and has published many articles on twentieth-century literature. In this essay, Aubrey discusses "Station" and other poems by Grennan in the context of the poet's interest in silence and stillness.

"Station" is one of a number of Grennan's poems that deal with family interactions, both happy and sad. Some of these poems are directly about Grennan's three children, Conor, Kate, and Kira. *As If It Matters*, the collection in which "Station" first appeared, is framed by two such poems. The first poem in the book, "Two Climbing," is as much about fulfillment between father and son as "Station" is about awkwardness and loss. The poet and the twelve-year-old boy climb Tully Mountain in Ireland. Just as in "Station," not many words pass between them, but in the climbing expedition the silence is one of pleasure and fulfillment, not of confusion. Man and boy are pleased with themselves for having done "some dumb male thing," and this time Conor has no difficulty in finding the right word: "*adventure*."

Grennan's poem "Two Gathering" is about a trip made by the poet and his then nearly sixteen-year-old daughter Kate to gather mussels from a seashore in Ireland. It is a poem of celebration, both of Kate and of the beauty of the landscape. Once again, few words are exchanged between father and child. It seems that words are hardly needed as they go about their purpose: "In our common silence we stay / aware of one another, working together." As in "Two Climbing," the silence is broken not by the poet but by the child, who exclaims about the variety of colors in the mussels. The daughter's voice also breaks into the "wide silence" of nature earlier in the expedition. Both "Two Climbing" and "Two Gathering" are poems in which spoken words emerge out of contented silence and express the joy of discovery. How different is the silence between father and child in "Station," which describes a silence of suppression, of the word stopped in the throat, paralyzed in the mind, not flowing out sweetly on a bed of silence as in the happier poems, both of which, incidentally, are set outside, in nature, rather than in the enclosed stifling space of a crowded railroad station.

Grennan is a poet sensitive to silence and stillness, two words that appear often in his work. In his observation of nature, this perception of still moments in the midst of ongoing natural processes sometimes has an almost Wordsworthian or Keatsian quality. Grennan's appreciation of the deep meanings inherent in stillness and silence also draw him to paintings, especially those by the Dutch masters and the French painter Pierre Bonnard. It is Bonnard who supplies the inspiration for "The Breakfast Room," a poem in which the still life is presented as a kind of nothing on the verge of becoming something: "this stillness, this sense / that things are about to achieve illumination." And typically, since Grennan is a poet of family and ordinary domestic moments, he extrapolates from the painting into real life, suggesting that in anyone's kitchen at breakfast time there might be "a pause / on the brink of something always / edging into shape, about to happen."

"The second kind of silence is a negative one. It is the silence of suppression, the silence that marks a breakdown in the flow of life between people. Instead of a kind of fullness-in-potential there is emptiness, a gap, an absence."

It is this moment of "pause" in which there is silence that holds Grennan's attention. He is highly attuned to it and finds it in a wide variety of situations, often simple, domestic ones. In "Weather," for example, after the weather changes for the better after days of persistent rain, "the house is spinning / its own sure silence round your lives." In "Song," the poet listens to his daughter singing solo at her junior-high-school graduation and manages to access a still point within, which they both share, and in which he is able to communicate with her: "while into / our common silence I whisper, / *Sing, love, sing your heart out!*"

These silences are always positive. They suggest the connections between people and between people and things. They point toward a kind of ground of being that all life shares and that is apparent in moments when people cease their

What Do I Read Next?

- Grennan's *Still Life with Waterfall* (2002) is filled with observations of the natural world, animal life, and human relationships. Some critics have identified a feeling of foreboding in many of these poems, as well as a search for continuity. Other critics have remarked on the subtle eroticism of some of the poems in this collection.

- *Modern Irish Poetry: An Anthology* (1995), edited by Patrick Crotty, includes selections from Seamus Heaney, Eavan Boland, Derek Mahon, Michael Longley, Paul Muldoon, Medbh McGuckian, Paul Durcan, Nuala Ni Dhomhnaill (in translation from Irish), and others. Crotty argues that much twentieth century Irish writing can be interpreted as a quarrel with the dominating figure of W. B. Yeats.

- Seamus Heaney's *Opened Ground: Selected Poems, 1966–1996* (1998) is a large, representative selection of poems made by the poet himself. Heaney includes poems from his previous twelve books of poetry, as well as some previously uncollected poems. The book also includes his Nobel lecture, "Crediting Poetry."

- Paul Muldoon is one of the most celebrated contemporary Irish poets and his *Poems 1968–1998* (2001) illustrates the rich variety of his work, including the erotic as well as the political, and notably also his hundred haiku about suburban New Jersey.

---

perpetual busyness. In an essay on the work of his fellow Irish poet Derek Mahon (in *Facing the Music: Irish Poetry in the Twentieth Century*), Grennan writes of Mahon's "recurrent preoccupation with silence," a phrase that might equally well describe Grennan's own work.

Perhaps the best example of this aspect of Grennan's poetry comes in the poem "Morning: the Twenty-second of March." The scene is once again the family home. On a spring morning, the poet listens to the various natural sounds outside, in particular the sound of a dove that sings and then falls silent. Something about the silence makes it transformative; it suddenly shifts the poet's consciousness into an object-less, timeless dimension of being:

> —our life together hesitating in this gap
> of silence, slipping from us and becoming
> nothing we know in the swirl that has
> no past, no future, nothing
> but the pure pulse-shroud of light, the dread
> *here-now*—reporting thrice again
> its own silence. The cup of tea
> still steams between your hands
> like some warm offering or other
> to the nameless radiant vacancy at the window,
> this stillness in which we go on happening.

There are, then, two kinds of silence in Grennan's poetry. The first might be thought of as silence-as-being, a silence in which all life is embedded, even as it lives in its world of flux ("this stillness in which we go on happening"). It can be discerned in the most ordinary moments of the day by those who happen to be alert to it. It is a "regenerative silence" (again, this is a phrase used by Grennan to characterize Mahon's work but applies equally well to his own), which promotes life, union, happiness.

The second kind of silence is a negative one. It is the silence of suppression, the silence that marks a breakdown in the flow of life between people. Instead of a kind of fullness-in-potential there is emptiness, a gap, an absence. Something should be there—speech, communication, continuity of life—but is not. It is a silence of desolation. It can be heard in Grennan's several poems about family separations, the radical breaks that occur in the lives of two or more people. These poems include "Station," as well as two poems Grennan wrote about divorce. (He was divorced from his wife of fourteen years in 1986.) In "Women Going," Grennan writes of the aftermath of divorce as "this absence beating its stone wings / over every ordinary corner of the day." One can imagine the father in "Station" feeling the same way after the departure of his son. In fact, he feels it even before the son steps on the train (the waiting train fills the station "with aftermath and longing," the word "aftermath" suggesting the desolation that will immediately follow the parting).

The second poem about divorce, "Breaking Points," is a searing examination of the despair felt by the husband (or anyone in a similar situation) as he leaves the house for the last time following the divorce: "we say / *What now? What else? What?*" It is as if life has come to a sudden halt. Everything stops, or seems to, in this void. The arrangement of the poem on the page emphasizes this blank void, since the next line containing only the two words "And now" is so deeply indented on the page that the unanswered questions in the previous line seem almost to hang in the air, alone. How different is this silence-as-void from the moments of generative silence and stillness that the poet experiences in calmer, more serene moments.

Both poems about divorce emphasize the pain and desolation of parting. These feelings are also apparent in "Station," although the implications of the final lines of the poem need some elucidation. In the last sentence, the father imagines his son sitting in the second train on his journey:

> that pale face of his
> carried along in the dark glass, shining
> through shadows that fill the window
> and fall away again
> before we're even able to name them.

The alliterative music created by the phrase "shining through shadows," in combination with "fill the window / and fall," which further develops the play on the "i" and "a" as well as "f" sounds, is typical of Grennan's style. As far as meaning is concerned, at the literal level the observation is simple. As the train rushes on, the father imagines seeing not only his son's face in the window but also all the fleeting reflections from whatever the train is passing outside. There is surely an undertone of regret and even melancholy here also. The use of the word "shadows" recalls the earlier occurrences of "shade," "ghostly faces," and "pale face," all referring to the train station or the people inside the train. It is as if the father is losing his son to a realm of shadows, where nothing has substance anymore. The switch from singular to first-person plural in the last line expands the thought from the personal to the general; the shadows vanish "before we're even able to name them," just as earlier the thoughts that should have been expressed were not; they too were like shadows in the mind and heart, felt but never articulated, never finding proper form. Also, the vanishing shadows in the last line suggest the frustrated human desire to categorize things and thereby to understand life. And hovering behind this meaning is perhaps yet another: the father's wistful feeling that his son has departed before he has been able to get to know him fully. There is a sadness in these concluding lines, however obliquely that sadness may be expressed. As such, it is a rather untypical conclusion from a poet who usually tries to emphasize the positive things that can be retrieved from daily existence and relationships. The situation of the father in "Station" is that he wants something to hold onto as he says goodbye to his son, but he cannot do it; he finds only shadows.

Source: Bryan Aubrey, Critical Essay on "Station," in *Poetry for Students*, Thomson Gale, 2005.

Ben Howard

In the following review, Howard praises Grennan's attention to the nuances and melodies of language and cites a commonality between Grennan and James Joyce.

Eamon Grennan's considerable resources include an eye for the elusive detail and an ear for the most reclusive sound. Like many Irish poets, bardic and modern, he is keenly aware of aural phenomena, be it the "joyous contralto barking / of geese going over," or the "intimate rustle / of this woman's loose skirt," or the assonantal splendors of the mother tongue. Among the great Irish modernists Grennan's forbear is not Yeats so much as Joyce, with whom he shares a love of the fabric of words and a willing immersion in quotidian realities. With graceful precision Grennan can speak of "the daily / ineluctable clutter of our lives" or describe the "glistering layers of olivebrown bladderwrack." Alert to the nuances and melodies of language, he is also attuned to the darker resonances of domestic life and the "secular depths" of ordinary things.

Grennan was born in Dublin in 1941, holds degrees from University College, Dublin and Harvard University, and is currently teaching at Vassar College. *As If It Matters* is his second collection to be published in this country, and in style and content it has something in common with recent books by male American poets of Grennan's generation, most notably Stephen Dunn. Writing in a slow exploratory line that sometimes approaches prose, Grennan examines the tensions and banalities of middle-class life, the dynamics of marriage and parenthood, the trauma of divorce, the pain of separation from a son and daughter. A pair of tender narrative poems frames the collection, the first recounting a walk with his "solicitous" twelve-year-old son and the second

"Eamon Grennan's considerable resources include an eye for the elusive detail and an ear for the most reclusive sound."

celebrating a mussel-gathering expedition with his exultant teenaged daughter. Between those symmetrical poles Grennan has arrayed some thirty meditative-descriptive poems of medium length, most of them cast in the first-person, present-tense mode and many commemorating privileged moments. Grennan's concerns lie chiefly with personal relationships, but he also embraces the natural world, including some of its homelier inhabitants:

> And something Dutch
> about that recumbent mass, their couchant
> hefty press of rumination, the solid globe
> folded round the ribs' curved hull,
> barrelling that enormous belly. The close
> rich smell of them
> grinding down grass to milk
> to mother us all, or the childhood smell of stalls
> all milk and piss and dungy straw:
> what that umbered word, *cowshed,* conjures.
> "COWS"

For this reader the appeal of these lines lies less in their perceptions than in their aural felicities—the artful deployment of liquid consonants, the quasi-rhyme of *hull, smell,* and *all,* the subtle chiming of *umbered word, barrelling,* and *belly.*

Not all of Grennan's successes are so unalloyed. At their weaker moments these poems lapse into sententiousness and cliché ("courting disaster"; "tight as a drum") or engage in minute description for its own sake. Like others of his generation Grennan has not fully absorbed the influence of Seamus Heaney, whose voice can be heard in particular lines ("bodies all curve and urgency") or, more pervasively, in the overworked technique of suspending paired modifiers over a line break ("the close / rich smell of them"; "their couchant / hefty press"). But it would be unfair to regard Grennan as another gifted son of Heaney or to overlook the distinction of his voice and outlook. Resisting the ideological grievance and the backward look, his poems reflect a sensibility tempered by experience but ready for the next uncommon moment. Watchful, expectant, and respectful of "things . . . about to achieve / illumination," this open-handed poet has kept faith with his own poetic credo: "To love the scrubbed exactitudes / and the dimmer thing / that shivers at the brink."

Source: Ben Howard, Review of *As If It Matters*, in *Poetry*, Vol. 161, No. 4, January 1993, pp. 233–34.

Richard Tillinghast

In the following review, Tillinghast praises Grennan's spiritual openness and places his work within the context of Irishness.

Reading for the first time Eamon Grennan's "Men Roofing" in *The New Yorker* a couple of years ago, I experienced the same sense of unqualified assent I felt at the age of seventeen when I first read Richard Wilbur's great lyric, "Love Calls Us to the Things of This World" in the Untermeyer anthology. It would be extravagant to claim that Grennan's poem was the best I had read in thirty-five years; but "Love Calls Us to the Things of This World" is a touchstone for me. Since no one reads Matthew Arnold anymore, it might not be out of place to quote William Butler Yeats's version of what Arnold meant by a touchstone (I ran across Yeats's sentence in Seamus Heaney's essay, "Sense of Place"): "The final test of the value of any work of art to our particular needs, is when we place it in the hierarchy of those recollections which are our standards and our beacons."

Why Eamon Grennan's poetry reminds me of Richard Wilbur's is that both poets have a largeness, a generosity, an unforced openness to experience that affirms what we have in common rather than the barriers we erect to divide us. The conventional wisdom of the moment is, to quote Wendy Steiner in the April 5, 1992, *New York Times Book Review* (though the sentiment may be found in practically every contemporary literary-critical forum), that "the path to a common voice nowadays runs through the partisan."

Grennan's inclusive, non-partisan embrace of "the things of this world" hints at a spiritual openness reminiscent of the early Chinese Buddhist teachers, whose attitude is summed up in P'ei Hsiu's preface to a ninth-century text by Huang Po: "To those who have realized the nature of Reality, there is nothing old or new, and conceptions of shallowness and depth are meaningless. . . . That which is before you is it." Aware that meaning inheres in that border zone where the "scrubbed exactitudes" of our world give way to that "dimmer thing," the ambient world that haloes what is perceptible to our senses, Grennan dwells sometimes exuberantly, sometimes grievingly, but always intently, in both worlds.

"Men Roofing" is first of all a poem about work. Why is it that the activity in which we expend most of our lives has been the subject for so little poetry? The great examples of this genre that we do have, come across with the force of inevitability, with a levelness of tone not found in poems about, for example, love and ambition. Frost's "Two Tramps in Mud Time" glows with a healthy physicality:

> Good blocks of beech it was I split,
> As large around as the chopping block;
> And every piece I squarely hit
> Fell splinterless as a cloven rock.

As does Seamus Heaney's "Digging," with its "Under my window, a clean rasping sound / When the spade sinks into gravelly ground: / My father, digging." The same poet's "Thatcher" exudes a great sense of pleasure derived from craft: "Bespoke for weeks, he turned up some morning / Unexpectedly, his bicycle slung / With a light ladder and a bag of knives." "Men Roofing" is dedicated to Seamus Heaney, and I take the dedication as encouragement to think of this poem as an homage to "Thatcher."

"Why Eamon Grennan's poetry reminds me of Richard Wilbur's is that both poets have a largeness, a generosity, an unforced openness to experience that affirms what we have in common rather than the barriers we erect to divide us."

First an extended meditation on air and sky, where "Overhead / against the gentian sky a sudden first flock whirls / of amber leaves and saffron, quick as breath, fine / as origami birds." How light a touch the man has! "What a sight between earth and air they are," Grennan says of the roofers, "drenched / in sweat and sunlight, relaxed masters for a moment / of all our elements!" Again like Heaney, he gives us figures of mastery. Important because all of us, whether we think about it often or have grown to take it for granted, concern ourselves with the question of how we will get along in this world.

Men working. But not only that. The poem shows us the essence of their activity: "men roofing, taking pains to keep the weather / out. . . ." If one sympathizes with Gary Snyder's belief that "As a poet I hold the most archaic values on earth. They go back to the late Paleolithic," one is struck with the realization that the provision of shelter must surely be one of the most ancient human endeavors. Paradoxically the "brink" between earth and heaven also suggests a metaphor for the unseen frontier between the physical and the spiritual, and this is the frontier to which this poem takes us: "Briefly they stand balanced / between our common ground and nobody's sky." What is, I suppose, most "Irish," if one cares to venture out into that treacherous bog, about this poem is its startling illumination of ordinary action as a form of ritual. We feel ourselves gently nudged in the direction of seeing the "plume of blue smoke" which "feathers up / out of a pitch-black cauldron" as ritual censing, like the bonfires lit in the British Isles on All Hallows' Eve, or the American Indian's offering of tobacco to the spirits. "Odorous," the poem concludes, "their column of lazuli smoke loops up from the dark / heart of their mystery. . . ." The mention of "lazuli," associated in one's mind with the mystical Byzantium evoked by Yeats, transports us into a world of liturgy and acts of propitiation. By this point in the poem the men have become mediators between earth and sky, between the physical and the spiritual: "they ply, they intercede."

Eamon Grennan has justly been praised as a poet of the domestic—and of the domestic in its fullness, including a place for eros within the complete domestic configuration. Another poem from *What Light There Is*, "Jewel Box," delves into the contents of the poet's wife's jewelry box:

> Morning and evening
> I see you comb its seawrack tangle of shell,
> stone, wood, glass, metal, bone, seed
> for the bracelet, earring, necklace, brooch
> or ring you need.

The various ornaments, from Africa, Nepal, the Mediterranean, are talismans of the woman's exotic appeal. The bathroom, where the jewel box—a treasure-trove of more than material value—is kept and where the couple perform their ablutions before going out into the world, becomes in the poem a sort of nest from which they issue forth.

Her washed bras, hung up to dry, look oddly like "the skinned Wicklow rabbits I remember / hanging from hooks outside the victuallers' / big windows." The comment that follows is worth pausing over: "We've been domesticated strangely, / love, according to our lights...." The poem catches the poised instant of departure, where the man and the woman stand balanced between their private, erotic selves and the identities they must assume in their workaday lives. The moment of departure is, like many a moment in this poet's work, epiphanic and luminous: "Going down the dark stairs and out / to the fogbound street, you light my way."

In "All Souls' Morning" the day dawns rainy, and the scene inside the poet's house comes into focus so perfectly that we recognize at once where we are, aware at the same time, perhaps, of having the scene evoked for us with a remarkable ease: "Rain splatting wet leaves; citrine light; the cat / scratching the sofa; the house dead quiet / but for the furnace thumping in the cellar. . . ." A scene so familiar we are startled to see it evoked so deftly. As a man passes by, out walking his dog in the rain, suddenly "my father comes leaning as he always did / up Clareville Road, not far from where he's buried, bent / against the bitter wind. . ." Here's how the poem ends:

> *All night,*
> you said when we wakened warm by one another, *I*
> *was*
> *seeing shapes widen round the room, hearing them*
> *whisper in the wall.* And now my hungry children
> come
> clattering to the kitchen for breakfast. The house
> quickens.

The dead appear—as they are perhaps more likely to do in Ireland than in the United States—but they appear within the context of the family and the home, which is where almost everything happens in Grennan's poetry. Everything is contained within the nest. Even the dream about the dead is narrated "when we wakened warm by one another" and when the children were about to appear for breakfast. Perhaps it is these two qualities that make Grennan a palpably "Irish" poet: the hearth as the focus for life's dramas; and the willingness to admit the existence of presences other than the human.

Earlier in this essay I invoked Buddhism. "Morning: the Twenty-Second of March," another poem from *What Light There Is*, again opening itself to a moment when, though seemingly nothing is happening, Grennan's alert senses are able to register an essence:

> our life together hesitating in this gap
> of silence, slipping from us and becoming
> nothing we know in the swirl that has
> no past, no future, nothing
> but the pure pulse-shroud of light...

While this bit of metaphysics is being spun out,

> The cup of tea
> still steams between your hands
> like some warm offering or other
> to the nameless radiant vacancy at the window,
> this stillness in which we go on happening.

These lines come about as close as anything I can think of to capturing *the moment itself,* the essence of what we call for lack of a better word, life.

Again like Richard Wilbur, Grennan is at home in the natural world. Moving from his first American collection, *What Light There Is*, to the 1992 book, *As If It Matters*, here are lines from "Cows":

> I love the way a torn tuft
> of grassblades, stringy buttercup and succulent
> clover
> sway-dangles towards a cow's mouth, the mild
> teeth
> taking it in—purple flowers, green stems and yel-
> low petals
> lingering on those hinged lips
> foamed with spittle. And the slow chewing sound
> as transformation starts: the pulping roughness
> of it, its calm deliberate solicitude, its
> entranced herbivorous pacific
> grace, the carpet-sweeping sound of breath
> huffing out of pink nostrils.

Listen to the word-music at play here: how the short *u*'s in "love," "tuft," "buttercup" and "succulent" create a looping melody, separated as they are by differing vowels that intervene, reminiscent of Gerard Manley Hopkins's rhythms. "Sway-dangles" gets the sloppy motion just right: there's nothing prim about a cow's table manners. Not just description, though, as the idea-word "transformation" tells us. One feels how intent an observer is at work here in the almost passionate accumulation of adjectives: "its / entranced herbivorous pacific / grace," suggestive of something Elizabeth Bishop wrote in a letter to Anne Stevenson on the subject of Darwin's journals. "What one seems to want in art, in experiencing it, is the same thing that is necessary for its creation, a self-forgetful, perfectly useless concentration."

In *As If It Matters*, observations of the physical world sometimes open out into analogies to the world of the emotions, as in "Breaking Points," where the poet watches a friend chop a huge maple into firewood, "hoisting / the wedgehead heavy axe and coming down with it / in one swift glittering arc: a single *chunk,* / then the gleam of two half moons of maple / rolling over in the driveway." The tree being split triggers a remembrance of the time his earlier marriage and family broke apart:

> . . . this is the way it is
> in the world we make and break
> for ourselves: first the long green growing, then
> the storm, the heavy axe, those shining remnants
> that'll season for a year
> before the fire gets them. . .

The eye of these poems is not averted from breakage and loss. The jumble of unstacked firewood "from this Babylonian distance looks like / a pattern of solid purposes or the end of joy."

One feels the losses recorded in some of these poems suffered and sustained, but never relished or displayed to advantage, as in Confessional Poetry. In "Compass Reading" the poet rescues a cat from the jaws of a bird, "the broken neck, closed eyes, the tuft, / the ruffled wings—the chest / still soft and warm—and placed them / out of harm's way, as if it mattered. . ." And it *does* matter in the larger balance, one feels, because the cat, "tasting a salt smear of blood / across tongue and teeth," becomes in the economy of the poem an emblem of death writ large: "And she will not /—for all her satisfactions— / be appeased."

Let me now go into more detail as to what there is about Grennan's poetry to distinguish it as Irish rather than American or English. Perhaps the distinction is ultimately not important. But I have already mentioned three emphases: a sense that life approaches at times the significance of ritual, which readers will be familiar with from Yeats; the centrality in Irish life of the hearth, which links Grennan to poets of the land, most notably Patrick Kavanagh—still not widely known in this country, but revered by Irish readers and considered by many Irish poets to be, rather than Yeats, their true progenitor; And thirdly, the weather eye that the poet keeps out for presences other than the physical and earthly—an orientation that links him to the entire history of spirituality without which it would be impossible to conceive of Irish letters from the earliest folk tales of the supernatural and saints' lives, to the *aisling* or dream vision poems of the Irish-language tradition, the otherworldly terror of Sheridan Le Fanu, Joyce's "The Dead," the spirits Heaney evokes in *Station Island,* and on and on.

Starting with the Irish nationalist movement that began in the 19th century, Ireland went from being, in Shaw's words, "John Bull's other island" to a country very much aware, often in an excruciatingly self-conscious way, of its unique history and culture. Nationalistic pride and self-assertion still of course flourish: a foreign reader of *The Irish Times* or a listener to the cultural programs on Radio Eireann will often find himself amazed at the Irish passion for self-definition. Things are changing, however. Anyone who reads widely in contemporary Irish literature or who visits the island and gets some sense of its cultural life, will know that Ireland no longer experiences the isolation that fostered many of the myths that have defined it both for outsiders and for the Irish themselves. While finding itself still culturally entangled, often unwillingly, with Britain, Ireland now looks east to continental Europe and west to the United States.

Membership in the European Community has meant not only an influx of tourists and development money—much of it to be used for cultural projects—but a greater respect in Europe for Ireland as an autonomous country and people than it was traditionally accorded under British rule; at the same time, Ireland has become more susceptible to continental European trends. As for the United States, Ireland has a tremendous vulnerability to American culture—the good, the bad, and the ugly. Immigration, often to America, has been a fact of Irish life ever since the Famines of the 19th century. Many Irish people are culturally mid-Atlantic, and this is especially true of Grennan. A round dozen of the poems in *As If It Matters* appeared first in *The New Yorker.* Irish poetry, despite its many excellences, is not really so "foreign" as what comes to us from Poland, Latin America, or even Britain, for that matter, where ever since Larkin there has been a retreat into provinciality in the face of the "global village" mentality. There is in addition the phenomenon of the Irish poet in the American university—with Seamus Heaney, Derek Mahon, Paul Muldoon, and Eamon Grennan all teaching part- or full-time in the States. Perhaps these sociocultural factors have at least something to do with Grennan's accessibility to the American audience.

"The Cave Painters" seems to me typical of Grennan's ability to tap into experiences that compel the assent of a wide range of readers. "They've left the world of weather and panic / behind them," he writes of these imagined prehistoric artists, "and gone on in, drawing the dark / in their wake. . . ." Living as we do in a culture that positions the human being at the center of the universe, it is good to be reminded of a time when the balance of power was differently disposed. The "one unbroken line" of the cave painters' art encompasses

> the speed of the horse, the bison's fear, the gentle
> arch
> that big-bellied cow throws over
> its spindling calf, or the lancing dance of death

that bristles out of the struck buck's
flank. In this one line they place
a beak-headed human figure of sticks
and one small, chalky, amputated hand.

That hand, seen here as amputated, has disappeared into the picture it has painted. The modest position of the human, the artist, within the economy of observed life in this picture has immense appeal. Though I have just claimed that Grennan typifies a generation of writers where "Irishness" is less determining than it was in the past, one might go so far as to say that nothing is so Irish as the craft, the care, the lack of egocentricity evident here. These artists "must have had," the poem concludes, "one desire we'd recognise," and this is a desire with whose intent every artist, every writer will concur:

they would, before going on
beyond this border zone, this nowhere
that is now here, leave something
upright and bright behind them in the dark.

Source: Richard Tillinghast, "Eamon Grennan: To Leave Something Bright and Upright Behind," in *New England Review*, Vol. 11, No. 2, Spring 1993, pp. 189–95.

Sources

Cotter, James Finn, Review of *As If It Matters*, in *Hudson Review*, Vol. XLV, No. 3, Autumn 1992, pp. 524–26.

"Eamon Grennan," in *Salon*, at http://archive.salon.com/weekly/grennan.html, (last accessed May 17, 2004).

Grennan, Eamon, *Facing the Music: Irish Poetry in the Twentieth Century*, Creighton University Press, 1999, pp. xiv, 262–63.

———, *Relations: New and Selected Poems*, Greywolf Press, 1998.

Hosmer, Robert E., Jr., Review of *Relations: New and Selected Poems*, in *America*, Vol. 180, No. 11, April 3, 1999, p. 23.

Howard, Ben, Review of *As If It Matters*, in *Poetry*, Vol. CLXI, No. 4, January 1993, pp. 233–34.

Further Reading

Brophy, James D., and Eamon Grennan, eds., *New Irish Writing: Essays in Memory of Raymond J. Porter*, Twayne Publishers, 1989.

Sixteen essays cover various aspects of modern Irish literature, including poetry, drama, and short stories. Grennan contributes an introduction and an essay on the poetry of Paul Duncan and Paul Muldoon.

Campbell, Michael, ed., *The Cambridge Companion to Contemporary Irish Poetry*, Cambridge University Press, 2003.

This guide to contemporary Irish poetry covers major figures such as Heaney as well as his precursors, including Louis MacNeice and Patrick Kavanagh, as well as other leading contemporary figures such as Thomas Kinsella, Nuala Ni Dhomhnaill, and Paul Muldoon. The book includes cultural and historical backgrounds, a chronology, and guide to further reading.

Fleming, Deborah, "The 'Common Ground' of Eamon Grennan," in *Eire-Ireland: A Journal of Irish Studies*, Vol. 28, No. 4, Winter 1993, pp. 133–49.

Fleming discusses a wide range of Grennan's poetry, examining his treatment of universality and the ordinary.

Tillinghast, Richard, "Eamon Grennan: 'To Leave Something Bright and Upright Behind,'" in *New England Review*, Vol. 15, No. 2, Spring 1993, pp. 189–95.

In this review of Grennan's collections *What Light There Is* and *As If It Matters*, Tillinghast discusses Grennan's concern with family, home, and the natural world; his spirituality that sometimes resembles Buddhism; and the presence of epiphanies in the ordinary moment. Tillinghast likens Grennan to American poet Richard Wilbur, but he also discusses what makes Grennan's poetry Irish rather than American or English.

Wrigley, Robert, Review of *Still Life with WaterFall*, in *Nation*, Vol. 277, No. 8, December 1, 2003, p. 38.

This review of Grennan's most recent collection is one of the most substantial treatments of the poet's work to date. Wrigley has nothing but praise for Grennan's artistry in presenting the natural world.

Ten Years after Your Deliberate Drowning

Robin Behn

1993

Robin Behn's "Ten Years after Your Deliberate Drowning" is a poem about life and love as well as about death. It incorporates images of a benevolent nature and also nature gone awry. It is about love that transcends physicality and flows into eternity. It is simple, and it is complex.

Through her use of extended metaphor, which in this poem centers on two moths, Behn tries to make sense of death while simultaneously trying to make sense of love and the loss of it. The poem is personal and from that most intimate point of view becomes universal, for who has not experienced, or at least pondered, the emotions that emanate from the incomprehensible concepts of love and death? As Behn delves into these two abstractions, she takes her readers with her, gently inviting them to look at both the wonder and the pain.

A copy of the poem can be found in Behn's second collection of poetry, *The Red Hour* (1993).

Author Biography

Robin Behn was born in 1958. She is a prize-winning poet and author of three collections of poetry. Behn is also a distinguished professor of English and creative writing and was honored with the Burnum Distinguished Faculty Award at the University of Alabama, where she began teaching since the 1980s. Behn has stated that she comes

Robin Behn

from a family of teachers. Her father also taught English and instilled in her a love of language.

Behn received her bachelor's degree from Oberlin College. She then continued her studies at the University of Missouri-Columbia and was granted a master's degree from the University of Iowa. She has been awarded several major grants, including the prestigious John Simon Guggenheim fellowship.

Her first collection of poetry, *Paper Bird*, was published in 1988 and won the Associated Writing Programs Award in poetry. Her poem "Ten Years after Your Deliberate Drowning," which appears in the collection *Red Hour*, was published in 1993. In 2001, her third collection of poetry, *Horizon Note*, was published and awarded the Brittingham Prize in poetry from the University of Wisconsin Press. Behn has also coedited a book that emphasizes her skills as a teacher, *The Practice of Poetry: Writing Exercises from Poets who Teach* (1992).

Behn has won numerous honors for her writing, including a National Endowment for the Arts individual artist grant, an Alabama State Council on the Arts individual artist grant, and the Pushcart Prize for poetry. Her poems have been published in many literary magazines including *American Poetry Review*, *Kenyon Review*, and the *Iowa Review*. Her work has been anthologized in the *Pushcart Prize Anthology*, *Best American Poetry*, and *Poets of the New Century*.

Poem Text

Since then, I work at night.
Against the glass the identical moths

open themselves to me. The lamp
illumines the decorative eyes

evolution has granted them.
So don't think I'm alone.

To them I am *the* light.
Days I don't come with flowers,

please think of these white petals
pressed into this pane.

Pale shapely trapezoids—
they too remember your shoulders.

If I don't light the light
for *x* nights in a row . . .

Tell me what *x* is.
You must be in *x* by now.

Sometimes one travels several inches
on its thready legs—

an old idea alighting
on a new ledge in the brain.

I used to think—what thing was it
that I had failed to do?

Now I just see your body,
filled almost up with water,

harden in my arms, then break
—so much does it desire to be filled—

against the real river for good.
The eyes through which I see this

are impervious to light.
This I have learned from the moths:

open your wings when you must
and flash the inner eyes

of a creature so big it could eat
both you and the thought that would eat you.

Most of what follows I see:
How there are more and more,

how they never fly away.
Nor do they rest in pairs.

Whatever made these wings
is remaking yours now

somewhere in the workshop where the thing is
extracted
that leaves behind the dark.

Out there their clustered shadows
spill darker kissmarks on that dark.

Poem Summary

Lines 1–6

Behn's poem "Ten Years after Your Deliberate Drowning" is obviously about a suicide, but it is also about love. This is made evident in the first six lines of the poem. The speaker is feeling left behind. As she sits at her desk working, she thinks about her loss. There are two moths on the window in front of her, which, in the mind of the speaker, might symbolize the speaker and the person she has lost. The phrase "identical moths" might be a reference to the closeness the speaker and the person who passed away had. These moths are separated from the speaker, though. There is a glass between them and her. The glass could represent the invisible shield that a person feels when someone she loved has died. The memories and emotions tied to that person still linger, although the person's physical body is gone. Then, the speaker writes that the moths "open themselves to me." When something opens itself, it implies a new understanding may have been reached. Possibly the speaker, in watching the moths, comprehends something new about the way she feels. Or else, maybe she has come to an acceptance of her friend's death.

The speaker makes reference to a lamp that "illumines the decorative eyes." These eyes to which she is referring could be the markings on the moths' wings. But, they also could be symbolic eyes, such as the so-called inner eyes of revelation. The speaker could be referring to an insight she has received, while pondering her friend's death in the past decade. She says "So don't think I'm alone." The decorative eyes on the moths' wings were given to them, the speaker states, through "evolution." Like the moths, the speaker has also evolved, she implies, from someone who was lonesome to someone who is no longer alone.

Lines 7–12

In line seven, the speaker sends the reader back to the mention of a lamp in line 4, when she writes: "to them I am *the* light." She is the light, and the moths now become the "petals" of the flowers the speaker did not take to her friend's grave. In some ways, the speaker and the moths have once again traded places, as they do earlier when the speaker figuratively "sees" through the decorative eyes on the moths' wings. As the reader progresses to the last two lines in this section (lines 11 and 12), the moths are transferred to the image of the friend, when the speaker compares the "trapezoids," the shapes of the two opened wings on each moth as they spread themselves flat. The "trapezoids" cause memories to stir in the speaker, reminding her of the shape of her friend's shoulders.

Lines 13–16

The word *light* is presented again, this time as a candle (conjuring the image of the moth being drawn to the fire, and thus to its death), but also representing a small memorial ritual, such as when a person lights a candle in memory of someone who has died. If the speaker does not "light the light / for *x* nights in a row . . ." the poem continues, using *x* as an unknown number. However, the use of *x* in this case might signify that the speaker has forgotten how long she has lit the candle or perhaps suggesting that she will light the candle forever. Then in the next two lines, she again uses *x*, first to allude to whatever is unknown or unanswered and then to imply heaven or whatever exists after death. In these lines, the speaker intimates that once a person dies, all answers are forthcoming; all answers are known. Although all references to *x* on one level represent the same thing—the unknown—there are layers of meanings implied, which make the symbol *x* represent a different meaning in each use. For instance, on a surface level, the first *x* implies an amount, a number. The second *x* suggests the unknown. And the third, depending on a person's religious or spiritual beliefs, hints at a heaven or afterlife.

Lines 17–20

Line 17 abruptly brings the reader back from the abstract *x* to the concrete "thready legs" of the moths on the speaker's windowpane. The thready legs first appear to be characteristics of the moths: "Sometimes one travels several inches." This concrete image shifts in the next line when the speaker uses an abstract concept: "an old idea alighting / on a new ledge in the brain." Here, the speaker turns the moth into an insight, just as she has previously done with her insinuation that she sees through the moths' eyes. This time, though, the movement of the moths is compared to the movement of a thought, as if when a person is inspired with an idea, it is similar to a moth "alighting" on a "new ledge."

Lines 21–27

These lines are once again concrete images. They are also a bit morbid, as the speaker recalls vivid images of the last night she saw her friend. First, she remembers that after his death, she used to blame herself for the things she "had failed to do." In other words, she wonders if she had only done such and such, maybe he would not have taken his life. She wonders how she might have saved him. Now that ten years have passed, it is possible that she no longer worries about that. Those questions, although they may not have been answered, have faded away. In their place, she has only the image of his bloated body, stiffened by rigor mortis. The speaker uses this stiffened after-death state to play on words, making the body appear, in her mind at least, to "break." Then, she says that it broke because it desired "to be filled," suggesting that her friend could not find what he wanted in this world, so he died (or broke) in order to be filled. In the next line, she continues her thought, stating that his body broke "against the real river for good." The "real river" could be a suggestion of life or maybe the afterlife. Either life broke him apart or else she is implying that he was reborn in the afterlife, broken away from physicality to allow his soul to escape and be free.

Lines 28–34

Her eyes, the speaker states, are "impervious to light." This could mean that she is blind or that the eyes through which she now "sees" her friend's death are not the eyes through which she sees the present moment. In other words, in this instance she might be talking about her inner eyes, the eyes of intuition or of memory. Looked at in another way, she could be saying that her eyes do not see the light she mentions earlier in the poem—the light of inspiration or revelation. But then, she says "This I have learned from the moths: / open your wings when you must / and flash the inner eyes." Again, this is a little ambiguous. Opening wings could suggest a flying away or a fleeing. However, to "flash the inner eyes" suggests the opposite. Instead of just looking with the physical eyes, the speaker seems to be saying that a person must look deeper, with the inner eyes. It is these inner eyes, the eyes "of a creature so big" it could devour not only the speaker but her thoughts, which are so powerful they themselves could completely consume her. In some ways, the speaker could be saying that a person must become something that he or she is not. Just as the moths can scare away predators by opening their wings and pretending, with their decorative eyes, to be much bigger than they really are, so too a person must close his or her outer eyes and look at the tragic loss of a friend through the eyes of his or her spiritual self, something much bigger than his or her ego. If the speaker does not do this, she contends, her loneliness and longing for her friend will eat her up.

Lines 35–38

The next four lines are a continuation of what the speaker learns from the moths. The lines "how there are more and more, / how they never fly away" could suggest, on a figurative level, that even when someone dies, life goes on for those left behind. But the next line, "Nor do they rest in pairs," is a little more troublesome. The reader wonders if the speaker is making reference to the fact that people cannot live as "pairs," or is she speaking from a deeper level and therefore expressing her thoughts that both in life and in death a person is really all alone. A person is born alone and must face death alone. The concept of pairs is an illusion, the speaker might be saying. Although paired physically, a couple is never paired on a spiritual level.

Lines 39–44

Here the speaker begins with the concept of a creator. She leaves the definition of a god to the reader. Her only mention of a greater being is through the word "whatever." The "whatever" created the moth and is now recreating her friend's body—spiritual body, in this case, as she mentions wings, an allusion to the concept of an angel. This "whatever" is in the "workshop where the thing is extracted / that leaves behind the dark." She is thinking of her friend's death and wondering what it is that escapes from the body that takes the "light" of life, the spirit force, and leaves behind only the darkness of death. What is death, she seems to be asking. At the same time, she wants to know what that thing is that has been taken away. Then the final two lines of this work appear, the most abstract and vague lines in this poem. Questions arise here as to what the speaker is referring when she describes "their clustered shadows." Is she talking about the moths? Or does she mean death? Possibly, she is talking about what remains when the light has been "extracted" from a person's loved one when he dies. Or could she be referring to all of these concepts at once? The "out there" mentioned in the line "Out there their clustered shadows / spill darker kiss-marks on that dark" could mean the space on the other side of her window, the night, or it could be the unknown, which infers death. The "darker kiss-marks" could be the form of the moth with its body fluttering around the light, or they could be the memories of the love that the speaker once shared with her friend. The speaker could be saying that the dark of the night as well as the dark of the unknown are made darker still because she has been touched by death, by having been in love with someone who has passed into that darkness.

Themes

Death

Death is an obvious theme in Behn's poem "Ten Years after Your Deliberate Drowning." The title of this poem is the first mention of death, and from there, the reader is constantly reminded that the speaker of this poem has lost a loved one. The speaker is trying to come to grips with death, trying not only to console herself about her loss but to understand what death is. The passage of time may have changed her sense of loneliness and longing, but she still does not fully comprehend what death is. She has witnessed it, which has forced her to face her own mortality. She too will one day die, and she wants to know what awaits her on the other side. "Tell me what *x* is," the speaker asks. She also wants to know if she is responsible for her friend's death. Was there something that she did not do that made this person want to die? Could she have postponed this person's death? Is there something that she missed? She wants to know the answers to these questions not only to hypothetically bring her friend back but also so she will never do that same thing again and cause someone else's death.

Throughout most of the poem, death is an abstraction. The speaker talks around it, talks of the emotions that death has caused. But in the middle of the poem, death becomes concrete, as the speaker remembers the physicality of death: "Now I just see your body, / filled almost up with water, / harden in my arms." Physical death is real. She saw the distorted body of her friend and cannot forget the image. It is that concrete image of death that haunts her as her mind constantly returns to that scene. It is because she was there, because she saw the physical death that she knows her friend is gone forever. Having physically seen death makes the abstract concept of death concrete. Although she does not fully comprehend death, she knows that her friend is definitely gone. Her friend's death is not some nightmarish memory; it is real.

Love

This poem concentrates, on the surface, on the theme of death. Below the surface are many other themes. One of the major themes is that of love. Without ever using the word *love*, there is no doubt that the speaker of this poem loved the person who died. Her reference to "identical moths" in the beginning of the poem insinuates how close she felt to the person who has drowned. They were once together, but now she is alone, even though she tries to deny that by stating "so don't think I'm alone." Later the speaker writes, "Days I don't come with flowers," which implies that there are also days when she does bring flowers, even ten years after this person's death. The speaker also insinuates that she misses her friend tremendously, for she has often thought about how she might have done something differently and maybe her friend would still be there. There is also the reference to the speaker having given her friend a last embrace when the body was found. "Harden in my arms," the speaker writes as she remembers the last time she saw her friend. The embrace of a bloated and stiffened body could only reflect a strong love. Further into the poem, the speaker mentions "the thought that would eat you," suggesting a psychological torment such as the death of a friend would cause. If this were only a casual relationship, there would not be a thought remaining that would be big enough to eat the speaker. She is suffering from the loss because of the depth of the love she feels. Finally, the speaker refers to "kissmarks," which may suggest the kisses she and this person may have shared. She remembers their kisses, which have marked her, making the darkness that she feels after her friend's passing that much darker.

Loneliness

Although the speaker of the poem denies she is alone, her denial actually accentuates her loneliness. Loneliness is on her mind; otherwise she would not have mentioned it. Also, relating to a chance encounter with two moths as keeping her company emphasizes that loneliness. The reader wonders if the moths are her only friends. The speaker makes no more direct comment about her loneliness. She only alludes to it. The reader must insinuate it from the images she presents. Those images include the fact that she still takes flowers to the grave, suggesting her strong memories of a relationship. There is also the mention of her friend's shoulders, a symbol of comfort. She makes no mention of any other pair of shoulders having taken her friend's place. Also, the fact that she recalls her friend's shoulders implies she has a need to be comforted, an allusion to loneliness. She continues to try to "fix" her friend's death, wondering what she could have done to prevent it. Her longing to bring her friend back suggests she is not moving forward, which also suggests a person who is lonesome. Whether she is surrounded by friends or not, her thoughts are not in the present moment. They are snagged on an event in the past, which fills a person with a sense of loneliness, a sense of something missing in life. The speaker also states,

Topics For Further Study

- Research suicide in the United States. Are the major causes known? What is the breakdown in age groups in the statistics? Read Dr. Kay Redfield Jamison's study *Night Falls Fast: Understanding Suicide* and write a report on her findings.
- Research the various forms of contemporary American poetry, such as feminist poetry, language poetry, and postmodern poetry. How do these forms differ? In which category do you believe Behn's poetry belongs. Use reference statements to back up your theory.
- Write a poem using one specific image (e.g., Behn used moths). Tie this image to some powerful event that has occurred in your life. You can use any form of poetry you would like, but concentrate on using that image throughout your poem as Behn has done.
- Write three letters to Behn's friend, conveying the same thoughts she conveyed in her poem. What is it that she is trying to say to him? What do you think she might have said to him in the first letter, written shortly after his death? In the second letter, written to him after one year has passed? How have her emotions changed? The third letter should be in the same timeframe as Behn's poem, ten years after his death.

"they do not rest in pairs," a reference to an empty bed, perhaps. She now "rests" at night in a bed all alone. In the closing lines of the poem, the speaker refers to an ever-deepening darkness, something a person who feels alone could see or feel.

Spirituality

Behn makes several references to "the light" in this poem, which suggests spirituality or enlightenment. There is "the lamp" that "illumines," "*the* light," and "light the light," along with other images of light. This light not only illumines, it draws things to it, such as the moths. So the reader could easily read into these references a sense of the spiritual light, a light that helps the person understand, or a light that guides. In the phrase "light the light," the reader could infer a sense of practicing a spiritual ritual. The speaker also refers to a kind of generic godhead when she mentions the "whatever," a being or energy that she believes creates all things and then takes life away. The speaker also makes many statements about the inner eye, or a way of looking at life beyond the physical and the practical. She refers to going deeper inside herself to seek the spiritual explanation of life and death. "Flash the inner eyes," Behn writes, then she recalls what she sees when she uses her inner eyes. It is through her spiritual beliefs that she is able to understand the metaphor of the moths.

There is also a place, which she cannot name and only refers to as *x*. It is in this place, she suggests, that questions that persist will one day be answered, an allusion to a final place of paradise or heaven. In another place in the poem, this place becomes the "workshop." It is through the speaker's allusions that the reader can infer her spiritual belief in a creator, a possible final explanation of what life is all about, and a final place of illumination where a person is granted a "remaking" of wings or a spiritual understanding.

Style

Imagery

Behn uses the imagery of moths throughout this poem. The moths, then in turn, acquire other images, such as the "inner eyes." It is through the moths that the speaker of the poem learns to accept her friend's death. She talks to her friend through the moths. And in some way, the moths also represent her friends—she is not alone because the moths alight on her window. There are also hidden aspects or symbols associated with the moths that are not explicitly mentioned but are subliminally expressed through an accepted cultural understanding. These include the metaphor of rebirth. A moth was once a caterpillar, so it becomes a symbol of life and death. Behn does not mention this in any part of her poem. But readers may associate the moths with life and death. There is the life of the speaker and the death of the friend. There is also the longing of the speaker for the friend to return or be reborn. The speaker also talks about an afterlife, which is another form of the life/death/life metamorphous that the caterpillar/moth enacts. In another way, the moth also suggests suicide, as moths may be drawn to their deaths when they see lit candles and fly toward the flame. Therefore, the moth and the suicidal friend are connected.

Light is also used as an image. Light may be death to the moth, but it is also illumination or a type of spiritual awakening. The speaker states that the light illumines the moths parallel to her own spiritual awakening, in which "an old idea" is placed "on a new ledge in the brain." In this sense, light is like the proverbial light bulb that turns on when a person is inspired. The speaker also mentions lighting the light, a practice of lighting candles for the dead. This is a memorial practice, with the candles lighting the way for the dead for the journey across the unknown. The candle also represents a reminder for those who remain alive. The candle's statement is that life is temporary. Eventually the candle is extinguished. In another place in the poem, the speaker says that she has become the light to the moths. Here she uses the light in a way that suggests friendship. The moths are drawn to her and keep her company, abating her loneliness. And finally, the speaker states that her inner eyes are impervious to the light. This time, light represents the outer world, the world of physicality. When she turns her eyes inward, to the darkness, she sees things that she cannot see in the light.

The river is used metaphorically as a crossing from life to death. The river called her friend just as the light called the moths. The river filled her love and smothered out life. Looked at in one way, the river (or nature in general) caused a tragedy. But the speaker goes further with this metaphor. Her friend desired "to be filled," and the river was what filled her friend. The river brought satisfaction. The friend was thirsty for knowledge of the other side and broke "against the real river for good." The "real river" represents the answers to the unknown or the promise of returning to a place of all-knowing. The river, in some myths, is a place of crossing from one world to another.

There is frequent mention of eyes in this poem. There are the decorated eyes on the wings of the moths, fake eyes that frighten away predators. There are the eyes that see memories and eyes that see the messages or the signs that are placed along the path of life, messages that help people better understand life.

Finally, there are the metaphors for death. These include the use of "*x*," which stands for the unknown. The aspect of darkness, or "darker kissmarks on that dark," suggests death. And the speaker also mentions the act of extraction, which implies the symbolic loss of spirit, or life.

Title

There are many interesting facets to the form of this poem. To begin with, the poet brings the title into the body of the poem by relating her first sentence directly to the title. The phrase "Since then" opens the poem, a phrase that would not make full sense without considering the title. This adds emphasis to the title, letting the reader know that it is not just the drowning that is the topic of this poem but also the time that has lapsed between the suicide of her friend and the time of the writing of the poem.

Couplet

The other obvious form is the use of the couplet, two lines placed on the page without space between them. These couplets are not rhymed and the phrases they contain are not always directly related to one another. For example, the couplet that reads, "To them I am *the* light. / Days I don't come with flowers," is not a complete thought. In order to finish the thought, the reader must continue to the next couplet. The couplet does, however, provide the opportunity to place a lot of space into this poem. Space is a form that is often used when a poet is expressing a particular emotion. The space offsets the words, intensifying them, reflecting how emotions intensify life. Also, since there is no rhyming scheme, the space provides a cadence, or a beat. If the cadence is not even within the couplets, there is still a regular beat presented, at least spatially, with the pattern of two lines then a space, two lines then a space.

Free Verse

The overall form is that of free verse, a poem that does not include rhyme or meter and in which the line is based on thought rather than on a syllabic beat. A free-verse poem reads a lot more like narrative than poetry. The thoughts and images of the poem influence the structure, which reads much like a person talking. Walt Whitman's "Leaves of Grass" (1855) is often cited as a classic form of American free verse. Modern poets, who are aware of traditional form, nonetheless choose to break all the rules and create a form that fits the images that are to be portrayed.

Historical Context

Economics, Fashion, and Politics in the 1990s

The 1990s were a mixed bag of good news and bad, with many of the events of the 1990s mirroring those of the first four years in the twenty-first century. For instance, in the 1990s there was a president in the White House named Bush, who was forced to deal with the then-Iraqi-head-of-state Saddam Hussein. There was a Gulf War broadcast live on television. Trouble on Wall Street was also present in the 1990s and came in part through Mikel Milken, who pleaded guilty to securities fraud. And another Middle Eastern country, Iran, was also in the news in the form of the Iran-Contra affair, a political/military circumstance that left Oliver North facing charges for attempting to cover up details about the U.S. government selling guns to the Iranians in exchange for hostages, charges that were later overturned.

In fashion, mini-skirts were back again; and very high-priced sneakers were the fad. Arnold Schwarzenegger was in the news, not because of politics but due to his box-office hits—the *Terminator* movie series. Another familiar name in the early years of the twenty-first century was also well known in the 1990s—that of Rush Limbaugh, who gained a lot of attention with his bestseller, *The Way Things Ought to Be*.

The 1990s stood alone, however, with its share of surprises. On a note of victory, the Berlin Wall was torn down, thus reuniting East and West Berlin; the Cold War was ended; and Apartheid in South Africa was eliminated, allowing Nelson Mandela to be freed after spending over thirty years as a political prisoner. The U.S.S.R. disintegrated, leaving the United States the sole superpower in the world. And in technology, the growth of the Internet made emailing one's friends more popular than talking on the phone.

Poetry in the 1990s

Poetry in the 1990s experienced a change in direction. Free verse and autobiographical, or personal poetry, began a trend that gained enthusiasm as the 1900s progressed. Then poets such as Philip Dacey (*What's Empty Weighs the Most: 24 Sonnets*, 1997), David Jauss (*Black Maps*, 1996), and Dana Gioia (*The Gods of Winter*, 1991), who are referred to as neo-formalist, turned the clock back to a time when poetry was written according to established rules of rhyme and meter, with subjects that were less personal and more universal. Neo-formalists are sometimes referred to as extremists on the right as they attempt to bring back a reliance on tradition. Those who write free verse, in contrast, are called centrists. Free-versers, some say, are more American because they are always looking for new forms, breaking with tradition. While, neo-formalists, some critics believe, rely too much on old European styles.

On the left extreme are what are referred to as language poets. These include Rae Armantrout (*Necromance*, 1991), Steve Benson (*Roaring Spring*, 1998), and Lyn Hejinian (*My Life*, 2002). Language poets are known for the exploration of words for their meaning. Language poets are said, in general, to invite the reader into the production of a poem. These poets often leave the meaning ambiguous so that the reader is not a passive partner. Instead, the reader must work on the poem to discover his or her own meaning.

Multicultural literature, which began its surge in the 1960s, continued to expand in the 1990s. The first ethnic group to receive a lot of attention was African American poets. Then Latino and Native American poetry gained in popularity. By the 1990s, poetry from Americans with Chinese, Japanese, and other Asian backgrounds flourished, as did poetry translated into English from poets from all over the world.

Critical Overview

Behn's most highly praised poetry collection is *Horizon Note*, published in 2002. As Craig Arnold puts it in *Poetry*, "There's much to envy in this book—Robin Behn's third, and her best to date." *The Red Hour*, Behn's second collection, which includes "Ten Years after Your Deliberate Drowning," also received praise, but the writing in *The Red Hour* is considered by many critics less mature than that in *Horizon Note*, which is no surprise given that it was published ten years prior. Mary Ann Samyn in *Cross Currents* finds *The Red Hour* sometimes difficult to read (because of the subject matter, not for the writing). Behn's poetry, Samyn writes, "demand[s] much from . . . readers," but in spite of this the "rewards are plentiful." Samyn continues, "the reader willing to stay with the difficult emotional material will arrive at final destinations full of everyday graces." A *Publishers Weekly* reviewer also notes that some of the material in *The Red Hour* is hard to face, including the suicide of Behn's friend in "Ten Years after Your Deliberate Drowning." This same critic enjoyed Behn's use of extended metaphors: "[Behn] proves herself highly adept in the use of simile and metaphor, giving already weighty subjects further depth." Although Fred Muratori in *Library Journal* thought Behn relied too much on metaphors, which "smothered" her "protagonists" with "zealous, awkward cleverness," he finds, overall, that Behn's poetry is "eager to separate itself from the flat musings of her contemporaries." Pat Monaghan, writing in *Booklist*, remarks on the spiritual aspect of Behn's poems. "Behn's spirituality is unorthodox," Monaghan noted and explained further that "Behn explores . . . the intersection between self and God."

Criticism

Joyce Hart

Hart has degrees in English and creative writing and is a freelance writer and author of several books. In this essay, Hart studies the subtle way Behn exposes her emotions in "Ten Years after Your Deliberate Drowning."

Behn's poem "Ten Years after Your Deliberate Drowning," given the poet's focused subject of suicide, could have been, at its worse, a melodramatic rendering. There is material in this poem, such as a vivid image of a corpse, which could have justified an overflow of sobbing phrases. But Behn did not allow that to happen. Maybe it was the ten-year lapse between the actual event and the writing of the poem that provided her the needed objectivity, the space and time to remove herself from personal saturation of her emotions. Nonetheless, the emotions are still evident, and possibly they are even more intense in her silence. The purpose of this essay is to look at the ways Behn exposes herself to her readers, the way she subtly hints at the deep love she feels for her departed friend and at what she has endured since her friend's death.

> *"Behn's monster is her emotions, which have been opened just as the moths' wings are open. And her struggle is not to close her emotions but rather to learn to live with them open without letting them consuming her."*

Right from the beginning, Behn causes the reader to pause with the wording of her poem's title. Behn does not use the word *suicide* nor does she use the word *death*. Instead, she has chosen to refer to her friend's passing as a "drowning." But it is not an ordinary drowning. It is a "deliberate" one. And from this point, Behn tells her readers that she is angry. If she had merely used either *suicide* or *death*, she would have implied that her friend was gone. And with the use of either of those words, her message would have been flat. But Behn raises the tension, because the word *deliberate* implies a lot more than a simple passing. Rather it suggests that there was premeditation involved, that her friend had decided to kill himself. And that is what has baffled the poet. Why would her friend do this? Why had she not seen the signs? What was her part in his drowning? The death of a friend from natural causes is heartbreaking enough. But to be left with these unanswered questions causes more tension. Behn wants the reader to know this right from the beginning. The word *deliberate* is explicit.

In the first line of the poem, there is another subtlety. The speaker states that since the drowning, she works at night. If the statement of her title had not preceded this line, little might have been made of it. After all, most readers would probably have considered that the speaker works a regular job during the day; therefore, the only time allotted to the poet's writing is at night. But there is another interpretation to ponder. If the first line is read along with the title, a fine twist might be implied. Holding the title in mind, one can infer that prior to her friend's drowning, the speaker did not write

What Do I Read Next?

- Behn's first collection of poetry, *Paper Bird* (1988), contains many poems that delve into the spiritual. She demonstrates her skill with figurative language as she stretches her images to their full without losing control of them.

- *Horizon Note* (2001) has been called Behn's best collection. She won the Brittingham Prize in poetry for this book. A consistent overtone in this collection is that of music, which Behn uses as a metaphor throughout.

- *Eyeshot* (2003) is a collection of highly praised poems by Heather McHugh, a prize-winning Canadian writer who was educated at Harvard and who has taught at many U.S. colleges. Her work is often described as witty, sensual, and outright funny.

- Beth Ann Fennelly's *Open House: Poems* (2002) won the Kenyon Review Prize in poetry and has been described as being witty and filled with unexpected insights. Fennelly states that she loves to write about those moments after which everything is changed. She also likes to write with a sense of humor.

- Catie Rosemurgy's first collection of poetry, *My Favorite Apocalypse* (2001), has won not only prestigious awards but also the affection of her readers for her outspoken voice and for her daring. Her poetry has been described as being somewhere between Yeats and Mick Jagger.

---

at night, that the suicide of her friend has caused this change. And from that point, one might question why this change occurred. The obvious would be to realize that while the friend was alive, the speaker of this poem and the friend kept company at night. There was no time to write at night. This would imply that the speaker is insinuating that she is now lonely at night. Taken a step further, it could also imply that she has trouble sleeping. She might even feel restless at night and is led to her writing as a way of trying to make sense of her emotions that are keeping her awake.

So in just the first two lines of her poem, Behn, with only a few words that normally would not allude to the extent of one's emotions, has exposed some of her innermost feelings. It is from this point that she begins her long metaphor through the symbol of moths. She states that on the glass in front of her, she has "decorative eyes" staring back at her, so she is not alone. Here, Behn employs understatement and tries to fool the reader into thinking this is an honest comment on her state of mind. It is as if someone had asked if she had food in the house, and she had looked up at her all-but-empty cupboard and seen a few crumbs of bread and therefore answered she would not go hungry. Of course, she is lonesome. If she is still trying to come to terms with the suicide of her friend ten years after it happened, she is still missing him. And his absence is causing more than loneliness.

In the next passage, the speaker claims that to the moths, she is "*the* light." Why would she say this? Could it be possible that she is mocking herself? She, who cannot see the light has become the light for these moths. They are drawn to her as if she were the beacon in the dark, a lighthouse. What a joke that must seem to her when she still feels so lost a long decade later.

Then the speaker begins to feel guilty, not for longing for her friend, clinging to his memory for so long. Rather, she feels bad about the days, in the past ten years, when she did not take flowers to her friend's grave. With these words, she implies that this has become a ritual. She does not say *months* or *years*. She says "days I don't come." If all she has missed is days during those ten years, why would she feel guilty? The only conclusion one can come to is that she still feels guilty about her friend's death. Again she implies her loneliness, because she frequents the cemetery as often as one would visit a close friend. No one has apparently replaced the camaraderie or maybe even the love that she still feels for this dead person. Even in death, her friend has not left her. Or at least, she has not yet left her friend.

The speaker says that when she does not bring flowers, her friend is to think of the "white petals / pressed into this pane." She is referring to the moths, whose flattened wings look like petals. But what else might she be thinking about? White can stand for death, such as the whiteness of one's skin after all the blood had drained from the surface. White is often used to imply the spirit or the ghost of someone who has died but white is also a color used in weddings. So is the speaker thinking of flowers at a funeral or the flowers she never received at a wedding ceremony? And in this same statement, Behn uses the word "pane" to refer to the window. Why did she not use the word *window* or *glass*? Could it be that Behn chose the word "pane" because it is a homophone (a word that sounds the same as another word with a different meaning) of the word *pain*? Readers might pass over this phrase quickly without realizing the relationship, but something subconsciously sinks in. There is real pain in this poem despite the fact that the poet tries very hard to disguise it.

Another good example of how expertly Behn camouflages her emotions is in the mention of her friend's "trapezoids"—her friend's shoulders. The common saying of having a shoulder to lean on is not lost on Behn. Of all the body parts she might have mentioned, her friend's hands or face or arms, she remembers the shoulders. These are broad shoulders, she implies, strong enough to hide her from the outside world, something she has been missing since her friend's demise. But even here, with this statement, the speaker does not come straight out and declare her longing. Instead, she transfers her emotions to the moths: "They too remember your shoulders."

The only other time the speaker mentions her friend's body is when she describes it in death. What could have given her the strength and courage to wrap her arms around a bloated and stiff body? How could anyone ever forget the deep emotions conjured up by that contact with a dead and disfigured body—a body that had previously been as warm and sheltering. What but the deepest love could have inspired that? And if Behn is telling her readers that is exactly what she did, then she is also confessing the deep sorrow that remains inside of her. If that is not enough proof of the depth of her emotions, then her reference to "the thought that would eat you" cinches it. Her "creature so big" is not something outside her. But it is a predator. And this whole poem might be about her struggle to tame it or to avert it. Behn's monster is her emotions, which have been opened just as the moths' wings are open. And her struggle is not to close her emotions but rather to learn to live with them open without letting them consuming her.

Source: Joyce Hart, Critical Essay on "Ten Years after Your Deliberate Drowning," in *Poetry for Students*, Thomson Gale, 2005.

Pamela Steed Hill

Hill is the author of a poetry collection, has published widely in literary journals, and is an editor for a university publications department. In the following essay, she discusses Behn's prolific use of light and dark to describe the conflicting emotions she experiences after the suicide of a loved one.

The stark title of Behn's poem is as deliberate as the intentional drowning of someone the speaker knew and cared about a decade before the work was written. Typical of Behn's style, the language is honest and uncomplicated throughout. Yet, it is also delicately woven with soft, provocative images that play against the harshness of the title. Her use of a light-versus-dark motif is made all the more powerful by the use of the moths through which she portrays it. These frail, elusive creatures that come out at night, drawn toward light bulbs and candle flame, provide a fitting and intriguing vehicle for expressing grief and complacence, sorrow and serenity. In short, they are the light and the dark of the speaker's mind as she struggles toward emotional balance.

"Ten Years after Your Deliberate Drowning" begins with an assertion for which no reason is given. The speaker addresses her deceased friend, saying that she has been working "at night" since the loved one's suicide. The work she refers to is likely composing poems, but it could be any night-shift position she holds. Regardless of which, she offers no explanation for what must be a considerable change in lifestyle if her work previously had been completed during daytime hours. These first words of the poem help define the difficult mind-set of the speaker who has responded to her grief with a drastic decision. After announcing it in the first line, she goes immediately to an image of "identical moths" that "open themselves" to her. Perhaps the sudden shift is only a creative effort to diminish reality through metaphor, thereby easing the conflict of emotions.

Light in various forms permeates the poem, from the "lamp" that "illumines the decorative eyes"

"After the grim depiction of her friend's corpse and her declaration that only impenetrable eyes can bear to see it, the speaker thinks again of the moths."

of the moths to "the light" lit for the dead to "an old idea alighting / on a new ledge in the brain." The speaker even suggests that the insects have bestowed an odd kind of divinity upon her, claiming that "To them I am *the* light." But she does not seem to consider herself a superior being to them. Instead, they provide companionship and comfort, keeping her from being lonely, as she assures her deceased friend. The relationship between the speaker and the moths is made even more complex when she compares their wings ("these white petals" and "Pale shapely trapezoids") to the shoulders of the dead friend. In doing so, she implies a desire to remember something good, something white and pretty to fend off the darker memories that are sure to follow.

Another quick shift in the speaker's thoughts occurs in the eighth and ninth stanzas when she says, "Tell me what *x* is." Whether *x* is a limitless number of "nights in a row" that she neglects to "light the light" for her dead friend or the eternity in which the loved one "must be . . . by now," the emotions stirred by either idea are too much to ponder. She suddenly returns to the moths, as before, describing one's movement across the windowpane as it "travels several inches / on its thready legs." The speaker again takes mental refuge in a comforting metaphor, still concentrating on the insects as lovers of light and brightness. She knows they represent the opposite side as well, however, and her attention cannot be swayed from it for long.

The second half of the poem is given more to the dark side of the speaker's thoughts and, therefore, the darkness suggested by the presence of moths at the window. People do not tend to see or pay attention to moths except after nightfall when the airy creatures flutter about outdoor lights or make their way inside to dart around lamps or television screens. This inevitable association with darkness intrudes upon the speaker's thoughts as she pictures the dead friend's body "filled almost up with water / harden in [her] arms." She claims that "The eyes through which I see this / are impervious to light," meaning it is impossible for light to penetrate them. Although her mind cannot escape the horror of the scene, her eyes will not allow full light to shine upon it. In essence, she takes comfort and cover in the darkness that comes when she closes her eyes to sights too painful to recall.

After the grim depiction of her friend's corpse and her declaration that only impenetrable eyes can bear to see it, the speaker thinks again of the moths. Here, though, the decorative eyes, pretty white petals, and shapely trapezoids of her earlier thoughts are changed into "the inner eyes / of a creature so big it could eat / both you and the thought that would eat you." Suddenly the moths are monstrous. What she has "learned" from them is that there are times when a human too must "open [her] wings" and defy the horrible emotions that would overcome her if she weakens. She must "flash" the secret eyes that are normally hidden in a last effort to combat the dark realm of sadness, grief, and depression.

In the end, the darker emotions seem to prevail in the speaker's mind. The moths do not revert to their airy, light character but exist in images of compulsion and loneliness. Instead of abating, the dark thoughts multiply ("there are more and more"), and, like the insects, they are helplessly compelled to bang at the glass and "never fly away." They also never "rest in pairs," implying a solitary existence, whether forced or self-imposed. One of the most striking images is of "the workshop where the thing is extracted / that leaves behind the dark." The moths have been there, their light taken from them, leaving them only "clustered shadows" that "spill darker kissmarks on that dark." But the workshop is for people too. The same being that made the wings of the moths is now making wings for the speaker's loved one. This picture is both haunting and depressing. One must assume that the dead will not only be given wings but will also have the "thing . . . extracted" that leaves behind their own darkness.

It is difficult not to read Behn's poem as a despairing and melancholy work, and, given the inspiration for it, one is not likely surprised by its gloominess. If anything saves it from being completely woebegone, however, it is the intriguing mechanism through which the poet relays its message. Her inventive use of moths and their natural association with both light and darkness move the poem away from pure pathos and sentimentality and toward a more thoughtful form of expression. The reader is not necessarily expected to sympathize with the speaker but to intellectualize her response to a friend's suicide. One is forced to ponder not just a grievous loss or a grim scene but the irony of despair and hope, surrender and determination.

Readers may also make a case for an ending that is not totally pessimistic. Even though the words "darker" and "dark" both appear in the final line of the poem, so does "kissmarks," a rather playful, light description of moths dancing about and touching the windowpane. It suggests a sweet, friendly relationship between the speaker and the creatures that come to visit her at night as she works. The first half of the poem, at least, supports this more pleasant scenario in which the moths are portrayed in a welcoming manner. But if the fluttering bugs actually represent a turmoil of emotions, one cannot be too sure of the friendship. After all, it is only the outer light of a burning lamp that draws them. Their inner light has apparently been extinguished.

Source: Pamela Steed Hill, Critical Essay on "Ten Years after Your Deliberate Drowning" in *Poetry for Students*, Thomson Gale, 2005.

Sources

Arnold, Craig, Review of *Horizon Note*, in *Poetry*, Vol. 180, No. 3, June 2002, pp. 170–73.

Behn, Robin, *The Red Hour*, HarperCollins, 1993.

Monaghan, Pat, Review of *The Red Hour*, in *Booklist*, Vol. 90, No. 3, October 1, 1993, p. 246.

Muratori, Fred, Review of *The Red Hour*, in *Library Journal*, Vol. 118, No. 18, November 1, 1993, p. 97.

Review of *The Red Hour*, in *Publishers Weekly*, Vol. 240, No. 38, September 20, 1993, p. 67.

Samyn, Mary Ann, "Through Loss to Gladness," in *Cross Currents*, Vol. 44, No. 3, Fall 1994, pp. 418–20.

Further Reading

Barnstone, Aliki, *Book of Women Poets: From Antiquity to Now*, rev. ed., Schocken Books, 1992.

This is a highly praised collection of more than 300 poets from all over the world. The editor of this collection is also a poet, and her poetic inclination is evident in the collection.

Behn, Robin, and Chase Twichell, *The Practice of Poetry: Writing Exercises from Poets Who Teach*, Harper Resource, 1992.

This is a collection of writing exercises from practicing poets and teachers to help aspiring poets. Several essays are also included to provide instruction and inspiration.

Jamison, Kay Redfield, *Night Falls Fast: Understanding Suicide*, Vintage, 2000.

Dr. Jamison once planned her own suicide, then recovered from her depression, went on to receive a degree in psychiatry, and taught at Johns Hopkins University. In her book, Jamison provides personal, professional, and scientific information on the topic of suicide.

Wooldridge, Susan G., *Poemcrazy: Freeing Your Life with Words*, Three Rivers Press, 1997.

Anne Lamott (*Bird by Bird*, 1995) helped fiction writers loosen up so they could write better, and now Wooldridge has done the same for poets. Wooldridge has run many successful writers' workshops and has put the knowledge she has gained as a teacher and poet into this book.

While I Was Gone a War Began

Ana Castillo

2001

On August 7, 1998, Al Qaeda operatives under the direction of Osama Bin Laden bombed two United States embassies in Africa. The truck bombing in Nairobi, Kenya, killed 213 people, injured approximately 4,000, and severely damaged the embassy. The other bombing, in Dar Es Salaam, Tanzania, killed twelve people and injured eighty-five others. Upon hearing about these bombings, Ana Castillo wrote the poem "While I Was Gone a War Began," and she notes in *I Ask the Impossible* (2001), the collection in which the poem appears, that the poem was originally written in 1998 in Chicago. The poem is thus a reaction to a specific (albeit unnamed within the poem) incident, but it addresses the violent state of the world in general.

Although Al Qaeda terrorist attacks against the United States have been numerous, the embassy bombings were the most notable until the World Trade Center and Pentagon attacks in the United States on September 11, 2001. The title of Castillo's poem, therefore, seems prophetic. The war against America had indeed begun, but the majority of the public did not realize it until the New York City and Washington, DC attacks on that date.

"While I Was Gone a War Began" is set in a vineyard and in Rome, Italy. The message of the poem seems to be that everyone is affected by world events, and everyone must do his part to improve the world in whatever way his talents enable him. The poem also questions the effectiveness of literature in combating social injustice and expresses frustration with the public's acceptance of violence as a norm in everyday life.

Author Biography

Born to Raymond and Raquel Rocha Castillo on June 15, 1953, Ana Castillo grew up speaking Spanish in a working-class Italian neighborhood in Chicago, where she first encountered the prejudice that led her to become active in the Chicano and feminist movements. She feels, however, that the urban environment was beneficial in that it exposed her to a range of cultures, beliefs, and customs. Her parents were great storytellers, but they took the practical road of sending their daughter to a secretarial high school. However, Castillo's lack of interest and poor typing skills led her to pursue higher education at Chicago City College and then Northern Illinois University. At first she studied art but was so discouraged by teachers who failed to understand her cultural and feminine perspective that she turned to writing for personal expression and finished with a bachelor's degree in liberal arts in 1975. Supporting herself by serving as a college lecturer and a writer-in-residence for the Illinois Arts Council, Castillo then worked toward her master's degree in Latin American and Caribbean studies at the University of Chicago and graduated in 1979. The years that followed were filled with a variety of short-term college teaching positions. In 1991, Castillo was granted a doctorate in American studies from the University of Bremen in Germany.

Castillo has said she never thought of writing as a way to make a living. Her topics have been such that she also did not expect to be noticed by the mainstream. Nevertheless, by the mid-1990s Castillo had won several prestigious awards and was able to become a full-time writer. Although Castillo started out as a poet, she has also written novels and short stories with themes that mirror her poetry: social consciousness, feminism, and life as a Chicana. Among her awards are two National Endowment for the Arts fellowships (1990 and 1995), and the Carl Sandburg Literary Award in 1993 for her novel *So Far from God* (1993). Other acclaimed works are *The Mixquiahuala Letters* (1986); *Peel My Love like an Onion* (1999); *My Father Was a Toltec and Selected Poems 1973–1988* (1995; originally published as *My Father Was a Toltec: Poems* in 1988); *Massacre of the Dreamers: Essays on Xicanisma* (1994), a collection of essays; and

Ana Castillo

Loverboys (1996), a collection of stories. In addition, Castillo's work appears in numerous anthologies, and she has published various articles. In April 2000, Castillo and other notable Chicagoans were depicted on a historical mural on the sky deck of the Sears Tower.

In 2001, Castillo published her fifth volume of poetry, *I Ask the Impossible*, which contains work written over the previous eleven years. Intended to express topics relevant to women, particularly poor or minority women, the poems are about death, social protest, love, and family relationships. Among the poems is "While I Was Gone a War Began," as well as several poems that focus on the childhood of Castillo's son, Marcel Ramon Herrera. The public can read about her activities at her Website: http://www.anacastillo.com.

Poem Text

While I was gone a war began.
Every day I asked friends in Rome
to translate the news.
It seems I saw this story
in a Hollywood movie,
or on a Taco Bell commercial,
maybe in an ad for sunglasses

or summer wear—shown somewhere
for promotional purposes.

Hadn't I seen it in an underground cartoon,
a sinister sheikh versus John Wayne?
Remembering Revelation I wanted to laugh,
the way a nonbeliever remembers Sunday School
and laughs, which is to say—
after flood and rains,
drought and despair,
abrupt invasions,
disease and famine everywhere,
we're still left dumbfounded
at the persistence of fiction.

While I was gone
continents exploded—
the Congo, Ireland,
Mexico, to name a few places.
At this rate, one day soon
they won't exist at all.
It's only a speculation, of course.

"What good have all the great writers done?"
an Italian dissident asked, as if
this new war were my personal charge.
"What good your poems,
your good intentions,
your thoughts and words
all for the common good?
What lives have they saved?
What mouths do they feed?
What good is your blue passport
when your American plane blows up?"
the Italian dissident asked in a rage.
"Forced out of his country,
the poor African selling trinkets in Italy,
does not hesitate to kill other blacks
not of his tribe.
Who is the bad guy? Who is the last racist?
Who colonizes in the twenty-first century best:
the Mexican official over the Indian
or the gringo ranchero over the Mexican illegal?
"I hope for your sake your poems become
missiles,"
the dissident said. He lit a cigarette, held it to
his yellowed teeth.
"I hope for my sake, too. I tried," he said.
"I did not write books or have sons
but I gave my life
and now, I don't care."

Again, I had nothing to give but a few words
Which I thought then to keep to myself
for all their apparent uselessness.
We drank some wine, instead,
made from his dead father's vineyard.
We trapped a rat getting into the vat.
We watched another red sun set over the fields.
At dawn, I left,
returned to the silence of the press
when it has no sordid scandal to report.
As if we should not be scandalized
by surprise bombing over any city at night,
bombs scandalizing the sanctity of night.

Poem Summary

Stanza 1

In the first line, the narrator states that while she "was gone a war began," but she does not divulge in this first stanza where she has been or where the war is. She notes that she is in Rome and that she has been seeking translations of daily news reports from her friends. The narrator feels as if she has heard the story before, perhaps in a movie or an advertisement. The scenes of war on television must appear like movies or commercials; they have been seen before so many times, but this time they are for real and the speaker is in disbelief.

Stanza 2

The narrator questions whether she has seen these images before in an underground cartoon, or perhaps in an old John Wayne film. John Wayne stands for the ideal American defender. Castillo may have chosen the phrase "sinister sheikh" because it is a stereotypical image that Americans have of Arab terrorists. Consequently, the "sinister sheikh versus John Wayne" is the classic bad guy versus good guy.

Turning then to a biblical reference, the narrator brings to mind the disasters recorded in the Book of Revelation. Comparing herself to a nonbeliever remembering Sunday school as just a bunch of stories and not true recordings or predictions, she wonders why people bother with such fiction when real life is much scarier. The fiction seems scarier than anything we can imagine from our comfortable little worlds, but it is not. For centuries, the apocalyptic events in Revelation have been considered the worst possible disasters. The narrator lists a number of such catastrophes that have already happened around the world, repeatedly and at the same time, and is at a loss to explain the continued existence of fiction. Reality is enough.

Stanza 3

In this stanza, the narrator discusses conflicts that have erupted around the world. The narrator mentions the Congo, Ireland, and Mexico, because in 1998 rebel forces took over large sections of the Congo from its relatively new ruler; the Good Friday Agreement in Ireland that was expected to bring long-sought peace to the country was met with continued violence by the IRA; and in the impoverished state of Chiapas, Mexico, Zapatista rebels and the Mexican Army continued to clash. The narrator suggests that the rate of conflict is such that in these parts of the world and presumably elsewhere humans may soon destroy everything and everyone. The line "It's only a speculation, of course" is a sarcastic touch added, possibly, for all the people who respond cynically to such a prediction.

Stanza 4

This long stanza is a conversation between the narrator and a person she calls "an Italian dissident." The dissident angrily asks her what good the great writers have done in terms of saving lives and feeding the hungry. He mocks her by asking what protection an American passport gives her "when your American plane blows up?" in a possible reference to the bombing of Pan Am flight 203 over Lockerbie, Scotland in 1988. He asks these questions, says the narrator, "as if / this new war were my personal charge." Considering Castillo's message in this poem that each person has to make a contribution to the world, perhaps she uses the word "personal" intentionally to indicate that the war is indeed her personal charge because every individual must take responsibility for what goes on in the world.

The dissident mentions that African refugees in Italy now selling trinkets would not hesitate to kill their enemy again if given the chance. The dissident asks if the African is the bad guy or the ones who drives him out of his country. He questions "Who is the last racist?" in a chain of racists, if the white colonialists killed blacks, but blacks now kill each other. And who exhibits the worst colonial behavior, the Mexican authority brutalizing the indigents or the white rancher taking advantage of the Mexican illegal immigrants?

The stanza concludes with the dissident saying he hopes that for both their sakes the narrator's pen will be mightier than the sword in its effectiveness at combating the world's problems. He says that he is not a writer or a father, but he still gives his life for a good cause until he no longer has the energy or will to care anymore. The description of the dissident as a smoker with yellowed teeth makes him more real in the reader's mind.

Stanza 5

The dissident's angry comments leave the narrator speechless at the realization of the possible futility of her words. She also may feel chastised for using words when he had just told her they do no good. The narrator and the dissident drink wine in silence and trap "a rat getting into the vat." She reveals that she and the dissident are at the vineyard that belonged to the dissident's late father. They watch the sun set together. These common actions are placed in the poem to indicate that life goes on. We have to keep living, so we eat and drink. We act as if there will be a future by preserving a vat from getting contaminated. Castillo's use of the word "another" in describing the red sunset reminds the reader that there have been many sunsets before and, most likely, there will be many more to come. At the end of the poem, the narrator returns to the world where the press is more concerned with "sordid scandal" than with reporting on the world's anguish, when in fact "surprise bombing over any city at night" is the worst scandal of all. "Any" and every bombing should be considered a violent assault on us all because, ultimately, we are all affected in some way or another. Such incidents are not someone else's problem, but a horror that should disturb us into action to preserve the "sanctity of the night."

Themes

War

The theme of war is obvious in this poem since the word "war" is in its title. First the narrator hears the news of the war, and then she describes her reaction. She names countries where violence is threatening to destroy the people entirely, and she gives examples of the universality of hatred and power struggles. After speculating about the value of literature in a war-torn world, she also points out how people have become so used to wars that they have perhaps accepted the violence as normal and turned their attention to more trivial matters.

Role of Literature

The Italian dissident in the poem asks, "What good have all the great writers done? . . . What good your poems, / your good intentions, / your thoughts and words." These questions have probably been asked for centuries, yet we know that every great civilization has had a body of literature and that poets, dramatists, and other storytellers have existed for thousands of years. The Greek tragedies show us that literature has more purpose than a pleasant way to pass the time; literature can be used as a vehicle for change. It can have the impact of Thomas Paine's essays that helped start a revolution. Literature can teach, advise, console, enlighten, and incite. Literature can help us to reflect upon the past and to envision the future. Literature can have a message of such impact that "poems become missiles," as the

Topics For Further Study

- One of Ana Castillo's influences has been Columbian author Gabriel Garcia Marquez, winner of the Nobel Prize for literature in 1982. Research the life and works of Garcia Marquez and comment on the impact he has had on Latin American and world literature.
- Another influence on Castillo is the "magical realism" movement made famous by a number of prominent Latin American writers. Describe magical realism and name some of the members of the movement from South America.
- Castillo is considered one of the best writers in Chicana literature. What is Chicana literature? What are its distinguishing features? In what time period has this literature been written?
- "While I Was Gone a War Began" is a poem about the violence in our world. Elsewhere in *I Ask the Impossible*, Castillo makes mention of Sister Dianna Ortiz, Anna Mae Aquash, and Comandante Ramona. Who are these women and what is their connection to violence in world affairs?
- It is often mentioned that Castillo participated in the Chicano Civil Rights movement of the 1960s and 1970s. What was this movement and how did it differ from that of African Americans?

dissident hopes in "While I Was Gone a War Began." Consequently, writers keep writing with the mission of proving that the pen is mightier than the sword and that the role of literature is vitally important to the question of whether civilization thrives or fails.

Fiction versus Reality

Perhaps it is a human defense mechanism to confuse fiction and reality. When the narrator of this poem hears the news about a war starting, she is not sure that the story she is hearing is real. "It seems I saw this story / in a Hollywood movie, / or on a Taco Bell commercial." The narrator is trying to point out that life in the modern world of television, movies, and other media has blurred the lines between reality and fiction and has deadened the reaction to real disaster by making people feel as if it is not real people who are suffering and dying.

The narrator in the poem goes on to question why people even bother with fiction when reality is always so much more amazing, "after flood and rains, / drought and despair, / abrupt invasions, / disease and famine everywhere." She mentions Revelation, which lists multiple catastrophes that will befall the earth just before the end of the world. The narrator is questioning why the gospel writer describes such terrors as a one-time event when such tribulations happen every day. How will people recognize Armageddon when such calamity is nothing new? The inference is that the horrors of reality can never be matched, and certainly not surpassed, by the inadequate imaginations of writers.

Apathy

The Italian dissident in the poem declares "and now, I don't care." After a lifetime of fighting for his cause, he probably still cares or else he would not complain to the narrator, but he probably feels as though he has given all he can and nothing has changed. In contrast, the people who are not "scandalized by surprise bombings" may not ever have cared. They may not want to put any effort into making the world a better place as long as their own little patch of the earth is reasonably comfortable. Why care about who is bombing whom on the other side of the world? But Castillo says a bombing over *any* city should be considered scandalous because it violates the "sanctity of night"—that is, the sanctity of peace and peace of mind. It is an old message: we are all members of the human family and what happens to one of us happens to all of us. However, not all people believe or understand this concept and that causes the narrator's sorrow at the end of "While I Was Gone a War Began."

Style

Free Verse

Free verse is the most popular poetic form used by twentieth and early twenty-first century poets, and it is the form Castillo uses in writing "While I Was Gone a War Began." Walt Whitman was perhaps the first poet to use this form, and it was quite a shock to readers in 1855 who were used to poems with strict metrical and rhyme patterns (for example, sonnets). Free verse avoids patterns and fixed line lengths. In fact, free verse varies line length to aid in achieving a desired impact. Rhythm and sound patterns are created by the use of assonance, alliteration, internal rhyme, and the like. Rhythm is also created within lines by designing phrases of about equal length and by repeating phrases that have the same syntactical structure. The result is a cadence similar to the balance of phrases in a musical composition. Castillo uses this cadence device in "While I Was Gone a War Began" when she makes her lists of places where she may have seen "this story" before (a Hollywood movie, a Taco Bell commercial, etc.) and of catastrophes (flood, drought, disease, etc.). The repetition of the "what" and the "who" questions in the fourth stanza also establish a connection and a cadence that unites the poem. The same effect is achieved in the last stanza with the repetition of "we" at the beginning of sentences. With the successful use of these free verse techniques, Castillo shows herself to be a skilled poet.

Narrative or Lyric Poetry

Lyric or narrative poems have characters, plot, setting, and a point of view similar to prose. They are not quite stories chopped into shorter lines, but they do have a story of sorts, a setting of time and place, a specific point of view, and characters dramatizing the message. Such is the case with Castillo's "While I Was Gone a War Began." The main character is the speaker in the poem, just as Castillo's narrator is the "I" in "While I Was Gone a War Began." The speaker may be the poet or a fictional character and may be speaking to another character, perhaps in a dialogue. Castillo has a second character in this poem, the Italian dissident. Their exchange about the value of literature expresses the frustration of the writer. Often, however, the speaker in a narrative poem is a lone character speaking about a personal concern.

Imagery

Imagery refers not only to the descriptive passages of a poem, but also to an appeal to the senses. The dominant sense in "While I Was Gone a War Began" is the visual sense, as seen through the mind's eye. Multiple "pictures" fill the poem: Hollywood, Taco Bell, sunglasses, summer wear, a sheikh, John Wayne, Sunday school, a flood, rains, a drought, a blue passport, a plane, a poor African selling trinkets, a Mexican official, a Mexican Indian, a white rancher, a Mexican worker, a vineyard, a vat, a rat, a red sunset over fields, and a city being bombed. Most of these are used for the purpose of comparison, but also to set the scene and to bring to mind instances of injustice that the reader knows.

Historical Context

In *I Ask the Impossible*, each of the poems is followed by a date and place indicating when the poem was written and in which city. Consequently, the reader immediately knows that "While I Was Gone a War Began" was written in 1998 in Chicago. The year 1998 was full of many noteworthy events. Castillo has revealed that she wrote this poem specifically in reaction to the August 7 bombings by Al Qaeda terrorists at two U.S. embassies in Africa. It was these bombings that first brought international notoriety to Osama Bin Laden and Al Qaeda. In response, the FBI put Bin Laden on its most-wanted list, and President Clinton, on August 20, ordered cruise missile strikes on a pharmaceutical plant in the Sudan, which was suspected of producing materials for chemical weapons. He also ordered an attack on an Al Qaeda camp in Afghanistan.

Although the specific event that inspired Castillo to write "While I Was Gone a War Began" is not mentioned in the poem, she does refer to three other hot spots in the world: the Congo, Ireland, and Mexico. In May 1997 the long-time and highly corrupt Congo ruler, Mobutu Sese Seko, was overthrown. His replacement, Laurent Kabila, soon proved to be not much better, so in August 1998 rebel forces began attacking Kabila's army and managed to take control of large portions of the country. Since this situation occurred in the same month as the embassy bombings, it was natural for Castillo to list the Congo when she declared in the poem that "continents exploded" during the time that she was gone.

Castillo also names Ireland as an explosive place. This may seem a strange choice since it was in April 1998 that the Good Friday Agreement was reached whereby the Protestants of Northern Ireland agreed to share power with the Catholics, and they

Smoking guns near the Syrian-Israeli border

gave the Republic of Ireland a voice in Northern Ireland affairs. However, it took a few years for the parties involved to follow through on the agreement and, in the meantime, the IRA, the radical opposition in Northern Ireland held responsible for multiple terrorist activities, refused to disarm. Thus, the violence continued even after the agreement was signed, and that is probably the reason Castillo mentions Ireland.

In Mexico, the third of Castillo's referenced countries, the conflict between the Mexican army and the Zapatistas escalated in June 1998. The Zapatistas are a group of mostly indigenous Mayan rebels who organized in 1994 in opposition to the Mexican government's treatment of indigenous people in the state of Chiapas. Although an agreement in 1995 gave the Mayans the right to govern themselves in autonomous communities within Mexico, the agreement was never really honored. Instead, the government built up military installations in Chiapas. In 1997, army raids into Zapatista communities resulted in multiple deaths and imprisonments. Then, in June 1998 two more massacres occurred. It is probably this terrible incident to which Castillo refers in the poem. After 1998, international support and massive demonstrations forced the Mexican government to meet some of the demands of the Zapatistas, but the situation was still not totally resolved and unrest continued.

Critical Overview

Ana Castillo enjoys a favorable reputation among critics writing for a number of prestigious publications. In an article for *MELUS*, Elsa Saeta depicts Castillo as "One of the most articulate, powerful voices in contemporary Chicana literature ... whose work has long questioned, subverted, and challenged the status quo." Janet Jones Hampton writes in an article for *Americas*, "Her poems, like her prose, recount the struggles and survival skills of marginalized peoples and sing of their dreams and hopes." Marjorie Agosin in *MultiCultural Review* praises Castillo as "lyrical and passionate" and "one of the country's most provocative and original writers."

In a critique specific to *I Ask the Impossible*, Donna Seaman in *Booklist* says Castillo's poems are "alight with stubborn love, crackling wit, and towering anger." A *Publishers Weekly* critic says of *I Ask the Impossible* that the point of Castillo's poetry is the "immediacy and the message" and that readers can bask in her "experiences and longings or get angry and motivated by her cries for justice." A review of *I Ask the Impossible* appearing in *Library Journal*, written by Lawrence Olszewski, calls Castillo "one of the most outstanding Chicanas writing today"; however, Olszewski feels the social-protest poems in this collection, which would include "While I Was Gone a War Began," are "the weakest and most routine of the lot."

Critic Norma Alarcon, in a chapter on Castillo for a collection of criticism called *Breaking Boundaries: Latina Writing and Critical Readings*, remarks on Castillo's expert use of irony as a trademark element in her poetry. Irony is also mentioned in a *Publishers Weekly* interview Samuel Baker conducted with Castillo. Baker describes Castillo as "one of the most prominent Latina writers in the U.S.," adding that "she couches passion for life and work in gentle ironies." There is little doubt that Castillo is considered an important and influential American writer of feminist, Chicana, and protest literature.

Criticism

Lois Kerschen

Kerschen is a freelance writer and part-time English instructor. In this essay, Kerschen explores the life experiences and political activism that led Castillo to writing and that are the background to "While I Was Gone a War Began."

"While I Was Gone a War Began" is a narrative or lyric poem, a type of poem that is noted for having a lone character speaking about a personal concern. This definition truly fits Ana Castillo's poem about war and other violence because she wrote the poem as a social activist in reaction to disturbing world events. Poetry is considered an ideal medium for protest because the structure of a poem requires that strong emotions be stripped to their barest expression. In "While I Was Gone a War Began" Castillo certainly achieves the expression of strong emotions and manages to tie together a number of issues in a short amount of space, including the relevance of her life as a writer.

It was almost inevitable that Ana Castillo would grow up to put a Chicana imprint on feminist and political causes. She was born in 1953, right at the beginning of a time in America when people began to rise up to claim their civil rights and question many social institutions. The Korean War was just ending, but social problems in the United States were stirring up the winds of dissent. During the summer of Castillo's birth in Chicago, there was a huge race riot in protest of integrated housing there. That same year, President Eisenhower authorized "Operation Wetback," which directed the Immigration Service to arrest and deport over 3.8 million Chicanos over the next five years. The use of the derisive term "wetback" in the name of the project indicates the extent of prejudice and discrimination directed at Mexican Americans at the time. This oppression is still evidenced in the relationship of the "gringo ranchero over the Mexican illegal" that Castillo mentions in the poem. As a Chicana activist, Castillo is very aware of the way that border ranchers take advantage of illegal immigrants from Mexico, using their status as a threat to enforce subjugation and exploitation.

When Castillo was a child, hers was the only Mexican family in an Italian neighborhood. Their Italian landlord would not allow them to use the front door and insisted that Castillo's mother scrub the front-entry stairs on her knees every Saturday morning as a condition of their lease. As Castillo later wrote in "A Chicana from Chicago" in *Essence*, she grew up with a "strange sense of ongoing vigilance and repression." Those circumstances made an indelible impression. From then on, being a member of a minority of color, being a member of a Hispanic culture, and being female defined her life and determined her mission in life as a writer.

As Castillo entered her teenage years, the situation for Chicanos was such that life was a struggle and social opportunities were limited. She remembers being subjected to police harassment because of being a Chicana. Considering the conditions Castillo experienced in Chicago, it is no wonder that the Mexican American communities in the Midwest agitated for change and joined the Chicano Civil Rights movement, even though their issues were different from those in the Southwest, where the movement was made famous. At the same time, the civil rights demonstrations by African Americans were grabbing the headlines. In her article for *Essence*, Castillo comments:

> I am very familiar with police-state mentality. I was a minor when I witnessed the riots after the Martin Luther King Jr. assassination [1968] and saw the city go up in flames from my back porch. I remember the national guard marching into my neighborhood shopping center.

"As part of the protest movement in the mid-1970s, Castillo learned that working toward social change meant making your own individual contribution of talent. For Castillo, that meant taking up the pen."

Castillo's memories of harassment, racial hatred, and a police state bring to mind the third stanza of "While I Was Gone a War Began," where the question is asked "Who is the last racist?" and references are made to the tyranny of colonial rule. The latter is illustrated in the poem by "the Mexican official over the Indian," a reference to the Mexican government treatment of the indigenous people in the state of Chiapas that has led to the Zapatista rebellion.

At the opening of "While I Was Gone a War Began," the narrator says, "Every day I asked friends in Rome / to translate the news." Even while away, apparently on a vacation, the narrator must know the news, indicating an intense interest in world affairs. This interest has resulted in an extensive knowledge about the world's hot spots as

What Do I Read Next?

- *Women Are Not Roses* (1984) is Castillo's third book of poetry. In it she explores the idea of women who feel disenfranchised in male-dominated cultures.
- *The Mixquiahuala Letters* (1986), Castillo's first novel, earned her an American Book Award from the Before Columbus Foundation. As the title indicates, the novel is composed of a series of letters, written in the 1970s and 1980s, between Teresa, a California poet, and Alicia, her college friend who has become an artist in New York City. The correspondence reveals how the roles these women have assumed differ from the traditional roles of Latina women and how the men in Teresa's and Alicia's lives—both Anglo and Chicano—resent this difference.
- In 1993 Castillo published *So Far from God*, a novel that garnered more public interest than any of her previous works. Written in the genre of magical realism, the story follows the life of a Latina woman and her four vastly different daughters. This book received the Carl Sandburg Literary Award.
- Castillo's first short-story collection was published as *Loverboys* (1996). Quirky characters, strong-willed women, and multiple variations of love and friendship fill these stories and reveal Castillo's talent for inventiveness, humor, and eroticism.
- *Peel My Love like an Onion* (1999) is a novel about a flamenco dancer who overcomes many challenges but is unlucky in love and life. This book exhibits Castillo's feminism at a new depth.
- Gabriel García Márquez is one of the Latin American authors who has influenced Ana Castillo. His book *One Hundred Years of Solitude* is world renowned and is considered one of the most influential novels of the twentieth century. It was republished in 2003.
- *MultiAmerica: Essays on Cultural Wars and Cultural Peace* (1997), edited by Ishmael Reed, is an anthology that includes essays by Castillo, Toni Morrison, Amiri Baraka, Frank Chin, Bharati Mukherhjee, Barbara Smith, and Miguel Algarin, among others.

---

indicted in the poem's references to the troubles in the Congo, Ireland, and Mexico. These references are expanded by the detail given to the "poor African selling trinkets in Italy." This African could be a refugee from the civil strife in the Congo or any of a number of conflicts that have driven Africans from their homelands, yet holding onto the tribal hatreds that cause them to "not hesitate to kill other blacks." For an activist such as Castillo, news is the daily motivation to keep working to solve the world's problems.

News is also an avenue for discovering others with whom one can identify. Just after high school, when Castillo was particularly searching for sisters in the cause, she read *As Tres Marias*, a book by three Portuguese women who broached issues affecting Latina women and for doing so were being censored and were in prison. As Castillo told Janet Jones Hampton in an interview for *Americas*, "That was a fundamental book for me that initiated my writing because it brought it all together for me." Castillo decided right then that she could also "bring all of that together in writing."

In college, Castillo (quoted in "Ana Castillo Painter of Palabras") says, the "negative social attitudes toward people of humble origins, as well as the institutional racism and sexism of the university discouraged me." This increasing awareness of the oppression subjugating her as a woman and a Mexican American led her to writing as a means of expressing her outrage. Her voracious reading of Latin American authors led her naturally to become a Chicana protest poet advocating that the image of American society should be multicultural and not just Anglo-American and decrying the economic inequality of Chicanos. In the process,

Castillo has introduced "Xicanisma," a specifically Mexican American brand of feminism. In an interview with Elsa Saeta in *MELUS*, Castillo said that, in the literature of women, we have had a void in the representation of women "who look and think and feel like me and who have had similar experiences in society. I wanted to fill that void."

As part of the protest movement in the mid-1970s, Castillo learned that working toward social change meant making your own individual contribution of talent. For Castillo, that meant taking up the pen. In "While I Was Gone a War Began," she says "I had nothing to give but a few words." Samuel Baker reports in *Publishers Weekly* that Castillo has said, "I was a Chicana protest poet, a complete renegade—and I continue to write that way." She has remarked that she wants her writing to engage the reader in a discussion of issues. A collection of Castillo's poetry written from 1973 to 1988 called *My Father Was a Toltec and Selected Poems, 1973–1988* demonstrates, sometimes in matter-of-fact statements, a political vision that has broadened and become more complicated as her career has progressed. Although Castillo is very much concerned with expressing herself as a feminist and Chicana, she seems to have come back in recent works to political subjects as well. *I Ask the Impossible* is proof of that. Once again with this poem, she is pointing out the struggles of victimized people. As previously mentioned, the third stanza gives examples of this struggle in the descriptions of the "poor African selling trinkets in Italy," "the Mexican official over the Indian," and "the gringo ranchero over the Mexican illegal." The Italian dissident with whom she has the conversation in the poem is also an example of one who struggles against injustice in that he is described as a dissident and says "I gave my life" for whatever was his cause.

In the same moment, the dissident says, "and now, I don't care." In the Saeta interview, Castillo emphasizes, "Refusing to participate is a political act" too, because not participating means that you have joined the mainstream or status quo. Thus, in this poem, Castillo presents both the act of involvement in the person of the narrator poet whose poems may have "become missiles" and the act of non-involvement as represented by the Italian dissident who no longer cares. However, it is also in this poem that she questions the value of a writer in solving these problems and expresses the frustration in trying:

> What good have all the great writers done? . . .
> What good your poems,
> your good intentions,
> your thoughts and words
> all for the common good?
> What lives have they saved?
> What mouths do they feed?

As a young woman, Castillo had trouble finding books by U.S. Latinas because Latina writers could not get published. Now, writers of all cultures and colors are being published. Some of the credit for this change can be given to Castillo who not only has written what needed to be said, but also has fought for the right to be heard. Her writings are a voice arising from her Chicana experience, but poems such as "While I Was Gone a War Began" have a universal message as well. Castillo's commitment to universal peace and justice can also be seen outside her literary works. She has written commentary in a number of articles, and she has served on the American Booksellers Association panel for Social Responsibility. As of 2004, the front page of her Website was focused on links to activist sites, to calls for action in some protest or political movement.

In the introduction to her collection of poetry *I Ask the Impossible*, Castillo says, "When I started taking writing in verse seriously nearly three decades ago, I wrote as a witness to my generation. . . . I hope that my poems still serve as testimony to the times." "While I Was Gone a War Began" is definitely a testimony to the early twenty-first century in its reaction to a violent deed, in its listing of hot spots in the world, in its questioning of the racism and oppression that continue around the globe. It also expresses a frustration with the seeming futility of efforts to better the human condition. In the opening of the fourth stanza of the poem, the narrator decides to keep her words to herself because of "their apparent uselessness." However, the despair expressed in this poem is atypical of Castillo's attitude. It is perhaps more of a barb at the apathy of others. The fact that the poem exists and was published is evidence that Castillo's political and social conscience continued its commitment to stay in the fray and fight the good fight, one poem at a time.

Source: Lois Kerschen, Critical Essay on "While I Was Gone a War Began," in *Poetry for Students*, Thomson Gale, 2005.

Ana Castillo and Samuel Baker

In the following interview, Castillo discusses her formative years, inspirations for her writing, and her upcoming projects.

The road from the nearest el stop to Ana Castillo's North Side Chicago home curves for

> "*Being of Mexican background, being Indian-looking, being a female, coming from a working-class background, and then becoming politicized in high school, that was my direction. I was going to be an artist, a poet.*"

several blocks alongside the solemn, deserted expanse of historic Graceland Cemetery and then enters an offbeat shopping district that features a fortune-teller's storefront, a shuttered nightclub and a Mexican restaurant incongruously named Lolita's. Far from seeming out of place, these picturesque locations mesh perfectly with the bustling everyday Chicago life that surrounds them. Such harmonies between the romantic and the mundane, manifest in Castillo's neighborhood, also resonate in the adventurous chords of her art—as heard most recently in the story collection *Loverboys*, out this month from Norton.

Castillo lives halfway down a side-street full of lush lawns and profuse sprinklers, in the ground-floor apartment of a tidy brick two-flat. Her son, Marcel, just out of seventh grade, ushers *PW* into a modest combination livingroom and study. Decorated in a subtle Southwestern style, the room is dominated by a series of striking paintings of Castillo—self-portraits, it turns out. Literary quarterlies share space on the coffee table with an issue of *USA Weekend* that features a Castillo story, "Juan in a Million."

The day has been a scorcher. When Castillo herself enters the room, however, her bold features set off by her long black hair and simple white sun dress, she appears totally imbued with cool. As she begins to hold forth, a wry sense of humor catalyzes energy together with reserve; she couches passion for life and work in gentle ironies. One of the most prominent Latina writers in the U.S., Castillo is already the author of three novels, several volumes of poetry and an essay collection. Today, however, our conversation starts with the latest events in her fast-moving career: the publication of her story in *USA Weekend*, with its circulation of nearly 40 million, and her appearances at the just-concluded 1996 Chicago ABA, where she did an autograph session and served on the Booksellers for Social Responsibility panel.

Talk of the ABA sparks an account of Castillo's interest in the independent bookstore scene. In the title story in *Loverboys*, Castillo draws on her experience with, and affinity for, booksellers to create a narrator who "runs the only bookstore in town that deals with the question of the soul." This protagonist handsells a volume of Camus to a philosophically inclined customer, who subsequently emerges as the main "loverboy" of the piece.

No particular store served as her model, but Castillo has long depended on independent bookstores to nurture her public. When she wrote "Loverboys" she was living in Albuquerque, writing her novel *So Far from God* and organizing occasional events at the Salt of the Earth bookstore. Castillo extols Salt of the Earth for its support of the writers' community in Albuquerque and across the country and laments its demise this past year. Owner John Randall originally coordinated the Booksellers for Social Responsibility panels at the ABA.

"As a writer whose books were published with small presses," Castillo says, "it was a natural for me to talk about the importance of bookstores." She speaks in rapid cadences of full sentences, given a musical lilt by her warm voice. "The kind of literature I write is not directed for the mainstream, although *So Far from God* did very well, and I'm hoping that we're entering a new era now where it will be more and more the case that writers from the fringes occupy the mainstream."

If *Loverboys* bids to occupy the mainstream of contemporary fiction, it nonetheless retains strong connections to Castillo's tremendously varied, and often quite radical, previous body of work. Born and raised in Chicago, Castillo began publishing poetry in the mid-1970s, when she was a college student. Norton's recent edition of her poetry, *My Father Was a Toltec and Selected Poems, 1973–1988* (1995), collects work from the period when writing was her calling, but not yet a career. It includes selections from two self-published chapbooks, *Otro Canto* (1977) and *The Invitation* (1979), together with many poems from *Women Are Not Roses* (Arte Publico, 1984) and all of *My Father Was a Toltec* (West End Press, 1988). Castillo's verse moves freely between English and

Spanish, interlacing unvarnished accounts of her life, her family and her friends with boldly erotic passages and matter-of-fact political statements.

Castillo links her impulse to write to idealism. "In the mid-'70s, the idea was to work towards social change. The call of the day for young people everywhere of all colors and backgrounds was to contribute in some way to a more just society. Being of Mexican background, being Indian-looking, being a female, coming from a working-class background, and then becoming politicized in high school, that was my direction. I was going to be an artist, a poet. Never once did I think of it as a career. I certainly never thought I could possibly earn a dime writing protest poetry. So all those years I went around like a lot of young poets—and a lot of old poets—going anywhere I could find an audience, getting on a soapbox and reading. I was a Chicana protest poet, a complete renegade—and I continue to write that way."

Even as Castillo continues to write as a renegade, however, her work—in particular, her fiction—has found a home with the reading public. Her first novel, *The Mixquiahuala Letters*, was published by Bilingual Review Press in 1986. It brought Castillo critical acclaim, an American Book Award from the Before Columbus Foundation and steady sales. Without consulting Castillo, Bilingual Review sold the rights to that novel and to Castillo's subsequent effort, *Sapogonia*, to Doubleday/Anchor, which brought them out in paperback in 1992 and 1994, respectively. This annoyed Castillo, who would have liked to have had more involvement in the publication (she eventually was able to make some revisions to *Sapogonia*). Her chief comment on the matter now is to urge young writers to have their contracts vetted, no matter how small and friendly the press.

Prospering at Norton

In the wake of the success of her first fiction efforts, Castillo signed up with agent Susan Bergholz, of whom she speaks warmly. Bergholz, Castillo says, played a key role in the genesis of what would become Castillo's debut publication with Norton, the novel *So Far from God*. In an emotionally bleak period during her sojourn in New Mexico, Castillo had happened upon an edition of *The Lives of the Saints*. Reading its spiritual biographies inspired her to write a story about a modern-day miracle that happens to a little girl known as La Loca. After dying, La Loca does not only rise from the dead: she ascends to the roof of the church that had been about to house her funeral and reproves the Padre for attributing her resurrection to the devil. Upon reading this story, Bergholz suggested that Castillo develop it into a novel.

"So I wrote two more chapters," she recalls; she sent it out and eventually Gerald Howard took it at Norton. The story grew to encompass the lives of four sisters, martyrs in different ways to the modern Southwest, and of their mother, Sofia, who turns her bereavements to positive account by organizing the community politically and by working to reconfigure the Catholic religion. Castillo speaks very highly of Howard's editing.

"When *So Far from God* came out," Castillo declares, "I started looking at writing as a career, because indeed, after 22 years, I began to earn my living from it." Having settled back into the very same apartment where, more than a decade ago, she wrote *The Mixquiahuala Letters*, she now plans to write full-time in Chicago, forgoing the itinerant writer-in-residence life that took her in recent years to colleges from Chico State in California to Mount Holyoke in Massachusetts.

Castillo has made forays into writing cultural criticism, collected in *Massacre of the Dreamers: Essays on Xicanisma*, which earned her a Ph.D. from the University of Bremen. While she speaks positively of the resident-writer experience, she is disdainful of fiction-writing workshops. This sentiment has its roots in her own formation. "By no means had I, as many young writers do these days, gone for an M.F.A. and said 'well, I want to be a writer,'" Castillo says. "I had wanted to be a painter, but I was discouraged in college. And so I thought, I'm not going to go through that with my writing." For Castillo, a more idiosyncratic, personal path is best.

Castillo does have a strong investment in pedagogy, however, a commitment currently finding its most direct expression in a children's book project, *My Daughter, My Son, the Eagle, the Dove*. This manuscript consists of two long poems based on Aztec and Nahuatal instructions to youths facing rites of passage. "These poems are teachings from my ancestry," she says, "hundreds of years old, from the time of the conquest of the Americas, and yet applicable today—we're going to package them with contemporary illustrations."

Also underway is a new novel, *Peel My Love like an Onion*. In this project, Castillo focuses on the Chicago gypsy community, for which a good friend serves her as native informant. Uncomfortable with the idea of fully assuming gypsy character in narrating this work, Castillo currently has the novel narrated by a Chicana woman who speaks with a gypsy.

Clearly, Castillo's social conscience continues to inform the choice and development of her projects. Forthcoming in October from Riverhead is *Goddess of the Americas,* an essay collection which she has edited on the Virgin of Guadalupe, beloved patron of the oppressed peoples of Latin America. Castillo's good friend Sandra Cisneros is one contributor; others include Elena Poniatowska and Luis Rodríguez. The idea for the book originated with its editor at Riverhead, Julie Grau. When Grau "asked if I was interested," says Castillo, "I couldn't say no to the Virgin of Guadalupe—I saw that as a discreet message to me." While Castillo herself is not a practicing Catholic, she feels that celebrating the Virgin can help redress the sad fact that "what we could call the feminine principle is too absent from—is too denigrated by—Western society.

"I don't particularly care if people want to worship the Virgin of Guadaloupe," she continues, "if they get the message that we need to respect the things that we call female, which we don't. You know, we put so much pressure on mothering, and as a single mother I understand that, but how much support and respect do we really give mothers in our society?" Castillo is not afraid to provoke controversy. "One of my goals in life is to get an encyclical from the church—if not from the pope, then from the bishops—to ban the book. I think that would be the best advertisement for the book, if a cardinal or someone would say that it definitely should not be read by any good Catholic in the world."

It might seem that Castillo's new offerings, *Loverboys* and *Goddess of the Americas* separate sexuality and spirituality into distinct packages. But this is not the case. For Castillo, "spirituality is a manifestation of one's energy, and that energy includes who you are as a total being"—including your sexuality. She sees the propinquity of the two publications as a clear message that "these are not two separate issues for me, but one issue for us to consider."

The spiritual epiphanies that sexual desires and experiences bring in *Loverboys* occur not as religious visions but rather as aesthetic fulfillment. Sometimes characters recognize such fulfillment themselves. More often, they remain confused, even lost, even while Castillo's rendering of their lives into stories touches them with grace. This grace works whether the story be a tragic one or more essentially comic. This graceful touch of Castillo's is a powerful and unique gift—as many readers of hers already know, and as many more readers will soon discover.

Source: Samuel Baker, "Ana Castillo: The Protest Poet Goes Mainstream," in *Publishers Weekly,* August 12, 1996, pp. 59–60.

Ana Castillo and Simon Romero

In the following interview, Castillo discusses how she came to New Mexico, the unique New Mexican Spanish spoke there, and the state of Chicana literature.

[*S.R.:*]*I understand you're originally from Chicago. How did you end up in Albuquerque? Why here?*

[A.C.:]People usually think I came here to teach at the University, but I didn't. I had visited here and been invited to talk here a few times...

...over at the university...

...yeah, so I'd met a few people like Rudy Anaya—he was instrumental in inviting me—but it was after a sweat that it came to me to come here, so I did. I got my adobe and I've lived here for three years and this is home.

Where else had you lived before coming to Albuquerque?

Five years in California, including three years in the Bay Area. I also taught up in Chico and then I was a fellow at UCSD for a year. Before that I lived nearly all my life in Chicago, aside from travelling extensively here and there.

You mentioned previously that you'd be interested in collaborating with someone on a film. How would you describe the current state of Chicano film-making?

We could say, finally, that in 1993 there is Chicano filmmaking. So I think the possibilities are endless in terms of what the genre would be like. However, in terms of looking for sources of money, I think we have to be very careful not to fall into Hollywood's commodification of Chicano culture. We could look at the example of Piri Thomas, a successful Puerto Rican writer now living in the Bay Area, who has received repeated offers from Hollywood ... and he said he's not going to write about his people doing drugs and going to jail. He mentioned that every time they wanted him to write something, they wanted him to do that, to portray the Puerto Ricans and the Latinos in a negative way.

What kind of film would you make?

A.C.:Well of course, if you think about the kind of books I've written, it would be different, coming from a woman's perspective, something like, say, Maria Novaro's "Danzon." I think it would be similar to a Maria Novaro film, with a Chicana protagonist, with Brown women, with the specificity of our culture. But, you know, I think the issues I have always dealt with are very contemporary and very "universal."

There's a certain trace of Baccaccio or Cervantes in So Far from God. *For example, you begin each chapter with a humourous summary. How important would you say humor is in your novels?*

It seems to be coming out more and more. When I devoted myself to poetry—and poetry is a very serious medium—I don't think the people that knew me as an individual with that tongue-in-cheek kind of humor . . . well, it didn't always lend itself to my poetry. When you're writing poetry, it's like working with gold, you can't waste anything. You have to be very economical with each word you're going to select. But when you're writing fiction, you can just go on and on; you can be more playful. My editor's main task is to cut back, not ask for more.

Not only do you use New Mexican Spanish in So Far from God, *but also the unique English that's spoken here, the long descriptive sentences. It appears that the syntax is Spanish, but the vocabulary is essentially English. How would you say that New Mexico's vernacular differs from Chicago's or California's?*

Well, I'm glad you observed that. Are you a native New Mexican?

Yeah. . .

Good, then maybe I can get an endorsement from you since the language here is very different. At first when you hear the speech here, you don't really know what to do with it, but then I just went with it, because as a writer as well as a translator I do believe that translated words are not different names for the same thing. They're different names for different things. If my novel was instead written in White standard English, I'm doing nothing more than writing a White standard novel with an ethnic motif. Here I started to listen very carefully, and the double negatives in fact drove some of the New York copyeditors crazy, they had to cut back. But it was fun for me. I tried to stay as true as I could, so I used Ruben Cobos' dictionary of Southwestern Spanish, and when I went into Spanish I never assumed the word I would use would be the word a nuevomexicano would use. Chicago Spanish, for example would be more reminiscent of Central Mexican Spanish. And the californios go back several generations, and many don't have Spanish. And if we're talking about L.A., there's been a huge migration of Mexicanos and Central

"*When you're writing poetry, it's like working with gold, you can't waste anything.*"

Americans. So it was very important to me to feel the aspirations of the northern New Mexicans and represent them correctly.

How would you describe the future of Chicano speech? Do you see language as something in a permanent state of change, as something maleable? What language will the next generation of Chicanos be writing in?

I definitely do see language serving its users, and when it no longer serves them we need to look for new words. I was a principal translator of *This Bridge Called My Back*, which is a groundbreaking feminist anthology of writing by women of color. The original title was *Este Puente, Mi Espalda,* and near the end of the project I decided on *Esta Puente, Mi Espalda,* so we had a debate and decided to put a note in the book, and what happened was that because we are Chicanas it was assumed that we don't know our English nor our Spanish. People would actually question us publicly if we knew that *puente* was a masculine noun. We felt like the White feminists who used herstory instead of history. We were doing the same thing. We will never have "a" Chicano English or Spanish because of regional differences. But I think that because of our bilingual history, we'll always be speaking a special kind of English and Spanish. What we do have to do is fight for the right to use those two languages in the way that it serves us. Nuevo-mexicanos have done it very well for hundreds of years, inventing words where they don't have them. I think the future of our language is where we claim our bilingualism for its utility.

How would you characterize the reception of Chicano literature abroad? There seems to be an interest in Germany and England. . .

Many European countries are fascinated with minorities from the United States. They still see this country as a world power and they covet that power. . . . I was approached by a professor once at the Sorbonne in Paris and asked about racism in this country, and when I reflected on racism on the streets of Paris—you know, I'd be considered an Arab there—well, she didn't want to address that. . . . It just goes to show it was easier for Europeans to study racism in the United States than it is from within the belly of the beast.

You mentioned that you have a young son, Marcel. How would you describe the schools here in Albuquerque?

I have him in San Felipe and I had him as a non-Catholic child, so I pay more. He was baptized by the Chicano/Native American community and not by the church. Anyway, when I first came I tried very hard to get him into Longfellow, a school with good programs, but it was very hard, I even offered to teach for free. . . . I had serious reservations about putting him in the public schools in my area. I think that the problems here in Albuquerque, especially in regards to the Chicano community, are as serious as those in any large city in this country. . . . The gang problem does not seem like it should be that serious, but it is for a Latino. I have a tremendous amount of fear for the future of my boy. He's nine-and-a-half and dark-skinned. By the time he's 12 or 13, who knows who he's going to be identifying with in these days when you get shot down for wearing expensive Nikes to school. . . . I've heard that if a Latino makes it to 19 years of age, he has a good chance of surviving into adulthood. Up until then, you don't know.

What significance does modern Latin American writing have for you and your work?

I've been writing and publishing now for almost 20 years, so when I began examining my reality, the closest examples I could find were the Latin Americans, especially the women. And I was especially influenced by a book called *As Tres Marias* written by three Portuguese women. That book came out when I was just coming out of high school. These women were in prison, they were being censored, and later I saw this story in New York as an experimental play. They were talking about all the issues that affect Latina women, from Catholicism to incest to patriarchy. At that time, we didn't have many books by U.S. Latinas; they were writing but not getting published. Anyone that came close to my experience was someone that I would read.

How would you describe the current state of American fiction? Is there a glut of themes? Is it getting repetitive now?

Well, you know, as time has gone on and we're at the end of the 20th century and major publishing is a big business, yes, of course we're going to get a lot of plain, mediocre trash. There are a lot of writers who get huge advances for books that don't go anywhere and they have to burn them somewhere or throw them away. I always think about all the poor trees that have been sacrificed. All it is is a mass-consumption for a brain-dead readership. The writers who have been serious about recreating American literature have always been far and few between. What we do have at the end of the 20th century that we didn't have at the beginning, at that time of the Lost Generation of rich white boys, is a mixture. We're now getting gay writers of color, let's say, and women of color being published. This is unprecedented.

How do you view the reception of your work in Mexico?

Among feminists, there's been an ongoing dialogue. For example, Elena Poniatowska has become a friend of mine and she's acknowledging Chicana literature. And in a month, I'll be attending a conference on Chicana writers at UNAM (Universidad Autonoma de Mexico). This exchange has been taking place for about 10 years. *The Mixquihuala Letters* should be translated into Spanish, I understand that my poetry has been studied, and *Esta Puente, Mi Espalda* has also been used in Mexico now for several years. I think, again, that it's the women who are taking the lead in establishing this communication. . . . As far as our language goes, I'm not exactly sure that the bilingualism that we use—though we have a stronger hold on it—isn't understood by Mexicanos once it crosses the border. You hear it a lot in the slang picked up by the Pop Culture. People like to think of themselves as purists, but there is no such thing as purity, when there exists so much contact.

Source: Simon Romero, "An Interview with Ana Castillo," in *NuCity*, June 18–July 1, 1993.

Ibis Gómez-Vega

In the following essay, Gómez-Vega discusses Castillo's struggle to realize and cultivate her talents as a poet and novelist, and the work she has done to combat racism and sexism.

Ana Castillo is one of a few Mexican American writers who have attracted the attention of the mainstream reading public. From her earliest writing she has tried to unite those segments of the American population often separated by class, economics, gender, and sexual orientation. Her success is a tribute to her self-discipline, her courage, and her considerable literary ability.

Castillo was born in Chicago on 15 June 1953 to Raymond Castillo and Raquel Rocha Castillo, struggling working-class people. In a 1997 interview Castillo told Elsa Saeta that she attended a "secretarial high school," studying to become a file clerk, which her parents considered a good job. Castillo, however, had other ideas. She said that she was "a lousy typist" and had an "aversion to authority," so she abandoned secretarial training. After attending Chicago City College for two years, she transferred to Northeastern Illinois University, where she majored in secondary education, planning to teach art. She received her B.A. in 1975.

Castillo's experience as a student at Northeastern Illinois was largely negative, she explained in the interview, because "the extent of the racism and the sexism of the university in a city like Chicago discouraged" her from becoming an art teacher. She went on: "by the time I was finishing my B.A.—and it took a lot of work to get scholarships and grants to get through the university system—I was really convinced that I had no talent. I couldn't draw and I had no right to be painting." As a result of these experiences, Castillo stopped painting. During her third year of college, however, she resumed writing poetry.

These first poems were a response to her grandmother's death. In the introduction to *My Father Was a Toltec* (1988) she claims to have been "possessed suddenly to compose from a place so deep within it felt like the voice of an ancestor embedded in a recessive gene." Appropriately written on the "ugly" yellow pages of a utilitarian notepad picked up at the factory where her mother worked, the poems, she says, "were short, roughly whittled saetas [couplets from a poem or song] of sorrow spun out of the biting late winter of Chicago" that allowed the child poet to work through her pain. "If it hadn't been that my mother got it for me, and at no cost, at the factory," she says, "I wouldn't have had a pad on which to give birth to my first poems." Her family's working-class status set the stage for a developing writer who throughout her literary career has examined pervasive social and economic inequities that affect women and Latinos in the United States.

Castillo's literary career began before she finished college. At twenty she gave her first poetry reading at Northeastern Illinois University, and in 1975 *Revista Chicano-Riqueña* published two of her poems, "The Vigil (and the Vow)" and "Untitled." That same year another poem, "Mi Maestro," was included in the anthology *Zero Makes Me Hungry*. The following year the *Revista Chicano-Riqueña* published a second group of her poems about racial injustice, particularly the fate of indigenous peoples in America. Mindful of her previous experience as a painter, Castillo told Saeta, she promised herself never to take writing courses "with anybody or any university . . . because I was so afraid that I would be discouraged and told that I had no right to be writing poetry, that I didn't write English well enough, that I didn't write Spanish well enough." Like many other Latino poets of her generation, Castillo felt that she had "no models that spoke to my experience and in my languages," and she admits in the introduction to *My Father Was a Toltec* that she felt compelled to "carve out for myself the definition of 'good.'" She wanted to be a good poet, but a poet on her own terms, with a political conscience and fluency in the two languages that she used to navigate through a predominantly Anglo world.

> *"From her earliest writing she has tried to unite those segments of the American population often separated by class, economics, gender, and sexual orientation."*

Despite her uncertainty about the value of her poems, Castillo continued to write and develop her poetic voice. Caught up in the political fervor of the 1970s and concerned by the plight of Latinos in the United States, she told Saeta in 1997 that she thought of herself as "a political poet, or what is sometimes called a protest poet talking about the economic inequality of Latino people in this country." One of her early poems, "Invierno salvaje" (Savage Winter), written in 1975 and published in the anthology *Canto al Pueblo* (1980), addresses the difficult lives of Latinos during a hard winter. When the worker-poet asks the harsh winter, "¿Intentas matarnos?" (Do you intend to kill us?), the answer is that winter, harsh as it may be, "No tendrás / el honor" (will not have the honor) because "Las fábricas / nos esperan / y la voz / del mayordomo / es aún más fuerte / que la tuya" (The factories / await us / and the voice / of the foreman /

is more powerful / than yours). "The New Declaration of Independence," published in *Revista Chicano-Riqueña* in 1976, celebrates the political awareness of "an entire people / who are coming together as ONE! / At last . . . At last!" Castillo's work should be read with an awareness of what Yvonne Yarbro-Bejarano describes in "Chicana Literature from a Chicana Feminist Perspective" (1988) as "the most important principle of Chicana feminist criticism . . . the realization that the Chicana's experience as a woman is inextricable from her experience as a member of an oppressed working-class racial minority and a culture which is not the dominant culture."

In 1975 Castillo moved to Sonoma County, California, where she taught ethnic studies for a year at Santa Rosa Junior College. Returning to Chicago in 1976, she pursued a master's degree in Latin American and Caribbean studies in 1978 and 1979. In 1977 she published a chapbook, *Otro Canto* (Other Song), in which she collected her earlier political poems, including "Napa, California," dedicated to migrant-labor activist César Chávez, and "1975," a poem about "talking proletariat talks." From 1977 to 1979 she was writer in residence for the Illinois Arts Council. In 1979 she published her second chapbook, *The Invitation*, a collection that exhibits for the first time Castillo's interest in sexuality and the oppression of women, especially Latinas. She also received her M.A. degree in 1979 from the University of Chicago and between 1980 and 1981 was poet in residence of the Urban Gateways of Chicago. A son, Marcel Ramón Herrera, was born on 21 September 1983.

In 1984 Arte Público Press published *Women Are Not Roses*, a collection of poems that includes some poems from her chapbooks. In 1986 her first novel, *The Mixquiahuala Letters*, which she had begun writing in 1979, was published by the Bilingual Press; it received the Before Columbus Foundation's American Book Award in 1987. Written as a series of letters from Teresa, a Latina, to her Anglo-Spanish friend Alicia, the novel reveals Teresa's complicated feelings for Alicia during their ten-year friendship. Castillo provides three tables of contents or reading strategies, labeled "For the Conformist," "For the Cynic," and "For the Quixotic."

Regardless of which reading strategy the reader chooses, *The Mixquiahuala Letters* begins with Teresa's description of three trips to Mexico taken by Teresa and Alicia, together or separately, and follows a narrative through which Teresa not only reminds her friend what happened during their time together but also admits her own feelings of love and hate. Anne Bower claims that *The Mixquiahuala Letters* "is very much a quest novel . . . with form and explanation taking us into the women's emotional and artistic searches," while Erlinda Gonzales-Berry argues that in Castillo's "letter writing project, the letter simultaneously functions as a bridge and as a boundary between subject and object." Gonzales-Berry believes that the letter "verbally links the receiver, (Other), to the sender, (Self), but it also posits the other as the impenetrable mirror that reflects the specular image of the speaking-writing subject." She argues that this binary opposition is necessary so that Teresa can exorcise "her rage . . . through the act of writing" because "in the act of sharing [her letters with Alicia], Teresa discovers her love for Alicia."

Castillo pointed out in a 1991 interview with Marta A. Navarro that Teresa compares and contrasts herself with Alicia throughout the novel because she is dealing with "a very real, painful reality for Mexicanas, brown women who don't fit into the aesthetic" of what is considered beautiful in North America. According to Castillo, Teresa's letters address "the fact that in patriarchy, all women are possessions, but the highest possession, . . . is the white woman." Thus, although in one letter Teresa admits to driving "sixteen and a half hours just to ask you to *dance* with me," in another she tries to explain "why I hated white women and sometimes didn't like you." Teresa's ambivalent feelings for Alicia gradually evolve into a homoerotic subtext that recurs throughout Castillo's work, although Castillo told Navarro that her female characters cannot identify themselves as lesbians because they are not "willing to give up that hope for identity through the male" that is so important to them.

By 1985 Castillo was once again in California teaching at San Francisco State University, becoming more and more involved as an editor for Third Woman Press and receiving early praise for *The Mixquiahuala Letters*. After the novel received the Before Columbus Foundation's American Book Award in 1987, Castillo was further honored by the Women's Foundation of San Francisco in 1988 with the Women of Words Award for "pioneering excellence in literature." Still needing money and finding it difficult to raise her son alone, she taught Chicano humanities and literature at Sonoma State University in 1988, creative writing and fiction writing at California State University at Chico as a visiting professor in 1988–1989, and Chicana feminist literature at the University of California at

Santa Barbara as a dissertation fellow/lecturer for the Chicano Studies Department during the same school year. In 1989 she received a California Arts Council Fellowship for Fiction and in 1990 a National Endowment for the Arts Fellowship.

Castillo's second novel, *Sapogonia: An Anti-Romance in 3/8 Meter* (1990), was written in Chicago in 1984 and 1985 while she was teaching English as a second language and taking care of her new baby. The novel springs from her passion for flamenco music, which had earlier led her to the Al-Andalus flamenco performance group, with which she performed in 1981 and 1982; Máximo Madrigal is the main male character in the novel and a second-generation flamenco artist. Although Castillo denies that the novel is autobiographical, several aspects of the female protagonist, Pastora Velásquez Aké, are reminiscent of the author's life. Pastora sings her own poems, becomes involved in liberation politics, and questions her Catholic faith. Toward the end of *Sapogonia*, she "rejoices over the child that was sprouting from her very soul," happy even though she has neither married Eduardo, the child's probable father, nor told him that she is with child. She plans to give birth to the child and "teach it to fly," expecting to rear him or her alone, an act of defiance even for a lapsed Catholic.

On the back page of the original Bilingual Press edition of 1990, Rudolfo A. Anaya called *Sapogonia* "a literary triumph." The novel is a complicated narrative about the love/hate relationship between Pastora and Máximo. Yarbro-Bejarano argues in "The Multiple Subject in the Writing of Ana Castillo" (1992) that *Sapogonia* "explores male fantasy, its potential for violence against women and the female subject's struggle to interpret herself both within and outside of this discourse on femininity," a discourse that, in *Sapogonia*, evolves through Pastora's web of connections with both men and women as well as through her commitment to Latino politics.

By the early 1990s Castillo was a fellow at the University of California at Santa Barbara, where she gave a seminar and researched her dissertation. She received her Ph.D. in American studies from the University of Bremen in 1991 with a dissertation on Xicanisma, or Chicana feminism, subsequently published as *Massacre of the Dreamers: Essays on Xicanisma* (1994). Patricia Dubrava describes the book as "a collection of essays on the experience of the 'Mexic Amerindian' (Castillo's term) women living in the United States and a meditation on the recent history of Mexic activism." In this book Castillo advocates "our own mythmaking from which to establish role models to guide us out of historical convolution and de-evolution," and she believes these myths should address "our spiritual, political, and erotic needs as a people." According to Rosaura Sánchez, Castillo is a "cultural feminist" whose book "for the most part focuses on cultural differences," but Sánchez sees "a running thread of biologism in the text that would be difficult to construe as other than deterministic and essentialist."

In August 1990, before completing her Ph.D., Castillo moved to New Mexico, where she began to write her third novel. According to Bill Varble, she "had been mourning the death of her father, and recently read a book on saints to research another novel" when she sat down to write "the first chapter of *So Far from God* one afternoon in September of 1990."

By far her best novel, *So Far from God* (1993) distinguishes itself through Castillo's use of the New Mexicans' English sprinkled with Spanish, a language whose rhythm often makes the characters' English sound like Spanish. In a 1993 interview with Robert Birnbaum, Castillo describes "listening very carefully [to the New Mexicans' speech patterns] because the way you use language is the way you're experiencing life." The characters in this novel use double negatives and "code switch" (alternate) between Spanish and English as they communicate. Reading *So Far from God* prompted Sandra Cisneros to exult on the jacket of Castillo's book,

> This Ana Castillo has gone and done what I always wanted to do—written a Chicana *telenovela*—a novel roaring down Interstate 25 at one hundred and fifteen miles an hour with an almanac of Chicanismo—saints, martyrs, t.v. mystics, home remedies, little miracles, *dichos*, myths, gossip, recipes—fluttering from the fender like a flag. Wacky, wild, y bien funny. *¡Dale gas*, girl!

Other Latino critics also praised the Spanish feeling of the novel, and Jaime Armín Mejía called the novel a "contagiously fast-moving, silly, irreverent, yet wise series of tales from Nuevo Méjico." Mejía also praised the voice of the female narrator, who calls herself a *"metiche mitotera,"* the equivalent of a busybody, who "is privy to all that transpires to everyone and everything ... [and] intrudes into the *novela's* postmodern narrative to fill it with *chisme* (gossip), *remedios* (remedies), and *recetas* (recipes)." This narrator's Latin voice provides "readers a not always reliable but certainly a culturally rich understanding of the *nueva mexicana* community" where the novel is set.

So Far from God, Castillo's best-known novel, focuses on the lives of a New Mexican mother, Sofia, and her four daughters, who seem doomed to live chaotic lives from page one when la Loca levitates during her own funeral and ascends to the roof of the church. What follows is an intricately developed story through which the four daughters—Fé (Faith), Esperanza (Hope), Caridad (Charity), and la Loca—live their lives and die young. Fé dies from exposure to chemicals at a job that promised to help her achieve the "American Dream" to which she aspired. Esperanza, the only one of the four sisters who leaves her hometown in Tome and, thereby, the safety offered by the family, disappears during Desert Storm as she covers the war for a news station. Caridad is first attacked and left disfigured by "la malogra," the evil that lurks out in the night, and then is miraculously healed during one of la Loca's seizures. Caridad not only becomes herself again but also becomes a healer; shortly after falling in love with a woman, she takes the woman's hand and plunges off a mountain to become, perhaps, a mythological character. La Loca, a character who never leaves home, contracts AIDS from no apparent source and dies, leaving Sofia, alone and angry, to become a radical political organizer.

So Far from God is simultaneously funny and sad, as Castillo examines several different issues at once. Fé's story illustrates what can happen to Latinas who turn their backs on their culture to pursue material possessions. Sofia's story is probably the most poignant; even before she loses all four daughters, she becomes a community activist, hoping to improve the lives of the people of Tome. Because spirituality also plays a significant role in this novel, many critics consider it Castillo's homegrown version of Mexican American magic realism, but *So Far from God* is actually a work in which the lives of five women are realistically defined not by their imaginations but by their connections to each other and the world around them. In 1993 the novel won the Carl Sandburg Literary Award in Fiction and the National Association of Chicano Studies Certificate of Distinguished Recognition for "Outstanding Contributions to the Arts, Academia, and to Our Community." The following year, *So Far From God* won the Mountains and Plains Bookseller Award, and Castillo also received a second National Endowment for the Arts Fellowship in fiction.

In 1996 Castillo published *Lover Boys*, an uneven but interesting collection of short stories. Brian Evenson, writing for the *Review of Contemporary Fiction* (Spring 1997), claims that "as intriguing as the book's cultural depictions is the complex way in which gender and desire are figured and refigured from story to story." Evenson recognizes in the stories a theme that runs through much of Castillo's work, "desire of all types, heterosexual and homosexual, from women who flirt with other women despite feeling themselves largely heterosexual, to the lesbian in the title story who finds herself drawn irresistibly to a young man." Reviewing the book in *Library Journal* (July 1996), Barbara Hoffert called the stories "terse, fragmentary pieces" but added that Castillo's "strength would seem to be in capturing character through a well-sketched situation." Likewise, Catherine Bush in *The New York Times Book Review* (8 September 1996) complained that Castillo has "grown a little too enamored of the sound of her own voice," which Bush described as a "discursive, conversational style," but she added that "this voice has a vibrancy that compels attention, jamming ribald humor up against pathos and melancholy desire." Donna Seaman in *Booklist* (August 1996) found Castillo's work "defiant, satirically hilarious, sexy, and wise," as well as "tirelessly inventive." Seaman also noted that "Castillo's strong women tend to be creative . . ., well traveled, independent, resourceful, sensual, given to drink and laughter and solitude, and wildly skeptical about the possibilities of finding happiness anywhere other than deep within their own vibrant souls."

In *Peel My Love Like an Onion* (1999), Castillo returns to one of her favorite themes: flamenco dancing and music. Castillo creates Carmen, "La Coja" ("the cripple"), whom she invests with an obsession to become a flamenco dancer although she is not a gypsy and one of her legs is afflicted by polio. As she laments at the beginning of the novel,

> Nothing sadder than a washed-up dancer. I was beyond sad. One day you turn thirty-six years old. The sum of your education is a high school diploma. No other skills but to dance as a gimp flamenco dancer, and your polio-inflicted condition is suddenly worsening. Nowhere to go but down.

The trip down, however, is filled with convoluted love stories about Carmen and Manolo and Carmen and Agustín, both dancers and gypsies as well. These two men dance in and out of Carmen's life without ever committing to much more than a good time. Máximo Madrigal, the main character from *Sapogonia*, makes an appearance as a flamenco musician who becomes Carmen La Coja's gallant, but temporary, lover. *Peel My Love Like an Onion* is the first of Castillo's novels to be deeply concerned with the erotic lives of its main characters.

Carmen is in many ways defined by her non-supportive, selfish family. They recognize her passion for dancing only when she becomes a singer earning good money. That she could become a flamenco dancer in spite of her "condition" escapes them, and they are not capable of giving her more than occasional reassurance, a lack of support that might explain why Carmen expects nothing of the men in her life. Her one purpose and joy in life is to be onstage dancing to flamenco music.

Castillo's novels, short stories, and poetry all emerge from a working-class, Latina sensibility; yet, her work has crossed social and ethnic lines to examine issues common to all people regardless of their cultural backgrounds or ethnicity. Her detailed descriptions of a specifically Latino culture are the backdrop for a body of literature that speaks to people of all cultures.

Source: Ibis Gómez-Vega, "Ana Castillo," in *Dictionary of Literary Biography*, Vol. 227, *American Novelists Since World War II, Sixth Series*, edited by James R. Giles and Wanda H. Giles, Gale, 2000, pp. 83-89.

Patricia De La Fuente

In the following essay, De La Fuente discusses Castillo's roles as a teacher, novelist, and poet, and her involvements in the Chicano and feminist movement.

Ana Castillo is a prominent and prolific Chicana poet, novelist, editor, and translator whose work has been widely anthologized in the United States, Mexico, and Europe. Beginning in 1977 with her first poetry chapbook, *Otro Canto* (Other Song), Castillo's literary credits include the Before Columbus Foundation American Book Award for her first novel, *The Mixquiahuala Letters* (1986), a nomination for the 1986 Pushcart Prize, and a 1988 nomination for the Western States Book Award for the manuscript of her novel *Sapogonia* (published in 1990).

Born on 15 June 1953 and raised in Chicago, where she lived with her parents, Raymond and Raquel Rocha Castillo, Ana Castillo attended public schools there and became involved with the Chicano movement in high school when she was seventeen. She credits her Mexican heritage with providing a rich background of storytelling and remembers writing her first poems at the age of nine after the death of her grandmother. Castillo received a B.A. in liberal arts in 1975 from Northern Illinois University and an M.A. in Latin-American and Caribbean studies from the University of Chicago in 1979. In 1985 Castillo moved to California, then later relocated in Albuquerque in 1990 with her young son, Marcel Ramón Herrera, born on 21 September 1983.

"Castillo's poetic voice speaks for all women who have at one time or another felt the unfairness of female existence in a world designed by men primarily for men."

In addition to creative writing, Castillo has taught a wide range of subjects—including U.S. and Mexican history, the history of pre-Columbian civilizations, Chicano literature, and women's studies—at various universities. She has been invited to lecture not only at U.S. universities but also at the Sorbonne in Paris and at schools in Germany, where she completed a university reading tour hosted by Germany's Association of Americanists in June 1987. In 1989 and 1990 Castillo was a dissertation fellow in the Department of Chicano Studies at the University of California, Santa Barbara.

Her awards include a National Endowment for the Arts Fellowship for poetry (1990) and a California Arts Council Fellowship for fiction (1989), and she was an honoree of the Women's Foundation of San Francisco annual celebration of women in the arts for "pioneering excellence in literature" (1988). She is the first Hispanic to be honored with a collection, the Archives of Ana Castillo, at the University of California, Santa Barbara. In Chicago she has served as writer in residence for the Illinois Arts Council and in San Francisco as a board member of Aztlán Cultural / Centro Chicano de Escritores.

Castillo's poetic voice speaks for all women who have at one time or another felt the unfairness of female existence in a world designed by men primarily for men. In *Otro Canto* this voice is raised in protest against "The heavy pressure of it all" in a poem that questions the way things are:

i see it all the way
god should and I'm
wonderin' why
he doesn't.

Her first collection of poems, *Women Are Not Roses* (1984), includes selections from *Otro Canto* and her second chapbook, *The Invitation* (1979), along with sixteen new poems in which Castillo continues to examine the themes of sadness and loneliness in the female experience.

The Mixquiahuala Letters, an epistolary novel based on forty letters written by the character Teresa to her friend Alicia, is a provocative examination of the relationship between the sexes. A farranging social and cultural exposé, the novel examines Hispanic forms of love and gender conflict. The conclusion of the novel leaves the reader with the distinct impression that the narrator's crusade for sexual freedom and self-determination is far from an unqualified success. In her 1989 study "The Sardonic Powers of the Erotic in the Work of Ana Castillo," Norma Alarcón suggests an interesting connection between Castillo's earlier poetry (in *Otro Canto* and *The Invitation*) and her epistolary novel in that "both reveal the intimate events in the life of the speaker, combined with the speaker's emotional response to them, thus exploring the personal states of mind at the moment of the event or with respect to it." Alarcón sees the epistolary novel as "Castillo's experimentations with shifting pronouns and appropriative techniques for the purpose of exploring the romantic/erotic" and suggests that the female narrator "is betrayed by a cultural fabric that presses its images of her upon her, and her response is to give them back to us, albeit sardonically."

In *Sapogonia*, Castillo hits her full-fledged and sophisticated stride in an intricately woven tale of the destructive powers of male-female relationships. Told from the viewpoint of the male narrator, Máximo Madrigal, whom critic Rudolfo Anaya has described (on the book cover) as "an anti-hero who relishes his inheritance as Conquistador while he agonizes over his legacy as the Conquered," the novel traces the obsessive relationship between the narrator and the woman he is unable to conquer, Pastora Aké.

A make-believe country, Sapogonia is "a distinct place in the Americas where all mestizos reside, regardless of nationality, individual racial composition, or legal residential status—or, perhaps, because of all these." As such, it both attracts and repels Madrigal, who was raised by his Spanish father and a wise Indian grandmother, Mamá Grande, who told him, "not once but many times, the stories related to her people, their history, and her own ideas about their traditions." In this novel the survival of the native culture is entrusted to the women and is symbolically represented by the little clay statues Mamá Grande insists on placing "alongside and at the foot of the statue of the Virgin." These Indian statues reappear in Aké's Chicago room on her dresser, where she lights candles to them and calls them spirit guides. Their influence persists, as does that of Mamá Grande and Aké's own Yaqui grandmother, a reminder of a nurturing, mythological background in the turbulence of the meaningless present.

Critic Patricia Dubrava called Aké "a kind of Joan Baez, a singer and songwriter [while] Max is a kind of anti-Don Quixote on a quest for fortune and dominion" (*Bloomsbury Review*, March 1991). Aké's role of protest singer defines her as a woman of vision and courage, forging her personal place in a chaotic world but with her feet firmly grounded in the traditions of her heritage. Madrigal is caught between the vices of two cultures, and unlike Aké, who remains true to herself throughout, he is torn between his dual roles of conqueror and conquered. His obsession with her, the one woman in his life he cannot conquer, suggests a deeper psychological trauma that prevents him from finding satisfaction.

"The ways in which we perceive and misperceive each other is one of Castillo's most important themes," Alarcón has pointed out. This observation is particularly true of *Sapogonia*, which is a study of the infinite ways men and women have of misreading each other. This concern with relationships between the sexes is concisely and expertly treated in an earlier, anthologized short story about the same characters, "Antihero" (1986), in which Madrigal reviews his obsession with "*her*, that cancerous sore of [his] existence." This woman who provokes, in turn, the narrator's surprise, rage, murderous instincts, and obsessive desire, is never named in the story but is certainly the same enigmatic, emancipated Aké. "Why couldn't she be like Laura?" Madrigal asks himself. But that is exactly the point; Aké is not another Laura, a woman Madrigal has easily conquered and imprisoned in a marriage of convenience—for him. Aké is a woman a man may experience, "twisted like live wires in an explosion of passion," but whom he may never be sure of, never really possess, and never truly understand. Unable to conquer her and place her among his other "victims," Madrigal recognizes "her intensity, her power of destruction" and, in a sense, allows himself to be destroyed by his frustration that "such a woman exists." In *Sapogonia*, Castillo expands and elaborates this basic conflict, but the essence of the novel may be found in "Antihero."

Castillo has completed a manuscript on Chicana feminist theory, a series of essays titled

"Massacre of the Dreamers: Reflections on Mestizas in the U.S. / 500 Years After the Conquest." She is working on a new collection of poems in English and Spanish from 1987 to the present, tentatively called "Guerillera Love Poems." Aside from this, she also has a new long work of fiction in progress, "Santos," and her novel *The Mixquiahuala Letters* was purchased by Doubleday for a 1992 reprint. Given the enthusiastic critical reception of her work to date, the addition of new contributions by Castillo to the increasingly prestigious canon of Chicana writers will be a welcome event indeed.

Source: Patricia De La Fuente, "Ana Castillo," in *Dictionary of Literary Biography*, Vol. 122, *Chicano Writers, Second Series*, edited by Francisco A. Lomeli and Carl R. Shirley, Gale, 1992, pp. 62-65.

Sources

Agosin, Marjorie, Review of *Massacre of the Dreamers*, in *MultiCultural Review*, March 1995, p. 69.

Alarcon, Norma, "The Sardonic Powers of the Erotic in the Work of Ana Castillo," in *Breaking Boundaries: Latina Writing and Critical Readings*, University of Massachusetts Press, 1989.

Baker, Samuel, "Ana Castillo: The Protest Poet Goes Mainstream," *PW* Interview, in *Publishers Weekly*, Vol. 243, No. 33, August 12, 1996, pp. 59–60.

Castillo, Ana, "A Chicana from Chicago," in *Essence*, Vol. 24, No. 2, June 1993, p. 42.

———, *I Ask the Impossible*, Anchor Books, 2001, pp. xvi-xvii.

———, "Introduction," in *I Ask the Impossible*, Anchor Books, 2001.

Hampton, Janet Jones, "Ana Castillo Painter of Palabras," in *Americas*, Vol. 52, January 2000, p. 48.

Olszewski, Lawrence, Review of *I Ask the Impossible*, in *Library Journal*, Vol. 126, No. 1, January 1, 2001, p. 111.

Review of *I Ask the Impossible*, in *Publishers Weekly*, Vol. 248, No. 1, January 1, 2001, p. 88.

Saeta, Elsa, "A *MELUS* Interview: Ana Castillo," in *MELUS*, Vol. 22, No. 3, Fall 1997, pp. 133–55.

Seaman, Donna, Review of *I Ask the Impossible*, in *Booklist*, Vol. 97, No. 3, March 1, 2001, p. 1219.

Further Reading

Anzaldúa, Gloria, *Borderlands/La Frontera: The New Mestiza*, 2d ed., Aunt Lute, 1999.

First published in 1987, *Borderlands* has become a classic in Chicano border studies, feminist theory, gay and lesbian studies, and cultural studies.

Edgerton, Robert, *The Troubled Heart of Africa: A History of the Congo*, St. Martin's Press, 2002.

Edgerton provides a thorough history of the Congo from the sixteenth century up through 2001, with a sensitive description of the land, its rich resources, and the many political struggles of its people.

Hayden, Tom, ed., *The Zapatista Reader*, Nation Books, 2001.

An anthology of essays, interviews, articles, and letters, this book contains some of the best writing about the Zapatista peasant rebellion in Chiapas, Mexico.

McKittrick, David, and David McVea, *Making Sense of the Troubles: The Story of the Conflict in Northern Ireland*, New Amsterdam Books, 2002.

An overview of the sectarian strife in Northern Ireland since the 1960s, this book gives a balanced presentation of the people and the issues involved.

Moya, Paula, *Learning from Experience: Minority Identities, Multicultural Struggles*, University of California Press, 2002.

This book discusses Chicana literature and literary criticism, examining ethnic, feminist, and contemporary literary studies.

Sandoval, Chela, and Angela Y. Davis, *Methodology of the Oppressed*, University of Minnesota Press, 2000.

This book describes the different forms of feminist practice employed to bring social justice out of cultural and identity struggles.

Words for Departure

Louise Bogan

1923

Louise Bogan's poem "Words for Departure" was published in her first book of poetry, *Body of This Death* (1923). In 1922, Bogan had spent six months in Vienna, immersing herself in her work and studying European poetry. When she returned from this period of study, she found a publisher, Robert M. McBride & Company of New York City and within months had published her first compilation of poems. The twenty-seven poems in this first collection of work often focus on romantic relationships and on sexual betrayal. This is true of "Words for Departure," as well, which, while offering advice for a departing lover, also reveals the depth of pain suffered at a lover's betrayal.

The poems in this first book reveal Bogan's study of classical lyrical poetry, with its emphasis on traditional themes. The author uses the classical lyrical motifs of love, time, nature, and rebirth in "Words for Departure" to suggest that all four of these themes are permanently interwoven when love is lost. Bogan studied the poetry of William Butler Yeats and was influenced by modern poetry, but she also adopted the ideas of English Renaissance poets such as John Donne, including some of the metaphysical poet's traditions.

"Words for Departure" was written only a few years after Bogan's husband died but, because the marriage was not a happy one, it is difficult to identify his death as a source for this poem. While Bogan used her poetry to tell stories, the narrative is never obvious and the source of the image not easily defined. Instead the reader must work at deciphering the meaning.

Many of the poems from *Body of This Death* were reprinted in Bogan's later books, though this is not true for "Words for Departure," which is contained only in this first collection. *Body of This Death* has been out of print for many years and as of 2004 was difficult to find; however, "Words for Departure" can be found online at some poetry Websites.

Louise Bogan

Author Biography

Louise Bogan was born August 11, 1897, in Livermore Falls, Maine. During her early childhood, the family moved frequently, although Bogan's education was not neglected during these moves. In 1910 Bogan enrolled in Boston's Girls' Latin School, where she studied Latin, Greek, and French, in addition to the more traditional high school subjects of mathematics, science, and history. While still in high school, Bogan began publishing her first poems, initially in her high school literary magazine, the *Jabberwock*, and later in the *Boston Evening Transcript*. In 1916, after her education at the Girls' Latin School was completed, Bogan enrolled at Boston University, but only studied there for a year. That same year, she married Curt Alexander, who was in the army. In 1917, the couple moved to New York City, and then Bogan's husband was transferred to Panama, where the couple's daughter Mathilde (Maidie) was born. Bogan was unhappy in Panama and with her marriage in general, and in 1918 she took her daughter and returned to her parents' home in Massachusetts. She briefly reconciled with her husband after the war ended but then left him again in 1919. Alexander died the following year, and Bogan used her army widow's pension to support her fledgling career as a writer in New York City.

In New York, Bogan quickly became active in the literary life of the city. She tried to make up for the lack of a formal education by reading, especially the works of early twentieth-century poets such as William Butler Yeats, whose work influenced her own. She used this time to develop her own writing skills, often publishing poems in literary journals such as *Poetry: A Magazine of Verse* and the *Measure*.

By 1923, Bogan had a publisher for her first book of poems, *Body of This Death* (1923), from which the poem "Words for Departure" is taken. Many of the poems in this collection reflect themes of sexual betrayal, which is not surprising considering that Bogan's mother's frequent sexual infidelity occupied much of the author's childhood. After the publication of her first book, Bogan also began to write poetry reviews and criticism, particularly for the *New Yorker*, an endeavor that continued for thirty-eight years.

In 1925, Bogan married again, this time to poet Raymond Holden. The marriage allowed Bogan to reclaim Maidie from her parents' home, where the child had been living since 1919. The marriage, however, was unsuccessful and, by 1931, a severely depressed Bogan had entered the New York Neurological Institute, hoping to find a cure for the depression that plagued her for the rest of her life. Bogan and Holden were divorced in 1937, and she never married again.

During the next thirty years, Bogan continued to write and publish. Her autobiography *Journey around My Room: The Autobiography of Louise Bogan* was published posthumously in 1980. Bogan received many awards in her lifetime, including the John Reed Memorial Prize in 1930 and the Helen Haire Levinson Memorial Prize in 1937. In 1933 and 1937, Bogan was awarded Guggenheim fellowships. In 1944 she received a Library of Congress fellowship in American Letters, and in 1945 she was awarded the Library of Congress Chair in

Poetry, a position she held until 1946. Additional recognition quickly followed with the Harriet Monroe Poetry Award in 1948 and a National Institute of Arts and Letters grant in1951. In 1955, Bogan received the Bollingen Prize in poetry for *Collected Poems, 1923–1953* (1954). During the next several years, she continued to earn honors for her poetry, receiving an Academy of American Poets fellowship in 1958, a Brandeis University Creative Arts Award in poetry in 1961, and a National Endowment for the Arts grant in 1967. Bogan died February 4, 1970, in her New York apartment.

Poem Summary

Overview

Bogan's lyrical poem "Words for Departure" offers instructions for a departing lover, but the poem goes beyond simple leave-taking to create an image of love found and then lost. The poem is divided into three sections, each containing several stanzas. The first section is one of oppositions and takes place in the present tense. The second section is focused on memories, recalling the lover as he was in the past. The final section pushes the lover away and looks to the future. The poem itself is filled with ambiguities that reveal the pain the speaker feels at her lover's betrayal. In the end, although she instructs him on how a lover should leave, her own grief at this loss is captured in her inability to watch him leave.

Lines 1–5

The first line of Bogan's poem begins with the word "nothing," a word that is repeated several times in the first section of the poem. With the first line, the author also creates an opposition that dominates the entire poem. Initially the first line suggests a stagnant existence, when time stops and nothing is remembered and nothing is forgotten. The speaker would like time to stand still, but the poem quickly moves into real time, as images of the passing day reveal that she cannot hold back time. The author recalls the early morning world outside the lovers' room, with the noise of wagons moving on the pavement and the evidence of recent rain still on the windowsill. The use of "we awoke" reveals they are lovers who have shared this room during the night.

There is a world beyond their room, and it is this world that will intrude. The town exists just outside the window. Bogan creates images of the town in only a few words. The chimney pots that grace the rooflines are compared to trees, only this image is a "grotesque" caricature of nature in which birds must nestle among the roofs in manmade perches rather then those created by nature's hand. In this instance, pavement and buildings have replaced nature, defiling what nature has constructed. The word "grotesque" also refers to the narrator's individual world, which is in turmoil because the loved one will leave that day for another love. The loss of the lover is a distortion of the author's own world, an incongruity in her natural world, where love has been replaced by treachery.

Lines 6–11

The second stanza of the first section repeats the opening of the first stanza, with the repetition of the word "nothing" and the same opposition of ideas and lack of movement that opened the poem. The moment of separation is approaching, but the poet has not yet accepted the end of the love affair, and she cannot look beyond this moment to a future without her lover. All she sees at this moment is *nothing*. In the next lines Bogan's focus shifts subtly from the lovers to the passage of time that marks their final hours together. The hours of the day are marked by "bells" that remind the speaker that only a few hours remain before the lover leaves her. The warm summer day begins to cool as evening approaches. While the first stanza noted the morning of their final day, the second stanza observes that time is continuing its unstoppable move toward the day's conclusion. The day wanes and the "streets" become "deserted." Soon the moon begins to light the dusk and the day is ending. The dark signals both the end of the day and the end of the relationship.

Lines 12–15

The last stanza of the first section develops a fuller picture of the lovers. While they were not described in the poem's opening lines, in these lines the lovers stand together, face-to-face, with hands clasped and foreheads touching. It is the moment of their parting. Once again the author uses *nothing* to describe this couple. Nothing remains of the love that once existed. In line 14 Bogan suggests that the woman never really possessed her partner's love and thus she cannot have lost what she has never had. In this moment of dissolution, she gains nothing and loses nothing, and in the final line of this section, she explains that he has not offered her the gift of love, nor has he denied his love for another. Initially it appears that in the nothingness of their love's finality, the lovers will part without words of love or recrimination. The speaker seems to accept that there is nothing that remains of the love they once knew, but the following sections of the poem reveal that she cannot walk away so easily.

Lines 16–18

The second section of the poem moves backward from the present tense of the first section to an image of the lovers' past. In lines 17 and 18 the narrator begins to reveal the depth of her attachment for her lover. He was not a brief moment in her life, a quick stop at an unfamiliar town. Her love for him was sure and steady and not a love, as she reminds the reader in line 18, from which she had fled. In these lines the author offers the first suggestion of the depth of pain with which she has been left. She was committed to loving him and did not deny him the fullness of her love. These lines also reveal a growing tone of bitterness that the poet is unable to mask.

Lines 19–23

In the final five lines of the second section of the poem, the author uses images from nature to explain the importance of the lover in her life. Lines 19 and 20 describe the newness of the relationship and the inexperience of the lover. Their initial time together was tentative, the hesitancy of new love described as "awkward as flesh." And yet how can flesh, nature's creation, be awkward? The tension created with the pairing of words such as "flesh" and "awkward" suggests the speaker is returning to the lovers' earliest days together, searching for signs of incompatibility that she might have missed. Perhaps she missed warnings of what was to come? She describes her lover's initial touch as uncertain and as weightless as early morning frost or the dusting of ash that adds no weight and yet covers and obscures a surface. Both the frost and the ash continue the oppositions the author favors in this poem: one image is of clean white purity, while the other image is the remains of something annihilated. Ash, so easily stirred by wind, is grey; it is nature's response to the fire that destroys life, and it hides what might remain after the fire has been extinguished. The lover's touch, once so light and pure, was really something darker that hid the betrayal that lay below.

Line 21 continues this image of something hidden. The rind of fruit hides what is concealed within, but the image is incomplete, and the rind is not pealed away to reveal the fruit. The lover is without substance. There is nothing below the surface, no depth of feeling. The next image focuses on the purity of an apple. The speaker is all interior, all emotion. She has no outer rind to protect her and is instead open to all the emotions that flow from her. The two fruits continue the opposition noted elsewhere in the poem. The cliché about the fundamental differences between apples and oranges is a familiar one, but Bogan uses this old cliché in a new manner. In this case the rind of the orange is paired with the white-juiced interior of the apple to demonstrate that the lovers never belonged together. In the final line of the second section, the author compares the lovers to music that has been written but never completed. The music that would have given voice to the lyrics is missing, just as the lovers were unable to find completeness in their relationship. Now that their relationship is ending, their song together will never be completed; their story is left unfinished.

Lines 24–28

At the beginning of the third section, the speaker tells her lover that there will be no further recounting of the past. He is told to "Go from mine," the speaker's world, "to the other," the world of a new lover. She tells him to create a new life with a new lover, and yet there is ambivalence in these final words. This ambivalence is present in the opposition of images relayed in this section of the poem. Initially the lover is told to "Be together" with his new love, to "eat" and "dance," but the contrast appears with the inclusion of the word "despair" in this line. The lover will know contentment initially, but the time with the new love will not be without its grief. This idea is continued in line 27, when the author instructs the lover to "Sleep, be threatened, endure." The speaker reminds the lover that his sleep will also be coupled with discord, just as it was when they were together. He will "know the way of that," since the lover experienced those same emotions of unhappiness when he was with the speaker. Although the lover is moving on to someone new, the patterns of the old relationship will not be lost, and happiness will continue to be elusive for someone who is so easily dissatisfied with a lover. In these lines the tone of bitterness that earlier crept into the poem becomes more obvious. Although the speaker suggested in line 15 there would be no recrimination, the lover's betrayal and the pain it has caused linger near the surface, and she is unable to let him walk away without pointing out his weaknesses.

Lines 29–34

In these next four lines, the speaker looks ahead to the end of her lover's next relationship. She is sure he will treat his next lover the same way he treated her, and so she offers him advice on how to leave the new lover. When that relationship ends, he is told to "be insolent." He should be impertinent and disrespectful as he departs, but he should also not linger. As he cuts off the relationship, he should do so quickly, with a quick "strike." And he should not be too serious, but instead be "absurd," and yet he is also instructed to "be mad." The opposition of images that began this poem continues in the final lines. Contrasting phrases such as "be absurd" but "be mad" suggest that this is how he treated the poet when he was preparing to leave her. There was no logic or fairness in how her lover treated her. He was absurd, then angry, and then disrespectful. Since he treated her so badly, he should continue this behavior with his new love and "be insolent" but not "talk." These commands reveal the depth of her pain. She has been betrayed, and love neither ends simply and easily, nor ends without pain. She predicts that this new love will soon lose the "bloom" of happiness and end with silence, just as their love ended with a lover's silence. The reader never hears the word of the lover in these lines. He is silent, but the poet's accusations serve to tell his story.

In the final two lines of the poem, the speaker moves from the future and her lover's next relationship back into the present and the moment of leave-taking. She tells her lover to walk away into the dark; he should not need a lantern to light the way. Rather than illuminate his departure, the speaker prefers this leave-taking to occur at night. If she cannot see him actually leave, there can be "some uncertainty" about his departure. If he walks into the darkness and completely disappears, she need not ever see him actually leave. There will be no need to imagine him with his new love. In the final two lines of "Words for Departure" the speaker reveals the depth of her pain at her lover's betrayal. She has used the previous seven lines to chastise him and to predict his inability to find happiness, but as he leaves all that is forgotten as she tries to grasp the enormity of his leaving.

Themes

Beginning and Ending

In "Words for Departure," Bogan offers many contrasting images, but one important aspect of the poem is the duel image of the lovers beginning and ending their relationship. In her descriptions of the lovers' earliest time together, the speaker gives voice to memories that are now clouded with pain. In line 19 the speaker describes the hesitancy of a new relationship. In the beginning her lover was unsure of himself. She describes his ineptitude as "awkward as flesh." The analogy reveals one of the tensions in the poem. Awkwardness with a new lover is understandable, and the uncertainty of action that accompanies new love is to be expected, but the speaker couples it with the word "flesh," a word that denotes something that is natural. Flesh cannot be awkward, but as the speaker looks back to the beginning, she searches for hints that might have anticipated this loss. The pairing of these words in the same phrase suggests that perhaps the awkwardness of flesh should have warned her that they did not belong together. The end of the relation actually occurs in lines 12 and 13, even though he does not walk away until line 34. The emotional parting is depicted in the image of the lovers "Hand clasped hand, / Forehead still bowed to forehead." This is their last touch, and it is the last moment before the author is swept away by the pain of her lover's leave-taking. The speaker continues to recount their time together and to offer bitter words about how the relationship has ended, but it is this last touching that signals the end of love. In the final section of the poem, the speaker tells her lover, "you have learned from the beginning." With this phrase the speaker brings the beginning forward to the end, and the cycle of beginnings and endings is complete.

Grief

Bogan's poem is filled with images of grief at the loss of love's promise. She begins with the simple phrase, "Nothing was remembered, nothing forgotten." The speaker cannot bear to remember, nor can she possibly forget. The repetition of the word *nothing* describes the emptiness of her life as her lover prepares to leave her. She has not yet accepted that her lover is leaving, and she cannot yet look beyond it. Instead there is only nothing. In line 14 she acknowledges she never really possessed him. This realization offers little relief for her grief, and so in the next several lines she gives voice to her pain. She questions whether she missed signs that they did not belong together, and in moments of pain and irony she instructs him how to break-up with his next lover. The depth of her grief is captured in the final two lines of the poem, when the speaker instructs her lover to go in darkness. If he leaves without light, she will not actually see him leave, and hence there will be "some uncertainty about [his] departure." In these final lines it becomes clear that she cannot sustain the anger of the previous lines, and all she feels now is grief.

Topics For Further Study

- Poetry should create images and pictures in the reader's mind. Using Bogan's poem, draw or illustrate one of the images her poem creates.
- Bogan's poem was published in the early 1920s. Her poem depicts unmarried lovers who are ending their relationship. Examine the cultural and social lives of women in the early 1920s. Pay close attention to the life of an unmarried woman living alone, and try to determine what options were available for women who did not wish to marry.
- The nineteenth amendment, giving women the right to vote, was finally approved in 1920. Research the suffrage movement and try to determine the reasons why so many people were opposed to allowing women to vote.
- Bogan was inspired by several poets, especially the seventeenth-century metaphysical poets, particularly John Donne. Compare Bogan's poem to one of Donne's poems. You might consider choosing "Woman's Constancy" or "The Sun Rising" as possible poems for this exercise. What similarities do you note? In what ways has Bogan altered Donne's ideas to fit her own poetic needs and style?
- It is often helpful when studying poetry to try and write a poem. Poems need not have a rhyme scheme or be of any predetermined length to be successful, and often imitating a poet's style is an effective way to get started writing poetry. Choose the topic of lost love and create your own poem, modeling it after Bogan's poem.

Light and Darkness

Bogan's poem begins with dawn, with the rain of the night still lingering on the windowsills and the chirping of early-morning birds outside. The lovers' day of parting begins in the light of morning. Traditionally dawn signals a new beginning, a rebirth. This dawn signals the end of one relationship and the beginning of the speaker's life without her lover. When the day ends and dusk begins to fall, the speaker begins to reflect on her time with her lover as she prepares for his departure. In this case darkness not only ends the day, it also ends their time together as a couple. She asks him to walk away in the dark. She wants no light to illuminate his going. Darkness signifies a conclusion, but for the speaker it also helps create an illusion that might sustain her for a few more hours.

Movement of Time

In "Words for Departure" the poet plays with time, slipping between present, past, and future tense. The poem opens in the present tense; it is the morning of the last day. Even though she would like to hold time static, the day marches on. She hears the bells ringing the time, "separated hour from hour." The heat of the summer wanes and the coolness of dusk approaches, and the day is nearly gone as the first section of the poem ends. In the second section, the author recalls the past. She reflects on the lovers' time together, remembering hints from time past that might have portended this ending. In the final section, she tells her lover to learn from the past, even as she looks to a future in which he will be as dissatisfied with his new lover as he was with the old one whom he leaves this day. At the end of the poem, the speaker reverts to present tense as she bids her lover to leave. In shifting time from present to past to future and back again to the present, the speaker uses manipulation of time to paint a complex picture of this final day with her lover. The poet adds a depth to the narrative that a straightforward chronological story would lack, and the reader is allowed to experience both the speaker's pain and the lover's duplicity in a series of images.

Nature

Lyric poetry uses nature to depict images of order and disorder. In Bogan's poem, the messiness of the break-up of this love affair is reflected in the images of nature that are present. The birds that scatter in line 4 settle in "chimneypots" that mirror "grotesque trees." Rather than find haven in a tree, the birds look to manmade perches. This reversal of nature is what the poet finds in the disorder of her own life. What she thought was the naturalness of love has now been revealed to be as false as the birds' perches. Initially the oranges and apples in lines 21 and 22 might suggest the perfection of nature that the poet thought analogous to the lovers, and yet on close examination, the orange is revealed as a rind with no center, while the apple contains a center with no covering. These fruits are imperfect examples of nature, just as her love affair was imperfect. Earlier the love seemed ideal, but now the speaker notices the differences and the disruptions in nature that had been hidden.

Rememberance

The center section of Bogan's poem is occupied with the speaker's remembrance of the lovers' past. In line 16 she recalls, "I have remembered you." These words reveal that she will not forget him. He was not a brief moment in her life, not "the town visited once." She loved him deeply and did not withhold herself. Rather than protect herself from love, she welcomed love and did not run from it. She was not "the road falling behind running feet." She stood still and embraced him in love. The speaker uses these memories to probe for reasons why their love did not last. She reflects on the lovers' time together and acknowledges their differences. In recalling these memories, the speaker is able to begin grieving for what is being lost.

Style

Analogy

Analogy is a common element of poetry, used to suggest a similarity between things that appear on the surface to be dissimilar. For example, the lover is "a rind" with no substance inside. The speaker, on the other hand, is the fruit of the apple, all emotion with no thick skin to protect her. The use of analogy in Bogan's poem is subtle, which means that the reader needs to read the poem carefully to understand all the analogies.

Imagery

Simply put, imagery refers to the images in a poem. The relationships between images can suggest important meanings in a poem, and with imagery, a poet uses language and specific words to create meaning. For instance, Bogan includes images from nature to illustrate the disruption in her natural world. She also includes an image of the lovers' parting, with hands clasped and foreheads touching, an image that reveals the depth of loss that shakes her being. The contrasting images Bogan includes help create tension in the poem and add to its complexity.

Lyric Poetry

Lyric poems are strongly associated with emotion, imagination, and a song-like resonance, especially when associated with an individual speaker or speakers. Lyric poetry emerged during the Archaic Age, around the eighth century B.C. The poems of this time period were shorter than the previous narrative poetry of Homer or the didactic poetry of Hesiod. Since lyric poetry is so individual and emotional in its content, it is by its very nature also subjective. Lyric poetry is also the most common form of poetry, especially since its attributes are common to many other forms of poetry. Bogan's poem combines many of the attributes of lyric poetry, with its emphasis on love and loss and on nature and chaos.

Metaphysical Poetry

Metaphysical poetry began in the seventeenth century as a revolt against the conventions of the Petrarchan poetry so popular in the Elizabethan period. Metaphysical poetry is notable for its use of psychological analysis of love, its depiction of the poet's complexity of thought, and its imagery of the disillusionment of love. The seventeenth-century poet John Donne is most often associated with metaphysical poetry. Bogan studied Donne's work carefully, and her poem "Words for Departure" contains effective images of disillusionment, as well as a psychological analysis of what went wrong in the love affair.

Narrative Poetry

A narrative poem is a poem that tells a story or recounts events. Bogan's poem tells the story of her lover's departure from her life. However, Bogan makes this structure her own by refusing to tell the story in a straight chronological form. Instead she shifts time in her narrative and creates tension and complexity in her story. The story ends with the poet's recognition that she cannot change what is happening. Her lover will leave in spite of her words and neither her love for him nor her anger at his actions will change what is happening.

Parallelism

Paralelism is a grammatical device that conveys equal importance of two or more ideas by using the same syntax for each idea. For example, Bogan uses parallelism to describe the emptiness she feels as her lover is preparing to leave her. In line 1 she explains, "Nothing was remembered, nothing forgotten." She again repeats this structure in line 6 with "Nothing was accepted, nothing looked beyond." Bogan returns to this structure in line 14 with "Nothing was lost, nothing possessed." All three lines have exactly the same structure. This use of parallelism focuses the reader's attention on these lines and on specific words and signifies that they are important elements of the poem.

Poetic Form

The word poem is generally assigned to mean a literary composition distinguished by emotion, imagination, and meaning. But the term *poem* may also fit certain designated formulas, such as a sonnet or a sestina, which are defined by a specific length and/or a particular rhyme scheme. A poem may also include divisions into stanzas, a sort of paragraph-like division of ideas, and may also include a specific number of stressed or unstressed syllables in each line. Bogan's poem is divided into separate sections, with each section also divided into stanzas of varying lengths. Every word in Bogan's poem suggests an image or idea, and nothing is wasted. Modern poetry has moved away from the strict formulas used by early poets, but even contemporary poets still strive for an impassioned response to their poems. Bogan studied the Renaissance lyric poets, and she is able to make effective use of traditional poetic forms.

Historical Context

Cultural and Societal Changes

The early 1920s was a period of clashing ideals and traditions, of contradictions and sometimes frightening possibilities. The end of World War I resulted in a *carpe diem* attitude, an eat-drink-and-be-merry view of the world. The loss of life from the war, followed by the flu epidemic of 1918, left many people frightened and unsure about the future. Many people just wanted to be happy and have fun after this terrible period in history. During this same time, women won the right to vote in 1920, after a seventy-two-year struggle. Although they often voted as the men in their lives instructed, winning the right to vote suggested to women that perhaps they were equal to men. And there were other changes afoot that would set women free from the household duties that consumed their time. Apartments were being built, and smaller apartments did not require much work to keep clean. The sale of canned and convenience foods was growing, and as a result, some of the drudgery of cooking was eliminated. Bakeries and commercial laundries opened. There were washing machines and irons to aid with cleaning, and many houses had telephones and radios. It was easier to keep in touch with the outside world. New inventions permeated every aspect of people's lives. Automobiles made transportation available to many people, who now used cars to journey beyond their towns, whereas in the past most people lived and died within only a few miles of their birthplace. The car also led to greater sexual freedom. In the past, few young men and women had the opportunity to be alone. Most young people lived with their parents, and cars offered a privacy not previously experienced.

By July 1920 leading newspapers were reporting the scandalous news that women's skirts were now at least nine inches off the ground. For the first time, women were showing their ankles. Over the next few months, skirt lengths continued to rise. Suddenly women were wearing thin, shapeless dresses that stopped well above the woman's shin-bone. Women were no longer strapped-in by corsets. Suddenly the softness of a woman's body was available to be touched. Women were also wearing cosmetics and cutting their hair and letting it hang loosely. The new hairstyles and clothing were easier to maintain. Women were also dancing, and it was not the ladylike waltz that had been considered so proper in the past. In the new dances, women were pressed close to their partners and no stiff corset separated the dancing pair. Moreover, young women were smoking in public and drinking, although the latter occurred somewhat more privately. Prohibition, after all, had supposedly outlawed drinking.

This youthful rebellion by young women did not go unnoticed. Parents were appalled, but most thought the descriptions that filled the newspapers were of other people's children. There were attempts to curtail women's freedom and return them to the repressive old days. Religious journals denounced the new kind of freer dancing as carnal, and parents were lectured from pulpits to take better control of their children, especially their daughters. Additional opposition to women's freedom came from leading women who proposed that a society be created to monitor women's clothing styles. Across the United States, local clergymen were asked to submit their ideas for the proper female dress. In several states, bills were proposed that

Compare & Contrast

- **1920s:** In the United States, women finally have the right to vote. The nineteenth amendment to the Constitution is approved August 26, 1920. It has taken more than seventy years of hard work, beginning with a women's rights convention in 1848, for women to finally achieve this right.

  Today: The bitter and lengthy fight for the right to vote seems far removed for women today.

- **1920s:** In January 1921 in London, the first women to serve on a divorce-court jury are sworn in. Divorce, however, is still rare and is still considered scandalous, particularly for women.

  Today: Divorce is much more common, and few cases go to trial. A woman's ability to divorce is no longer decided by men, and society is much more accepting of divorce.

- **1920s:** By 1922, the flapper girl has changed the image of women. A woman can now smoke and drink in public, wear lipstick, and wear short skirts. She no longer has to cover her body from neck to toes. Sexual freedom for women is also a part of this movement, although the double standard that condemns women's sexuality remains in effect.

  Today: Women in Western countries show even more of their bodies in public, and there is no hesitancy about smoking and drinking or wearing cosmetics. Many women feel free to express their individuality in whatever way they choose.

- **1920s:** T. S. Eliot publishes *The Waste Land* in October 1922. Eliot's long poem moves poetry in a new direction, incorporating a variety of poetic forms, languages, and references to older works. His poem also captures the despair of World War I and proves a counterpoint to the recklessness that otherwise grips the early 1920s.

  Today: Poetry is less regimented by formulas and is more individualistic. Eliot's poem, now largely relegated to classroom study, no longer seems so shocking, unless it is studied within its historical context.

would make wearing skirts more than three inches above the ankle a crime; in one state even two inches above the ankle would be illegal. Bills were also introduced that would make the exposure of more than three inches of a woman's throat a crime.

The changes in women's clothing and behavior signaled huge changes in society. Women were demanding more independence, and not just from corsets, but from antiquated rules that repressed and defined women as chaste and pure and as destined only for marriage and motherhood. Bogan's poem "Words for Departure" depicts a woman being abandoned by her lover. There is no suggestion that the couple is married, although a divorce would still have been considered scandalous. This freedom for young women was every parent's nightmare, but it was independence that women craved. The early 1920s marks a time when women escaped from their traditional roles and sought the opportunity to express themselves, a freedom of expression evidenced in Bogan's poem.

Critical Overview

Bogan's poem "Words for Departure" was included in her first published collection of poems, *Body of This Death.* Although she was a young poet at the time of its publication, Bogan had already published poems in poetry magazines and so there was some notice paid in 1923 to this thin book of twenty-seven poems. As Martha Collins observes in her study of Bogan's work titled *Critical Essays on Louise Bogan*, critics in general found her first collection to be a "small book" filled with rather short poems. Collins states that "Bogan's strongest admirers have almost always been poets."

Perhaps Collins's observation helps explain the mixed reviews that greeted Bogan's first book. In a letter written March 1, 1924, and included in Ruth Limmer's collection of Bogan's personal letters (*What the Woman Lived: Selected Letters of Louise Bogan, 1920–1970*), Bogan mentions several unfavorable reviews. She writes, "*The Dial* certainly gave [*Body of This Death*] a rotten smack, didn't it?" Bogan also notes, "Johnny Weaver in the *Brooklyn Eagle* put me down as *very slight* and wanted to know why all the hosannas had been raised." Bogan then mentions a third critic, John Gould Fletcher, who "in *The Freeman* said my 'lack of thought' was painful." Bogan's attitude seems to be nonchalant about these negative reviews, however, perhaps because she has more confidence in her own work than did the critics.

Although Bogan did not highlight any positive reviews of *Body of This Death* in her letters of this period, there were reviews that praised the book's many strengths. Two of the first reviews of Bogan's early poetry are included in Collins's book. In a review originally published in the *Nation*, Mark Van Doren suggests that Bogan's poems "take effect directly upon the imagination." Van Doren acknowledges that Bogan's poems are not easily understood, but he observes, "Miss Bogan has always spoken with intensity and intelligent skill." He concludes his review with high praise, writing the book "may be a classic."

Collins also includes an essay originally contained in Llewellyn Jones's *First Impressions: Essays on Poetry, Criticism and Prose*. Jones writes of Bogan's first book that the poetry in this collection depicts the struggle "against all that stifles, diverts, and disarms life." According to Jones, Bogan's poems also portray the struggle "against the pettiness that haunts the footsteps of love." Jones compares Bogan's work to that of William Butler Yeats, whose work Bogan admired. Like Yeats, says Jones, Bogan "has not sacrificed beauty to ... austerity." Jones finds Bogan "is not afraid to deck her beauty in imagery, natural or classical." It appears Jones had read earlier criticism of Bogan's work because the critic urges readers to "make allowances" for those poems that seem obscure to the reader, since the poet "is giving us subjective poetry distilled from what is evidently intense experience."

As Lee Upton notes in his essay "The Re-Making of a Poet: Louise Bogan," "whether poets are born or made, surely they are remade by their critics." While Bogan's first work may not have achieved overwhelming critical acclaim, she did eventually hold an important place in critical discussions of modern poetry.

Criticism

Sheri E. Metzger

Metzger has a doctorate in English Renaissance literature. Metzger teaches literature and drama at the University of New Mexico, where she is a lecturer in the University Honors Program. In this essay, Metzger explores the fractured depiction of self in Bogan's "Words for Departure," which she suggests can be read as an icon of the poet's own childhood experiences.

In composing poetry, Bogan used a variety of poetic forms, but the poems in *Body of This Death*, and the poem that is the subject of this essay, "Words for Departure," are lyric poems, often defined by their emotional response to the grief, chaos, and betrayal associated with love. Bogan writes in her autobiography *Journey around My Room* that lyric poetry is "the most intense, the most condensed, the most purified form of language," and thus it is to be expected that she would turn to lyric poetry to express the fabric of emotion that is rendered by the betrayal of love. Bogan was an intensely private person, who rarely revealed the personal details of her own life. The posthumous publication of her autobiography and letters opened her life to study and to the inevitable rereading of her poetry in a search for the connections between her poems and the events and people depicted in her autobiographical writings. As only one example of what might be constructed from an examination of these connections, Bogan's poem "Words for Departure" can be examined as illustrating an effort by Bogan to locate herself in her poems of betrayed love.

Many critics have cited Bogan's turbulent childhood, her mother's infidelity, and Bogan's first marriage as explanation of why Bogan's many poems in her first collection of poetry, *Body of This Death*, are so centered on betrayal. In her autobiography, Bogan recounts episodes of her life, always presented as brief vignettes, like photos in an album that reveal the incongruity of her life. Many of the episodes that involve her mother are marked by tumult and discord. As a response to all this strife, Bogan also notes something as simple as her mother sewing, the click of a needle against a thimble, as a moment "that meant peace." There must

> *"As Bogan notes in her autobiography, separations, secrets, and deception defined her childhood. Her poetry is charged with her personal story of betrayal."*

have been much discord for Bogan, who, writing so many years after the events that are recalled, remembers a needle click as a particular sound that suggested peace in this stormy household. Bogan also writes of her mother's friend Dede, whose presence scared the child and who brought disruption to the house as she acted as "go-between" between Bogan's mother and her lover. Bogan knew that her mother had lovers, had even walked in unexpectedly and caught her mother with her lover. Thus, it is easy to appreciate Bogan's comments that when her mother "dressed to go to town, the fear came back." These trips meant "going to the city; it meant her other world; it meant trouble." Bogan's mother was prone to sudden anger, blaming everyone, and presumably her daughter, when things went wrong. Her mother would suddenly disappear for weeks and then just as suddenly reappear, creating tumult and tension in her daughter's life.

Still another betrayal occured in 1909 when Bogan's family moved to Boston. Bogan was only a teenager when she began to study drawing with a Miss Cooper, whom the young girl began to idolize as genteel and refined—the qualities that Bogan's mother most lacked and that the young girl most admired. Miss Cooper was thought to be perfect, for about two years. Bogan was about fifteen years old when she discovered that her idol was human, and she writes in her autobiography that Miss Cooper betrayed her. The betrayal was as simple as a sigh, a moment that signaled dissatisfaction or discontent, or perhaps boredom. Whatever the meaning of the sigh, the perfection of Miss Cooper's persona was disrupted, never to reappear. Bogan's days at the drawing studio had given her a peaceful retreat from her mother's chaotic world, and so the betrayal was all the more painful. She describes angry tears, disillusionment, and dismay. Bogan's reaction was extreme, but this disillusionment, coupled with all the chaos and betrayal of her early life, eventually led a very young Bogan to marry an unsuitable older man as a means of escape. She did not write of the marriage in her autobiography, but when asked what she has sought in her life, she replied that she sought love. She explains that she has sought love because she "worked from memory and example." Her mother constantly sought reassurance of her own worth in love affairs, and Bogan experienced her father's anger and the fighting between parents. Bogan writes in her autobiography how all the agony of her childhood "has long been absorbed" into her work. It is this absorption of agony that Bogan captures and reveals in "Words for Departure."

In her essay "Lethal Brevity: Louise Bogan's Lyric Career," Marcia Aldrich says, "[l]ike many other writers early in the century, Bogan turned cultural and personal disappointments into modernist poetry." In her discussion of *Body of This Death*, Aldrich charges that the subject of "women in the throes of love" is a traditional one for poets, but that in this instance "the volume finds that the literary life of feeling is one of depersonalization and disillusionment." The poems in *Body of This Death* provide no happy endings, as the title certainly suggests. The poems contained within, according to Aldrich, "define a possessive love between unequal lovers." This critique is certainly true of "Words for Departure." In the poem, it is the male lover who holds all the power. Regardless of the depth of her love for him, the speaker cannot prevent his leaving. All control rests with the male lover and not with the female narrator, and as Aldrich suggests, these lovers are unequal. And yet, as Christine Colasurdo notes in "The Dramatic Ambivalence of Self in the Poetry of Louise Bogan," Bogan's poems are not victim poems. Colasurdo suggests that "What appear to be victim poems are in fact celebrations of the self's emergence from family constraints, failed love, and rigid gender roles." Bogan is a woman who has survived her family and her husband. It is not easy for Bogan to reveal herself, and as Colasurdo observes, Bogan was "a poet who vigorously avoided self-display in her life and work." And yet, she is a poet who also created poems that use the language of suppression and silence.

Although Bogan does use the language of self-suppression, especially in her multiple uses of the word "nothing" in "Words for Departure," she also reveals the painful experience of love, especially in the last line of the poem: "Let there be some

What Do I Read Next?

- *Collected Poems, 1923–1954* (1954), by Louise Bogan, is a collection of her early poems. Also included are three poems written after World War II ended. Bogan was awarded the 1955 Bollingen Prize for this collection.
- *The Blue Estuaries: Poems, 1923–1968* (1968) was Bogan's final work of poetry. This collection earned Bogan the best reviews she ever received for a book of poetry.
- *The Metaphysical Poets* (1960, 3d ed.), edited by Helen Gardner, provides a good introduction that helps explain the characteristics of metaphysical poetry. The collection of poetry included provides a selection of poets, over many years.
- *The Poetry of John Donne and the Metaphysical Poets*, reissued in 1989 and edited by Joseph E. Grennen, includes a comprehensive selection of Donne's work. Donne is considered the most important of the metaphysical poets, and he had an influence on Bogan's poetry.
- *Sleeping on the Wing: An Anthology of Modern Poetry with Essays on Reading and Writing* (1982), by Kate Farrell and Kenneth Koch, is a collection of poetry selected from among twenty-three modern poets. In addition to a collection of wonderful poems, the authors also provide guides to help fledgling writers create their own poems.
- *Sound and Form in Modern Poetry* (1996, 2d ed.), by Harvey Seymour and Robert McDowell, is a good basic text to help the student understand form and function in modern poetry. One strength of this book is its emphasis on metrical structure and stanza forms.

---

uncertainty about your departure." As a child and as a young wife, Bogan experienced many departures. Her ambivalence at these many comings and goings is part of what creates so much tension in her poetry. In his essay "The Re-Making of a Poet: Louise Bogan," Lee Upton points out that Bogan seems to present "a closed face" to critics. Consequently, Bogan emerges as stern and limited and perceived as a poet who depicts "female victims without imagining a more compelling conception of women." Noting that Bogan's poems are "profoundly oppositional," Upton explains that "[s]eparation rather than unity propels her poetics." In "Words for Departure," a lover leaves. He also leaves behind anger, grief, and betrayal. These are mismatched lovers; one, perhaps a man, but equally possibly a woman, is secretive. This lover is the "rind"; nothing is known of the interior, what this lover is feeling or thinking. This lover has mysteries to unlock, words and feelings that remain hidden. The other lover is the opposite, the interior, the "white-juiced apple"; everything is known and nothing is hidden. As Bogan notes in her autobiography, separations, secrets, and deception defined her childhood. Her poetry is charged with her personal story of betrayal. Bogan, whose public "closed face" gives away nothing of her personal life, gives voice to a lover's betrayal in "Words for Departure." Her mother had "her fantasies, her despairs, her secrets, her subterfuges." She was like the rind, the lover whose secrets and whose departure brings such pain.

Upton also indicates that it is Bogan's position as an outsider that leads to many of the oppositional forces found in her poems. Bogan writes in her autobiography that she was "a member of a racial and religious minority." She knew this from a young age; she experienced the bigotry directed against Irish Catholics, and she understood that she "was a 'Mick,'" regardless of her other "faults or virtues." Her status as an outsider, says Upton, can be found in her poetry: "[d]ivided voices dominate her work and require that we read her poems not as simple polemics but as explorations of multiple levels of psychological crisis." The opposition noted in "Words for Departure," the countering of "Nothing was remembered, nothing forgotten," the repetition of this parallelism throughout the poem—these are Bogan's divided voice. She creates divisions and breaks in unity in her poetry, just as her life was a series of moves, separations, betrayals, and broken attachments. In exploring meaning in Bogan's poetry, Upton suggests that for Bogan "separation became a means of survival." While still quite young, she removed herself from her parents and husband and even her young daughter, and moved to New York City to live on her own. This leaving is what she understands as normal, given her own childhood experiences.

Bogan, who had so little control over her childhood existence, tried as an adult to control her own life. In her essay "Music in the Granite Hill," Deborah Pope suggests that the women in Bogan's poems "struggle to establish a sense of selfhood and control over their emotional and social environments, which constantly operate to defeat them." Pope proposes that "Words for Departure" is part of a poetic sequence that reveals the emotional turmoil of Bogan's failed marriage. As Pope also notes, with so much turmoil in her own early life, Bogan sought control in her poetry. "Words for Departure" reveals a stasis in the poet's world. Each movement of the poem is balanced; lines and phrasing are parallel, the oppositions counterpoised and the symmetry clear. Nothing is out of control, and yet, one lover is leaving and another is in pain. Yet even that inequity is equal. The lover does leave, but the other lover assumes control also. It is this lover's voice that is heard in the poem and this lover who demands that her lover leave in the dark. It is the abandoned lover who issues warning and it is this lover who commands the reader's attention. Like Bogan, this lover is a survivor. Upton suggests that Bogan's poetry "explores the unconscious dynamics of women's experience." It may also reveal the dynamics of Bogan's own life.

Source: Sheri E. Metzger, Critical Essay on "Words for Departure," in *Poetry for Students*, Thomson Gale, 2005.

Marcia Aldritch

In the following essay excerpt, Aldrich places Bogan's career within the context of an aesthetic of romantic crisis and argues that Bogan did not evolve into a mature poet due to her status as a feminine lyric poet of the time.

The modernist poet Louise Bogan never wrote poetry easily or voluminously. Over her lifetime she published 105 collected poems, most of them written while she was in her twenties or thirties. *The Sleeping Fury*, published in 1937 when Bogan was forty years old, was her last book of new poems. She wrote no poetry from 1941 to 1949, and the *Collected Poems, 1923–1953* added but three lyrics to the work gathered in *Poems and New Poems*, published in 1941. In her twenties Bogan was already contrasting her own writing blocks with Keats's "sitting down every morning and writing 200 lines, fully and easily" (*Letters*). In middle age she wrote poetry with still greater difficulty and infrequency, reaching an impasse that persisted for some thirty years, even while she remained active as a translator and critic until her death in 1970. "The woman who died without producing an oeuvre" was the harsh epitaph Bogan wrote for herself when still in her thirties; she was haunted by the possibility that history would remember her only for what she did not accomplish (*Journey*).

One reason for Bogan's small output, offered by many of those who have written about her, is strict standards of artistic excellence, which created an anxious perfectionism that approached self-censorship. Bogan felt, as she herself recognized, "the knife of the perfectionist attitude at my throat" (*Letters*). But if such standards—based in a modernist, originally masculine aesthetic of impersonality—help account for Bogan's limited production overall, they do not in themselves explain the shape of her creative career, the decline and disappearance of poetry in her middle and late years. After all, Bogan worked in a modernist idiom from the start. In *Louise Bogan's Aesthetic of Limitation*, Gloria Bowles provides a more adequate explanation of the volume of poetry Bogan produced—or did not produce—at different stages of life. Along with the psychoaesthetics of perfectionism, Bowles cites biographical and vocational factors. The "burden" of Bogan's reviewing for the *New Yorker*, "her precarious psychological balance, her perfectionism, her sense of being unappreciated, and her idea of the innate limitations of the woman poet combined to effectively put an end to her art in her early forties." All of these factors are comprised in Bogan's sense of the vocation of the feminine lyric poet, which was shaped by an ideology of youthful romantic love, traditionally both the subject matter of the feminine lyric and the source of the woman poet's inspiration. It is this sense of vocation that most directly enforced change over the course of her career. For what does such a complex of assumptions leave to the middle-aged feminine lyricist?

The Traffic in Pleasure: Early Careers

Bogan was one of a number of women writers of the 1920s, including Sara Teasdale, Elinor Wylie, and Edna St. Vincent Millay, who redefined and modernized the feminine lyric. Their signature was established forms like the sonnet, and they retained the traditional concentration on intense personal feeling. In renewing the feminine lyric, however, they replaced celebrations of religious faith and the domestic sphere, predominant in poetry of the nineteenth century, with powerful sensual experience as the chosen means of transcendence. Bogan and her contemporaries still relied on love, but now it was the engine of physical sensation. Teasdale reported in a letter that she had set up a shrine to Aphrodite and declared, "She is more real to me than the Virgin." Whereas Eliot had advanced a universal, ideal order of European tradition, Bogan and her compatriots acknowledged a specific line of women's poetry leading into their own. Teasdale's anthology of love poetry by women, *The Answering Voice,* distills this tradition as it developed up to World War I, emphasizing idealistic yearning, disappointment, and memory. Although Bogan disdained the exaggerated posturing of sentimental nineteenth-century verse on the subject of love, she credited women with maintaining the line of feeling in American poetry against any exclusive modernist impulse toward irony and impersonality. Bogan identified herself with a lyric of emotion because it derived from the valid foundation of women's art: "Women's feeling, at best, is closely attached to the organic heart of life"; to women belonged the functions of "security, receptivity, enclosure, nurturance." Albeit ambivalently, Bogan accepted the sentimental tradition as one that sustained her own poetry. The headline of her obituary in the *New York Times*—"Louise Bogan, Noted Poet Who Wrote about Love, Dead"—dramatizes the extent to which she was identified with the one subject.

It was not a subject free from impediments. Indeed, Bogan's struggle as a writer was from the outset contingent on the identification of the female poet with heterosexual love, the well of feeling. Remarks in "The Heart and the Lyre," Bogan's evaluation of the female tradition, suggest why. Here she links strength of emotion with the feminine lyric gift: "In women, more than in men, the intensity of their emotions is the key to the treasures of the spirit." How and when could one find special strength of feeling? It was available in moments of crisis, in the throes of romance. Of "Zone," first published in *Poem and New Poems*, Bogan noted, "I wrote a poem which derives directly from emotional crisis, as, I feel, a lyric must" (*Journey*). This belief, too, was an inherited feature of the feminine lyric; Teasdale, for example, placed herself in a tradition based in the inevitability of women's frustration in love. But the conviction that the lyric derives from moments of crisis creates difficulties in composition, for crisis is not a sustainable form of experience. As Malcolm Cowley emphasized, Bogan's theory made it impossible for her to write a great deal. Even in her youth, a reliance upon extreme feeling limited Bogan's opportunities to create poetry.

"Perhaps the most economical means to sketch the cultural pressures prevailing in the 1920s is to show that the female lyric poet responded to what produced like results in two great contemporary film actresses, Greta Garbo and Louise Brooks."

An aesthetic of romantic crisis does permit a certain production of poetry if one has a supply of crises—such as was provided to Bogan by her biography through her twenties. She was born in 1897 into an Irish Catholic family then residing in Livermore Falls, Maine. After several other shifts, her parents moved to Boston when she was still a young girl. Her mother was, in Bogan's account, a handsome but vain woman who derived her sense of identity through attracting the romantic interest of men, however fleeting and destructive. Her energies were compulsively channeled into a traffic in pleasure—the upkeep of her figure and dress, endless arrangements of liaisons. These sexual adventures dominated Bogan's life as a young girl. On one occasion she suffered an episode of blindness lasting two days; she was never able to recall what scene had precipitated this symptom. She was "the highly charged and neurotically inclined product of an extraordinary childhood and an unfortunate early marriage, into which last state [she] had rushed to escape the first" (*Letters*). Living with her family during her freshman year at Boston College, Bogan won a scholarship to Radcliffe but chose to marry Curt Alexander, a corporal in the army, rather than remain at home and attend college. Shortly after the marriage, Alexander was transferred to the Canal Zone, and Bogan, by this time pregnant, followed. She found the exotic Panamanian landscape "alien and hostile" and the marriage an even stranger threshold: "All we had in common was sex" (*Journey*). After the birth of their daughter, Alexander refused sexual relations with Bogan, and the marriage quickly deteriorated.

Like many other writers early in the century, Bogan turned cultural and personal disappointment into modernist poetry. Her first book, *Body of This Death*, published in 1923 and dedicated to her mother and daughter, takes as its subject women in the throes of love. The subject is fully traditional, but the results are not promising, for the volume finds that the literary life of feeling is one of depersonalization and disillusionment. *Body of This Death* studies the bourgeois family and marriage; the latter is sought to escape the former, but it proves an equivalent entrapment. Figures who seek to detach themselves from family through romantic passion discover that it provides no ultimate remedy. The mother's power over the daughter's fate frames many of her attempted escapes, and marital rites of passage fail. Women are identified with beautiful, often aestheticized, objects—stones, marble girls who hear "no echo save their own." The volume builds a spiral of betrayals, each ending in an image of arrest.

> To love never in this manner!
> To be quiet in the fern
> Like a thing gone dead and still.
> ("Men Loved Wholly beyond Wisdom")

Female destiny is the experience of "being trapped—of being used, of being made an object" (*Journey*).

Body of This Death begins on a note of hope. Heterosexual consummation, romantic love, would be the means to Bogan's self-creation; sexual love and fertility would empower her. The book's lead-off poem, "A Tale," expresses a longing for love as a means of control, as well as transcendence in the manner of the feminine lyric. Bogan, in the person of the poem's youthful protagonist, hopes for "a land of change" away from the suffocatingly familiar props of her New England childhood. Outwardly she succeeds in severing ties to her family, breaking apart what had shut her in "as lock upon lock." But the allegiance to passion under conditions of inequality, what amounts to women's objectification in male desire, can be debilitating and cruel. The body, for all its sensory power, betrays women who are conventionally young and desirable in a man's world.

> nothing dares
> To be enduring, save where, south
> of hidden deserts, torn fire glares
> On beauty with a rusted mouth.
> Where something dreadful and another
> Look quietly upon each other.
> ("A Tale")

The metonymy of the mouth, rusted and partial, paves the way to the subjects of the last couplet. There the dehumanized "something and another" figure the depersonalizing effect of the youth's fate. "A Tale" initiates the pattern of sexual quest and failed release in *Body of This Death*. In the dramatic disappointment of Bogan's journey's end, we find the source of the projected landscapes:

> Here I could well devise the journey to nothing,
> At night getting down from the wagon by the black barns,
> The zenith a point of darkness, breaking to bits,
> Showering motionless stars over the houses.
> Scenes relentless—the black and white grooves of a woodcut.
> ("A Letter," Journey)

The "withered arbor" in "Statue and Birds" is another sample of disillusionment, the statue representing the results of the transformation of strong experience into the lyric, the essence of Bogan's sense of her poetic process.

> Here, in the withered arbor, like the arrested wind,
> Straight sides, carven knees,
> Stands the statue, with hands flung out in alarm
> Or remonstrances.
>
> Over the lintel sway the woven bracts of the vine
> In a pattern of angles.
> The quill of the fountain falters, woods rake on the sky
> Their brusque tangles.
>
> The birds walk by slowly, circling the marble girl,
> The golden quails,
> The pheasants, closed up in their arrowy wings,
> Dragging their sharp tails.
>
> The inquietudes of the sap and of the blood are spent.
> What is forsaken will rest.
> But her heel is lifted,—she would flee,—the whistle of the birds
> Fails on her breast.

The marble girl occupies the center of the arbor, around which the birds slowly circle and from which they depart. Their motion is opposed to the marble girl's stasis; art as static perfection opposed to the freedom of the birds. Against their natural movements we can measure the girl's beautiful but frozen gesture.

The emphasis on "Here" suggests that the text we read, the poem, is also an arbor of sorts. It, too, is a sanctuary, a shady recess enshrining the female statue. But in the poem's process, the statue erodes as statue. It becomes "the marble girl" and finally the "she" of the closing stanza. This final pronoun is a composite of the statue and the depersonalized poet. The walls soften with the poet's late discovery of herself within them. Thus Bogan places her own female beauty in a withered arbor, suggesting an unnatural enervation, the loss of freedom for and by the figuration of art. Enshrinement in an artificial recess becomes another entrapment. The female statue suggests the aesthetic imperatives of Keats's Grecian urn: to attain final perfection, the marble girl must become "an object, in the double sense of being dead and also an object for aesthetic contemplation." In the marble girl's arrested form, Bogan encodes her own self-defeat and complicity within the tradition that objectifies women.

The persistence of the subject of love in the feminine lyric, whether in the traditional moods or with Boganian bitterness, exemplifies a dependence common among women on youthful heterosexual ties for self-definition. The rite of passage theme in "Betrothed" shows how thoroughly the conventional female of Bogan's period was still defined by heterosexual love relationships. The betrothal song, as a set piece of nineteenth-century poetry, celebrates a young woman's passage into marriage. Bogan represents the young woman as an elegiac figure of feminine dismay.

> You have put your two hands upon me, and your mouth,
> You have said my name as a prayer.
> Here where trees are planted by the water
> I have watched your eyes, cleansed from regret,
> And your lips, closed over all that love cannot say.
>
> My mother remembers the agony of her womb
> And long years that seemed to promise more than this.
> She says, "You do not want me,
> You will go away."
>
> In the country whereto I go
> I shall not see the face of my friend
> Nor her hair the color of sunburnt grasses;
> Together we shall not find
> The land on whose hills bends the new moon
> In air traversed of birds.

The lover's hands and mouth, placed or imposed on the female, silence rather than caress, and this imposed silence seems linked to the daughter's failure to deliver herself cleanly from her mother's womb. The "you" of "Betrothed" makes proprietary claims upon the female, wrenching possession from the mother. Thus the poem emphasizes the continuity of possession from mother to husband, from daughter to wife, "lock upon lock." It is through relationship with the husband that Bogan discovers the crucial fact about women's sexual identity: they are defined by their relations with others. The female's identity never stands alone, cut free from the mother's claims of birth or from the husband's future rights.

If love as subject connects Bogan's lyric to the nineteenth century, it is still possible to distinguish women's relationships during the period of Bogan's first publications from those prevailing in the nineteenth century. The poems in *Body of This Death* define a possessive love between unequal lovers. Although the woman is often absorbed and transformed by such love, she must give up friends, family, home, and landscape, even her prior sense of self, to achieve her exaltation. The 1920s, when Bogan's volume was published, saw a shift away from a greater identification of women with women in the nineteenth century. The invention of the category of homosexuality late in the nineteenth century stands as a watershed between the two periods, creating that which is proscribed. A contemporary indicator of this shift is a group of essays compiled in the *Nation* under the title *These Modern Women.* Attempting to ascertain what distinguished contemporary women's experiences, the essays describe a reorientation away from the homosocial ties of girlhood toward heterosexual relationships.

Perhaps the most economical means to sketch the cultural pressures prevailing in the 1920s is to show that the female lyric poet responded to what produced like results in two great contemporary film actresses, Greta Garbo and Louise Brooks. Their appeal to the film audience—by means of beauty, passion, and suffering—resembled the specifications for the desired and desiring female in the lyric. Garbo personified glamour, sensual expression, and inaccessibility to the general audience, a version of the closed poem encoding sexual appetite. Her film characters sacrificed themselves—to one man, for love. Brooks, on the other hand, exemplified the unbridled pleasure principle. In critical tributes her acting is a matter of instinctual physicality: she "needed no directing, but could move across the screen causing the work of art to be born by her mere presence." Directors made similar observations about Garbo, believing she embodied what Roland Barthes in "The Face of Garbo" called the "lyricism of women." The impulse is to locate the basis of the actress's art in her youthful desirability. The same impulse exhibits itself in the critical response to lyric poets, whose art was the gesture of overflowing emotion. Their reception in the 1920s was not generally a matter of analysis; instead it was suffused in romance and infatuation. Many were celebrated beauties whose photographs accompanied their poems in print. Millay cut a romantic figure, rising to notice through public readings that captivated numbers of men, intensifying the propensity to collapse distinctions between poet and poetry. Wylie's much-publicized romantic life, in combination with the austere form of her beauty, was a considerable factor in the reception of her poems. In reviews, descriptions of her physical appearance and of her poems overlap.

Of course the most obvious ideal of physical beauty for women in this century has been youthfulness. As Lois Banner remarks, "An unlined face, hair neither gray nor white, a slim body with good muscle tone have been the signs of beauty achieved." After the 1920s the focus on youth came to include sophistication, glamour, and experience; however, a deepening of sensual experience was still contained within a paradigm of youth and beauty. Garbo quit the screen at age thirty-seven; Brooks's career began before she was twenty-one and lasted but thirteen years. Withdrawal from the public eye was necessary for the actresses to preserve their images from the revisions that would have accompanied their aging. They grew older behind closed doors and sunglasses. The assumption that the aging body is, in Kathleen Woodward's phrase, the "sign of deformation" links these retirements to Bogan's career. In her medium Bogan was as deeply immersed in a process of youthful passion, a romantic objectification of women. The lyric, in the hands of young women, embodied qualities of youth—compression, intensity, passion, and longing—without the marks of decline associated with old age.

The allotted role of women poets, a concern with romantic love, satisfied Bogan's youthful sense of the kind of poetry she aspired to write, even if the outcome of love, as represented in *Body of This Death*, was destructive. Many writers embraced their identification with love, youth, and desirability because of the opportunities offered but never imagined their fate when they no longer were young. In Western culture, certain forms of power pass swiftly from the old to the young. Marketability in the positions historically open to women, from waitressing to acting, depends upon youthfulness. Women experience anxiety in aging because, quite simply, they may be superseded; women poets were troubled by the process of aging because it seemed to deny them their subject—passion. Valuing love, women poets of the period simultaneously valued youth. When Bogan arrived in middle age, she was faced with alternative prospects: to change the focus and process of her writing or to retire from poetry.

Source: Marcia Aldritch, "Lethal Brevity: Louise Bogan's Lyric Career," in *Aging and Gender in Literature: Studies in Creativity*, edited by Anne M. Wyatt-Brown and Janice Rossen, University Press of Virginia, 1993, pp. 105–20.

Lee Upton

In the following essay, Upton discusses recent critical analyses of Bogan's work and how modern readings have come to recognize the ways that her poetry explores the unconscious dynamics of women's experience.

Reputation, that fitful wind, changes direction often for a poet. After poets die their reputations may shift even more wildly; for whether poets are born or made, surely they are remade by their critics. Louise Bogan's is a curious case in point. Although respected by her peers and in later life at last highly awarded, she nevertheless remains absent or nearly so from many contemporary discussions of modern poetry. Yet although this poet is not fully secured within descriptions of the modernist project, in recent years some measure of attention has been directed to her work. Surely Elizabeth Frank's meticulous biography has generated increased interest. Martha Collins has gathered the central critical essays on the poet and places critical reaction in focus, and a number of other readers have constructed analyses that reevaluate Bogan, particularly in regard to feminist issues. Ruth Limmer's "mosaic" of Bogan's autobiographical writing has been of inestimable value, and Jacqueline Ridgeway has written a useful introduction to this poet. In turn, Gloria Bowles has written a study that argues for Bogan as a "major modernist" (1). Deborah Pope includes a chapter on Bogan in her exploration of isolation in women's poetry, and Mary K. DeShazer has written compellingly of Bogan's muse.

Yet, despite re-evaluations of Bogan's poetry, many discussions have begun to form an edifice that may compromise our appreciation of her work. Her poems, challenging and resistant to much interpretation, remain displaced by an image of their creator, a woman whose proclivities were, in such readings, poised against her own growth. As Martha Collins suggests, we must freshly attempt to understand the "pleasure" that these poems may arouse (20). Unfortunately, Bogan too often appears in critical narratives as the joyless negative of the feminist poet and a maimed point of departure for the woman who is a poet today. In her seemingly cool and highly ordered art, it would seem that Bogan presents a closed face and a brittle completion. This, at any rate, is the poet who has emerged, early as well as late, in many estimations.

In much of the earliest criticism, Bogan is placed (even when compared with female contemporaries) as largely an exception among women. Allen Tate's discussion may serve as an example: "Women, I suppose, are fastidious, but many women poets are fastidious in their verse only as a way of being finical about themselves. But Miss Bogan is a craftsman in the masculine mode" (41–42). In his review of *Dark Summer*, Louis Untermeyer argues that the book's "quality lifts it high above the merely adequate writing published in such quantities by women in these so literate states" (36). In the most often cited account of Bogan's poetry, Theodore Roethke similarly chooses to make her an exception to her sex. After running through the supposed faults of women poets, including "lamenting the lot of the woman; caterwauling; writing the same poem about fifty times, and so on," he argues that "Louise Bogan is something else" (87). What that "something else" might be has puzzled critics before and since.

In more recent critical reconstructions, the criticism I am particularly interested in here, Bogan appears problematic for reasons that, paradoxically, prove similar to those which Tate, Untermeyer, and Roethke establish. In the re-making of the poet, Bogan again serves as an exception of sorts, an isolated and unusually gifted poet, yet one removed from healthy self-affirmation, excluded not only by patriarchy but limited, as Gloria Bowles in particular argues, by her own internalization of male modernism's disdain of women's poetry and rejection of "'female emotion'" (1). The Louise Bogan of much recent criticism would seem a victim identified with her oppressors, narrow and yet intent on universalizing her themes, devoted to a male structure of values, and yet confined within the lyric as women's traditional province. In different mixtures, such criticism reconfigures Bogan through three principal positions. First, there is a tendency to view her work through metaphors of ingestion, particularly in terms of a suspect growth, the cancer of an internalized male value system that consumes her scope and accomplishment; second, there exists a critical repulsion from Bogan's autobiographical reticence, a reticence that counters that strain within Anglo-American feminist criticism which prizes directness and sincerity; and, finally, there arises an evolutionary frame placing Bogan as a stern and repressed ancestor from whom contemporary poets must diverge in style and viewpoint.

"In the recent re-making of Louse Bogan this poet's aesthetics too often remain obscured by critics who seek directness, unity, and affirmation. As a consequence, Bogan becomes our puzzling Athena of modern American poetry."

The construction of Bogan's poetry in the light of self consumption may be especially revealing. We might consider Deborah Pope's analysis. Pope describes Bogan's poetry written after her first book, *Body of This Death* (1923), as "distrustful, cynical. . ., built on a reduction of the human and natural landscape" (40). Bogan's work is described as "a poetry of no return" (52) in which the poet makes "femaleness itself . . . a constitutional flaw" (*Separate* 10). Repeatedly the poet is viewed as distanced from her actual body and victimized by an alien value structure which she has, in a sense, internalized. As a consequence, Bogan and her poetry would seem to have little "body" left: "Tragically, what seems least to fit [in this poetry] is the female body itself" (*Separate* 52). In somewhat similar terms, Patrick Moore begins his essay by remarking that "Styles are symptoms" (67) and finds much of Bogan's poetry to be "a wasteland of anxiety and repression." Furthermore, he argues that "true feelings are blurred by symbol, distanced by masks, muted by form." Hers is a style, he observes, that is "rare, if not impossible, in a feminist poet" (79). Dominating these symptoms is a suspect "maleness," a value structure which dismisses women's achievement and constrains Bogan to a dubious goal of masculinized perfection. Although sensitive to and appreciative of many elements in Bogan's poetic, Bowles maintains that Bogan's poetry proves "an extreme example of a woman's internalization of male ideas of the woman poet" (2). In her turn, DeShazer, despite her sympathetic treatment of Bogan's poetry and a revisionary account of the poet's employment of silence, finds her subject to be similarly problematic because of "a male-defined concept of the woman artist . . . " (46).

A word frequently heard in many estimates is "limitation." Bogan's body of just over 100 poems, her conception of the woman poet's role, and her refusal of self-disclosure are summoned in recent criticism as limitations. Earlier critics also found the concept of limitation to be a useful one. Over fifty years ago Allen Tate depicted Bogan as a poet who practices "a strict observance of certain limitations" (42). Yvor Winters described her "subject-matter, or rather attitude" as "central . . . as any attitude so limited could be" (33). On a less ambiguous note, Lewellyn Jones argued that Bogan pits her poetry "against the limitations, imposed and self-imposed, on women; and at the same time [creates] a cry for something positive, for something compelling" (27). More recently, Bowles titled her study *Louise Bogan's Aesthetic of Limitation,* defining the poet's working practice as limitation, or "a strict idea of what a woman poet could and could not permit herself" (1).

Repulsion toward Bogan's insistence on privacy further focuses criticism. Although actual autobiographical circumstances are purged or seldom become part of Bogan's working materials, such omissions of the personal strike critics as repressive. Bowles argues that Bogan's "compacted forms, her suppressions and obscurities, are her declaration of the near impossibility—even in the twentieth century—of being both woman and poet" (51–52). Implicit in such criticism is an appetite for revealed context and direct autobiography. In her turn, Pope maintains that Bogan's poems reflect "the exclusion and suppression of any nature and life that does not fit her frame" and declares that Bogan developed "a style and stance pared to the bone: the granite hill that is both imprisoning and terrible" (*Critical* 165).

In other discussions, Bogan's poetry serves as symptomatic of oppression, and the poet becomes a deadening ancestor in an evolutionary struggle. Bogan is reduced to a variation of the critic's theme of isolation in Pope's study. Representing victimhood, her work is characterized by "powerless and extreme bitterness," "alienation from the body," and "a posture of renunciation" (*Separate* 10). Sandra Gilbert and Susan Gubar, drawing on Bowles and a brief portion of Bogan's correspondence, consign her situation to that of a "paradigm." As such, the poet is rhetorically effective, a trope for women's repressive past and "self-loathing" (xxiii). Bogan then becomes a disempowered figure, a doomed ancestor in an evolutionary struggle whose supposed failure in self-affirmation serves as a point of departure for theory.

In another brief discussion that presents Bogan emblematically, Paula Bennett follows an evolutionary rubric. Bennett examines the emergence of Medusa in women's poetry—the mythological figure upon whom one of Bogan's central poems focuses. Bennett argues that women poets validate through Medusa "those aspects of their being that their families and society have invalidated by treating such qualities as unfeminine and unacceptable" (246). Recast in contemporary poetry, Medusa becomes Bennett's symbol of self-empowerment. Yet such an empowered self is seen as beyond the focal experience of Bogan. In fact, Bogan's "Medusa," the earliest poem that Bennett draws upon, emerges in her analysis as devoid of "life" and "tragically appropriate for a poet of extraordinary gifts who believed only 105 of her poems worthy of permanent record and who appears to have despised the very idea that she might be considered a woman poet" (247). In Bennett's brief discussion, Bogan becomes a psychological victim of the gorgon's paralysis. Citing a contemporary poet whose poem on Medusa "hurts to read" and reveals "ugliness," Bennett casts Bogan (whose poems apparently do not impress upon Bennett their own rage) as a petrified specimen of repression. In an extension of the critical emphasis on symptoms, she argues that the new woman poet must "heal the internal divisions that have historically distorted and controlled her relationship to her craft." As such, Bogan's exploration of psychological rupture awaits a redemtive "healing." Repeatedly, Bogan emerges as a bad patient of sorts, recalcitrant to the medicine of acceptance and neglectful of "the true self within" (6).

In such discussions, a strangely split figure arises. Particularly in the analyses of Pope and Bennett, Bogan becomes an exemplar of repression despite her considerable achievement. Lingering behind their criticism is a ghost image of a projected Louise Bogan—a healed and generous figure, a foremother whose "true self within" might emerge at last.

Through such reconstructions, Bogan assumes the position of a stern, limited (and limiting) predecessor. She is perceived as internalizing maleness, circumscribing her own emotional range, and depicting female victims without imagining a more compelling conception of women. Yet such descriptions of Bogan's poetry fail fully to contend with the vital complexity of her poetics. The challenge of her work is more often commented upon rather than contended with in much recent discussion, and ultimately Bogan becomes a figure virtually encased within an oppressive past. Nevertheless, we should note that Bogan's subject matter remains crucial and, indeed, fruitfully disturbing for contemporary readers and particularly for poets who might find her example of striking use. The subjects of violent stasis, betrayal, unity and rupture, gender impositions, and release from obsession (the latter most clearly within her final poems, laboriously wrested from silence) inform her poetry.

Beginning with an examination of threatening violence and pervasive separation in her first book, *Body of This Death*, published when she was twenty-six, Bogan creates an arena in which an externalized and oppressive force must be withstood. She invests in a poetics that exposes difference. While we might here explore a number of features in her work—her investigation of repression and her investment in counter-violence, for instance—in this context I wish to call attention in brief form to Bogan's animated separations, her poetics of rupture and difference.

Bogan's poetry is profoundly oppositional. Separation and juxtaposition are her methods of composition. As in one of her earliest poems, "A Tale," she too "cuts what holds [her] days together / And shuts [her] in, as lock on lock" (3). The act of separating yoked conceptions creates "A fine noise of riven things" (5). Separation rather than unity propels her poetics. Separation clarifies by making extreme, and as such reveals modes of alienation, especially between women and men. In particular Bogan is interested in the exclusion of men from women's intimate concerns. In other contexts separation serves to revive psychological health, for separation proves a means to disengage from oppressive forces. Most often her emphasis on separation does not prove inviting, but resistant, and Bogan's poetry cannot readily comfort its critics. She creates divisions between self and reader that might in some ways account for the critical unease toward her work—a poetry that is itself a form of criticism in its avidity for distinctions. Unless we invert our usual categories of response, her poems would repel our readings. Separation, rather than unity, is a perceived good—a good that has consequences for the ways in which we may read and respond to this poetry.

An early poem, "The Alchemist," is especially important for what I am suggesting as a means of perceiving Bogan—realizing that I too am asking for a "re-making" of this poet's reputation, yet one that I hope may avoid collapsing her work into a trope for oppression. In the poem, the alchemist-poet experiments upon herself through a willed separation between body and mind. When her experiment fails to meet her expectations, she must make another discovery: "unmysterious flesh."

I burned my life, that I might find
A passion wholly of the mind,
Thought divorced from eye and bone,
Ecstasy come to breath alone.
I broke my life, to seek relief
From the flawed light of love and grief.

With mounting beat the utter fire
Charred existence and desire.
It died low, ceased its sudden thresh.
I had found unmysterious flesh—
Not the mind's avid substance—still
Passionate beyond the will.

Significantly, the alchemist's rediscovery of her flesh proves her reward, for by violently attempting to sever mind from body she is returned to the province of her own desires. In dyadic thinking the flesh's alliance with the feminine suggests that the triumph of the flesh in "The Alchemist" is, at last, a triumph for the feminine itself. Bogan rejects the cultural repudiation of the body and, as a consequence, the cultural rejection of women's bodily selves as desiring subjects. In other poems ironically inviting chastity and at least superficially resisting bodily desire, Bogan suggests that the flesh as female province continually must be recovered. As an alchemy of sorts, her depiction of extremes is carried out experimentally.

In her frequent sense of exclusion from her contemporaries, in her exile as a woman in patriarchal culture, and in her ethnic (Irish-American) self-consciousness, Bogan presents us with divided responses. She declares in her essay, "The Springs of Poetry," that the poet "should be blessed by the power to write behind clenched teeth, to subsidize his emotion by every trick and pretense so that it trickles out through other channels, if it be not essential to speech,—blessed too, by a spirit as loud as a houseful of alien voices, ever tortured and divided with itself." Divided voices dominate her work and require that we read her poems not as simple polemics but as explorations of multiple levels of psychological crisis. Her explorations do not simply embody the dominant aesthetic. For all their classic order, her poems attest to the lyric as a province for creative struggle and creative rupture. She proves a poet deeply aware of the ways in which male and female experience may be culturally segregated. And she is aware as well of the ways in which romantic symbiosis thwarts intimacy. In another context Bogan writes that "Women still have within them the memory of the distaff and the loom—and, we must remember, the memory of the dark, cruel, wanton goddesses. But because woman rarely has gone over, in the past, to a general and sustained low complicity or compliance in relation to her companion, man, we can hope for her future" (*Journey*). Against a "sustained low complicity," Bogan erects the poem.

The aesthetic technique of separation is particularly evident in this poet's most controversial poem "Women." If a body of work could be said to contain a culprit, "Women" is that perversely seductive culprit, for readings of the poem have contributed to a calcified presentation of Bogan's poetics as inimical to women. Nevertheless, the poem refuses a stable position—which may in some measure account for a plethora of contradictory readings. The poem might be viewed as a burlesque of gender, a broadside of self-hatred, a declaration of difference, a critique of culture, a disguised rebuttal to men, and, of course, as a savage criticism of women. No doubt the poem retains its power because it holds such possibilities in tension, refracting its conceptual hues broadly for each reader. The poem may be seen as compelling for its aesthetically sustained framing of the assignment of women's and men's roles in culture and especially for its enactment of the externalization of male presence within women's lives:

Women have no wilderness in them,
They are provident instead,
Content in the tight hot cell of their hearts
To eat dusty bread.

They do not see cattle cropping red winter grass,
They do not hear
Snow water going down under culverts
Shallow and clear.

They wait, when they should turn to journeys,
They stiffen, when they should bend.
They use against themselves that benevolence
To which no man is friend.

They cannot think of so many crops to a field
Or of clean wood cleft by an axe.
Their love is an eager meaninglessness
Too tense, or too lax.

They hear in every whisper that speaks to them
A shout and a cry,
As like as not, when they take life over their door-
sills
They should let it go by.

Frequently, "Women" has been cited as symptomatic of Bogan's adoption of assumptions that denigrate women. Pope finds the poem "devastating" (*Separate* 10) and argues that Bogan proposes "the utterly bleak proposition that women are by gender unable to love, to move, to be free, that it is neither landscapes, partners, nor roles, but women's very selves that are ultimately 'the body of this death'" (*Critical*). Elizabeth Frank suggests that the poem depicts women as "by nature tinged with defective wills" and cites the poem for "its obvious *envy* of maleness" (67). Taking a different tack altogether, Ronald Giles proposes an ironic reading, noting that Bogan's speaker "while appearing to catalogue the inadequacies of women, actually ridicules the accepted superiority of men" (34). The speaker shows women to be "provident, sentient, benevolent," and "more sophisticated" than men (40). Giles's reversals call attention to the poem's ostensible values ("If men *can think* 'of so many crops to a field' or of 'clean wood cleft by an axe,' so what?") (39). While his essay counters critics who present the poem as emblematic of Bogan's sympathies with patriarchy, Giles's reading strains the poem's rhetoric and largely overlooks its genuine denunciation of women's acculturated status. Although the poet's position as a woman problematizes our reception of the poem, her gender may not annul her actual uneasiness about women's status. While Bogan is an accomplished ironist, objections to women's strategies of accommodation inform the poem and provide for much of its critical power.

Bogan interrogates women's physical, emotional, and social positions. In the logic of the poem, women occupy an internal realm, men an external one. Ironically, as the poem's assumed "other," men, like women, "have no wilderness in them," for their activities revolve around rural domesticating occupations; they tend cattle, plant fields, chop wood. Although representing the feminine gender superficially as "content in the tight hot cells of their hearts," she portrays discontent and restless sensitivity on women's parts: "they hear in every whisper that speaks to them / A shout and a cry." The object of their love (presumably men) cannot satisfy, for the love men offer proves "an eager meaninglessness." The suggestions of maleness (is men's love the "dusty bread" women eat in their cells? Are men simply to be "let . . . go by?") are specific only in regard to men's avoidance of generosity: "Women use against themselves that benevolence / To which *no man* is friend" (emphasis mine). The one quality explicitly repudiated by men, benevolence is placed in critical focus as Bogan indicts cultural constriction that leads to women's self-sacrifice. If employed against self-hood, such negative benevolence allows any "life" to enter, even that which should be rejected. Cultural expectations of women's kindness are repudiated—kindnesses that women are discouraged from practicing toward themselves. Significantly, "Women" reveals maleness as exteriorized by a speaker who exaggerates oppositions between the sexes and finally renders women as the principal gender whose benevolence toward men is misplaced. "Women," then, is a portrayal of men as an absence, continually exterior to women. Finally, men are expelled from the site of the poem, presumably as "life" itself that should be "let go . . . by."

"Women," I am arguing, is both a critique of women's acculturated behavior and an implicit critique of men's. Bogan excoriates existing orders between the sexes. In particular she exposes the psychological constriction of women and the psychological externalization of men in regard to women's intimate concerns.

Bogan's reliance on strategies of extraction and separation reflects legitimate conflict—and a strategy for psychological survival that she learned early in life. In recent years we have had much of Bogan's private history opened to us through her vivid and revealing letters; Ruth Limmer's remarkable "mosaic" of autobiographical material; and Elizabeth Frank's carefully composed and insightful biography. Most readers are now aware of Bogan's difficult childhood, including the specter of familial violence and her mother's extramarital affairs and prolonged absences. Critics have reconstructed this life in ways that illuminate Bogan's conflicts and, most particularly, Frank has memorably revealed Bogan's embattled progression toward maturity. Bogan's autobiographical accounts suggest that, with whatever difficulty, she separated herself from overwhelming and capricious others; separation became a means of survival and integrity. She separated herself from her family, from two husbands, and from low cultural expectations of women's lyrics. Nevertheless, her life in some analyses becomes largely an exemplar of stern self-repression. In re-making the poet, her critics often focus on the hobbling nature of her childhood handicaps, neglecting the triumph of her audacious exploration of obsession.

We might consider in this context an early poem in which a woman must be extracted from a ruling conception—indeed, extracted in a way that must have been piercingly familiar to the young Bogan. In "The Romantic" a male figure would "name" a woman "chaste," denying her physical desire, that trope in Bogan's work for independence and life energy. Ascribing to a woman a purity that nullifies her experience, and attempting "to fix and name her," the romantic proves adept only at illusion and denial. The woman eludes his ultimate plans and entirely escapes figuration in the present. At best, her past may be described (and surely someone will be glad to describe "what she was") but neither her present nor her future may be narrated. Both resist interpretation:

> In her obedient breast, all that ran free
> You thought to bind, like echoes in a shell.
> At the year's end, you promised, it would be
> The unstrung leaves, and not her heart, that fell.
>
> So the year broke and vanished on the screen
> You cast about her; summer went to haws.
> This, by your leave, is what she should have been,—
> Another man will tell you what she was.

No longer a victim, the woman has fled the romantic's ideological constraints. A traditional romantic conception would limit the woman, and yet she is already an absence within the poem, for she refuses to be divorced from her own bodily experience. Through separation between the romantic and the object of his desire, Bogan reveals not only conflicts between the sexes but the absence of actual relationship.

In this context, mirroring, explored in a number of Bogan's poems, proves significant. Without clear psychological boundaries we simply reflect others, and a crippling symbiosis occurs. "Portrait" presents a woman coming into poetic and emotional maturity, for she need not "be a glass, where to foresee / Another's ravage." No longer reflecting her lover's desire, she is "possessed by time." If the latter phrase suggests sudden mortality and erotic devaluation, in turn it initiates another possibility: the woman may now more fully experience the mutable world and her own presence within it. In "The Crows" a passionate older woman may "hear the crows' cry" and gain knowledge. If the crows cry for aged and young, jeering "over what yields not, and what yields," the mature woman may hear enough to suspect romantic fusion. In a later poem, "Man Alone," a dominating sensibility is rendered exterior: a man who would only "read" his being through feminine presence must find himself continually estranged. For him, the feminine does not exist other than as a projection. As such the speaker remains a "stranger" to the narcissist who seeks his reflection through her:

> The glass does not dissolve;
> Like walls the mirrors stand;

The printed page gives back
Words by another hand.

And your infatuate eye
Meets not itself below:
Strangers lie in your arms
As I lie now.

Pointedly, the narcissist has no identity; the woman he seeks must effectively separate herself from him or she threatens to become, as myth would have it, his echo.

Within poems that are addressed most pointedly to women, stern lessons in perception are granted, one woman to another. Such lessons involve separation as a discipline that prompts new knowledge. As we have seen in "The Alchemist" separation proves a means of discovering the flesh—and, by extension—the feminine. In "Women" Bogan examines cultural law that renders men extraneous to women. In "The Romantic" she extracts the feminine from an overwhelming conception that denies the body. In "The Crossed Apple" she reveals suffering mandated within romantic love and refuses it for her speaker. The latter poem may prove particularly illuminating. Presumably an older woman (as women frequently bear apples in myth and fairy tale) presents a younger woman with a divided apple: a choice between peaceful nurturance, "Meadow Milk," or the suffering of passionate love, "Sweet Burning":

Oh, this is a good apple for a maid,
It is a cross,

Fine on the finer, so the flesh is tight,
And grained like silk.
Sweet Burning gave the red side, and the white
Is Meadow Milk.

Eat it; and you will taste more than the fruit;
The blossom, too,
The sun, the air, the dark at the root,
The rain, the dew,

The earth we came to, and the time we flee,
The fire and the breast,
I claim the white part, maiden, that's for me.
You take the rest.

Dividing experience into extremes ("this side is red without a dapple, / And this side's hue / Is clear and snowy"), the speaker's offering contains, if the maiden will interpret her gift correctly, a lesson in self-interest. Whether a wizened Eve or a revisionary witch, the speaker refuses self-illusion; she divides as a means to clarify. The maiden must refuse extremes of experience or—if she prefers—she might follow the speaker's example and "claim" the apple half that is "clear and snowy" for herself.

In later poems this poet dissolves urgent confrontation, investing her poetry with effects of ephemerality and translucence. One of her crossed gifts to readers may be a map of release. From enacting obsession she moves to the repudiation of obsession. The later poem "After the Persian" is especially interesting in this sense. Her speaker immediately opens with a quiet refusal, for any state of being that she has judged to be sterile and deceptive must be abjured. She rejects a "terrible jungle" of infertility and illusion precisely because she has already understood its nature. The jungle's "sterile lianas" and "serpent's disguise" signal self-betrayal:

I do not wish to know
the depths of your terrible jungle:
From what next your leopard leaps
Or what sterile lianas are at once your serpents'
disguise and home.

Bogan projects mature experience as that of dwelling, inhabiting a threshold of plenitude in which living beings are not hardened into facile artifice or static conception. In this paradisal landscape of the psyche, creatures are in continual flux. Through flashing, jewel-like lines, Bogan renders an uncategorizable state. Moving from the wilderness of the youthful quester to the garden of mature knowledge, the dweller has triumphed over fruitless obsession and needless sorrow:

Here the moths take flight at evening;
Here at morning the dove whistles and the pigeons
coo.
Here, as night comes on, the fireflies wink and
snap
Close to the cool ground,
Shining in a profusion
Celestial or marine.

Each of the poem's five sections presents an engaged progression toward psychological release and an effect of discipline rather than escape. The first establishes a benevolent site; the second reviews the past; the third honors the "treasure" of the poem itself; the fourth contrasts present fulfillment with past suffering; and the fifth enacts departure and release. For Bogan, "the shimmer of evil" must be replaced by "the shell's iridescence / And the wild bird's wing." As her fluctuating images thwart possessiveness, conflict is supplanted by release for a speaker who herself must progressively disappear from the poem:

Goodbye, goodbye!
There was so much to love, I could not love it all:
I could not love it enough.

Some things I overlooked, and some I could not
find.
Let the crystal clasp them
When you drink your wine, in autumn.

Just as the treasure of experience rendered into poetry must prove "weightless," so too the speaker must become a disembodied spirit freed of confines. The poem proves a paean to the possibility of securing an inner life that reflects peaceful self-nurturance by separating the self from oppressive and deceptive forces.

A spirit of criticism animates many of Bogan's poems. We might recall that Bogan wrote meticulous and wide-ranging criticism, serving as poetry critic for the *New Yorker* for thirty-eight years. For some readers during her lifetime she was more widely known as a critic than as a poet. The fine lens of analytical discernment that she focused upon her contemporaries' poetry clarified in turn the relationship that her poems explore. Externalizing an alien value structure rather that absorbing it. Bogan is not a comfortable figure, aggrandized easily into any critical view, including that of much recent criticism in which she too often emerges as either a repressed mandarin or a stricken victim. Questioning romantic illusion, symbiosis, and self-sacrifice in love, she presents a "crossed" gift to women: a poetry of profound criticism rather than simple affirmation.

Bogan remains a poet who will continue to be read—perhaps even more so as we come to recognize the ways that her poetry explores the unconscious dynamics of women's experience. We may recall that in "The Crossed Apple" the action of the witch-like speaker—her claim to tranquility and her refusal to embrace the destructive experience of "Sweet Burning"—constitutes a lesson of sorts, a counter to the excesses of culture that define women as self-destructively benevolent. We might in turn recall Adrienne Rich's observation that Bogan's poetry proves "a graph of the struggle to commit a female sensibility, in all its aspects, to language." Rich further observes, "We who inherit that struggle have much to learn from her." Bogan's poetry of separation offers an invigorating challenge to her readers. In the recent re-making of Louse Bogan this poet's aesthetics too often remain obscured by critics who seek directness, unity, and affirmation. As a consequence, Bogan becomes our puzzling Athena of modern American poetry. But before casting her poetics as a "paradigm" of oppression and self-hate, we might do well to remember Bogan's repudiation of suffering and the example that she dramatizes of positive self-concern:

I claim the white part, maiden, that's for me.
You take the rest.

Source: Lee Upton, "The Re-Making of a Poet: Louise Bogan," in *Centennial Review*, Vol. 36, No. 3, Fall 1992, pp. 557–72.

Brett C. Millier

In the following essay, Miller discusses Bogan's education, her passionate nature, and her contributions to poetry.

The critic Malcolm Cowley remarked in a review of Louise Bogan's slim volume *Poems and New Poems* (1941) that she had "done something that has been achieved by very few of her contemporaries: she has added a dozen or more to our small stock of memorable lyrics. She has added nothing whatever to our inexhaustible store of trash." Bogan's reputation as a poet is secure on exactly that scale. She is remembered and studied as one of the finest lyric poets America has produced, though the fact that she was a woman and that she defended formal, lyric poetry in an age of expansive experimentation made evaluation of her work, until quite recently, somewhat condescending. Her achievement in poetry has also been overshadowed by her extensive critical writings; for thirty-eight years she was the poetry critic for *The New Yorker* magazine, the arbiter of taste in such matters for a literate and influential audience.

Louise Bogan was born of the unhappy marriage of Daniel and May Shields Bogan in Livermore Falls, Maine, a bustling mill town on the Androscoggin River. In 1897, the year of Louise's birth, Daniel Bogan was superintendent in a pulp mill in the town, the first of many such relatively white-collar mill jobs he would hold during her childhood. Louise was their third child; a son, Charles, had been born in 1884, and a second son, Edward, had died in infancy. Bogan grew up in the Irish communities of deepest New England, moving often with her family to a variety of hotels and boardinghouses and other temporary dwellings: to Milton, New Hampshire, in 1901; to Ballardvale, Massachusetts, in 1904; to Roxbury, near Boston, in 1909. These moves were prompted both by economics and by the family's unhappiness. May Shields Bogan was a beautiful and unstable woman prone to flaunting her many extramarital affairs (on at least one occasion witnessed by her daughter) and to mysterious and lengthy disappearances.

Despite these disruptions, Bogan was quite well educated, in a New Hampshire convent (1906–1908) and at Boston's excellent Girls' Latin School (1910–1915), where she received a classical education in Latin, Greek, French, mathematics, history, science, and the arts. Having fallen under the poetic spell of A. C. Swinburne and the French Symbolists, she was a constant contributor to Latin's literary magazine, *The Jabberwock*, until

> *"She is remembered and studied as one of the finest lyric poets America has produced, though the fact that she was a woman and that she defended formal, lyric poetry in an age of expansive experimentation made evaluation of her work, until quite recently, somewhat condescending."*

she was told by the headmaster to trim her ambitions: "No Irish girl could be editor of the school magazine." Such prejudice was prevalent in Boston at the time, and Bogan never ceased to resent it. She transcended these limitations, however, and continued to publish her high school poems, including four in the *Boston Evening Transcript*, and was named class poet. She was a wide and constant reader who followed her own tastes and developed early and intense literary ambitions.

The difficulties and instabilities of her childhood produced in Bogan a preoccupation with betrayal and a distrust of others, a highly romantic nature, and a preference for the arrangements of art over grim, workaday reality. She would suffer for most of her life from serious depression, which resulted in three lengthy hospital stays for treatment. She would drink heavily, and her work would suffer from what Elizabeth Frank in *Louise Bogan: A Portrait* (1985) has called "a principle of arrest": "Something stopped Louise Bogan dead in her tracks, not once, but many times." But her fine early education would form the foundation of her poetry and criticism, as would, in some sense, her unhappiness.

Sent by her parents to Boston University in 1916, Bogan did extremely well and earned a scholarship to Radcliffe for her sophomore year. She turned it down, however, for the chance to leave home in the company of a husband, Curt Alexander, a soldier of German origin nine years her senior. She moved with her husband to New York City, and then, when war was declared in 1917, to Panama, where she gave birth to their daughter, Mathilde (Maidie) Alexander. Miserable in the role of military wife and in the heat and humidity of Panama, Bogan wrote poems about her condition, including "Betrothed" (which appeared in her first collection) and "The Young Wife" (which she never collected) and schemed to get back to New England. She left Panama with her child in May 1918 and moved in with her parents in Massachusetts. At the end of the war she was briefly reconciled with her husband, and they lived for a time on army bases near Portland, Maine, and near Hoboken, New Jersey. In the summer of 1919 she left Alexander for good, delivering her daughter to her parents and finding herself an apartment in New York from which to launch her career as a woman of letters. Alexander died in 1920, and his army widow's pension enabled Bogan to stay in the city.

From her temporary job at Brentano's bookstore in New York, Bogan quickly became involved in the city's active literary community. Her earliest friendships included Lola Ridge, Malcolm Cowley, William Carlos Williams, Mina Loy, Maxwell Bodenheim, John Reed, Louise Bryant, Conrad Aiken, and, most important, Edmund Wilson. At the fringes of, but deeply skeptical about, the leftist politics common in the group, Bogan nonetheless found herself in an intense love affair with a young radical named John Coffey, who would shoplift (his speciality was furs) and then plead the cause of the poor in his courtroom appearances. Bogan drove the getaway car on one of these escapades, a fact that embarrassed her from time to time for the rest of her life. When Coffey finally succeeded in making his motives clear to a judge, he was committed to a hospital for the insane.

Bogan set about educating herself and honing her writing skills with great seriousness and dedication. Ever conscious of her educational deficiencies (she carried a lifelong resentment toward people with advanced degrees), she sought to make up for them by reading. In this period she discovered the poetry of William Butler Yeats, who, like Rainer Maria Rilke and W. H. Auden later, would become a poetic touchstone and an important influence on her work. Bogan's poems appeared in the best journals of her day, almost from the beginning of her stay in New York. She published often in Harriet Monroe's influential *Poetry: A Magazine of Verse* and was involved from the start with *The Measure*, a "little magazine" devoted to the formal lyric. She became acquainted with the work of the most important female poets of the day, including Elinor Wylie and Edna St. Vincent Millay, as well as the poetry of Edward Arlington Robinson, perhaps her most direct American influence. Also through her work on *The Measure* (and a brief stint as a card filer in the office of the anthropologist William Fielding Ogburn) she met and became friendly with Margaret Mead and the poet Léonie Adams. In 1922 Bogan spent six months alone in Vienna, absorbing European culture and writing, and by the fall of 1923 she had secured a publisher, Robert M. McBride, for her first book of poems.

Body of This Death (1923) contains several of Bogan's most memorable poems and in general reveals its author's preoccupations and tastes. Betrayal, particularly sexual betrayal, is a constant theme, though the poems are in no way "confessional." In private writing included in *Journey Around My Room: The Autobiography of Louise Bogan* (1980), Bogan echoes Emerson's charge that the poet tell his life story in "cipher": "The poet represses the outright narrative of his life. He absorbs it, along with life itself. The repressed becomes the poem. Actually, I have written down my experience in the closest detail. But the rough and vulgar facts are not there."

Like Emily Dickinson's "gift of screws," Bogan's poems are made of meticulously distilled experience, distanced from the source by objective language. Often presented by their titles as songs or chants or arias, her poems call attention to themselves as rhetorical acts in a common language. Such commitment to public discourse did not protect Bogan from occasional obscurity—the distillation sometimes reduced emotion to indecipherable symbolism. But Bogan saw herself in the tradition of sixteenth-and seventeenth-century English lyric poetry, and she disciplined her poetic emotion to the formal rhyme and meter she instinctively preferred. Her well-known poem "The Alchemist" speaks to the method:

> I burned my life, that I might find
> A passion wholly of the mind,
> Thought divorced from eye and bone,
> Ecstasy come to breath alone.
> I broke my life, to seek relief
> From the flawed light of love and grief.

The poem's concluding second stanza admits the necessity of "unmysterious flesh" after all.

Several of the poems in *Body of This Death* address specifically female concerns and point to Bogan's ambivalent relationship with the tradition of female lyric poets. Her poems are by no means dogmatically feminist; Bogan held a deep distrust for all ideological commitment. In fact, she has been castigated somewhat unfairly by contemporary feminists for the dry pronouncements of her much-anthologized lyric "Women": "Women have no wilderness in them, / They are provident instead, / Content in the tight hot cell of their hearts / To eat dusty bread." Missing the ironic self-criticism in the poem ("As like as not, when they take life over their door-sills / They should let it go by"), feminist critics have read it as general condemnation of women and their ways of viewing experience. While the situation of women in Bogan's poems is rarely preferred to the situation of men, she is capable of wise and penetrating insight. "Betrothed," "Portrait," "My Voice Not Being Proud," "Medusa," "The Crows," "The Changed Woman," "Chanson Un Peu Naïve," and "Fifteenth Farewell" are all strong poems with female speakers or subjects. She saw herself and her work as arising from that definite tradition of female lyricists, represented in the generation just older than Bogan herself by the strong figures of Sara Teasdale, Millay, and Wylie. For Marianne Moore and Hilda Doolittle, the more typically modernist women poets of the period, she felt less affinity.

Early in 1924 Bogan's close friend Edmund Wilson suggested that she try her hand at criticism. That spring she published her first book review, of D. H. Lawrence's *Birds, Beasts and Flowers* (1923), in *The New Republic*. She would continue to write poetry reviews for the rest of her life, and as poems came to her less and less frequently as she grew older, Bogan became better known as a critic than as a poet. In 1931 she wrote her first review for *The New Yorker*, and twice a year until 1969 she presented the season's new poetry books to that magazine's discriminating audience while also continuing to write for *The New Republic* and the *Nation*.

Bogan's predilections in her criticism are similar to those in her poems: she showed a marked preference for crafted eloquence over free-verse expansiveness; she directed her readers away from contemporary fashions and toward what she called in the February 1925 issue of *The Measure* "the heft and swing of English poetry in the tradition"; and she would tolerate no slackness in thought or expression. She thought of herself as educating her audiences and shared with them the enthusiasms of her own reading, particularly William Butler Yeats, Rainer Maria Rilke, and W. H. Auden. She was critical when she saw the need to be, regardless of her relationship to the writer, and she lost friends in the process. In 1932 she reviewed her friend Allen Tate so harshly that he wrote to protest. Her reply, in a private letter dated 1 April, defended her objective view: "I was reviewing a book of poetry which aroused in me respect and irritation in about equal measure. If you objected to the tone of my review, I objected, straight down to a core beyond detachment, to the tone of some of the poems."

In 1925 Bogan married Raymond Holden, a sometime poet and novelist who had been a friend of Robert Frost. She retrieved her daughter from her parents and moved with Holden to Boston. Although Holden came from a wealthy family, he was in financial straits by the time he married Bogan. From the start their marriage suffered from economic strain, but for a time the relationship was relatively happy. They moved in a social and literary circle that included Rolfe Humphries and Adams, both of whom would be lifelong friends to Bogan. In 1926 they moved back to New York but spent the winter in Sante Fe, New Mexico, for Holden's health. In 1928 they bought a farmhouse in Hillsdale, New York, and amid the chaos of renovations Bogan found a measure of happiness and new poems. But in December 1929 the house burned to the ground (including almost all of Bogan's books, letters, and manuscripts). While the insurance money enabled the couple to set up a new life in New York, the happiest period in Bogan's life had clearly come to an end.

Dark Summer (1929), her second volume of poetry, marks Bogan's first work with her most helpful editor, John Hall Wheelock of Scribners. In what would become a pattern in Bogan's publishing life, the volume includes a selection of poems from *Body of This Death* as well as new work, which included the only two long poems she ever published: "The Flume," an autobiographical narrative based on the many waterways of her mill-town childhood (which she never again included in a collection); and "Summer Wish," a moving argument between two voices concerning the possibility of spring's renewal and the necessity for acceptance in fall. "Summer Wish" reflects the contemplative happiness of Bogan's stay in the house in Hillsdale and as such was almost anachronistic by the time it saw print.

The shorter lyrics of *Dark Summer* again show Bogan's mastery of observation, diction, meter, and rhyme in poems that generally emphasize acceptance and fulfillment rather than the disappointment and betrayal of her earlier work. "Cassandra" captures the mythical figure's sorrowing mood: "To me, one silly task is like another. / I bare the shambling tricks of lust and pride. / This flesh will never give a child its mother." "Winter Swan" and "The Cupola" show the poet's descriptive powers, reminiscent of those of Moore. Other poems such as "The Crossed Apple" recall the language and tone of Robert Frost:

This apple's from a tree yet unbeholden,
Where two kinds meet,—
. . . .
Eat it; and you will taste more than the fruit:
The blossom, too,
The sun, the air, the darkness at the root,
The rain, the dew,
The earth we came to, and the time we flee,
The fire and the breast.
I claim the white part, maiden, that's for me.
You take the rest.

The seasons and the passage of time are the subject of several of the strongest lyrics in the book, including "Division," "Girl's Song," "Feuer-Nacht," "Fiend's Weather," and "Come, Break with Time." The lovely first stanza of "Simple Autumnal" illustrates Bogan's preoccupation:

The measured blood beats out the year's delay.
The tearless eyes and heart, forbidden grief,
Watch the burned, restless, but abiding leaf,
The brighter branches arming the bright day.

In the year following the publication of *Dark Summer*, the marriage between Bogan and Holden began to fail, and Bogan fell ill with severe depression. In the spring of 1931 she checked herself into New York's Neurological Institute in hopes of finding a cure. "I refused to fall apart," she wrote to Wheelock, "so I have been taken apart, like a watch." In the mood of self-reflection following her release from the hospital, she wrote the autobiographical essay "Journey Around My Room," which would become the basis of the "autobiography" edited by her friend Ruth Limmer in 1980.

In 1932 Bogan was awarded a Guggenheim Fellowship "for creative writing abroad" and set sail alone for Italy in April 1933. While she was away in Italy, France, and Austria, struggling to write and often depressed, her marriage fell apart completely. When she returned home several months early to remake her life, the enterprise was not immediately successful. In November 1933 she checked herself into New York Hospital's Westchester Division, this time admitting a "bad nervous crack-up."

She stayed at the hospital for nearly seven months and returned home a good deal healthier than when she had left. She divorced her husband, gathered her good friends—Edmund Wilson and Morton Dauwen Zabel in particular—around, and set about to do her work. Though she was able to write only a few poems, she took up her critical prose with enthusiasm and began to write short stories and autobiographical prose, which she hoped to make into a novel tentatively titled "Laura

Dailey's Story." An excellent prose stylist and storyteller, Bogan eventually published thirteen stories in *The New Yorker*, but she did not complete her novel. She gave up writing both fiction and autobiography after 1936.

The years between 1935 and 1941 or so were some of the most fulfilling in Bogan's life, despite financial troubles (she was evicted from her apartment in September 1935 and had to retrieve her possessions from the street). She continued to write critical prose and began to prepare her third book of poems, *The Sleeping Fury* (1937). In June 1935 she began a happy love affair with the young poet Theodore Roethke, a dozen years her junior. She wrote to Wilson of her enthusiasm:

> I, myself, have been made to bloom like a Persian rose-bush, by the enormous love-making of a cross between a Brandenburger and a Pomeranian, one Theodore Roethke by name. He is very, very large (6 ft. 2 and weighing 218 lbs) and he writes very very small lyrics. 26 years old and a frightful tank. We have poured rivers of liquor down our throats, these last three days, and, in between, have indulged in such bearish and St. Bernardish antics as I have never before experienced. . . . Well! Such goings on! A woman of my age! The affair lasted several months, and the two remained friends. Bogan had much to teach Roethke about lyric poetry, and she quickly assumed that role in his life. Several poems came to Bogan during this relationship, perhaps the last such spell of extended creativity she would experience. The new poems enabled her to publish *The Sleeping Fury*, which was then generally regarded as her strongest volume.

The lyrics of *The Sleeping Fury* reflect the hard-won wisdom of Bogan's psychological recovery as well as her renewed health and vitality. Its reviewers remarked the collection's "sparseness" but praised its integrity. Her friend Zabel noted in the 5 May 1937 *New Republic* the book's freedom from the fashionable ideologies of the day and defended its "old fashioned" values:

> It is because they show so firmly what this depth can yield that these poems bring the finest vitality of the lyric tradition to bear on the confusions that threaten the poets who, by satire or prophecy, indignation or reform, have reacted against that tradition and cast it into contempt. . . . Her work, instinctive with self-criticism and emotional severity, speaks with one voice only; her rewards and those of her readers have a common source in the discipline to which the clarity of her music and her unsophistic craftsmanship are a testimony. It should be a model for poets in any decade or of any ambition.

The book opens and closes with "songs" and in between contains a handful of Bogan's finest lyrics. The opening of "Roman Fountain" reflects her memories of Italy and, perhaps, some of the sexual vitality of her affair with Roethke:

> Up from the bronze, I saw
> Water without a flaw
> Rush to its rest in air,
> Reach to its rest,
> and fall.
> Bronze of the blackest shade,
> An element man-made,
> Shaping upright the bare
> Clear gouts of water in air.

Several poems offer advice to an imagined reader who has suffered what Bogan has. "Henceforth, from the Mind" counsels acceptance of the diminished emotional intensity of a healthy adult life. "Exhortation" repudiates that resolution through painful irony: "Give over seeking bastard joy / Nor cast for fortune's side-long look. / Indifference can be your toy; / The bitter heart can be your book."

In her title poem, "The Sleeping Fury," Bogan looks mental torment in the face:

> Your hair fallen on your cheek, no longer in the
> sem-
> blance of serpents,
> Lifted in the gale; your mouth, that shrieked so,
> silent.
> You, my scourge, my sister, lie asleep, like a child,
> Who, after rage, for an hour quiet, sleeps out its
> tears.
> . . . .
> And now I may look upon you,
> Having once met your eyes. You lie in sleep and
> forget
> me.
> Alone and strong in my peace, I look upon you in
> yours.

"Kept" shows a mature denial of sentimentalized memories of childhood and youth:

> Time for the wood, the clay,
> The trumpery dolls, the toys
> Now to be put away:
> We are not girls and boys.
> . . . .
> Time for the pretty clay,
> Time for the straw, the wood.
> The playthings of the young
> Get broken in the play,
> Get broken, as they should.

Bogan also looks hard at alcohol, the friend and sometime nemesis of her life. In "To Wine" she ironically exhorts the "Cup, ignorant and cruel," to

> Take from the mind its loss:
> The lipless dead that lie
> Face upward in the earth,
> Strong hand and slender thigh;
> Return to the vein
> All that is worth
> Grief. Give that beat again.

In 1937 Bogan applied for and was granted the remainder of her Guggenheim Fellowship, which she had been unable to complete in 1932. In April she sailed for Ireland. From the start the trip was a struggle for Bogan, who was frequently depressed and anxious. In the country of her ancestors she was unable for find a place for herself, and she sailed home several weeks later in a state of near collapse. A man on the boat train to Southampton came to her rescue and cared for her throughout the voyage home. After a week of recovery Bogan, who had remarked in her notebook three years before that "There can be no new love at 37, in a woman," began a relationship with the man, an electrician from the Bronx, that would last eight years. She kept it largely a secret from her friends, but by her own account the relationship was as happy and fulfilling as any she would ever have.

In the spring of 1938 Bogan moved into the apartment on West 169th Street where she would live for the rest of her life, engaging in a lively and energetic career as a literary critic and a woman of letters, squabbling with her fellow poets and critics, and publishing many incisive and insightful reviews and essays. She championed the cause of W. H. Auden as he arrived in the United States in 1939 and did a great deal in bringing public attention to his work. But poems came to her only occasionally. She struggled to produce enough work for a new book, and *Poems and New Poems* included old work as well as what Bogan called her "light verse," clever occasional poems on contemporary topics. In this category is the memorable couplet titled "Solitary Observation Brought Back from a Sojourn in Hell": "At midnight tears / Run into your ears."

The group of new poems in the volume opens with "Several Voices Out of a Cloud," a sharp attack on the ideological hacks Bogan saw dominating the world of poetry. The poem is uncharacteristically contemporary, in a manner reminiscent of Auden: "Come, drunks and drug-takers; come, perverts unnerved!" she invites and concludes by naming the pretending poets:

> Parochial punks, trimmers, nice people, joiners
> true-blue,
> Get the hell out of the way of the laurel. It is
> deathless
> And it isn't for you.

Other new poems have a variety of subjects: "Animal, Vegetable and Mineral" is a contemplation of the glass flowers exhibit at Harvard's Museum of Natural History; "To Be Sung on the Water" is a tender and playful love lyric; and "Zone" captures with icy accuracy the disquieting ambiguity of New England in the month of March: "Now we hear / What we heard last year, / And bear the wind's rude touch / And its ugly sound / Equally with so much / We have learned how to bear."

Bogan wrote no poems between the publication of *Poems and New Poems* in 1941 and 1948. The horror of World War II discouraged her about the power of poetry against such hatred, and she was troubled by what she saw as the obscurity of her own position. In hopes of finding a publisher that would promote her work more forcefully, Bogan left Scribners and Wheelock, with unfortunate results. She would not find a new publisher until 1954, and the sense of being on her own made writing poems more difficult. She once remarked to Wheelock that "A woman writes poetry with her ovaries." As she entered middle age Bogan began to feel that her time had past.

Bogan's essays and reviews did much to keep her name before the public in the war years and their wake. She began new, lasting friendships among young admirers of her work, including William Maxwell, a novelist and *New Yorker* staffer when he met Bogan in 1938; May Sarton, an established poet whom Bogan invited to her apartment in 1953; and Ruth Limmer, an English professor whom Bogan met in 1956 when she received an honorary doctorate from the Western College for Women (Limmer would become her literary executor). With the winding down of the war, literature could once again command attention, and Bogan began to be asked to serve on various poetry-prize juries. In 1944 she gave the Hopwood lecture at the University of Michigan. She also began to read her poems in public and accepted the position as Consultant in Poetry to the Library of Congress (1945–1946). She was in the Library Fellows group that, amid controversy, awarded the first Bollingen Prize to Ezra Pound, then incarcerated in a mental institution in Washington, D.C., having been judged incompetent to stand trial for treason at the end of the war. She accepted a teaching position at the University of Washington and went on to teach at the University of Chicago and New York University, among other places. Bogan also began her work as a translator, working with Elizabeth Mayer on works by Johann Wolfgang von Goethe and Ernst Juenger and with Elizabeth Roget on works by Jules Renard. In 1951 she published her critical study, *Achievement in American Poetry, 1900–1950*, which included an anthology with her selection of worthy poems from the period.

Bogan found a publisher in the new Noonday Press in the early 1950s and set about preparing her

Collected Poems 1923–1953 (1954). She had only three new poems to add to the whole: "After the Persian," her contemplation of Persian art at New York's Metropolitan Museum; the light poem "Train Tune"; and, most remarkably, "Song for the Last Act." This poem is built around a refrain, varied to marvelous effect in each of its three stanzas: "Now that I have your face by heart, I look"; "Now that I have your voice by heart, I read"; "Now that I have your heart by heart, I see." The poem links desire and memory in a tone unmistakably valedictory, "O not departure, but a voyage done!" A year later Bogan published a volume of *Selected Criticism: Prose, Poetry* (1955). Both volumes were respectfully reviewed, and she shared the 1955 Bollingen Prize with Léonie Adams.

Bogan's last years were a combination of honors, continued hard work, dark depression, and alcoholism. Between 1957 and 1964 she went annually to the MacDowell Colony in Peterborough, New Hampshire, where she found the time and peace to write poems as well as critical prose. Her collection *The Blue Estuaries: Poems 1923–1968* (1968) includes a dozen new poems, most of which had been begun much earlier. Most of her last poems are in free verse, as Bogan grew more willing to accept poems in the forms in which they came to her. Notable among these last works is "The Dragonfly," written on commission from the Corning Glass Company, which had a Steuben glass dragonfly carved to illustrate it. The poem "Night" provided the title for the collection. It recalls in both setting and sound poems by Elizabeth Bishop, Bogan's somewhat younger contemporary:

The cold remote islands
And the blue estuaries
Where what breathes, breathes
The restless wind of the inlets,
And what drinks, drinks
The incoming tide;
. . . .
—O remember
In your narrowing dark hours
That more things move
Than blood in the heart.

The Blue Estuaries received strong reviews. William Meredith in the 13 October 1968 *New York Times Book Review* called Bogan "one of the best woman poets alive" and wondered at how her "reputation has lagged behind a career of stubborn, individual excellence." Hayden Carruth in the August 1969 issue of *Poetry* praised the poems despite their small number: "this book's best pages make it fundamentally irreducible." That assessment seems accurate; perhaps the forces or frailties that prevented Bogan from writing more afforded her marvelous control over her art.

Louise Bogan died at her apartment of a coronary occlusion on 4 February 1970. A memorial service, arranged by her friend William Jay Smith, was held at the Academy of Arts and Letters on 11 March, attended by 120 of her friends and admirers. At the service W. H. Auden noted Bogan's personal strength. "Aside from their technical excellence," he said of her poems, "what is most impressive . . . is the unflinching courage with which she faced her problems, and her determination never to surrender to self-pity, but to wrest beauty and joy out of dark places."

Source: Brett C. Millier, "Louise Bogan," in *Dictionary of Literary Biography*, Vol. 169, *American Poets Since World War II, Fifth Series*, edited by Joseph Conte, Gale, 1996, pp. 54–62.

Carol Shloss

In the following essay, Shloss discusses Bogan's personal struggles with her family, the passionate, often painful tones of her poetry, and her success as a writer and critic.

In 1970, at a memorial service for Louise Bogan, W.H. Auden identified what he thought to be the most enduring qualities of her lyric poetry: "aside from their technical excellence, [what] is most impressive about her poems is the unflinching courage with which she faced her problems, and her determination never to surrender to self-pity, but to wrest beauty and joy out of dark places." Auden had first met Bogan in 1941 when she was well established as a critic of poetry at the *New Yorker* and had already written four of the six books of verse on which her reputation as one of America's finest lyric poets was to rest. For almost thirty years, he had watched the unfolding of a talent. His appreciation of her gifts as poet, essayist, fiction writer, and autobiographer was shared by many of Bogan's friends, who also saw the violence of feeling which her work expressed and subdued through the regularities of form. Classical in their adherence to the laws of traditional poetic structure, romantic in their tendency to embrace the extremes of passionate experience, her best lyrics can stand with the work of the poets she most admired: Yeats, Rilke, and Auden. As Theodore Roethke had earlier written in honor of his friend, teacher, and mentor, "The best work will stay in the language as long as the language survives."

Bogan's journey to a place of prominence in American letters had been wrested from unpromising beginnings. Born on 11 August 1897,

> *"Classical in their adherence to the laws of traditional poetic structure, romantic in their tendency to embrace the extremes of passionate experience, her best lyrics can stand with the work of the poets she most admired: Yeats, Rilke, and Auden."*

the daughter of Daniel Bogan, a clerk in a paper mill in Livermore Falls, Maine, and Mary Helen Murphy Shields Bogan, she was more properly destined for married life in the mill towns of New England. Her mother was a reckless, violent, and undependable woman who handled the disappointments of her marriage through numerous love affairs. The Bogan children, Louise and her brother, Charles, were raised in a succession of rooming houses and exposed to an equally consistent succession of their mother's lovers. These childhood circumstances would never leave Bogan's memory, and they account for one of the predominant emotional constellations in both her life and art: the belief that love was inextricably bound with rage, guilt, and betrayal. By the age of six or eight she had become "what I was for half my life: the semblance of a girl, in which some desires and illusions had been early assassinated: shot dead."

If her parents served as the source of Bogan's early grief, they also provided her, indirectly, with the resources for coping with that sorrow. Eventually Daniel Bogan moved his family to Boston. where Louise was given piano lessons and then sent to Girls' Latin School. She was trained in Greek and Latin, and in the classical structures of versification. These few years were almost the whole of her formal education. Although she wrote constantly (by the age of eighteen, she "had a thick pile of manuscripts in a drawer in the dining room"), she chose not to pursue a full college career. After one year at Boston University (1915–1916), she abandoned plans to go on to Radcliffe in favor of marriage, on 4 September 1916, to a young soldier of German origin, Curt Alexander. In part she married as an escape from the domestic traumas of her parents' household, but she proved to be more of her mother's child than she could comfortably admit; for in later years, she reenacted the cycle of lust and betrayal that she so regretted in her parent. It was as if she were drawn to recapitulate her position as a helpless, violated child until, with the help of psychoanalysis, she broke through the cycle of damage to a superior awareness.

Nowhere does her poetry discuss these painful experiences; nonetheless they underlie and explain the dynamics of many of her early lyrics. Later in life, she was able to formulate a theory about the relationship between poetry and the experiences in life which empower it: in *Journey Around My Room* (1980) she said, "The poet represses the outright narrative of his life. He absorbs it, along with life itself. The repressed becomes the poem. Actually, I have written down my experience in the closest detail. But the rough and vulgar facts are not there." Yet initially, in her poetry and in her life, she sought passion for its own sake and was dismayed when it offered her so little that she wanted.

On 19 October 1917 Mathilde (Maidie), her only child, was born; several months later, two of her first poems were published in *Others*, a little magazine edited by Alfred Kreymborg in New York City. By May 1918 she had left Alexander at his station in Panama and returned to the home of her parents. This, too, was a temporary move, a prelude to a life of uncommon transience in which moving represented or expressed an underlying restlessness of spirit. Years later, her emotions governed by a hard-won and mature perspective, she wondered if she had eradicated the deepest sources of her own creativity in the course of mastering her otherwise self-destructive conflicts. To Morton Zabel she wrote in December 1935, "I don't recommend to you, this calm I have reached. It may be spiritual death or spiritual narcosis." But in the midst of young adulthood, she did not pause to analyze. She was pulled toward New York City, where she hoped to find a context for herself among the bohemians of Greenwich Village.

New York in 1919 did, in fact, nurture her talent and provide her with the friends who remained closest to her in later life: William Carlos Williams, Malcolm Cowley, Maxwell Bodenheim, Edmund Wilson, Léonie Adams, Margaret Mead, Ruth Benedict, and Rolf Humphries were among her earliest acquaintances. Leaving Maidie with her parents, she found a lover; she worked and wrote. In 1920 she learned of Curt Alexander's death. Whatever remorse she may have felt about their broken relationship and the temporary abandonment of their child was seasoned with the rewards of poetic achievement. By 1921 Harriet Weaver had published five of her poems in *Poetry*; by 1923 Bogan had found a publisher for her first book of verse. Robert M. McBride and Company brought out *Body of This Death*.

The title of the book is taken from Rom. 7:24: "O wretched man that I am! who shall deliver me from the body of this death?" Its themes are those that would absorb her for her entire career: the betrayal of beauty by the flesh, the antipathy between passion and wisdom, the tension between time and the "crystal clasp" of art. Strongly influenced by Yeats, Bogan found highly personal and deeply feminine ways to express the yearning for transcendence which must succumb to the limitations of time and human error. "Knowledge" can stand as an example of themes whose variations are worked out by "A Tale," "Medusa," "A Letter," "Sonnet," and the other poems of this collection: "Now that I know / Now passion warms little / Of flesh in the mould, / And treasure is brittle,—I'll lie here and learn / How, over their ground, / Trees make a long shadow / And a light sound."

When Robert Frost read "A Tale," the opening poem of *Body of This Death* , he remarked, "That woman will be able to do anything." Other critics shared his appreciation of Bogan's technical mastery and commented on the intensity, fierceness, and pride which seemed to motivate the writing. But not everyone was as discerning or generous. Often reviewers were puzzled, finding the language "only obscurely significant" (*Dial*). The worst review came from John Gould Fletcher, who considered the book to have "an emptiness of thought that is positively painful" (*Freeman*).

Bogan took what she could from both praise and blame. Her allegiance to the life of letters was too deeply ingrained to let adverse reactions discourage her. Among those whose opinions she valued, the book's publication established her as a serious new talent. She would continue to write and to grow closer to Wilson and Humphries and the small group of writers who published in the *Measure* the *New Republic*, and the *Nation*.

In 1924 she met Raymond Peckham Holden, the son of a wealthy New York family, a man who aspired to the life of poet and novelist, and who later became the managing editor of the *New Yorker*. On 10 July 1925 they were married; and after living briefly in Boston, New York, and Santa Fe, they bought a farmhouse in Hillsdale, New York. This house became for Bogan the place of harmony and abundance which her own childhood had denied her. Here she cooked, gardened, raised her child, and learned to see the patterns of nature which life in the city had rendered obscure. Here, too, she wrote most of the lyrics for *Dark Summer* (1929), sending them, finally, to Edmund Wilson for criticism and advice about publication.

By recommending that she forward a copy of *Body of This Death* to Charles Scribner's Sons, Wilson initiated the strongest and most enduring publishing relationship of Bogan's career. Maxwell Perkins was favorably impressed with her work and John Hall Wheelock even more so. He offered Bogan a contract, asked for more work, and eventually published her next three volumes of poetry.

With these prospects before her, Bogan settled into one of the still, certain interludes of her life. Domestic order mirrored a psychic order that was all too rare in her experience of intimate relationships. It was precisely the fragility of this balanced, pastoral life that made its subsequent destruction so grim. After Christmas 1929, the Holdens returned to Hillsdale only to see their house on fire, manuscripts and notebooks—indeed all their possessions—destroyed in the blaze. Posed as she was between desire and rage, Bogan could not help but read the fire emblematically; and in fact, the equanimity of her marriage seems to have dissipated along with her more tangible belongings. Although *Dark Summer* had come out the previous September, the pleasure of its publication could not offset another kind of interior disintegration.

The middle period of Bogan's creative life is marked by a dichotomy between the increasing solidity of her reputation as a poet and the seeming vulnerability of her emotions. Even as she received the accolades of critics, she lapsed into a deepening depression. In public life, Yvor Winters reviewed *Dark Summer*, singling out "Come, Break with Time" and "Simple Autumnal" for special praise. They could, he said, stand "with the best songs of the sixteenth and seventeenth centuries, whether one selects examples from Campion, Jonson, or Dryden." From a much later vantage point, Elizabeth Frank named "Simple Autumnal" "one of the great lyrics in American poetry." She saw it as the effort of a writer to ally herself with the seasonal cycles of ripening and decay that Bogan's earlier poetry had tried to escape. Like Hart Crane's "Voyages," it is a song of reconciliation and acceptance, which moves toward integration of the personal and natural worlds. "Summer Wish" is even more accomplished and brings Bogan's work into the company of Yeats's "The Tower" and Wallace Stevens's "Sunday Morning." It is a meditative eclogue, a dialogue in which two voices confront the problem of despair.Although the second voice overwhelms the first, offering it a vision of stasis ("See now / Open above the field, stilled in wingstiffened flight, / The stretched hawk fly"), Bogan, in private life, was less and less able to find those quiet moments.

In April 1931 she submitted herself for a rest cure at the Neurological Institute in Manhattan. Once again, her private struggle was carried on amid an otherwise flourishing career. In 1933 when she was awarded a Guggenheim Foundation grant for travel in Europe, Bogan seized the opportunity, for she sensed that distance and change would grant her a perspective valuable both to her craft and to her domestic situation. In the first goal, she succeeded, but her marital problems were not so easily resolved. Very shortly after she returned from Europe, she once again admitted herself to a hospital for rest and personal reflection. By 1935, when she divorced Raymond Holden, the period of greatest turbulence in Bogan's life was over.

It is probably not fortuitous that the 1930s were also the time of Bogan's greatest achievements in prose writing. The self-reflection required by psychoanalysis may have spurred her autobiographical trilogy: "Journey Around My Room" (*New Yorker*, 1932), "Dove and Serpent" (*New Yorker*, 1933), and "Letdown" (*New Yorker*, 1934). All of these pieces constitute Bogan's inquiry into those steps that "started me toward this point, as opposed to all other points on the habitable globe." Her *New Yorker* stories, influenced by Viola Meynell, Ivan Turgenev, and Anton Chekhov, often seemed to work through the issues that were most pressing in her actual experience—the destructiveness of romantic attachment, the need for private sources of strength and grace.

This belief in the value of turning inward can also explain Bogan's resistance to the social movements of the 1930s. She placed her faith in the lessons of psychoanalysis and in individual responses to fate; she gave no credence to solutions posed in terms of collective destiny. If one were "to lift the material world to the ideal," she said (*New Republic*, 1936), "it would be just as well to clear up the ideal, to know the human springs that feed it." Freud, with his discovery of the unconscious, was more important to her than Marx, with his belief in economic determinism; and as the 1930s passed, and as more and more of her intimate friends—Rolf Humphries, Léonie Adams, Edna St. Vincent Millay, and Edmund Wilson—came to sympathize with the Communist cause, Bogan found herself increasingly isolated.

To Rolf Humphries and Edmund Wilson she proposed a political truce, since she needed their help in preparing her next book of poems. *The Sleeping Fury*, once again published by Scribners, appeared in 1937. The title of the book is also the name of a relief sculpture Bogan had seen in Rome at the Museo Nazionale delle Terme, "L'Erinni Addormentata"; and to some extent, this image of rage and grief, exhausted and given over to sleep, informs the entire collection of poems. Where Bogan's first two books had shown the influence of Yeats, *The Sleeping Fury* showed most clearly the influence of Rilke, whom she had been reading avidly for several years. When she had needed a language for anger, indignation, and bitter disappointment, Yeats's high blown rhetoric had been an adequate guide; now that she sought to transcend suffering and to express emotional equanimity, the German poet served her better. The most beautiful lyrics in this collection, "Henceforth from the Mind," "The Sleeping Fury," and "Sóng for a Lyre," have the quiet authority of a poet in full command of her art.

The Sleeping Fury was essentially Bogan's last full book of original verse; the books that followed it were collections of previously published works with new poems added to them. *Poems and New Poems*, which came out in 1941, was the last book Bogan published with Scribners before her break with John Hall Wheelock. *Collected Poems, 1923–1953* was brought out by Cecil Hemley of Noonday Press in 1954. *The Blue Estuaries: Poems 1923–1968* which Farrar, Straus, and Giroux published in 1968, served as a summary of her poetic achievement as it stretched from youth to age.

Although the years after 1937 were years of declining productivity, they were years when Bogan consolidated her reputation and reaped the fruits of an earlier devotion to letters. Others were anxious to know her opinions. If it was as a poet that Bogan made her reputation, it was as a critic that she made her living. Her work for the *New Yorker* continued until shortly before her death. Twice a year she provided the magazine with omnibus reviews of the most interesting poetry of the previous months, and she wrote countless brief notices. On her resignation from the magazine in 1969, William

Shawn, then editor in chief, wrote, "for thirty-eight years we have been in the extraordinary position of knowing beyond all question that no other magazine's reviewing of poetry was as perceptive or trustworthy or intelligent as our own."

Awards and requests for readings, talks, and teaching posts started coming in the 1940s. In 1944 she became a Fellow in American Letters at the Library of Congress; in the same year, she gave the Hopwood Lecture at the University of Michigan. In 1945 she went to Washington, D.C., as the Consultant in Poetry to the Library of Congress. The year 1948 was filled with invitations to universities, and though she remained acutely aware of her own lack of formal education and convinced that the academy had slighted her, a catalogue of her activities in this one year alone belies her own assessment: she went to a poetry conference at Sarah Lawrence College, gave a reading at the New School for Social Research with Robert Lowell, Marianne Moore, and Allen Tate, taught summer school at the University of Washington, and spoke at Bard "On the Pleasures of Formal Verse."

In 1951 she was elected to the National Institute of Arts and Letters; in 1954 she was elected to the Academy of American Poets. In 1955 she shared the Bollingen Prize for poetry with Léonie Adams. In 1957 she was invited to the MacDowell Colony, and in the following year she participated in the Salzburg Seminar in American Studies. An award from the Academy of American Poets came in 1959, and she received the Creative Arts award from Brandeis University in 1962. In 1969, a year before her death, she was elected to the American Academy of Arts and Letters. On the more personal level, she had sustained the lifelong friendships of people she respected and had found room, at an age when other lives are often narrowing in scope, to admit new intimacies: William Maxwell, the new poetry editor for the *New Yorker*; Elizabeth Mayer, a German translator; and May Sarton, a younger writer and poet, are several examples.

Bogan's final years were lived in a kind of secular monasticism. Weaned from the destructive passions that had governed her youth, she lived alone and with the dignity of a hard-won victory over private terrors. To her lifelong friend, Morton Zabel, she wrote, "It is as though I had, after thirty years, really come into my whole being. . . . I can feel rage, but I am never humiliated, any more, and I am never lonely." Despite her brave words, her struggle was never simple and success never to be assumed. She could relapse into depressions until the end of her life. But she had, on the whole, found admission to the "temperate threshold" so avidly sought in and through her verse.

Poetry, to Bogan, was wrought from "rhythm as we first experience it . . . within the heartbeat, pulse and breath." Certainly, in her own case, it was an extension of self so vital that its excision would have left her vulnerable to inner demons and, as Stanley Kunitz put it, to "the deep night swarming with images of reproach and desire." But language did not fail her nor she it; and in her devotion to poetry she found forgiveness and personal reconciliation. To others she gave some of the most austere, searing, and beautiful lyrics written in America in this century.

Louise Bogan died on Wednesday, 4 February 1970. At her memorial service, Richard Wilbur, who spoke along with Auden, observed that "she remained faithful to the theme of passion." William Meredith, writing during her lifetime, was more encompassing in his praise: Louise Bogan was "one of the best women poets alive."

Source: Carol Shloss, "Louise Bogan," in *Dictionary of Literary Biography*, Vol. 45, *American Poets, 1880–1945, First Series*, edited by Peter Quartermain, Gale, 1986, pp. 52–59.

Sources

Aldrich, Marcia, "Lethal Brevity: Louise Bogan's Lyric Career," in *Aging and Gender in Literature*, edited by Anne M. Wyatt-Brown and Janice Rossen, University Press of Virginia, 1993, pp. 105–20.

Bogan, Louise, *Body of This Death*, Robert M. McBride, 1923, pp. 10–11.

———, *Journey around My Room: The Autobiography of Louise Bogan*, written with Ruth Limmer, Viking Press, 1980, pp. 29–31, 34–35, 40–43, 48–50, 52–53, 68.

Colasurdo, Christine, "The Dramatic Ambivalence of Self in the Poetry of Louise Bogan," in *Tulsa Studies in Women's Literature*, Vol. 13, No. 2, Autumn 1994, pp. 339–61.

Collins, Martha, ed., *Critical Essays on Louise Bogan*, G. K. Hall, 1984, pp. 2, 27–31.

Limmer, Ruth, ed., *What the Woman Lived: Selected letters of Louise Bogan, 1920–1970*, Harcourt Brace Jovanovich, 1973, p. 5.

Pope, Deborah, "Music in the Granite Hill: The Poetry of Louise Bogan," in *A Separate Vision: Isolation in Contemporary Women's Poetry*, Louisiana State University Press, 1984, pp. 15–53.

Upton, Lee, "The Re-Making of a Poet: Louise Bogan," in *Centennial Review*, Vol. 3, No. 36, Fall 1992, pp. 557–72.

Van Doren, Mark, "Louise Bogan," in *Nation*, October 31, 1923, p. 494.

Further Reading

Allen, Frederick Lewis, *Only Yesterday: An Informal History of the 1920s*, 1931, reprint, Perennial, 2000.
Allen's book is a social history of the 1920s. It is a very readable and entertaining history of a period of great social change.

Clift, Eleanor, *Founding Sisters and the Nineteenth Amendment*, John Wiley & Sons, 2003.
This book chronicles the struggle for women to be given the right to vote. Clift's book is very readable, filled with interesting anecdotes that provide a glimpse into history.

Frank, Elizabeth, *Louise Bogan: A Portrait*, Knopf, 1985.
Frank won the 1986 Pulitzer Prize for this biography. She provides a good overview of Bogan's life, including insights into Bogan's childhood and rocky relationship with her mother.

Ruiz, Vicki L., and Ellen Carol DuBois, eds., *Unequal Sisters: A Multicultural Reader in U.S. Women's History*, 3d ed., Routledge, 2000.
This book is a collection of thirty essays that provide a multicultural view of women's history. The essays cover all aspects of women's lives, including political, religious, social, racial, and sexual.

Glossary of Literary Terms

A

Abstract: Used as a noun, the term refers to a short summary or outline of a longer work. As an adjective applied to writing or literary works, abstract refers to words or phrases that name things not knowable through the five senses.

Accent: The emphasis or stress placed on a syllable in poetry. Traditional poetry commonly uses patterns of accented and unaccented syllables (known as feet) that create distinct rhythms. Much modern poetry uses less formal arrangements that create a sense of freedom and spontaneity.

Aestheticism: A literary and artistic movement of the nineteenth century. Followers of the movement believed that art should not be mixed with social, political, or moral teaching. The statement "art for art's sake" is a good summary of aestheticism. The movement had its roots in France, but it gained widespread importance in England in the last half of the nineteenth century, where it helped change the Victorian practice of including moral lessons in literature.

Affective Fallacy: An error in judging the merits or faults of a work of literature. The "error" results from stressing the importance of the work's effect upon the reader—that is, how it makes a reader "feel" emotionally, what it does as a literary work—instead of stressing its inner qualities as a created object, or what it "is."

Age of Johnson: The period in English literature between 1750 and 1798, named after the most prominent literary figure of the age, Samuel Johnson. Works written during this time are noted for their emphasis on "sensibility," or emotional quality. These works formed a transition between the rational works of the Age of Reason, or Neoclassical period, and the emphasis on individual feelings and responses of the Romantic period.

Age of Reason: See *Neoclassicism*

Age of Sensibility: See *Age of Johnson*

Agrarians: A group of Southern American writers of the 1930s and 1940s who fostered an economic and cultural program for the South based on agriculture, in opposition to the industrial society of the North. The term can refer to any group that promotes the value of farm life and agricultural society.

Alexandrine Meter: See *Meter*

Allegory: A narrative technique in which characters representing things or abstract ideas are used to convey a message or teach a lesson. Allegory is typically used to teach moral, ethical, or religious lessons but is sometimes used for satiric or political purposes.

Alliteration: A poetic device where the first consonant sounds or any vowel sounds in words or syllables are repeated.

Allusion: A reference to a familiar literary or historical person or event, used to make an idea more easily understood.

Amerind Literature: The writing and oral traditions of Native Americans. Native American literature was originally passed on by word of mouth, so it consisted largely of stories and events that were easily memorized. Amerind prose is often rhythmic like poetry because it was recited to the beat of a ceremonial drum.

Analogy: A comparison of two things made to explain something unfamiliar through its similarities to something familiar, or to prove one point based on the acceptedness of another. Similes and metaphors are types of analogies.

Anapest: See *Foot*

Angry Young Men: A group of British writers of the 1950s whose work expressed bitterness and disillusionment with society. Common to their work is an antihero who rebels against a corrupt social order and strives for personal integrity.

Anthropomorphism: The presentation of animals or objects in human shape or with human characteristics. The term is derived from the Greek word for "human form."

Antimasque: See *Masque*

Antithesis: The antithesis of something is its direct opposite. In literature, the use of antithesis as a figure of speech results in two statements that show a contrast through the balancing of two opposite ideas. Technically, it is the second portion of the statement that is defined as the "antithesis"; the first portion is the "thesis."

Apocrypha: Writings tentatively attributed to an author but not proven or universally accepted to be their works. The term was originally applied to certain books of the Bible that were not considered inspired and so were not included in the "sacred canon."

Apollonian and Dionysian: The two impulses believed to guide authors of dramatic tragedy. The Apollonian impulse is named after Apollo, the Greek god of light and beauty and the symbol of intellectual order. The Dionysian impulse is named after Dionysus, the Greek god of wine and the symbol of the unrestrained forces of nature. The Apollonian impulse is to create a rational, harmonious world, while the Dionysian is to express the irrational forces of personality.

Apostrophe: A statement, question, or request addressed to an inanimate object or concept or to a nonexistent or absent person.

Archetype: The word archetype is commonly used to describe an original pattern or model from which all other things of the same kind are made. This term was introduced to literary criticism from the psychology of Carl Jung. It expresses Jung's theory that behind every person's "unconscious," or repressed memories of the past, lies the "collective unconscious" of the human race: memories of the countless typical experiences of our ancestors. These memories are said to prompt illogical associations that trigger powerful emotions in the reader. Often, the emotional process is primitive, even primordial. Archetypes are the literary images that grow out of the "collective unconscious." They appear in literature as incidents and plots that repeat basic patterns of life. They may also appear as stereotyped characters.

Argument: The argument of a work is the author's subject matter or principal idea.

Art for Art's Sake: See *Aestheticism*

Assonance: The repetition of similar vowel sounds in poetry.

Audience: The people for whom a piece of literature is written. Authors usually write with a certain audience in mind, for example, children, members of a religious or ethnic group, or colleagues in a professional field. The term "audience" also applies to the people who gather to see or hear any performance, including plays, poetry readings, speeches, and concerts.

Automatic Writing: Writing carried out without a preconceived plan in an effort to capture every random thought. Authors who engage in automatic writing typically do not revise their work, preferring instead to preserve the revealed truth and beauty of spontaneous expression.

***Avant-garde*:** A French term meaning "vanguard." It is used in literary criticism to describe new writing that rejects traditional approaches to literature in favor of innovations in style or content.

B

Ballad: A short poem that tells a simple story and has a repeated refrain. Ballads were originally intended to be sung. Early ballads, known as folk ballads, were passed down through generations, so their authors are often unknown. Later ballads composed by known authors are called literary ballads.

Baroque: A term used in literary criticism to describe literature that is complex or ornate in style or diction. Baroque works typically express tension, anxiety, and violent emotion. The term "Baroque Age" designates a period in Western European literature beginning in the late sixteenth century and ending about one hundred years later.

Works of this period often mirror the qualities of works more generally associated with the label "baroque" and sometimes feature elaborate conceits.

Baroque Age: See *Baroque*

Baroque Period: See *Baroque*

Beat Generation: See *Beat Movement*

Beat Movement: A period featuring a group of American poets and novelists of the 1950s and 1960s—including Jack Kerouac, Allen Ginsberg, Gregory Corso, William S. Burroughs, and Lawrence Ferlinghetti—who rejected established social and literary values. Using such techniques as stream-of-consciousness writing and jazz-influenced free verse and focusing on unusual or abnormal states of mind—generated by religious ecstasy or the use of drugs—the Beat writers aimed to create works that were unconventional in both form and subject matter.

Beat Poets: See *Beat Movement*

Beats, The: See *Beat Movement*

Belles-lettres: A French term meaning "fine letters" or "beautiful writing." It is often used as a synonym for literature, typically referring to imaginative and artistic rather than scientific or expository writing. Current usage sometimes restricts the meaning to light or humorous writing and appreciative essays about literature.

Black Aesthetic Movement: A period of artistic and literary development among African Americans in the 1960s and early 1970s. This was the first major African American artistic movement since the Harlem Renaissance and was closely paralleled by the civil rights and black power movements. The black aesthetic writers attempted to produce works of art that would be meaningful to the black masses. Key figures in black aesthetics included one of its founders, poet and playwright Amiri Baraka, formerly known as LeRoi Jones; poet and essayist Haki R. Madhubuti, formerly Don L. Lee; poet and playwright Sonia Sanchez; and dramatist Ed Bullins.

Black Arts Movement: See *Black Aesthetic Movement*

Black Comedy: See *Black Humor*

Black Humor: Writing that places grotesque elements side by side with humorous ones in an attempt to shock the reader, forcing him or her to laugh at the horrifying reality of a disordered world.

Black Mountain School: Black Mountain College and three of its instructors—Robert Creeley, Robert Duncan, and Charles Olson—were all influential in projective verse. Today poets working in projective verse are referred to as members of the Black Mountain school.

Blank Verse: Loosely, any unrhymed poetry, but more generally, unrhymed iambic pentameter verse (composed of lines of five two-syllable feet with the first syllable accented, the second unaccented). Blank verse has been used by poets since the Renaissance for its flexibility and its graceful, dignified tone.

Bloomsbury Group: A group of English writers, artists, and intellectuals who held informal artistic and philosophical discussions in Bloomsbury, a district of London, from around 1907 to the early 1930s. The Bloomsbury Group held no uniform philosophical beliefs but did commonly express an aversion to moral prudery and a desire for greater social tolerance.

***Bon Mot*:** A French term meaning "good word." A *bon mot* is a witty remark or clever observation.

Breath Verse: See *Projective Verse*

Burlesque: Any literary work that uses exaggeration to make its subject appear ridiculous, either by treating a trivial subject with profound seriousness or by treating a dignified subject frivolously. The word "burlesque" may also be used as an adjective, as in "burlesque show," to mean "striptease act."

C

Cadence: The natural rhythm of language caused by the alternation of accented and unaccented syllables. Much modern poetry—notably free verse—deliberately manipulates cadence to create complex rhythmic effects.

Caesura: A pause in a line of poetry, usually occurring near the middle. It typically corresponds to a break in the natural rhythm or sense of the line but is sometimes shifted to create special meanings or rhythmic effects.

***Canzone*:** A short Italian or Provencal lyric poem, commonly about love and often set to music. The *canzone* has no set form but typically contains five or six stanzas made up of seven to twenty lines of eleven syllables each. A shorter, five- to ten-line "envoy," or concluding stanza, completes the poem.

***Carpe Diem*:** A Latin term meaning "seize the day." This is a traditional theme of poetry, especially lyrics. A *carpe diem* poem advises the reader or the person it addresses to live for today and enjoy the pleasures of the moment.

Catharsis: The release or purging of unwanted emotions—specifically fear and pity—brought about by exposure to art. The term was first used by the Greek philosopher Aristotle in his *Poetics* to refer to the desired effect of tragedy on spectators.

Celtic Renaissance: A period of Irish literary and cultural history at the end of the nineteenth century. Followers of the movement aimed to create a romantic vision of Celtic myth and legend. The most significant works of the Celtic Renaissance typically present a dreamy, unreal world, usually in reaction against the reality of contemporary problems.

Celtic Twilight: See *Celtic Renaissance*

Character: Broadly speaking, a person in a literary work. The actions of characters are what constitute the plot of a story, novel, or poem. There are numerous types of characters, ranging from simple, stereotypical figures to intricate, multifaceted ones. In the techniques of anthropomorphism and personification, animals—and even places or things—can assume aspects of character. "Characterization" is the process by which an author creates vivid, believable characters in a work of art. This may be done in a variety of ways, including (1) direct description of the character by the narrator; (2) the direct presentation of the speech, thoughts, or actions of the character; and (3) the responses of other characters to the character. The term "character" also refers to a form originated by the ancient Greek writer Theophrastus that later became popular in the seventeenth and eighteenth centuries. It is a short essay or sketch of a person who prominently displays a specific attribute or quality, such as miserliness or ambition.

Characterization: See *Character*

Classical: In its strictest definition in literary criticism, classicism refers to works of ancient Greek or Roman literature. The term may also be used to describe a literary work of recognized importance (a "classic") from any time period or literature that exhibits the traits of classicism.

Classicism: A term used in literary criticism to describe critical doctrines that have their roots in ancient Greek and Roman literature, philosophy, and art. Works associated with classicism typically exhibit restraint on the part of the author, unity of design and purpose, clarity, simplicity, logical organization, and respect for tradition.

Colloquialism: A word, phrase, or form of pronunciation that is acceptable in casual conversation but not in formal, written communication. It is considered more acceptable than slang.

Complaint: A lyric poem, popular in the Renaissance, in which the speaker expresses sorrow about his or her condition. Typically, the speaker's sadness is caused by an unresponsive lover, but some complaints cite other sources of unhappiness, such as poverty or fate.

Conceit: A clever and fanciful metaphor, usually expressed through elaborate and extended comparison, that presents a striking parallel between two seemingly dissimilar things—for example, elaborately comparing a beautiful woman to an object like a garden or the sun. The conceit was a popular device throughout the Elizabethan Age and Baroque Age and was the principal technique of the seventeenth-century English metaphysical poets. This usage of the word conceit is unrelated to the best-known definition of conceit as an arrogant attitude or behavior.

Concrete: Concrete is the opposite of abstract, and refers to a thing that actually exists or a description that allows the reader to experience an object or concept with the senses.

Concrete Poetry: Poetry in which visual elements play a large part in the poetic effect. Punctuation marks, letters, or words are arranged on a page to form a visual design: a cross, for example, or a bumblebee.

Confessional Poetry: A form of poetry in which the poet reveals very personal, intimate, sometimes shocking information about himself or herself.

Connotation: The impression that a word gives beyond its defined meaning. Connotations may be universally understood or may be significant only to a certain group.

Consonance: Consonance occurs in poetry when words appearing at the ends of two or more verses have similar final consonant sounds but have final vowel sounds that differ, as with "stuff" and "off."

Convention: Any widely accepted literary device, style, or form.

***Corrido*:** A Mexican ballad.

Couplet: Two lines of poetry with the same rhyme and meter, often expressing a complete and self-contained thought.

Criticism: The systematic study and evaluation of literary works, usually based on a specific method or set of principles. An important part of literary studies since ancient times, the practice of criticism has given rise to numerous theories, methods, and "schools," sometimes producing conflicting, even contradictory, interpretations of literature in general as well as of individual works. Even such basic issues as what constitutes a poem or a novel have been the subject of much criticism over the centuries.

D

Dactyl: See *Foot*

Dadaism: A protest movement in art and literature founded by Tristan Tzara in 1916. Followers of the movement expressed their outrage at the destruction brought about by World War I by revolting against numerous forms of social convention. The Dadaists presented works marked by calculated madness and flamboyant nonsense. They stressed total freedom of expression, commonly through primitive displays of emotion and illogical, often senseless, poetry. The movement ended shortly after the war, when it was replaced by surrealism.

Decadent: See *Decadents*

Decadents: The followers of a nineteenth-century literary movement that had its beginnings in French aestheticism. Decadent literature displays a fascination with perverse and morbid states; a search for novelty and sensation—the "new thrill"; a preoccupation with mysticism; and a belief in the senselessness of human existence. The movement is closely associated with the doctrine Art for Art's Sake. The term "decadence" is sometimes used to denote a decline in the quality of art or literature following a period of greatness.

Deconstruction: A method of literary criticism developed by Jacques Derrida and characterized by multiple conflicting interpretations of a given work. Deconstructionists consider the impact of the language of a work and suggest that the true meaning of the work is not necessarily the meaning that the author intended.

Deduction: The process of reaching a conclusion through reasoning from general premises to a specific premise.

Denotation: The definition of a word, apart from the impressions or feelings it creates in the reader.

Diction: The selection and arrangement of words in a literary work. Either or both may vary depending on the desired effect. There are four general types of diction: "formal," used in scholarly or lofty writing; "informal," used in relaxed but educated conversation; "colloquial," used in everyday speech; and "slang," containing newly coined words and other terms not accepted in formal usage.

Didactic: A term used to describe works of literature that aim to teach some moral, religious, political, or practical lesson. Although didactic elements are often found in artistically pleasing works, the term "didactic" usually refers to literature in which the message is more important than the form. The term may also be used to criticize a work that the critic finds "overly didactic," that is, heavy-handed in its delivery of a lesson.

Dimeter: See *Meter*

Dionysian: See *Apollonian and Dionysian*

Discordia concours: A Latin phrase meaning "discord in harmony." The term was coined by the eighteenth-century English writer Samuel Johnson to describe "a combination of dissimilar images or discovery of occult resemblances in things apparently unlike." Johnson created the expression by reversing a phrase by the Latin poet Horace.

Dissonance: A combination of harsh or jarring sounds, especially in poetry. Although such combinations may be accidental, poets sometimes intentionally make them to achieve particular effects. Dissonance is also sometimes used to refer to close but not identical rhymes. When this is the case, the word functions as a synonym for consonance.

Double Entendre: A corruption of a French phrase meaning "double meaning." The term is used to indicate a word or phrase that is deliberately ambiguous, especially when one of the meanings is risque or improper.

Draft: Any preliminary version of a written work. An author may write dozens of drafts which are revised to form the final work, or he or she may write only one, with few or no revisions.

Dramatic Monologue: See *Monologue*

Dramatic Poetry: Any lyric work that employs elements of drama such as dialogue, conflict, or characterization, but excluding works that are intended for stage presentation.

Dream Allegory: See *Dream Vision*

Dream Vision: A literary convention, chiefly of the Middle Ages. In a dream vision a story is presented as a literal dream of the narrator. This device was commonly used to teach moral and religious lessons.

E

Eclogue: In classical literature, a poem featuring rural themes and structured as a dialogue among shepherds. Eclogues often took specific poetic forms, such as elegies or love poems. Some were written as the soliloquy of a shepherd. In later centuries, "eclogue" came to refer to any poem that was in the pastoral tradition or that had a dialogue or monologue structure.

Edwardian: Describes cultural conventions identified with the period of the reign of Edward VII of England (1901–1910). Writers of the Edwardian Age typically displayed a strong reaction against the propriety and conservatism of the Victorian Age. Their work often exhibits distrust of authority in religion, politics, and art and expresses strong doubts about the soundness of conventional values.

Edwardian Age: See *Edwardian*

Electra Complex: A daughter's amorous obsession with her father.

Elegy: A lyric poem that laments the death of a person or the eventual death of all people. In a conventional elegy, set in a classical world, the poet and subject are spoken of as shepherds. In modern criticism, the word elegy is often used to refer to a poem that is melancholy or mournfully contemplative.

Elizabethan Age: A period of great economic growth, religious controversy, and nationalism closely associated with the reign of Elizabeth I of England (1558–1603). The Elizabethan Age is considered a part of the general renaissance—that is, the flowering of arts and literature—that took place in Europe during the fourteenth through sixteenth centuries. The era is considered the golden age of English literature. The most important dramas in English and a great deal of lyric poetry were produced during this period, and modern English criticism began around this time.

Empathy: A sense of shared experience, including emotional and physical feelings, with someone or something other than oneself. Empathy is often used to describe the response of a reader to a literary character.

English Sonnet: See *Sonnet*

Enjambment: The running over of the sense and structure of a line of verse or a couplet into the following verse or couplet.

Enlightenment, The: An eighteenth-century philosophical movement. It began in France but had a wide impact throughout Europe and America. Thinkers of the Enlightenment valued reason and believed that both the individual and society could achieve a state of perfection. Corresponding to this essentially humanist vision was a resistance to religious authority.

Epic: A long narrative poem about the adventures of a hero of great historic or legendary importance. The setting is vast and the action is often given cosmic significance through the intervention of supernatural forces such as gods, angels, or demons. Epics are typically written in a classical style of grand simplicity with elaborate metaphors and allusions that enhance the symbolic importance of a hero's adventures.

Epic Simile: See *Homeric Simile*

Epigram: A saying that makes the speaker's point quickly and concisely.

Epilogue: A concluding statement or section of a literary work. In dramas, particularly those of the seventeenth and eighteenth centuries, the epilogue is a closing speech, often in verse, delivered by an actor at the end of a play and spoken directly to the audience.

Epiphany: A sudden revelation of truth inspired by a seemingly trivial incident.

Epitaph: An inscription on a tomb or tombstone, or a verse written on the occasion of a person's death. Epitaphs may be serious or humorous.

Epithalamion: A song or poem written to honor and commemorate a marriage ceremony.

Epithalamium: See *Epithalamion*

Epithet: A word or phrase, often disparaging or abusive, that expresses a character trait of someone or something.

Erziehungsroman: See *Bildungsroman*

Essay: A prose composition with a focused subject of discussion. The term was coined by Michel de Montaigne to describe his 1580 collection of brief, informal reflections on himself and on various topics relating to human nature. An essay can also be a long, systematic discourse.

Existentialism: A predominantly twentieth-century philosophy concerned with the nature and perception of human existence. There are two major strains of existentialist thought: atheistic and Christian. Followers of atheistic existentialism believe that the individual is alone in a godless universe and that the basic human condition is one of suffering and loneliness. Nevertheless, because there are no fixed values, individuals can create their own characters—indeed, they can shape themselves—through the exercise of free will. The atheistic strain culminates in and is popularly associated with the works of Jean-Paul Sartre. The Christian existentialists, on the other hand, believe that only in God may people find freedom from life's anguish. The two strains hold certain beliefs in common: that existence cannot be fully understood or described through empirical effort; that anguish is a universal element of life; that individuals must bear responsibility for their actions; and that there is no common standard of behavior or perception for religious and ethical matters.

Expatriates: See *Expatriatism*

Expatriatism: The practice of leaving one's country to live for an extended period in another country.

Exposition: Writing intended to explain the nature of an idea, thing, or theme. Expository writing is often combined with description, narration, or argument. In dramatic writing, the exposition is the introductory material which presents the characters, setting, and tone of the play.

Expressionism: An indistinct literary term, originally used to describe an early twentieth-century school of German painting. The term applies to almost any mode of unconventional, highly subjective writing that distorts reality in some way.

Extended Monologue: See *Monologue*

F

Feet: See *Foot*

Feminine Rhyme: See *Rhyme*

Fiction: Any story that is the product of imagination rather than a documentation of fact. Characters and events in such narratives may be based in real life but their ultimate form and configuration is a creation of the author.

Figurative Language: A technique in writing in which the author temporarily interrupts the order, construction, or meaning of the writing for a particular effect. This interruption takes the form of one or more figures of speech such as hyperbole, irony, or simile. Figurative language is the opposite of literal language, in which every word is truthful, accurate, and free of exaggeration or embellishment.

Figures of Speech: Writing that differs from customary conventions for construction, meaning, order, or significance for the purpose of a special meaning or effect. There are two major types of figures of speech: rhetorical figures, which do not make changes in the meaning of the words; and tropes, which do.

***Fin de siecle*:** A French term meaning "end of the century." The term is used to denote the last decade of the nineteenth century, a transition period when writers and other artists abandoned old conventions and looked for new techniques and objectives.

First Person: See *Point of View*

Folk Ballad: See *Ballad*

Folklore: Traditions and myths preserved in a culture or group of people. Typically, these are passed on by word of mouth in various forms—such as legends, songs, and proverbs—or preserved in customs and ceremonies. This term was first used by W. J. Thoms in 1846.

Folktale: A story originating in oral tradition. Folktales fall into a variety of categories, including legends, ghost stories, fairy tales, fables, and anecdotes based on historical figures and events.

Foot: The smallest unit of rhythm in a line of poetry. In English-language poetry, a foot is typically one accented syllable combined with one or two unaccented syllables.

Form: The pattern or construction of a work which identifies its genre and distinguishes it from other genres.

Formalism: In literary criticism, the belief that literature should follow prescribed rules of construction, such as those that govern the sonnet form.

Fourteener Meter: See *Meter*

Free Verse: Poetry that lacks regular metrical and rhyme patterns but that tries to capture the cadences of everyday speech. The form allows a poet to exploit a variety of rhythmical effects within a single poem.

Futurism: A flamboyant literary and artistic movement that developed in France, Italy, and Russia from 1908 through the 1920s. Futurist theater and poetry abandoned traditional literary forms. In their place, followers of the movement attempted to achieve total freedom of expression through bizarre imagery and deformed or newly invented words. The Futurists were self-consciously modern artists who attempted to incorporate the appearances and sounds of modern life into their work.

G

Genre: A category of literary work. In critical theory, genre may refer to both the content of a given work—tragedy, comedy, pastoral—and to its form, such as poetry, novel, or drama.

Genteel Tradition: A term coined by critic George Santayana to describe the literary practice of certain late nineteenth-century American writers, especially New Englanders. Followers of the Genteel

Tradition emphasized conventionality in social, religious, moral, and literary standards.

Georgian Age: See *Georgian Poets*

Georgian Period: See *Georgian Poets*

Georgian Poets: A loose grouping of English poets during the years 1912–1922. The Georgians reacted against certain literary schools and practices, especially Victorian wordiness, turn-of-the-century aestheticism, and contemporary urban realism. In their place, the Georgians embraced the nineteenth-century poetic practices of William Wordsworth and the other Lake Poets.

Georgic: A poem about farming and the farmer's way of life, named from Virgil's *Georgics.*

Gilded Age: A period in American history during the 1870s characterized by political corruption and materialism. A number of important novels of social and political criticism were written during this time.

Gothic: See *Gothicism*

Gothicism: In literary criticism, works characterized by a taste for the medieval or morbidly attractive. A gothic novel prominently features elements of horror, the supernatural, gloom, and violence: clanking chains, terror, charnel houses, ghosts, medieval castles, and mysteriously slamming doors. The term "gothic novel" is also applied to novels that lack elements of the traditional Gothic setting but that create a similar atmosphere of terror or dread.

Graveyard School: A group of eighteenth-century English poets who wrote long, picturesque meditations on death. Their works were designed to cause the reader to ponder immortality.

Great Chain of Being: The belief that all things and creatures in nature are organized in a hierarchy from inanimate objects at the bottom to God at the top. This system of belief was popular in the seventeenth and eighteenth centuries.

Grotesque: In literary criticism, the subject matter of a work or a style of expression characterized by exaggeration, deformity, freakishness, and disorder. The grotesque often includes an element of comic absurdity.

H

***Haiku*:** The shortest form of Japanese poetry, constructed in three lines of five, seven, and five syllables respectively. The message of a *haiku* poem usually centers on some aspect of spirituality and provokes an emotional response in the reader.

Half Rhyme: See *Consonance*

Harlem Renaissance: The Harlem Renaissance of the 1920s is generally considered the first significant movement of black writers and artists in the United States. During this period, new and established black writers published more fiction and poetry than ever before, the first influential black literary journals were established, and black authors and artists received their first widespread recognition and serious critical appraisal. Among the major writers associated with this period are Claude McKay, Jean Toomer, Countee Cullen, Langston Hughes, Arna Bontemps, Nella Larsen, and Zora Neale Hurston.

Hellenism: Imitation of ancient Greek thought or styles. Also, an approach to life that focuses on the growth and development of the intellect. "Hellenism" is sometimes used to refer to the belief that reason can be applied to examine all human experience.

Heptameter: See *Meter*

Hero/Heroine: The principal sympathetic character (male or female) in a literary work. Heroes and heroines typically exhibit admirable traits: idealism, courage, and integrity, for example.

Heroic Couplet: A rhyming couplet written in iambic pentameter (a verse with five iambic feet).

Heroic Line: The meter and length of a line of verse in epic or heroic poetry. This varies by language and time period.

Heroine: See *Hero/Heroine*

Hexameter: See *Meter*

Historical Criticism: The study of a work based on its impact on the world of the time period in which it was written.

***Hokku*:** See *Haiku*

Holocaust: See *Holocaust Literature*

Holocaust Literature: Literature influenced by or written about the Holocaust of World War II. Such literature includes true stories of survival in concentration camps, escape, and life after the war, as well as fictional works and poetry.

Homeric Simile: An elaborate, detailed comparison written as a simile many lines in length.

Horatian Satire: See *Satire*

Humanism: A philosophy that places faith in the dignity of humankind and rejects the medieval perception of the individual as a weak, fallen creature. "Humanists" typically believe in the perfectibility of human nature and view reason and education as the means to that end.

Humors: Mentions of the humors refer to the ancient Greek theory that a person's health and personality were determined by the balance of four basic fluids in the body: blood, phlegm, yellow bile, and black bile. A dominance of any fluid would cause extremes in behavior. An excess of blood created a sanguine person who was joyful, aggressive, and passionate; a phlegmatic person was shy, fearful, and sluggish; too much yellow bile led to a choleric temperament characterized by impatience, anger, bitterness, and stubbornness; and excessive black bile created melancholy, a state of laziness, gluttony, and lack of motivation.

Humours: See *Humors*

Hyperbole: In literary criticism, deliberate exaggeration used to achieve an effect.

I

Iamb: See *Foot*

Idiom: A word construction or verbal expression closely associated with a given language.

Image: A concrete representation of an object or sensory experience. Typically, such a representation helps evoke the feelings associated with the object or experience itself. Images are either "literal" or "figurative." Literal images are especially concrete and involve little or no extension of the obvious meaning of the words used to express them. Figurative images do not follow the literal meaning of the words exactly. Images in literature are usually visual, but the term "image" can also refer to the representation of any sensory experience.

Imagery: The array of images in a literary work. Also, figurative language.

Imagism: An English and American poetry movement that flourished between 1908 and 1917. The Imagists used precise, clearly presented images in their works. They also used common, everyday speech and aimed for conciseness, concrete imagery, and the creation of new rhythms.

***In medias res*:** A Latin term meaning "in the middle of things." It refers to the technique of beginning a story at its midpoint and then using various flashback devices to reveal previous action.

Induction: The process of reaching a conclusion by reasoning from specific premises to form a general premise. Also, an introductory portion of a work of literature, especially a play.

Intentional Fallacy: The belief that judgments of a literary work based solely on an author's stated or implied intentions are false and misleading. Critics who believe in the concept of the intentional fallacy typically argue that the work itself is sufficient matter for interpretation, even though they may concede that an author's statement of purpose can be useful.

Interior Monologue: A narrative technique in which characters' thoughts are revealed in a way that appears to be uncontrolled by the author. The interior monologue typically aims to reveal the inner self of a character. It portrays emotional experiences as they occur at both a conscious and unconscious level. Images are often used to represent sensations or emotions.

Internal Rhyme: Rhyme that occurs within a single line of verse.

Irish Literary Renaissance: A late nineteenth- and early twentieth-century movement in Irish literature. Members of the movement aimed to reduce the influence of British culture in Ireland and create an Irish national literature.

Irony: In literary criticism, the effect of language in which the intended meaning is the opposite of what is stated.

Italian Sonnet: See *Sonnet*

J

Jacobean Age: The period of the reign of James I of England (1603–1625). The early literature of this period reflected the worldview of the Elizabethan Age, but a darker, more cynical attitude steadily grew in the art and literature of the Jacobean Age. This was an important time for English drama and poetry.

Jargon: Language that is used or understood only by a select group of people. Jargon may refer to terminology used in a certain profession, such as computer jargon, or it may refer to any nonsensical language that is not understood by most people.

Journalism: Writing intended for publication in a newspaper or magazine, or for broadcast on a radio or television program featuring news, sports, entertainment, or other timely material.

K

Knickerbocker Group: A somewhat indistinct group of New York writers of the first half of the nineteenth century. Members of the group were linked only by location and a common theme: New York life.

***Kunstlerroman*:** See *Bildungsroman*

L

***Lais*:** See *Lay*

Lake Poets: See *Lake School*

Lake School: These poets all lived in the Lake District of England at the turn of the nineteenth century. As a group, they followed no single "school" of thought or literary practice, although their works were uniformly disparaged by the *Edinburgh Review.*

Lay: A song or simple narrative poem. The form originated in medieval France. Early French *lais* were often based on the Celtic legends and other tales sung by Breton minstrels—thus the name of the "Breton lay." In fourteenth-century England, the term "lay" was used to describe short narratives written in imitation of the Breton lays.

***Leitmotiv*:** See *Motif*

Literal Language: An author uses literal language when he or she writes without exaggerating or embellishing the subject matter and without any tools of figurative language.

Literary Ballad: See *Ballad*

Literature: Literature is broadly defined as any written or spoken material, but the term most often refers to creative works.

Lost Generation: A term first used by Gertrude Stein to describe the post-World War I generation of American writers: men and women haunted by a sense of betrayal and emptiness brought about by the destructiveness of the war.

Lyric Poetry: A poem expressing the subjective feelings and personal emotions of the poet. Such poetry is melodic, since it was originally accompanied by a lyre in recitals. Most Western poetry in the twentieth century may be classified as lyrical.

M

Mannerism: Exaggerated, artificial adherence to a literary manner or style. Also, a popular style of the visual arts of late sixteenth-century Europe that was marked by elongation of the human form and by intentional spatial distortion. Literary works that are self-consciously high-toned and artistic are often said to be "mannered."

Masculine Rhyme: See *Rhyme*

Measure: The foot, verse, or time sequence used in a literary work, especially a poem. Measure is often used somewhat incorrectly as a synonym for meter.

Metaphor: A figure of speech that expresses an idea through the image of another object. Metaphors suggest the essence of the first object by identifying it with certain qualities of the second object.

Metaphysical Conceit: See *Conceit*

Metaphysical Poetry: The body of poetry produced by a group of seventeenth-century English writers called the "Metaphysical Poets." The group includes John Donne and Andrew Marvell. The Metaphysical Poets made use of everyday speech, intellectual analysis, and unique imagery. They aimed to portray the ordinary conflicts and contradictions of life. Their poems often took the form of an argument, and many of them emphasize physical and religious love as well as the fleeting nature of life. Elaborate conceits are typical in metaphysical poetry.

Metaphysical Poets: See *Metaphysical Poetry*

Meter: In literary criticism, the repetition of sound patterns that creates a rhythm in poetry. The patterns are based on the number of syllables and the presence and absence of accents. The unit of rhythm in a line is called a foot. Types of meter are classified according to the number of feet in a line. These are the standard English lines: Monometer, one foot; Dimeter, two feet; Trimeter, three feet; Tetrameter, four feet; Pentameter, five feet; Hexameter, six feet (also called the Alexandrine); Heptameter, seven feet (also called the "Fourteener" when the feet are iambic).

Modernism: Modern literary practices. Also, the principles of a literary school that lasted from roughly the beginning of the twentieth century until the end of World War II. Modernism is defined by its rejection of the literary conventions of the nineteenth century and by its opposition to conventional morality, taste, traditions, and economic values.

Monologue: A composition, written or oral, by a single individual. More specifically, a speech given by a single individual in a drama or other public entertainment. It has no set length, although it is usually several or more lines long.

Monometer: See *Meter*

Mood: The prevailing emotions of a work or of the author in his or her creation of the work. The mood of a work is not always what might be expected based on its subject matter.

***Motif*:** A theme, character type, image, metaphor, or other verbal element that recurs throughout a single work of literature or occurs in a number of different works over a period of time.

***Motiv*:** See *Motif*

Muckrakers: An early twentieth-century group of American writers. Typically, their works exposed the wrongdoings of big business and government in the United States.

Muses: Nine Greek mythological goddesses, the daughters of Zeus and Mnemosyne (Memory). Each muse patronized a specific area of the liberal arts and sciences. Calliope presided over epic poetry, Clio over history, Erato over love poetry, Euterpe over music or lyric poetry, Melpomene over tragedy, Polyhymnia over hymns to the gods, Terpsichore over dance, Thalia over comedy, and Urania over astronomy. Poets and writers traditionally made appeals to the Muses for inspiration in their work.

Myth: An anonymous tale emerging from the traditional beliefs of a culture or social unit. Myths use supernatural explanations for natural phenomena. They may also explain cosmic issues like creation and death. Collections of myths, known as mythologies, are common to all cultures and nations, but the best known myths belong to the Norse, Roman, and Greek mythologies.

N

Narration: The telling of a series of events, real or invented. A narration may be either a simple narrative, in which the events are recounted chronologically, or a narrative with a plot, in which the account is given in a style reflecting the author's artistic concept of the story. Narration is sometimes used as a synonym for "storyline."

Narrative: A verse or prose accounting of an event or sequence of events, real or invented. The term is also used as an adjective in the sense "method of narration." For example, in literary criticism, the expression "narrative technique" usually refers to the way the author structures and presents his or her story.

Narrative Poetry: A nondramatic poem in which the author tells a story. Such poems may be of any length or level of complexity.

Narrator: The teller of a story. The narrator may be the author or a character in the story through whom the author speaks.

Naturalism: A literary movement of the late nineteenth and early twentieth centuries. The movement's major theorist, French novelist Emile Zola, envisioned a type of fiction that would examine human life with the objectivity of scientific inquiry. The Naturalists typically viewed human beings as either the products of "biological determinism," ruled by hereditary instincts and engaged in an endless struggle for survival, or as the products of "socioeconomic determinism," ruled by social and economic forces beyond their control. In their works, the Naturalists generally ignored the highest levels of society and focused on degradation: poverty, alcoholism, prostitution, insanity, and disease.

Negritude: A literary movement based on the concept of a shared cultural bond on the part of black Africans, wherever they may be in the world. It traces its origins to the former French colonies of Africa and the Caribbean. Negritude poets, novelists, and essayists generally stress four points in their writings: One, black alienation from traditional African culture can lead to feelings of inferiority. Two, European colonialism and Western education should be resisted. Three, black Africans should seek to affirm and define their own identity. Four, African culture can and should be reclaimed. Many Negritude writers also claim that blacks can make unique contributions to the world, based on a heightened appreciation of nature, rhythm, and human emotions—aspects of life they say are not so highly valued in the materialistic and rationalistic West.

Negro Renaissance: See *Harlem Renaissance*

Neoclassical Period: See *Neoclassicism*

Neoclassicism: In literary criticism, this term refers to the revival of the attitudes and styles of expression of classical literature. It is generally used to describe a period in European history beginning in the late seventeenth century and lasting until about 1800. In its purest form, Neoclassicism marked a return to order, proportion, restraint, logic, accuracy, and decorum. In England, where Neoclassicism perhaps was most popular, it reflected the influence of seventeenth-century French writers, especially dramatists. Neoclassical writers typically reacted against the intensity and enthusiasm of the Renaissance period. They wrote works that appealed to the intellect, using elevated language and classical literary forms such as satire and the ode. Neoclassical works were often governed by the classical goal of instruction.

Neoclassicists: See *Neoclassicism*

New Criticism: A movement in literary criticism, dating from the late 1920s, that stressed close textual analysis in the interpretation of works of literature. The New Critics saw little merit in historical and biographical analysis. Rather, they aimed to examine the text alone, free from the question of how external events—biographical or otherwise—may have helped shape it.

New Journalism: A type of writing in which the journalist presents factual information in a form usually used in fiction. New journalism emphasizes description, narration, and character development to bring readers closer to the human element of the story, and is often used in personality profiles and in-depth feature articles. It is not compatible with "straight" or "hard" newswriting, which is generally composed in a brief, fact-based style.

New Journalists: See *New Journalism*

New Negro Movement: See *Harlem Renaissance*

Noble Savage: The idea that primitive man is noble and good but becomes evil and corrupted as he becomes civilized. The concept of the noble savage originated in the Renaissance period but is more closely identified with such later writers as Jean-Jacques Rousseau and Aphra Behn.

O

Objective Correlative: An outward set of objects, a situation, or a chain of events corresponding to an inward experience and evoking this experience in the reader. The term frequently appears in modern criticism in discussions of authors' intended effects on the emotional responses of readers.

Objectivity: A quality in writing characterized by the absence of the author's opinion or feeling about the subject matter. Objectivity is an important factor in criticism.

Occasional Verse: Poetry written on the occasion of a significant historical or personal event. *Vers de societe* is sometimes called occasional verse although it is of a less serious nature.

Octave: A poem or stanza composed of eight lines. The term octave most often represents the first eight lines of a Petrarchan sonnet.

Ode: Name given to an extended lyric poem characterized by exalted emotion and dignified style. An ode usually concerns a single, serious theme. Most odes, but not all, are addressed to an object or individual. Odes are distinguished from other lyric poetic forms by their complex rhythmic and stanzaic patterns.

Oedipus Complex: A son's amorous obsession with his mother. The phrase is derived from the story of the ancient Theban hero Oedipus, who unknowingly killed his father and married his mother.

Omniscience: See *Point of View*

Onomatopoeia: The use of words whose sounds express or suggest their meaning. In its simplest sense, onomatopoeia may be represented by words that mimic the sounds they denote such as "hiss" or "meow." At a more subtle level, the pattern and rhythm of sounds and rhymes of a line or poem may be onomatopoeic.

Oral Tradition: See *Oral Transmission*

Oral Transmission: A process by which songs, ballads, folklore, and other material are transmitted by word of mouth. The tradition of oral transmission predates the written record systems of literate society. Oral transmission preserves material sometimes over generations, although often with variations. Memory plays a large part in the recitation and preservation of orally transmitted material.

***Ottava Rima*:** An eight-line stanza of poetry composed in iambic pentameter (a five-foot line in which each foot consists of an unaccented syllable followed by an accented syllable), following the *abababcc* rhyme scheme.

Oxymoron: A phrase combining two contradictory terms. Oxymorons may be intentional or unintentional.

P

Pantheism: The idea that all things are both a manifestation or revelation of God and a part of God at the same time. Pantheism was a common attitude in the early societies of Egypt, India, and Greece—the term derives from the Greek *pan* meaning "all" and *theos* meaning "deity." It later became a significant part of the Christian faith.

Parable: A story intended to teach a moral lesson or answer an ethical question.

Paradox: A statement that appears illogical or contradictory at first, but may actually point to an underlying truth.

Parallelism: A method of comparison of two ideas in which each is developed in the same grammatical structure.

Parnassianism: A mid nineteenth-century movement in French literature. Followers of the movement stressed adherence to well-defined artistic forms as a reaction against the often chaotic expression of the artist's ego that dominated the work of the Romantics. The Parnassians also rejected the moral, ethical, and social themes exhibited in the works of French Romantics such as Victor Hugo. The aesthetic doctrines of the Parnassians strongly influenced the later symbolist and decadent movements.

Parody: In literary criticism, this term refers to an imitation of a serious literary work or the signature style of a particular author in a ridiculous manner. A typical parody adopts the style of the original and applies it to an inappropriate subject for humorous effect. Parody is a form of satire and could be considered the literary equivalent of a caricature or cartoon.

Pastoral: A term derived from the Latin word "pastor," meaning shepherd. A pastoral is a literary composition on a rural theme. The conventions of the pastoral were originated by the third-century Greek poet Theocritus, who wrote about the experiences, love affairs, and pastimes of Sicilian shepherds. In a pastoral, characters and language of a courtly nature are often placed in a simple setting. The term pastoral is also used to classify dramas, elegies, and lyrics that exhibit the use of country settings and shepherd characters.

Pathetic Fallacy: A term coined by English critic John Ruskin to identify writing that falsely endows nonhuman things with human intentions and feelings, such as "angry clouds" and "sad trees."

Pen Name: See *Pseudonym*

Pentameter: See *Meter*

***Persona*:** A Latin term meaning "mask." *Personae* are the characters in a fictional work of literature. The *persona* generally functions as a mask through which the author tells a story in a voice other than his or her own. A *persona* is usually either a character in a story who acts as a narrator or an "implied author," a voice created by the author to act as the narrator for himself or herself.

***Personae*:** See *Persona*

Personal Point of View: See *Point of View*

Personification: A figure of speech that gives human qualities to abstract ideas, animals, and inanimate objects.

Petrarchan Sonnet: See *Sonnet*

Phenomenology: A method of literary criticism based on the belief that things have no existence outside of human consciousness or awareness. Proponents of this theory believe that art is a process that takes place in the mind of the observer as he or she contemplates an object rather than a quality of the object itself.

Plagiarism: Claiming another person's written material as one's own. Plagiarism can take the form of direct, word-for-word copying or the theft of the substance or idea of the work.

Platonic Criticism: A form of criticism that stresses an artistic work's usefulness as an agent of social engineering rather than any quality or value of the work itself.

Platonism: The embracing of the doctrines of the philosopher Plato, popular among the poets of the Renaissance and the Romantic period. Platonism is more flexible than Aristotelian Criticism and places more emphasis on the supernatural and unknown aspects of life.

Plot: In literary criticism, this term refers to the pattern of events in a narrative or drama. In its simplest sense, the plot guides the author in composing the work and helps the reader follow the work. Typically, plots exhibit causality and unity and have a beginning, a middle, and an end. Sometimes, however, a plot may consist of a series of disconnected events, in which case it is known as an "episodic plot."

Poem: In its broadest sense, a composition utilizing rhyme, meter, concrete detail, and expressive language to create a literary experience with emotional and aesthetic appeal.

Poet: An author who writes poetry or verse. The term is also used to refer to an artist or writer who has an exceptional gift for expression, imagination, and energy in the making of art in any form.

Poete maudit: A term derived from Paul Verlaine's *Les poetes maudits* (*The Accursed Poets*), a collection of essays on the French symbolist writers Stephane Mallarme, Arthur Rimbaud, and Tristan Corbiere. In the sense intended by Verlaine, the poet is "accursed" for choosing to explore extremes of human experience outside of middle-class society.

Poetic Fallacy: See *Pathetic Fallacy*

Poetic Justice: An outcome in a literary work, not necessarily a poem, in which the good are rewarded and the evil are punished, especially in ways that particularly fit their virtues or crimes.

Poetic License: Distortions of fact and literary convention made by a writer—not always a poet—for the sake of the effect gained. Poetic license is closely related to the concept of "artistic freedom."

Poetics: This term has two closely related meanings. It denotes (1) an aesthetic theory in literary criticism about the essence of poetry or (2) rules prescribing the proper methods, content, style, or diction of poetry. The term poetics may also refer to theories about literature in general, not just poetry.

Poetry: In its broadest sense, writing that aims to present ideas and evoke an emotional experience in the reader through the use of meter, imagery, connotative and concrete words, and a carefully constructed structure based on rhythmic patterns. Poetry typically relies on words and expressions that have several layers of meaning. It also makes use of the effects of regular rhythm on the ear and may make a strong appeal to the senses through the use of imagery.

Point of View: The narrative perspective from which a literary work is presented to the reader. There are four traditional points of view. The "third person omniscient" gives the reader a "godlike" perspective, unrestricted by time or place, from which to see actions and look into the minds of characters. This allows the author to comment openly on characters and events in the work. The "third-person" point of view presents the events of the story from outside of any single character's perception, much like the omniscient point of view, but the reader must understand the action as it takes place and without any special insight into characters' minds or motivations. The "first person" or "personal" point of view relates events as they are perceived by a single character. The main character "tells" the story and may offer opinions about the action and characters which differ from those of the author. Much less common than omniscient, third person, and first person is the "second-person" point of view, wherein the author tells the story as if it is happening to the reader.

Polemic: A work in which the author takes a stand on a controversial subject, such as abortion or religion. Such works are often extremely argumentative or provocative.

Pornography: Writing intended to provoke feelings of lust in the reader. Such works are often condemned by critics and teachers, but those which can be shown to have literary value are viewed less harshly.

Post-Aesthetic Movement: An artistic response made by African Americans to the black aesthetic movement of the 1960s and early 1970s. Writers since that time have adopted a somewhat different tone in their work, with less emphasis placed on the disparity between black and white in the United States. In the words of post-aesthetic authors such as Toni Morrison, John Edgar Wideman, and Kristin Hunter, African Americans are portrayed as looking inward for answers to their own questions, rather than always looking to the outside world.

Postmodernism: Writing from the 1960s forward characterized by experimentation and continuing to apply some of the fundamentals of modernism, which included existentialism and alienation. Postmodernists have gone a step further in the rejection of tradition begun with the modernists by also rejecting traditional forms, preferring the antinovel over the novel and the antihero over the hero.

Pre-Raphaelites: A circle of writers and artists in mid nineteenth-century England. Valuing the pre-Renaissance artistic qualities of religious symbolism, lavish pictorialism, and natural sensuousness, the Pre-Raphaelites cultivated a sense of mystery and melancholy that influenced later writers associated with the Symbolist and Decadent movements.

Primitivism: The belief that primitive peoples were nobler and less flawed than civilized peoples because they had not been subjected to the corrupt influence of society.

Projective Verse: A form of free verse in which the poet's breathing pattern determines the lines of the poem. Poets who advocate projective verse are against all formal structures in writing, including meter and form.

Prologue: An introductory section of a literary work. It often contains information establishing the situation of the characters or presents information about the setting, time period, or action. In drama, the prologue is spoken by a chorus or by one of the principal characters.

Prose: A literary medium that attempts to mirror the language of everyday speech. It is distinguished from poetry by its use of unmetered, unrhymed language consisting of logically related sentences. Prose is usually grouped into paragraphs that form a cohesive whole such as an essay or a novel.

***Prosopopoeia*:** See *Personification*

Protagonist: The central character of a story who serves as a focus for its themes and incidents and as the principal rationale for its development. The protagonist is sometimes referred to in discussions of modern literature as the hero or antihero.

Proverb: A brief, sage saying that expresses a truth about life in a striking manner.

Pseudonym: A name assumed by a writer, most often intended to prevent his or her identification as the author of a work. Two or more authors may work together under one pseudonym, or an author may use a different name for each genre he or she publishes in. Some publishing companies maintain "house pseudonyms," under which any number of authors may write installations in a series. Some authors also choose a pseudonym over their real names the way an actor may use a stage name.

Pun: A play on words that have similar sounds but different meanings.

Pure Poetry: poetry written without instructional intent or moral purpose that aims only to please a reader by its imagery or musical flow. The term pure poetry is used as the antonym of the term "didacticism."

Q

Quatrain: A four-line stanza of a poem or an entire poem consisting of four lines.

R

Realism: A nineteenth-century European literary movement that sought to portray familiar characters, situations, and settings in a realistic manner. This was done primarily by using an objective narrative point of view and through the buildup of accurate detail. The standard for success of any realistic work depends on how faithfully it transfers common experience into fictional forms. The realistic method may be altered or extended, as in stream of consciousness writing, to record highly subjective experience.

Refrain: A phrase repeated at intervals throughout a poem. A refrain may appear at the end of each stanza or at less regular intervals. It may be altered slightly at each appearance.

Renaissance: The period in European history that marked the end of the Middle Ages. It began in Italy in the late fourteenth century. In broad terms, it is usually seen as spanning the fourteenth, fifteenth, and sixteenth centuries, although it did not reach Great Britain, for example, until the 1480s or so. The Renaissance saw an awakening in almost every sphere of human activity, especially science, philosophy, and the arts. The period is best defined by the emergence of a general philosophy that emphasized the importance of the intellect, the individual, and world affairs. It contrasts strongly with the medieval worldview, characterized by the dominant concerns of faith, the social collective, and spiritual salvation.

***Repartee*:** Conversation featuring snappy retorts and witticisms.

Restoration: See *Restoration Age*

Restoration Age: A period in English literature beginning with the crowning of Charles II in 1660 and running to about 1700. The era, which was characterized by a reaction against Puritanism, was the first great age of the comedy of manners. The finest literature of the era is typically witty and urbane, and often lewd.

Rhetoric: In literary criticism, this term denotes the art of ethical persuasion. In its strictest sense, rhetoric adheres to various principles developed since classical times for arranging facts and ideas in a clear, persuasive, appealing manner. The term is also used to refer to effective prose in general and theories of or methods for composing effective prose.

Rhetorical Question: A question intended to provoke thought, but not an expressed answer, in the reader. It is most commonly used in oratory and other persuasive genres.

Rhyme: When used as a noun in literary criticism, this term generally refers to a poem in which words sound identical or very similar and appear in parallel positions in two or more lines. Rhymes are classified into different types according to where they fall in a line or stanza or according to the degree of similarity they exhibit in their spellings and sounds. Some major types of rhyme are "masculine" rhyme, "feminine" rhyme, and "triple" rhyme. In a masculine rhyme, the rhyming sound falls in a single accented syllable, as with "heat" and "eat." Feminine rhyme is a rhyme of two syllables, one stressed and one unstressed, as with "merry" and "tarry." Triple rhyme matches the sound of the accented syllable and the two unaccented syllables that follow: "narrative" and "declarative."

Rhyme Royal: A stanza of seven lines composed in iambic pentameter and rhymed *ababbcc.* The name is said to be a tribute to King James I of Scotland, who made much use of the form in his poetry.

Rhyme Scheme: See *Rhyme*

Rhythm: A regular pattern of sound, time intervals, or events occurring in writing, most often and most discernably in poetry. Regular, reliable rhythm is known to be soothing to humans, while interrupted, unpredictable, or rapidly changing rhythm is disturbing. These effects are known to authors, who use them to produce a desired reaction in the reader.

***Rococo*:** A style of European architecture that flourished in the eighteenth century, especially in

France. The most notable features of *rococo* are its extensive use of ornamentation and its themes of lightness, gaiety, and intimacy. In literary criticism, the term is often used disparagingly to refer to a decadent or overly ornamental style.

Romance:

Romantic Age: See *Romanticism*

Romanticism: This term has two widely accepted meanings. In historical criticism, it refers to a European intellectual and artistic movement of the late eighteenth and early nineteenth centuries that sought greater freedom of personal expression than that allowed by the strict rules of literary form and logic of the eighteenth-century Neoclassicists. The Romantics preferred emotional and imaginative expression to rational analysis. They considered the individual to be at the center of all experience and so placed him or her at the center of their art. The Romantics believed that the creative imagination reveals nobler truths—unique feelings and attitudes—than those that could be discovered by logic or by scientific examination. Both the natural world and the state of childhood were important sources for revelations of "eternal truths." "Romanticism" is also used as a general term to refer to a type of sensibility found in all periods of literary history and usually considered to be in opposition to the principles of classicism. In this sense, Romanticism signifies any work or philosophy in which the exotic or dreamlike figure strongly, or that is devoted to individualistic expression, self-analysis, or a pursuit of a higher realm of knowledge than can be discovered by human reason.

Romantics: See *Romanticism*

Russian Symbolism: A Russian poetic movement, derived from French symbolism, that flourished between 1894 and 1910. While some Russian Symbolists continued in the French tradition, stressing aestheticism and the importance of suggestion above didactic intent, others saw their craft as a form of mystical worship, and themselves as mediators between the supernatural and the mundane.

S

Satire: A work that uses ridicule, humor, and wit to criticize and provoke change in human nature and institutions. There are two major types of satire: "formal" or "direct" satire speaks directly to the reader or to a character in the work; "indirect" satire relies upon the ridiculous behavior of its characters to make its point. Formal satire is further divided into two manners: the "Horatian," which ridicules gently, and the "Juvenalian," which derides its subjects harshly and bitterly.

Scansion: The analysis or "scanning" of a poem to determine its meter and often its rhyme scheme. The most common system of scansion uses accents (slanted lines drawn above syllables) to show stressed syllables, breves (curved lines drawn above syllables) to show unstressed syllables, and vertical lines to separate each foot.

Second Person: See *Point of View*

Semiotics: The study of how literary forms and conventions affect the meaning of language.

Sestet: Any six-line poem or stanza.

Setting: The time, place, and culture in which the action of a narrative takes place. The elements of setting may include geographic location, characters' physical and mental environments, prevailing cultural attitudes, or the historical time in which the action takes place.

Shakespearean Sonnet: See *Sonnet*

Signifying Monkey: A popular trickster figure in black folklore, with hundreds of tales about this character documented since the nineteenth century.

Simile: A comparison, usually using "like" or "as," of two essentially dissimilar things, as in "coffee as cold as ice" or "He sounded like a broken record."

Slang: A type of informal verbal communication that is generally unacceptable for formal writing. Slang words and phrases are often colorful exaggerations used to emphasize the speaker's point; they may also be shortened versions of an often-used word or phrase.

Slant Rhyme: See *Consonance*

Slave Narrative: Autobiographical accounts of American slave life as told by escaped slaves. These works first appeared during the abolition movement of the 1830s through the 1850s.

Social Realism: See *Socialist Realism*

Socialist Realism: The Socialist Realism school of literary theory was proposed by Maxim Gorky and established as a dogma by the first Soviet Congress of Writers. It demanded adherence to a communist worldview in works of literature. Its doctrines required an objective viewpoint comprehensible to the working classes and themes of social struggle featuring strong proletarian heroes.

Soliloquy: A monologue in a drama used to give the audience information and to develop the speaker's character. It is typically a projection of the speaker's innermost thoughts. Usually delivered while the speaker is alone on stage, a soliloquy is intended to present an illusion of unspoken reflection.

Sonnet: A fourteen-line poem, usually composed in iambic pentameter, employing one of several rhyme schemes. There are three major types of sonnets, upon which all other variations of the form are based: the "Petrarchan" or "Italian" sonnet, the "Shakespearean" or "English" sonnet, and the "Spenserian" sonnet. A Petrarchan sonnet consists of an octave rhymed *abbaabba* and a "sestet" rhymed either *cdecde, cdccdc,* or *cdedce.* The octave poses a question or problem, relates a narrative, or puts forth a proposition; the sestet presents a solution to the problem, comments upon the narrative, or applies the proposition put forth in the octave. The Shakespearean sonnet is divided into three quatrains and a couplet rhymed *abab cdcd efef gg.* The couplet provides an epigrammatic comment on the narrative or problem put forth in the quatrains. The Spenserian sonnet uses three quatrains and a couplet like the Shakespearean, but links their three rhyme schemes in this way: *abab bcbc cdcd ee.* The Spenserian sonnet develops its theme in two parts like the Petrarchan, its final six lines resolving a problem, analyzing a narrative, or applying a proposition put forth in its first eight lines.

Spenserian Sonnet: See *Sonnet*

Spenserian Stanza: A nine-line stanza having eight verses in iambic pentameter, its ninth verse in iambic hexameter, and the rhyme scheme *ababbcbcc.*

Spondee: In poetry meter, a foot consisting of two long or stressed syllables occurring together. This form is quite rare in English verse, and is usually composed of two monosyllabic words.

Sprung Rhythm: Versification using a specific number of accented syllables per line but disregarding the number of unaccented syllables that fall in each line, producing an irregular rhythm in the poem.

Stanza: A subdivision of a poem consisting of lines grouped together, often in recurring patterns of rhyme, line length, and meter. Stanzas may also serve as units of thought in a poem much like paragraphs in prose.

Stereotype: A stereotype was originally the name for a duplication made during the printing process; this led to its modern definition as a person or thing that is (or is assumed to be) the same as all others of its type.

Stream of Consciousness: A narrative technique for rendering the inward experience of a character. This technique is designed to give the impression of an ever-changing series of thoughts, emotions, images, and memories in the spontaneous and seemingly illogical order that they occur in life.

Structuralism: A twentieth-century movement in literary criticism that examines how literary texts arrive at their meanings, rather than the meanings themselves. There are two major types of structuralist analysis: one examines the way patterns of linguistic structures unify a specific text and emphasize certain elements of that text, and the other interprets the way literary forms and conventions affect the meaning of language itself.

Structure: The form taken by a piece of literature. The structure may be made obvious for ease of understanding, as in nonfiction works, or may obscured for artistic purposes, as in some poetry or seemingly "unstructured" prose.

Sturm und Drang: A German term meaning "storm and stress." It refers to a German literary movement of the 1770s and 1780s that reacted against the order and rationalism of the enlightenment, focusing instead on the intense experience of extraordinary individuals.

Style: A writer's distinctive manner of arranging words to suit his or her ideas and purpose in writing. The unique imprint of the author's personality upon his or her writing, style is the product of an author's way of arranging ideas and his or her use of diction, different sentence structures, rhythm, figures of speech, rhetorical principles, and other elements of composition.

Subject: The person, event, or theme at the center of a work of literature. A work may have one or more subjects of each type, with shorter works tending to have fewer and longer works tending to have more.

Subjectivity: Writing that expresses the author's personal feelings about his subject, and which may or may not include factual information about the subject.

Surrealism: A term introduced to criticism by Guillaume Apollinaire and later adopted by Andre Breton. It refers to a French literary and artistic movement founded in the 1920s. The Surrealists sought to express unconscious thoughts and feelings in their works. The best-known technique used for achieving this aim was automatic writing—transcriptions of spontaneous outpourings from the unconscious. The Surrealists proposed to unify the contrary levels of conscious and unconscious, dream and reality, objectivity and subjectivity into a new level of "super-realism."

Suspense: A literary device in which the author maintains the audience's attention through the buildup of events, the outcome of which will soon be revealed.

Syllogism: A method of presenting a logical argument. In its most basic form, the syllogism consists of a major premise, a minor premise, and a conclusion.

Symbol: Something that suggests or stands for something else without losing its original identity. In literature, symbols combine their literal meaning with the suggestion of an abstract concept. Literary symbols are of two types: those that carry complex associations of meaning no matter what their contexts, and those that derive their suggestive meaning from their functions in specific literary works.

Symbolism: This term has two widely accepted meanings. In historical criticism, it denotes an early modernist literary movement initiated in France during the nineteenth century that reacted against the prevailing standards of realism. Writers in this movement aimed to evoke, indirectly and symbolically, an order of being beyond the material world of the five senses. Poetic expression of personal emotion figured strongly in the movement, typically by means of a private set of symbols uniquely identifiable with the individual poet. The principal aim of the Symbolists was to express in words the highly complex feelings that grew out of everyday contact with the world. In a broader sense, the term "symbolism" refers to the use of one object to represent another.

Symbolist: See *Symbolism*

Symbolist Movement: See *Symbolism*

Sympathetic Fallacy: See *Affective Fallacy*

T

***Tanka*:** A form of Japanese poetry similar to *haiku.* A *tanka* is five lines long, with the lines containing five, seven, five, seven, and seven syllables respectively.

***Terza Rima*:** A three-line stanza form in poetry in which the rhymes are made on the last word of each line in the following manner: the first and third lines of the first stanza, then the second line of the first stanza and the first and third lines of the second stanza, and so on with the middle line of any stanza rhyming with the first and third lines of the following stanza.

Tetrameter: See *Meter*

Textual Criticism: A branch of literary criticism that seeks to establish the authoritative text of a literary work. Textual critics typically compare all known manuscripts or printings of a single work in order to assess the meanings of differences and revisions. This procedure allows them to arrive at a definitive version that (supposedly) corresponds to the author's original intention.

Theme: The main point of a work of literature. The term is used interchangeably with thesis.

Thesis: A thesis is both an essay and the point argued in the essay. Thesis novels and thesis plays share the quality of containing a thesis which is supported through the action of the story.

Third Person: See *Point of View*

Tone: The author's attitude toward his or her audience may be deduced from the tone of the work. A formal tone may create distance or convey politeness, while an informal tone may encourage a friendly, intimate, or intrusive feeling in the reader. The author's attitude toward his or her subject matter may also be deduced from the tone of the words he or she uses in discussing it.

Tragedy: A drama in prose or poetry about a noble, courageous hero of excellent character who, because of some tragic character flaw or *hamartia,* brings ruin upon him- or herself. Tragedy treats its subjects in a dignified and serious manner, using poetic language to help evoke pity and fear and bring about catharsis, a purging of these emotions. The tragic form was practiced extensively by the ancient Greeks. In the Middle Ages, when classical works were virtually unknown, tragedy came to denote any works about the fall of persons from exalted to low conditions due to any reason: fate, vice, weakness, etc. According to the classical definition of tragedy, such works present the "pathetic"—that which evokes pity—rather than the tragic. The classical form of tragedy was revived in the sixteenth century; it flourished especially on the Elizabethan stage. In modern times, dramatists have attempted to adapt the form to the needs of modern society by drawing their heroes from the ranks of ordinary men and women and defining the nobility of these heroes in terms of spirit rather than exalted social standing.

Tragic Flaw: In a tragedy, the quality within the hero or heroine which leads to his or her downfall.

Transcendentalism: An American philosophical and religious movement, based in New England from around 1835 until the Civil War. Transcendentalism was a form of American romanticism that had its roots abroad in the works of Thomas Carlyle, Samuel Coleridge, and Johann Wolfgang von Goethe. The Transcendentalists stressed the importance of intuition and subjective experience in communication with God. They rejected religious dogma and texts in favor of mysticism and scientific naturalism. They pursued truths that lie beyond the "colorless" realms perceived by reason and the senses and were active social reformers in public education, women's rights, and the abolition of slavery.

Trickster: A character or figure common in Native American and African literature who uses his ingenuity to defeat enemies and escape difficult situations. Tricksters are most often animals, such as the spider, hare, or coyote, although they may take the form of humans as well.

Trimeter: See *Meter*

Triple Rhyme: See *Rhyme*

Trochee: See *Foot*

U

Understatement: See *Irony*

Unities: Strict rules of dramatic structure, formulated by Italian and French critics of the Renaissance and based loosely on the principles of drama discussed by Aristotle in his *Poetics.* Foremost among these rules were the three unities of action, time, and place that compelled a dramatist to: (1) construct a single plot with a beginning, middle, and end that details the causal relationships of action and character; (2) restrict the action to the events of a single day; and (3) limit the scene to a single place or city. The unities were observed faithfully by continental European writers until the Romantic Age, but they were never regularly observed in English drama. Modern dramatists are typically more concerned with a unity of impression or emotional effect than with any of the classical unities.

Urban Realism: A branch of realist writing that attempts to accurately reflect the often harsh facts of modern urban existence.

Utopia: A fictional perfect place, such as "paradise" or "heaven."

Utopian: See *Utopia*

Utopianism: See *Utopia*

V

Verisimilitude: Literally, the appearance of truth. In literary criticism, the term refers to aspects of a work of literature that seem true to the reader.

***Vers de societe*:** See *Occasional Verse*

***Vers libre*:** See *Free Verse*

Verse: A line of metered language, a line of a poem, or any work written in verse.

Versification: The writing of verse. Versification may also refer to the meter, rhyme, and other mechanical components of a poem.

Victorian: Refers broadly to the reign of Queen Victoria of England (1837–1901) and to anything with qualities typical of that era. For example, the qualities of smug narrowmindedness, bourgeois materialism, faith in social progress, and priggish morality are often considered Victorian. This stereotype is contradicted by such dramatic intellectual developments as the theories of Charles Darwin, Karl Marx, and Sigmund Freud (which stirred strong debates in England) and the critical attitudes of serious Victorian writers like Charles Dickens and George Eliot. In literature, the Victorian Period was the great age of the English novel, and the latter part of the era saw the rise of movements such as decadence and symbolism.

Victorian Age: See *Victorian*

Victorian Period: See *Victorian*

W

***Weltanschauung*:** A German term referring to a person's worldview or philosophy.

***Weltschmerz*:** A German term meaning "world pain." It describes a sense of anguish about the nature of existence, usually associated with a melancholy, pessimistic attitude.

Z

***Zarzuela*:** A type of Spanish operetta.

***Zeitgeist*:** A German term meaning "spirit of the time." It refers to the moral and intellectual trends of a given era.

Cumulative Author/Title Index

C

D

E

F

G

H

I

J

K

L

M

N

O

P

Q

R

S

Cumulative Nationality/Ethnicity Index

Australian

Canadian

Canadian, Sri Lankan

Chilean

Chinese

Egyptian, Greek

English

French

German

Ghanaian

Greek

Hispanic

Indian

Indonesian

Iranian

Irish

Italian

Jamaican

Japanese

Jewish

Kiowa

Lithuanian

Mexican

Native American

Osage

Polish

Romanian

Russian

St. Lucian

Scottish

Senegalese

Spanish

Swedish

Vietnamese

Welsh

Subject/Theme Index

R

S

T

U

W

Cumulative Index of First Lines

A

B

C

D

E

F

G

H

I

J

L

M

N

O

P

Q

R

S

T

W

Y

Cumulative Index of Last Lines

A

B

C

D

E

F

G

H

I

J

L

M

N

O

P

R

S

T

U

W

Y